Professional SQL Server Development with Access 2000

Rick Dobson

Wrox Press Ltd. ®

Professional SQL Server Development with Access 2000

© 2000 Wrox Press

Published by Wrox Press Ltd,
Arden House, 1102 Warwick Road, Acocks Green,
Birmingham, B27 6BH, UK
Printed in the United States
ISBN 1-861004-83-4

Trademark Acknowledgements

Wrox has endeavored to provide trademark information about all the companies and products mentioned in this book by the appropriate use of capitals. However, Wrox cannot guarantee the accuracy of this information.

Credits

Author
Rick Dobson

Additional Material
Robin Dewson
Hope Hatfield
Ian Herbert
Helmut Watson

Managing/Development Editor
Dominic Lowe

Technical Architect
Ian Blackham

Technical Editors
Catherine Alexander
Claire Brittle
Sarah Drew
Mark Waterhouse

Author Agent
Tony Berry

Project Manager
Cilmara Lion

Proofreader
Christopher Smith

Technical Reviewers
Stuart Brown
Greg Clark
Robin Dewson
Damien Foggon
Tony Greening
Ian Herbert
Roberta Townsend
Helmut Watson

Production Project Coordinator
Pip Wonson

Additional Layout
Tom Bartlett
Mark Burdett
Maryse Guichaoua

Cover Design
Shelley Frasier

Production Manager
Laurent Lafon

Figures
Shabnam Hussain

Index
Adrian Axinte
Alessandro Ansa
Andrew Criddle

About the Authors

Rick Dobson

Rick Dobson is an experienced author/trainer/developer who specializes in Access, SQL Server, Web, and Microsoft Office development techniques. He got the urge to write this book as he was completing "Programming Microsoft Access 2000" for Microsoft Press. As he was preparing that book, the monumental advance in SQL Server programmability from Access became apparent to him. This revelation urged him to write this book to serve the many Access developers who will benefit from a solid introduction to professional SQL Server development techniques that build on the great tools in Access 2000. At the urging of Wrox editors and with the help of Microsoft program managers, he designed the book so that it addresses both SQL Server 7 and SQL Server 2000. Rick's regular column in SQL Server Magazine taught him that many SQL Server developers and database administrators can also find value in Access RAD techniques for building SQL Server solutions. So, he wrote the book with these folks in mind as well.

Rick's writing experience is substantial. In addition to this book and the one for Microsoft Press, he contributed to several Que books. Beyond that, he is a contributing editor to SQL Server Magazine. His articles regularly appear in a broad selection of print and web-based publications that target developers and IT professionals, including Microsoft Office & VBA Developer, Visual Basic Programmer's Journal, Microsoft Technet, and msdn online. You can find a list of Rick's publications at http://www.programmingmsaccess.com/Access2000Seminar/RDPubs.htm.

Rick is also an accomplished trainer. He has delivered training sessions in England, Australia, Canada, and throughout the US. His consulting practice sponsored the Access 2000 Development Seminar in 1999. This three-city seminar tour offered two days of advanced training on Access 2000 development techniques. In 2000, his practice expands the scope, duration, and number of cities visited by the tour. The scope grows to encompass both SQL Server and Access development issues. In addition, a heavy web focus emerges. The seminar lasts three days with a separate day of presentations and demonstrations on Access and SQL Server and a third day of hands-on training. The site travels to six cities in 2000.

One of the best ways to get to know Rick is by sampling the content at the two web sites that his practice maintains. The practice's most current and up-to-date site is ProgrammingMSAccess.com (http://www.programmingmsaccess.com). It contains hundreds of pages of code samples, demonstrations, tutorials, presentations, book excerpts, and links to full-length magazine articles. Another site with some older and generally simpler content that will still be of interest to some developers is Cabinc.net (http://www.cabinc.net).

I start the process of acknowledging those who made this book possible with two caveats. First, I received so much help in so many different ways that I honestly do not feel that I can develop a comprehensive list. If there is something that you like in this book, chances are someone else made it possible. However, I take full responsibility for anything you do not like about the book. I had plenty of great advice, and somebody must have told me not to do whatever you don't like – I just failed to respond to the advice.

Wrox is the book's publisher, and you would naturally expect their staff to play a major role. Here's a highly abbreviated list of some of the Wrox persons with whom I interacted.

Dominic Lowe engaged me to do the book. Without his efforts, this book would not be in the Wrox library. Cilmara Lion and Tony Berry worked with me during the many months that it took to write this book. Their patience, encouragement, and gentle prodding are gratefully recognized.

Ian Blackham and Sarah Drew are two lead members on the Wrox editorial team who worked on transforming my text into a Wrox book. With the help of an army of other editors, they went on a search-and-destroy mission to eradicate fuzzy and potentially inaccurate statements in my initial draft of the book. I hope you concur the result is comprehensible, engaging, and accurate material on how to build professional SQL Server solutions with Access 2000 projects.

Aside from the Wrox, I thank Microsoft and its PR firm Waggener Edstrom. Several employees went way beyond the call of duty to help me get you timely, authoritative information in this book.

Bill Ramos was especially helpful in clarifying how Access projects worked with SQL Server 2000. This was challenging for Microsoft since SQL Server 2000 released after Access 2000.

Rich Dickinson assisted me to verify bug reports and in identifying ways of working around them.

Eric Foster from Waggener Edstrom helped to make it possible for me to attend two special events on SQL Server 2000. The book's demonstration of innovative SQL Server 2000 functionality would have been much weaker were it not for his efforts.

My wife, Virginia Dobson, encouraged me to undertake the book. Then, she assisted with proof reading, handling administrative interactions with Wrox, and kind understanding throughout the project.

Writing a book is a statement of faith. You spend months of your life finishing hundreds of pages of content that you hope will help others. I do not believe that I could sustain this expectation without the author and finisher of my faith – Jesus Christ. Thank you, Lord.

Robin Dewson

Having been a consultant for many years on mainframe systems, finally broke away over 4 years ago to become a software consultant on PC systems, to which I am eternally grateful to Annette Kelly for the opportunity and having the faith. Also to Daniel Tarbotton for having to put up with me for 3 years. Currently at a major investment bank working on a trading system called "Kojak" using a number of technologies from Visual Basic and Visual FoxPro, through to Sybase. Thanks to all at Wrox, especially Tony Berry, and Cilmara Lion, a nicer couple of people you may never meet. Also my wife, Julie, and 3 kids, Scott, Cameron and Ellen for allowing me to ruin their holiday with this book. Good luck to the Bedford Blues.

Dedicated to my mum and dad, for pushing me when I needed to be pushed, being very understanding of their troublesome son, and helping me stick with my Sinclair zx80 , and beyond.

Hope Hatfield

Hope has over 12 years of IT experience and currently owns a software development company, Hatfield Consulting, Inc. Hatfield Consulting specializes in developing Web and Windows based software using Visual Basic, Access, SQL Server, ASP and FrontPage. Hope enjoys the changes, challenges, and diversity that are required in the IT field. She lives in Indianapolis, Indiana with her husband Rich, and their two dogs.

Ian Herbert

Ian is director of Swifton Databases Limited (www.swifton.co.uk), based in Birmingham, UK. Swifton specializes in delivering database solutions for small and medium sized businesses, especially those operating in the chemical and chemical analysis sector.

I am indebted to a number of people at Wrox Press for their help, including Tony Berry, Ian Blackham, and Sarah Drew. However, special thanks are reserved for Cilmara Lion for her encouragement and professionalism throughout.

Helmut Watson

Helmut started his IT career nearly 20 years ago writing games for the BBC micro. Soon after that he had to get a proper job so he moved into databases, initially using PC-Oracle v1.0. He quickly decided to change to DBMS' that actually worked - Dbase, Clipper, Paradox, Informix, SQL-Server, etc. etc. etc. After 20 years there aren't many on the list left to try now.

Helmut specializes in database analysis and GUI design and runs a consultancy called "Nearly Everything" from his home in Essex, England.

Known as Woof! to his friends (or anyone else who buys him a beer) he is a keen cyclist and a finalist in the 2000 British Marbles-on-Sand championships. Most people think he's a bit odd until they meet him – then they're sure!

Table of Contents

Table of Contents

Table of Contents

Introduction

Microsoft Access has generated a large following among developers seeking to build powerful, easy-to-use, cost effective database solutions and applications. Traditionally these applications have been aimed towards the small or medium sized business, or restricted size applications in larger organizations. The advent of Access 2000 has changed the development landscape – while the default database engine is still Jet, Access 2000 developers now have the option of using a feature called Access projects, and either using the Microsoft Data Engine (MSDE), which is now distributed with Access 2000, or even a SQL Server database (the Microsoft database engine for enterprise applications).

The MSDE is effectively a scaled down (optimized for supporting 5 users) version of SQL Server – it can be distributed freely, is compatible with SQL Server and is a great tool for developing client-server applications. Significantly the use of Access projects in conjunction with the MSDE represents a great way of building solutions which start small, have a well known and familiar front-end, but can easily be scaled up into a larger and more sophisticated database when the need arises.

Access projects present a superb route for Access developers to make a transition to working with SQL Server engines and effectively migrating their skill set. Conversely experienced SQL Server developers may wish to make use of the rapid application development features of Access and Access projects for quickly demonstrating aspects of their database.

This book will give you a great grounding in the use of Access projects with MSDE or SQL Server 7.0, and will introduce SQL Server 2000. It will address both core constituencies of Access project users – the Access developer wishing to migrate to SQL Server, and the SQL Server developer looking to make use of Access.

Regardless of the niceties of the design, one of the most crucial aspects of database solutions is their ability to deliver to the user the required data in a suitable format. The development of distributed computing and the Internet has meant new technologies must be leveraged to meet new user demands. Access 2000 both offers new features, such as data access pages, and tight integration with the FrontPage 2000 Web development tool to rise to these challenges. In the latter part of the book this subject area will be fully covered enabling you to employ the latest approaches in the provision of application functionality.

Who Should Read this Book

This book is a *Professional...* series book, and thus isn't aimed at the novice Access 2000 user. Indeed as we discussed above, we think that most readers will be either intermediate to advanced Access developers, with a grasp of VBA coding and SQL, looking to build scalable solutions with a MSDE/SQL Server database, or SQL Server developers or administrators looking to rapidly build accessible user interfaces. In both cases you'll be looking to dig into the features of

Access 2000 projects, and maybe also use more advanced Access 2000 features for delivering data over the Web.

As you'll see from the rear cover, this book forms the link in a Wrox learning tree and we would expect you to be reasonably conversant with the type of topics covered in *Professional Access 2000 Programming* (*ISBN 1-861004-08-7*), while this book will give you a good foundation for moving on to *Professional SQL Server 7.0 Programming* (*ISBN 1-861002-31-9*).

How to Get the Most from this Book

The detailed software requirements for building getting the most out of the book are outlined in Chapter 1, which we advise looking at before going much further, but as a short list we suggest:

- ❑ Either Windows NT 4.0 (SP 4 or greater) with the Windows NT 4.0 Option Pack, or Windows 2000 (Windows 9x users with the Windows NT 4.0 Option Pack can easily use the book, but have restricted options)
- ❑ A copy of Access 2000 as distributed through Office 2000
- ❑ A copy of MSDE (available with Access 2000), or a copy of SQL Server 7.0 or SQL Server 2000
- ❑ A copy of FrontPage 2000

The Windows NT 4 Option Pack can be ordered (or downloaded free) from Microsoft's web site at http://www.microsoft.com/ntserver/nts/downloads/recommended/NT4OptPk/default.asp. A downloadable evaluation version of SQL Server 7.0 is available at http://www.microsoft.com/sql/productinfo/evalcd.htm.

What's Covered in this Book

To start the book, in **Chapter 1** we introduce the idea of Access projects and look at how this feature in Access 2000 fits into the various models of application development. To set the book in context we then revise and review some of the underlying concepts in relational database development, and comment on the products and technologies we'll working with. Throughout the book we'll be making substantial use of T-SQL, VBA and ADO, ASP, and SQL-DMO to interact with databases – in many places comparing and contrasting the options and possibilities each of these offers.

Chapter 2 looks at the installation issues surrounding the various database engines (MSDE, SQL Server 7.0, and SQL Server 2000) that we have the choice of using Access 2000 projects with. From there we introduce and review the utilities these products have, before finally moving on to opening up an Access project and familiarizing ourselves with the interface we are presented with.

In **Chapter 3** we start delving into using Access projects to manipulate and handle databases. The primary goal for the chapter is to discuss the design, creation, and manipulation of tables. Straight off in the chapter we'll see the increased flexibility and sophistication of MSDE/SQL

Server engines over the Jet engine, with the increased variety of data types on offer. This is the first point at which we get stuck into using T-SQL, ADO with VBA, and SQL-DMO. This is a substantial chapter and we follow it with the slightly lighter (and more visually based) **Chapter 4** where we discuss database diagrams.

We return to looking at database objects in **Chapter 5** where we look at views and **Chapter 6**, which covers stored procedures. Both of these chapters will serve to deepen our knowledge of T-SQL, both in the area of query development and programming using variables.

The focus changes slightly from the database engine towards the user in **Chapter 7** where the use of Access forms within Access projects is looked at, and in **Chapter 8** where Access reports are highlighted. This represents familiar ground for the Access developer, but here we need to discuss the features in the context of interaction with a new database engine. For those familiar with SQL Server databases it will provide an insight into how to use Access 2000 as a rapid application development tool.

While staying with the issues surrounding presentation of data to the user, the spotlight turns towards the Web in the next three chapters – **Chapter 9** covers publishing datasheets, while **Chapter 10** investigates creating forms with ASP. Here we'll start to stray into the area of programming for the Web and we'll be looking at using Microsoft FrontPage as a development tool alongside Access 2000. These chapters will show just how easy it is for Access developers to leverage their skills in a new arena. To round off the section we'll talk about another new feature in **Chapter 11**; data access pages which present, for certain environments, a convenient way of developing highly functional Web based applications.

Finally, in **Chapter 12**, the main body of the book ends with a round-up of some of the programming approaches that developers working with Access projects may well find useful, but didn't fall into the main thrust of our coverage.

That's not all though, because we have a number of appendices that provide useful reference material to support the main material:

- ❑ **Appendix A** covers aspects of SQL Server security
- ❑ **Appendix B** provides a detailed look at the issues surrounding moving Access Jet engine database solutions up to a MSDE/SQL Server installation
- ❑ **Appendix C** shows two ways in which databases can be copied between installations
- ❑ **Appendix D** provides background information for the Web-oriented chapters as here we'll provide a reference section on the creation of DSNs
- ❑ **Appendix E** further complements the Web section by giving background information on using files for logging information
- ❑ **Appendix F** gives a reference to the objects, methods, and properties present in the ADO 2.1 object model.

Conventions Used

You are going to encounter different styles as you are reading through this book. This has been done to help you easily identify different types of information and to help you keep from missing any key points. These styles are:

> **Important information, key points, and additional explanations are displayed like this to make them stand out. Be sure to pay attention to these when you find them.**

General notes, background information, and brief asides look like this.

❑ Keys that you press on the keyboard, like *Ctrl* and *Delete*, are displayed in italics

❑ If you see something like, `BackupDB`, you'll know that it is a filename, or function name

❑ Names of objects in Access projects or SQL Server databases, such as database names like pubs, or table names like Categories are displayed as shown here

❑ The first time you encounter an **important word**, it is displayed in bold text

❑ Words that appear on the screen, such as menu options, are in a similar font to the one used on screen, for example, the File menu

This is how code samples look the first time they are introduced:

```
Private Sub Command_Click
    MsgBox "Don't touch me"
End Sub
```

Whereas code that you've already seen, or that doesn't relate directly to the point being made, looks like this:

```
Private Sub Command_Click
    MsgBox "Don't touch me"
End Sub
```

Customer Support

We want to know what you think about this book: what you liked, what you didn't like, and what you think we can do better next time. You can send your comments, either by returning the reply card in the back of the book, or by e-mail (to feedback@wrox.com). Please be sure to mention the book title in your message.

Source Code

Full source code for the sample databases and associated code used in this book, can be downloaded from the Wrox web site at: http://www.wrox.com.

Errata

We've made every effort to make sure that there are no errors in the text or the code. However, to err is human, and as such we recognize the need to keep you informed of any mistakes as they're spotted and corrected. Errata sheets are available for all our books at www.wrox.com. If you find an error that hasn't already been reported, please let us know.

P2P.WROX.COM

For author and peer support we have a number of mailing lists you may find useful. Our unique system provides **programmer to programmer™ support** on mailing lists, forums and newsgroups, all *in addition* to our one-to-one e-mail system. Be confident that your query is not just being examined by a support professional, but by the many Wrox authors and other industry experts present on our mailing lists. At p2p.wrox.com you'll two different lists specifically aimed at developers working with the SQL language and SQL Server databases that will support you, not only while you read this book, but also as you start to develop your own applications.

To enroll for support just follow this four-step system:

1. Go to p2p.wrox.com.

2. Click on the SQL button.

3. Click on the type of mailing list you wish to join.

4. Fill in your e-mail address and password (of at least 4 characters) and e-mail it to us.

We are constantly adding to the number of lists as demand grows – we suggest you keep an eye out for new lists that may help you in your development efforts.

Why this System Offers the Best Support

You can choose to join the mailing lists or you can receive them as a weekly digest. If you don't have the time, or facility, to receive the mailing list, then you can search our online archives. Junk and spam mails are deleted, and your own e-mail address is protected. Any queries about joining or leaving lists, or any other queries about the list, should be sent to listsupport@p2p.wrox.com.

1

Access 2000 and SQL Server

Microsoft Access has, over its various versions, proved itself to be a powerful, user-friendly product for delivering database solutions. The latest version – Access 2000 – presents a number of exciting new features to developers, and the primary aim of this book is to highlight one of these features: the use of **Access projects** to build custom SQL Server solutions. Access projects are a new file type introduced with Access 2000 that facilitate SQL Server data definition tasks, and the integration of SQL Server database objects, such as tables, with Access objects, such as forms.

Previous versions of Access only used the Jet database engine; however, Access 2000 allows users to choose between the default Jet engine and the **Microsoft Data Engine** (**MSDE**). This latter engine is essentially a "cut down" version of SQL Server – it is optimized to support 5 users, can be freely distributed, and is a great tool for developing small user base **client-server** applications. Importantly, since the MSDE is compatible with SQL Server 7.0, applications developed with MSDE can be easily upgraded to an environment suitable for handling large amounts of data and substantial numbers of users.

> This book will discuss the use of Access 2000 with three SQL Server versions – the MSDE, SQL Server 7.0, and SQL Server 2000. At the time of writing SQL Server 2000 was moving from beta testing to the release candidate stage. It is possible there may be some differences between the details of SQL Server 2000 presented in the book and the final version.

As the Internet becomes ever more important, the need for applications to be Web-enabled is increased; a second purpose of this book is to show how Access 2000 can be used to deliver information over the Internet both by using the new feature of **data access pages**, and to introduce other Web technologies like **Active Server Pages** (**ASP**).

The aim of this chapter is to prepare you for building SQL Server solutions with Access 2000 and as such the main areas this chapter will cover are:

❑ Different models of Access and SQL Server solutions – client-server models, n-tier architectures and the Internet

❑ A quick review many of the basic ideas behind relational databases

❑ A summary of the technologies we'll encounter of the course of the book

❑ The software requirements for making best use of this book

We'll encounter far more about the various relational database concepts and the software technologies as we progress through the book and this chapter is just aimed at quickly introducing or revising the terminology.

Before we go any further, let's highlight who we think may benefit from building SQL Server solutions via Access 2000.

❑ Why Develop SQL Server (looking either to move onto building scalable solutions or progress their skill set), the tight integration between Access 2000 and SQL Server means they can quickly, and easily, start to build solutions. For example, with the AutoForm wizard, developers can build an Access form based on a SQL Server table with a single click. So, if you've previously worked solely with Jet-based solutions, you now have the opportunity to build more scalable solutions while still retaining some of the familiar Access objects, such as forms, reports, and modules.

❑ SQL Server administrators will find many rapid application development tools in Access 2000 to help them make their databases more useful to their clients.

As we'll show over the course of this book, Access project functionality enables the easy development of interesting, cost effective business solutions. In addition, the tight integration between Access 2000 and the FrontPage 2000 Web development tool means that Access 2000 developers can move easily on to building Web based solutions using the functionality available through Access projects. Furthermore, Access developers conversant with VBA will find it relatively straightforward to develop more sophisticated Web applications utilizing **Active Server Page** (**ASP**) technology.

Now, let's move on to putting Access 2000 solutions into perspective.

Application Architecture

This book concerns the use of Access 2000 in conjunction with SQL Server and, over the course of the book, we'll move from looking at solutions that could potentially be based on one computer through to Internet oriented applications – **distributed** applications involving more than one computer.

We'll begin with the most basic application.

Single-Tier Architecture

Traditionally, most Access solutions tended to have one or only a few users. The Access database tended to sit on a local machine where the Access forms and modules directly accessed the data and all the forms and code were in the actual Access database itself:

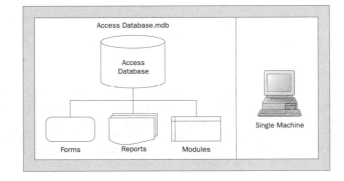

As you can see, the whole solution is within the Access .mdb database. All the code for the **presentation layer** (the interface the user interacts with), and the **business logic** (the code that implements the business rules associated with the application such as data validation, data processing, and so on) is contained in the same Access project and there are no separate modules or code held outside of this project.

There may be some separation of code to perform business functions placed into modules; however, it is still contained within the Access database. All data access is also within the database and the whole solution is self-contained. Access is the perfect vehicle for single-tier solutions and a single tier is perfect for small applications with only one or a few users, where the data is held locally with no need for any interaction with any data or processes outside the module, and the solution is relatively straightforward and not too complex.

Once we start to consider a network of machines we start to consider forms of distributed computing; the simplest example being the **client/server** or **two-tier** architecture.

Two-Tier Architecture

A two-tier architecture enables the presentation layer to be located on a client computer with the data (termed the data layer or tier) located separately. If the business logic is bundled with the presentation code on the client we have a so-called **fat** client (also called **thick** or **rich** client), whereas if it resides on the server, with the data, we have a so-called **thin** client.

> *It's worth noting that the tiers we refer to are logical not physical – thus both tiers (the client part and the server part) may reside physically on the same machine although normally they would be on different units.*

This brings us on to a difference between using the standard Access 2000/Jet data engine combination and using Access 2000 projects with MSDE/SQL Server. The first allows the formation of a file-server architecture whereas the second gives a client/server architecture. Let's examine the difference.

File-Server Architecture

In this system the Access database is split into two separate databases:

❑   A back-end database file that holds just tables and data for the database solution

❏   A front-end database file that includes queries, forms, and reports that link to the back-end database – a copy of this file must be placed onto each client workstation

When a user performs data access, their front-end query requests data from the back-end file. The processing of the back-end database takes place on the user's workstation, thus if a query retrieves 100,000 records all of these would be sent across the network to the client. If there are several clients attempting to query the database at the same time, among other problems, network traffic may become intolerable.

This architecture may be set up by splitting a database via the Access database splitter wizard.

Client/Server Architecture

When Access 2000 builds a solution with Access projects and a MSDE or SQL Server database, it switches to a client/server database model. With this approach, each client has an Access project file with an `.adp` extension (rather then the usual `.mdb` extension for the Access database file). The Access project issues a request to the database server (namely, SQL Server with Access projects) and receives a reply from it. In this scenario, however, the data processing is carried out on the server, and only the results of the request are returned to the client.

This brings a number of important benefits:

❏   Network traffic is reduced

❏   The superior computing resources of a server machine can be leveraged efficiently

❏   A more sophisticated SQL Server based database can be developed – for instance SQL Server has a more sophisticated query processor, and can handle larger volumes of data and more concurrent users as well as having more advance recovery and security features

This book is concerned with the client/server (and more complex architectures discussed below) and we won't be discussing the pros and cons of database splitting. Generally Access projects may be thought of as giving fat client applications.

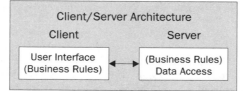

Now that the data is split from the application, giving a two-tier architecture, you could consider breaking out the business logic into a separate logical tier giving a **three-tier** architecture. This moves us away from Access projects but will serve as a lead into considering Internet based applications.

Three-Tier and N-Tier Architectures

In a three-tier application the presentation layer is on the client, the data resides on the database server and the logic concerning business rules is built into a separate layer, which could potentially reside on a different machine again. The tiers still work in the same way – the client obtains data from the database *via* the business logic. Here, however the business tier has the opportunity to manage database access for multiple clients so enhancing the scalability, flexibility, and efficiency of the application. Thus, in this layer there is now logic governing both the precise business rules and the operation of the application.

Another benefit of this type of architecture is that the tasks involved in developing the application can be logically sub-divided and code relating to different tasks can be localized in one place. Thus, if the business rules change only code in one tier needs changing without any requirement for the presentation layer and database to be affected. The business logic may be contained in COM components coded in a language such as Visual Basic or C++ : development of business tier components lies outside the scope of this book. As but this architecture won't be specifically considered furhter.

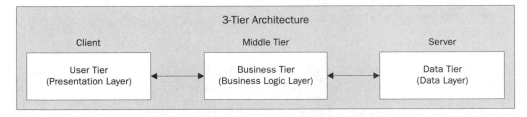

Of course this approach can be extended – further sub-division of the business logic into different units may leads to an **n-tier** architecture. Distributed computing is now extremely common due to the Internet and some of the really exciting material found later in this book shows how Access can be used to develop Internet based applications.

Internet Applications

In an Internet application, information is presented to the client via a browser running HTML or scripts. As we'll see later there are several ways in which Access can be used in this context:

- ❑ **Datasheets** can be published giving either static or dynamic information via a browser
- ❑ **Data access pages** may be used to allow the client to interact with the database
- ❑ **Active Server Page** (**ASP**) technology can also be employed to allow dynamic interaction with a database

All these different approaches fit into the 2-, 3-, and n-tier models of application architecture in slightly different ways, for example data access pages involve processing on the client side, while the use of ASP technology involves a browser invoking processing on a web server that will then access the database. This might sound confusing at the moment, but all will become clear as we explain the approaches in more detail later.

We'll be using another Microsoft product – FrontPage 2000 – to aid us in our development of Web based information delivery. As we'll see in later chapters this tool can help us deliver advanced solutions without a great deal of coding effort.

Relational Databases

As developers you'll already have a considerable knowledge and awareness of relational database management and design issues on which to draw. But since this book is bringing together two separate database technologies, we're going to run through a brief revision of the fundamental terminology of relational databases, from the perspective of a SQL Server database, to get up to speed before we actually get down to building SQL Server solutions with Access projects.

As a basis for this summary we're going to look at:

- ❑ Structured Query Language (SQL)
- ❑ The constituents of a SQL Server database such as tables, views, and stored procedures
- ❑ Aspects of database design like entities, relationships, and normalization
- ❑ Miscellaneous related topics like replication and security

SQL

Structured Query Language (**SQL**) was born out of the development, at IBM, of relational database design theory in the late 1960s and has become the industry standard language for creating, querying, and maintaining databases. The specification for the language has been defined by the American National Standards Institute (ANSI), with the most recent version being known as ANSI SQL-92.

This language can be used with all major databases like SQL Server and Oracle; however, these products support features that go beyond those in the standard specification, and thus use their own slightly enhanced versions of SQL (although as they meet the basic ANSI SQL-92 standards they are termed **entry level SQL 92 compliant**). The proprietary extension of ANSI SQL-92 used by Microsoft in SQL Server is called **Transact-SQL** (**T-SQL**).

Microsoft has leant towards ANSI SQL-92 as its standard in Jet based databases, and although a few features aren't supported, Access 2000 more closely supports ANSI-92 than any previous version of Access.

Throughout the book, our approach will be to introduce SQL statements and functions as we need them. We'll first encounter them in detail in Chapter 3 where we'll use T-SQL to create, populate, and modify tables.

Database Fundamentals

For the Access developer working with SQL Server we need to consider the following:

- ❑ Tables
- ❑ Stored Procedures
- ❑ Views
- ❑ Diagrams

Tables

Tables are the fundamental building blocks of any relational database system whether it be an Access database, a SQL Server database, or an Oracle one.

Access tables are very easy to build, and give a wide range of functionality. There is even some in built intelligence once a table is built that prompts the developer if they don't define a key. There are, however, differences between tables in Access and SQL Server – this will be discussed in detail in Chapter 3, which discusses all aspects of table handling; here we'll just briefly highlight some of the main aspects of tables and highlight one obvious difference between Access and SQL Server.

Data Types

When defining a table one of the first tasks is to set the data type for a column. In Access, a `text` defined field covered every occasion when you wanted to hold any sort of character string, whereas in SQL Server there is a choice six data types giving a considerable amount of flexibility. The first two data types are `char` and `nchar`. They are both very similar, with the exception that `nchar` holds the Unicode representation of the contents of the field, rather than the ASCII. `Char` and `nchar` are directly related to the Access `text` data type. The field is of fixed length and can hold any alphanumeric character. However, `varchar` and `nvarchar` will probably be used more. These data types are very much like `char` and `nchar`, in that they have a maximum length that the field can be.

Where they gain their usefulness, is in their ability to save space if the contents of the field doesn't reach that maximum length. If the field is defined as 50 characters long, but only 20 are used, then 30 bytes are saved on that field for that record. Over a large number of records, where an average space saving is 30 characters, you could save a lot of space, and hence reduce backup times. `Text` and `ntext` are exactly like `varchar` and `nvarchar`, but don't have the 8000 character limit of `varchar`. Thess data types are usually used to hold very large amounts of data, up to 2GB.

Identifying Rows

In Access, the AutoNumber field is generally used to define each row in a table uniquely. Each time a new record is created, it is given a new and unique number, almost like a record counter. The equivalent within SQL Server is the **Identity** column property. The starting point for the numbering is set by a **seed** value and increases for each row by an **increment**. For example, you could get a row identity to start at 5000 and increment in multiples of any number you wish. In Access, you are restricted that the increment is in single units.

An alternative possibility in SQL Server is to assign the row a **Globally Unique Identifier** (**GUID**). GUIDs are 128 bit values, generated using a combination of information, which are statistically guaranteed to be globally unique (as opposed to identity values that are just unique within the table).

By ensuring your record is unique you can enforce entity integrity for a particular table, and so ensure that records that have to be unique remain so.

NULLs, Defaults and Check Constraints

To indicate an indeterminate value in a row the special value termed **NULL** maybe used. For example, a column in a table containing personal information about customers may have a number of columns for data (such as gender) that may only be optionally volunteered by the customer. In the case that the gender of the customer is unknown a NULL value may be attributed to the column. As NULL represents an unknown value then NULL values are not equal to each other or any non-NULL value. Columns in SQL Server have to be specifically allowed to contain NULL values.

Instead of allowing NULL values there are occasions when it is felt preferable to use a default value for a field that has no data – for instance, in the above example a default of "Unknown gender" could be used if the customer didn't elaborate. In addition to what may be termed **default constraints** there are also **check constraints** that can be used to restrict the data that a field in a table can accept. These constraints allow some form of data validation and are analogous to placing a validation rule on a field in Access.

Primary Keys and Foreign Keys

The **primary key** of a table identifies the column(s) of the table whose values *uniquely* identify a row (and thus cannot be NULL). The use of primary keys allows references to a row to be made from another table in the database – so allowing relationships between data to be set up.

Implementing relationships between tables involves using **foreign keys** – a foreign key is a column (or set of columns) in one table that references the primary key of another table.

These relationships help (alongside the constraints and data types we've just discussed) to ensure **data integrity**, for instance ensuring that, in a database containing customer information, if the tables holding the customer personal details (name, address etc.) and customer credit details (store card number, credit limit) are different, each row containing card numbers is always associated with a customer name and address (in other words there are no records of card numbers without a name to go with them), and that the store card fields hold valid card numbers.

The use of foreign keys in setting up table relationships implements what is termed **declarative referential integrity** (**DRI**), – in SQL Server 7.0 DRI does not support **cascading** updates or deletes and **triggers** (see below) have to be used. A cascading delete is when a deletion made in one table automatically causes deletion of dependent information in other tables.

Another type of key is the **alternate key** – these are also known as **UNIQUE constraints**. These are much like primary keys in that if a UNIQUE constraint is applied to a column (or columns), then every entry in the column must be unique. However, unlike a primary key, there can be more than one UNIQUE constraint per table and that column (or columns) doesn't act as *the* unique identifier for the table.

Triggers

There are times when manipulating (inserting, deleting, or updating) rows in a database, it's useful to get something else to happen automatically. For example, when changing a row it may be necessary to copy some information about that change to an audit trail, or to enable changes made in one table to be cascaded to another.

This can be achieved by using a **trigger** – SQL code that is attached to the table and executes when the appropriate action occurs. Access doesn't have triggers as such, without you having to program them explicitly; SQL Server on the other hand, is very adept at using triggers. Indeed triggers themselves can be used to enforce referential integrity – in this case termed **code-based referential integrity**.

We'll look at triggers in more detail in Chapter 6.

Indexes

An **index** is used in a relational database to provide fast access to data in the rows of a table. Indexes work like the index does in the back of, say, an encyclopedia – it's faster to look up a subject in the index than trawl through the entire book trying to find it. There are two types of index, **clustered** and **non-clustered**, which order the information they hold in different ways – this leads to different benefits and drawbacks for a production database.

Stored Procedures

A **stored procedure** is an ordered series of T-SQL statements collected into a unit that is precompiled and stored as part of the database. Stored procedures can accept parameters as input, perform logical decisions, call other stored procedures, and return a value or a set of results, if required. Programming languages like Visual Basic, C++, VBA, or many others can be used as the starting point for calling a stored procedure, or, as quite often happens, one stored procedure can call another, and so allow good code reuse. Indeed to perform many administrative tasks SQL Server comes with a large number of ready coded stored procedures – **system stored procedures**.

Stored procedures are tremendously powerful and Chapter 6 is devoted to covering them in detail.

Views

As you become more adept at using SQL Server, and as your application expands, security of your data will become more and more of an issue. There will be situations where the business demands are such that the viewing of certain parts of a table's content should be restricted (such as when you have a table containing employees' details and wish to hide salary information).

Views are one solution to this problem. A view can be thought of as a virtual table in that it may behave like a table but doesn't actually contain any data itself. As we'll find in Chapter 5, they represent stored queries managed by the database engine and are comparable to Access queries and querydefs.

An additional benefit of views, apart from security, is that they can be used to improve efficiency by only delivering to the user the information they need.

Diagrams

Database diagrams are graphical representations of the underlying structure of the database and can be used to show the relationships between tables (as well as the design of the tables themselves). They can be especially useful during database design, and may be used as part of the documentation of a database. Additionally, they present a convenient visual route into database modification. We discuss the use of database diagrams in Chapter 4.

Aspects of Database Design

When designing a database we can easily identify two distinct phases – the **logical design** and the **physical design**. The logical design stage is the concept stage, where the constituents of the scenario being addressed are identified as **entities**, which have properties and can be related to each other. The physical design stage involves translation of the logical design into a relational database design.

Let's dig into this a bit further and look at entities, relationships, and normalization.

Entities

An **entity** is any person, place, object, or concept for which data will be collected. Entities have **attributes** that define the characteristics of the entity and will have **identifiers** that allow them to be uniquely identified. Interactions between entities are described by **relationships**. In the physical design entities become tables, attributes map to fields (columns), and relationships map to relationships. The unique identifier of an entity is a primary key.

So, returning to the example of a table containing employee details – in the original logical design employees were identified as entities that data was going to be collected about, and fields such as first name, last name, social security number, telephone number, etc. were identified as attributes describing the entities. In the case of such a table, since a social security number uniquely identifies a person, that attribute would make a good candidate for becoming the primary key of the table.

The relationships that the employees table may be involved in depend on the other tables; let's now look at relationships in more detail.

Relationships

No matter how large or how small the database you are building, there must be at least one relationship between two tables within it, otherwise, it is just a collection of unrelated data.

A relationship can be defined as a link in between data in two tables, where the link is a mutual connection of information.

For example if there are 2 tables in a database containing a field that holds the ID of a customer, then a relationship could, and probably does, exist between these 2 tables. In a database relationships are links between tables where the foreign key of one table maps to the primary key of another.

There are three types of relationship to consider:

- ❑ One-to-one
- ❑ One-to-many
- ❑ Many-to-many

One-to-one Relationship

A **one-to-one** relationship is the easiest relationship to understand, although probably the least used within databases. This is where one record in one table has a single matching record in another table.

One potential scenario for a one-to-one relationship is in dividing the information held about customers into frequently and infrequently used data. So the MainCustomerDetails table may contain details like name, address, and phone number, while the InfrequentCustomerDetails table may hold details about when the customer opened a credit account and the amount of money they spent at the store last month. Splitting the data like this could allow better management of data and improved database performance by ensuring tables aren't carrying extraneous data.

We can represent a one-to-one relationship by:

One-to-many Relationship

One-to-many relationships are the most common type within a database. This is when one record in one table, is related to no one, or many records in a second table. There are several well documented scenarios in many books, so let's take the banking system situation where a main (or **parent**) table, called CustomerDetails, is related to a second (**child**) table, called Transactions. The parent/child definition demonstrates to a developer which table controls which other table, and in the logical structure, which table, the parent, sits topmost.

The CustomerDetails table has fields BankAccountNumber, CustomerName, BranchCode, and CurrentBalance. The Transaction table has fields BankAccountNumber, TransactionType, Date, Reference, and Amount. There will of course, only be one customer record; however, as each regular payment, or cash withdrawal takes place, a transaction record is created.

So, for any given customer one set of customer details will be linked to many transactions, unless of course they are a brand new account holder who has made just the one transaction, or hasn't made any transactions. Thus the relationship encapsulates the whole range of possibilities.

One-to-many relationships can be represented by:

Many-to-many Relationship

Many-to-many relationships are less frequent, but still common within most database applications. A many-to-many relationship occurs when each record in a table may be associated with one or more records in another table, and that each record of the latter table may be associated with one or more records in the former table.

Let's consider the well-known situation of a publishing house keeping track of it's output in a database. If author details are kept in one table and title details are kept in another we have a classic many-to-many relationship. One author may be linked to one, or several different titles, while any given title may have been written by multiple authors. The veracity of such an observation can easily be checked by looking at a shelf full of Wrox books.

A many-to-many relationship, is depicted:

However since these relationships can't be physically created in a database, many-to-many relationships are resolved into two one-to-many relationships by creating a new table called a **link entity** (or **junction table**) containing the primary keys from each of the involved tables. We'll come across this in Chapter 4.

After we've developed a logical design, to ensure it's optimal we'll need to consider refining it via the process of normalization.

Normalization

We can summarize **normalization** as the process of eliminating duplicated data from the database by refining tables, columns, and relationships to create a consistent database design. The process of normalization via refining data through different **normal forms** should lead to an optimum database design with little chance of data integrity being compromised and addition of data being handled in the best possible manner.

We won't go into normalization in detail here, but will just remind you that generally database designers stop refining their design after getting their tables into **third normal form** (**3NF**) and indeed may actually **denormalize** some tables for specific reasons to improve database performance and usability or decrease database complexity.

Just to revise the first three normal forms, we have:

❏ **First normal form** (**1NF**) – each column should store only one value (not a list), all the data in the table should be related and there should be no duplicate rows so a primary key may be assigned. There should be no repeating attributes in multiple columns – repeating data groups need to be moved to another table.

❏ **Second normal form** (**2NF**) – a table is in 2NF if it is in 1NF *and* every non-key column is fully dependent on the entire primary key.

❏ **Third normal form** (**3NF**) – a table is in 3NF if it is in 2NF *and* all non-key columns are mutually independent.

Miscellaneous Topics

While we've discussed many general and practical aspects of databases there are two administrative topics that we still need to cover:

❏ Replication

❏ Security

Replication

We won't be discussing **replication** in this book in any great detail, although the topic is alluded to occasionally. Replication is the process of creating and maintaining one or more copies of a master database on different computers.

Replication becomes essential where there are issues about having distributed data. One such example of where replication is important is where a traveling salesperson needs to have access to a copy of a company database that can both be queried and updated. The salesperson can carry a local copy of the database on a portable computer and, to ensure data consistency within the company, use replication techniques to communicate any changes they make to the local database back to the central database. At the same time they can receive changes that have been made to the central database.

It should be noted, however, that SQL Server has a different replication model from Access.

Security

Paying attention to database security is crucial to ensuring that the data stored is kept safe, that it isn't modified without appropriate permission, and that unauthorized personnel aren't allowed to access sensitive information. Our discussion of SQL Server security is deferred to Appendix A where we'll take an in-depth look at **logins** (account names that can access the server), **users** (account names that can access a database), **roles** (collections of rights that users have assigned to them – a user may belong to one or more roles) and **permissions** (what actions certain roles may perform).

Now we've revised and maybe even introduced a few database terms, let's turn our attention to the various technologies we'll be using throughout the book.

Technologies

In this section we'll briefly discuss the following:

❏ Visual Basic for Applications (VBA)

❏   ActiveX Data Objects (ADO)

❏   SQL Distributed Management Objects (SQL-DMO)

❏   Active Server Pages (ASP)

As with T-SQL, this book doesn't aim to provide a definitive guide to any of these technologies (indeed Wrox Press has books devoted specifically to each of the subjects), but aims to show how they can be used to perform typical tasks in the context of Access projects and SQL Server databases. In some cases we'll show how tasks can be accomplished with a variety of approaches using different technologies.

Visual Basic for Applications (VBA)

VBA is the programming language used in all Office products including Access and allows us to extend the scope of our Access projects. We'll be encountering a lot of VBA, in conjunction with the other technologies in this section, as we look at programmatically controlling our databases.

Within the book we'll show how to use VBA to manipulate Access objects, such as forms, reports, and their controls in Access projects alongside database access. VBA is not restricted to just the data within a table, as we'll see when we look in detail at stored procedures and see how to find out what columns and structures are returned from data in a stored procedure.

Since VBA is used in all Office products we'll be also be using it in FrontPage 2000 when we look at publishing datasheets onto the Web.

ActiveX Data Objects (ADO)

ADO is the current Microsoft data access technology standard for accessing data through **ODBC** (**Open Database Connectivity**) or **OLE DB** providers. It provides the developer with a common interface to data, no matter what the provider of the data to the application. For example, if you had an Access poject that was accessing SQL Server data via ADO, and you decided to move to Oracle, the only code changes would be to the connection to the database, and to the data provider. All the calls to stored procedures, SQL statements, etc, would remain the same.

It's worthwhile taking a step back and putting ADO in perspective. Before ADO came along, Access developers (or Visual Basic developers accessing a Jet database), would, and some may even still, use a technology called **Data Access Objects** (**DAO**) as the method for retrieving information. Then Microsoft brought along **Remote Data Objects**, (**RDO**) which was designed specifically for accessing data on remote servers, but also as an eventual replacement for DAO. However, RDO from an Access developer's viewpoint is not a good choice of data extraction (and hence many may not have come across it) as RDO goes through all the relevant data access of DAO, as well as its own data layer.

Both DAO and RDO sit on top of ODBC. ODBC was designed to access relational data, and either didn't have any methods to access any other data, or made use of complex and cumbersome methods. For example, to use ODBC to access a flat file (like a .txt file), you have to define what each column is, its (limited) data type and length, and whether the data is comma or tab delimited.

By the late nineties, it was clear that developers wanted a common interface to retrieve data, and did not want to limit themselves to Microsoft databases, and furthermore also wanted to be able to access data on other platforms, for example, data on a mainframe, or Web-based information.

To allow access to non-relational data, OLE DB was released and with it ADO, which provides an interface between languages like VB and OLE DB. As the diagram overleaf shows we could consider OLE DB to be the glue that binds ADO and the data together.

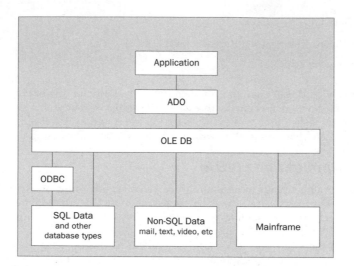

An OLE DB **provider** is required for each specific data source, and so if you moved an application from a SQL Server database to an Oracle one, you would need to change the data provider, ADO would need to point to an OLE DB provider for Oracle, and no longer need to point to an OLE DB provider for SQL Server. Having the data access commands separate from the actual data access itself, allows programmers to ensure that their code is as close to 100% transportable as possible.

There are ADO samples throughout the book – in the chapters on tables, views, and stored procedures, ADO facilitates data definition or manipulation tasks. ADO can be used to link Access objects, such as forms and reports, with data sources as well as returning data for web pages.

As the diagram below shows, ADO has a very simple object model, and a reference to the objects and collections is provided in Appendix F.

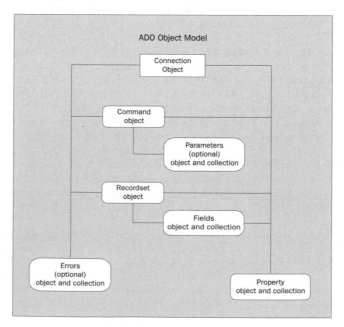

For the moment let's highlight the three objects we'll use most frequently:

- ❑ The Connection object represents a connection to a data source. When that data source is the Access project, ADO provides a very simple syntax for designating the connection string (as discussed Chapter 3). However, when SQL Server is being used with Web servers, another connection string syntax is especially convenient (as seen in Chapter 10).

- ❑ The Recordset object is used for manipulating the data returned from an OLE DB provider.

- ❑ The Command object is used for passing queries or data (or database) manipulation commands to the database.

More advanced uses of VBA and ADO are covered in Chapter 12.

SQL Distributed Management Objects (SQL-DMO)

SQL-DMO is an object model for SQL Server database and replication management (*not* data access). Each and every SQL Server object, database object, and so forth is represented by, and can be manipulated through, SQL-DMO objects. For example the tables of any given SQL Server database are accessible via the SQL-DMO Tables collection. Each table in this collection has collections and objects representing all its components and attributes such as column definitions, constraints, keys, and triggers.

A moment's reflection on the composition of a database may lead you to the, correct, conclusion that the SQL-DMO object model is rather large – it contains 60 different objects and over 1000 different properties and methods. Accordingly, as we use SQL-DMO (in relation to tables, views, and stored procedures), only the particularly relevant objects will be discussed. These snippets will, however, give you a fair flavor of how to use SQL-DMO in the context of Access projects.

Active Server Pages (ASP)

ASP technology is used to create and run interactive web applications built on server-side scripting. It works on the principle of building an HTML template for a page into which VBScript (or JavaScript) functionality is embedded. This functionality can be used to perform a variety of tasks including data access and manipulation (maybe via COM components) and the results are used to dynamically generate more HTML, which is returned to the browser requesting the page.

As ASP is processed at the server, rather than the client, this leads to two huge benefits:

- ❑ The script that is processed on the server is not returned to the client and thus sensitive data (such as connection strings to databases) can be kept secure.

- ❑ The HTML that is returned will be compatible with different sorts of browser.

Of course as the ASP page outputs HTML to the browser there is always the opportunity for embedding client side-script in the page as well giving the flexibility to execute client side.

We'll be considering ASP in more detail in Chapters 9 and 10 when publishing data to the Web is covered.

So the obvious question before we actually get started, is which database engine should I plump for?

Software Requirements

To use this book there are a number of possibilities depending on the precise Windows operating system you're running. Basically, you'll need either Windows 9x, NT 4.0 (with Service Pack 4), or Windows 2000 operating system and a copy of Access 2000 as distributed through Office 2000, which will make a MSDE available. As detailed below, to gain full benefit from the chapters devoted to publishing data on the Web, FrontPage 2000 and Web Server software will be required.

As we've previously mentioned, we do have choices to make about the database we choose to connect to and let's explore these before discussing other software requirements and the approach we take to sample code.

Database Engines

All three of the database engines we explore in this book – SQL Server 7, SQL Server 2000, and MSDE – are attractive since SQL Server 7.0 and MSDE are highly compatible. All of them are programmed with the same SQL syntax and it's straightforward to attach the database files from a MSDE solution to a SQL Server and run without any further changes.

Although MSDE and versions of SQL Server 7.0 will run on Win 9x operating systems, their functionality will be somewhat diminished (particularly as regards security matters) as compared to if they are installed on an NT 4.0 (with SP 4) or Windows 2000 operating system. SQL Server 2000 will not install on Windows 95, but will allow a connectivity capability to be configured. SQL Server 2000 will install on Windows 98 2nd edition, with reduced functionality.

Installation of the various database engines is discussed in detail in Chapter 2; at which point the differing client tool options, sample databases available, and auxiliary resources will be fully explored.

Let's have a look at each of them in slightly more detail.

MSDE

It's highly likely that many Access developers will start with MSDE – its free availability provides a simple no-cost way for Access developers to learn more about SQL Server development techniques. It's versatile because it does not require a SQL Server license, and it's included with Access in all versions of Office 2000.

There are two versions available:

❑ The version, mentioned above, that is available in any Office 2000 edition that includes Access 2000 – this version works with the Access project interface.

❑ A second MSDE version for Office targets applications that require a royalty-free version of MSDE. A license to deploy solutions based on this version is gained with the Microsoft Office 2000 Developer edition (MOD) or any Visual Studio 6.0 professional or enterprise tool. This MSDE version does not include hooks into the Access project interface, and it requires special Office Package and Deployment Wizard adaptations to accommodate the distribution of solutions built with it. Just as with applications that use the Access run-time component, you must build your own custom interface for this version – see http://msdn.microsoft.com/vstudio/MSDE/genfaq.asp for more details.

MSDE is aimed at small workgroup solutions with 5 or fewer concurrent users with less than 2Gb data.

As Access developers gain experience with MSDE, and start building solutions with Access projects, some may find it beneficial to switch to one of the full-scale versions of SQL Server. At the time of writing SQL Server 2000 was entering release candidate stage.

SQL Server 7.0

Access 2000 was released slightly after SQL Server 7 and Access projects are compatible with all versions of the product. As we'll see in the next chapter, SQL Server comes with a richer set of administration tools than MSDE and scales to larger database sizes and more users. It comes in a number of different flavors (Desktop, Standard, and Enterprise) all with slightly different capabilities. SQL Server 7.0 has proven to be an extremely popular and powerful product and has proved popular with VB developers.

A free 120 day downloadable evaluation version of SQL Server is available at www.microsoft.com/sql/productinfo/evalcd.htm.

SQL Server 2000

SQL Server 2000 represents enhancements over SQL Server 7 in several areas, but information at this present time of writing suggests the newer edition is not supposed to change the fundamental interface between Access 2000 and SQL Server. The installation section in Chapter 2 details the patches that needed to be installed at the time of writing to resolve some minor incompatibilities between SQL Server 2000 and Access projects. It additionally appears that there has been some change in the database format, and at the time of writing SQL Server 2000 database files do not install on SQL Server 7.0/MSDE installations.

The coverage of SQL Server 2000 aims to provide a slight taster of the forthcoming enhancements in SQL Server 2000 that will be of particular interest to Access developers – we won't attempt to provide details of new features (such as XML support) that aren't currently directly relevant to Access projects.

Additional Software

The other technologies and products we need to have available to make full use of the book are:

ADO

This is academic, as Access 2000 ships with ADO 2.1 although there are more recent versions of ADO available through the Microsoft Web site.

SQL-DMO

Again, academic as the libraries are installed during the MSDE or SQL Server set up.

FrontPage 2000

The chapters concerning Web publishing make reference to FrontPage 2000 because it is a Web development tool that ships as part of the Office 2000 Premium and the Office 2000 Developer editions. As part of that suite of tools it integrates well with Access and uses VBA to extend its functionality.

To utilize FrontPage 2000 with any of the Web servers discussed below, the FrontPage 2000 Server Extensions (available during FrontPage 2000 installation) will need to be installed. More details on their use can be found at http://officeupdate.microsoft.com/frontpage/wpp/serk/inwindow.htm. Note, to take advantage of the full functionality of FrontPage 2000, these extensions will need to be installed on any server a site is eventually deployed to – for ISP hosting or use within an Intranet environment this should be checked with the system administrator.

ASP

This server-side technology is available through the relevant Microsoft Web Server for your platform:

❑ Windows 95 and 98 use **Personal Web Server** (**PWS**). PWS is available on the FrontPage 2000 CD. Alternatively, Windows 95 users can obtain it from the **Windows NT 4 Option Pack** while Windows 98 users can find it on their original installation disc.

❑ Windows NT 4.0 Workstation and Server – in both cases the NT 4 Option Pack is required. On Workstation this will enable **Peer Web Sever** (**PWS**) to be installed, while on Server this will install **Internet Information Server** (**IIS**) **4.0**.

❑ Windows 2000 Professional, Server, and Advanced Server have **Internet Information Services** (**IIS**) **5.0** included on the installation discs. If it isn't installed use the Add/Remove Programs option on Control Panel.

The Windows NT 4 Option Pack can be downloaded from www.microsoft.com.

Configuring PWS and IIS can *sometimes* be a complicated process – detailing the various options lies outside the scope of this book, and here we'll be leveraging the settings in the default configuration (which generally suffice).

Like ADO there are slightly different versions of ASP in use (although the evolutionary differences between versions need not concern us) – Win 9x, NT 4.0 based Web servers make use of ASP 2.0 while IIS 5.0 on Windows 2000 uses ASP 3.0.

Databases and Sample Code

The best way to build SQL Server solutions in Access projects is with new projects. However, many developers will want to migrate data and other solution elements from Jet databases. Appendix B explores two tools that can facilitate this effort – the Access Upsizing Tool, which is an integrated Access component, and the SQL Server Data Transformation Wizard. Note that at the time of writing there is currently no upsizing to SQL Server 2000.

This book often uses one database per chapter, where the database is frequently an adaptation of the three sample databases generally available to Access developers (see Chapter 2 for a discussion on the precise availability of different sample databases). As all the code listings, whether T-SQL, ADO, or VBA for Access objects, appear within the book it is an easy task to follow the methodology and apply it to whatever database you have available.

Additionally, the code samples, Access projects, and adapted databases are available for download from www.wrox.com.

Due to the apparent change in file formats between MSDE/SQL Server 7.0 and SQL 2000, if using the downloadable amended databases, be careful about which sample database file is used. However, although the file formats are different the T-SQL code used to develop database objects can still be downloaded and executed to give the same results.

Summary

This book is about using Access 2000 with SQL Server database engines and is designed primarily to help experienced Access developers migrate their applications and skill sets to the more powerful engine offered by SQL Server. A subsidiary aim will be to show SQL Server developers the reverse process – how to use Access to build easily accessible database solutions rapidly. Apart from using Access in a traditional closed network environment we'll be showing how to use Access 2000 projects in publishing data to the Web.

The nature of the book as a stepping stone between databases, means that we are going to focus on the issues faced in transitioning, and will not attempt to provide complete coverage of the features in either Access 2000 or SQL Server 7.0 – for that aspect we respectively recommend *Professional Access 2000 Programming, ISBN 1-861004-08-7* and *Professional SQL Server 7.0 Programming, ISBN 1-861002-31-9*, both from *Wrox Press.*

To set us up for the rest of the book, this chapter has supplied some general background on three main areas – the architectural issues surrounding software application development (particularly as related to Access), a quick review of much of the basic terminology associated with relational databases, and a brief overview of the software technologies we'll be using throughout the book. To complete the chapter we reviewed the software products we'll specifically need to make effective use of the forthcoming chapters.

Right, enough of the introductions, let's get down to business and start to look at installing a SQL Server type database engine.

Installing Engines and Starting Projects

This chapter aims to get us ready for the rest of the book, by providing all the information that we'll need to get started with Access projects. We'll start by looking at the typical installation process for the **Microsoft Data Engine** (**MSDE**), **SQL Server 7**, and **SQL Server 2000**. After you've installed your chosen engine, a number of configuration options and utilities will become available, and part of the job of this chapter is to provide some grounding in the use of these tools. This will help in our familiarization with these database engines. Throughout the chapter we'll highlight points at which the versions differ from each other.

After that we'll make a start on Access projects themselves by setting up a project, connecting to a database, and having a look around the Access project interface. At this point, we'll also briefly discuss the **Visual Basic Editor** (**VBE**), which we'll be using during the coding sections of the book.
So in summary we'll look at:

- ❑ Database engine installation
- ❑ Getting started with MSDE and SQL Server
- ❑ Getting started with Access Projects

Without more ado, let's begin on the hard work.

Software Installation

As we saw in the last chapter we have three basic choices, and the first part of this chapter will provide installation details for all three. In order, we'll be looking at:

- ❏ Microsoft Data Engine (MSDE)
- ❏ SQL Server 7.0
- ❏ SQL Server 2000

Additionally, we'll look at a couple of related topics:

- ❏ Installation of associated utilities
- ❏ SQL-DMO library compatibility issues between SQL Server versions

Microsoft Data Engine (MSDE) Installation

As we pointed out previously, MSDE provides the same database engine as SQL Server, but has been optimized for use by five users. Additionally, there are a few MSDE distribution issues to be aware of:

- ❏ Only one MSDE can be installed per machine.
- ❏ Only one MSDE can be running per machine.
- ❏ When packaging an MSDE solution, be very careful with the MSDE DLLs as they may already be on the distributed machine, and uninstalling our application could make any remaining applications fail.
- ❏ While an MSDE installation on our machine can come from either the Office 2000 Premium or Office 2000 Developer suite of programs, MSDE can only be distributed from the Office 2000 Developer Edition – it *cannot* be distributed from the Office 2000 Premium Edition.

MSDE does *not* install with the rest of the Office 2000 files and has to be completed separately and manually. The installation process is straightforward and consists of the following steps:

- ❏ Launching the setup program from the installation CD – run `Setupsql.exe` from the `SQL\x86\Setup` folder
- ❏ Responding to a series of screens that allow setting configuration and changing default settings
- ❏ Waiting for the automatic installation to finish

Let's look at this in a bit more detail. The first screen gives the choice of installing MSDE to a local machine or one installed elsewhere on a network. After making the selection, click Next twice to go past a welcome screen and bring up the registration screen. After progressing past this screen, we'll be presented with a Setup screen, which offers us the opportunity to change the installation folders in which MSDE stores its programs and our data. Unless we've a compelling reason to alter the default settings, click Next to move onto the Character Set/Sort Order/Unicode collation screen:

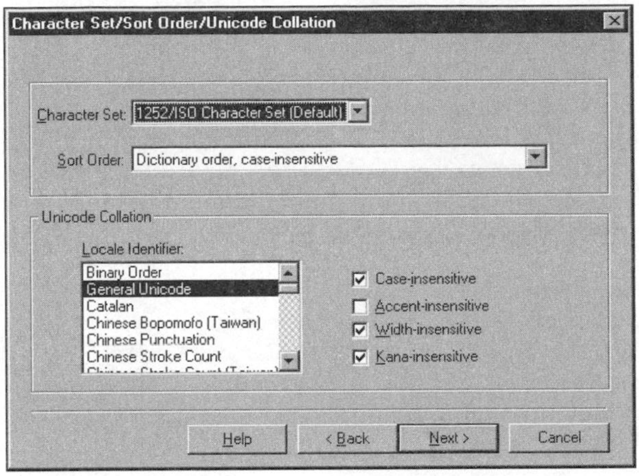

Here another set of default settings are presented, together with a number of choices:

❑ **Character Set** – different character sets are available for supporting different languages.

❑ **Sort Order** – the default choice here (**Dictionary order, case insensitive**) means that when data is sorted it should be returned in A-Z order. If the case sensitive option is selected then data will be returned in the order Aa, Bb, Cc, and so forth. Be careful here though, because selecting this latter option will make all the objects in SQL Server case sensitive, meaning that a table titled **Categories** will not be accessed if referred to as **categories** in a SQL statement.

❑ **Unicode Collation** – Unicode is an international character set and, as it provides codes for more than 65,000 characters, allows storage of characters from a number of different languages (such as Russian, German, Japanese, etc.) apart from the installed one.

Again, unless we have a very good reason, accept the defaults and advance to the next screen:

After choosing the sort order that we want, we then move on to the set up for the default SQL Server network library:

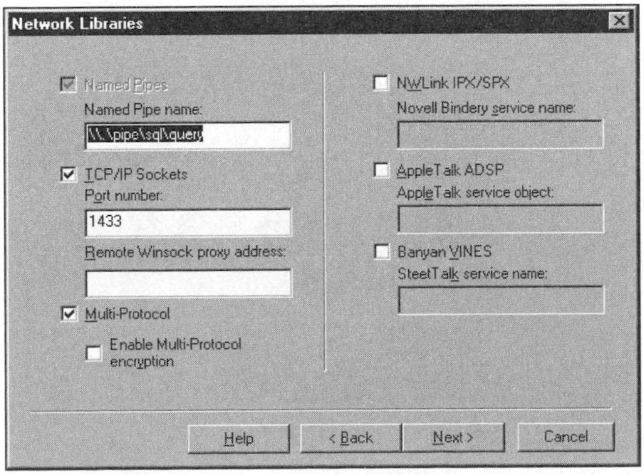

MSDE uses **network libraries**, each network having its own DLL, to pass pieces of information, known as **packets**, across the network from the client software to the database. The great thing about SQL Server is that it can listen to several network connections and libraries at the same time. In most installations, the defaults work fine. However, a database server must listen on the same network protocol that a client uses issues to requests. These network libraries do vary with the operating system of the server: Windows 9x computers use TCP/IP and Multi-Protocol libraries. Windows NT and Windows 2000 computers use Named Pipes as the default network library, although we can use TCP/IP or MultiProtocol. Alter the settings on this screen with care.

If the installation is being carried out on an NT 4.0/2000 platform, the next task is to set up a service account. A SQL Server Service Account needs to be created so that the SQL Server Agent has an account to log on to SQL Server, and if we want MSDE to automatically start when the operating system boots. Both services login to the system they're running on – the default is to have them login to the same account, but you can, as shown here, give the MSDE Service and the SQL Server Agent (the task scheduler for SQL Server) separate logins if you really want.

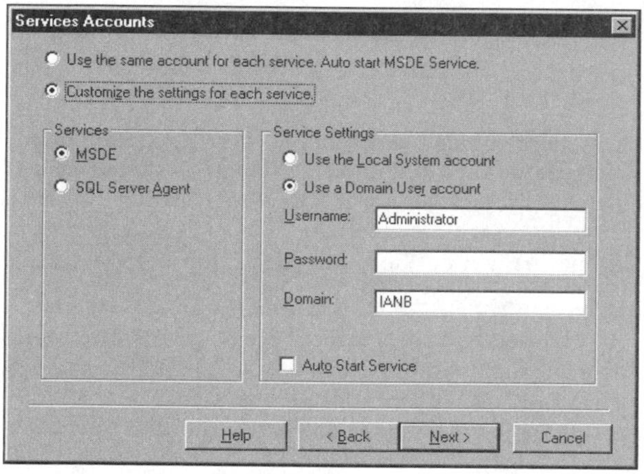

After pressing Next, and waiting for the automatic installation to finish, on Windows NT and Windows 2000 computers MSDE starts automatically. On Windows 9x computers MSDE must be initialized by selecting Start | Programs | MSDE | Service Manager to open the SQL Server Service Manager:

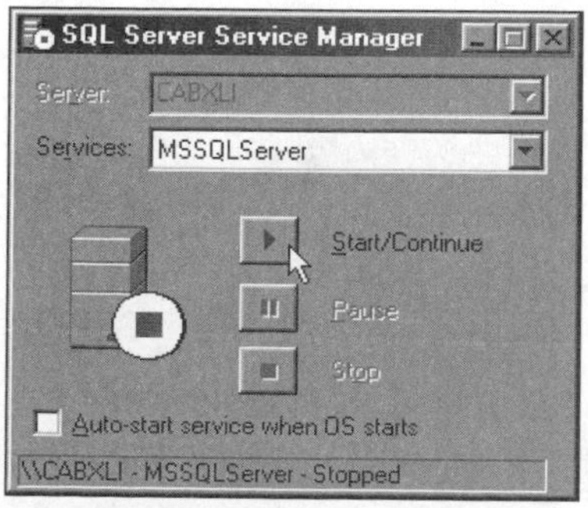

Notice the dialog's name refers to SQL Server although we are working with MSDE – the fact that Microsoft uses the same dialog for MSDE and SQL Server underscores the similarity of the products. To launch MSDE click the Start/Continue control and, to ensure it automatically starts on computer boot check **Auto-start service whenever OS starts.** Without selecting the **Auto-start** check box, you must open the **Service Manager** dialog and start MSDE the first time MSDE is needed in any Windows session. After starting MSDE from the Service Manager it's ready to use.

For selected T-SQL commands, it's necessary to know the location in which MSDE stores data and log files for databases (SQL Server engines use data and log files jointly to manage databases for client requests). For example the sp_attach_db and sp_detach_db stored procedures, which we discuss at the end of this chapter, require the Data folder location when a database is migrated from a SQL Server type engine on one computer to a SQL Server on a second. In MSDE, the default location for programs and databases is the MSSQL7 directory.

Immediately after installation, MSDE provides no built-in sample databases – the details for creating a new SQL Server database or connecting to an existing one appear later in this chapter. Don't forget that when developing MSDE solutions, Microsoft has designed the server so that performance declines after more than a handful of concurrent connections.

SQL Server 7.0 Installation

SQL Server 7 is available in Desktop, Standard, and Enterprise editions, which can be summarized thus:

❑　The Desktop version is the only option available for the Windows 9x and ME platforms. It can also run on Windows NT and 2000 and, although it uses the same engine as the other versions of SQL Server, it offers reduced functionality. Users of the Desktop version miss out on **Online Analytical Programming functionality** (**OLAP**) and **Microsoft Search Services**, which gives the ability for facilities like full text searches and other options that can speed up the processing of data.

❑　The Standard edition of SQL Server runs on Windows NT and Windows 2000, and contains the full functionality of SQL Server.

❑　The Enterprise edition is designed for Windows NT Enterprise edition and has support for high level database services using large numbers of processors and server clustering.

As a sophisticated product, aimed at supporting applications in an enterprise environment (the Enterprise edition can scale to handle multi-terabyte sized databases for hundreds of concurrent users), SQL Server has a variety of installation options. To aid installation choices, the SQL Server 7.0 installation CD enables the browsing of **Books Online** (the online help system for SQL Server, which we'll cover later) from the CD.

For a typical installation start the installation process by clicking Install SQL Server 7.0 Components on the welcome screen and choose the appropriate edition for your purposes.

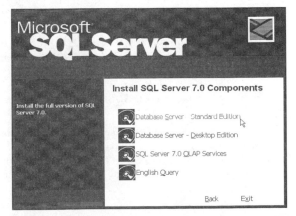

The only dialog we are going to concern ourselves with (we are going to accept the defaults from the others) is the Choose a Licensing Mode dialog, that permits you to specify how a SQL Server accepts client access licenses. Client licensing can be designated on a **per server** or a **per seat** basis:

❑ Per seat licenses go with the connection device (for example, a laptop) – required where there are *static* users and the same users are connecting to the same server all the time

❑ Per server licenses go with the server, and so each connection to the server is counted – useful when you have many users but only a few are connected at any one time

When the automatic installation process loads all the files and performs its associated tasks, click Finish on the Setup Complete screen to exit the setup application. Before SQL Server can be used the first time, the SQL Server Service Manager must be used (as for the MSDE installation) – select Start | Programs | Microsoft SQL Server 7.0 | Service Manager and click Start/Continue. The installation process automatically selects Auto-start service when OS starts control on Windows NT and Windows 2000 computers.

SQL Server 7.0 installations contain two sample databases – pubs and Northwind. These are excellent for testing database and application designs, and each has been used by Microsoft for demonstrating its products for a number of years. Most readers will be very familiar with Northwind as it has shipped with Access in previous version, and pubs has always shipped with SQL Server. We will discuss the sample databases later this chapter.

The data and log files for user created databases, and those that SQL Server automatically installs can again be found in the Data folder of the MSSQL7 directory if the default locations are selected during installation.

SQL Server 2000 Installation

As pointed out previously, at the point of writing SQL Server 2000, was just entering Release Candidate stage – details on some early patches and fixes are given at the end of this section. It is possible the situation may change at full release. It additionally appears that there has been some change in the database format and at the time of writing SQL Server 2000 database files do not install on SQL Server 7.0/MSDE installations.

SQL Server 2000 has similar versioning to SQL Server 7.0 with a Personal edition, Standard edition and Enterprise edition. The Personal Edition in SQL Server 2000 corresponds to the Desktop Edition in SQL Server 7.

Unlike SQL Server 7, SQL Server 2000 does not install on Windows 95 computers. However, you can install SQL Server 2000 Personal Edition on Windows 98 computers running the Second Edition version of that operating system. SQL Server 2000 does support a new option for the installation of a connectivity capability for Windows 95 computers. Installing this capability enables Windows 95 computers to connect to SQL Server 2000 database servers running on other computers.

Installing SQL Server 2000 is very similar to installing SQL Server 7, but there are a few variations. The starting point is to insert the CD for the desired SQL Server 2000 edition, and then, for a typical installation, select SQL Server 2000 Components to start the process. This screen offers the opportunity to browse a help file covering setup and upgrade issues.

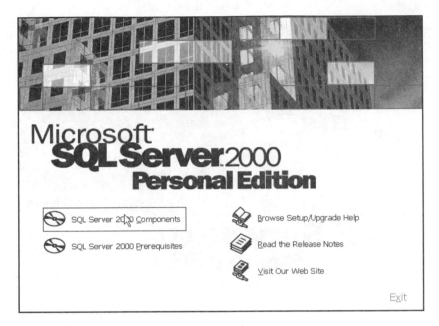

Click **Install Database Server** on the second installation screen to enter the setup process for a SQL Server. As with the installation for MSDE and SQL Server 7.0, a typical installation, with the standard defaults, can be created merely by clicking **Next** or **Yes** to nearly all setup screens although it is worth highlighting two screens:

The Authentication Mode Dialog

This dialog allows us to choose authentication via Windows logon accounts exclusively (not available when SQL Server 2000 runs on a Windows 98 computer) or through mixed mode Windows and SQL Server logon accounts.

If mixed mode is chosen, the **Authentication Mode** dialog requires a password to be set for the system administrator (**sa**) account unless the **Blank password** (**not recommended**) option is specifically checked. While a blank password is clearly undesirable for production environments since it poses a significant security risk, it speeds logon and relieves the burden of tracking a password in a development environment.

The Choose Licensing Mode Dialog

This screen functions similarly to that shown in the SQL Server 7.0 installation. Again, the per seat option allows client access licenses to be assigned to connection devices, but there is no longer a per server option. A new per processor option replaces the per server option. With this option, each processor license can legally support an unlimited number of users, but a license is required for each processor on a server.

After the automatic process for loading files and associated tasks completes, click **Finish**. As with SQL Server 7, the SQL Server Service Manager must be opened and the server started for its initial use unless the system is restarted. SQL Server 2000 installs with the two standard sample databases – **pubs** and **Northwind**.

If your computer is running Windows 95, recall that SQL Server 2000 supports only connectivity functions and you will not be able to create database objects in SQL Server 2000.

Indeed even to enable connectivity to SQL Server 2000, prerequisite software must be installed. To do this, from the initial installation screen (see above) choose **SQL Server 2000 Prerequisites**. Then, on the next screen choose Install Common Controls Library Update (Windows 95 only). Without these prerequisites installed, you would be running old versions of the DLLs leading to an unusable SQL Server installation. After the prerequisites install, backup one screen and exit the installation process.

The default destination folder for SQL Server programs and databases changes with the migration from SQL Server 7.0 to SQL Server 2000; With SQL Server 2000, the installation program creates a Microsoft SQL Server folder under the Program Files directory. This new folder under Program Files contains two sub-folders named 80 and Mssql. The Mssql sub-folder, in turn, has a Data sub-folder, which SQL Server 2000 uses, as a repository for the data and log files of its databases. As with SQL Server 7, this is a default location, which can be overridden if necessary.

Access Project and SQL Server 2000 Compatibility Issues

As we've already indicated Access 2000 is compatible with SQL Server 7.0, and the MSDE that ships with Microsoft Office 2000. However, at the point of writing it appears that there are some incompatibilities between Access projects and the SQL Server 2000 release candidate version being used.

The incompatibilities that we are aware of, and the solutions offered, fall into three areas:

❑ Difficulties in running stored procedures in SQL Server 2000 databases from an Access project should be addressed by installing the Office 2000 SR-1a Update (available from the Office Update web site – http://officeupdate.microsoft.com/). A further concern regards the ability of Access 2000 running on a computer with SQL Server 7.0 to create stored procedures on a SQL Server 2000 computer. At the time of writing, this was unresolved.

❑ Access 2000 projects allows SQL Server 2000 tables, views, and database diagrams to be opened and viewed, however, design changes to these database objects cannot be made. At the time of writing, it was reported a partial solution could be obtained by installing the client tools for the release version of SQL Server 2000 on the workstation along with Access 2000.

❑ At the time of writing we were unable to visually create new databases or upsize Access 2000 databases to SQL Server 2000. It is likely a patch will be made available through the Office Update web site after the release of SQL Server 2000 to address this issue.

It must be stressed that these issues were found with the early versions of SQL Server 2000 used during production of the book and the situation will probably be resolved by the time you are actually reading this.

Installing SQL Server 7.0 Client Components with MSDE

We established at the beginning that this book is for developers and database administrators who want to build SQL Server solutions with Access projects, and it addresses three versions of SQL Server. But while MSDE and SQL Server 7.0 are highly compatible, there are some important differences. The SQL Server client tools, such as **Enterprise Manager** and **Query Analyzer** (which we'll be looking at later in the chapter) are missing from MSDE.

The general approach of the book is to use Access projects whenever possible and these projects offer much of the functionality that is found in those client tools, as they provide a framework for managing database objects and writing and running T-SQL code. However there are points in the book where for convenience, or other reasons we may use the tools.

If you have a SQL Server 7.0 client pack with an uncommitted license, you can use the license to endow a MSDE server with selected SQL Server client components. Of course, you may well be better to install SQL Server rather than MSDE with this license, but don't forget that there are a number of advantages to MSDE, smaller footprint perhaps being the greatest advantage. This can substantially enhance productivity with MSDE and help you to become familiar with SQL Server.

Before installing the SQL Server client components, MSDE will appear on the Windows Start menu. In addition, MSDE will show as a distinct program in the Add/Remove Program Properties dialog accessible through the Control Panel. After installation of the SQL Server client components, SQL Server will replace MSDE on the Start menu and this menu provides access to the client tools. Note that the Add/Remove Program Properties dialog will change to add a new line item for Microsoft SQL Server even while the MSDE option remains. SQL Server client components tightly integrate with MSDE so that you cannot remove the client components without also losing your MSDE installation. Therefore, you should have a recovery plan if you envision a need to return to a stand-alone MSDE installation without the SQL Server client tools.

To install the SQL Server Client Components begin the installation by choosing to install the Standard or Desktop Edition of SQL Server 7.0, as we discussed previously. Eventually the Select Components dialog will be reached and at this point choose the desired components.

Clicking Next on the dialog prepares the installation program to complete the installation of the client components. Choose Next on the Start Copy Files dialog to start the update of an MSDE server installation with SQL Server client tools.

SQL-DMO Compatibility Across SQL Servers and MSDE

As we briefly mentioned in Chapter 1, SQL-DMO is a programmatic interface for managing a SQL Server installations. SQL-DMO installs along with an installation of the server or client utilities for MSDE, SQL Server 7.0, and SQL Server 2000. A successful installation places `sqldmo.dll` in the `\Mssql7\Binn` folder (in the case where SQL Server 7.0 was installed) and `sqldmo.rll` in the `\Mssql7\Binn\Resources\xxxx` folder where xxxx represents the language identifier, such as 1033 for English, US. In addition, SQL-DMO requires the SQL Server ODBC driver, version 3.7 or later.

There are, however, important differences between the files as SQL Server 2000 installs a different version of `sqldmo.dll` and `sqldmo.rll` from those installed with SQL Server 7 and the MSDE shipping with Office 2000. The features that SQL-DMO exposes change between versions because SQL Server 2000 adds functionality not available in the prior version. However, the program file names implementing SQL-DMO for both versions are the same.

Beyond that, any VBA programs will work in one version or the other, but not both.

Additionally, the help file name differs between engines; for SQL Server 7 it is `sqldmo.hlp` while for SQL Server 2000 the file is `sqldmo80.hlp`.

The MSDE installation process does not make available a SQL-DMO Help file.

Getting Started with SQL Server and MSDE

After installing SQL Server or Microsoft Data Engine (MSDE), a new menu becomes available from the Windows Start menu which can be exposed by choosing Start | Programs and highlighting either Microsoft SQL Server (7.0 or 2000) or MSDE (depending on which database is installed). The options available on the new menu fall into three broad classes:

- ❑ Those that either have used once or typically used very infrequently – these are utilities for configuring a server or client or uninstalling the database server
- ❑ Those for specialized tasks, such as importing data to or exporting from the database server
- ❑ Those for database administration and management

In this section we're going to familiarize ourselves with some of these options (some of which won't be available to those using MSDE) and tools to see what these new databases offer us, before we move on to the Access projects themselves. Additionally we'll dig a little deeper into the databases that are installed during the database installation process.

So within this section we're going to look at:

- ❑ Client and server network utilities
- ❑ The uninstall utility

- ❑ Service manager
- ❑ Importing and exporting data
- ❑ Enterprise Manager
- ❑ Query Analyzer
- ❑ Resources
- ❑ Sample Databases
- ❑ System Databases

Client and Server Network Utilities

The Client Network Utility and Server Network Utility enable communications between a database server and its clients to be adjusted. This is an area where a little knowledge can be a dangerous thing so our coverage here will be, by necessity extremely brief. Generally, if you've installed Access and the database of choice on a stand-alone machine and accepted the defaults, all should work just fine.

If you are operating in a network situation and problems occur, and you don't have network support, we advise that the resources (see later) for MSDE, SQL Server, and those for the Windows platforms being used, are consulted carefully.

Essentially these utilities provide a way into adjusting the **NetLibs** (**Network Libraries**) that MSDE/SQL Server uses to communicate with network protocols. The same NetLib must be available on both the client and the server computers so that they can communicate via the network protocol (such as Named Pipes or TCP/IP). If the server and client network settings are not compatible, applications on client workstations will fail to connect with their server (you can start to see the can of worms that may develop here – this is one topic where we definitely feel 'tinkering' is not advisable). Just as an example, one potential area of incompatibility in a Windows based system is when SQL Server database servers are running on NT 4.0/Windows 2000 and clients are using Windows 9x (a subject we touched on when we talked about MSDE installation).

Uninstall Utility

The Uninstall command is used to remove a failed, or redundant database server. The option appears on the menu with the name of the specific type of server (such as Uninstall MSDE).

The Uninstall command leaves the database and log files in place so that they can be re-attached to another database server (see later).

Service Manager

We've already encountered the Service Manager when we discussed database installation and pointed out that we have to ensure our MSDE or SQL Server is running if we actually want to do anything with it.

The dialog can be called up using either the Start menu option or its icon on the lower right portion of the status bar. While previously we concentrated on the MSSQLServer service, the dialog also allows other services to be controlled such as:

- ❑ SQLServerAgent – the task scheduler for SQL Server

- ❏ MS DTC (Distributed Transaction Coordinator) – monitors transactions
- ❏ Full Text Search – the engine that provides full text search capabilities in SQL Server

These other options are selected through the Services: drop-down although, depending on the installation type, not all of them may be available.

As we saw previously, the purpose of this dialog is to control the running of services and also determine whether a service starts automatically when a computer boots.

Import and Export Data

The Import and Export Data option launches the **Data Transformation Services** (**DTS**) Wizard when selected.

DTS facilitates the copying or moving of data from one location to another. At the same time it also presents the option of transforming the data from one format to another. Thus DTS can be used for getting data into and out of SQL Server.

While data is being moved between formats, various transformation functions can also be performed, such as converting a NULL to a 0, or concatenating information like house number and street. Its data pump features work for other data repositories besides SQL Server, for example we can use DTS to move data between other products such as Oracle and Excel or Sybase and DB/2.

We'll be looking at how DTS can help us in Appendix B. Incidentally this feature was introduced with SQL Server 7.0 and its functionality is going to be upgraded further in SQL Server 2000.

Enterprise Manager

Enterprise Manager and **Query Analyzer** are two tools that are used for a vast amount of the time by SQL Server developers, and it would be remiss to pass them by without comment. In the context of this book we won't be seeing so much of them because the Access project user and programmatic interfaces offer an alternative route into the same functionality. We should also re-iterate that these options aren't available through MSDE – the following discussion also leverages databases that aren't available in MSDE.

Enterprise Manager can be thought of as an easy-to-use graphical front-end to SQL Server administrative and database development functions. It can be used to administer security, backup databases and transaction logs, create scripts, and manage tables, views, stored procedures, and all the other objects in a SQL Server database. Access 2000 developers using MSDE will probably want to adapt the Access project interface to simulate as much of the Enterprise Manager functionality as possible.

Opening Enterprise Manager via Start | Programs | Microsoft SQL Server | Enterprise Manager brings up the initial window. To inspect a database expand the icons for the SQL Server Group, the required SQL Server, its Databases, and the specific database required. This brings up a list of objects within the database. So in the screenshot at the top of the next page we have drilled down to the Tables collection within the pubs database and have exposed a list of tables:

Right-clicking on any table name opens a context-sensitive menu that enables a number of options to be selected – for example from here the design of the table can be viewed and edited, and the contents of the table viewed.

It is also possible to create a schematic view of the pubs, or any database that is within SQL Server. By right-clicking Diagrams and choosing New Database Diagram the Create Database Diagram Wizard is opened – this allows diagrams like that shown below to be developed (we'll be seeing more of diagrams in Chapter 4):

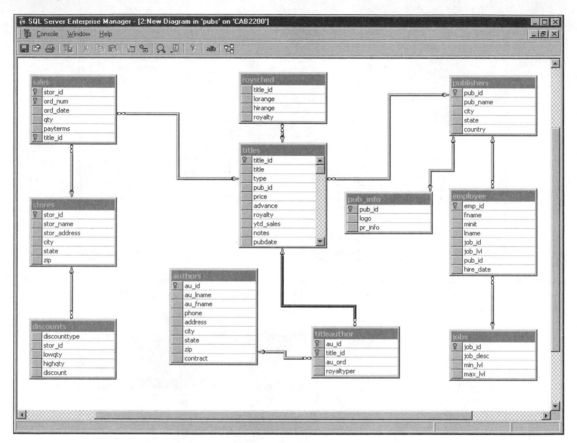

Query Analyzer

Query Analyzer opens a window with a single pane for entering and executing ad hoc T-SQL statements (but there is the potential for multiple panes and sometimes tabs). This tool is tremendously useful when developing T-SQL queries. When it is opened a dialog requesting connection details is shown; once this is completed the Query Analyzer window comes up. One tiny gotcha, which often catches brand new users of the tool out, is that the database against which the queries are being executed needs to be selected from the drop-down box in the icon bar.

SQL Server Query Analyzer

File Edit View Query Window Help

Query - ianb.pubs.WROX_UK\ianb - (untitled) - select * from a...

DB: pubs

```
select * from authors
```

au_id	au_lname	au_fname	phone	address	city	state	zip	contract
172-32-1176	White	Johnson	408 496-7223	10932 Bigge Rd.	Menlo Park	CA	94025	1
213-46-8915	Green	Marjorie	415 986-7020	309 63rd St. #411	Oakland	CA	94618	1
238-95-7766	Carson	Cheryl	415 548-7723	589 Darwin Ln.	Berkeley	CA	94705	1
267-41-2394	O'Leary	Michael	408 286-2428	22 Cleveland Av. #14	San Jose	CA	95128	1
274-80-9391	Straight	Dean	415 834-2919	5420 College Av.	Oakland	CA	94609	1
341-22-1782	Smith	Meander	913 843-0462	10 Mississippi Dr.	Lawrence	KS	66044	0
409-56-7008	Bennet	Abraham	415 658-9932	6223 Bateman St.	Berkeley	CA	94705	1
427-17-2319	Dull	Ann	415 836-7128	3410 Blonde St.	Palo Alto	CA	94301	1
472-27-2349	Gringlesby	Burt	707 938-6445	PO Box 792	Covelo	CA	95428	1
486-29-1786	Locksley	Charlene	415 585-4620	18 Broadway Av.	San Francisco	CA	94130	1
527-72-3246	Greene	Morningstar	615 297-2723	22 Graybar House Rd.	Nashville	TN	37215	0
648-92-1872	Blotchet-Halls	Reginald	503 745-6402	55 Hillsdale Bl.	Corvallis	OR	97330	1
672-71-3249	Yokomoto	Akiko	415 935-4228	3 Silver Ct.	Walnut Creek	CA	94595	1
712-45-1867	del Castillo	Innes	615 996-8275	2286 Cram Pl. #86	Ann Arbor	MI	48105	1
722-51-5454	DeFrance	Michel	219 547-9982	3 Balding Pl.	Gary	IN	46403	1
724-08-9931	Stringer	Dirk	415 843-2991	5420 Telegraph Av.	Oakland	CA	94609	0
724-80-9391	MacFeather	Stearns	415 354-7128	44 Upland Hts.	Oakland	CA	94612	1
756-30-7391	Karsen	Livia	415 534-9219	5720 McAuley St.	Oakland	CA	94609	1
807-91-6654	Panteley	Sylvia	301 946-8853	1956 Arlington Pl.	Rockville	MD	20853	1
846-92-7186	Hunter	Sheryl	415 836-7128	3410 Blonde St.	Palo Alto	CA	94301	1
893-72-1158	McBadden	Heather	707 448-4982	301 Putnam	Vacaville	CA	95688	0
899-46-2035	Ringer	Anne	801 826-0752	67 Seventh Av.	Salt Lake City	UT	84152	1
998-72-3567	Ringer	Albert	801 826-0752	67 Seventh Av.	Salt Lake City	UT	84152	1

Results Grid / Messages

Query batch completed.   Exec time: 0:00:00   23 rows   Ln 2, Col 1

NUM

Incidentally, Query Analyzer is generally felt to be a more hospitable environment for running **Books Online** (see the *Resources* section below) samples than the stored procedure template in Access projects. However, we'll be using the latter extensively in this book because that is the feature presented through the Access project interface, which is our primary focus.

Resources

While our aim is that you will find this book enormously helpful, there is no way that it can (or should) attempt to take the place of the reference material that is supplied with Access and SQL Server. Thus in this section we're going to have a look at **Books Online** and Access help.

These two sources also have the admirable quality of being *free* to Access developers. The Books Online resource ships with SQL Server but not MSDE. It is however available from either the MOD MSDN library or the Microsoft web site (http://www.microsoft.com/sql/downloads/p51745.htm).

Of course this book is designed to be part of a Wrox learning tree and two other books you may find particularly useful are *Professional SQL Server 7.0 Programming* (*ISBN 1-861002-31-9*) and *Professional Access 2000 Programming* (*ISBN 1-861004-08-7*) from Wrox Press and my own practice's web site at www.programmingmsaccess.com.

Books Online (BOL)

Books Online is, in fact, a comprehensive resource on SQL Server. It contains information on installation, administration, data access, programming, and special add-on capabilities, such as English Query, which enables developers to build custom applications that allow users to ask questions in English rather than SQL. Books Online should be available with the other tools discussed here, through the Start | Programs | SQL Server menu. Within the MOD MSDN Library, Books Online has the name Microsoft SQL Server Programmer's Toolkit and is accessible by sequentially expanding the Platform SDK, Database and Messaging Services, and finally Microsoft SQL Server Programmer's Toolkit.

In the context of the material covered in this book, Books Online may be found especially useful for both its T-SQL and SQL-DMO samples.

The interface for Books Online is intuitive and straightforward, so we won't go into it here apart from highlighting the Search tab – it allows us to type a search term and click List Topics to have Books Online return a list of all its pages with that term. If the term has spaces, enclose it in quotes to return just those pages with all the words in the term and not pages with any word in the term. This application of Books Online is especially handy for finding code samples. The following screenshot shows a T-SQL code sample that creates a stored procedure:

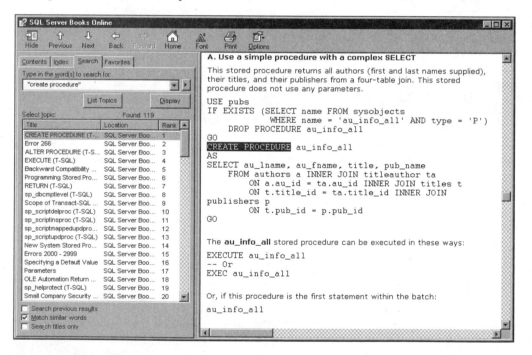

Looking at code samples brings us on to an important point for Access developers, in that the code samples shown in BOL will run fine in Query Analyzer, but some editing is necessary before it will run from a stored procedure template in an Access project.

An Aside – Using Samples from Books Online

The issues with this sample are representative of many samples throughout Books Online and the crucial thing here is to think carefully about what you are copying before you run it as stored procedure inside an Access project.

We're jumping the gun a bit here, as we're alluding to things we're not going to encounter until the end of the chapter (or later in the book), but now seems a reasonable point to introduce the general approach.

Firstly, the GO keyword is used to separate T-SQL scripts into batches of commands that can be executed – it isn't a T-SQL command, but is a command that is recognized by Query Analyzer. Thus when transferring the code into an Access stored procedure template this needs to either be removed or commented out (we can comment out either by using -- on a single line, or encapsulating a number of lines between an opening /* and a closing */. These latter instructions need to each be on a line of their own).

Secondly, the USE command is used to show which database to connect to; again this isn't needed in an Access project environment, because as we'll see, the database is already defined.

These first two points indicate there are keywords used in Query Analyzer which are not applicable to Access stored procedures.

Thirdly, the script actually consists of two operations – it starts with a script conditionally removing a stored procedure named au_info_all if it exists. This kind of statement is not necessary within stored procedures created in Access projects and will not be required.

> *In short when using samples from BOL we need to have a careful understanding of precisely what elements we are after, and we need to edit out the rest.*

Access Help

Access Help has good documentation on T-SQL – it can be found under Getting Started with Transact-SQL.

This documentation is worth mentioning for a couple of reasons:

- ❑ It is available directly from Access projects.

- ❑ The documentation presents an alphabetical list of the T-SQL keywords – many of these keyword descriptions include code samples that demonstrate interesting coding techniques, but those that do not often include links to other keywords which usually do.

Sample Databases

As we pointed out during the installation section, while SQL Server comes with two sample databases – pubs and Northwind – the MSDE is without a sample database after installation (in fact as we'll see below the Access sample project file does give us some help). At the end of this chapter we'll highlight routes to bring databases into MSDE, and information on moving databases to MSDE is covered in Appendices B and C.

Access developers who focused exclusively on Jet-based solutions and other developers new to SQL Server may be unfamiliar with pubs. However, it is a SQL Server sample database in much the same way that the Northwind.mdb file is the standard sample Access database file. The pubs database design includes tables with names, such as authors, titles, publishers, and sales, which represent the entities in a book business.

The SQL Server Northwind database that ships with SQL Server 7 and SQL Server 2000 has the same relationships among tables as the one that ships with Access 2000. Therefore, many Access developers will be familiar with the data and be able to use it as a convenient learning model for discovering how to do tasks in SQL Server that they already know how to do in Access.

Over the course of the book we'll be working with both pubs and Northwind to provide illustrations of the concepts and coding we're discussing.

System databases

When you install SQL Server or MSDE, the database server will automatically start to use four databases. Whether you know about them or not, these databases manage user-created databases and the operation of the database server. The database names are master, model, msdb, and tempdb. These are all **system databases**.

> One word of warning, which cannot be overstated: under *no* let's repeat that – *No*, circumstances should you alter the master database or the msdb database.

The master Database

Every SQL Server must have a master database. The master database is the most crucial database within SQL Server. It records all the system level information about the whole server system. The master database records the existence of each database within the server, but it is up to each database to then look after its own tables and information.

Under no circumstances should you consider altering any information within the master database. You should also keep an up to date database backup of the master database, just in case of corruption.

The model Database

The model database does what its name suggests – it acts as a model for all user-created databases on a database server and is installed with SQL Server with default settings. If you are a sophisticated administrator who will be installing SQL Servers for use by less experienced administrators, it *may* be worthwhile customizing the model database. There are a number of customization issues that can be dealt with within the model database. For example, you can create user-defined data types, or define the initial sizes of databases, along with many other options, and these will automatically appear in all new, user-created databases. This avoids the need for new or inexperienced database administrators to re-create the user-defined data type in each new database.

Initially, it may be wise to leave the model database alone, because any mistakes, or even an inappropriate value for a setting, will repeat with each new database. For example, setting the initial size of a database to a value that is too large for most user-created databases will waste disk storage.

The msdb Database

The msdb database stores information about scheduled tasks, alerts and operators, as well as backup history – SQL Server Agent and Task Manager rely on this database to perform their functions. Unlike the two preceding system databases, the accidental deletion of this database will not *usually* cause your database server to fail. However, the removal of the database will disable SQL Server Agent and leave it in a corrupt state. Since the database is so small we *strongly* recommend it's left alone.

The tempdb Database

The tempdb database has two primary roles. First, SQL Server uses it to store temporary tables as it develops return sets for complex queries. Second, it can hold any temporary tables the user creates (a topic outside the scope of this book).

Not only are the objects it holds temporary, but tempdb is itself temporary, and is completely reconstructed each time SQL Server is restarted.

Getting Started with Access Projects

As we've previously mentioned, Access projects are a new type of Access file (having the .adp extension). This file type seamlessly integrates SQL Server database objects, such as tables, views, and stored procedures, with Access objects, such as forms and reports, and delivers three significant benefits:

- ❑ Access developers can graphically create SQL Server solutions with much of the ease and familiarity of building traditional Jet database solutions.

- ❑ Access projects simplify the task of displaying result sets from SQL Server database objects in traditional Access forms and reports as well as data access pages, (a new feature in Access 2000).

- ❑ The Database window menu in Access projects facilitates administrative database functions – a useful feature for MSDE developers who don't necessarily have Enterprise Manager.

Access project files make use of OLE DB technology to access MSDE/SQL Server data; these project files are *not* database files – they merely connect to a database and allow the objects in the database to be manipulated through the Access interface and allow Access features (forms, reports) to work with data in the data store.

In this section we'll:

- ❑ Introduce Access project files

- ❑ Quickly familiarize ourselves with the **Database** window

- ❑ See how to open and create Access projects

- ❑ Look at the database utilities accessible through the project interface

- ❑ Quickly review the Visual Basic Editor

Database designers can manually tap the benefits of Access projects from two interfaces. Firstly we have the **Database** window to create new databases and Access projects as well as examine and edit existing database and Access objects. Secondly, the Access project menu can be used to perform many of these tasks and additional ones such as managing security, and importing data.

To start with we need a project to work with.

Introducing Access Project Files

As we saw previously, while users of SQL Server have sample databases installed with their data engine, MSDE users have none. They can however install a sample Access project named

NorthwindCS.adp. This is found on the Office 2000 installation disc 1 under the Access option and can be installed via the custom installation option (expand the Access node, expand the Sample Databases node and select Northwind SQL Project File).

Once the project file is loaded, it is available to use within Access – the first time that the NorthwindCS.adp project is opened it runs a script that automatically loads the NorthwindCS database. Since NorthwindCS.adp ships with Office 2000, the NorthwindCS database can be loaded into a database server running either MSDE or SQL Server.

The NorthwindCS.adp Access project contains forms and reports that build on the database objects in the NorthwindCS database, which can be used as models for the forms and reports in your own custom solutions. On starting to work with this project, the Show Me menu command may be found especially useful. It opens the Show Me window, which contains information and links providing a useful overview of a number of topics such as:

❑   How the NorthwindCS.adp project manages its database and Access objects

❑   The design techniques used to create the forms and reports in the NorthwindCS project

❑   Using **data access pages** as a simplified technology for building web-based database solutions

Now let's move on to have a look at the interface we're presented with.

An Overview of the New Database Window

When an existing .adp file is opened, it shows a Database window that is similar to one that appears when you open a traditional Access database file with a .mdb extension. The following screenshot depicts the NorthwindCS.adp file with its Database window open in an Access session:

Access projects integrate two disparate sets of object classes in the Database window. The first four object classes on the Objects bar – tables, views, database diagrams, and stored procedures – denote database objects. Access project files connect to these objects via the OLE DB component architecture and the database server (MSDE or SQL Server), manages the objects. Note that the .adp file itself does *not* hold or maintain these objects – it merely connects to them via its OLE DB link.

Over the course of the book we'll be looking into each of these objects in turn. As we'll see, SQL Server tables are generally similar to those in traditional Access database files (those with a .mdb extension). Views and stored procedures enable functionality similar to stored queries and QueryDef objects in traditional Access database files, and a shorthand way of understanding Database diagrams is to think of them as a more powerful version of the Relationship window from earlier versions of Access. The remaining five object classes in the Database window Objects bar – forms, reports, pages, macros, and modules – do reside in the Access project file.

Access projects offer developers graphical means for using forms, reports, and data access pages (referred to as Pages) to expose the contents of tables and views. The Access project interface refers to data access pages as Pages. We can programmatically use stored procedures as the record source for these Access objects. Additionally, custom solutions can be developed to enable user interaction with the data both graphically and through VBA code behind forms and reports as well as well as in stand-alone and class modules (similar results for data access pages can be achieved using VBScript, or JavaScript code behind the page). To further enhance programmatic access and user interaction with SQL Server data sources macros can be used. Subsequent chapters deal with all of these topics (except for macros, which are generally inappropriate for the kind of database solutions that merit the use of Access projects).

> *Let's just re-iterate this important point – an Access project is not a database file, it merely connects to a database managed by SQL Server or MSDE. By integrating database objects and Access objects in a common interface, Access projects create a rapid application development environment for building SQL Server solutions. This makes it easier and less expensive for businesses to achieve the scalability advantages that SQL Server brings to database chores.*

No matter where an object class resides, Access projects offer a consistent way of viewing the members of the class, which are exposed when the appropriate object is selected in the Objects bar (as shown above for the tables in the NorthwindCS database). Similarly clicking on Modules would expose the two modules that belong to the NorthwindCS Access project.

Database Window Icons

The Database window offers four modes of viewing object lists (List view, Large Icons, Small Icons, and Details), which can be switched between by clicking the right four icons at the top of the Database window. The Details view works slightly differently for database objects than for Access objects. For Access objects, it presents the object name along with its creation and last-modified dates, its class type, and any description for the object, while for database objects just the object name and its class type are presented (although the other column headings show).

The three left-most buttons on the Database window change function depending on the type of object selected. In the example shown for Tables the screen shows their labels as Open, Design, and New. Unsurprisingly, these allow you to open an existing table to display its data, open an existing table to show its design, or start to create a new table. Views, Forms, and Pages have the same labels for these buttons, whereas for stored procedures, the Database window labels the buttons Run, Design, and New.

The Access 2000 menu for the Database window includes collections of commands that help to create and administer database solutions. These commands are particularly prevalent on the File and Tools menus. Other commands, such as many of those on the View and Insert menus, duplicate the role of controls on the Database window. Our next section will generally concentrate on commands found on the File menu.

Opening and Creating Access Projects

In this section we're going to be looking at:

❑ Setting up an Access project

❑ Connecting to an existing database including looking at attaching databases

❑ Creating a new database

> **The section on attaching databases is extremely important if you intend to download and use any of the sample database files.**

Setting up an Access Project

The File menu includes several commands for getting a database into the Database window. The easiest route for starting out is to open an existing Access project. For example, after installation, the NorthwindCS.adp file can be opened via File | Open command, and if the installation was typical, it should be found at c:\Program Files\Microsoft Office\Office\Samples.

Choosing File | New opens the New dialog with two icons on its General tab that pertain to Access projects – for the moment let's satisfy ourselves with looking at the icon with the label Project (Existing Database). This creates a new Access project that can be linked to an existing database and is useful in situations such as:

❑ Experimenting with new Access objects for an existing database

❑ Developing two or more Access projects for the same database

If you have different communities of users for a database, you can control their access and functionality to the database, in part, by developing different Access projects for each community of users.

The Project (Existing Database) icon opens the File New Database dialog. This name for the dialog is actually a misnomer since really a new Access project is being created that eventually connects to an existing database. After providing a suitable name, clicking Create generates the new Access project. It also opens the Data Link Properties dialog.

Connecting to an Existing Database

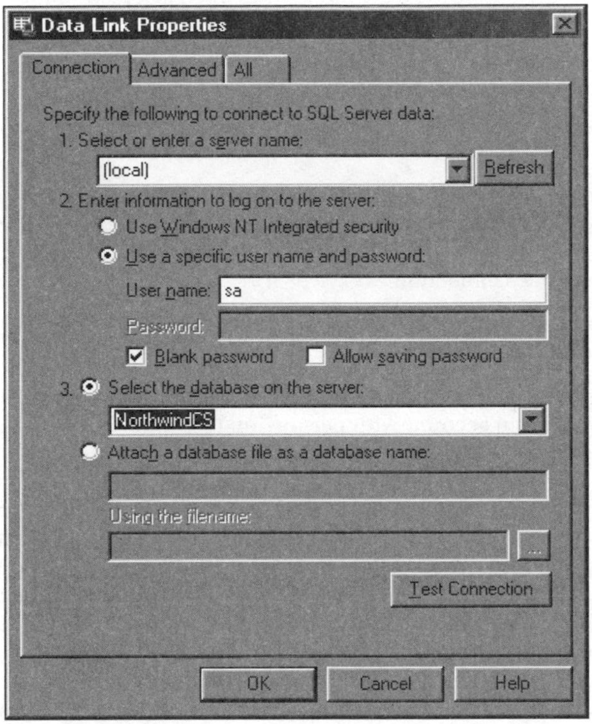

The Data Link Properties dialog (also available via File | Connection) is where parameters are specified for linking the new project to an existing database. There are three areas we have to consider on the Connection tab:

❑ Server Name – we need to specify a SQL Server or MSDE name (often this is the name of the computer running the database server). If the database that you want to link your new project to is on the machine being worked upon then (local) can be selected for the server's name, otherwise the drop-down box will give a list of possibilities. In fact one of the easiest ways to find your SQL Server name is bring up the SQL Server Service Manager.

❑ Server log on – Select either Windows NT Integrated security or Use a specific user name and password (the former option may be possible depending on the machine configuration and if the platform is NT 4.0 or Windows 2000). If using the second option either check with the SQL Server system administrator for user name and password details, or if the installation was performed by yourself and no other changes have been made, you can log in as the system administrator (sa) with no password (as illustrated). Of course this is highly insecure and should *never* be used in a production environment.

The logon information for the Data Link Properties *dialog ties critically to the SQL Server security model (covered in Appendix A). For simplicity all samples in the main body of the book will use a* sa *logon with no password. In Appendix A information on how to develop a more secure server is detailed.*

❑ Database – Once the first two options have been completed, clicking on the drop-down box should reveal a list of the databases managed by the server named in the first step. In the example shown the NorthwindCS database has been selected, but depending on the database installed pubs or Northwind may be the initial options.

Once all the boxes have been completed, to verify the connection click Test Connection. If a Test connection succeeded message is received then we can OK the message dialog and the Data Link Properties dialog.

If our database connection fails, we'll need to search for problems and resolve them. Typical problems when initially starting to work with SQL Server include:

❑ No physical network connection.

❑ The server not running – we discussed starting the servers via the SQL Server Service. Manager earlier in the chapter

❑ An invalid login account – the login has to be valid for the particular database we've selected (we have to use a login account with permission to create tables). The sa login will always have this authority (if we are in a position to use it).

Once we've got a successful connection and pressed OK on the Data Link Properties dialog we'll open up an Access project with the Database window pointing at the selected database (in this case we would get the display shown previously when we discussed the Data Base window). Remember that while the database objects accessible through this project are those of the underlying database, the Access objects (such as forms and reports) can, and will probably, be different to those residing in any other Access project that happens to connect the same database.

One interesting point to note at this stage is that, while the Northwind database distributed with Access comes complete with forms and reports, on creating and opening an Access project connected to a SQL Server based version of Northwind, these won't be available because forms and reports are not SQL Server database objects.

Remember that if you wish to change the connection in a project, the Data Link Properties *dialog can be accessed via* File | Connection.

Now it may be that we wish to look at a database, that has been developed on another MSDE/SQL Server, but for which we've been given the files (for instance the sample databases available for download from www.wrox.com). To do this we'll have to **attach** those files to our database installation. A second approach is to copy databases between servers – that is covered in Appendix C.

Attaching and Detaching Databases

This section on attaching databases is extremely important if you intend to download and use any of the sample database files. Although this section uses stored procedures and relies on using the stored procedure template, neither of which subjects are covered until later in the book, we include the section here, because of its relationship to setting up Access projects. Even if you're unfamiliar with T-SQL the steps are pretty self–explanatory.

As we'll see in Chapter 6, stored procedures are compiled series of T-SQL statements that can be used to carry out some function. MSDE and SQL Server have many system stored procedures that can be leveraged by the developer and administrator to make their lives easier and in this section we'll be looking at two such procedures – `sp_attach_db` and it's sister procedure `sp_detach_db`. This pair of system stored procedures enables database files to be attached to (or detached from) a server with a single command.

So, apart from the purpose we have here of attaching the download databases these procedures come in handy when:

- ❑ There is no network connection between, say, the database development machine and a test or production unit. This is where the 'sneaker net' returns – we have to manually detach a database from its server, physically transport the data to the other computer and then re-attach it to the new server.

- ❑ We want a cheap and easy way to deploy a SQL Server application based on an Access project. This scenario calls for shipping a client community both the database and `.adp` files for an application. A local administrator can run a stored procedure to attach the database to the local server and then e-mail, or otherwise distribute, the `.adp` file to registered users.

Database servers are always monitoring their database files and this means that we cannot freely copy them without first detaching them from the server. After detaching the database, it remains on the hard disk of the server it was previously attached to – the data is not deleted although the server will be unable to access the data until the database has been re-attached. To re-attach a file we can use the `sp_attach_db` stored procedures.

> *The `sp_attach_db` system stored procedure will work for the vast majority of databases you may build for SQL Server using Access, however if you have a really complex database this method may fail. SQL Server does have an alternative technique based on the* CREATE DATABASE *statement with the* FOR ATTACH *clause for building databases. As this is beyond the scope of this book please refer to Books Online for details. If you are attaching the database to a new server and the database participated in replication at its former server, then you must also run the* `sp_removedbreplication` *system stored procedure. Again this is beyond the scope of this book.*

By default, SQL Server databases have two files associated with them:

- ❑ The primary physical database file (`.mdf`), which is where the data for the database is ultimately stored

- ❑ The log file (`.ldf`), which contains a record of the operations that have taken place on the database since the last time the data was "committed"

We won't get any further into this structural issue; suffice to point out that both files are needed for the database to operate successfully. For confirmation of the existence of these files, if you've used a default installation one of these files can be found for each database on your server, in the Mssql7/Data folder.

To attach (or detach) database files we just need to be working inside an Access project that is connected to the MSDE/SQL Server installation we wish to attach the database to. Create a new stored procedure (click on the **Stored Procedures** icon in the **Object** list then double-click **Create Stored Procedure in Designer** in the object list pane). Into the template that is revealed, add the following code:

```
Alter Procedure "attach_a_db"
AS

--You can use @filename1 for the primary database file and
--@filename2 for the log file

EXEC sp_attach_db @dbname = N'db_Wrox_trial',
  @filename1 = N'c:\mssql7\data\Wrox_trial.mdf',
  @filename2 = N'c:\mssql7\data\Wrox_trial.ldf'

Return
```

> *If it's not already familiar, the T-SQL used here will be explained over the course of the book, especially in Chapter 6 where we take a detailed look at stored procedures.*

The script shows the format for the sp_attach_db system stored procedure. The command takes three parameters that are specified as indicated:

> *In each case the leading N followed by a single quote denotes Unicode formatting for the database and file names.*

- ❑ @dbname – The name for the database formed by attaching the files; file names can be up to 260 Unicode characters in length.
- ❑ @filename1, @filename2 – The file name parameters for the database files to be attached including the name of the file and its path. Note this pathname should not contain spaces.

So, in this example we are attaching the two files from a hypothetical database called **Wrox_trial** and will attach it to the server using the same name. If you're downloading sample databases from www.wrox.com you'll see they all come as two files – the database file and the log file.

Execution of the script is quite straightforward. Firstly close the template window and give the procedure a name when requested. If you accepted the default here you would be given attach_a_db. On giving a name the template window will close and the **Database** window will be revealed – together with, under the **Objects** icon, the new stored procedure. Then highlight the stored procedure and click the **Run** (exclamation mark) icon at the top left of the **Database** window. This should execute the stored procedure returning a message (if all went swimmingly) that the stored procedure executed successfully but did not return records. At this point the database should be attached and ready to connect to (this could be checked via **File | Connections** and the **Data Link Properties** dialog.

Similarly the script for detaching a database can:

```
Alter Procedure "detach_a_db"
AS

--You can optionally set the database name in single quotes
EXEC sp_detach_db 'Wrox_trial'

return
```

In order for detach_a_db to succeed you must be sure that nobody is using the database in any way whatsoever (this includes applications, SQL Server scheduled tasks, etc.) Remember that this operation will make the database completely inaccessible to the server until it is re-attached!

Creating New Projects and New Databases

Perhaps the most interesting feature of the File | New command is its ability to create both a new Access project with a matching, new SQL Server or MSDE database. This permits a developer to start with an empty database and project, which can either be populated from scratch or with objects from previously created databases and projects. In order to create a new database for a new Access project, you must be able to connect to an MSDE or SQL Server on a remote or local computer and have a login account with the permission to create a database on the server (the system administrator – sa – login has this authority).

The process is started by selecting the Project (New Database) icon on the General tab of the New dialog. This, again, opens the File New Database dialog, but as we'll see, the name is not a misnomer in this instance.

Verify that the Save in drop-down list box points at the folder in which you want to store your Access project and insert the file name for the new project. Clicking Create makes the new Access project, and launches the Microsoft SQL Server Database Wizard.

The Microsoft SQL Server Database Wizard enables a developer to create a new database in either MSDE or SQL Server by completing a couple of text boxes and clicking a couple of buttons.

By default, the initial wizard dialog assigns the new database its project's name with a SQL suffix. For example, for a project named MyNewDatabase.adp, the wizard names its matching database **MyNewDatabaseSQL** but any other unique name consistent with SQL Server database naming conventions will be OK (the name should start with any letter in the Unicode 2.0 specification – this encompasses all upper and lower case letters from A – Z, but any names which are the same as SQL Server keywords, or contain embedded spaces, must be enclosed in double quotes (" ") or square brackets ([ ]).

On the initial dialog the SQL Server name, the login ID (and password, if there is one) need completing (again if the database is running on the machine you're working on (local) can be used). On an NT 4.0 or Windows 2000 platform the drop-down box will give a choice of all the accessible MSDE/SQL Server installations, while a Windows 9x platform requires the server name to be entered.

Again, whatever login ID is used must have database creation permission on the SQL Server. After that click Next and progress to the point at which Finish can be clicked and the wizard will create the new database.

We won't consider how to populate a new database at this point – the body of the book will show how to create all the database objects we need to build a fully functioning database, while Appendix B discusses moving Access data into SQL Server databases by upsizing, and also indicates how **Data Transformation Services** (**DTS**) can be used to import data (from a variety of sources). This same service can be used to export data.

Next let's move on to some more miscellaneous topics that are essential for us to administer our databases properly, and are generally found under the Tools menu.

Database Utilities

In this section we're going to be looking at three areas:

❑   File maintenance – including backups and restores of databases as well as improving the storage efficiency of Access projects, using the Compact database utility (this doesn't actually compact SQL Server, but compacts the Access project file)

❑   Security – both for the database objects and the code within an Access project

❑   Replication – this represents a means of synchronizing multiple copies of a database

> *To use these database utility commands on a computer, it must have a local installation of either SQL Server or MSDE – the commands are only for the local installation.*

File Maintenance Utilities

Here we'll look at backing up, moving or copying, dropping, and compacting databases.

Backing Up

SQL Server is a very robust database manager, but it is still possible for a database to fail. A traditional recovery strategy from a failed database is to restore it from a recent backup.

Backups can be created using Tools | Database Utilities | Backup giving a file with a .dat extension. The backup file takes a snapshot of a database at a point in time and thus using this backup method the process must be repeated at appropriate intervals. The Backup command only saves a copy of the database objects – not the Access objects, such as forms and reports (to create a backup of these, use the file system to create a copy of the Access project file).

Users of SQL Server have another option – they can use the SQLServerAgent to schedule such jobs as backups. This is a SQL Server administration tool that lies outside the scope of this book.

In the event of a database failure, the database can be restored via Tools | Database Utilities | Restore. This command replaces the current copy of a database with the backup file that's referenced. As we may expect this process does not recover the Access objects in a project file. However, this command can be used to restore a database to a *new* Access project. Therefore, if you have a backed up copy of an Access project, the backed up project with the Access objects can be connected to the restored database – giving a recovered Access project with both restored database objects and backed up Access objects.

Moving or Copying

One common chore with database servers is to move or make a copy of a database from one server to another, and the backup commands present an approach to this (there are several of ways to do this –

we've already discussed the attach and detach stored procedures and Appendix C will show a programmatic method). The method outlined below does have the merit of not requiring any programming, being easy to follow, and operating from an Access project:

❑ First, create a backup of a database on one server

❑ Second, create a new Access project on a second database server with its own empty database

❑ Third, restore the database for the new Access project on the second server with the backup file created in the first step

These simple steps can create a new database on the second server with the contents of the original database.

Dropping

To retire a database that is no longer required use **Tools | Database Utilities | Drop SQL Database**. Invoking this command is equivalent to detaching a database from a server and erasing its files, permanently. Therefore, be absolutely sure that any database objects to be preserved have been copied before dropping the database.

The command will fail unless you have the database open exclusively and will produce an error message saying the database can't be dropped because it is in use. After clearing the error message, the Access project disconnects its database although the command does not remove database from the database server. Thus the database can be reconnected to via the **Data Link Properties** dialog.

> *To open an Access project exclusively, from* **File Open** *dialog instead of simply clicking* **Open** *after the relevant file has been found, click the drop-down button control next to* **Open** *and choose* **Open Exclusive**.

Compacting or Repairing

The **Tools | Database Utilities | Compact and Repair Database** command is especially useful after deletion of several Access objects. This behavior fragments an Access project file and compacting an Access project improves the efficiency of how an Access project stores its objects to disk. It has no impact at all on database objects maintained by a database server. The command is again somewhat of a misnomer for an Access *project* as the command actually does nothing at all to the database connected to an Access project; however, when Access is working in a standard mode with a Jet engine the database is compacted as well.

Security Utilities

The **Tools** menu offers a couple of avenues for securing Access projects and the database objects they expose. Access project security can be considered on three separate planes, with different security procedures required for each level:

❑ The first level is database object security

❑ The second level is the code behind forms and reports

❑ The third level is the collection of Access objects, such as forms and reports, in an Access project

This section identifies the menu commands and the general types of functionality that they provide within Access projects – Appendix A talks in more detail about SQL Server security.

Selecting Tools | Security | Database Security exposes dialogs that facilitate the addition, editing, and deletion of server logins, database users, and database roles. These are the basic building blocks of SQL Server security. In order to open the SQL Server Security dialog, MSDE must be installed on the computer – even if the Access project connects to a SQL Server database (whether local or remote).

One of the great advantages of developing SQL Server solutions with Access projects is the chance to use Access' rapid application development techniques, such as putting code behind forms as well as placing VBA code in stand-alone and class modules. There are a couple of options for protecting this code:

❑ Put a password on all the modules in a project – this restricts entry to any VBA code in a project as we'll see below.

❑ Convert the .adp file to an .ade file (via Tools | Database Utilities | Make ADE File). Converting a file from .adp to .ade format compiles all modules, strips the modules of any editable source code, and it compacts the Access project. An .ade file loads faster with optimized memory usage for improved performance than its .adp counterpart.

The major security advantage with this latter approach is that it makes tampering with the code less trivial, although there are some downsides:

❑ The source code or references cannot be edited anymore since there are none in the project

❑ Forms and reports cannot be opened in Design view

❑ Forms, reports, or modules cannot be imported or exported from the Access project

If there is a chance that the source code will need editing, an editable copy of the Access project file will have to be retained. Microsoft cautions in its documentation that Access 2000 .ade files will not be able to be opened in future versions of Microsoft Access. Therefore, if you anticipate your application's life cycle extending through the release of the next version of Access, keep a copy of the .adp file.

Replicating Data Between Servers

In Chapter 1 we briefly alluded to the subject of replication, which has great use in a wide variety of circumstances, especially where there is use of distributed copies of the same database.

The details of how replication works are beyond the scope of this book, but is worth alluding to here as the capability is available through Tools | Replication. Note that there are some *major* differences in the way Jet empowers replication versus SQL Server and for more details refer to a specialist SQL Server book.

Our final topic for the chapter is the Visual Basic editor.

The VBE User Interface

As a seasoned Access developer it is more than likely that you're conversant with the **Visual Basic Editor** (**VBE**) for implementing your programming solutions. Although most features within the VBE for Access 2000 remain unchanged, there have been a few alterations that we should familiarize ourselves with. So, to get up to speed we'll take a moment to review, briefly, the essential features of the Access 2000 VBE.

You will already know that the VBE is accessed either by the shortcut, Alt+F11, or from the Database window, Tools | Macros | Visual Basic Editor.

OK, so we know that the VBE is the development environment used for entering any VBA code that a project requires, including the creation of modules, or class modules. It can also be used to access the code behind any Access forms.

Access automatically bundles event procedures and other procedures behind forms and reports into a single module per form or report. A form has modules, also known as functions or subroutines, which sit as code behind the form. A stand-alone module, also known as a program, or a routine within a program, has no direct association with any other code. Custom classes can also feature in VBA code; these are in essence, hybrid modules, but more powerful and flexible than plain stand-alone modules. We can create properties and methods in these classes to give them the functionality and ease of manipulation we require.

The VBE permits us to manage all modules, both standard Access, and user-created, and the VBA code they contain.

The stand-alone modules in an Access project appear in the **Database** window when **Modules** is selected on the **Objects** bar. Double-clicking the module opens it within the VBE. Modules can also be selected in the **Database** window; they can be renamed or removed here. New, blank, stand-alone modules can also be created from the **Database** window by selecting **modules** as the object within the **Objects** bar, and then clicking **New** on the **Database** window.

Clicking the **Code** button on the **Database** window tool bar, opens the VBE at the code for the currently selected object.

The same control is available on the Form and Report Design view tool bars, and opens the VBE at the code for that form or report.

The VBE Windows

The **View** menu in the VBE offers the **Code**, **Project**, and **Properties** windows along with selected other windows to help monitor the performance of the VBA code in modules.

❑ The **Code** window – This is the most important window in the VBE, allowing the input of new code and editing of existing code. This window also has many built-in debugging features.

❑ The **Project** window – This is an explorer that displays and lists all the forms and modules within an Access project, and enables navigation from one form or module to another. When another form or module has focus, any existing code created for that form or module is displayed within the VBE, or an empty code window is displayed if there is no code at that point.

The Window menu also enables navigation between open Code windows.

❑ The **Properties** window – This offers an interface similar to the **Properties** dialog for forms, reports, and their controls. An object must be selected before the **Properties** window will display its properties. To see the properties of a specific control, we need to go to the layout mode, taking us back to Access, by clicking on the **View Object** button in the **Project** window To return to the code, we would use the **Code** button, on the tool bar. On returning to the VBE, the properties window will be populated.

You can use the Alt+Tab *shortcut to navigate to any other open window, such as the Database window, from the VBE. However, the VBE offers a direct path back to the last open window in Access. Simply press Alt+F11. You can also choose* View | Microsoft Access *from the standard VBE menu bar or click the* View Microsoft Access *control on the VBE standard tool bar.*

To add a new procedure to an existing module, we choose Insert | Procedure or we can simply select an entry point for a new procedure, and just begin to type. When using the menu command, Access prompts for the name of the procedure and other information in the Add Procedure dialog. On clicking OK, Access creates the shell for a procedure and inserts it into the code module ready for the new code.

Each Access project has its own corresponding **VBA project**. A VBA project is a collection of modules (and other containers for VBA code) associated with an Access project.

The NorthwindCS icon at the root of the Project window, which is in bold and is the top-most entry, denotes the internal VBA project name for the Access project named NorthwindCS. The name in parentheses is the Access project name as saved to the hard drive. The two need not match.

Right-clicking the icon opens the VBA Project Properties dialog.

From the General tab, we can alter the VBA project's name, and place a project description to provide information for the next person who needs to use it. If a project has a custom Help file, the General tab of this Properties dialog enables the insertion of the file name, and the Context ID information for it. The Protection tab allows us to specify whether a project should be locked for viewing:

Checking the Lock project for viewing check-box restricts viewing and editing of code and properties associated with a VBA project. We can also password-protect the project so by entering a password in the two password boxes in the bottom half of the tab.

.ade Files

.ade files can also be used to secure the VBA code in Access projects. This file is a compiled version of the code in the VBA project associated with an Access project. The conversion reduces the file size, resulting in more efficient memory use than .adp files; it also increases the speed of running the code. Since .ade files only contain compiled code, the code cannot be edited, so an .ade file is totally secure as far as VBA code is concerned. The conversion also extends security to forms and reports.

> *An .ade file does nothing to affect the security of tables, views, stored procedures, or database diagrams. These reside on the server, and you should invoke SQL Server security to protect them from unauthorized access. Appendix A deals with SQL Server security.*

.ade files are useful for distributing Access applications. In order to revise an application, however, you must recover the original .adp file and then edit it as required.

We create .ade files based on .adp files with the Tools | Database Utilities | Make Ade File command in the Database window. This command opens a Save As dialog that allows us to specify a folder and a file name for the .ade file. Doing this results in a completely new version of the Access project with the code compiled.

> **If you ever make a .ade file, it is imperative that you keep a copy of your Access project and code, otherwise you may find that you will not be able to get back to your Access project to complete any alterations.**

The Object Browser

When writing VBA code, there will be times, when you will be including objects that are not part of Access. These are added into code by selecting Tools | References from the VBE. The Object Browser displays all the methods and properties of these objects, exposes all the objects referenced within Access, including Access itself.

To open the Object Browser, we select View | Object Browser, or press *F2*. Once the Object Browser is open, it displays a set of classes that we can determine, by altering the top combo box (the Project/Library drop-down).

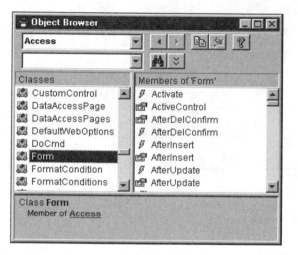

In the screenshot, the classes have been restricted to those found and contained within Access. The Form class has been selected from the Classes list so that all of the properties, methods and events available for a form within an Access project appear in the pane Members of 'Form'. Icons also enable speedy identification of how each member is defined. The grey area below the Classes list displays the name of the class that is selected, and the library to which the class belongs. If we were to scroll down, we'd see that events and methods are also displayed, along with the parameters required to be passed to them.

> *The Object Browser also provides help on objects and methods. Selecting any member and then clicking the* Help *button (or the keyboard shortcut F1) opens VBA documentation for that topic in a separate window.*

In addition to the Classes and Members of windows, the Object Browser also includes Project/Library and Search Text drop-down controls. The drop-down Project/Library contains an entry for each library to which a VBA project has a reference. For example, if you previously added a reference to the Microsoft ADO Object Library within your VBA code, then that library appears in the control's list.

We can use the Project/Library and Search Text controls to search for objects for methods, events, properties, parameters, or constants. You can specify a search in one library or all libraries. When the Search button is clicked, the Object Browser automatically opens a Search Results window, and then searches through the library for the entered string. Any items found are listed in the search results for you to then make your choice.

We can click an item in the Search Results window to select the corresponding item automatically in the Classes window. This will cause the Members of window to show the members appropriate to our selection.

Debugging VBA Procedures

Even the best programmers make mistakes and need to debug their code. The Visual Basic Editor offers multiple tools for debugging VBA code.

When debugging, one of the biggest problems can be identifying where an error occurs in the code. **Breakpoints** enable us to stop the action in a procedure and examine intermediate results on the way to a procedure's conclusion. The procedure in the following screen shot includes a For loop that the author wants to run 7 times. At the end, int2 should equal 1+2+3+4+5+6+7, or 28. To check the result of the mathematics, there is a Debug.Print statement at the end. When we run the program normally, without any breakpoints, the program returns a value of 36 for int2.

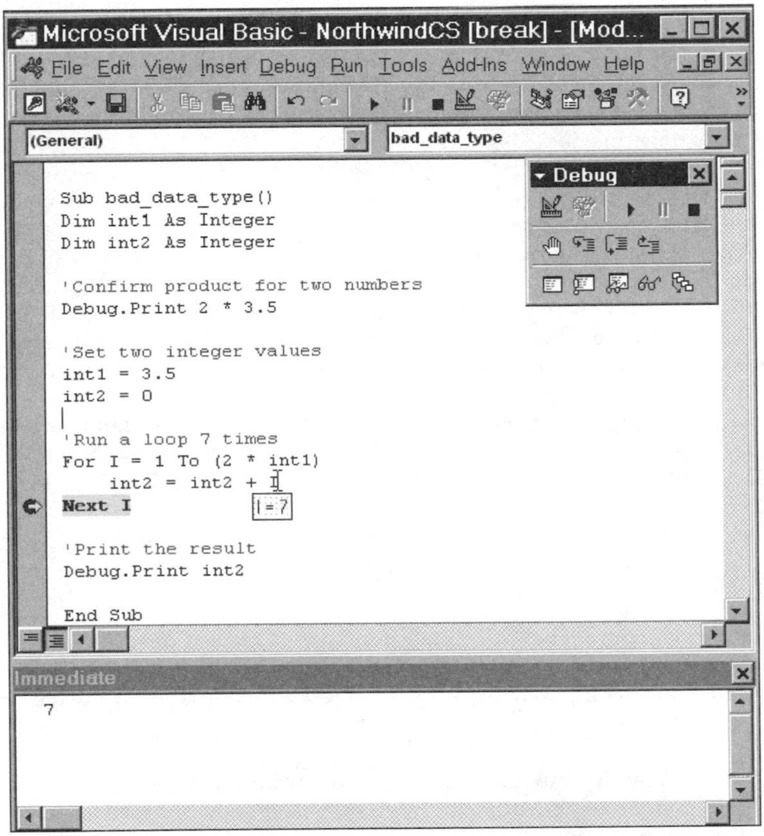

If we wanted to step through the code, and stop at the end of each loop, we could set a breakpoint. We do this by placing the cursor on the appropriate line of code where the execution should pause, and pressing *F9* to set the breakpoint. The graphic shows this breakpoint on the Next I statement. A breakpoint is defined by a red dot in the left hand column.

You can add as many breakpoints to a procedure as you wish, by clicking in the margin wherever you want the breakpoint to be set. Clicking the same point again toggles off the breakpoint. Once a program is in operation, you can toggle the breakpoint setting for lines of code with the Toggle Breakpoint tool (it looks like a hand) on the Debug tool bar.

61

Examining the code, we find that two variables at the start are each defined as an `Integer`. Then there is a `Debug.Print` to demonstrate what 2 * 3.5 results in, which is 7. The first variable, `int1`, is set to 3.5. However, we know that `int1` only holds whole numbers. so Access has rounded up the value to 4.

Before starting to test the code, we can expose the **Immediate** window by choosing **View | Immediate Window** from the VBE menu bar, so that any debug statements can be viewed, or we can enter any code to run outside the procedure.

To test the code, we place the cursor at any point within the procedure, and either press *F5*, which will run the code to the first breakpoint, or press *F8*, to execute one line of code at a time; we can also use the three controls to the right of the **Toggle Breakpoint** control on the **Debug** toolbar.

On reaching the breakpoint in the code, it behaves exactly as it sounds; it halts the procedure at that point.

The yellow arrow in the left hand column, which is currently over the breakpoint, represents the current point which has yet to execute demonstrating that the code has run up to the breakpoint, and has now stopped before executing this line

If we were to step into the next line of code from the preceding screenshot, which has been taken part way through debugging, we would see that control passes again to the `int2 = int2 + 1` statement. This indicates the loop is operating more than 7 times. Resting the mouse cursor near `int1` in the `For` statement reveals that `int1` has a value of 4. This, as we identified earlier, is problem because 2 times 4 is 8 rather than 7. Obviously there are several possible workarounds for this little bug (for example, declaring `int1` as a `Single` instead of an `Integer` data type), which we've created merely to review the debugging features of the VBE.

We haven't gone in to depth here as you will already, no doubt, be very familiar with these features but we have provided a quick revision. For detailed information on debugging in the VBE, however, Professional Access 2000 Programming from Wrox Press (ISBN 1-861004-08-7) is recommended.

Summary

This chapter has hopefully provided the practical information you'll need for getting stuck into the rest of the book with minimal further software installation required (apart from attaching any databases from the code download available from www.wrox.com, and the web-oriented software detailed in Chapters 9, 10, and 11).

In this chapter we've examined the installation procedures for the Microsoft Data Engine (MSDE), SQL Server 7.0, and SQL Server 2000. Additionally we've looked at the differences in capabilities between different versions of the same product and highlighted what utilities and samples we may expect to find after installation of each product.

From there we moved on to to introduce the main focus of this book – Access projects. These new files (with the `.adp` extension) aren't database files but do have a defined connection to a database and:

❑ Allow objects in the database to be worked with through the Access interface

❑ Allow Access functionality (forms and reports) to use the underlying data in the database

While introducing Access projects we also considered a number of related issues, such as connecting databases to Server installations and using database utilities, and carried out a quick review of the Visual Basic Editor.

Now we've made a start with Access projects, we now need to begin the task of examining how we can effectively employ them to build and supply database solutions. The logical place to start is the building blocks of relational databases – tables.

Designing SQL Server Tables with Access 2000

With Access 2000, more developers than ever before can build their own custom solutions from the ground up. The three major sections of this chapter will equip us with the skills to start building our own SQL Server database solutions. We will see how to populate our databases with custom tables, through both the user interface and a mix of programmatic approaches.

This is a long chapter, which will provide us with much of the basic grounding we need for the rest of the book. It is split into three very precise sections:

❑ Data types

❑ Creating and managing tables

❑ Constraints

We will now look in more detail at what each of these sections covers.

First, this chapter drills down into SQL Server **data types**. We will divide the data types into three sets:

❑ A core set of data types, generally similar between traditional Access database files and SQL Server

❑ Several important data types unique to SQL Server, and a few data types only available for Access database files

❑ SQL Server 2000 new and exclusive data types

Happily, when we use Access projects to build SQL Server tables, we can assign SQL Server data types to the columns of our tables. Building great database solutions starts with using the right data type for each column in every table.

Second, we will explore ways of building, editing, and modifying tables. In this section, we focus on adding columns to a table and populating tables with values. There is an especially rich array of tools for performing these tasks, including **T-SQL**, **ADO** via **VBA**, and **SQL–DMO**.

It is generally easier to add tables and populate them with columns manually. However, programmatic approaches have the advantage of providing code that documents our table designs for better documentation and easier maintenance.

In addition, the same programmatic tools we use to build tables will help us customize our SQL Server solutions in other areas. T-SQL is very convenient for building stored procedures and SQL-DMO is useful for looping through collections of SQL Server `Database` objects.

Third, this chapter presents a series of techniques for adding **constraints** to tables. Selected constraints include:

- ❑ Whether a column can contain `NULL`s
- ❑ `CHECK` constraints for controlling the values that go into a column
- ❑ `UNIQUE` constraints (also referred to as alternate keys)
- ❑ Primary keys
- ❑ Foreign keys

The fact that SQL Server solutions typically address larger databases with more users than traditional Access database file solutions, increases the significance of proper and flexible table design, along with controlled referential integrity. This chapter equips us with the skills to create powerful databases with precisely defined tables that are easy to fine-tune over time.

> There are a variety of examples in this chapter – the code for which can be downloaded from **http://www.wrox.com**. Some examples require Query Analyzer and Enterprise Manager; most do not. Readers with these tools installed will be able to carry out all of the code samples. Everyone else will still gain information from reading those examples they cannot complete.

SQL Server Data Types

If tables are the building blocks of database applications, then **data types** are the building blocks of tables. Data types tell us far more than just the type of data the object contains. They also show the length of the stored value or its size, and for numeric data types, the precision and scale of the number.

> *Precision is the number of digits the number can contain and scale is the number of digits that can be stored after the decimal point.*

Data types can be applied to the following objects:

- ❑ Columns in tables and views
- ❑ Parameters in stored procedures

❑ Variables

❑ T-SQL functions returning one or more values of a specific data type

❑ Stored procedures with a return code – always integer data type

The enlarged set of data types in SQL Server versus Access enables a database developer to more finely tune a database to match the real-world systems they model, thus enabling computer resources to be used more effectively.

Happily, all of our essential Access database data types are in SQL Server, in one form or another. We can even assign data types to columns with a designer-friendly grid that resembles the one in Access. This section reviews data types in three parts:

❑ First, we will look at SQL Server data types that are analogous to Access database data types. In several cases, this is just a matter of learning the new name. In other cases, the differences relate to the capabilities of the data type, such as the maximum number of characters.

❑ Second, we review several data types that are in SQL Server 7 and MSDE, but are missing from Access databases, and vice versa. We can use these to tap into some of the unique capabilities of SQL Server.

❑ Third, and finally, we review three new data types that are available exclusively with SQL Server 2000. If you have been waiting for a reason to upgrade from SQL Server 7, these may help you make the decision.

Data Types in Access and SQL Server

The following table enumerates the SQL Server data types that correspond to Access database file data types.

The Bit data type in SQL Server provides the same type of capability as the Yes/No data type in Access databases. Both data types represent Boolean values, but they take different approaches. From a raw data perspective, SQL Server represents True and False with values of 1 and 0, respectively, but Access uses values of -1 and 0 for the same purposes. Access developers should update their query design techniques to reflect this distinction when they use the Bit data type to replace their prior use of the Yes/No data type.

Access Name	SQL Server Name	Size in Bytes	Comments
Yes/No	Bit	Varies (dynamically sized)	For fields with binary values. As small as 1 Bit. This depends on the number of fields with this data type. The first Bit data type takes up 1 byte; the next 7 make use of the same byte. If there are 9 to 16 Bits, they are stored as 2 bytes etc. Allows nulls for the first time in SQL Server 7.0 – although allowing nulls uses an additional byte. Columns of type bit cannot have indexes on them.

Table continued on following page

Access Name	SQL Server Name	Size in Bytes	Comments
Number (Byte)	Tinyint	1 byte	For numeric fields with values from 0 through 255.
Number (Integer)	Smallint	2 bytes	For numeric fields with values ranging from -32,768 through 32,767.
Number (Long Integer)	Int	4 bytes	For numeric fields with values ranging from -2,147,483,648 through 2,147,483,647.
Number (Single)	Real	4 bytes	For numeric fields that can efficiently store large numbers with some approximation. The range of values is -3.40E + 38 through 3.40E + 38. Both Float and Real data types are known as approximate data types, as they do not store the exact number specified for many numbers – they store a very close approximation of the value. Therefore, these data types should not be used when exact numbers are required, such as in financial applications; the Integer, Decimal, Money, or Smallmoney data types should be used instead.
Number (Double)	Float	Various. For n is 1-24, 4 bytes. For n is 25-53, 8 bytes. These give us precision levels of 7 and 15 digits respectively.	For numeric fields that can efficiently store very large numbers with some approximation. The range of values is -1.79E + 308 through 1.79E + 308. Accepts an argument, Float(n), that determines size and precision. n must be a value between 1 and 53 – the synonym for double precision is Float(53) and for Real is Float(24).
Number (Decimal) (p,s)	Decimal(p,s)	Varies (dynamically sized)	For numbers up to a total of p digits with s digits after the decimal point, total no more than 38. Fields with this data type perform integer arithmetic like those with a money data type. The range for this data type varies depending on which version of SQL Server you are using, and how it is started. Access database files can represent Decimal data type numbers in the range -2^{28} through $2^{28} - 1$.

Access Name	SQL Server Name	Size in Bytes	Comments
Number (Replication ID)	Unique identifier	16 bytes	For uniquely identifying rows in replicated table applications and other scenarios where you need a number unique in space and time.
Currency	Money	8 bytes	For numeric fields representing currency where the rounding associated with Real and Float data types is not acceptable. Range of values is from -2^63 through 2^63 - 1. Accurate to within a ten-thousandth of a monetary unit.
Date/Time	Datetime	8 bytes	For fields that hold dates and times. In SQL Server, the beginning date is January 1, 1753. The last date is December 31, 9999. The finest resolution between any two dates or times is 3.33 milliseconds. In Access database files, dates can extend from January 1, 100 through December 31, 9999 with a resolution of 1 second.
AutoNumber	Int (with Identity property)	4 bytes	This data type is often convenient for uniquely identifying the rows in a table. Access database files have an explicit data type that increments by 1 starting at a seed of 1. SQL Server offers parameters for setting the seed and increment values of an IDENTITY column. Access database files do not offer control of the seed and increment through its user interface, but you can manipulate these values through Jet SQL.
Text(n)	Varchar(n) or Nvarchar(n)	Varies (dynamically sized)	For variable-length text fields. Text(n) in an Access database stores up to 255 characters, but it is always in Unicode format. Varchar(n) is non-Unicode format; it stores up to 8,000 characters. Nvarchar(n) is Unicode format; it stores up to 4,000 characters.

Table continued on following page

Access Name	SQL Server Name	Size in Bytes	Comments
Memo	Ntext and Text	Varies (dynamically sized)	SQL Server uses the Text data type for text fields up to $2^31 -1$ characters in non-Unicode format. The ntext data type holds up to $2^30 -1$ characters in Unicode format. Access database files permit up to $2^16 -1$ characters in its Memo data field with a Unicode format. Starting with Access 2000, Access recognizes Unicode formatting.
Ole Object	Image	Varies (dynamically sized)	For binary objects from other applications, such as Excel spreadsheets or Paint images. This data type is not for images only – it's an all purpose kind of data type. Maximum size is $2^31 -1$ bytes.

We will now categorize these data types and examine each group in more detail.

Numeric Data Types

The Number data type for Access databases has several subtypes, such as Double, Single, Long Integer, Integer, and Byte. SQL Server treats these subtypes as separate data types. We need to pay close attention to the name changes because they can be confusing.

The Decimal data type is yet another Number subtype in Access and a regular data type in SQL Server. This data type behaves slightly differently in Access compared to SQL Server, and also in different versions of SQL Server. When SQL Server 7.0 starts with the -p switch and unconditionally with SQL Server 2000, this data type can represent numbers in the range from -10^38 through $10^38 - 1$. A SQL Server column with the full 38 digits requires 17 bytes.

When you install SQL Server, SQL Server setup writes a set of default startup options in the registry under a specific key.

SQL Server offers a number of startup options that we can use to override the default options. To do this we need to create and store a new key in the registry (using the Registry Editor), then edit the registry entry to include the relevant startup option. Note that each startup option is stored as a separate parameter in the Parameters of the MSSQL key.

For the new options to take effect, restart SQL Server from the command prompt using: sqlservr -c -s<new key name>.

The -p *option is used to specify the maximum level of precision of decimal (up to a maximum of 38 decimal places) and numeric data types – for other possible startup options, see Books OnLine.*

Note that caution should be taken when editing the registry, as incorrect changes can cause serious problems. Only more experience users should consider carrying out the above procedure.

SQL Server 7.0 without the -p startup parameter can represent numbers in the same range as Access (-2^28 through 2^28 -1). This is the default.

This data type requires two parameters to complete its specification.

❑ The **p** parameter designates the total number of digits that a column reserves to represent numbers. SQL Server calls this **precision**, and has a maximum value of 38.

❑ The second parameter, **s**, specifies the number of digits to the right of the decimal point. SQL Server calls this **scale**.

Access has one more Number subtype – the Replication ID; so named for its role in uniquely identifying rows in the replicas of a replica set. SQL Server names this data type Uniqueidentifier, although it is actually a **Globally Unique ID number (GUID)**. This number is unique across both space and time, which is why it is so appropriate for replication applications. Copies of the database in different locations can enter records at different times, fully assured that they can have one column with values that are unique across all the database copies participating in the replication application.

The Money and Datetime data types in SQL Server match the Currency and Date/Time data types in Access. The main point to note with these data types is that the name changes as you move from Access to SQL Server.

The AutoNumber data type is a Long Integer number that Access starts at one and automatically increments by one for each record added to a table. Microsoft Access documentation recommends this data type for primary keys in several situations. SQL Server offers the same functionality with the IDENTITY property for its Int data type. By default, SQL Server starts an IDENTITY property column with 1, and increases the column by 1 for each new record. In addition, the SQL Server table design grid makes it easy to change both the seed and increment value for an IDENTITY column. As with Access, making a column act like an AutoNumber does not automatically make it a primary key.

Therefore, after creating an IDENTITY column we need to designate it as the table's primary key if we wish to use it that way. SQL Server allows us to name this column how we wish, unlike Access where it defaults to AutoNumber.

Data Types for Text

Access databases represent text data exclusively with a variable-length data type, Text. Table designers can specify an upper limit for the field, but the length of each row in a Text column reflects the actual text in that specific column up to the set limit. Access does not allow this limit to exceed 255 characters. SQL Server 7.0 and later provide the Varchar data type for variable-length text data. The upper limit for this data type can be set for the table, up to a maximum of 8,000 characters.

There is also the Nvarchar data type, which is another variable-length text data type, but with a maximum upper limit of 4,000 characters. This difference stems from the fact that the Nvarchar data type represents characters in a dual-byte Unicode format while the Varchar data type relies on a single-byte format.

> As a reminder, Unicode is an international character set that supports over 650 of the world's languages, such as French, German, Japanese, Chinese, and Russian. To keep character coding easy and effective, the Unicode standard allocates a unique 16-bit value (instead of an 8-bit value used by other character sets) to each character and does not use complex modes or escape codes to specify modified characters or special cases. This provides codes for more than 65,000 characters – over 200 times the capacity allowed by 8-bit code sets (256 characters). For further information see http://www.unicode.org.

The Unicode format eliminates the reliance on SQL Server code pages for character representation and sorting when using multiple languages. **Code pages** are conventions that SQL Server uses for interpreting and encoding character strings. Different countries, such as Japan and the US, can have different character sets, with associated code pages, for encoding characters. If we know that our database will be holding exclusively one style of text, the Varchar format represents our data more compactly, making it faster to retrieve and smaller to store. If our database includes characters from multiple countries with different character sets, then the flexibility of the Unicode format can offset the advantages of the traditional single-byte format for representing characters with a unified character set for countries with different character sets.

Be careful, however. You cannot create a mail merge in Access with either Nvar, char, or Nchar character types. This is because the information doesn't get put in. See the next section, *SQL Server Data Types Not in Access*, for more on the Nchar data type.

The Text and Ntext data types in SQL Server allow the storage of very long text fields in a way that parallels the Memo data type in Access. The distinction between Text and Ntext corresponds to that between Varchar and Nvarchar. The Unicode format for the Ntext data type makes it appropriate for applications that have data from multiple countries with different character sets, other than the default on your machine. However, the maximum number of characters for an Ntext field (1,073,741,823) is only half that for a Text field (2,147,483,647).

Aside from allowing the storage of more characters, Text and Ntext data types differ from their shorter variable-length data types in another way. SQL Server does not always store these data types as part of a data row – instead it stores a pointer to the data. Note that Text and Ntext (and Image) data types in SQL Server 2000 can store their data in a row if:

❑ Text in row is enabled. To enable this option, we need to use the sp_tableoption stored procedure (see below), specifying text in row as the option_name and ON as the option value.

```
sp_tableoption [@TableNamePattern = ] 'table'
             , [@OptionName = ] 'option_name'
             , [@OptionValue = ] 'value'
```

❑ The length of the string is shorter than the limit specified in @OptionValue. To specify a maximum size that is not the default, specify an Integer value, within the range 24 to 7000, as the option value.

❑ There is enough space in the data row. Maximum size is 256 bytes.

When storing data in the data row, reading and writing the Text, Ntext, or Image strings can be as fast as reading or writing character and binary strings, as SQL Server does not have to access separate pages to read or write the data.

Otherwise, the data row contains a 16-byte pointer to the storage location of the Text or Ntext data. There must be enough space in the data row to hold the pointer. This design speeds the retrieval of records containing Text or Ntext columns with many rows, each with many characters. The pointer is often smaller than Text and Ntext fields, which can often have many more than 16 bytes. The retrieval unit is smaller, so retrieval goes faster. Image columns save and retrieve like Text and Ntext columns.

External Data Types

The Image data type holds binary files, such as Excel spreadsheets and .gif files. SQL Server does not interpret the contents of Image columns, but it stores and retrieves those contents as a string of Bits. This requires your application to recognize the format for a string of Bits and apply the correct file reader to decipher the string. Like `Text` and `Ntext` columns, `Image` columns in a data row do not always contain actual data, but merely a pointer to the location of the data.

Why does SQL Server have so many more Data Types than Access ?

The purpose of this diversity in data types is to enable database architects to match the behavior of a real-world system while they conserve computer resources. For example, if you have a table column that only holds `Integers` in the range from 0 through 255, then it makes no sense to assign a `Float` data type to that column. This is for two reasons:

❑ The `Float` data type is an approximate data type; it does not store the exact number specified, but instead stores a very close approximation of the `Integer` values from 0 through 255. Therefore, these data types should not be used when exact numbers are required. The `Bit` data type precisely represents all integers from 0 through 255.

❑ The `Float` data type takes 4 or 8 bytes per row (depending on the level of precision), but the `Bit` data type takes just 1 byte per row.

Because of SQL Server's capability to deal with much larger databases with more users, compared to Access solutions, using the wrong data type can have a more profound negative impact on performance. Assigning excessively large data types can waste storage and slow data retrieval. For these reasons, when we migrate from Access to SQL Server databases, we can improve our databases by paying more attention to getting the data type right.

Let us now look at SQL Server 7.0 data types that have no counterpart in Access.

SQL Server 7.0 Data Types Not in Access

In addition to the data types that SQL Server and Access jointly share, eight additional data types are available to SQL Server 7.0 and MSDE users. These extra data types point the way to new opportunities for enhancing the SQL Server applications that we build with Access projects. We need to be careful though, if our data has to be exported back to Access tables for any reason. The table below points to selected properties for these data types – in the *Size in Bytes* and *Comments* columns. Obviously, there is no column for Access names, as these data types do not exist in Access.

SQL Server Name	Size in Bytes	Comments
Smallmoney	4 bytes	For numeric fields representing currency. Use this data type instead of `Money` when the range of data values extends over the smaller range of -2^{31} through $2^{31} - 1$. Accurate to within a ten-thousandth of a monetary unit.
Smalldatetime	4 bytes	For date and time fields that hold dates in the range from January 1, 1900 through June 6, 2079 to an accuracy of within one minute.
Char(n) or Nchar(n)	Varies	For fixed-length text fields. `Char(n)` is non-Unicode format; it stores up to 8,000 characters. `Nchar(n)` is Unicode format; it stores up to 4,000 characters. SQL Server uses blank characters to pad from the right fields holding less than n characters. Fields specified with more than n characters are truncated at the limit of n characters.

Table continued on following page

SQL Server Name	Size In Bytes	Comments
Binary(n)	Varies	For fixed-length binary data fields; you can hold any fixed-length bit stream of n bytes. The maximum size is 8,000 bytes. With ANSI PADDING on, SQL Server pads fields with less than n bytes with zeroes.
Varbinary(n)	Varies	For variable-length binary data fields, such as a small .gif file, of up to n bytes. The maximum size is 8,000 bytes. In contrast to binary data types, Varbinary types accept NULLs. In the case of Varbinary data type values, their length can range from 0 through 8,000 bytes, but binary data types values can have lengths of 1 through 8,000 bytes.
User-defined	Varies	For custom fields, such as social security number or part number. This data type builds on system-defined data types by adding a nullability setting and binding Rules and Defaults (these are discussed below).
Cursors	N/A	This data type allows for the creation and manipulation of cursors on a server. This data type does not pertain to table columns, but instead is a data type for stored procedure output based on a SELECT statement.
Timestamp	8 bytes	A unique number for tracking INSERTs and UPDATEs throughout a database. This is not a datetime field, but more like an AutoNumber for INSERTs and UPDATEs. Any table can have at most one column with a Timestamp data type.

We will now examine these data types in more detail.

Small Data Types

The Smallmoney data type complements the Money data type by offering a smaller storage container for holding currency values. Both currency data types can express currency to the nearest ten-thousandth unit. When our currency data fits within the limits of the Smallmoney data type, its use can reduce the size of our database and speed data retrieval. You can specify a Smallmoney or Money data type with a leading currency symbol, followed by the currency value without commas. The Smallmoney and Money data types support 18 currencies, including the US dollar, the UK pound, and the Japanese yen.

The Smalldatetime data type complements the Datetime data type in a manner that generally parallels the roles of Smallmoney and Money (see above). The Smalldatetime data type represents a smaller range of dates than the Datetime data type. In addition, Smalldatetime columns denote time only to the nearest minute. Due to this diminished extent and resolution, the Smalldatetime saves 4 bytes per record. You can format Datetime and Smalldatetime data with either the CAST or the CONVERT function, but CONVERT offers an array of special display options that include truncating the time, showing the milliseconds, and presenting dates and times in international formats. We will discuss these functions later in the chapter.

Text Data Types

The Char and Nchar data types are for fixed-length text fields. Nchar data is a Unicode-formatted version of the Char data type. The upper limit in characters per records for Char and Nchar fields are 8,000 and 4,000 respectively.

Char and Nchar columns store their data – not just a pointer to the data – in the rows of a table. Note that, as we stated earlier, Text and Ntext (and Image) data types in SQL Server 2000 only store their data in a row under certain conditions.

These data types are appropriate whenever we have fixed-length text fields. An example might be a person's social security number. In this case, the length of the text field is identical for all entries in a table. SQL Server can retrieve fixed-length text faster than variable-length text since it does not have to determine when a field ends. Therefore, when the data in a column is not all of the same length, SQL Server's default is to use ANSI_PADDING (by setting this option to ON or OFF with the SET keyword – SET ANSI_PADDING {ON|OFF}) to pad Char and Binary (see below) fields. Char fields are padded with blanks and Binary columns with zeros to the length of the column.

External Data Types

Binary and Varbinary data types hold binary data, such as .gif and .jpg files, of the same sort as the Image data type. The Binary data type holds fixed-length binary data, and the Varbinary data type holds variable-length data. Both Binary and Varbinary data types have an upper limit of 8,000 bytes. When the data in a Binary column is not all the same length, SQL Server pads the field with zeroes to the length of the column as we discussed above.

These data types need careful use, as a lot of space can be wasted with very few rows.

Binary and Varbinary columns hold actual data and not just pointers to binary data outside the table.

User Defined Data Types

User-defined data types enable us to create custom data types from the built-in system data types discussed above. We would need to invoke a **system stored procedure** called sp_addtype to create a new custom data type.

Microsoft has included a large number of built-in, system stored procedures, which we can use as if they were, or as part of, our own user-defined, procedures. They also serve as useful examples of T-SQL code, which we can use as an aid to learning the language or to help write our own code. Chapter 6 discusses system stored procedures in greater detail. However, system stored procedures are so important that we will be referring to them between now and then.

This system stored procedure permits us to name our user-defined data type, designate its base system data type, and specify its length, precision, and scale. We can additionally designate its default status for accepting NULL values.

After creating a user-defined data type, it becomes available for use just like any system data type, with one exception. User-defined data types are valid only for the database in which we create them. One workaround for this problem is to update the model database with a custom user-defined data type. Recall from Chapter 2 that the model database serves as a template for all new databases created with a SQL Server.

Some companies/development groups have there own standard "model" database to encourage best practices and conformance to design standards.

Therefore, if we add a `user-defined` data type to this database, all new databases created after the changes on that server will have the custom data type available. Existing databases will still need to have the `user-defined` data types added.

We can further constrain a `user-defined` data type by creating `Rule` and `Default` objects – these are not ANSI compliant (bringing about portability issues), and they do not perform as well as constraints. Microsoft describes these objects as backward compatible; therefore we will give you an overview of them below, and not discuss them again after this chapter.

Defaults and Rules

`Defaults` and `Rules` are two traditional classes of database objects that parallel the functionality of `DEFAULT` and `CHECK` constraints. They apply to the individual columns of a table.

A `Default` is a value inserted into a column automatically, if a user does not enter one. In a RDBMS, every data element (a particular column in a particular row) must contain a value, even if it is NULL. Some columns do not accept NULL values, and hence either the user or SQL Server must add another value.

`Rules` are T-SQL expressions that define the acceptable data that can be entered into a column. After binding a `Rule` to a column, SQL Server checks each `INSERT` or `UPDATE` statement against the most recent `Rule` for that column. Note that data entered before the creation and binding of a `Rule` is not checked. We will meet `Rules` again later in the chapter, when we use them to solve a particular programmatic problem. `Defaults` and `Rules` are very similar to constraints, which we will discuss later in the chapter. `Rules` and `Defaults` are independent `Database` objects – much like `Tables` – while constraints are just features of a table (they have no existence of their own).

As they are independent objects, we need to bind our `Rules` and `Defaults` to specific columns as our needs dictate. They can also be bound to user-defined data types, using two system stored procedures, `sp_bindrule` and `sp_binddefault`. This vastly improves our ability to produce highly functional user-defined data types. While a `DEFAULT` *constraint* for a table is the same in all situations, we can bind different `Default` *objects* to a column, depending on special circumstances. We can bind `Defaults` to several columns in a database to force adherence to a standard that goes beyond data typing. `Rules` and `Defaults` are also reusable without being redefined, due to their independent object nature. The same `Rule` can be bound separately to multiple columns in a table, but the `Rule` will work independently with each column. We can also apply different `Rules` to a column depending on the context.

Cursors

The `cursor` data type enables an application to work with a server-side cursor. This is not a data type for a table. Instead, the `cursor` data type makes a row set available for processing on a row-by-row basis on the server. This enables an application to take advantage of the more powerful server-side computer resources and pass back a small set of essential information to a client workstation.

Timestamps

The `Timestamp` data type applies to columns that increment a value monotonically for each `INSERT` and `UPDATE` to a database, as we will discuss later. Each table in a database can have at most one column with a `Timestamp` data type. Within a database, there is a global timestamp value, which is a binary number reflecting the date and time the data was last modified. A major use of `Timestamps` is to check whether one user has modified a record, before another user applies a change. Timestamp columns are not appropriate for primary keys since they change during an UPDATE.

Each INSERT or UPDATE in tables with a Timestamp column copies the current global Timestamp value to the Timestamp column for the current row and then updates that global value for its next use. SQL Server stores Timestamp values in a Binary (8) format. In order to view the contents of a Timestamp column in a readable format, you must convert it (for example, to an Int data type). Use the CAST function, as discussed below, for this purpose in Query Analyzer. Query Analyzer will display Binary Timestamp values for viewing with a SELECT statement, but an Access project requires a transformation before it will display the values in a Timestamp column.

The T-SQL code in this section is to explore general design principles for creating tables programmatically and to highlight the behavior of the Timestamp field in particular. Some of the example (see below) runs in Access projects, but other portions do not. This is because Microsoft did not implement all of Query Analyzer's features in Access projects. We got some hint of this in the preceding chapter's discussion of guidelines for converting Books Online code for use in Access projects. In the following T-SQL sample, Access projects do not return binary data type values. Many samples in this book demonstrate how to use T-SQL code in Access projects. In this section, we focus on the T-SQL syntax for specifying a table and the behavior of Timestamp fields as demonstrated by the output.

Using a Timestamp Column With IDENTITY and Datetime Columns

We will now look at an example of using of a Timestamp column along with IDENTITY and Datetime columns. Don't worry if anything seems a little confusing at the moment, we will be examining this again later. You can also try it out in Query Analyzer, if you have the client tools installed on your machine. We will learn more about the details of using specific T-SQL statements later in this chapter and throughout the book.

```
--Suppresses messages about records processed
SET NOCOUNT ON
-- Remove table1 if it exists already
IF EXISTS (SELECT * FROM sysobjects WHERE id = object_id('table1')
    and OBJECTPROPERTY(id, N'IsUserTable') = 1)
DROP TABLE table1

-- Create table1 with
-- identity, datetime, and timestamp fields
CREATE TABLE table1
(
    myidentity int IDENTITY,
    mydatetime datetime DEFAULT getdate(),
    mytimestamp timestamp
)

-- Insert six records into table1 with
-- default values
INSERT INTO table1 DEFAULT VALUES
INSERT INTO table1 DEFAULT VALUES
INSERT INTO table1 DEFAULT VALUES
INSERT INTO table1 DEFAULT VALUES
INSERT INTO table1 DEFAULT VALUES
INSERT INTO table1 DEFAULT VALUES

Display inserted values
```

```
SELECT myidentity,
    CONVERT(varchar,mydatetime,109) AS 'mydatetime', mytimestamp,
    CAST(mytimestamp AS int) AS 'mytimestamp2'
FROM table1
```

The code is split into three sections. We will now examine each of these in more detail. The initial section includes a SET NOCOUNT ON statement that suppresses messages about how many records are affected by each INSERT and SELECT statement. The main task we perform in the initial section is to remove table1 if it already exists in the database. This is so that we can create it in next section without any errors.

```
--Suppresses messages about records processed
SET NOCOUNT ON
-- Remove table1 if it exists already
IF EXISTS (SELECT * FROM sysobjects WHERE id = object_id('table1')
    and OBJECTPROPERTY(id, N'IsUserTable') = 1)
DROP TABLE table1
```

In the second section, we create table1, and then populate the table with six new records. IDENTITY and Timestamp columns automatically populate themselves with values for each INSERT. The DEFAULT constraint for the field named mydatetime causes it to use the GETDATE() function to populate its rows with the current date and time. The default is used, as we do not supply any values of our own in the following INSERT statements. If we did, these would be used in place of the default value.

```
-- Create table1 with
-- identity, datetime, and timestamp fields
CREATE TABLE table1
(
    myidentity int IDENTITY,
    mydatetime datetime DEFAULT getdate(),
    mytimestamp timestamp
)

-- Insert six records into table1 with
-- default values
INSERT INTO table1 DEFAULT VALUES
INSERT INTO table1 DEFAULT VALUES
INSERT INTO table1 DEFAULT VALUES
INSERT INTO table1 DEFAULT VALUES
INSERT INTO table1 DEFAULT VALUES
INSERT INTO table1 DEFAULT VALUES
```

In the third section, we use a SELECT statement to display the mytimestamp field in both Binary and Int format. Notice that we use both the CAST and CONVERT functions to carry out data conversions. We use CAST to display mytimestamp in Int, and CONVERT to choose the display style of the Datetime column.

```
-- Display inserted values
SELECT myidentity,
    CONVERT(varchar,mydatetime,109) AS 'mydatetime', mytimestamp,
    CAST(mytimestamp AS int) AS 'mytimestamp2'
FROM table1
```

The CONVERT and CAST Functions

Both the `CONVERT` and `CAST` functions perform data type conversions. (Note that `CAST` is ANSI compliant and `CONVERT` isn't). In many cases they do the same thing, except that `CAST` doesn't offer some of the date formatting options provided by `CONVERT`. `CAST` can still do date conversion; it just doesn't offer the control over formatting that the `CONVERT` function does. You need to specify the style of the date format you want in the `style` argument. See Books Online for the different formats available.

The syntax for these functions is as follows:

```
CAST (expression AS data_type)
```

```
CONVERT (data_type [(length)], expression [, style])
```

In our example above the `SELECT` statement uses the style parameter value `109` at the end of the `CONVERT` function to display a `Datetime` column with millisecond values.

The screen shot below illustrates the output generated when the above code is run from Query Analyzer. Using Query Analyzer enables the display of both the `Binary` and `Int` values for a `Timestamp` column.

> *We can use the Windows calculator (choose the Scientific view) to confirm that the values of the mytimestamp VarBinary (8) column correspond to the converted values in the mytimestamp2 Int column.*

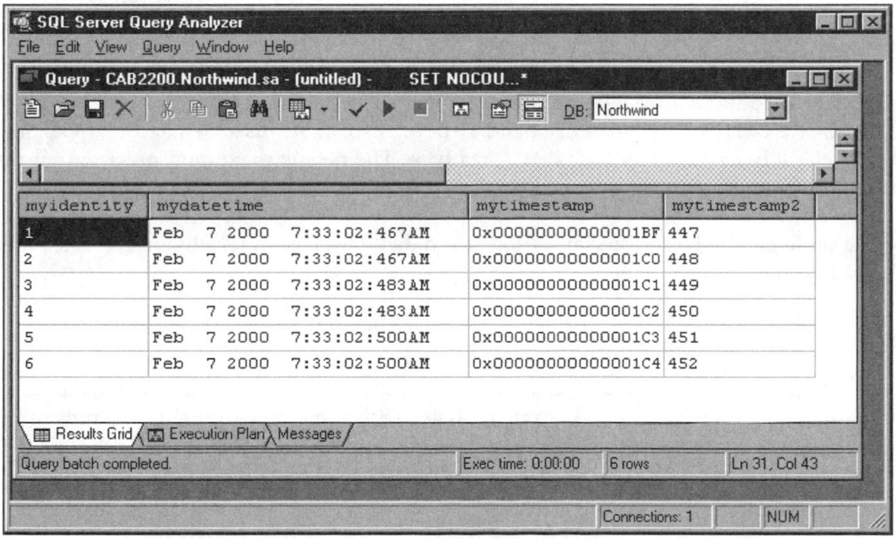

Let us now quickly look at Access data types that have no counterpart in SQL Server.

Access data types not in SQL Server

Two Access data types do not align well with any of the SQL Server data types:

Access Name	SQL Server Name	Comments
Lookup	No equivalent	We can achieve some of this functionality by creating a view that simulates the Lookup field behavior and by specifying the view as the record source for a combo box control on a form. Chapter 7 will also demonstrate this approach.
Hyperlink	Text and Ntext (hyperlinks inactive)	Note that SQL Server provides Text and Ntext data types, but hyperlinks are inactive. Nevertheless, Access projects offer similar functionality through the Hyperlink form control property. Chapter 7 discusses the property and demonstrates its use.

We will now look at data types unique to SQL Server 2000. We cover these data types for background knowledge. When using Access projects as the primary development platform for SQL Server we will not be able to use these data types, since it does not support them. In addition, since SQL Server 2000 introduces these data types, developers using the MSDE that ships with Office 2000 or SQL Server 7 will not be able to use these functions either.

SQL Server 2000 Data Types

SQL Server 2000 introduces three new system data types to further enrich our database development options. These are Bigint, Sql_variant, and Table. Also, as we discussed earlier, SQL Server 2000 upgrades the default behavior of the Decimal data type. The default maximum precision for this data type grows from 28 to 38 digits, without the need for the -p switch when starting SQL Server.

The following table gives a brief overview of the new data types. Again, for obvious reasons, there is no column for Access data types.

SQL Server Name	Size in Bytes	Comments
Bigint	8 bytes	For integer fields with values exceeding the bounds of the int data type. Use Bigint to represent values in the range from -2^{63} through $2^{63}-1$. SQL Server 2000 converts Bigint data type values to Numeric (19,0) data types when sending results to SQL Server versions 6.0 through 7.0. Versions prior to 6 requesting Bigint data get it back with a Float data type.
Sql_variant	Varies	For fields that can hold multiple other data types, such as Int, Decimal, Char, Binary, and Nchar. Sql_variant columns cannot hold Text, Ntext, Image, and Timestamp data type values.
Table		Use this data type for variables or as the return from a user-defined function to temporarily store results for future use.

Bigint

The Bigint data type makes available an Integer data type with the same value limits as the Money data type, but it does not assign any digits to a position after the decimal point (it's an Integer after all!). Int remains SQL Server's primary Integer data format.

SQL Server 2000 updates selected T-SQL functions to accommodate Bigint data. These include ABS, AVG, MAX, MIN, POWER, and SUM. In other cases SQL Server attempts to convert Bigint data to Int data. When the Bigint value falls outside the range of legitimate Int values, a conversion error results. For this reason, consider explicitly converting Bigint to Decimal(19,0) data before using functions not explicitly upgraded for Bigint. You can perform explicit conversions to and from Bigint with the CAST and CONVERT functions.

In addition, two new functions explicitly target the Bigint data type. COUNT_BIG operates like the COUNT function to return the number of items in a group, except that it returns a Bigint value. The ROWCOUNT_BIG function stops processing a query after processing the specified number of rows. Readers familiar with SQL Server functions will recognize this as similar to the ROWCOUNT function. The difference is that the ROWCOUNT function limits processing to the highest Int value; but the ROWCOUNT_BIG function extends the limit to the highest Bigint value.

Sql_variant

The Sql_variant data type behaves similarly to the Variant data type in VBA. Sql_variant columns can concurrently hold multiple different data types. The only data types not permitted in a Sql_variant column are Text, Ntext, Image, and Timestamp. A Sql_variant column cannot serve as a primary or foreign key, and it cannot have an IDENTITY property. Each instance of a column with a Sql_variant value has two supporting items. One is the actual data value, and the other is the meta-data description of the data. This description includes a specification of the base data type, its maximum length, precision, scale, and collation. The **collation** in SQL Server determines the sorting and comparison of data values.

As with Variant data types in VBA, you can derive confusing results when comparing Sql_variant column values with different base data types, such as a Char value of '123' and an Int value of 111. The '123' value appears greater than 111, but the native Sql_variant comparison returns 111 as greater than '123'. To avoid potentially confusing results, transform Sql_variant data to a standard data type before making comparisons. Sql_variant data types cannot participate as operands with numeric or string concatenation operators, such as +. We have to insert the CAST function based on a Sql_variant data type, rather than the native Sql_variant data type as the operand in concatenation expressions.

Table

User-defined functions can return values or tables. When a user-defined function returns a Table, it is in the new data type format introduced with SQL Server 2000. In essence, the Table data type is like a temporary table created in SQL Server's temp database. However, using the Table data type means you can access the result set faster, as it is in memory, rather than within a database and on a hard drive.

That concludes our examination of data types. We will now move on to the second major section of the chapter and focus on creating and managing tables using various techniques.

Creating and Managing Tables

When we work with Access projects, there are five ways to make or edit a database table. Many developers are familiar with the notion of treating a table as a class of entities, such as employees, orders, or authors. When database designers model real-world systems with a database, they create tables to represent entities in the real world. The columns or fields of a table represent properties of an entity. Therefore, an Employees table can have fields such as a first name, last name, hire date, and so on. An Orders table is more likely to have columns that denote an order's date, an ID for the customer making the order, and other information that helps to characterize a particular order. The rows of a table represent instances in a domain. The rows of the Employees table in the pubs database denote the employees of a publisher, and the Orders tables in the Northwind database has a separate row for each order.

In this section we will review four separate techniques we can use to create, and work with, the contents of a table in a SQL Server database. Again, don't worry if you don't grasp every concept presented here. We aim in this section to give you a hands-on feel for the basics of how to create and manage tables. Subsequent material in this chapter and the remainder of the book will build on the foundations presented here, so there will be ample opportunities to master all these techniques. The four techniques for creating and managing tables covered here are:

- ❑ Manually
- ❑ Using T-SQL
- ❑ Using VBA and ADO
- ❑ Using SQL–DMO

In a later chapter, we look at a fifth technique for creating and managing tables, using the database diagram.

Creating and Managing Tables Manually

The Tables collection on the Access project **Database** window offers a graphical means of creating and managing tables. With SQL Server, there are some distinct advantages to creating tables programmatically. However, we will create them manually first, as this is a good approach for starting to learn about SQL Server tables.

This section works with an Access project named Chapter03Pubs.adp with a connection to the pubs database.

Many of the examples and samples for the remainder of this chapter refer to the pubs database. Not all readers will necessarily have a copy of the pubs database. However, we will mostly be discussing the creation of our own tables rather than the use of existing pubs tables.

Creating Tables Manually

In this section, we will run through the basic steps needed to create a SQL Server table manually, using an Access project. For ease of reading, this information is split into the following sections:

❏ A quick look at the `Authors` table

❏ Creating your own tables

First we need to establish a connection to the **pubs** database, as discussed in Chapter 2. Now let's examine one of the tables in this database to see what this can tell us about SQL Server tables.

A Quick Look at the Authors Table

One excellent way to learn about SQL Server tables is to examine the tables in a sample database. The following screen shot reveals the **Design** view of the **Authors** table in the **pubs** database. To create this, we start by selecting the `Authors` table in the **Database** window of an Access project connected to the **pubs** database. Then, we click **Design** on the toolbar.

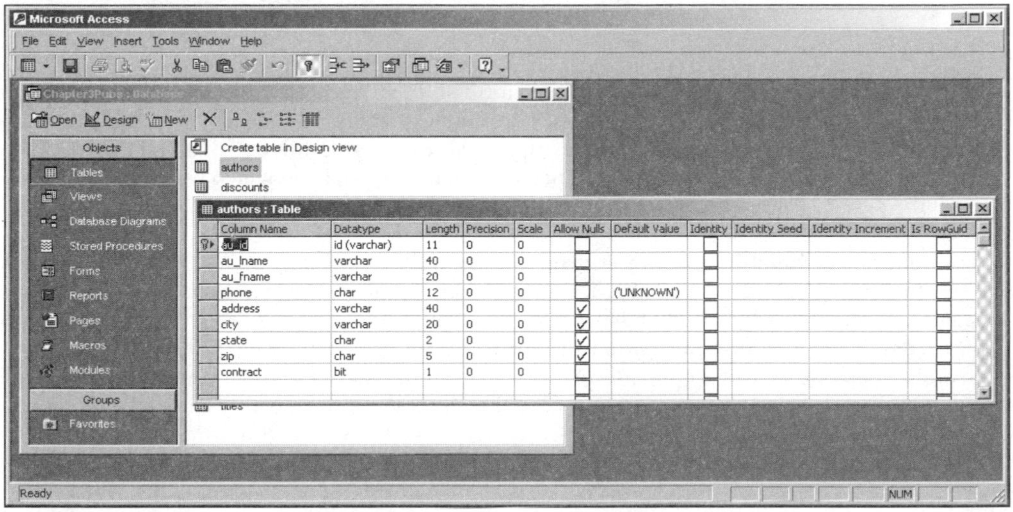

We depict the **Authors** design grid inside an Access project **Database** window to emphasize the relationship between them. Each row in the grid designates a column in the `Authors` table. Therefore, we can see from the grid that we have an `Authors` table with 9 columns.

The cursor rests in the au_id row. We can tell that this column has a user-defined data type, as the **Datatype** column shows the au_id row does not have a standard name. Instead, its data type name appears as id (varchar). The user-defined data type name is id, and its base system type is `varchar (11)`. Whenever we specify an `id` data type for a column in any table within the **pubs** database, Access automatically enters 11 into the **Length** column, and 0 in the **Precision** and **Scale** columns. `Varchar` data values do not have precision or scale, since they are variable-length text strings. Access does this because the **pubs** database has a user-defined data type id, which all tables in **pubs** can use. The definition for the id user-defined data type designates that the column is initially not NULL.

The au_id column serves as the primary key for the `Authors` table. Notice the depressed icon on the toolbar across the top of the **Database** window toolbar set. Moving off the au_id row de-selects the **primary key symbol** on the toolbar. The primary key symbol looks like the one Access uses for its own databases.

By looking at the other rows in the grid we can ascertain that:

❏ Aside from au_id and contract, all the other columns either use the `varchar` or `char` data types.

❑   For fields that have highly variable lengths, such as first and last names, the design specifies `varchar` data types.

❑   The application assumes five-digit zip codes. Therefore, it uses a `char` data type with a length of 5.

❑   Notice that in the **Default Value** column for the **phone** field the grid has an entry of ('UNKNOWN'). If the user does not enter a phone number, SQL Server will assign its default value.

❑   The **contract** field uses a `Bit` data type to represent whether an **author** is under contract. In **Datasheet** view, the values in this column appear as **True** or **False**, but they have values of **1** and **0** for the two states of the `Bit` data type. Don't forget that this is different from how Access represents these states, as **-1** and **0**.

Let's move immediately on, and use this knowledge to create our own tables.

Creating Tables

We start the creation of our own new table by selecting **Tables** in the **Objects** bar of an Access project, then clicking **New** and selecting **Design View**. Access imaginatively names the new table **TABLE1** and opens a blank design grid. We type a name for our first field, in this case **myidentitycol**, then tab from **Column Name** to **Datatype**. Click the down arrow to open a list of data types from which we can choose. This list includes all the system data types as well as any user-defined data types for this database.

As we want our first column to serve as a primary key, we will need to clear its **Allow Nulls** check box and click the **Primary Key** button on the **Table Design** toolbar. We also want to use an `IDENTITY` property with our primary key, so we need to check the **Identity** check box. Recall that this property is applied to a column with an `Int` data type; it works similarly to the Access `AutoNumber` data type. With SQL Server, we have more flexibility because we can set the `Identity Seed` and `Identity Increment` values for the column. Set both of these to 4 for **myidentitycol**, so that the column starts with a value of **4** and increases it by **4** for each new record.

We now continue to populate the grid, adding one row for each additional column in our table. As a minimum, we must specify the column's name. We will typically need to change the data type from its default setting as well. By leaving the **Allow Nulls** check box selected, we make it possible to commit the row without a value for the column. If our application requires a value for the column, clear the **Allow Nulls** check box and consider assigning a default value for the column. See the discussion of the **phone** column settings in the preceding screen shot for an example of how to do this.

In general (unless our application requires replication), we will not be using the **Is RowGuid** check box in the far right column of the design grid. In order to select this box, the column's data type must be a `Uniqueidentifier`. When we select the **Is RowGuid** check box, Access automatically inserts **(newid())** in the **Default Value** column. This function creates a new `GUID` for the row whenever a user inserts a new record. Since a `GUID` is a 16-byte number, we should not use it unless our application requires a unique value in both space and time for each and every row in the table.

The top panel in the following pair of screen shots shows the **Design** view for **TABLE1**:

Column Name	Datatype	Length	Precision	Scale	Allow Nulls	Default Value	Identity	Identity Seed	Identity Increment	Is RowGuid
myidentitycol	int	4	10	0			✓	4	4	
fname	varchar	20	0	0						
lname	varchar	40	0	0						
ext	char	4	0	0						

TABLE1 : Table

myidentitycol	fname	lname	ext
4	Rick	Dobson	8629
8	Virginia	Dobson	3743
12	Tony	Hill	9294
(AutoNumber)			

Record: 1 of 3

We manually enter three new records for our table into the Datasheet view, as shown in the lower panel of the above screen shot. We can toggle between the two views by clicking the first tool on the toolbar in either view.

In order for us to enter records manually, our table must have a primary key. Interestingly, the primary key is not necessary when an application programmatically enters records. After typing the first and last names along with the extension number and moving off the record, SQL Server automatically assigns the myidentitycol value. We can see that TABLE1 has three records with myidentitycol values of 4, 8, and 12.

Easy as it is to enter data manually, we might need to restrict the type of data that is added to a given column. The topic of defining constraints to limit data input to a column is looked at in depth in the section *Creating Constraints*.

Now that we have seen how to create and mange tables manually, let's see how we would do this using T-SQL. As Access projects do not have a built-in version of Query Analyzer, we can only run our T-SQL scripts using the stored procedure template provided.

Creating and Managing Tables with T-SQL

As we saw previously with the `Timestamp` example, tables can be created and managed using T-SQL in stored procedures.

In order to do this, we need to know two key statements:

❑ When we create a table, using the CREATE TABLE statement, we need to give it a name and designate one or more columns for the table's design.

❑ We can use the ALTER TABLE statement to modify a table's design by adding and dropping design features. For example, we can create a CHECK or PRIMARY KEY constraint.

Both of these statements have very rich syntax. Even a table's name can require up to four levels.

At this point it is useful to discuss some important issues concerning the naming of our tables:

❑ If we do not name a table correctly, our applications can fail, as the table will not be referenced properly.

❑ If the name contains embedded spaces or reserved words, then we will need to use delimiters.

Concepts for Naming Tables

The four parts of a table's name are:

```
servername.databasename.ownername.tablename
```

The default server and database names are the current ones. For example, if our application is running in the **pubs** database on the cab2200 server, and we reference the Authors table created by John, then our code can call the table by:

```
cab2200.pubs.John.authors
```

On the other hand, if our code is running from the **pubs** database on the cab2200 server, it can reference the table as:

```
John.authors
```

If the user named John is running the application, then the application can reference the table as:

```
authors
```

Users in the **sysadmin fixed server role** (see Appendix A for a discussion on fixed server roles) can create tables that do not require an explicit ownername qualifier. Any member of this role is mapped to a special user inside each database called dbo; any object created by any member of this role belongs to dbo automatically. For example, if the user account named Henry belongs to the sysadmin fixed server role, then code run by other users with a connection to the database containing tablename can refer to a table created by Henry with either:

```
tablename
```

or:

```
dbo.tablename
```

If Henry created a table called Customers in the **Northwind** database on the cab2200 server and Henry belongs to the sysadmin fixed server role in that database too, then other users can refer to the table with either this syntax:

```
cab2200.Northwind.Customers
```

or:

```
cab2200.Northwind.dbo.Customers
```

Appendix A drills down on SQL Server security with in-depth discussions of fixed server roles. There we will tell see how to create users and assign them to SQL Server roles. In this chapter, all databases are created by **sa** (system administrator), who is a member of the sysadmin role.

> *This approach is going to be used throughout the book – in the chapters we'll try to present the basic concepts, without the extra layer of security considerations, then we'll collect security matters together in Appendix A*

If the name for our tables or its qualifiers includes blank spaces or SQL Server reserved words, then we must delimit the name using square brackets, although generally speaking we should avoid embedded spaces. For example, if Henry created a table named `table by Henry`, then code referencing that table could have this format:

```
[table by Henry]
```

We can, optionally, use double quotes as delimiters instead of left and right brackets, for example:

```
"table by Henry"
```

If we use double quotes, then we must set the `QUOTED_IDENTIFIER` option to `ON`. This setting determines what meaning SQL Server gives to double quotation marks. One of the most straightforward approaches to controlling the option is with the `SET QUOTED_IDENTIFIER` statement. We can toggle the status of the `QUOTED_IDENTIFIER` option with `ON` or `OFF` parameters. If this is set to `OFF` double quotation marks delimit a character string, as do single quotes. When it is set to `ON`, double quotation marks delimit an identifier, such as a column name, and character strings must be delimited by single quotation marks.

For example, the meaning of `SELECT "J" FROM Table_A` would change depending whether `QUOTED_IDENTIFIER` was set to `ON` or `OFF`. If `ON`, we are selecting the column named J; if it is `OFF`, `"J"` is equivalent to the letter J (a character string).

Connections through the Microsoft OLE DB provider and ODBC driver for SQL Server automatically turn the option `ON`. In addition, several T-SQL statements permit you to manage this option.

In an effort to keep the focus away from naming conventions so that we can concentrate on more advanced programmatic issues, this chapter typically uses names that do not require delimiters.

Many Access developers will feel more comfortable with quotes because it is somewhat similar to using single quotes in Access database files. Others, for example database administrators learning Access so they can build applications rapidly for their clients, may prefer the more common convention of embracing a table name in brackets. Either approach works when we use T-SQL in Access projects.

Creating Tables with T-SQL

Before we start creating tables with T-SQL, let's get a feel for T-SQL script by looking at an example.

Not all readers of the book will have Enterprise Manager. If you do not, don't panic, just miss out the next few screen shots and move to the end of this section to review the T-SQL code sample and its related discussion.

T-SQL Script for Tables in pubs

When we create a table with a stored procedure that invokes the `CREATE TABLE` statement, we need to think carefully about the syntax that we are using. The statement requires a name for the table, as well as one for each column. After specifying the column names, we can specify their data type, whether they will accept `NULL`s, default value, and constraints.

One excellent way to learn more about the correct syntax before we create our own tables is to use the sample databases and the script generation capabilities of Enterprise Manager. This same approach is useful for examining the T-SQL code that generates any `Database` object in our own databases. So let's look at an example. We'll take a look at the script for the `Authors` table on the pubs database.

Start by opening Enterprise Manager and expanding the server and database, in this case pubs, with the table for which we wish to view the script. Next, we double-click on the Tables collection, so that all the tables in the database are displayed on Enterprise Manager's right pane. Then, right-click on the Authors table, and choose All Tasks | Generate SQL Scripts to present the following dialog:

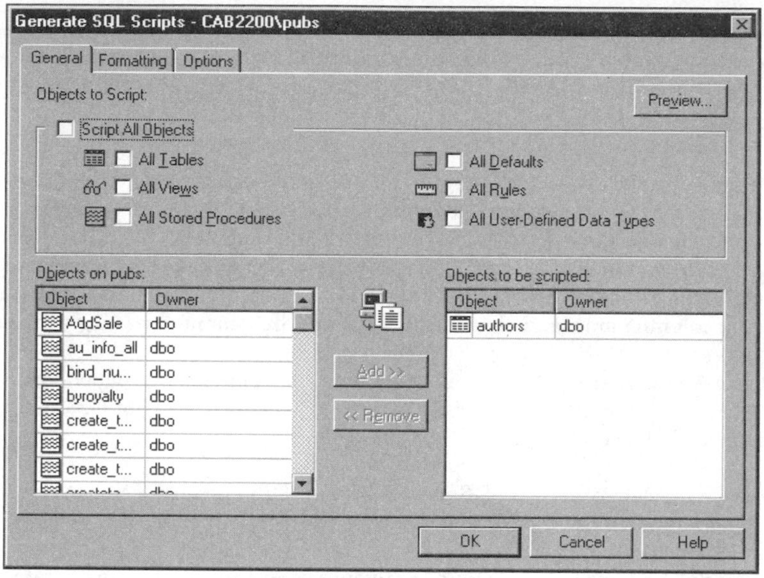

Click the Options tab to reveal the options shown in the next screen shot. We can select whatever items related to the table we want to expose in the script. Our options include indexes, full text indexes, and triggers, along with PRIMARY and FOREIGN keys and check constraints. For our example chose indexes and PRIMARY keys, FOREIGN keys, defaults, and check constraints. We can also select the output format of the file, which is useful when we want to view the file in Notepad.

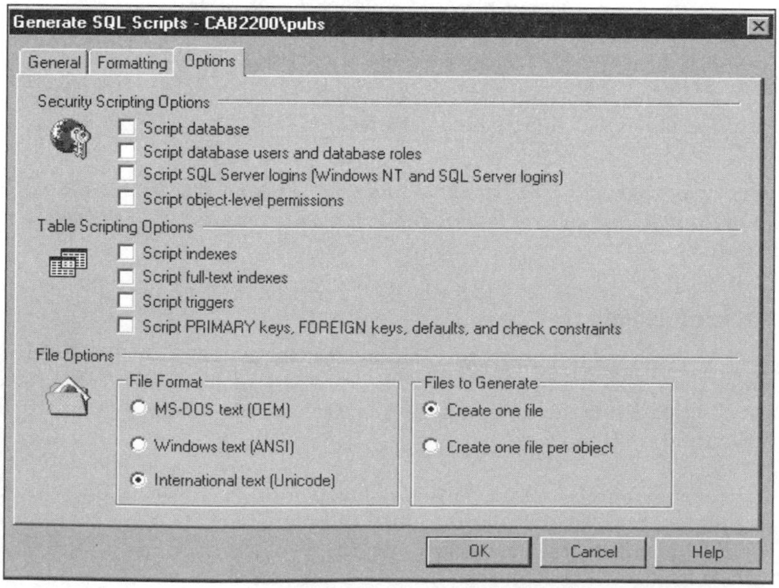

Next, on the **Formatting** tab, select the options shown in the screen shot below and also check the Include descriptive headers in the script files box.

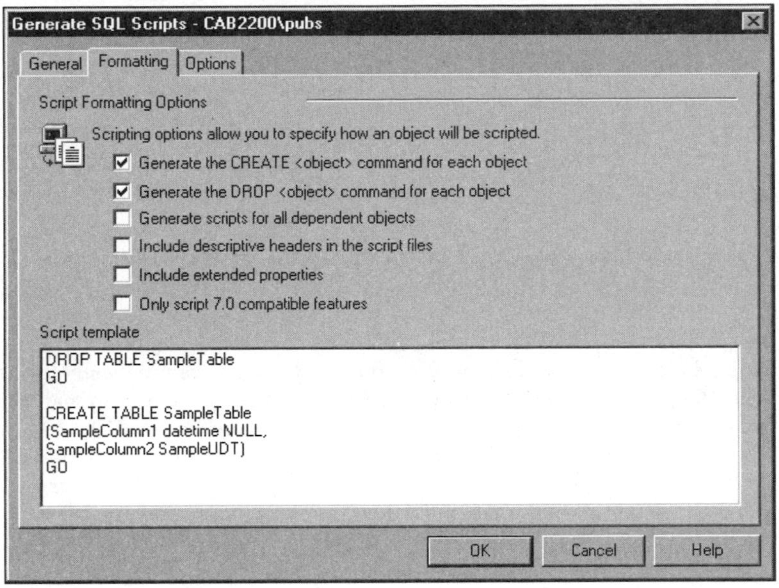

After making our selections on the **Formatting** and **Options** tabs, return to the **General** tab and click **Preview** on. This creates the script shown below for the `Authors` table of the **pubs** database in an **Object Scripting Preview** window.

```
ALTER TABLE [dbo].[titleauthor] DROP CONSTRAINT FK_titleauth_au_id_164452B1
GO


/****** Object: Table [dbo].[authors] Script Date: 2/10/2000 4:23:42 AM ******/
if exists (select * from sysobjects where id = object_id(N'[dbo].[authors]') and
OBJECTPROPERTY(id, N'IsUserTable') = 1)
drop table [dbo].[authors]
GO


/****** Object: Table [dbo].[authors] Script Date: 2/10/2000 4:23:48 AM ******/
CREATE TABLE [dbo].[authors] (
    [au_id] [id] NOT NULL ,
    [au_lname] [varchar] (40) NOT NULL ,
    [au_fname] [varchar] (20) NOT NULL ,
    [phone] [char] (12) NOT NULL ,
    [address] [varchar] (40) NULL ,
    [city] [varchar] (20) NULL ,
    [state] [char] (2) NULL ,
    [zip] [char] (5) NULL ,
    [contract] [bit] NOT NULL
)
GO


ALTER TABLE [dbo].[authors] WITH NOCHECK ADD
```

```
       CONSTRAINT [UPKCL_auidind] PRIMARY KEY CLUSTERED
       (
           [au_id]
       ) ON [PRIMARY]
    GO


    ALTER TABLE [dbo].[authors] WITH NOCHECK ADD
       CONSTRAINT [DF__authors__phone__09DE7BCC] DEFAULT ('UNKNOWN') FOR [phone],
       CHECK (([au_id] like '[0-9][0-9][0-9]-[0-9][0-9]-[0-9][0-9][0-9][0-9]')),
       CHECK (([zip] like '[0-9][0-9][0-9][0-9][0-9]'))
    GO

     CREATE INDEX [aunmind] ON [dbo].[authors]([au_lname], [au_fname]) ON [PRIMARY]
    GO
```

We can study the code in the window for interesting coding approaches, such as testing for the existence of a table and dropping it before trying to create it. If we do not check programmatically for a table that already exists, our script can fail to execute and generate a message prompting the user to manually remove a table. The sample script above also reveals the syntax for declaring columns in a CREATE TABLE statement. Objects related to the Authors table, such as its PRIMARY KEY, Default values, and CHECK constraints for selected columns appear in a series of ALTER TABLE statements. These supplementary ALTER TABLE statements complete the definition of the table.

Notice also the GO statements, which signal the end of a batch of T-SQL statements. Access stored procedure templates do not know how to process these statements, although they function in Query Analyzer. Therefore we need to comment out the GO statements if we want to attempt to run this code from within an Access project stored procedure template. Comment out the GO statements by inserting two dashes (--) before each one, which denotes a single-line comment in T-SQL.

While we will probably want to code our solutions with a slightly different syntax, these code samples represent a valuable resource for ramping up the T-SQL learning curve. Subsequent samples in this section demonstrate various adaptations and extensions of the techniques in this example.

Let's apply this knowledge and create our own table.

Creating a Table

We will use a simple stored procedure to create a telephone directory table. As mentioned previously we can use a stored procedure template to run a CREATE TABLE statement in an Access project.

The procedure starts with an ALTER PROCEDURE statement followed by a name for the stored procedure and the AS keyword. We will examine the CREATE and ALTER PROCEDURE statements in more detail at the end of this section, along with the EXECUTE statement. Two comment lines are identified with /* and */ markers.

Next, we use a CREATE TABLE statement to indicate that we will create a table named table4. If a table of the same name already exists, we will have to manually remove it before the procedure runs to a normal end. We will see shortly how this can be done programmatically.

The script generates a table with four columns:

❑ The table's first column has the name myid. It has an Int data type an IDENTITY property, so the first record will start with a value of one. Subsequent records will grow their value in the myid column by one with each new INSERT to the table.

❑ The second and third columns, fname and lname, have Varchar settings, as there is likely to be substantial variability for the length of these columns.

❑ The last column, ext, represents the extensions for the employees in the directory. The sample assumes a four-character length for this field.

```
Alter Procedure create_table4
As

/*
Create a table without a PRIMARY KEY,
but include a column with an IDENTITY property
*/
CREATE TABLE table4
(
myid int IDENTITY,
fname varchar(20),
lname varchar(40),
ext char(4)
)
```

The sample shows us further syntactical features of the CREATE TABLE statement:

❑ The column names must appear within a pair of parentheses.

❑ Commas separate the column declarations from one another.

❑ There is no comma delimiter after the last column declaration.

❑ We have placed the column declarations on separate lines for readability. This is not necessary, but it makes our code easier to read.

After running the create_table4 stored procedure from the Access project **Database** window, we can open the table. To do this we select the **Tables** collection on the **Objects** bar in the **Database** window. If **table4** does not appear in the **Tables** collection, we will need to choose **View | Refresh** to reveal the new table. Then, double-click on **table4** to open it. As we can see from the screen shot below there is no empty row to permit the manual entry of data into **table4**. This is always the case whenever we specify a table that does not possess a PRIMARY KEY.

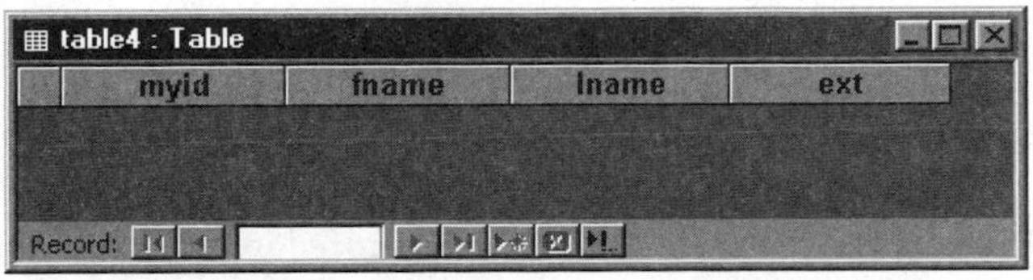

To add a row to facilitate the entry of data manually, we need to change the declaration for the myid column of our script to add a PRIMARY KEY. We chose this column as it has an IDENTITY property. Recall that this data type behaves like an AutoNumber field in Access database files. Replace the myid declaration line in the preceding ALTER PROCEDURE statement with the syntax that appears below:

```
myid int IDENTITY PRIMARY KEY,
```

91

This screen shot shows **table4** after the change:

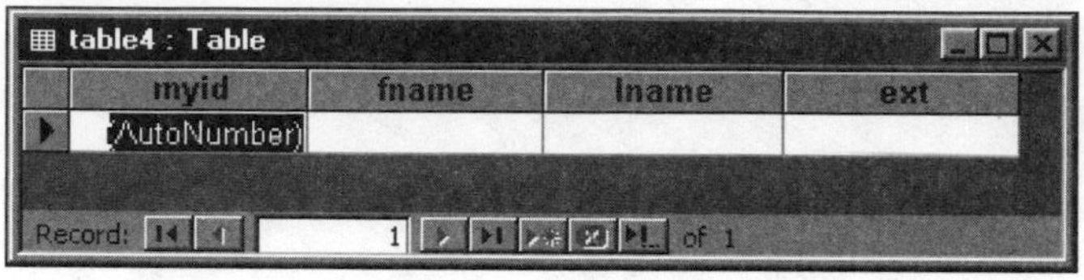

CREATE PROCEDURE and ALTER PROCEDURE

We use the CREATE PROCEDURE statement to initialize the definition of a new stored procedure. The T-SQL syntax allows us to assign a name to the procedure at the time of creation, for example:

```
Create Procedure "list_all_tables"

As

Exec sp_tables

Return
```

This name (list_all_tables in this case) is how we reference our custom stored procedures. We should always change the default name that the template provides to something more meaningful – assign a name according to the rules for SQL Server Identifiers. System stored procedure names begin with **sp_**, so it's a good idea to start our stored procedure names differently to avoid confusion. These rules vary depending on a number of factors, including our compatibility settings with prior versions of SQL Server.

Our CREATE PROCEDURE statements will fail if a procedure already exists with the same name as the statement specifies. We must first drop the old one from the project's **Database** window or by using Query Analyzer as follows:

```
Drop Procedure Test_One
```

Note that re-creating a stored procedure after dropping it does not automatically restore its permissions or startup property setting.

> *Developers grant the ability to execute stored procedures through permission assignments. Appendix A explains permission assignments and other security issues. With a stored procedure's startup property, we can specify whether to run a stored procedure automatically whenever SQL Server starts.*

As an alternative to dropping and then re-creating a stored procedure when we need to modify it, we can use the ALTER PROCEDURE statement:

```
Alter Procedure "list_all_tables"

As

--Modified code goes here

Return
```

This statement re-writes the new stored procedure over the old version and, because it retains the startup property setting and permissions, it is usually preferable.

When we build stored procedures in the Access stored procedure template it automatically defaults to this approach. The first time we create a stored procedure, the template automatically uses the CREATE PROCEDURE statement. Any time we open the procedure in Design view after that, Access replaces the CREATE PROCEDURE statement with an ALTER PROCEDURE statement.

Procedures can include just about any T-SQL statement. In fact, the only statements we cannot use within a procedure body (the lines between the CREATE PROCEDURE statement and the RETURN statement) are more CREATE statements as this confuses the compiler. We can, however, use an ALTER statement within a procedure body.

EXECUTE

The EXECUTE statement (we can also use the shorter EXEC) permits us to run a system or user-define stored procedure from within another procedure.

```
Create Procedure "list_all_tables"

As

EXEC sp_tables

--more code to do something interesting goes here

Return
```

This will invoke the system procedure sp_tables, which we have already seen. When sp_tables has finished, control will return to the calling procedure (list_all_tables) and any statements following EXEC will then be run.

Note that, within Query Analyzer, the EXECUTE keyword before an individual system stored procedure is good practice but optional. Within a template it is always mandatory, however.

Managing Tables with T-SQL

In order to manage a table programmatically using T-SQL, there are several key statements we need to grasp. These are

- ❑ INSERT
- ❑ UPDATE
- ❑ DELETE
- ❑ TRUNCATE

We will begin by looking at these statements one by one, then go on to combine the three in a series of manipulations to a table with a Timestamp column. The Timestamp column will allow us to track the changes we make. Then, we'll take a brief look at three particularly relevant system stored procedures.

Let's begin with the INSERT statement.

INSERT Statements

We use the INSERT statement to generate new rows in a SQL Server table. This statement works whether or not the table has a PRIMARY KEY setting.

To examine the syntax of this statement, we will look at an example script:

```
Alter Procedure insert_into_table4
As

/*
Enter two rows into table4
Notice that the row contents are identical
*/
INSERT INTO table4 (fname, lname, ext)
   VALUES('Rick', 'Dobson', '8629')
INSERT INTO table4 (fname, lname, ext)
   VALUES('Rick', 'Dobson', '8629')
```

The statement can have up to three parts:

❑   First, the target table. Notice that the INTO part of the INSERT statement is optional. This means that INSERT will run as well without INTO.

❑   Second, a list of field names identifies the fields into which we want to insert data.

❑   Third, a VALUES clause designates the precise values to add to those fields. We will generally not designate values for columns with an IDENTITY property, as SQL Server typically generates values for columns with this property automatically.

Motivated readers and those with prior development experience will wish to know about the SET INDENTITY_INSERT *statement. We can use this statement to gain permission to insert values into* IDENTITY *columns. The syntax is as follows:*

```
SET IDENTITY_INSERT [database.[owner.]]{table} {ON|OFF}
```

Note that only one table in a session can have IDENTITY_INSERT *set to* ON. *If one table already has* IDENTITY_INSERT *set to* ON, *and a another table requests to set this property to* ON, *an error message is generated to report that* IDENTITY_INSERT *is already* ON, *and the table that it is set to* ON *for.*

Notice that both rows contain identical values – the IDENTITY property column, myid, distinguishes the rows.

This screen below shows the results of running this script:

The data is intentionally duplicated to create the need for an UPDATE operation, which we will now look at.

UPDATE Statements

We use the UPDATE T-SQL statement with a SET statement to assign a new value to the rows within a column.

Again, let us examine the syntax of this statement by utilizing a script that will UPDATE the second record in table4, so that its first name and extension columns are different from the first row.

```
Alter Procedure update_row_in_table4
As
--Update the fname column
UPDATE table4
SET table4.fname = 'Virginia'
WHERE table4.myid = 2

--Update the ext column
UPDATE table4
SET table4.ext = '3743'
WHERE table4.myid = 2
```

Notice that it is common practice to use a separate SET keyword for each column that we want to revise. We determine the scope of the UPDATE statement with a WHERE clause.

The following screen shows how our UPDATE has changed the table:

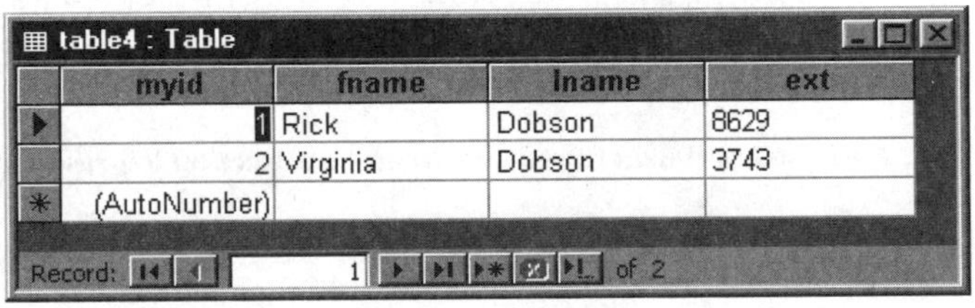

myid	fname	lname	ext
1	Rick	Dobson	8629
2	Virginia	Dobson	3743
(AutoNumber)			

We will continue by looking at how we can delete rows, first by using a DELETE statement.

DELETE Statements

T-SQL offers two statements for removing all the records from a table:

`DELETE <table> FROM <table_source> WHERE <search_condition>`

`TRUNCATE TABLE<name>`

We apply the DELETE statement to remove all records and leave the value for the next record in a column with an IDENTITY property unchanged. We can use the DELETE statement with a WHERE clause to selectively remove records from a table as well. The syntax for removing both of the records from our table4 with the DELETE statement is:

`DELETE table4`

If we invoked the insert_into_table4 stored procedure after this statement, it would now generate two rows with myid values of 3 and 4, as the IDENTITY property does not change when we delete our rows.

We will next examine how to delete our records using the second of these statements – TRUNCATE – instead.

TRUNCATE Statements

We can also remove all the records from a table with the TRUNCATE statement.

The syntax for removing all the records from table4 with the TRUNCATE statement appears below:

```
TRUNCATE TABLE table4
```

While the TRUNCATE statement and the DELETE statement without a WHERE clause are functionally identical and empty a table of records, the TRUNCATE statement has a three special side effects:

❑ The TRUNCATE statement resets the next value in a column with an IDENTITY property to its seed. Therefore, if you re-ran insert_into_table4 after a TRUNCATE statement, the myid column values would be 1 and 2 instead of 3 and 4.

❑ The TRUNCATE statement cannot not fire a trigger (similar to an Access event) as it is not logged. If we need to have a coordinated function occur as we remove the records from a table we should apply the DELETE statement instead because it does fire a trigger. We describe and demonstrate triggers in Chapter 6.

❑ The TRUNCATE statement does not update the log file as it removes records from a table. If we need the capability to restore our table from the log file, we must use the DELETE statement. Because TRUNCATE does not update the log for individual records removed, it is faster than the DELETE statement.

You cannot use TRUNCATE TABLE on a table referenced by a FOREIGN KEY constraint; we must use a DELETE statement without a WHERE clause.

> **TRUNCATE TABLE is faster and uses fewer system and transaction log resources than DELETE.**

Remember that DROP removes the table – DELETE and TRUNCATE remove the rows (only).

Now that we have an understanding of our three statements, let's move on to use them in a series of manipulations on a table with a Timestamp column.

Using INSERT and UPDATE Statements with a Timestamp Column

Let's examine another script that applies the CREATE TABLE statement. We will use the create_table6 stored procedure opposite to illustrate the programmatic use of the user-defined id data type from the pubs database, as well as the Timestamp data type. We have already seen both of these in action in this chapter. In addition, we will see the syntax for assigning a default value of the current date to a Datetime column.

Despite the similarity in their names, recall that the Timestamp and Datetime data types have nothing in common:

❑ A Timestamp column increments its value with each new INSERT, and it also increments its value by 1 with each UPDATE of the value in a row. In other words, a Timestamp column will assume different values after its initial INSERT and a subsequent UPDATE.

❑ A column with a Datetime data type stores a number that represents both a date and a time. In fact, we can selectively extract the date and time separately from a single Datetime value as we will see in this example. Chapter 5 includes a further sample that demonstrates a technique to do this.

The sample demonstrates the behavior of `Timestamp` columns and shows one approach to viewing the date and time values in a `Datetime` column value separately using the `CONVERT` function – we'll consolidate this knowledge later in this example.

```
Alter Procedure create_table6
As
--Drop table, if it exists, before creating it
IF EXISTS (SELECT * FROM sysobjects WHERE id = object_id('table6')
    and OBJECTPROPERTY(id,'IsUserTable') = 1)
DROP TABLE table6

--Create table6
CREATE TABLE table6
(
myid id PRIMARY KEY,
fname varchar(20),
lname varchar(40),
ext char(4),
mydatetime datetime DEFAULT getdate(),
mytimestamp timestamp
)
```

> *Don't forget that we need to have defined* id *as a* user-defined *data type if we don't run this procedure inside the* pubs *database.*

Another interesting feature of the `create_table6` stored procedure is that it drops `table6`, if `table6` already exists, before invoking our `CREATE TABLE` statement. The checking logic examines the `sysobjects` table in the `pubs` database and looks for a user-defined table named `table6`. If the table exists, the code drops the table. Otherwise, it skips directly to the `CREATE TABLE` statement. Remember that our earlier `create_table4` sample did not have this code before the `CREATE TABLE` statement. Therefore, if `table4` already existed, the system prompted us to remove the table by indicating that the table already exists. We then needed to respond to this message by removing the previously created version of the table from the database.

When we looked at the `Authors` table, we revealed the following code:

```
/****** Object: Table [dbo].[authors] Script Date: 2/10/2000 4:23:42 AM ******/
if exists (select * from sysobjects where id = object_id(N'[dbo].[authors]') and
OBJECTPROPERTY(id, N'IsUserTable') = 1)
drop table [dbo].[authors]
GO
```

The syntax for this logic is based on the knowledge we gained from looking at the `Authors` table; however, it is considerably less complex in format. Some of the simplicity builds on the fact that we know the table name is not a reserved word and that it has no spaces. In addition, we purposely used non-Unicode format for the table name and `id` values in the `EXISTS` condition expression. This makes the code inappropriate for applications that function in an international environment.

We will now develop a pair of stored procedures to demonstrate the operation of a `Timestamp` column. We should run each separately. The `insert_into_table6` stored procedure inserts two records into `table6`. While the records have different `id` column values, the other fields we add are the same. The `update_row_in_table6` stored procedure modifies the `fname` and `ext` columns for the record with an `id` value of `123-45-6780`.

```
Alter Procedure insert_into_table6
As
INSERT INTO table6 (myid,fname, lname, ext)
   VALUES('123-45-6789','Rick', 'Dobson', '8629')
INSERT INTO table6 (myid,fname, lname, ext)
   VALUES('123-45-6780','Rick', 'Dobson', '8629')


Alter Procedure update_row_in_table6
As

--Update the fname column
UPDATE table6
SET table6.fname = 'Virginia'
WHERE table6.myid = '123-45-6780'

--Update the ext column
UPDATE table6
SET table6.ext = '3743'
WHERE table6.myid = '123-45-6780'
```

In order to track the behavior of our two preceding stored procedures, we will prepare one more stored procedure, called show_tables6, which displays the table values:

```
Alter Procedure show_table6
AS
SELECT myid, fname,lname,ext,
   CONVERT(varchar,mydatetime,101) AS 'myusdate',
   CONVERT(varchar,mydatetime,108) AS 'myhhminss',
   CAST(mytimestamp AS int) AS 'mytimestamp'
FROM table6
```

It is a simple SELECT query from table6, except that we use the CONVERT function with two different style parameters for the mydatetime column. One parameter extracts the date from a column, and the other parameter pulls the time from the same column value. By running this stored procedure after insert_into_table6 and update_row_in_table6, we can see how they affect the Timestamp field.

The following pair of screen shots illustrates the output from show_table6 after the initial INSERT into table6 and again after the UPDATE of the fname and ext columns:

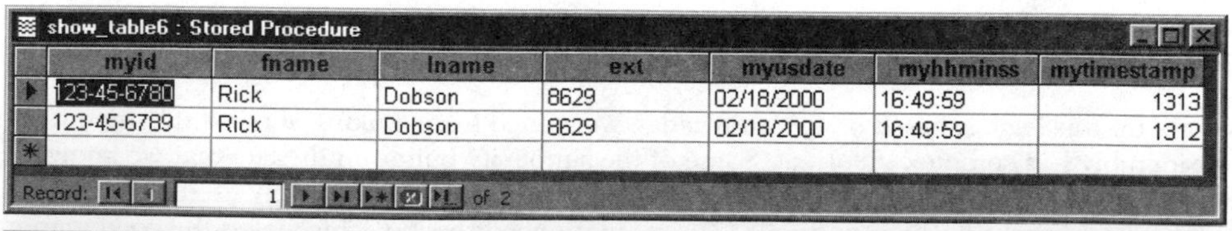

show_table6 : Stored Procedure

myid	fname	lname	ext	myusdate	myhhminss	mytimestamp
123-45-6780	Rick	Dobson	8629	02/18/2000	16:49:59	1313
123-45-6789	Rick	Dobson	8629	02/18/2000	16:49:59	1312

Record: 1 of 2

show_table6 : Stored Procedure

myid	fname	lname	ext	myusdate	myhhminss	mytimestamp
123-45-6780	Virginia	Dobson	3743	02/18/2000	16:49:59	1315
123-45-6789	Rick	Dobson	8629	02/18/2000	16:49:59	1312

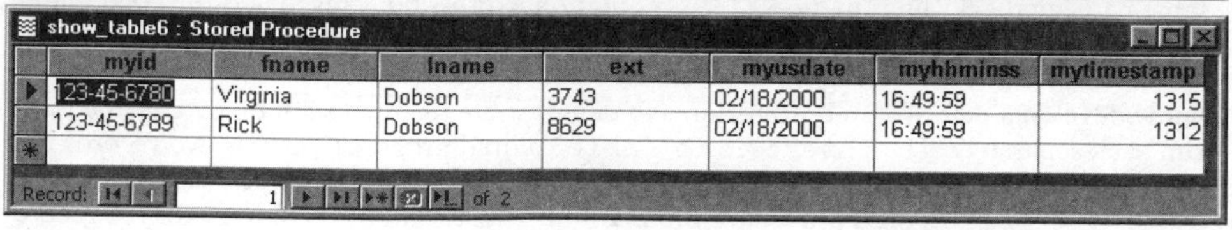

Record: 1 of 2

After our initial inserts the `Timestamp` values are **1313** and **1312**. Since we entered the record with a `myid` value of `123-45-6780` second, it has the larger `Timestamp` value. The second screen shot demonstrates that the `Timestamp` value, after our two UPDATE statements for the record with a `myid` value of `123-45-6780`, grows by 2. This is an increment of 1 for each UPDATE – once for the `fname` column and a second time for the `ext` column. We can also see that a single `Datetime` column can generate two separate fields in a SELECT query. One shows the date, namely **myusdate**, and the other represents the time with the **myhhminss** field.

Before closing the chapter's presentation on managing tables with T-SQL, let us examine three system stored procedures that can be especially useful when working with tables. Recall that system stored procedures receive focus in Chapter 6.

Three Useful System Stored Procedures

The `sp_tables` procedure can enumerate the table objects in a database.

```
sp_tables[[@name=]'name']
    [,[@owner=]'owner']
    [,[@qualifier=]'qualifier']
    [,[@type=]"type"]
```

Actually, this procedure returns information on three types of tables: system tables, user-defined tables, and views, which act as virtual tables. The `sp_tables` system stored procedure can list all the tables in a database with four columns of information about the tables, including qualifier, owner, name, and type. There's a fifth column in the procedure's return set, named REMARKS; SQL Server does not return a value for this column, so it is always blank. This is a Microsoft feature and not a bug. We can specify parameters when we call it to limit the type of items in its return set. We will discuss system stored procedures in more detail in Chapter 6.

The `sp_columns` system stored procedure returns information on 19 columns on the table, specified with its `@table_name` parameter.

```
sp_columns[@table_name=] object
    [,[@table_owner=] owner]
    [,[@table_qualifier=] qualifier]
    [,[@column_name=] column]
    [,[@ODBCVer=] ODBCVer]
```

The return set provides the following information:

- ❑ Table qualifier name
- ❑ Table owner name
- ❑ Table name
- ❑ Integer code for ODBC data type
- ❑ String representing a data type
- ❑ Number of significant digits (precision)
- ❑ Transfer size of the data (length)
- ❑ Scale
- ❑ Base for numeric data types (radix)

- Remarks
- Default value of the column
- Value of the SQL data type as it appears in the `TYPE` field
- Subtype code for `datetime` and `interval` data types
- Maximum length of a character or integer data type column (in bytes)
- Ordinal position of the column in the table
- Nullability of the column in the table

The `sp_help` system stored procedure reports information about a database object:

```
sp_help[[@objname=] name]
```

`sp_help` will report information about any `Database` object, user-defined data type or SQL Server data type, so it can be very useful when we want to explore a table in a database. To have it provide information about our `table6`, we need to run these two lines of code in Query Analyzer:

```
Use pubs
EXEC sp_help "table6"
```

The following screen shot shows selected Query Analyzer output from the `sp_help` sample we used above:

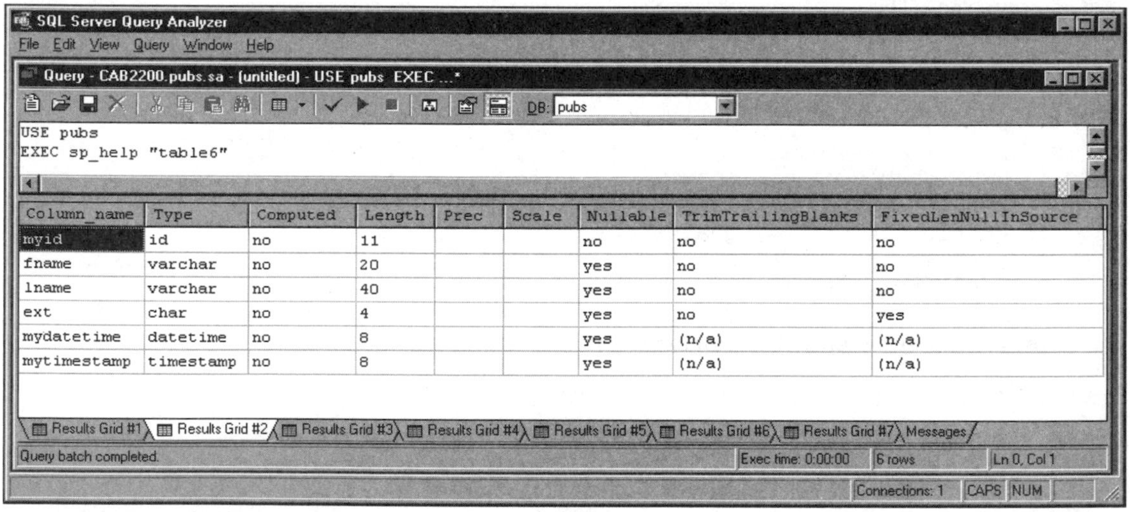

Column_name	Type	Computed	Length	Prec	Scale	Nullable	TrimTrailingBlanks	FixedLenNullInSource
myid	id	no	11			no	no	no
fname	varchar	no	20			yes	no	no
lname	varchar	no	40			yes	no	no
ext	char	no	4			yes	no	yes
mydatetime	datetime	no	8			yes	(n/a)	(n/a)
mytimestamp	timestamp	no	8			yes	(n/a)	(n/a)

The `sp_help` system stored procedure is different from `sp_tables` and `sp_columns` in that it returns multiple `Recordsets` – one for each return set. This creates special challenges when we run it from a VBA procedure with ADO. Specifically, we have to write our VBA procedure to extract multiple recordsets. If we run `sp_help` from a stored procedure template in an Access project, it will return just the first `Recordset`. We will see later in this chapter how to tackle the problem of returning multiple `Recordsets`.

Let's now examine another way we can create and manage tables – by using VBA and ADO.

Creating and Managing Tables with VBA and ADO

In order to create and manage SQL Server tables from an Access 2000 module we can use **VBA** (**Visual Basic for Applications**) and **ADO** (**ActiveX Data Objects**). Access developers are likely to find it very useful to draw on and extend a basic understanding of T-SQL with the VBA projects associated with Access projects. A VBA project can contain a stand-alone module, Form and Report Class modules, and stand-alone class modules. All these module types, in turn, serve as containers for VBA procedures.

When programming solutions, less is often more. With that attitude in mind, we will draw on just two core ADO constructs in this section – namely, Commands and Recordsets.

One convenient place to start exploring the management of SQL Server tables via ADO with Access projects is the creation of a table.

Creating Tables

This involves elements similar to those we used to build a table from an Access project template. Managing tables from VBA offers tighter integration with our Access project, including integration of SQL Server data with Access forms and reports. However, using ADO puts another layer between us and SQL Server.

To build a table we need to use only one ADO object, the Command object, and a few of its properties:

- ❑ The CommandText property. This property contains the CREATE TABLE statement.

- ❑ The ActiveConnection property. When we build a table in the database for the current Access project, we can specify the Command's ActiveConnection property as the Connection object for the current project. This is the Connection designated in the Data Link Properties. Remember that we open this with the File | Connection command on the Database window menu.

- ❑ The CommandType property. For all the samples in this section we use the adCmdText setting for the CommandType property. This setting specifies a T-SQL script. We do not have to set the CommandType property, but setting it can speed up the execution of our code, as the ADO interpreter does not have to work out what we are passing it in the CommandText property. Other CommandType property settings point at items such as stored procedures and previously saved Recordsets. We then invoke the Command's Execute method to create the table.

Refer to Chapter 12 for a more comprehensive review of programming VBA projects with ADO objects. We'll be illustrating the topics discussed here in multiple samples reinforcing these issues in the remainder of this chapter and in forthcoming chapters.

We run our VBA procedures that reference ADO Command and other objects from the **Visual Basic Editor** (**VBE**) environment associated with an Access project. We open the VBE by choosing Tools | Macro | Visual Basic Editor or typing the keyboard short cut of *Alt+F11*.

In order to use either an ADO Command object or Recordset object, we need to set up a reference to the Microsoft ActiveX Data Objects 2.1 Library (ADODB library). Access 2000 creates this reference by default (assuming we have created a link to SQL Server), but it can be manually turned off by us or a user. We can check that there is a reference to the ADODB library by choosing Tools | References from the VBE menu. Verify that there is a check next to the ADODB library name in the References dialog. If not, place one there, as in the screen on the following page:

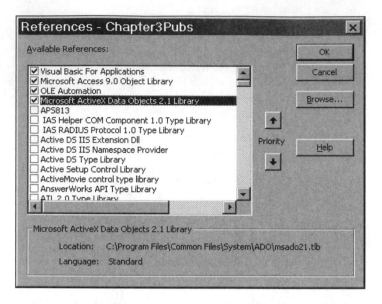

The code we're going to examine for creating a table is as follows. As discussed in Chapter 2, this can just be entered straight into the **Code** window of the VBE; alternatively it's available in the download in the Access project Chapter3Pubs.adp.

```
Sub call_create_table5_from_script()
Dim str1 As String

'Assign string with T-SQL statement
'to create table5
str1 = "CREATE TABLE table5 " & _
 "(" & _
 "myid int IDENTITY PRIMARY KEY, " & _
 "fname varchar(20), " & _
 "lname varchar(40), " & _
 "ext char(4)" & _
 ")"

'Call a procedure to run the T-SQL
'script in the string
create_table5_from_script str1

End Sub


Sub create_table5_from_script(str1 As String)
Dim cmd1 As ADODB.Command
On Error GoTo ct5fs_Errortrap

'Instantiate cmd1 pointer and assign
'selected properties
Set cmd1 = New ADODB.Command
cmd1.ActiveConnection = CurrentProject.Connection
cmd1.CommandType = adCmdText
```

```
'Assign T-SQL string to command's
'CommandText property and Execute the command
ct5fs_Startover:
cmd1.CommandText = str1
cmd1.Execute

'Release cmd1 pointer and exit sub
ct5fs_Exit:
Set cmd1 = Nothing
Exit Sub

ct5fs_Errortrap:
Debug.Print "VBA Error Report"
If Err.Number = -2147217900 Then
'-2147217900 = VBA error code for object already
'exists, so drop existing table and start over again
 Debug.Print Err.Number, Err.Description
 cmd1.CommandText = "DROP TABLE table5"
 cmd1.Execute
 Debug.Print "I dropped the previous version of table5."
 Resume ct5fs_Startover
Else
'Print VBA error message in Immediate window and
'alert user about error with a message box
 Debug.Print Err.Number, Err.Description
 MsgBox "Check Immediate window for error number and description.", _
   vbInformation, "My Custom Error Message"
 Resume ct5fs_Exit
End If

End Sub
```

Our first procedure, `call_create_table5_from_script`, defines a string variable containing a T-SQL statement with the code to create the table. We then call the second procedure, `create_table5_from_script`, as it passes the string variable. This second procedure instantiates the `Command` object for running the T-SQL statement and assigns its properties, before invoking the `Execute` statement. In the second procedure we also perform a coarse level of SQL Server error trapping. There is a better approach for detecting and diagnosing SQL Server errors, which we will look at later.

Let's now step through our second procedure to see what is happening. We start with a `Dim` statement to declare the `Command` object, which will be used to run the `CREATE TABLE` statement passed to it. Next, we instantiate the `Command` with a `Set` statement and assign values to the three properties we discussed at the beginning of this section.

We assign the OLE DB connection for the Access project to the `Command's` `ActiveConnection` property, in order to point the `Command` at the `Connection` for the current project. For the remaining two property assignments, we set `CommandType` to `adCmdText`, as discussed previously; then define the `CommandText` property as a text string to accept a specific string value from the first procedure in order to create our table.

Finally, we use the `Execute` statement to run the procedure. If all goes well, the procedure closes by setting the `Command` object to `Nothing`. In general, we should conserve resources by closing any open ADO objects and removing them from memory when we no longer need them (this would be done automatically, but it is better to do it in code). Note that the `Command` object does not have a `Close` method, but the `Connection` and `Recordset` objects do.

Let's now examine what can go wrong in our code. One of the errors that we trap occurs if the table already exists. If this is the case, then trying to create another table of the same name causes an error. In response to a VBA error code of -2147217900, the procedure drops the previous version of the table from the database and resubmits the Command. If we detected the right SQL Server error, the fix works and a new version of the table is created. If another VBA error occurs, the procedure detects that, prints the error to the Immediate window, and presents a message box telling the user to check the Immediate window.

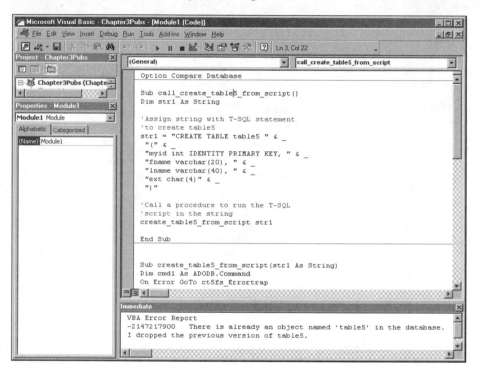

Now that we have considered some coarse error trapping, let's see how we can trap errors more effectively.

Trapping Errors More Effectively

One big problem with the error trapping in the preceding sample is that it only checks for VBA errors. However, SQL Server can return errors as well. Furthermore, multiple SQL Server errors appear with the same VBA error code. Therefore, we cannot properly diagnose SQL Server errors by looking exclusively at the VBA error code represented by err.Number. SQL Server passes its errors back to VBA through the ADO Errors collection of the Connection object.

While our sample does not explicitly declare a Connection object, recall that it does implicitly use the Access project's OLE DB connection to specify the ActiveConnection property for the Command:

```
Set cmd1 = New ADODB.Command
cmd1.ActiveConnection = CurrentProject.Connection
```

Therefore, our code can iterate through the Errors collection of CurrentProject.Connection.

We will now modify the code from our previous procedure, create_table_from_script, to check for ADO as well as VBA errors. The new code appears with shading.

```
Sub create_table5_from_script(str1 As String)
Dim cmd1 As ADODB.Command
Dim err1 As ADODB.Error
On Error GoTo ct5fs_Errortrap

'Instantiate cmd1 pointer and assign
'selected properties
Set cmd1 = New ADODB.Command
cmd1.ActiveConnection = CurrentProject.Connection
cmd1.CommandType = adCmdText

'Assign T-SQL string to command's
'CommandText property and Execute the command
ct5fs_Startover:
cmd1.CommandText = str1
cmd1.Execute

'Release cmd1 pointer and exit sub
ct5fs_Exit:
Set cmd1 = Nothing
Exit Sub

ct5fs_Errortrap:
Debug.Print "SQL Server Error Report"
For Each err1 In cmd1.ActiveConnection.Errors
 Debug.Print err1.NativeError, err1.Description
 If err1.NativeError = 2714 Then
'2714 = Native error code for object already
'exists, so drop existing table and start over again
  cmd1.CommandText = "DROP TABLE table5"
  cmd1.Execute
  Debug.Print "I dropped the previous version of table5."
  Resume ct5fs_Startover
 End If
Next
Debug.Print "VBA Error Report"
 Debug.Print Err.Number, Err.Description
'Alert user about error messages with a message box
 MsgBox "Check Immediate window for Native and VBA error " & _
   "numbers and descriptions.", _
   vbInformation, "My Custom Error Message"
 Resume ct5fs_Exit
End Sub
```

The sample again uses two procedures, the first of which, `call_create_table5_from_script`, *remains unchanged from our previous example and therefore isn't shown here.*

The processing of the string in the second ADO sample is identical to its predecessor. However, our error processing follows a different logic. We start with a loop that passes through the members of the Errors collection for CurrentProject.Connection (cmd1.ActiveConnection). In order to loop through the Errors collection, the procedure needs an ADO Error object, which we declare with a Dim statement at the beginning of the procedure. The loop checks for an ADO error number of 2714. This error number corresponds to the VBA error number of −2147217900, which we looked at earlier. It specifically identifies a case in which T-SQL attempts to create a new object when an object of that name already exists in the database. In this case, as previously, it drops the table. However, other ADO errors can correspond to this same VBA error number, which could cause the first sample to fail when the second one succeeds.

The way to work out which error codes we want to trap for is to generate the obvious ones and print their numbers to the Immediate window. Then, we can trap for selected errors and either correct them before rerunning the code or exit gracefully if we cannot conveniently recover from the error. We can also log them in a table or text file and build up a list of the ones that occur most commonly in our work.

Now that we have created a table, our next job is to manage its contents. Let's see how we do this with ADO.

Managing Tables with ADO

Firstly, we need to be able to easily add and delete content.

Adding Content to a Table

The basic model of specifying string parameters in one procedure and then calling a second procedure as our application passes those parameters is a very robust and flexible one for developing ADO solutions to SQL Server table management. Therefore, we will use that approach again for this and the next example. We adapt the two procedures from the above sample in order to INSERT records into our table.

> We will not examine error trapping here as the previous pair of samples explored that technique sufficiently.

Notice that syntax for the INSERT statement is the same as we used in the Access project stored procedure template – although we will just use INSERT here instead of the INSERT INTO used previously. As stated earlier, the INTO portion of the statement is optional.

As before, our application defines a T-SQL statement in the first procedure, then the second procedure assigns the statement into a Command object, and Executes the statement.

```
Sub call_insert_into_table5_from_script()
Dim str1 As String

'Assign string with T-SQL statement
'to insert values into table5
str1 = "INSERT table5 " & _
 "(fname, lname, ext) " & _
 "VALUES('Rick', 'Dobson', '8629') " & _
 "INSERT table5 " & _
 "(fname, lname, ext) " & _
 "VALUES('Jenny', 'Dobson', '3743')"

'Call a procedure to run the T-SQL
'script in the string
insert_into_table5_from_script str1

End Sub


Sub insert_into_table5_from_script(str1 As String)
Dim cmd1 As ADODB.Command

'Instantiate cmd1 pointer and assign
'selected properties
Set cmd1 = New ADODB.Command
```

```
    cmd1.ActiveConnection = CurrentProject.Connection
    cmd1.CommandType = adCmdText

    'Assign T-SQL string to command's
    'CommandText property and Execute the command
    cmd1.CommandText = str1
    cmd1.Execute

    'Release command resource at close
    Set cmd1 = Nothing

End Sub
```

The same basic design techniques apply to the use of UPDATE and DELETE statements. Chapter 6 will revisit syntax issues for these statements, as it describes how to work with tables inside stored procedures.

We also need to be able to examine the contents of our tables – from data and meta-data perspectives.

Examining Table Contents

After we carry out database maintenance with INSERT, UPDATE, or DELETE statements, our thoughts turn to printing out the records, so that we can verify the outcome of our maintenance actions.

The following sample shows the syntax to implement this. In the first procedure we just pass a single string value that completes the T-SQL statement. The statement in the second procedure presents all the records for all the columns in a table. At runtime, the first procedure passes the name of a specific table from which to select the data.

```
Sub call_list_all_records_in_a_table()
Dim tablename As String

'Assign a table name and invoke
'the second procedure
tablename = "table5"
list_records_in_a_table tablename

End Sub


Sub list_records_in_a_table(tablename As String)
Dim cmd1 As ADODB.Command
Dim rst1 As ADODB.Recordset

'Instantiate cmd1 pointer and assign
'selected properties
Set cmd1 = New ADODB.Command
cmd1.ActiveConnection = CurrentProject.Connection
cmd1.CommandType = adCmdText

'Concatenate the table name to the end of
'the T-SQL statement
cmd1.CommandText = "SELECT * FROM " & tablename
cmd1.Execute

'Instantiate a recordset, open it
'on the return set from the SELECT statement
```

```
'print the results in the Immediate window
'Verify the  contents returned by
'the SELECT statement
Set rst1 = New ADODB.Recordset
rst1.Open cmd1
Debug.Print rst1.GetString

'Release resources for ADO objects
rst1.Close
Set rst1 = Nothing
Set cmd1 = Nothing

End Sub
```

We start our second procedure by instantiating not only the `Command` object, but also a `Recordset` object. We do this so that, after selecting the records in the first part of the second procedure, we can pass those records from the `Command` object to the `Recordset` object. We then send the `Recordset` contents to the Immediate window by invoking the `GetString` method on the `Recordset` object within a `Debug.Print` statement. While using the `GetString` method avoids the need to write a loop, it does not give us as much formatting flexibility as we would have with the loop method.

> *When we execute the `Command` object, it invokes the `SELECT` method. However, the `Command` object has no way to expose its return set. Therefore we need to use a `Recordset` object, which opens with the `Command` as its record source. This allows us to utilize the full functionality of the `Recordset`.*

> *We could open the `Recordset` directly on the `SELECT` statement. However, this approach gives us exposure to how different ADO objects behave and demonstrates some basic functionality of `Command` and `Recordset` objects, which incidentally pass back the contents of a `SELECT` statement.*

> *When a T-SQL statement requires parameters, we would generally use the `Command` object since the `Recordset` object does not have a `Parameters` collection.*

By now, the robustness of passing a T-SQL string from one procedure to another should be very evident. However, how do we generalize this ADO computing model? The power of the technique grows as we are able to use it with many different kinds of statements without any recoding. In the spirit of more is less, it is desirable to devise an ADO T-SQL processor that trades off simplicity in favor of generality.

Making the Code More Flexible

We use the next sample to illustrate these principles. We call the second procedure, `run_a_script`, multiple times from the first procedure. In these multiple calls, the first procedure passes the second one a variety of different T-SQL statements. Some use `INSERT`. Others apply the `DELETE` statement, and one invokes the `TRUNCATE` statement. The first procedure does not rely exclusively on the `run_a_script` procedure to process a database. The `list_records_in_a_table` procedure from the proceeding sample also receives calls, so that we can enumerate the contents of our table.

Let's first examine the code and then run an example to see how these calls reveal the outcome of the database maintenance tasks.

```
Sub demo_run_a_script()
Dim str1 As String

'Use DELETE to remove all records from table5
str1 = "DELETE table5"
```

```
    run_a_script str1

    'Use INSERT to add new records into table5
    str1 = "INSERT table5 " & _
     "(fname, lname, ext) " & _
     "VALUES('Rick', 'Dobson', '8629') " & _
     "INSERT table5 " & _
     "(fname, lname, ext) " & _
     "VALUES('Jenny', 'Dobson', '3743')"
    run_a_script str1

    'Enumerate contents of table5
    list_records_in_a_table "table5"

    'Use TRUNCATE TABLE to remove all records from table5
    str1 = "TRUNCATE TABLE table5"
    run_a_script str1

    'Use INSERT to add new records into table5
    str1 = "INSERT table5 " & _
     "(fname, lname, ext) " & _
     "VALUES('Rick', 'Dobson', '8629') " & _
     "INSERT table5 " & _
     "(fname, lname, ext) " & _
     "VALUES('Jenny', 'Dobson', '3743')"
    run_a_script str1

    'Enumerate contents of table5
    list_records_in_a_table "table5"

    End Sub


    Sub run_a_script(myscript As String)
    Dim cmd1 As ADODB.Command

    'Instantiate cmd1 pointer and assign
    'selected properties
    Set cmd1 = New ADODB.Command
    cmd1.ActiveConnection = CurrentProject.Connection
    cmd1.CommandType = adCmdText

    'Assign T-SQL string to command's
    'CommandText property and Execute the command
    cmd1.CommandText = myscript
    cmd1.Execute

    'Release command resource at close
    Set cmd1 = Nothing

    End Sub
```

We will invoke the demo_run_a_script procedure immediately after populating table5 with its first pair of records, using the previous INSERT example. We repeat this code below to make the example easier to follow.

```
    Sub call_insert_into_table5_from_script()
    Dim str1 As String

    'Assign string with T-SQL statement
```

```
'to insert values into table5
str1 = "INSERT table5 " & _
 "(fname, lname, ext) " & _
 "VALUES('Rick', 'Dobson', '8629') " & _
 "INSERT table5 " & _
 "(fname, lname, ext) " & _
 "VALUES('Jenny', 'Dobson', '3743')"
```

These records will have myid values of 1 and 2 because of their IDENTITY property settings. The demo_run_a_script procedure starts by sending a DELETE statement to the run_a_Script procedure. This removes the two records in table5 and leaves table5 empty.

Next, we specify a pair of INSERT statements for submission to run_a_script. This inserts two records, which will have myid values of 3 and 4 because the DELETE statement leaves the IDENTITY property values intact.

The following screen shot shows the records that appear in the Immediate window after this and our next call to list_records_in_a_table. The top two records are the result of our above actions, and show that we have two records with myid values of 3 and 4.

We then proceed to use a TRUNCATE statement to remove the two new records from table5.

> *As we have already seen earlier in the chapter, the TRUNCATE and DELETE statements both remove records from a Recordset, but the TRUNCATE statement restores the IDENTITY property to its initial values.*

Once again, we use exactly the same code as seen after the DELETE statement to insert duplicate records and print out their values. However, in this case, the myid values for the new records are 1 and 2. This is because TRUNCATE resets the IDENTITY property to its initial seed and increment value. We can confirm this by looking at the bottom two records in the above screen shot.

One of the weaknesses of the Access project stored procedure template is its inability to display more than one Recordset in a return set. Query Analyzer performs this task by providing a separate tab for each Recordset. When we use ADO in our Access project applications, we can capture multiple Recordsets. Let's look at an example.

Returning Multiple Recordsets

The main technique we will introduce here is how to use the NextRecordset method for the Recordset object. Many analysts routinely loop through the columns within a row and the records within a Recordset until they exhaust the available rows. We can still follow this approach or we can use a more compact method, such as the GetString method illustrated above.

In any event, we must nest our procedure for returning the rows of a `Recordset` inside of another loop that advances to the next `Recordset` when it completes the previous one. We can have our code exit the outer loop when the `NextRecordset` method returns `Nothing`. Since this procedure empties the `Recordset` object, we do not have to release the `Recordset` resource explicitly, although it is advisable to do so. This is because there are cases when the loop may be broken by code, which would leave the `Recordset` open.

We will illustrate how to apply the `NextRecordset` method in the following `print_multiple_recordsets` procedure. It initially creates a query string that designates two `Recordsets`. The first of these specifies all the records in the `Authors` table of the pubs database; the second returns all the `Publishers` table records from pubs.

Next, we open a `Recordset` object on the query string. Notice that we do not strictly need a `Command` object to process the string. We can have the `Recordset` object process the query and make the results available to our application.

The body of the `print_multiple_recordsets` procedure consists of three nested loops:

❑ The outer loop manages the `Recordsets`.

❑ The next loop in passes through the records within the currently active `Recordset`.

❑ The innermost loop iterates through the columns within a row.

We include some minor formatting touches to mark the ends of records and `Recordsets` – this does not detract significantly from the utter simplicity of this technique.

```
Sub print_multiple_recordsets()
Dim str1 As String
Dim rst1 As ADODB.Recordset
Dim irs As Byte
Dim i As Integer

'Create string to produce multiple recordsets
str1 = "SELECT * FROM authors; " & _
 "SELECT * FROM publishers"

'Instantiate recordset and open it
'for multiple recordsets
Set rst1 = New ADODB.Recordset
rst1.Open str1, CurrentProject.Connection, _
 adOpenKeyset, adLockOptimistic, adCmdText

irs = 0
'Move through recordsets
Do Until rst1 Is Nothing

 Debug.Print "Results from recordset " & irs
'Move through rows in current recordset
 Do Until rst1.EOF

'Move through columns in current row
  For i = 0 To rst1.Fields.Count - 1
   Debug.Print rst1(i).Name & " = "; rst1(i)
  Next i
```

```
    rst1.MoveNext
    Debug.Print " ---"
    Loop


    Set rst1 = rst1.NextRecordset
    irs = irs + 1
    Debug.Print " --- " & vbCrLf
    Loop


End Sub
```

We can use this technique with multiple SELECT statements based on many more than two Recordsets. For example, we can use it to enumerate the values of all the columns in every record from each table in the Northwind database.

However, it does fail reliably in one scenario. This is when an ADO procedure attempts to retrieve all the return sets from the sp_help system stored procedure that we looked at earlier in the chapter.

```
sp_help[[@objname=] name]
```

The argument for this stored procedure can be the name of any table in the current database. Additionally, we need to precede the stored procedure name with the EXEC keyword. This rule holds for all system stored procedures that we run from ADO. When we run sp_help for any table, such as table5, we can consistently get back five return sets. Query Analyzer retrieves seven return sets. If we try to get either of the last two return sets with an ADO procedure, our VBA program fails.

This is not a problem for a couple of reasons:

❑ First, alternative system stored procedures exist for gathering the information in the last two return sets. System stored procedures are covered in more detail in Chapter 6. Also, all the system stored procedures are detailed in Books Online.

❑ Second, when we know that the procedure will end abruptly as soon as it tries to retrieve the sixth return set, we can code our procedure to halt just before the failure.

We use the following code sample to illustrate the technique to list the contents of the first five return sets from sp_help:

```
Sub sp_help_table5()
Dim cmd1 As New ADODB.Command
Dim rst1 As ADODB.Recordset
Dim irs As Byte
Dim i As Integer


'Specify command
cmd1.ActiveConnection = CurrentProject.Connection
cmd1.CommandText = "EXEC sp_help table5"
cmd1.CommandType = adCmdText
cmd1.Execute

'Use the default cursor on return set from cmd1
Set rst1 = New ADODB.Recordset
```

```
    rst1.Open cmd1

    irs = 0

    'While Not rs Is Nothing
    Do Until rst1 Is Nothing

      Debug.Print "Results from recordset " & irs

    'Move through rows in current recordset
     Do Until rst1.EOF

    'Move through columns in current row
      For i = 0 To rst1.Fields.Count - 1
        Debug.Print rst1(i).Name & " = "; rst1(i)

      Next i
     rst1.MoveNext
     Debug.Print " ---"
     Loop

     Set rst1 = rst1.NextRecordset
     irs = irs + 1
     Debug.Print " --- " & vbCrLf
     If irs = 5 Then Exit Sub
    Loop

  End Sub
```

Let's move on to our final technique for creating and managing tables – SQL-DMO.

Managing Tables with SQL–DMO

SQL Distributed Management Objects (**SQL–DMO**) enable developers working in any development environment that can control a COM object to programmatically administer SQL Server and MSDE database servers. Since VBA in Access projects can control COM objects, this means we can build applications for granularly managing SQL Server. Enterprise Manager, which Microsoft developed with SQL–DMO, provides very granular (fine-grained) control over SQL Server. Since we can program SQL-DMO, we can achieve the same granular control in our custom applications.

Before we start drilling down into the details, let us understand that SQL–DMO is the Object Model for SQL Server. Therefore, we can use it to control SQL Server just as we use the Microsoft Access Object Library to control classic Access functions.

In the introduction we examined why SQL-DMO is a viable option for Access developers. We return to SQL-DMO in at least two subsequent chapters to illustrate the breadth of what we can accomplish with it. Personally, I prefer its object model design and think that developers who like object models will possibly find it more appealing than T-SQL, especially those who do not have prior exposure to T-SQL.

A VBA project associated with an Access project must have a reference to the **Microsoft SQLDMO Object Library**. This reference points at `sqldmo.rll`. As we saw earlier, we can set a reference by choosing Tools | References in the VBE window. We then select the SQLDMO library, as in the screen shot overleaf:

113

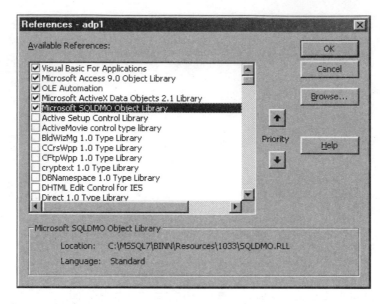

Since SQL–DMO is an object model, we will manipulate objects with properties and methods as we work with it. Many SQL–DMO applications will start by making a connection to a server.

Connecting to Servers and Enumerating Collections

We need to declare a `SQLServer` object, instantiate it, and then invoke its `Connect` method. We reference SQL Server and MSDE database servers by their network computer name. After we have our connection to a server, our application can manipulate the objects on that server. For example, we can enumerate the databases, tables, and columns that the server manages. As we enumerate objects, we can list selected properties. This section reinforces your skills in this area with three examples – starting with the enumeration of a database.

Enumerating Databases

We will use this first code sample as a vehicle to familiarize us with the basics of building a SQL–DMO application. We begin by making a connection to a server and enumerating its databases. The sample works with a SQL Server named `cab2200`. However, the sample's design will readily work with any server, as we specify a server name in the first procedure, and then pass that name to a second procedure, which opens a `Connection` on the server and loops through the members of the `Databases` collection on the server.

In any environment, we should really have a password for the `sa` login; alternatively, we may use another login altogether. Any login that we use must be a member of either the sysadmin or dbcreator fixed server roles. Recall that Appendix A discusses these roles under the heading *SQL Server Security*.

```
Sub call_list_databases()
Dim srvrname As String

'Name server and call database lister
srvrname = "cab2200"
list_databases srvrname

End Sub
```

```
Sub list_databases(srvrname As String)
Dim srv1 As New SQLDMO.SQLServer
Dim dbs1 as New SQLDMO.Database

'Connect to server
srv1.Connect srvrname, "sa", ""

'List database names with their owners
Debug.Print "The databases and their owners in " & srv1.Name & " are:"
For Each dbs1 In srv1.Databases
 Debug.Print dbs1.Name & String(25 - Len(dbs1.Name), " ") & dbs1.Owner
Next

End Sub
```

The second procedure shows the syntax for declaring a SQL Server and invoking its `Connect` method. We begin with a `Dim` statement for the server, which reserves space for the object and instantiates the `Server` object by using the `New` keyword. We can alternatively instantiate the `SQLServer` object with a `Set` statement outside its `Dim` statement.

> *This fails if we have a database with a name longer than 25 characters.*

Our `Connect` method takes three parameters, all of which are strings:

❑   The first denotes the server's name.

❑   The second specifies the login name

❑   The third is the password for the login. We can use two contiguous double quotes (`" "`) to represent a blank password.

`For…Each` loops are common VBA structures for enumeration tasks, and our sample uses such a loop to pass through the members of the `Databases` collection. We explicitly declare a `Database` object (`dbs1`) to hold the current database reference for each iteration through the loop.

We then use a `Debug.Print` statement to print out the name and the owner for each database. The VBA `String` function pads spaces after a database name, so that the owner names line up, all starting in the 26th column. We set the padding factor based on the names of the databases on the `cab2200` SQL Server. If our database names are longer, we will need to adjust the `String` function accordingly.

Let's consider another example – this time involving the enumeration of tables.

Enumerating Tables

The SQL–DMO model is a classic **hierarchical object model** and we can represent the portion of the SQL-DMO object model that we're interested here by:

As we can see the `Databases` collection resides within individual `SQLServer` objects. Similarly, the `Tables` collection is one of the collections within a specific database. The `Tables` collection contains `Table` objects, and these objects in turn have collections and objects that define the database, and enforce data and referential integrity.

> *You can probe the SQL-DMO object model with the Object Browser in a VBA project – we won't be discussing the object model in detail, just what we need to achieve our objectives.*

We will take advantage of this hierarchical structure in our second example, to enumerate the tables within the Northwind database on the `cab2200` SQL Server. This procedure runs within an Access project connected to the pubs database, but our SQL-DMO code references the objects in another database – the Northwind database – in a very straightforward manner.

```
Sub call_list_tables()
Dim srvrname As String
Dim dbsname As String

'Name server and database
'and call table lister
srvrname = "cab2200"
dbsname = "Northwind"
list_tables srvrname, dbsname

End Sub


Sub list_tables(srvrname As String, dbsname As String)
Dim srv1 As New SQLDMO.SQLServer
Dim tab1 As New SQLDMO.Table

'Connect to server
srv1.Connect srvrname, "sa", ""

'List table name and column count for user-defined tables
Debug.Print "User-defined tables with their column counts for the " & _
  dbsname & " database are:"
For Each tab1 In srv1.Databases(dbsname).Tables
  If tab1.TypeOf = SQLDMOObj_UserTable Then
    Debug.Print tab1.Name & String(25 - Len(tab1.Name), " ") & _
      tab1.Columns.Count
  End If
Next

End Sub
```

Again, we utilize two procedures. Our first procedure specifies the server and database names, and then calls the second procedure. In the second procedure, we begin by declaring `SQLServer` and `Table` objects. The `SQLServer` object is necessary to make a connection with a database server. The `Table` object is optional, but it serves to hold a reference to each table in the `For...Each` loop that we use to iterate through the tables in the Northwind database. The `For...Each` loop knows which collection to use as the `Columns` collection is a child of the `Table` we are looping through, which we specify in the first procedure.

This sample has more logic in its loop than our previous example:

❑ First, we filter tables before passing them to the Debug.Print statement, so that only user-defined tables are printed.

❑ Second, our print statement references a hierarchical collection of the Table object – its Columns collection. By using the Count property, we can display of the number of columns in each table.

When developing solutions with databases designed by other developers, or even by ourselves a while ago, it is often desirable to refresh our recollection of the design of a table. Our third example displays the column names with their data types and lengths for any specified table in a database.

Enumerating Columns

SQL-DMO is ideal for this kind of task. We begin in the first procedure by designating the server, database, and table names. Then, we invoke the second procedure and pass it the name parameters. The For...Each loop references the Columns collection from its parent object – the table which we specified in the first procedure. Similarly, the Table object depends on its parent – the database which we designated in the first procedure. Our Debug.Print statement simply prints the values of the name, datatype, and length properties for each column, as the loop passes through the table's columns.

```
Sub call_list_columns()
Dim srvrname As String
Dim dbsname As String
Dim tabname As String

'Name server, database, and table
'and call column lister
srvrname = "cab2200"
dbsname = "Northwind"
tabname = "Shippers"
list_columns srvrname, dbsname, tabname

End Sub

Sub list_columns(srvrname As String, dbsname As String, _
 tabname As String)
Dim srv1 As New SQLDMO.SQLServer
Dim col1 As New SQLDMO.Column

'Connect to server
srv1.Connect srvrname, "sa", ""

'List column name, datatype, and length for specified table
Debug.Print "Column names, datatypes, and widths for the " & _
 tabname; " table in the "; dbsname & " database."
For Each col1 In srv1.Databases(dbsname).Tables(tabname).Columns
 Debug.Print col1.Name & String(25 - Len(col1.Name), " ") & _
  col1.DataType, col1.Length
Next

End Sub
```

To confirm what the output from these samples looks like, we will examine the Immediate window output from the third sample. As with all the samples in this section, it starts with a brief header explaining the subsequent output. Then, this sample generates a table with three rows – one for each of the columns in the Northwind.Shippers table. We only need to use the String function to pad the first field in the table, as the other two align automatically due to their length and data type.

```
Immediate                                                                          
Column names, datatypes, and widths for the Shippers table in the Northwind database.
ShipperID            int              4
CompanyName          nvarchar         40
Phone                nvarchar         24
```

Microsoft designed SQL-DMO such that we could perform a full range of SQL Server administrative functions. The main sample in the next section adds a computed column to a table. In the process of implementing the task, we will demonstrate techniques for trapping errors with SQL-DMO programming.

Adding Objects, Trapping Errors, and Removing Objects

This sample performs a task that we could accomplish by using a T-SQL ALTER TABLE statement, but SQL-DMO integrates more tightly with traditional VBA programming techniques. This is primarily because the SQL-DMO model is highly structured and hierarchical, but the T-SQL programming model has a host of system stored procedures and T-SQL statements for getting directly to a result. In other words, T-SQL does not offer an object model for SQL Server, but SQL-DMO does.

A **computed column** is a virtual column in a table. It does not hold nor require data storage. Instead, an expression, such as Salesqty*Price, designates the value of the computed column, such as Revenue. Computed columns can appear in SELECT statement lists, as well as in their WHERE and ORDER BY clauses.

> *The SELECT statement in SQL Server works similarly to the one in Access with a few exceptions, such as computed fields, which are not available in Access for tables.*

Although there is only one real sample in this section, for ease of reading we'll break it into four subsections. We will start by examining how to count the number of columns in the table.

Counting the Columns

We will use the sample in this section to illustrate how to program a pair of Sub procedures that manage concurrently a connection to the same SQLServer object with an identical login. Notice from the preceding samples that it is normal for a procedure using SQL-DMO to open a Connection at the beginning of a procedure and to close the Connection and related objects just before the procedure closes. When we have two procedures that can open and close the same Connection, but one of those procedures needs to manage the Connection differently from the other, Connection conflicts can occur.

The following pair of procedures counts the columns in a table. Using the first procedure, we specify the database and the table. In the second procedure, count_columns_in_a_table, we open a Connection to the server maintaining the database that contains the target table. Then, we print out the count of columns to the Immediate window, just before closing the Connection.

The second procedure will count the columns in any table within any database on the cab2200 server. Therefore, it is a good candidate for use with other procedures besides the first procedure in this sample.

```
Sub call_count_columns_in_a_table()
Dim dbsname As String
Dim tabname As String

'Name server, database, and table
dbsname = "pubs"
tabname = "table5"
count_columns_in_a_table dbsname, tabname

End Sub


Sub count_columns_in_a_table(dbsname As String, tabname As String)
Dim srv1 As New SQLDMO.SQLServer
Dim dbs1 As SQLDMO.Databases
Dim tab1 As SQLDMO.Table

'Connect to server
Set srv1 = SQLServers("cab2200")
srv1.Connect "cab2200", "sa", ""

'Specify table name in database on cab2200 server
Set tab1 = SQLServers("cab2200").Databases(dbsname). _
 Tables(tabname)
Debug.Print "Column count for table5 is " & _
 tab1.Columns.Count & "."

'Release resources
srv1.Disconnect
Set srv1 = Nothing

End Sub
```

Now, we'll look at adding a computed column to a table.

Adding a Computed Field

The following procedure, `add_computed_field_to_titles`, presents the main sample of this section. At its core, this sample adds a computed column to the `Titles` table of the **pubs** database.

By calling the `count_columns_in_a_table` procedure, we set up the possibility for `Connection` conflicts between this and the called procedure. This is because the `count_columns_in_a_table` procedure can try to open a `Connection` that the `add_computed_field_to_titles` already has open. Likewise, `count_columns_in_a_table` can close a `Connection` that `add_computed_field_to_titles` needs open. Within the context of VBA programming, we can use simple error trapping as one relatively standard way of detecting and correcting these conflicts. Our sample and its discussion highlight this technique.

Another application of error trapping in the sample is in the case in which we try to add a new computed column to replace the previous one. If our purpose is truly to replace the old column, the error is merely a reminder to remove the old column and then try again to add the new column. We will demonstrate the syntax for this technique as well.

```
Sub add_computed_field_to_titles()
Dim srv1 As SQLDMO.SQLServer
Dim col1 As SQLDMO.Column
On Error GoTo add_trap
```

```
'Connect to server
Set srv1 = New SQLDMO.SQLServer
srv1.Connect "cab2200", "sa", ""

'Print column titles before adding new column
Debug.Print "Titles columns before add."
count_columns_in_a_table "pubs", "titles"
For Each col1 In srv1.Databases("pubs").Tables("titles").Columns
 Debug.Print col1.Name & String(25 - Len(col1.Name), " ") & col1.DataType
Next

'Add new, computed column to the table
Set col1 = New SQLDMO.Column
col1.Name = "SubTotalNoDiscount"
col1.DataType = "money"
col1.ComputedText = "CONVERT(money, ytd_sales * price)"
col1.IsComputed = True
srv1.Databases("pubs").Tables("titles").Columns.Add col1

'Print columns after adding new column
'Print computed column's formula if there is one
Debug.Print vbCrLf & String(25, "-")
Debug.Print "Titles columns after add."
count_columns_in_a_table "pubs", "titles"
For Each col1 In srv1.Databases("pubs").Tables("titles").Columns
 If col1.IsComputed = False Then
  Debug.Print col1.Name & String(25 - Len(col1.Name), " ") & _
      col1.DataType
 Else
  Debug.Print col1.Name & String(25 - Len(col1.Name), " ") & _
      col1.DataType, col1.ComputedText
 End If
Next

'Release resources
add_exit:
Set col1 = Nothing
srv1.Disconnect
Set srv1 = Nothing
Exit Sub

add_trap:
'Clear comment prefix on next line for a trace of error processing
'Debug.Print Err.Number, Err.Description
If Err.Number = -2147201024 Then
'Disconnect if already connected
 srv1.Disconnect
 Resume
ElseIf Err.Number = -2147201022 Then
'Connect if necessary
 srv1.Connect "cab2200", "sa", ""
 Resume
ElseIf Err.Number = -2147200500 Then
'Remove field if it exists already and refresh table
'Refresh permits Add method to see the column is removed
 srv1.Databases("pubs").Tables("titles").Columns. _
  Remove ("SubTotalNoDiscount")
 srv1.Databases("pubs").Tables("titles").Refresh
 Debug.Print "Removed old version of 'SubTotalNoDiscount'."
 Resume
```

```
  Else
   Debug.Print "Ended with unresolved error." & vbCrLf & _
    Err.Number, Err.Description
   Resume add_exit
  End If

  End Sub
```

A quick scan of the comments within the procedure confirms that much of the sample does other things besides add a column. Let's review the sections sequentially before examining the output from the procedure, to further reinforce our understanding of the techniques presented in this sample.

❑   We start the procedure with two Dim statements to declare a pair of SQL-DMO objects. One of these denotes the SQLServer object that all SQL-DMO applications need. The second is the Column object, which the procedure needs to append a column to the Titles tables

❑   Our first operational code in the sample instantiates the SQLServer object. Then, we use this object to open a Connection to the cab2200 server. This is standard operating procedure for most SQL-DMO applications. We cannot do anything until we have a connection to a server.

❑   Next, we take a snapshot of the table columns before adding our column. In particular, we report the total number of columns in the table and list the column names and datatypes. To compute the number of columns in the Titles table, we call the count_columns_in_a_table procedure. This call generates an error because the called procedure tries to open the same Connection that the calling procedure already has open. The code to resolve this conflict appears in the error trap section of add_computed_field_to_titles. In this particular instance, it is relatively easy to avoid the error. We could insert the code to take a snapshot of the Titles columns before invoking opening a Connection for the current procedure. However, sometimes we cannot readily bypass the error, and the error processing logic here equips us to deal with such situations.

❑   In the third section we add our column. We begin by instantiating a Column object. Next, we assign name, datatype, and expression values to the computed column. We also set the column's IsComputed property to True. After creating the column specification, we invoke the Add method to append it to the Columns collection for the Titles table in the pubs database.

❑   Once we execute the code to add a new column to the table, we take another snapshot of the columns in the Titles table. This snapshot is similar to the preceding one, except that it adds a new column to its output – the expression for computed columns. We use the IsComputed property in an If condition to determine if we should print just a column's name and datatype, or these two properties plus the column's ComputedText property.

❑   If all goes well up to this point in the procedure, we close the application by releasing resources and exiting the Sub procedure.

Beyond the code to close the procedure is the logic for processing errors. This section traps four types of errors.

Trapping the Error

The first error trap we use detects an attempt to open a Connection to a server on a login that already exists. In this case, we close the current connection and return control to the point that generates the error, so that it can make its Connection. This approach is simple. If we have a system with many users that generate this error, we will probably want to code a more advanced solution that reuses the existing Connection.

Our second error trap detects a case in which the code assumes a `Connection` that is not there (for example, another procedure closed it). In this scenario, we reconnect with a login appropriate for the current procedure.

We use the third error trap to catch cases in which we try to add a column to the `Titles` table when it is already there. The solution here is to drop the old column. We can accomplish this with the `Remove` method. We will also need to `Refresh` the `Titles` table before returning control to the statement that generated the error. Without the `Refresh` method, the code trying to add the new version of the column will still see the old version of the column. We can learn more about the `Refresh` method by looking in the **Object Browser** in the VBA project or just by clicking on `Refresh` in the above sample and pressing *F1*. A `Debug.Print` statement identifies that the procedure detected this error.

Finally, if an error occurs that is not one of the preceding three, the last path prints the error number and description to the **Immediate** window before exiting the procedure normally.

We present below the contents of the **Immediate** window output from running the procedure the first time. It contains two snapshots of the `Titles` table columns. We leave uncommented the line that prints each error number and description, so that we can view the normal flow of the program. The top snapshot shows the columns before the addition of our new computed column. Notice that it detects 10 columns in the `Titles` table. A series of 25 dashes separate the first and second snapshots. The bottom snapshot reports 11 columns in the `Titles` table. In addition, it shows the expression for the computed column.

```
Titles columns before add.
−2147201024 [SQL−DMO]This server object is already connected.
Column count for table5 is 10.
−2147201022 [SQL−DMO]This server object is not connected.
title_id    tid
title    varchar
type     char
pub_id    char
price    money
advance    money
royalty    int
ytd_sales    int
notes    varchar
pubdate    datetime

-------------------------

Titles columns after add.
−2147201024 [SQL−DMO]This server object is already connected.
Column count for table5 is 11.
−2147201022 [SQL−DMO]This server object is not connected.
title_id    tid
title    varchar
type     char
pub_id    char
price    money
advance    money
royalty    int
ytd_sales    int
notes    varchar
pubdate    datetime
SubTotalNoDiscount  money   (convert(money,([ytd_sales] * [price])))
```

The first error (number -2147201024) traps the case when the `count_columns_in_a_table` procedure tries to open a `Connection` that the `add_computed_field_to_titles` procedure already has open.

The second error (number -2147201022) detects the case when `count_columns_in_a_table` returns control to `add_computed_field_to_titles` at the point that it references `srv1`. This reference fails since the other procedure closed the `Connection`.

We see the same pair of errors again when the procedure takes the second snapshot of the `Titles` table `Columns` collection. If we run the `add_computed_field_to_titles` procedure a second time, it will typically generate a new error when we invoke the `Add` method for the `Columns` collection in the `Titles` table. This error appears between the first and second snapshots along with a custom message to further clarify the problem. It will show in the output as follows:

> –2147200500 [SQL–DMO]Column 'SubTotalNoDiscount' already exists.
> Removed old version of 'SubTotalNoDiscount'.

Our exploration of this sample will benefit from one more procedure, which show us how to remove the computed column.

Removing the Column

We use the `remove_field_from_titles` procedure to unconditionally drop the computed column from the `Titles` table. This restores the version of the table before we added the column. If the column that we are trying to remove is not there, then it generates an error with number –2147199728, which means that our code tried to drop a column that is not there. In this case, we should clear the message. The column has already been removed from the table.

```
Sub remove_field_from_titles()
Dim srv1 As SQLDMO.SQLServer

'Connect to server
Set srv1 = New SQLDMO.SQLServer
srv1.Connect "cab2200", "sa", ""

'Remove a column
srv1.Databases("pubs").Tables("titles").Columns. _
 Remove ("SubTotalNoDiscount")


'Release resources
srv1.Disconnect
Set srv1 = Nothing

End Sub
```

Let's finish off this section by examining SQL-DMO with SQL Server 2000.

SQL-DMO with SQL Server 2000

SQL-DMO is the object model for SQL Server. Therefore, SQL-DMO for SQL Server 2000 reflects all the administrative enhancements and innovations introduced with SQL Server 2000. These are too many to for us to enumerate here, but there are some issues worthy of special mention.

Note the object models are different between SQL Server 7.0 and SQL Server 2000 and this will be exemplified below. As a developer, it means we cannot connect to a SQL Server 2000 server from a SQL Server 7.0 server, as the models are incompatible.

There are some totally new objects and many other cases where objects are supersets of the version introduced with SQL-DMO for SQL Server 7.0. SQLServer2 is the name of the object running SQL Server 2000. Enhanced object names generally follow the convention of using the old object name with 2 as a suffix. The SQLServer2 object inherits all the properties and methods of the SQLServer object from SQL Server 7.0.

One of the new features of SQL Server 2000 is its ability to run multiple instances of SQL Server on a single computer. SQLServer2 has the ability to enumerate the multiple instances of SQL Server running on a computer as well as connect to any particular instance. SQL Server 2000 uniquely identifies instances of SQL Server by the combination of a **Service name** and an **Instance name**. SQLServer2 exposes InstanceName and ServiceName properties to enable developers to reference individual instances of SQL Server 2000 running on a computer.

The Collation property designates the collation of the items in a column. This new property pertains directly or indirectly to SQLServer2, Database2, Column2, UserDefinedDataType2, and SystemDataType2 objects. The new ListCollations method for the SQLServer2 object returns all valid collation names.

When we read the Collation property for an object, it identifies the default collation for string data types in that object. We can designate the Collation property for the Database2 and UserDefinedDataType2 objects at the time we create them. The Collation property setting for a Database2 object overrides the Collation setting in the model database. This enables us to establish unique collations for individual databases on a SQL Server. Similarly, a UserDefinedDataType2 object can have a unique collation from other data types in a Database2 object. Without any special settings, SQL Server 2000 automatically aligns its collation with the Windows collations, removing the need to specify separately a code page for string data at installation.

We will now complete the chapter with our third and final main section, which will examine the creation of constraints.

Creating Constraints

A constraint is a restriction. Placed at either column or table level, a constraint helps us to maintain the integrity of our database, by ensuring that our data meets certain integrity rules. There are six basic kinds of constraints:

- ❏ The nullability of a column
- ❏ A DEFAULT constraint for a column
- ❏ A CHECK constraint that limits the values a column will accept
- ❏ A UNIQUE constraint that forces the uniqueness of one or more columns across all rows
- ❏ A PRIMARY KEY that identifies one or more columns to serve as a unique key for all rows
- ❏ A FOREIGN KEY that points to unique or primary key values in another table and supports referential integrity

With Access 2000, we can program constraints using T-SQL in stored procedures from stored procedure templates, or VBA with either ADO or SQL-DMO from VBA projects. In this chapter we have already presented samples illustrating how to set nullability options and designate a primary key. If our tables require a substantial design effort or we only have a few of them, we may be more likely to create and edit constraints with a graphical design component, such as the Design view for database diagrams. This topic is discussed further in Chapter 4. However, there can be a decided attraction to creating our constraints programmatically. The programmatic approach provides an automatic way to re-create the table design, if necessary. In addition, if we find our application requires many tables with a relatively standard design, we can create them programmatically to reduce tedium and improve consistency.

Let's begin by examining the first two types of constraints in our list – Nullability and DEFAULT constraints.

Nullability and DEFAULT Constraints

Many database developers are familiar with a NULL value. It denotes a missing value in the sense that a field's value is not available at the time a record is entered into a database. This assignment results from one of two conditions. Either the user does not specify a value for a column or the user explicitly specifies a NULL value. By default, SQL Server allows NULL values for most data types, but we can explicitly override this with settings for individual columns, using the CREATE TABLE and ALTER TABLE statements.

It is good programming practice to set the nullability with either the NULL or NOT NULL keywords when initially declaring or altering a column. However, it is not strictly necessary if we know how the defaults work and what the settings are for a SQL Server. Columns with a Timestamp data type or an IDENTITY property cannot contain NULLs. The Default value for columns with a Datetime data type is also NOT NULL. If a Datetime column has no explicit setting, the default time is 12 midnight and the default date is January 1, 1900.

> *NULL is different from a zero-length string or blank and the numeric value of zero. A NULL value represents the non-entry of data in a column.*

The create_table4 stored procedure (see below for the reminder of the code) creates a table with four columns – three of which accept the default nullability setting.

```
Alter Procedure create_table4
As

/*
Create a table without a PRIMARY KEY,
but include a column with an IDENTITY property
*/
CREATE TABLE table4
(
myid int IDENTITY,
fname varchar(20),
lname varchar(40),
ext char(4)
)
```

The IDENTITY setting for the myid column forces it to have an integer value. Therefore, it cannot be NULL. We can force the fname and lname column values in a new version of table4 to be NOT NULL by following their data type specification with the NOT NULL keyword:

```
Alter Procedure create_table4_new
As

/*
Create a table without a PRIMARY KEY,
but include a column with an IDENTITY property
*/
```

```
CREATE TABLE table4_new
(
myid int IDENTITY,
fname varchar(20) NOT NULL,
lname varchar(40) NOT NULL,
ext char(4)
)
```

With a NOT NULL setting, SQL Server will not allow us to insert records having the value NULL for that row. With the default NULL or an implicit nullability setting, we can enter records into a table even if they do not have a value for a column (that is it accepts NULL values).

Notice that the code sample accepts the default setting for the nullability constraint with respect to the ext field (that is, it does not explicitly set the constraint). Programming is an art and not a science. For every rule that we state, good reasons and special circumstances can merit an exception. This book targets those developing SQL Server solutions with Access 2000. As professional developers, we will gain the experience to know under which circumstances it is acceptable to deviate from conventions.

We can also change the nullability for the ext column in the new version of table4 from its default setting of NULL to NOT NULL with the following stored procedure. We can copy it into the stored procedure template of an Access project and run it from there to modify the nullability of a column.

```
Alter Procedure make_ext_not_null
As
ALTER TABLE table4_new ALTER COLUMN ext CHAR(4) NOT NULL
```

We may find it easier to just open the table in **Design** view and clear the Allow Nulls check box for the ext column. However, this does not leave an audit trail of modifications to the table. The make_ext_not_null stored procedure is a reminder of the change made to table4.

As long as we are just specifying the design of a table not populated with data, the preceding approach works. If we are working with data that complies with the constraint, then we need to run make_ext_not_null. If the data in table4_new contains data non-compliant with the NOT NULL specification, then Microsoft Access informs us that the update to the table design fails.

We can run a WITH NOCHECK clause in such a situation. This clause of the ALTER TABLE statement disables the existing value check when adding a constraint to a table containing data. When creating constraints on existing tables with SQL-DMO, use DoAlterWithNoCheck to force WITH NOCHECK behavior and optimize constraint implementation. Subsequent samples in this chapter demonstrate the use of this clause.

It is worth here again comparing the Default objects we discussed earlier in the chapter and DEFAULT constraints. A Default is an object that we actually bind to our table, whereas a DEFAULT constraint is a non-object based solution, which is an integral part of the table definition.

A DEFAULT constraint defines what to do when a new row is inserted that does not include data for the column on which we have defined the DEFAULT constraint. We can define it as a literal value or as one of several system values, such as GETDATE(). The basic points to note are:

- ❑ Defaults are only used in INSERT statements – they are ignored for UPDATE and DELETE statements
- ❑ If any value is supplied in the INSERT, then the default is not used
- ❑ If no value is supplied, the default will always be used

Default values for a column override the default NULL setting for columns with another specific value. If a user does not specify a value for a column with a DEFAULT setting, SQL Server assigns the column the default value instead of a NULL. While NULL is technically an option for a DEFAULT value setting, we do not need it unless the default nullability setting changes.

Let's move on to our next constraint.

CHECK Constraints

CHECK constraints help ensure the integrity of data by limiting the values that are accepted by a column. To do this we specify a CHECK constraint with a logical (Boolean) expression that returns TRUE or FALSE based the logical operators. For example, to limit the range of values for a salary column to being between $20,000 and $80,000 we can use the logical expression: salary >= 20,000 AND salary <= 80,000.

Column-level constraints have expressions related to a single column. Note that we can apply multiple CHECK constraints to a single column, which will be evaluated in the order that they were created. We can also apply a single CHECK constraint to multiple columns by creating it at the table level. Table-level constraints can also be used to check one column against another, as long as all the columns are within a single table. Tables can have any number of CHECK constraints, and we can use virtually any expression that we could put use in a WHERE clause in our constraint.

New records with Boolean expressions evaluating to TRUE pass the check and enter the table. Records that fail the check will generate an error message informing us which constraint caused the record to be rejected. T-SQL syntax enables us to suspend the operation of a CHECK constraint. This is handy when we want to apply a constraint to a table that includes data that will violate the constraint.

We can specify a constraint at the same time that you we create a table using a stored procedure. Note that the constraint is added to the table and not the individual column. The constraint specification can have multiple elements.

To designate a CHECK constraint we use they two keywords CONSTRAINT and CHECK. We begin with the CONSTRAINT keyword accompanied by the name for our constraint. If we do not specify a name, SQL Server automatically generates an arbitrary name. This is followed by the CHECK keyword and an expression to represent the constraint:

```
CONSTRAINT <constraint_name> CHECK (<expression>)
```

Now that we have examined the basics of the CHECK constraint, let's look at some examples.

Specifying a Check Constraint at Table Creation

We will use the stored procedure script overleaf to demonstrate how we can specify a CHECK constraint within an Access project template. We begin by looking to see if we have a previous version of table4, and then drop it if necessary. Then, we use a CREATE TABLE statement to define table4. The table has a CHECK constraint named ext_numbersonly on the last column. We set the requirement that each of the four characters for the ext column be in the range from 0 through 9. Our initial version of `table4` generated by the `create_table4` stored procedure did not mandate that ext characters be numbers – therefore, a user could type an extension such as **abcd**. With the `ext_numbersonly` constraint as part of the definition of `table4`, attempting to insert an ext value that isn't all numbers will generate an error message.

```
Alter Procedure create_table4_ext_numbersonly
As
/*
Create a table without a PRIMARY KEY,
but include a column with an IDENTITY property for myid
and a check constraint for ext
*/

--Drop any previous version of table4
IF EXISTS (SELECT * FROM sysobjects WHERE id = object_id('table4')
    and OBJECTPROPERTY(id, 'IsUserTable') = 1)
DROP TABLE table4

--Create table4
CREATE TABLE table4
(
myid int IDENTITY,
fname varchar(20),
lname varchar(40),
ext char(4)
CONSTRAINT ext_numbersonly CHECK (ext LIKE '[0-9][0-9][0-9][0-9]')
)
```

We need to check that the constraint has been added. Open `table4` in **Design** view and use the **Properties** button on the Access toolbar to display the **Properties** dialog.

We will now attempt to `INSERT` a record into `table4` with non-numeric characters in the ext field, by using a stored procedure in an Access project stored procedure template:

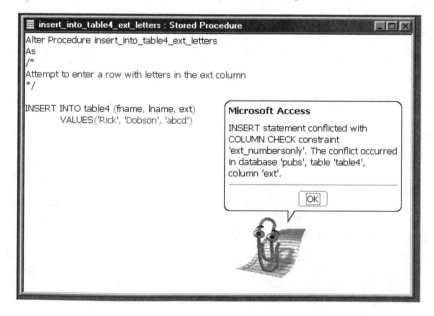

When we run the stored procedure (by clicking the **Datasheet view** button), we get an error message, as shown. This particular message explains that the value for the `ext` column within `table4` of the pubs database conflicts with the `ext_numbersonly` CHECK constraint. If our purpose is to block the entry of records with any characters other than numbers in the `ext` column, this constraint does the job. However, users can still enter records that do not satisfy the constraint by failing to enter any value at all for the `ext` column. This is possible as the preceding script fails to make the `ext` column NOT NULL.

We are not restricted to using CHECK constraints that are included in the initial design of a table. We can use the ADD statement within an ALTER TABLE statement to add a CHECK constraint to an existing table. Let's apply such a constraint to `table4`.

Adding a Check Constraint Programmatically

This technique works whether or not the existing table contains any CHECK constraints. When we build a CHECK constraint this way, some existing records may not satisfy our new constraint. If this is the case, we have three options:

- ❑   We can revise our existing data to bring it into compliance with the new constraint
- ❑   We can change the constraint
- ❑   We can add the constraint with a NOCHECK condition. This condition permits us to add a CHECK constraint to a table that only affects the entry of new records. Existing records can remain in the table even if they violate the constraint. We will use this option in our example.

This can, however, cause users serious problems if they later edit these records. They might intend to edit a field which has no constraints currently applied and be unable to save the record because a field they didn't want to edit fails to satisfy its constraint conditions. This can be frustrating for a user who may not even know what constitutes a valid value for this second field.

We will use the following script to examine the syntax for adding a CHECK constraint to `table4`. We require the first character of an `ext` column value to be odd. Note that this constraint is for the first digit only, while our earlier constraint is for all four digits.

```
Alter Procedure alter_table4_ext_add_firstodd
As
/*
Add a check constraint to table4 that
requires the first digit to be odd
*/

ALTER TABLE table4 WITH NOCHECK
ADD CONSTRAINT ext_firstodd_added
    CHECK (ext LIKE '[1,3,5,7,9]')
```

Before the addition of the `ext_firstodd_added` CHECK constraint, we could enter a value such as 8629 for an `ext` column value. However, after adding the constraint, if we attempt to add an `ext` value with an even digit for the first character, we will receive an error message saying our value conflicts with the constraint. The message fails to convey the expression behind the CHECK constraint.

As we add more CHECK constraints to a table, it can become difficult to keep track of the precise impact of each of them. What we need is a way to survey all our constraints. The `sp_helpconstraint` system stored procedure returns information for all types of constraints on a table. We can invoke it inside of an EXEC statement and pass the system stored procedure a table name, such as `table4`. This stored procedure returns information in multiple `Recordsets`. Therefore, we will need to extract the `Recordsets`. We saw how to do this earlier with the `print_multiple_recordsets` procedure, in the section on *Managing Tables with ADO*.

Alternatively, we can type `sp_helpconstraint`, followed by the table name, in Query Analyzer, as shown in the following screenshot for `table4`:

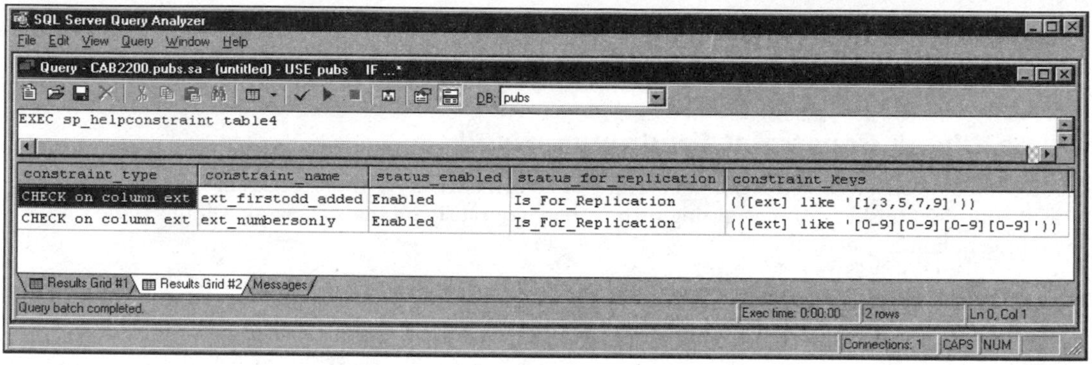

Recall that this table now has two `CHECK` constraints. We can see in the above screenshot the contents of the **Results Grid #2** tab, which displays specifications for column-level `CHECK` constraints. The **Results Grid #1** tab displays specifications for table-level `CHECK` constraints. Since we have no table-level `CHECK` constraints in this example, that tab will have no contents to display.

The column-level `CHECK` constraint names appear in the **constraint_name** column, and the expressions that define their constraints are in the **constraint_keys** column. Other columns in the grid give additional clues about the behavior of our `CHECK` constraints. One column reveals whether `CHECK` constraints participate in SQL Server replication applications. Another column identifies the **Enabled** status of constraints. We can temporarily disable a constraint if we need to add records from another table that violate the constraint. After entering the records, we can re-enable the constraint. Users cannot enter any column values into the database that violate an enabled `CHECK` constraint; users can modify other columns in the new records that do not conflict with the `CHECK` constraint.

We use the following syntax to disable the `ext_firstodd_added` constraint:

```
ALTER TABLE table4 NOCHECK CONSTRAINT ext_firstodd_added
```

It is even simpler to restore a disabled constraint. We run a stored procedure with the following line to re-enable the `ext_firstodd_added` constraint:

```
ALTER TABLE table4 CHECK CONSTRAINT ext_firstodd_added
```

We will finish our discussion on `CHECK` constraints by looking at how we can add them manually to a table.

Adding Constraints to a Table Manually

The following screenshot shows a variation of the table design we looked at when we first introduced manually creating tables. Our new table has the name **TABLE2**. Instead of using an `IDENTITY` property to uniquely mark records in its telephone directory, we use social security numbers. Since the **pubs** database already has a user-defined data type for social security numbers, we use the `id` data type used for the `au_id` column, which we saw earlier, in the `Authors` table.

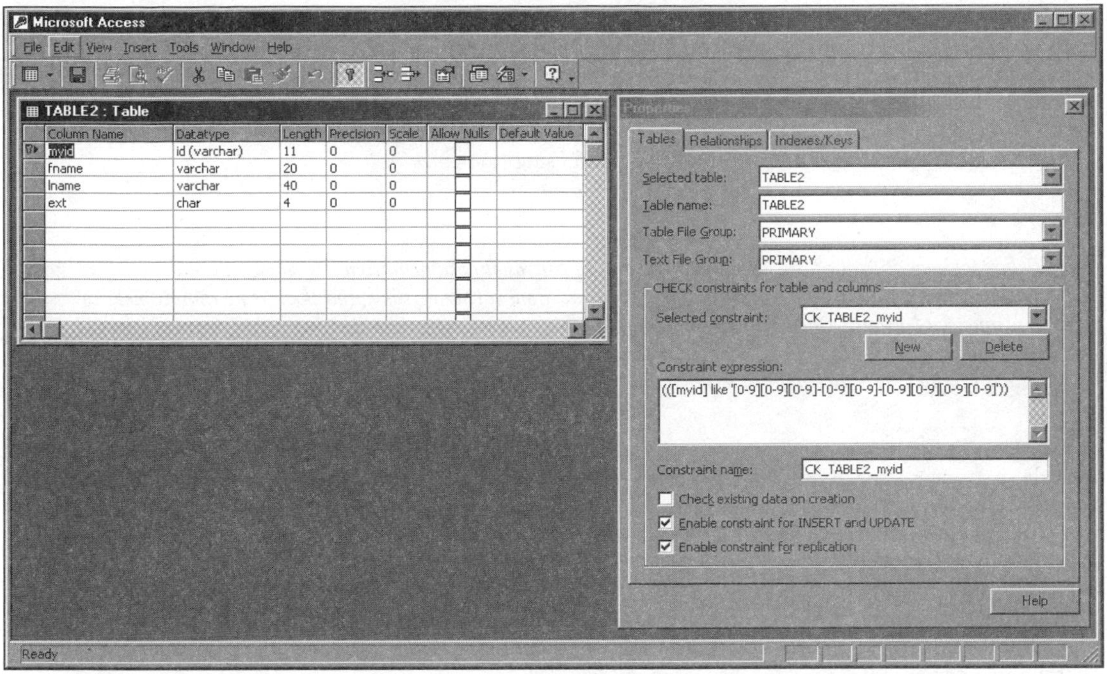

There are no built-in constraints on the characters in an `id` field, so users can enter letters as easily as numbers. Therefore, we need to add a constraint through the Properties dialog that appears on the right in the preceding screen. We open the Properties dialog for TABLE2 by choosing View | Properties. To add a constraint, we chose the Tables tab of the Properties dialog, then click on the New button. We then enter the syntax for our constraint and its name into the Constraint expression and Constraint name boxes. In our example, the Constraint expression contains the `LIKE` keyword and pattern rules to designate a field comprised entirely of digits and hyphens. The Constraint name is an `id` for our constraint. We can use it to recall our constraint later for editing or deleting. Access developers will recognize the syntax for specifying constraints with the `LIKE` keyword because it is similar to that used with an Access database file (`.mdb`).

When we save the table design, SQL Server compiles our Constraint expression(s). If there are no errors, it saves the table with any constraints we added. Otherwise, we have the opportunity to revise our expression or remove the constraint. Chapter 4 drills down on the Properties dialog more extensively as part of a discussion on database diagrams and related issues, such as indexes and table relationships.

If we attempt to insert a record with a social security field of `abc-de-fghi` it will violate the `CK_TABLE2_myid` constraint. This is because the constraint restricts the social security field to having numbers only, organized into three-two-four groups by hyphens, since this is the general form of a US Social Security number. Access responds to this attempt by issuing a message that states: INSERT statement conflicted with COLUMN CHECK constraint 'CK_TABLE2_myid'. The conflict occurred in database 'pubs', table 'TABLE2', column 'myid'. We click on OK to return to the Datasheet view, from where we can change our `myid` column value to one comprised of numbers and hyphens instead of letters and hyphens. Or we could just abort the attempt to add a new record.

Adding a CHECK constraint as illustrated in the preceding example solves the problem of non-numeric input for TABLE2, but what about other tables that use the user-defined id type?

If we limit our application development tools to CHECK constraints, we must re-enter the same constraint for each new table. This is because the syntax for adding a user-defined data type does not accept CHECK constraints. Rules represent one solution to the problem of having to re-create a CHECK constraint for each new table that applies a user-defined data type.

Let's have a look at some examples of creating and using Rules.

Rules

Before looking at Rules, we should remember that Microsoft documentation describes Rules as "backward compatible" – meaning they are preserved from earlier versions and there is no commitment to continue implementing them in future versions. This may leave users with databases that cannot be moved to the new server without being changed. Nevertheless, Rules offer an elegant solution for limiting the values accepted by a user-defined data type in any table within a database.

A Rule, unlike a CHECK constraint, is an independent object. However, both Rules and CHECK constraints include expressions specifying what the legitimate values we can use are. Since a Rule is an independent object, we can bind it to one or more other objects, such as user-defined data types and columns in one or more tables. As both user-defined data types and Rules are independent database objects, they work especially well together.

Access projects offer no direct means of creating or editing Rules, but we can manage them after they are created from an Access project stored procedure template. We create a Rule with the CREATE RULE statement. The general syntax for the statement is:

```
CREATE RULE rule_name
AS
condition_expression
```

Note that for the condition_expression:

❑   We can use any valid expression appropriate for the WHERE clause of a SELECT statement.

❑   The expression cannot reference anything external to itself.

❑   The expression must include a local variable name that starts with an @ sign (Chapter 6 explains how to declare and use local variables in SQL Server solutions). The name is an internal variable that is used to hold the value that we are attempting to add to the table. Any legitimate SQL Server identifier is allowed (for example, @foo). It doesn't matter what name we assign to the local variable.

Alternatively, we can just as easily create and manage Rules from Enterprise Manager. To create a new Rule in Enterprise Manager, we expand the database that we wish to create a Rule for, right-click on **Rules**, and choose **New Rule**.

The only reason that we are creating our rule in Enterprise Manager is because we CANNOT create Rules in an Access project.

The screenshot below demonstrates how we would add a new Rule to the **pubs** database:

Clicking **New Rule** presents a **Rule Properties** dialog, as in the following screenshot:

To get to this point, we need to open the **pubs** database on our server (in this case CAB2200), and follow the steps for creating a new Rule. Next, we enter a name for our new Rule, and type the expression for the Rule in the text box. We click **OK** to create the Rule.

After creating our Rule, we need to bind it to the id data type before it will impact on the values entered into a column with this data type. We accomplish this using the sp_bindrule system stored procedure. Remember that we can bind more than one Rule to a database object.

In the following figure we see a stored procedure in an Access project named bind_numbersonly_rule_to_id that does exactly what its name implies. To do this it runs the sp_bindrule system stored procedure with two parameters. The first of these names the Rule. The second parameter specifies the database object to which to apply the Rule – namely, the id user-defined data type.

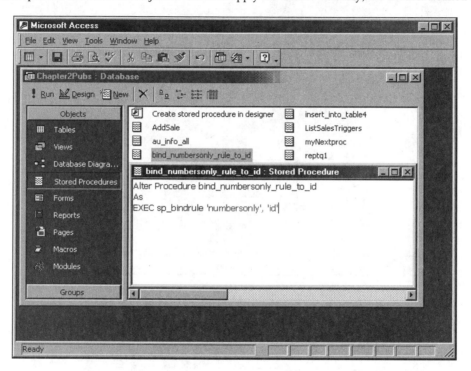

When we use a Rule, there are a couple of other stored procedures we will want to have available.

First, we will learn how to unbind a Rule from a database object. We can use this to temporarily disable a Rule. If we want to unbind a Rule from a table, then we can use this syntax:

```
EXEC sp_unbindrule tablename.rulename
```

To unbind our numbersonly Rule from the user-defined id data type:

```
Alter Procedure unbind_numbersonly_rule_from_id
As
EXEC sp_unbindrule 'id'
```

We also need to unbind a Rule before we can permanently remove it from our database. We can use the DROP statement for a rule that is not bound to any database object. For our current example the syntax would be:

```
Alter Procedure drop_numbersonly_rule
As
DROP RULE numbersonly
```

Notice that the preceding two stored procedures start with ALTER PROCEDURE instead of CREATE PROCEDURE – this is an Access project convention. Chapter 6 drills down on the coding and use of stored procedures in Access projects.

Let's move on to examine our next two constraints – UNIQUE constraints and PRIMARY KEYS.

UNIQUE Constraints and PRIMARY KEYS

UNIQUE and PRIMARY KEY constraints can both uniquely identify the rows of a table. Either type of constraint can pertain to a single column or a set of two or more columns. In addition, both the PRIMARY KEY and UNIQUE constraint can be either **clustered** or **non-clustered**. A clustered key has its values ordered on the disk according to the index value to speed up retrieval. However, there can be only one clustered index per table for obvious reasons. We can create foreign keys in another table, as we will discuss later, which point back to the current table by referencing either the PRIMARY KEY or a UNIQUE constraint in the current table.

Despite these similarities, there are important differences between the PRIMARY KEY and UNIQUE constraints.

❑   First, there can be only one primary key per table. There is no limit to the number of UNIQUE constraints.

❑   Second, a primary key must contain no NULL values at all. It requires a distinct value for each record. A UNIQUE constraint can contain one row with a NULL value.

❑   Third, a primary key defaults to creating a clustered index, and a UNIQUE constraint defaults to a non-clustered index.

A standard principle of relational database design is that every table should have a primary key. We can create the primary key at the same time that we create a table or we can alter a table after its creation to add a primary key. Unlike with CHECK constraints, we cannot suspend the enforcement rules for a primary key. The primary key must always uniquely identify the records in a database. Applications can distinguish between otherwise duplicate records by adding an IDENTITY property column based on an Int, or other acceptable, data type. The IDENTITY property will force uniqueness within a table at a site by incrementing each record a fixed amount from the preceding record starting at a seed value. If we have a replicated application that must run independently at two or more sites, we can create a primary key based on two columns – one of which identifies the site and the other of which has an IDENTITY property. As long as our site identifiers are unique across sites, our primary key will be unique across sites. Alternatively, we can base a primary key in a replicated application based on a Uniqueidentifier data type.

SQL Server automatically creates indexes to support the PRIMARY KEY and UNIQUE constraints. There can be no more than 249 non-clustered indexes per table, and only one clustered index. SQL Server will not add a PRIMARY KEY or UNIQUE constraint that violates these limits.

Let's look at an example of creating a table with a primary key.

Creating a Table with a Primary Key Using the IDENTITY Property

If we have a single column, such as an `Int` column with an `IDENTITY` property that serves as the primary key, we can create our table as usual, except that we include the words `PRIMARY KEY` after the `IDENTITY` keyword.

We will first examine the full syntax for the `CREATE TABLE statement`, so we can see how this all fits together. Don't get too caught up in all the details shown here, we present the code in full mostly for general interest and reference – there won't be a test at the end of the chapter!

```
CREATE TABLE
[ database_name.[owner].| owner.] table_name
({<column_definition> | column_name AS computed_column_expression
   | <table_constraint>} [,...n]
)
[ON {filegroup | DEFAULT} ]
[TEXTIMAGE_ON {filegroup | DEFAULT} ]

<column_definition> ::= { column_name data_type }
[ [ DEFAULT constant_expression ]
   | [ IDENTITY [(seed, increment ) [NOT FOR REPLICATION] ] ] ]
   [ ROWGUIDCOL ]
   [ <column_constraint>] [ ...n]
   <column_constraint> ::= [CONSTRAINT constraint_name]
{
   [ NULL | NOT NULL ]
   | [ { PRIMARY KEY | UNIQUE }
     [CLUSTERED | NONCLUSTERED]
     [WITH FILLFACTOR = fillfactor]
     [ON {filegroup | DEFAULT} ]]
     ]
   | [ [FOREIGN KEY]
     REFERENCES ref_table [(ref_column) ]
     [NOT FOR REPLICATION]
     ]
   | CHECK [NOT FOR REPLICATION]
     (logical_expression)
}
<table_constraint> ::= [CONSTRAINT constraint_name]
{
   [ { PRIMARY KEY | UNIQUE }
     [ CLUSTERED | NONCLUSTERED]
     { ( column[,...n] ) }
     [ WITH FILLFACTOR = fillfactor]
     [ON {filegroup | DEFAULT} ]
   ]
   | FOREIGN KEY
     [(column[,...n])]
     REFERENCES ref_table [(ref_column[,...n])]
     [NOT FOR REPLICATION]
   | CHECK [NOT FOR REPLICATION]
     (search_conditions)
}
```

Now let's look at an example, using just the relevant pieces of this syntax. Since SQL Server by default creates clustered indexes for `primary keys`, we do not have to explicitly include the `CLUSTERED` keyword after `PRIMARY KEY`. Note that we can add the `PRIMARY KEY` keywords to all the columns (if we have more than one) that we want to be part of our primary key.

```
Alter Procedure create_table4_identity_primary_key
As
/*
Using the PRIMARY KEY keyword to designate
a primary key based on a column with an
IDENTITY property; drop table_4 if it exists already
*/

CREATE TABLE table4
(
myid int IDENTITY PRIMARY KEY,
fname varchar(20),
lname varchar(40),
ext char(4)
)
```

If we want to add our primary key after the table's creation, this technique is not appropriate.

Incidentally, SQL Server assigns an arbitrary name to the index when we designate it with the PRIMARY KEY keyword. It is an arbitrary name that appears in the collection of indexes. The index has a name, which is different from the column(s) on which it is based.

We can also use a CONSTRAINT declaration in a CREATE TABLE or ALTER TABLE statement to create a primary key – which makes this method more flexible than using the PRIMARY KEY keyword. Let's look at a couple of examples.

Using the CONSTRAINT Syntax to Create a Primary Key

We will use the following T-SQL code sample to show a stored procedure that creates a table with a primary key using the CONSTRAINT syntax:

```
Alter Procedure create_table4_pk
As
/*
Create a table with a PRIMARY KEY based on two columns,
and a pair of check constraints --
    one created with the table
    another created after the table
*/

--Drop any previous version of table4
IF EXISTS (SELECT * FROM sysobjects WHERE id = object_id('table4')
    and OBJECTPROPERTY(id, 'IsUserTable') = 1)
DROP TABLE table4

--Create table4
--with a primary key and a check constraint
CREATE TABLE table4
(
myid int NOT NULL,
fname varchar(20),
lname varchar(40),
ext char(4) NOT NULL,
CONSTRAINT PK_table4 PRIMARY KEY CLUSTERED (myid,ext)
CONSTRAINT ext_numbersonly
    CHECK (ext LIKE '[0-9][0-9][0-9][0-9]')
```

```
)

--Add another check constraint to table4 after its creation
ALTER TABLE table4
ADD CONSTRAINT ext_firstodd_added
   CHECK (ext LIKE '[1,3,5,7,9]')
```

Again, we can specify a primary key based on one or more columns (up to as many as 16). Here, we base our primary key on the myid and ext columns – neither of which can contain NULLs. We can also name our primary key. In this case, it is called PK_table4. This is convenient when we need to refer back to it by name in order to delete it, or to change it by adding/deleting columns from its definition. The CONSTRAINT declaration for the primary key explicitly specifies that SQL Server should build a clustered index for the primary key. We can replace CLUSTERED with NONCLUSTERED to force the creation of a primary key on a non-clustered index.

Using the CONSTRAINT syntax helps us to see the similarity between a PRIMARY KEY and other types of constraints – for example, the two CHECK constraints we have added to the table. The first CHECK constraint declaration is in the CREATE TABLE statement. The second CHECK constraint declaration is in a separate ALTER TABLE statement. We can also add a primary key to a table after its initial creation, as we will see in our next example.

Adding a Primary Key to a Table

We will use the create_table4_pk_added stored procedure to demonstrate the syntax for adding a primary key to a previously created table. We begin by dropping the current version of table4; then executing the create_table4 stored procedure to created the initial version of the table. We then invoke an ALTER TABLE statement with the ADD CONSTRAINT keyword combination.

```
Alter Procedure create_table4_pk_added
As
/*
A sample demonstrating the addition of a primary key
after the initial creation of a table
*/

--Drop any previous version of table4
IF EXISTS (SELECT * FROM sysobjects WHERE id = object_id('table4')
   and OBJECTPROPERTY(id, 'IsUserTable') = 1)
DROP TABLE table4

--Restore initial version of table4 with no primary key
EXECUTE create_table4

--Add a primary key to table4
ALTER TABLE table4
ADD CONSTRAINT table4_pk_added
   PRIMARY KEY (myid)
```

As we can see from our sample above, we specify five things:

- ❑ That we are adding something to the table
- ❑ That we are adding a constraint

- ❏ That the constraint is called `table4_pk_added`

- ❏ That the constraint is of type `PRIMARY KEY`

- ❏ The column(s), `myid`, which the constraint applies to and on which the index for the primary key will be built

If we execute the `sp_helpconstraint` system stored procedure immediately after running this sample, we will see a primary key for `table4` with a constraint name of `table4_pk_added`.

We need to make sure that all the columns contributing to the definition of the primary key are explicitly or implicitly not nullable. Our applications can follow the `ADD` keyword with more than one `CONSTRAINT`. Use a comma to separate successive `CONSTRAINT`s.

Now let's look at an example of adding `UNIQUE` constraint.

Adding UNIQUE Constraints

We follow the same general syntax as for adding primary keys, except that we change the keyword in the `CONSTRAINT` declaration from `PRIMARY KEY` to `UNIQUE`. The following stored procedure sample defines `UNIQUE` constraint for `table4` based on the `ext` column:

```
Alter Procedure alter_table4_ext_ukfromtsql
As
/*
A sample that demonstrates adding a unique
constraint to a table
*/
ALTER TABLE table4
ADD CONSTRAINT ext_ukfromtsql
    UNIQUE (ext)
```

Recall that the index for a `UNIQUE` constraint will be non-clustered unless we explicitly designate a clustered index (and there is not already a clustered index on the table). It is not necessary for us to explicitly use the `NOT NULL` keyword in the column declaration, since SQL Server can build an index for `UNIQUE` constraint with no more than one `NULL` value.

Adding a clustered `PRIMARY KEY` or `UNIQUE` constraint to a large table requires re-sorting the data on disk according to the values of the `PRIMARY KEY` or `UNIQUE` constraint. For a database with a large number of rows or very wide rows, this can consume substantial amounts of time.

Experienced VBA developers may find SQL-DMO a comfortable environment for manipulating primary keys and `UNIQUE` constraints. For this reason, we present the following sample, which will help us extend the SQL-DMO skills we developed earlier in the chapter.

Using SQL-DMO to Add Primary and Unique Keys

We will build a primary key based on the `myid` column in `table4`, and `UNIQUE` constraint for the `ext` column. Our VBA procedure below assumes any version of `table4` with an `IDENTITY` or `NOT NULL` keyword for `myid`. This is a requirement, since we cannot build a primary key on a nullable column.

```
Sub add_primary_and_unique_keys_to_table4()
Dim srv1 As SQLDMO.SQLServer
```

139

```
Dim tab1 As SQLDMO.Table
Dim PK1 As New SQLDMO.Key
Dim nams1 As SQLDMO.Names
Dim tabname As String
Dim pkname As String
Dim ukname As String
Dim nams2 As SQLDMO.Names
Dim UK1 As New SQLDMO.Key
Dim intCount As Integer

'Assign table and key names
tabname = "table4"
pkname = "table4_pk_fromsqldmo"
ukname = "ext_uk"

'Connect to SQLServer
Set srv1 = New SQLDMO.SQLServer
srv1.Connect "cab2200", "sa", ""

'Create reference to table4
Set tab1 = _
 srv1.Databases("Pubs").Tables(tabname)

'Specify clustered, primary key and name it
PK1.Clustered = True
PK1.Type = SQLDMOKey_Primary
PK1.Name = pkname

'Specify nonclustered, unique constraint and name it
UK1.Clustered = False
UK1.Type = SQLDMOKey_Unique
UK1.Name = ukname


'Name table columns for primary key and unique constraint
Set nams1 = PK1.KeyColumns
nams1.Add ("myid")
Set nams2 = UK1.KeyColumns
nams2.Add ("ext)

'Remove table's current primary key and unique constraint if they exist
'and add in replacements
intCount = tab1.Keys.Count
For i = intCount To 1 Step -1
 If tab1.Keys(i).Type = SQLDMOKey_Primary Then
  tab1.Keys(i).Remove
 ElseIf tab1.Keys(i).Type = SQLDMOKey_Unique And tab1.Keys(i).Name = ukname Then
  tab1.Keys(i).Remove

 End If
Next i
tab1.Keys.Add PK1
tab1.Keys.Add UK1

'Release resources
Set tab1 = Nothing
srv1.Disconnect
Set srv1 = Nothing

End Sub
```

We begin with a series of declarations to support the procedure's tasks.

- In particular, we want to focus on the declarations for PK1 and UK1, the PRIMARY KEY and UNIQUE constraint that the procedure adds to table4.

- This sample introduces us to the SQL-DMO Names collection. This container facilitates the manipulation of a list of names. We use two of these collections to hold column names for the definition of the primary key and UNIQUE constraint.

- We also need a Table object, tab1, which points at the table to which we will add a primary key and UNIQUE constraint.

- The SQLServer object is necessary to help us make a connection to a server holding the database containing the table to which we want to add the constraints.

- The other declarations reserve memory for string and integer variables to help perform the procedure's tasks.

We define a few string constants and make a connection to a server, then point the Table object, tab1, at a table in the pubs database. We use the familiar table4 table, but we could re-orient the procedure at any other table in pubs (or, indeed, any other database). Two subsequent blocks assign specifications for the new primary key and UNIQUE constraint that we will add to the tab1 object. We explicitly set the primary key to have a clustered index and the UNIQUE constraint to have a non-clustered key. Next, we assign the KeyColumns collections for both keys to a Names collection. This design facilitates defining the keys over a range of columns, although this particular application uses a single column for each. We then define the primary key and UNIQUE constraint, respectively, on the myid and ext columns in table4.

Before adding the new keys, we must remove the existing primary key (if there is one) and any UNIQUE constraints with the same name as the one we are about to add. We use the For…Next loop with the nested If…ElseIf statement to accomplish this task. There is one trick to the loop worth noting. The loop uses a negative step of –1 and starts with the largest index for a Key object in tab1's Keys collection. Since the loop removes unwanted keys when it finds them, it can change the index values for the keys as it passes through the Keys collection members. Counting backward avoids an out-of-bounds error for the For loop's index value and also avoids not removing keys.

After removing any former versions of the primary key and UNIQUE constraint, we install the new keys with the ADD method for the Keys collection of tab1. We finish by releasing our SQL-DMO resources.

Let's finish with a look at FOREIGN KEY constraints.

FOREIGN KEY Constraints

All the other constraints we have considered up to this point refer to a single table. FOREIGN KEY constraints are a means of referencing or associating the records in one table with those in another. A foreign key in one table points at, or references, the primary key or UNIQUE constraint in another table.

The following diagram page depicts a foreign key relationship:

The foreign key in a related (referencing) table points back at or references the primary key in a main (referenced) table. The referenced and referencing tables must share a common field. For example, if our application tracks sales by employee, then it can have an `Employees` and a `Sales` table. The `Employees` table can have a primary key of `emp_id`, and the `Sales` table can have its own primary key of `sales_id`. Since each employee can have multiple sales, the `Sales` table relates to the `Employees` table. The way to tie each sales record back to one employee is to create a column in the `Sales` table that has the primary value for one employee. The `emp_id` column in the `Sales` table is a foreign key because it points back at the primary key in the `Employees` table.

Foreign keys enforce referential integrity, which pertains to the relationship between two tables. Referential integrity does not permit us to enter of a foreign key value in one table without a matching primary key value in a referenced table (unless a user leaves the foreign key value unspecified or enters a `NULL`). When a foreign key points back at a primary key, it can never be `NULL`. Similarly, traditional implementations of referential integrity do not allow cascading `DELETE`s and `UPDATE`s. In other words, changes, such as `UPDATE`s to the primary key, in one table do not propagate automatically to a second table with a foreign key that points back at it. In fact, classic referential integrity does not permit changes to a primary key value or record deletions if there are matching foreign keys in another table. Recent referential integrity implementations do support cascading `UPDATE`s and `DELETE`s – SQL Server 2000 does support the newer features, but SQL Server 7 does not.

Given this background, we present a couple of examples illustrating the use of foreign keys for referential integrity. The examples pull together content from this and the preceding chapter to illustrate how to piece together multiple skills.

Using Foreign Keys on an MSDE Server

Before we start writing code to specify foreign and primary keys, we need a database to work with. Since MSDE doesn't come with any sample databases, we'll have to build one. This is an easy task, using an Access project and the Microsoft SQL Server **Database Wizard**. Remember Chapter 2 describes using this wizard to build a new database. We specify the MSDE server `cabxli`, call the Access project file `Chapter03RI.adp`, and accept the default name of **Chapter03RISQL** for the corresponding database. As we saw in Chapter 2, the **Database Wizard** assigns the name. This database serves as a container for the `Customers` and `Orders` tables. We will build a `Foreign Key` constraint in the `Orders` table that points back to the `Customers` table.

Our first example explores the coding and operation of referential integrity on a computer running MSDE. This database engine is compatible with SQL Server 7, and it therefore does not support cascading `UPDATE`s and `DELETE`s. The first example also demonstrates how to copy data on the fly from a SQL Server database, namely the **Northwind** database, to an MSDE database, the one in the example. The same coding technique works between any pair of SQL Servers.

Creating and Populating a Table with a Primary Key

We will use the two stored procedures below to illustrate an approach to building the `Customers` table in the **Chapter3RISQL** database and populating it with values from the **Northwind** database on a SQL Server, `cab2200`. We should run these procedures on the server receiving the records.

```
Alter Procedure make_Customers
As
/*
This stored procedure builds a table in the Chapter03RISQL database on a MSDE
server (cabxli) and populates it with values from the Northwind database on a
SQL Server (cab2200). It executes a second stored procedure to assist in
```

```
copying records from the cab2200 server to the cabxli server.
*/

--Delete the table if it exists already
IF EXISTS (SELECT * FROM sysobjects WHERE id = object_id('Customers')
    and OBJECTPROPERTY(id, 'IsUserTable') = 1)
DROP TABLE Customers

--Create Customers for the Chapter03RISQL database
CREATE TABLE Customers
(
CustomerID    nchar(5)     NOT NULL    PRIMARY KEY,
CompanyName      nvarchar(40)    NOT NULL,
ContactName      nvarchar(30)    NULL,
Address        nvarchar(60)    NULL,
City        nvarchar(15)    NULL,
Region        nvarchar(15)    NULL,
PostalCode    nvarchar(10)    NULL,
Country        nvarchar(15)    NULL
)

--Populate the Customers table in the Chapter03RISQL database on the cabxli server
--with records from the Northwind database on the cab2200 server
INSERT INTO Customers
EXEC for_populate_customers


Alter Procedure for_populate_customers
As

--Select records from the Customers table in the Northwind database
--on the cab2200 server
SELECT CustomerID, CompanyName, ContactName, Address, City, Region,
    PostalCode, Country
FROM OPENROWSET('SQLOLEDB','cab2200';'sa';'',
 'SELECT * FROM Northwind.dbo.customers')
```

We start with the make_Customers stored procedure. First, we drop any previous version of the Customers table in the **Chapter03RISQL** database. Next, we use a CREATE TABLE statement to construct a new version of the Customers table. Except for two columns, all the columns in the Customers table are nullable. The columns that are not nullable are the PRIMARY KEY, CustomerID, and the CompanyName.

Immediately after we execute the CREATE TABLE statement, the Customers table is empty. We use the final two lines in the make_Customers stored procedure to insert the return set from the for_populate_customers stored procedure into the Customers table. In this second stored procedure, we use the OPENROWSET keyword to select records from another server without first creating a linked server. Chapter 5 explicitly discusses the OPENROWSET keyword. However, we can see in this example how to extract a subset of columns from the **Northwind** database on the cab2200 server. The order of our column list in the SELECT statement for the second stored procedure must match the order of the column declarations in the CREATE TABLE statement from the first stored procedure.

Our second example illustrates the operation of referential integrity on a computer running SQL Server 2000. With the SQL Server 2000 version, we can optionally enable cascading DELETEs and UPDATEs. Instead of using a code-based technique for transferring records between servers, we will populate our example database by manually importing records from the SQL Server 2000 version of the **Northwind** database. Some may prefer the code-based approach, but others may find it convenient to perform part of the task manually. The point of the contrasting examples is that either way works.

Creating and Populating a Table with a Foreign Key

The following code samples for creating the `Orders` table in **Chapter03RISQL** reveal that the same kind of logic applies when we create the `Orders` table as for the `Customers` table. Recall that when we work with a primary key that has an `IDENTITY` property, we do not normally copy values into the primary key column. Our application can turn off this default condition for the special cases in which it is necessary. Use the `SET_IDENTITY_INSERT` statement to enable the ability to write values into a column with an `IDENTITY` property. This feature is not necessary for our sample.

```
Alter Procedure make_Orders
As
/*
This stored procedure builds a table in the Chapter03RISQL database on a MSDE
server (cabxli) and populates it with values from the Northwind database. It
follows
the same approach as the preceding sample, but it is for the Orders table.
*/

--Drop table if it exists already
IF EXISTS (SELECT * FROM sysobjects WHERE id = object_id('Orders')
    and OBJECTPROPERTY(id, 'IsUserTable') = 1)
DROP TABLE Orders

--Create Orders in Chapter03RI
CREATE TABLE Orders
(
OrderID     int    NOT NULL  IDENTITY  PRIMARY KEY,
CustomerID     nchar(5)    NULL,
OrderDate     datetime    NULL
)

--Populate Orders with records from another source
INSERT INTO Orders
EXEC for_populate_orders


Alter Procedure for_populate_orders
As

--Select records from the Customers table in the Northwind database
--on the cab2200 server
SELECT CustomerID, OrderDate
FROM OPENROWSET('SQLOLEDB','cab2200';'sa';'',
  'SELECT * FROM Northwind.dbo.orders')
```

We use two additional `ALTER TABLE` statements to create and remove, respectively, the foreign key constraints.

```
Alter Procedure add_foreign_key
As

--Add the foreign key constraint to the Orders table
ALTER TABLE Orders
```

```
ADD CONSTRAINT fk_Customers_CustomerID FOREIGN KEY (CustomerID)
   REFERENCES Customers(CustomerID)


Alter Procedure drop_foreign_key
As

--Drop the foreign key constraint from the Orders table
ALTER TABLE Orders
DROP CONSTRAINT fk_Customers_CustomerID
```

We can use the two procedures to control the enforcement of referential integrity. By removing the constraint, we can add records that violate referential integrity. This could be desirable if, for example, we have historical data that used a different set of `CustomerID` values from those for more recent data.

When we add a foreign key constraint, we are establishing referential integrity between a pair of tables. We add the foreign key constraint to the table that references another table. The referencing table must point at either a primary key or `UNIQUE` constraint in the other table. Our code sample references the `CustomerID` from the `Customers` table. While the values in this column are unique in the `Customers` table, they repeat in the `Orders` table to represent a one-to-many relationship between the `Customers` table and the `Orders` table. This is typical for `FOREIGN KEY` constraints.

> *We can create foreign keys that reference their own table. This is not that common, but it can serve some database designs. We can look at the* Employees *table in the* **Northwind** *database for an example of this kind of foreign key. In particular, examine the syntax for the* FK_Employees_Employees *foreign key. In this context, a table references itself (for example, some employees can be both a direct report to another employee, but also a manager of other employees).*

Let's examine what we have achieved in our previous two examples.

What This Achieves

The following screen displays the Microsoft Access message that appears when a user tries to `UPDATE` a `CustomerID` value from **ALFKI** to **ALFZZ**:

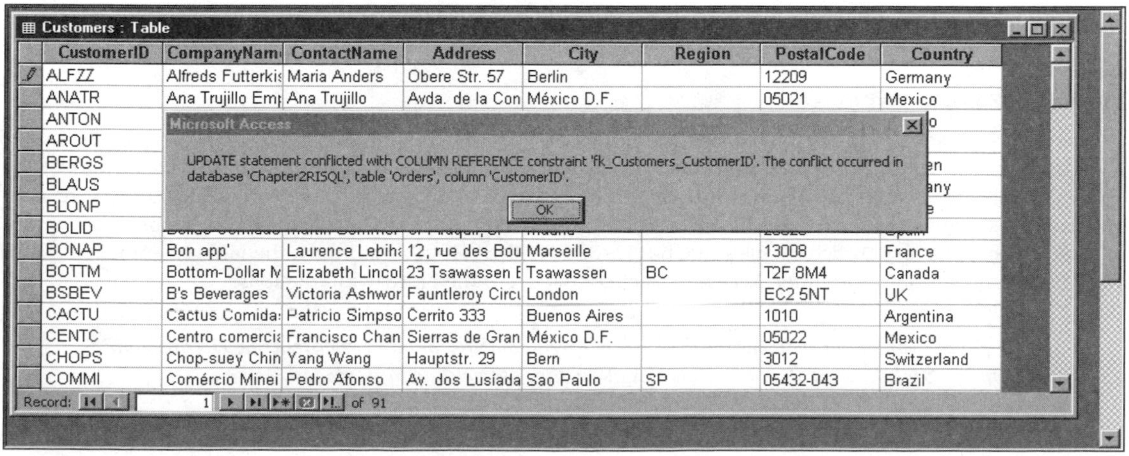

An identical message occurs if a user tries to DELETE the Customer record with ALFKI as a primary key. Notice that the message specifically mentions the FOREIGN KEY constraint created by our add_foreign_key stored procedure. Since the Orders table has records with ALFKI foreign key values, SQL Server through Access does not permit updates to the ALFKI value in the Customers table or a deletion of the Customer record with that CustomerID. If a user tries to UPDATE a foreign key value in the Orders table from ALFKI to ALFZZ, the error message above appears again. In this case, the reason is that users cannot change a record in the Orders table that results in a foreign key value without a match in the Customers table.

Enforcing referential integrity does not block us from updating and modifying our data, but it does place restrictions, such as those described above, on the kinds of changes that we can make.

One way we can change a primary key value in the Customers table with foreign key matches in the Orders table is to remove or disable the FOREIGN KEY constraint. Our drop_foreign_key stored procedure removes the foreign key. After running this, we can change CustomerID values in the Customers table even if they do have matches in the Orders table. We can then make matching changes to the corresponding foreign key values in the Orders table.

Finally, we can run the add_foreign_key stored procedure to re-establish referential integrity between the Customers and Orders tables. Our application requires a schema modify lock on the table when we invoke this stored procedure. Changing a primary key value with matching foreign key values can result in orphaned records. Orphaned records in this context correspond to Orders records that do not match any Customers records. To avoid this situation, we either UPDATE the foreign key values or move their records to another table.

Let's finish the chapter with a look at foreign keys and SQL Server 2000.

Foreign Keys in SQL Server 2000

SQL Server 2000 simplifies the management of referential integrity by adding the capability to enforce cascading UPDATEs and DELETEs. We may not want the cascading capabilities available for typical users, but database administrators and developers are likely to benefit from the features that these capabilities offer. As of the time of writing, we can only control these features programmatically from Access projects. We can graphically turn on and off cascading capabilities for a relationship from the Enterprise Manager in SQL Server 2000.

Before we examine the programmatic syntax for demonstrating cascading capabilities, we summarize the process used to create a sample database and tables for the demonstration.

Creating a Sample Database

We start this example identically to the preceding one with the creation of a new Access project file named Chapter03RIWithSS2000.adp, but we populate the database with tables differently. The Microsoft SQL Server Database Wizard creates a SQL Server database named Chapter03RIWithSS2000. The wizard runs on a computer named cab166 running the SQL Server 2000 beta. Instead of programmatically creating the Customers and Orders tables in Chapter03RIWithSS2000, we import the tables from the Northwind database. This requires another Access project connected to the Northwind database.

> *Note that we can do this without the third-party Access database, but that requires code. Here we will rely on the GUI, in order to demonstrate this alternative approach to the same task.*

We use the File | Get External Data | Import command to copy the Customers and Orders tables from the Northwind database to the Chapter03RIWithSS2000 database. Chapter 2 describes and demonstrates how to use the File | Get External Data | Import command. It also shows how to create an Access project that connects to a previously existing database, such as Northwind.

After we have created a new database with the Customers and Orders tables, we need to create a primary key in the Customers table before attempting to apply a FOREIGN KEY constraint to the Orders table.

Adding Primary and Foreign Keys

The File | Get External Data | Import command copies the data and most of the structure, but it does not translate a primary key. We can create a primary key for the Customers table by opening it in Design view, then selecting the row representing the CustomerID column, and clicking the Primary Key tool on the menu.

Our SQL Server 2000 example uses two FOREIGN KEY constraints – one that is identical to the previous example and another that uses cascading UPDATEs. The following code samples present the stored procedures that we will use to add and drop the constraints of both types. Note that we only show the new code.

```
Alter Procedure add_foreign_key_update
As


--Add a foreign key with a cascading update capability
ALTER TABLE Orders
ADD CONSTRAINT fk_Customers_CustomerID_update FOREIGN KEY (CustomerID)
    REFERENCES Customers(CustomerID) ON UPDATE CASCADE



Alter Procedure drop_foreign_key_update
As


--Drop a foreign key with a cascading update capability
ALTER TABLE Orders
DROP CONSTRAINT fk_Customers_CustomerID_update
```

All we need to do to enforce cascading UPDATEs is to include a short clause, namely ON UPDATE CASCADE, immediately after the standard CONSTRAINT syntax for a foreign key. A similar clause exists for implementing cascading DELETEs – namely, ON DELETE CASCADE. We require no change at all to remove a cascading versus a standard FOREIGN KEY constraint. In both cases, we follow the DROP CONSTRAINT phrase with the constraint's name. Microsoft also allows us to temporarily disable a cascading FOREIGN KEY constraint using the same WITH NOCHECK phrase that we saw earlier for PRIMARY KEY and CHECK constraints.

The screenshot on the following page demonstrates the cascading feature of an UPDATE from Customers flowing from the Customers table to the Orders table:

We change just one `CustomerID` in the `Customers` table – this affects six records in the `Orders` table. This demonstration confirms both the potential and pitfall of the cascading feature. One change in the right hands can productively UPDATE a series of records. In contrast, the poorly conceived UPDATEs of a novice database administrator or user can have a broader impact with the cascading feature – deleting one record in the main table can remove many records in a related table. Therefore, we may care to make its availability conditional on the status of the user. In any event, we should use cascading DELETEs very judiciously.

Summary

While this chapter nominally targets the building and maintenance of tables, we will discover that it helps us in other ways as well. One important area of this chapter is its introduction to T-SQL and SQL-DMO. This chapter specifically examines how to use these tools for building tables. In addition, this chapter also introduces how to use ADO with VBA projects to build tables. Much of this coverage targets using ADO objects as containers for T-SQL statements. However, there is also ample attention devoted to using SQL-DMO in VBA projects. Chapter 12 explores the special tasks that we can perform with VBA in the modules associated with Access projects. That chapter assumes we have a working knowledge of VBA in Access projects developed in the first part of the book.

Those new to SQL should check that a system stored procedure doesn't already exist that does what they want before coding their own – it's amazing how many applications out there have their own system stored procedures, and there's no point re-inventing the wheel.

Using Database Diagrams

Diagrams are a quick and easy way of representing relational database models, and documenting a database. It is a lot easier to understand a diagram of the data relationships between tables than the T-SQL code, particularly when your database is large. As well as presenting an easy means for us, the designer,s to grasp the scope of our databases, we can use database diagrams to show our clients what we've produced for them. Access projects provide a useful graphical tool to do just this, enabling you to create diagrams that actually generate the T-SQL code for tables in a database.

Up until Access 2000, it was difficult and tricky to build tables in a SQL Server database with Access. The addition of the **Database Diagram Designer** simplifies the specification of tables and the relationships between them in a SQL Server database model. This tool makes it easier for developers new to SQL Server to specify and maintain database designs. Because database diagrams are so easy to work with, we can dynamically revise a model while interacting with our clients, and maintain the documentation at the same time.

The chapter covers three main areas:

- ❑ An introduction to database diagrams

- ❑ How to effectively use the Database Diagram Designer

- ❑ Advanced topics – techniques for using database diagrams in Enterprise Manager not readily available in Access Projects and coverage of the new database diagram features introduced with SQL Server 2000

Introducing Database Diagrams

Database diagrams, also commonly called entity relationship diagrams or just entity diagrams, are not a substitute for good database design. Before you even start to use the Database Diagram Designer, you should think carefully about your database design.

Having said this, database diagrams do give developers a chance to step back and take in an overview of their database design. This is particularly useful for databases that we inherit from others, or when we're working on a large project with many tables and relationships. Diagrams can also be very helpful when communicating the important elements of a database's design to a client or to other developers employed by the client.

Database diagrams have an appearance that their name suggests. They graphically depict the relationships between tables. While database diagrams look similar to the Relationship window for Access database applications, database diagrams in Access projects can do an immense amount more.

With a Relationship window, we can define and edit relationships between existing tables. This includes the ability to designate cascading updates and cascading deletes. Aside from the relationship capabilities, we cannot define or edit tables in a Relationship window, although we can add existing tables to the window. Access 2000 enhances the capabilities of the Relationship window from earlier versions by letting us print it.

Database diagrams embrace and extend the functionality available from the Relationship window found in Access database files. With a database diagram in an Access 2000 project, we can create tables, columns, and indexes, and refine the relationships between them. Among the specific kinds of actions that developers can perform with database diagrams are:

- ❑ Add or drop existing tables into or from a database diagram
- ❑ Create new tables that update the database from inside a database diagram
- ❑ Add or drop tables in a database
- ❑ Add or drop columns in a table
- ❑ Add or drop a primary key to a table
- ❑ Designate or delete constraints for the columns within a table
- ❑ Assign or remove indexes on the columns within a table
- ❑ Declare or drop referential integrity (as well as cascading deletes and updates with Enterprise Manager in SQL Server 2000)

There can only be one Relationship window in an Access database file; however, an Access project permits multiple database diagrams. With the capability to manage multiple database diagrams, we can divide a database into logical parts that other people can manage independently. Conversely, we may sometimes wish to consolidate the individual parts into an overall depiction of a process or organization. Selected formatting tasks that you can perform with database diagrams include:

- ❑ Automatically arranging the boxes representing tables
- ❑ Altering the size of any selected subset of tables in a database diagram
- ❑ Adding and editing labels and annotations to a database diagram

❑   Showing labels for the relationships between tables

❑   Printing database diagrams

❑   Recalculating page breaks

❑   Saving and retrieving database diagrams

More General Properties of Database Diagrams

Individual database diagrams reside within the SQL Server database – just like tables, views, and stored procedures. SQL Server tracks the database diagrams within a database through the dtproperties table. This system table stores database diagram properties, and it resides in a user-defined database. The dtproperties table is somewhat similar to the sysobjects table, another table managed by SQL Server inside user-defined databases. We have no need to interact with the dtproperties table directly since we can manipulate database diagrams through the Database Diagram Designer window.

The Database window is used to open an existing database diagram or start a new one. We can then create or edit the properties of database objects in the database diagram from within the Database Diagram Designer window.

Experienced SQL Sever database administrators and developers will be pleased to know that data definitions for tables and their columns created in Enterprise Manager can be edited in Access and are 100% viewable from Access. Beyond that, database diagrams are 100% interchangeable between Enterprise Manager and Access projects. We can create a database diagram in Enterprise Manager and then edit in an Access project, and vice versa. SQL Server 7 does offer some enhanced functionality for working with database diagrams, such as the ability to save script changes, but these added features do not change the ability of Access projects to work with database diagrams developed with Enterprise Manager.

Unlike tables, views, and stored procedures, database diagrams have no Datasheet view, having only a Design view. They are great resources for graphically managing a database's structure. In addition, they tie seamlessly to the Access user interface. SQL Server 2000 allows database diagrams to expose the data in the tables it shows, a topic we'll come back to in the *Advanced Topics* section.

SQL Server 2000 and Access Projects

Since Access 2000 targets compatibility with SQL Server 7, new functionality for database diagrams introduced after SQL Server 7 is not available from within the Access project Database Diagram Designer. Therefore, the new database diagram features introduced with SQL Server 2000 that gain focus at the end of this chapter are not available from Access projects. The introduction of SQL Server 2000 has also created a series of incompatibilities between Access projects and the new SQL Server version that removed critical functionality that was present for both MSDE and SQL Server 7.

As we saw in Chapter 2, Microsoft has made several attempts to remedy the incompatibilities between Access projects and SQL Server 2000. Although these remedies fall into three areas, only one is relevant to this chapter. To remind you of this, if you install the Client Tools for the release version of SQL Server 2000, you should find that you will be able to design visually and save tables, views, and database diagrams in a SQL Server 2000 database from within an Access project.

Sample Database for the Chapter

In an effort to give you exposure to different sample databases that come with the various versions of SQL Server, this chapter will use a variation of the pubs database. We'll be adding database diagrams to this base sample over the course of the chapter. Remember, as we discussed in Chapter 1, if you're an Access developer using MSDE you won't have pubs by default.

Another thing we mentioned previously is that if you're using SQL Server 2000 you won't be able to create a table in the database graphically unless you have taken one of the steps outlined in Chapter 1.

Let's quickly have a look at a database diagram that you can create easily for the pubs database, to see some of the basic information that these tools can give us.

The Basic Pubs Database Diagram

The database diagram opposite depicts the pubs database tables and their relationships with one another. The tables describe entities such as publishers, authors, and titles, and the relationships between them.

Let's have a look at some of the features of this database diagram:

- ❑   Authors are in a many-to-many relationship with titles. The titleauthor table captures data unique to the intersection of authors and titles, including the order of the authors for a title and the percentage of the royalty that each author is to receive. As mentioned in Chapter 1, many-to-many relationships consist of two one-to-many relationships. The many-to-many relationship between authors and titles rests on a one-to-many relationship between authors and titleauthor and the one-to-many relationship between titles and titleauthor. Notice that the database diagram depicts the one-to-many relationship with a relationship line that has a key on the one side of the relationship and an infinity sign ( ) on the many side.

- ❑   The pub_info table is in a one-to-one relationship with the publishers table. Unlike other relationship lines between tables, the one between these two tables has a key on either end to characterize the one-to-one relationship.

- ❑   The pub_info table contains two potentially long data types – image for the logo column and text for the pr_info column.

Notice the display format for the pub_info table differs from the other tables in the database diagram. This illustrates the ability of a database diagram to display the detailed structure of a table. The detail the database diagram exposes is fully editable. When we close the database diagram and save our changes, any changes we made update the database design if we have security rights to makes those changes. This is a significant reason why database diagrams are such a potent design tool.

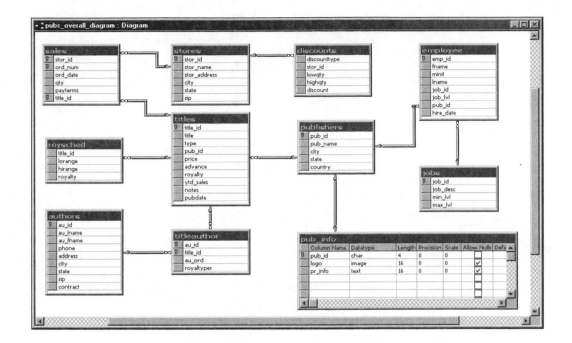

Using Database Diagram Designer

The Database Diagram Designer is the interface that Access projects offer for manipulating database diagrams. If an existing database diagram is opened from the Database window, it will likely show some subset of the tables in a database. If we choose to create a new database diagram from the Database window, the Database Diagram Designer will present a blank database diagram. In either case, we're going to need to know about the primary tools for managing the objects within a database diagram. These are:

❑ The Diagram Design toolbar

❑ The Diagram menu

❑ The Diagram window, and associated context-sensitive menus

The Diagram Design Toolbar

The Diagram Design toolbar, which is activated when we open a database diagram, supports four broad classes of functions:

❑ Populating a database diagram with new objects and hiding objects that don't need to be shown. When we add a database object to a database diagram, we can also elect to save the object to the database.

❑ Editing of objects that are in a database diagram.

❑ Management of the appearance of objects in a database diagram.

❑ Standard Windows tasks, such as printing, saving, and exchanging information with the Clipboard.

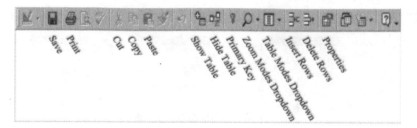

The two icons next to Help at the right hand end of the toolbar don't relate directly to the Database Diagram window. The New Object icon allows us to create a new database object, while the Database Window icon brings the Database window to the front. Let's examine those functions that do relate specifically to database diagrams, starting with Show Table.

Diagram Manipulation

The Show Table and Hide Table controls enable us to determine which tables appear in a database diagram. The Show Table control opens a dialog from which we can drag a table name to the Diagram window. This enables a blank database diagram to be populated, or tables to be added to an existing one. Access forbids us from entering two copies of a table in a single database diagram. However, it does permit the same table to appear in more than one database diagram. The following screenshot depicts a new database diagram in the process of having the authors table dragged on to it from the Show Table dialog. When the developer releases the mouse, the table opens on the database diagram. We can add multiple tables from the Show Table dialog by just dragging them one at a time onto the database diagram and releasing them.

Hide Table enables us to remove a table from a database diagram. However, the table still remains in the database.

156

Table Design

The Primary Key, Insert Rows, Delete Rows, and Properties controls permit the editing of the tables that appear in a database diagram. The Primary Key control assigns its namesake to the currently selected columns in a table. If there is already a primary key for a table, the control shows itself as selected when that row has focus in a database diagram. We can add and delete columns in a table with the Insert Rows and Delete Rows controls (the reference to rows indicates the way they appear in the database diagram). Clicking the Properties control opens a three-tabbed dialog that permits you to set properties for a table in a very granular way. A subsequent section in this chapter drills down on the Properties dialog.

Changing the Diagram Appearance

The Zoom Modes Dropdown and Table Modes Dropdown controls are used for refining the appearance of our database diagram. The Zoom Modes Dropdown control quite straightforwardly allows us to zoom in and out of our view of the database diagram. The Table Modes Dropdown control permits us to determine the appearance of any selected tables on the database diagram.

In the following screenshot, of a database diagram formed from a few tables in the pubs database, the five various options presented by the Table Modes Dropdown are illustrated. We've added labels to the database diagram so you can see which view is which. We'll see how easy it is to add our own labels in a later section. In the Keys view the table name is displayed along with any primary and foreign key columns for the table. In the Custom View, in its default format as seen here, the column name, data type, and Nullable setting of each column in a table are displayed. As we'll see in a moment the Custom view can be modified from the Diagram menu.

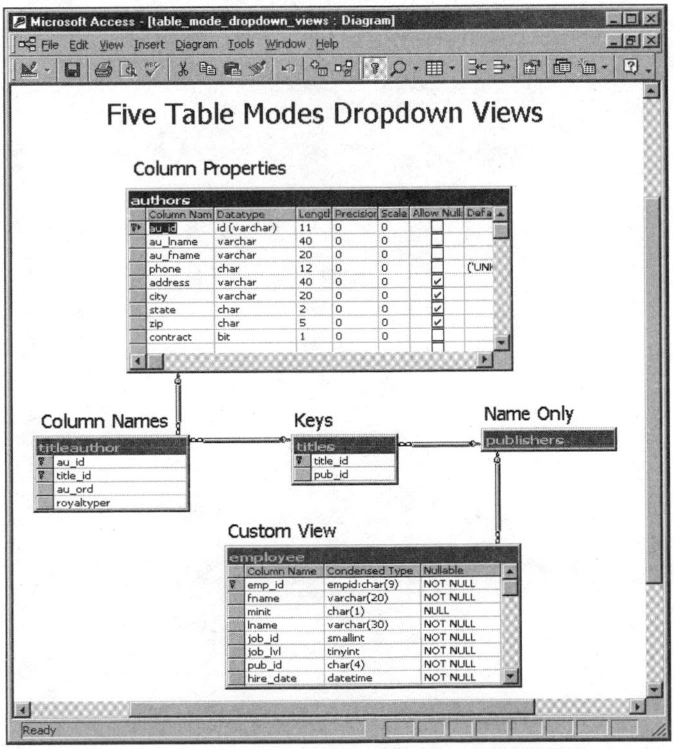

The Column Properties view reflects the current status of the table. In addition, we can edit the column properties directly from the view in the database diagram. For example, we can change identity seed and increment values.

The other views offer a reduced view of the table, showing only what their name would suggest. We can only edit what the views show us, so the less informative the view the less editing we will be able to do. Access does not commit our updates to the database until we save the database diagram.

Editing and Saving Diagrams

The Cut, Copy, and Paste controls allow objects in one database diagram to be moved or copied to another one. Save allows us to quickly save a database diagram with its current name or the default one that Access assigns it if we have not saved it previously. It is important to understand that saving a database diagram commits changes in the diagram to objects in our database. Be careful here. If structural changes do not fit together properly, then we won't be able to save any of the changes. Designing a database is like designing any complicated machine – you must think carefully about the impact even a small change can have.

In the following Database Designer window, we renamed the logo column in the pub_info table to logos, and clicked Save. The Save dialog indicates that the new table specification in the database diagram will replace the existing pub_info specification in the database. Clicking Yes performs the update to the column name in the database. Click No to decline updating the database and saving the database diagram. To leave the Database Diagram Designer without updating a database simply close the window and then decline the prompt to save changes. This leaves your database diagram unaltered as well.

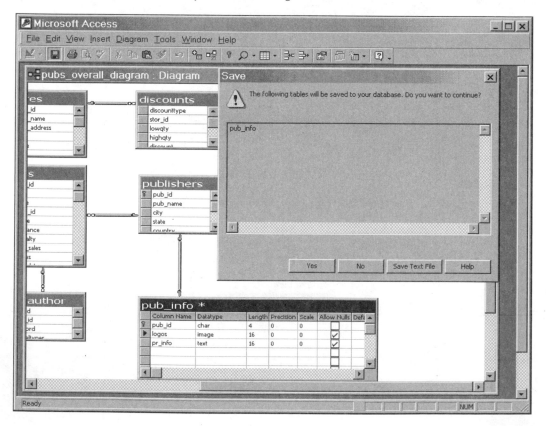

We can optionally click **Save Text File** on the **Save** dialog. This action creates a text file documenting when the file was created, our login ID as user, the SQL Server name, the database name, and a list of tables changed since the last time the database diagram was saved. The text file saves to the default folder for the Access project. Clicking **Save Text File** on the **Save** dialog does not actually save the changes to the database diagram. Access will tell us that it saved the text file to the same directory as your Access project. We must still click **Yes** on the **Save** dialog to commit our database diagram changes to database objects. The Notepad window below reveals the text file for the preceding change.

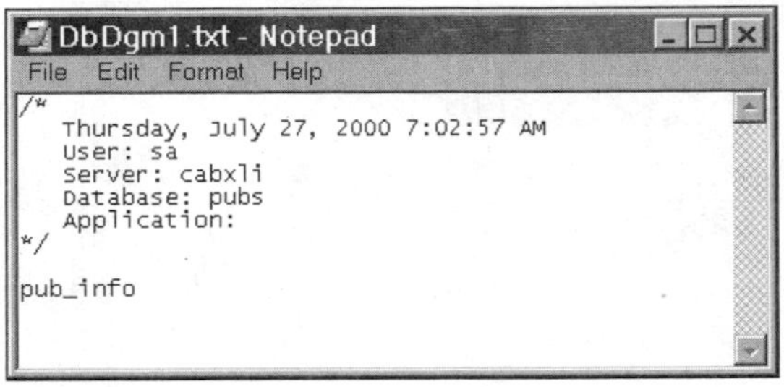

The Diagram Menu

When we open up a database diagram, be it new or existing, as well as the **Diagram Design** toolbar, Access adds a new menu. The options available through this new **Diagram** menu offer many of the commands on the toolbar plus some others that contribute to our ability to manage database diagrams and complement the available toolbar icons.

The **Diagram** menu has a rich selection of commands that enable us to populate database diagrams with database objects and format their appearance on the page. The commands are:

- ❏ New Table
- ❏ New Label
- ❏ Add Related Tables
- ❏ Show Relationship Labels
- ❏ Modify Custom View
- ❏ View Page Breaks
- ❏ Recalculate Page Breaks
- ❏ Autosize Selected Tables
- ❏ Layout Selection
- ❏ Layout Diagram

Let's illustrate the use of these commands to further highlight the usefulness and improved functionality that database diagrams offer in comparison to the **Relationship** windows previously available in Access.

Setting Up Diagrams

One quick way to populate a database diagram is by adding a table (via **View | Show Table**) that has relationships with several other tables. Then, we can choose the **Add Related Tables** command on the **Diagram** menu to populate the database diagram with these tables. So using the pubs database, and adding the stores and related tables yields:

159

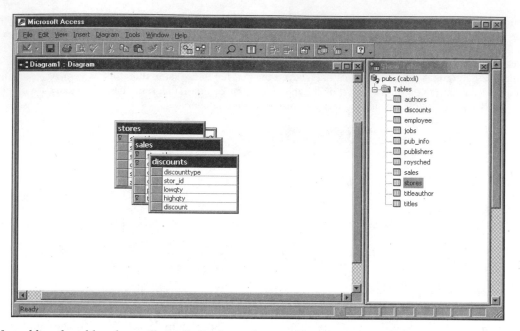

After adding the tables, they will usually not be easily viewable – we can use either the Layout Diagram or Layout Selection command to arrange the table icons for easy viewing:

To add clarity to a database diagram, we can added informative labels via the New Label command. Selecting this command creates an empty text box on our database diagram, into which we can type our label. Right-clicking within the text box opens the standard Font dialog, from where we can choose a custom font, style, and size for our text. Just like other text boxes, our new label can be resized by dragging handles on its border, and we can also position our label in much the same way. The following screen depicts the box for entering a new label in the preceding database diagram. The Font dialog is also shown, with an italic style selected for the label.

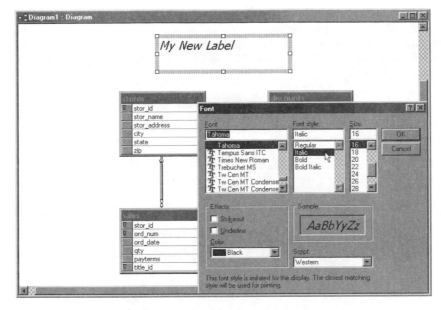

Adding New Tables

To add a new table to the database through the database diagram we use the Diagram | New Table menu. To illustrate this, the next screenshot shows the addition of a table named e-contacts. All the column properties are added manually, although stor_id may be added via copying and pasting from an existing table (specifications can be copied from within, but not between, databases). Note the contact_id column has been designated as the primary key.

To link the new table to the existing ones we'll establish a foreign key relationship with stores through the stor_id column. To do this, we select stor_id in stores and drag it to stor_id in e-contacts. This opens the Create Relationship dialog. If we want to specify declarative referential integrity, then we need to check the check box labeled Enable relationship for INSERT and UPDATE. We'll examine the options presented by these check boxes shortly.

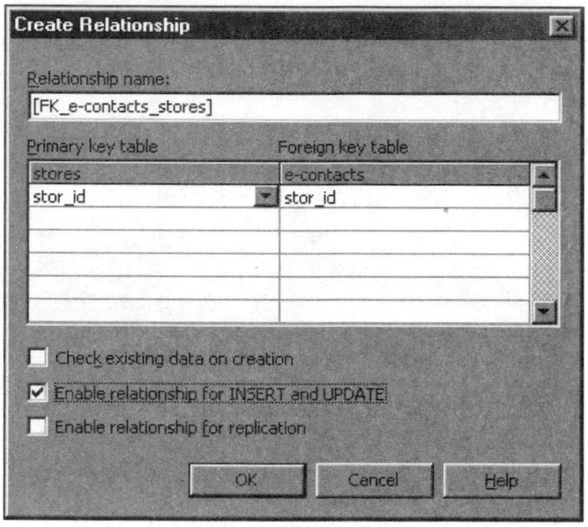

Clicking OK will give the following screenshot (after a few minor layout adjustments, including adding a new label). Incidentally, you'll probably notice the title bars for both the e-contacts and stores tables have asterisks following the table name. This indicates that they have changes that the Database Diagram Designer has not yet committed to the database design.

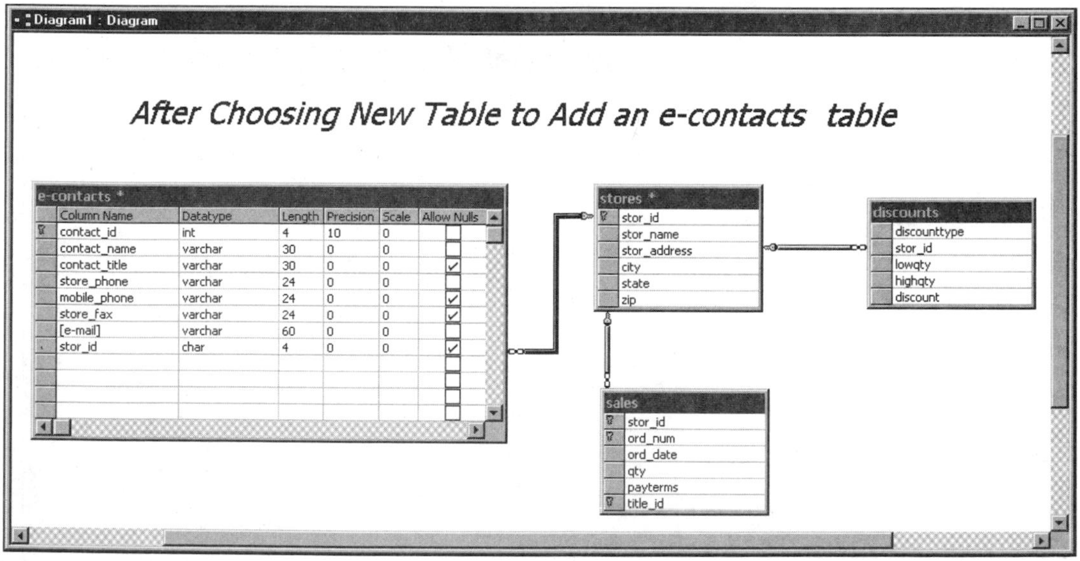

We're going to save the database diagram with the name add_e-contacts_table and click Yes on the Save dialog to commit the changes to e-contacts and stores. At the completion of the save command, the Tables collection in the Access project Database window includes a new member called e-contacts, indicating a new table in the database.

Modifying Appearances

The Modify Custom View command on the Diagram menu enables the Custom View formatting to be adapted. Invoking the Modify Custom View command opens the following Column Selection dialog. This dialog allows us to decide which columns to include in the custom view and the order in which they appear. We can select the columns to show using the arrows in between the two panes, and control their order with the Sort arrows.

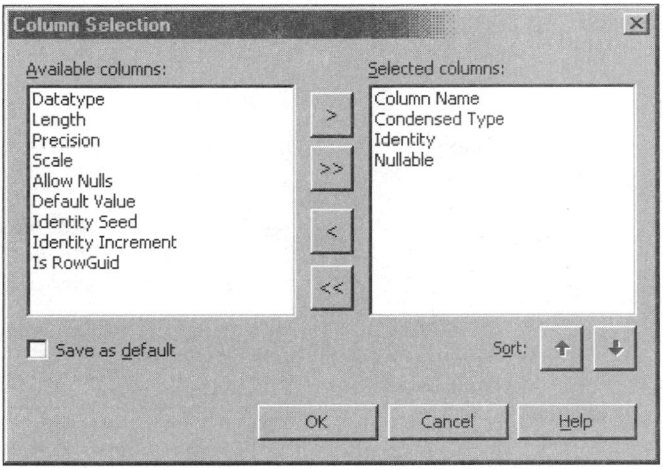

The settings in the Column Selection dialog apply to only one database diagram at a time. If we want settings to pertain to multiple database diagrams, then we have to repeat them in each diagram. On the other hand, settings do persist after we save a view. Therefore, if we add a new table in a Custom View, it continues to appear how it was last specified.

The Save as default check box might not perform as the online documentation suggests it should. The online help for the check box reads: "Replaces the current Custom View with the columns selected in this dialog box. If not selected, the column selection specified in the dialog box will be applied to the selected table in the Database Diagram." You might find that the Column Selection dialog settings apply to all tables in a database diagram whether or not you select the Save as default check box.

Printing Diagrams

The Database Diagram Designer does not have a Print Preview command, but does include the View Page Breaks and Recalculate Page Breaks commands. By using these commands in coordination with the File | Page Setup command, we can preview the appearance of a database diagram before printing.

To illustrate this the following screenshot shows the Database Diagram window for the pubs_overall_diagram database diagram immediately after invoking the View Page Breaks command. It displays the page breaks so that you can tell which parts of a database diagram will appear on each page.

We've switched back to the overall pubs database diagram so that you can see these commands for page layout work with a database diagram that has more tables than the Diagram1 we've just developed.

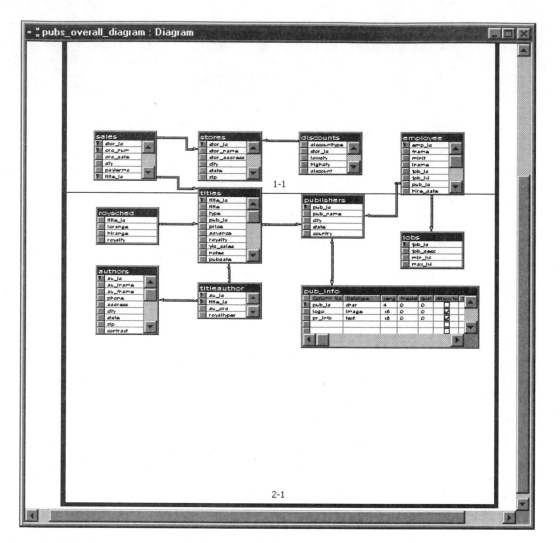

If we don't like the way our database diagram will print, we can either manually or automatically adjust the page layout. There are three things we can do to achieve this. We can change the orientation of the page in Page Setup, we can Recalculate Page Breaks, or we can move the tables around ourselves. In most cases, a mixture of these options produces the best results. The following screen reflects the outcome of altering the orientation of the page in Page Setup without moving any tables.

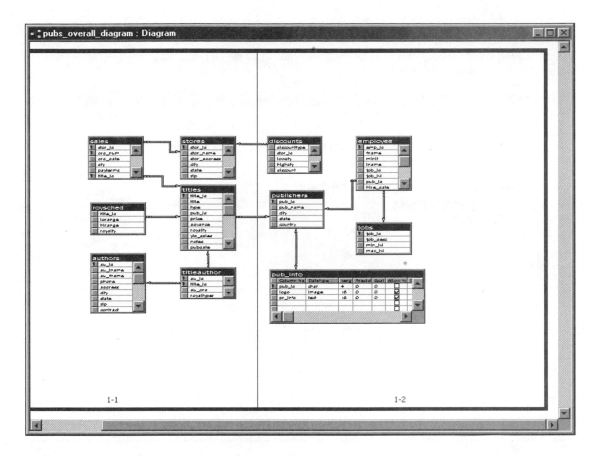

The Diagram Window and Menus

The Diagram window itself features three types of context-sensitive menu depending on whether a table, a relationship, or the window background itself is right-clicked upon.

Since most of the options are ones we've seen before (or are straightforward), the bulk of this section will be used to discuss the options available via the Properties dialog.

Diagram Window Context-Sensitive Menus

Let's move back to the smaller of the two diagrams we've been looking at, the add_e-contacts_table database diagram, and examine the context-sensitive menus the Database Diagram Designer provides. The next figure shows the context-sensitive menu for the e-contacts table in the add_e-contacts_table database diagram. The database diagram shows the row for the contact_id column highlighted. Right-clicking this table produces the menu in the database diagram. This menu shows the options available for that table with the contact_id column selected. Although we select a row in the table, the menu applies to the row and the table. For example, we can change the view from Column Properties to Column Names. This modification affects the table. You'll also notice that the menu shows the Primary Key command selected. We could clear that selection if we were going to use another column as the primary key for the table.

If you have a database diagram with a layout that is optimal for one task, consider saving it with a name that connotes its content and layout. Then, you can restore that format for the database diagram objects just by opening the saved version. This strategy can save time as you develop new database diagram layouts that build on previously created versions.

After Choosing New Table to Add an e-contacts table

If you do convert the **e-contacts** table format from Column Properties to Column Names, it will look a little peculiar. This is because the position of the top left corner of the table remains unchanged as the size of the **e-contacts** table changes. For at least this reason, a little manual editing is appropriate.

While we're manually editing the database diagram, it will be nice to have the relationship connectors point to the tables at the rows in the tables5 that designate the columns for a join. For instance, the connector between the **discounts** and **stores** tables points at the row for the **stor_address** column, but the **stor_id** column joins the two tables. Manually manipulating the table icons and connector lines can correct both problems. We can move tables by dragging their title bar, an action that can change the shape of connector lines. To get the more snake-like connectors without moving the table, drag one end of the connector to the corner of the table, and then around the edge.

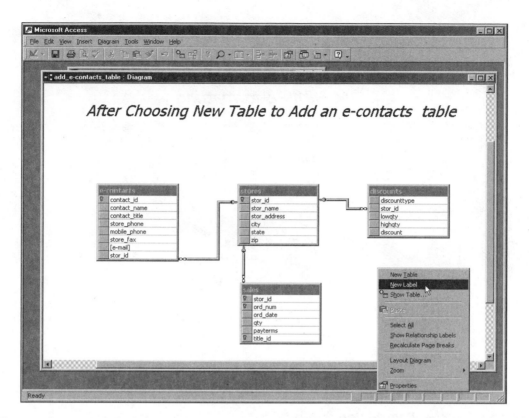

The next diagram, overleaf, depicts the re-formatted version of the add_e-contacts_table. The title bar indicates the name for the new diagram is add_e-contacts_table_with_re-format. Look for a moment at the new label; although it may look like one text box with centered text, it is in fact two that are aligned to give this impression. In addition, the screen portrays the context-sensitive menu for relationships. You can expose this menu by right-clicking the connector line between a pair of tables.

The relationships context-sensitive menu has two commands. First, we can delete the relationship from the database. Since we cannot undo this once we commit the action, Access prompts us to confirm our intention to do it before removing the relationship. This command does not just hide the relationship like the Hide Table command hides a table. Be certain before confirming your choice to delete a relationship. As with any change to a table, our user account must have the permission to perform the edit. See Appendix A for a discussion of security, including permissions.

Second, we can edit the relationship by choosing the Properties command. This opens the three-tabbed Properties dialog.

After Choosing New Table to Add an e-contacts table with Re-formatting

Working with the Properties Dialog

The tabs on the Properties dialog are, from left to right, Tables, Relationships, and Indexes/Keys. The dialog will generally open on the last tab selected. We'll go through these in the order of the tabs on the dialog. It is worth noting that the Properties dialog is not just for relationships, but can also be used to select any table in the database diagram.

To illustrate the use of the dialog we'll look at the database diagram containing the new e-contacts table. The Properties dialog allows you to specify constraints, deal with referential integrity, and specify indexes.

> **Remember to be careful when making changes to existing tables. Check to see if all records will comply with the new rules you're adding, or how many will be exceptions.**

Using the Tables tab to Specify Constraints

Using the Tables tab of the Properties dialog, we can designate either column or table check constraints.

A check constraint restricts the values in one or more columns by a Boolean expression. If the Boolean value is FALSE, then the check constraint blocks the entry of a new record or the updating of an existing record. Apart from the expression having to evaluate to TRUE or FALSE, check constraints can have the same form as the WHERE clause of a SELECT statement.

When a check constraint expression references a single column, it is a **column check constraint**. If the expression for a check constraint references two or more columns, then it is a **table check constraint**. We can optionally assign a check constraint to existing data in a table or to cases where we are replicating the data from one database server to another. The Tables tab enables us to temporarily turn off a check constraint so that we can enter critical data that fails to satisfy the constraint. This feature is convenient for working with existing data that may fail to meet a constraint. Users will not be able to update the old data because it does not comply with the constraint. However, the old data will be available for viewing.

Although opening the Properties dialog by right-clicking a table means the Selected Table control will automatically point to that table, any other table in the database diagram can be selected via this drop-down control. The Table name text box can be used to rename the table appearing in the Selected Table control. The Selected constraint drop-down control allows us to select any previously entered check constraint for editing. If we want to enter the name of a new constraint, we start by clicking New. Then, we type the expression representing our new constraint in the Constraint expression box. Finally, we type a new name in the Constraint name text box or we accept the default name that Access enters in the Selected constraint box.

Using the Tables tab to Specify Column Check Constraints

The following screen shotshows a column check constraint for the [e-mail] column. With this constraint, records entered or updated by users will not be accepted into the database unless their value for the [e-mail] column contains the @ character. Creating this constraint is as easy as clicking the New button, typing the constraint into the Constraint expression box, and maybe changing the name in the Constraint name box.

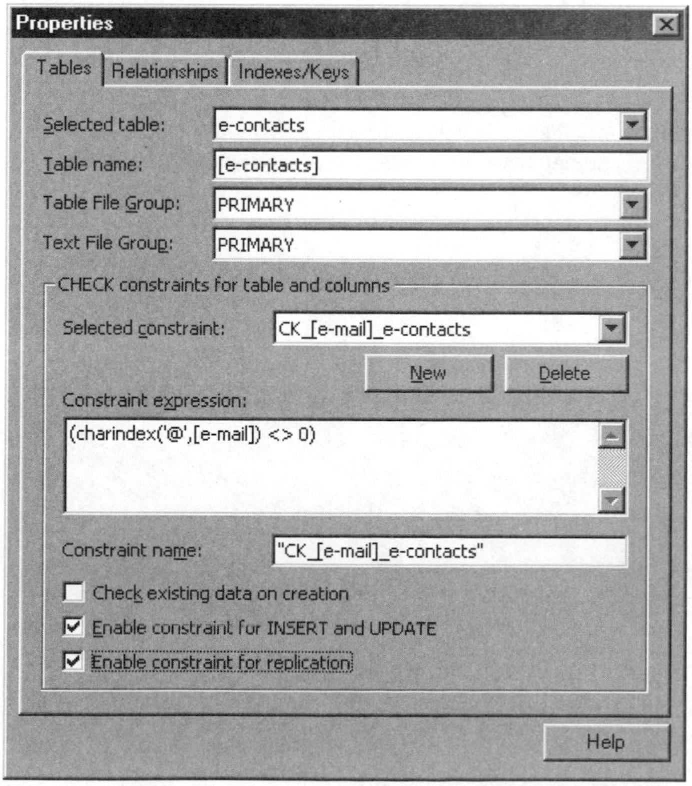

To create this constraint, we're using the CHARINDEX function. This returns the position of a string's initial character in another string expression. The syntax for this function is:

```
CHARINDEX('string_to_find',place_to_search , optional_start_location)
```

Since there is no way for us to know how many characters are in an e-mail address before the @, we haven't used an optional_start_location expression. The parameters as we've named them should be self-explanatory. The first tells the function what to look for, the second tells it where to look, and the optional last parameter tells it where in the second parameter to start looking.

If there is no match for the first string in the second string, the CHARINDEX function returns 0. This will happen only when a user enters an [e-mail] column value without an @. Therefore, the Boolean expression for the check constraint is TRUE only when @ is in the string containing the [e-mail] column value. The sample dialog selects both the **Enable constraint for INSERT and UPDATE** and the **Enable constraint for replication** check boxes.

> *There is a bug in the operation of the check boxes at the bottom of the **Properties** dialog **Tables** tab. In fact, the **Enable constraint for INSERT and UPDATE** only works reliably for INSERT. It fails to consistently detect updates that violate the constraint. The work-around is to check the **Enable constraint for replication** check box. This same bug and work-around works for MSDE and SQL Server 7.0 database diagrams opened from Access projects, and those opened from Enterprise Manager. This bug was also present in the beta versions of SQL Server 2000.*

> *While it would be nice to be able to tell you about every T-SQL function, such coverage is beyond the scope of this book. If you are interested in learning more about T-SQL, have a look at some of the resources in Chapter 2.*

Attempting to enter an [e-mail] column value without an @ (here a # was used instead) raises the following error message. The message pinpoints the source of the faulty data to the database, table, and even column. It further lists the name of the check constraint violated by the input. This makes resolving a data entry issue quick and easy.

Using the Tables tab to Specify Table Check Constraints

As we pointed out previously, a table constraint must reference two or more columns. The following screenshot presents a Properties dialog with a constraint expression that references both the [e-mail] and stor_id columns.

The constraint on the [e-mail] column is the same as in the preceding example. The new constraint specifies that the stor_id column cannot contain a NULL value. Recall that stor_id is a foreign key, and therefore NULL is normally a valid value for a foreign key. The new constraint therefore forces a user to enter a valid stor_id value from the stores table before it will let a new record into e-contacts. The Constraint Name text box assigns the name CK_[e-mail]_and_stor_id_e-contacts to the check constraint.

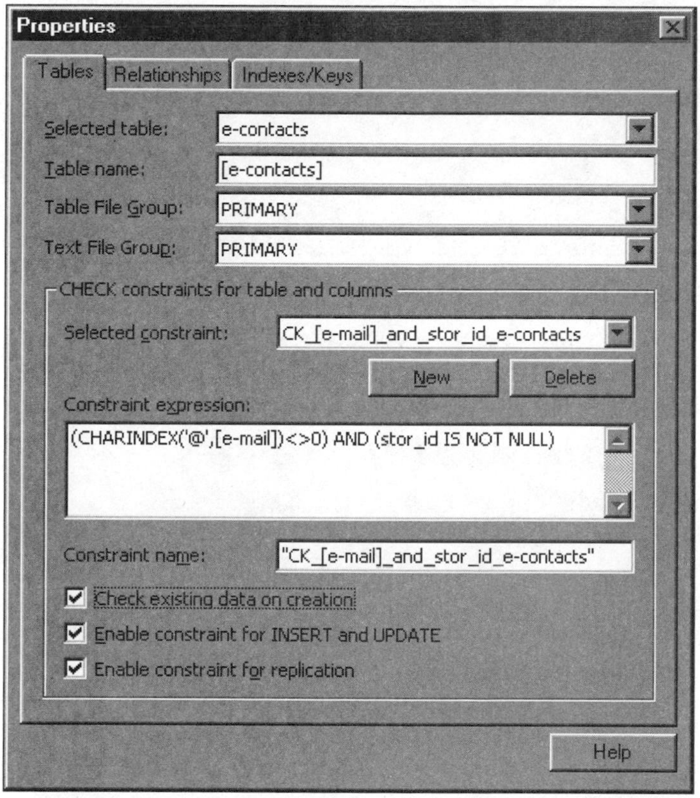

Normally, foreign keys can be left blank as data is entered into the table. This is a mixed blessing. On the one hand, we can enter a record even if we do not have a valid foreign key value, which is after all nothing but a lookup field. On the other hand, entering otherwise valid records with a NULL foreign key value can cause good data to get lost inside a database. Since we don't want to lose data, denying entry until a valid foreign key value is available allows the system to ensure that the record's parent will always be known.

The following screen depicts the error message that Access presents when a user attempts to input a new record with a missing stor_id value. Since the check constraint for missing stor_id values is part of a table check constraint, the message cannot tie the source of the error to a particular column. However, it does name the database, table, and table check constraint name that causes the error message to pop up. We can use this information to track down the source of the data entry rejection. To keep this job simple, we try to keep our table level check constraints simple.

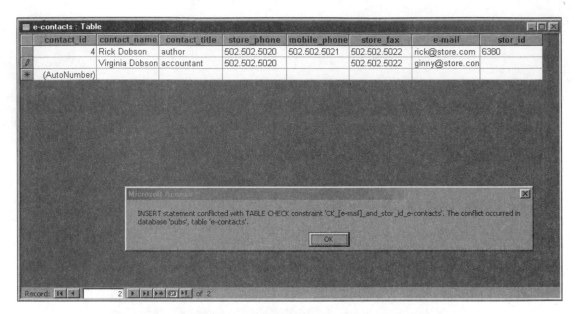

Using the Relationships tab to Specify Referential Integrity and Foreign Keys

By right-clicking the connector between the e-contacts and stores tables, we open the Properties dialog to reveal properties for the selected relationship. Clicking the Relationships tab identifies our options for managing relationships from the e-contacts table.

The tab confirms a relationship based on stor_id in both the e-contacts and stores tables. The selected Enable relationship for INSERT and UPDATE check box designates declarative referential integrity. You should remember that we said referential integrity ensures that keys are consistent between pairs of tables. The referential integrity is declarative because we specify it with a declaration – namely, by selecting the check box. If the e-contacts table had foreign keys pointing at more than one table, the Selected relationship: drop-down box would let us designate other relationships to display.

The two other check boxes help us manage the referential integrity between two tables in different contexts:

❑ The Check existing data on creation check box applies when we define referential integrity for tables that already have data. Leaving this check box blank allows our application to designate referential integrity for new records without requiring it for old records. This option is attractive when we want to apply referential integrity to a relationship and defer reconciling conflicts in historical data that violate referential integrity. Even with the Check existing data on creation check box clear, users cannot edit data that violates referential integrity. However, they can view it. The documentation for the database and the users needs to reflect the extent of referential integrity checking.

❑ The Enable relationship for replication check box applies to the operation of referential integrity when we are copying data between SQL Servers through their built-in replication functionality.

The following screen shows an attempt to enter a second record to the e-contacts table with a stor_id value that is not in the stores table. Notice that the error message explicitly references the foreign key named in the preceding screenshot. If we need to enter that record even though it violates referential integrity, we have to clear the Enable relationship for INSERT and UPDATE check box temporarily. If we take this action, then we must also leave the Check existing data on creation check box clear when we re-specify declarative referential integrity. This is because at least one existing record will violate referential integrity.

	contact_id	contact_name	contact_title	store_phone	mobile_phone	store_fax	e-mail	stor_id
	4	Rick Dobson	author	502.502.5020	502.502.5021	502.502.5022	rick@store.com	6380
		Virginia Dobson	accountant	502.502.5020		502.502.5022	ginny@store.co	5022
*	(AutoNumber)							

Microsoft Access: INSERT statement conflicted with COLUMN FOREIGN KEY constraint 'FK_e-contacts_stores'. The conflict occurred in database 'pubs', table 'stores', column 'stor_id'.

Using the Indexes/Keys tab to Specify Indexes and Keys

From the Column Properties and Column Names views, we can specify that one or more columns serve as the primary key for a table. However, those views in the Database Diagram window do not permit us to designate the primary key as a clustered index, neither do they allow us to create an index for the table. Chapter 3 looks at clustered primary keys. This capability is important because it can make retrieval on the primary key faster than it would be otherwise. The Properties dialog does permit us to specify a clustered index for a primary key. If we try to make a primary key have a clustered index after already designating another index for the table as clustered, the Properties dialog presents an error message. This reminds us to change the other index from a clustered index before designating the primary key as clustered.

To designate a primary key as clustered, we need to bring up the Properties dialog for the table with the key and select the Indexes/Keys tab. Then, we select the primary key from the Selected index: drop-down box. Finally, we click the Create as CLUSTERED check box towards the bottom of the dialog. The following screen shot depicts this dialog for the e-contacts table immediately after designating the index for contact_id as clustered:

If an application requires sorting or searching on a column or set of columns, we can often speed performance by creating an index for the column or set of columns. In the case of the e-contacts table, we might want an index for the contact_name. We can start the creation of the index by clicking New on the Indexes/Keys tab. Next, we select contact_name from the first line in the Column name list box. After specifying a column on which to build the index, we can optionally change the system default name for the index to something more meaningful.

If it is necessary to eliminate the possibility of duplicates in one column or a set of columns for which we are building the index, then choose the Create UNIQUE check box. In most Access applications, you should leave the Fill Factor and Pad index controls unspecified.

These controls relate to the structure of information in the index, and we'd recommend that, unless you have very good information about how a column will grow, you should probably leave these controls as they are. If you set the Fill Factor too high for a table which goes on to have large amounts of data added, the performance of the application will be degraded as SQL Server has to split existing data pages to make room for new index entries.

Microsoft recommends leaving the Don't automatically recompute statistics check box blank because it can degrade performance in many scenarios. This will be because the old statistics for the index may no longer be accurate. Old statistics could cause SQL Server to take longer searching the index.

The following screenshot illustrates the selections on the Indexes/Keys tab necessary to specify a new index on the contact_name column:

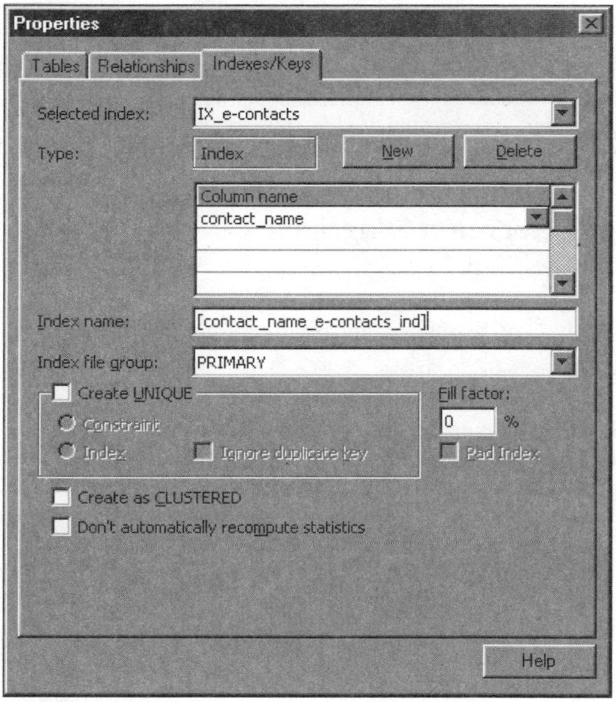

Advanced Topics

This section considers a couple of more specialized issues relating to database diagrams that are related to particular configurations, so not every section here will be applicable to everyone. More specifically we're going to look at:

- ❑ Subdividing and merging database diagrams
- ❑ Using database diagrams in Enterprise Manager
- ❑ SQL Server 2000 enhancements

Indeed, the latter two topics don't involve going through the Access project user interface at all, but they do provide useful related knowledge.

Subdividing and Merging Diagrams

There are lots of reasons for subdividing and merging database diagrams – especially when we're dealing with a database of more than ten or so tables. As a database application grows in complexity, it is likely to involve tables that represent entities related to the interests of multiple departments within an organization.

With Access 2000, we can readily subdivide our database diagrams into segments of the overall project according to the special interests of groups of users. It is quick and easy to consolidate the database diagrams for segments into an overall database diagram for full project reviews. This section shows how to perform these functions by creating two segments of database objects for the pubs database. Then, it rolls the database diagrams for those segments into a new master diagram that contains the objects from both segments.

> We examined the SQL-DMO object model for a Diagrams collection. However, there is no such collection in either the SQL Server 7.0 or SQL Server 2000 object models (at least for the 2000 beta version available as this chapter is being written). Therefore, you must perform these segmenting and consolidation tasks manually.

Creating and Merging Segment Diagrams

When creating a Segment Diagram, there are two options:

- ❑   Work from scratch – create a new database diagram and populate it as seen previously
- ❑   Segment an existing database diagram

To compose a Segment Diagram from an existing overall database design diagram, we'll need to start by opening two database diagram windows – a new one and one with the existing overall database design. Next, we select the tables from the current overall master database diagram that we want in our segment. Click the title bar of the first table to select it. Then, hold down the *Ctrl* key and click any additional tables for the new segment. After selecting the tables for our segment, we simply drag and drop them into the new blank database diagram. This action copies the table icons and their connectors into the new database diagram. This is our new Segment Diagram.

Consolidating the two Segment Diagrams follows the same process in reverse – open two segment diagrams and a blank diagram. Copying the appropriate tables from the two Segment Diagrams onto the new diagram will yield an appropriate merged database diagram.

Diagrams in Enterprise Manager

Database Diagrams work about the same in Access projects as they do in SQL Server's Enterprise Manager. However, there are at least two distinct advantages to working with database diagrams in Enterprise Manager:

- ❑   T-SQL scripts corresponding to the changes that are made in a database diagram can be created and saved
- ❑   Enterprise Manager has a wizard for building database diagrams

Creating Saved Scripts with Enterprise Manager

The Diagram Designer in Enterprise Manager includes a toolbar control for saving the T-SQL scripts associated with the changes to a database that we make in a database diagram. We do not have to save a change for the T-SQL recorder to save our actions. If we want to save a script, we have to do it before closing a database diagram. This is because the script only remains open within a Diagram Designer session or from the last script save, whichever is more recent. We can run these saved scripts in Query Analyzer or, with a little editing, in stored procedures from within Access projects.

There are three advantages to saving the changes in T-SQL scripts:

❑   Database changes do not have to be implemented immediately after making them in the Diagram Designer. This allows us to make the changes, save the scripts, and not save the updated database diagram. If we want to make the changes, we can always run the script later.

❑   The same database update can be easily performed on several different servers. Running saved scripts on different servers will save us the time of having to manually reproduce the editing changes on another server. Database architects can easily e-mail the scripts to an administrator or developer so they can apply the changes on another computer.

❑   Access developers migrating to SQL Server can readily learn T-SQL by making changes in a Diagram Designer and studying or editing the resulting code.

The following screenshot depicts Diagram Designer in Enterprise Manager after the creation of the new e-contacts table in the pubs database. This table has the same design as the one reviewed earlier in our Access project. Apart from having been created in Enterprise Manager, the sole distinction is that this example manually adds the e-contacts table to another server in Enterprise Manager. Being able to do this is critical for sites that have a production environment spread over various SQL Servers.

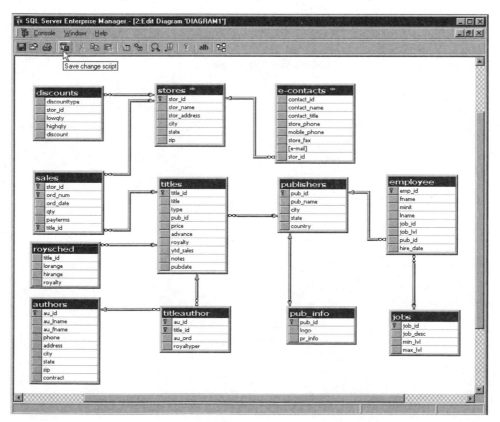

If you elect to update your database design using the saved scripts from Enterprise Manager, there is one disadvantage. The database diagram won't necessarily have been saved, and may not therefore reflect the script changes.

Adding a Table

Because this example creates the e-contacts table in Enterprise Manager, it is possible to save a T-SQL script that duplicates the effect of the manual design changes. Clicking the control highlighted in the previoius screen saves the script as DbDgm1.sql in the Binn folder of the SQL Server directory. Every time we save a new script, Enterprise Manager increments the number in the filename by one.

Before taking any other actions, we're going to save the database diagram after we've created the e-contacts table and saved the changes script for doing so. Saving the diagram resets the change log so we won't be able to save changes scripts until there are more changes made. Next, we'll drop the e-contacts table with the Delete Table from Database context-sensitive menu command and save the script for that action.

These actions create two scripts: one to add e-contacts to the database; and, a second to remove it from the database (DbDgm2.sql). However, the e-contacts table is still in the database until the changed database diagram is saved.

Since this example actually requires the e-contacts table in the database diagram, close the diagram without saving the changes.

The saved T-SQL script for adding the e-contacts table appears below. Notice that it is similar in appearance to the samples in Books Online in that it includes GO statements. Remember from Chapter 3 that Access stored procedure templates don't process GO statements, so you'll have to edit them out if you want to run these scripts from within an Access stored procedure template.

```
/*

  Monday, March 27, 2000 5:35:33 AM

  User:

  Server: CAB2200

  Database: pubs

  Application: SQL Server Enterprise Manager

*/



BEGIN TRANSACTION
SET QUOTED_IDENTIFIER ON
GO
SET TRANSACTION ISOLATION LEVEL SERIALIZABLE
GO
COMMIT
BEGIN TRANSACTION
CREATE TABLE dbo.[e-contacts]
```

```
    (
    contact_id int NOT NULL IDENTITY (1, 1),
    contact_name varchar(30) NOT NULL,
    contact_title varchar(30) NULL,
    store_phone varchar(24) NOT NULL,
    mobile_phone varchar(24) NULL,
    store_fax varchar(24) NULL,
    [e-mail] varchar(60) NOT NULL,
    stor_id char(4) NULL
    ) ON [PRIMARY]
GO
ALTER TABLE dbo.[e-contacts] WITH NOCHECK ADD CONSTRAINT
    [FK_e-contacts_stores] FOREIGN KEY
    (
    stor_id
    ) REFERENCES dbo.stores
    (
    stor_id
    )
GO
COMMIT
```

The code shown above contains an automatically generated comment section, and some information regarding transactions and SQL Server configuration options, in addition to the code defining the **e-contacts** table (which should be familiar from our discussion in the previous chapter). At this point, we only wish to highlight the fact that this feature enables us to quickly inspect the T-SQL for creating a table and, if you're unfamiliar with the language, could aid as a learning tool. We'll defer discussion of transactions until Chapter 6.

Dropping a Table

For completeness, the code for dropping the **e-contacts** table is shown below – again, at this point we're just interested in the DROP TABLE statement that appears in the midst of the transactional and configuration information.

```
/*

    Monday, March 27, 2000 5:45:28 AM

    User:

    Server: CAB2200

    Database: pubs

    Application: SQL Server Enterprise Manager

*/



BEGIN TRANSACTION
SET QUOTED_IDENTIFIER ON
GO
SET TRANSACTION ISOLATION LEVEL SERIALIZABLE
```

```
GO
COMMIT
BEGIN TRANSACTION
DROP TABLE dbo.[e-contacts]
GO
COMMIT
```

Using Saved Scripts

In order to access the new scripts we've just created, we need to use the File | Open command from within Query Analyzer. If we run the scripts from Query Analyzer, we must select pubs from the DB drop-down control. See the screenshot below for an illustration of how to select a database to use within Query Analyzer. You'll notice that this Query Analyzer window refers to a different SQL Server from the one in the code. This is to show you that you can transfer the script from one server to another, so you can recreate your table elsewhere.

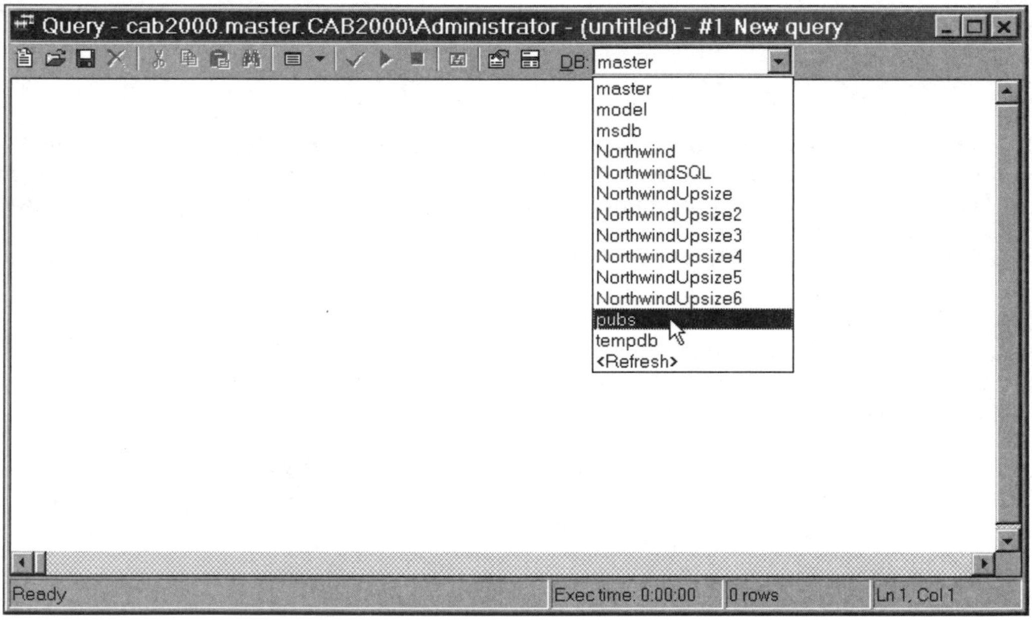

We'll start the example by running the script to delete the e-contacts table. We need to close any open version of the database diagram, and then open a new version of it. The e-contacts table should not show on the diagram (opposite). This is because the script removed the table from the database.

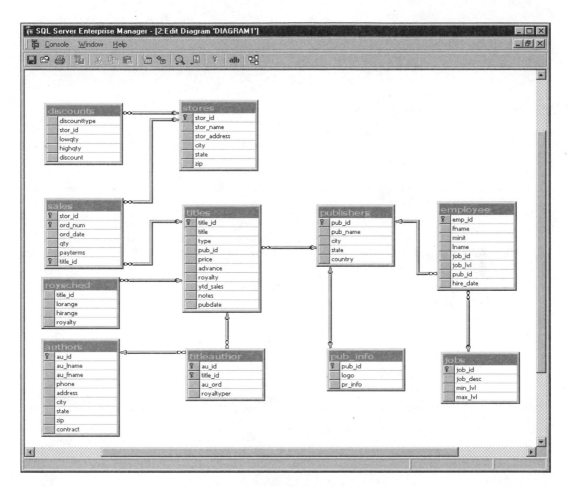

After confirming the unavailability of the e-contacts table, we'll close the database diagram. We're not going to accept the prompt to save any changes to the diagram. By not saving the changes, we leave the table's icon in the database diagram even though the table is missing from the database. From Query Analyzer, we run the script to add the e-contacts table back into the database. Then, when we open the database diagram again, the e-contacts table shows.

SQL Server 2000 Enhancements for Diagrams

SQL Server 2000 introduces enhancements for the management of database diagrams. There are three areas of improvement, and they all occur in the Enterprise Manager user interface. Therefore, Access developers will not be able to take advantage of the improvements from within Access 2000.

These enhancements are only available with Enterprise Manager for SQL Server 2000. Because of this, not all of the following enhancements can be used with the MSDE databases available at the time of writing.

Improvements appear in these areas:

❏   The new right-click menus offer more functionality than in earlier versions.

❑ The Relationships tab on the Properties dialog provides check boxes for specifying cascading updates and deletes.

❑ The Properties dialog offers two new tabs – Columns and Constraints, resulting from a change in the Tables tab.

Right-click Menu Enhancements

The right-click menu enhancements are most pronounced when we click on a table in a database diagram. The new menu lets us specify a selected tab when the Properties dialog opens and a new Task menu offers several interesting new commands:

❑ Manage Triggers enables a developer to examine the code in triggers or create new ones (we'll discuss triggers in Chapter 6).

❑ Manage Permissions allows database administrators to grant, revoke, or deny SELECT, INSERT, UPDATE, and DELETE permissions for users and roles. In addition, the command allows the granting, revoking, or denying of declarative referential integrity against an object. See Appendix A for a closer look at SQL Server security.

❑ Display Dependencies is intriguing since it shows objects that depend on a table as well as objects on which a table depends, such as user-defined data types. This function doesn't have as many options when applied to an MSDE database compared to an object in a SQL Server 2000 database.

❑ Generate SQL Scripts command lets us examine the T-SQL scripts for an object. This is not just a change script, but also a list of all the code behind an object.

❑ Open Table enables us to view the data in a table directly from the database diagram.

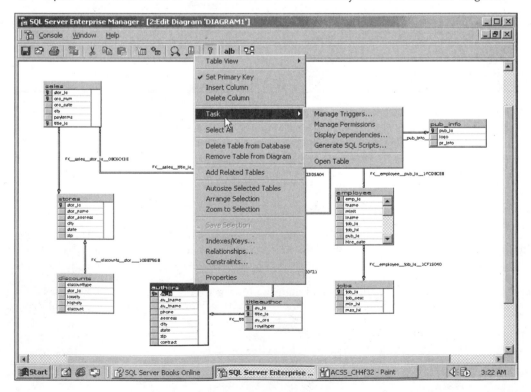

The right-click menu for the relationship connector between tables also picks up a new command named Show Relationship Labels. With this new menu, we can choose to label the connector lines in a database diagram with their relationship name, much as in the previous screenshot.

Cascading Updates and Deletes

Prior to SQL Server 2000, developers commonly wrote triggers for cascading updates and deletes associated with referential integrity. Starting with SQL Server 2000, we can use new T-SQL clauses to specify cascading updates or deletes without developing custom triggers. Chapter 3 demonstrates the syntax for using these new clauses. Access 2000 developers can take advantage of this inside of stored procedure templates. In addition, SQL Server offers two check boxes on the Relationships tab of the Properties dialog that allow us to specify cascading updates and deletes. These two new check boxes makes this task a lot easier because they no longer require us to write any code at all. They don't appear on the Properties dialog for an MSDE database diagram.

The Columns and Constraints Tabs on the Properties Dialog

The new Columns and Constraints tabs can work together. We can use the Tables tab to select a table from a drop-down list. We can view and set selected table properties from this dialog, including a description text string. We can also change the name of a table from this dialog. Information about check constraints that was formerly on the Tables tab is moved to a new Constraints tab. There is no new functionality on the Check

Constraints tab. It just holds items moved from the old version of the Tables tab. The Columns tab allows us to examine and set the properties of columns for the active table from a dialog. The Column Name box offers a drop-down list from which we can select any column in the currently selected table. This capability is roughly analogous to the Column Properties view, except that we see one column at time.

The following screenshot shows the titles table selected in a database diagram from the pubs database and the exposed properties for the title column:

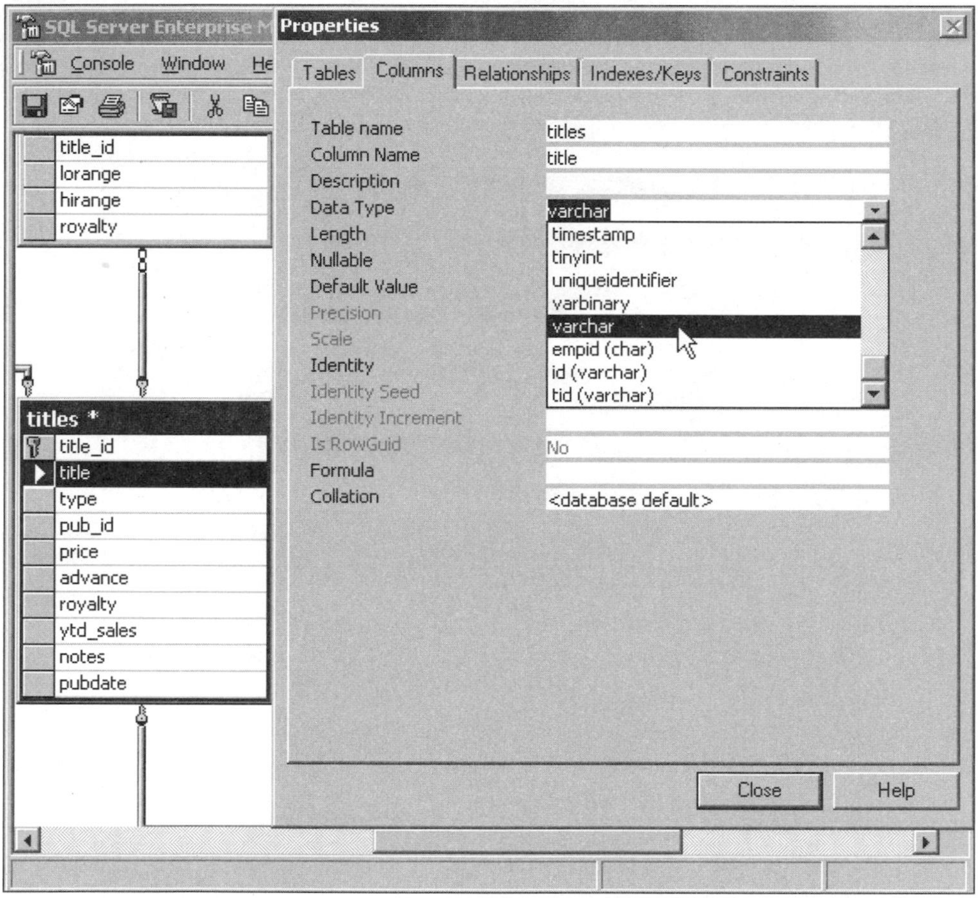

Summary

Database diagrams can simplify building and fine-tuning your database models, and represent a useful tool for examining the structure of your database. Because they are so easy to change and can dynamically update a database, they are especially valuable for interacting with clients who want to participate in the design of their database. You can also use database diagrams to document database design revisions that you make with them.

What have we learned in this chapter? We've thoroughly reviewed the Database Diagram Designer, and in doing so have seen how to create simple diagrams using existing tables. We have seen how simple it can be to create relationships and specify constraints on a table. We've also seen how to create new tables within our diagram, and that these new tables update the database. This has provided complementary information to that from Chapter 3. In addition, we've begun to pave the way for later chapters where we look in more depth at other ways of specifying indexes and triggers.

Because there is a new version of SQL Server released around the time this book is written, we've looked at the new functionality it provides.

Designing SQL Server Views with Access 2000

This chapter is all about **views**. It focuses on specifying, using, and examining SQL Server views. We'll learn how to create views with T-SQL, ADO, and SQL-DMO. There is also thorough coverage of how to build views graphically with the Query Designer.

The chapter systematically examines the different types of queries that can underlie views. Beyond that, we will discover techniques for processing the return set from a view. New view capabilities introduced with SQL Server 2000 are also considered. Subsequent chapters build on the knowledge we gain in this chapter by using views as data sources for forms, reports, and web pages. In order to master the techniques of those chapters we will need an intimate understanding of SQL Server views.

In its main sections, this chapter explores views from four distinct perspectives.

❑   In the first section, *What are SQL Server Views*, we describe the different types of views and the T-SQL statements for expressing them. This initial section also examines how to retrieve data from another database without importing the data. Access developers are likely to find this capability roughly equivalent to linking tables with Jet applications. The technology is different, but the result is similar.

❑   The second section, *Using the Views Collection,* drills down on the Views collection exposed by the **Database** window. The focus of this section is the graphical design of views with the Query Designer. Another major thrust of this section is exposing the T-SQL behind views. This section expands our grasp of T-SQL beyond the horizons of the first section. We also learn how to manipulate return sets from views in **Datasheet** view.

❑   In the third section, *Programmatically Manipulating Views with ADO*, the coverage shifts to working with views via ADO and T-SQL. We learn how to access the return sets from views. In addition, this section covers how to enumerate views and their T-SQL scripts. We also learn how to create views programmatically. One code sample in this section presents a type of view that Access only permits us to create programmatically.

❑   Finally, we describe how to process views with SQL-DMO in the section entitled *Programmatically Manipulating Views with SQL-DMO*. This section also contrasts ADO and SQL-DMO techniques for working with views. There are also performance comparisons on Windows 98, Windows NT, and Windows 2000 platforms.

The code samples for this chapter reside in the `Chapter5NorthwindCS.adp` file. For the sake of brevity, we'll refer to the `Chapter5NorthwindCSSQL` database as the **Northwind** database throughout the chapter. Please keep in mind, though, that the `Chapter5NorthwindCSSQL` database is slightly different from the default **Northwind** database, as it already contains all the views we will look at during the course of this chapter.

> *We can import tables into the SQL Server database to which an Access project connects through the File | Get External Data | Import command. Chapter 2 describes how to use this command to copy tables from the SQL Server database behind one project into the database behind a second project.*

What are SQL Server Views?

We can reasonably characterize views with several distinct kinds of comparison. It is common to describe SQL Server views as virtual tables, or sometimes as stored queries. A view can display data like a table, but it can be more flexible than a table. It permits filtering its underlying data sources by both columns and rows. We can also aggregate data within a view and group rows in different ways. The data source for SQL Server views, which can include more than one table in more than one database, other views, and multiple external data sources (Oracle, Access, Excel, etc.), is one of the main ways that a view differentiates itself from a table.

In a very broad sense, SQL Server views are like queries or querydefs in Access, in that they all represent stored query statements managed by a database engine. In addition, SQL Server views and Access queries and querydefs enable standard SELECT queries with joins and groupings. Despite striking similarities between SQL Server views and Access queries, there are some important differences as well:

❑   SQL Server provides richer joining options than Access

❑   Queries in Access support the ORDER BY clause, but SQL Server views do not

❑   Access queries directly support UPDATE, INSERT, and DELETE operations, but SQL Server views do not

❑   Access queries support parameter queries, but SQL Server views do not

SQL Server does, of course, offer these capabilities – just not with its views; instead we run a batch of T-SQL statements in Query Analyzer or run a stored procedure.

> *SQL Server views are virtual tables; they correspond to SELECT queries in Access. We can modify the table(s) behind a SQL Server view with INSERT, DELETE, and UPDATE T-SQL statements. Access action queries can actually contain INSERT, DELETE, and UPDATE Jet SQL statements. SQL Server stored procedures, rather than views, correspond to Access action queries.*

If we look carefully at the Access 2000 querying abilities with Jet, we will discover that Access 2000 supports a `Views` collection. While the `Views` collection for Jet is closer to SQL Server views than Access queries, there are some significant distinctions as well. Despite the similarity in their names, the Jet and SQL Server `Views` collections are not the same. For example, we can create and edit the properties of a Jet-based view with the ADOX library in a VBA project, but we must use the SQL-DMO library to perform comparable tasks with a SQL Server view. Another difference is that the `Append` method for the `Views` collection in the ADOX library does not work with SQL Server. The SQL-DMO library has a much richer (and different) set of properties and methods than the ADOX library. In SQL-DMO, we invoke the `Add` method for the `Views` collection to create a new view in a SQL Server database. All of these approaches are covered in the appropriate sections of this chapter.

These commands are unavailable for a Jet-based view. Jet SQL's own `CREATE VIEW` statement naturally enough creates a Jet view, but there is no `ALTER VIEW` statement in Jet SQL. On the other hand, Jet-based views support the `ORDER BY` clause, but recall that this clause is not available for SQL Server views.

> While SQL Server views do not support the `ORDER BY` clause, developers and end users can sort view return sets in a variety of ways. The Access project Datasheet view toolbar includes two buttons for sorting a return set: one in ascending, and the other in descending order. Additionally, we can readily sort an Access report based on a view's return set. Finally, we can embed the T-SQL for a view in a stored procedure where we can use the `ORDER BY` clause.

This section looks at the following areas:

❑   What Views Do

❑   Types of Views

What Views Do

Views can serve many purposes in an application. They are able to filter data – by columns and by rows. This makes it possible to expose a subset of a database that targets the needs of a particular application. For example, if clerks must enter hours billed by employees, a view can help by presenting just employeeid, date, clientid, and [billable hour] columns. It is common in SQL Server databases to denote object names with embedded spaces within brackets, for example [billable hours], although generally speaking we should avoid embedded spaces. Other confidential information such as employee salary, which may be in the employees table, can be missing from the view. We use the list in a `SELECT` statement to determine which columns a view shows.

Similarly, a view can filter by row. Include a `WHERE` clause in a `SELECT` statement to designate a criterion specifying which rows to include in a view. We can refine the previous example about billable hours. Let's consider an organization with multiple groups organized by major account(s). In this scenario, assistants only need to see the list of billing employees for their department – not all the rows in the employees table. By matching the [major accountid] of the entry clerk with the client's [major accountid] in a `WHERE` or `JOIN` clause, a `SELECT` statement can restrict the list of clients showing in a view to those appropriate to a specific clerk. SQL Server offers a graphical designer for views that can help us get started designing SQL Server views without immediately becoming familiar with all the nuances of T-SQL view statements.

By not granting permissions to select against base tables, but instead assigning select, update, insert, and delete permissions for views, an application can secure a database. With a carefully designed security model based on multiple views, employees can gain access to just the subset of a database that pertains to their responsibilities – without gaining permissions for other parts of a database. This chapter illustrates how to create restrictive views. Appendix A describes how to work with SQL Server security.

In a decision support environment, flexible and easy data access is a critical issue. By creating views that are reasonably complex but commonly needed, an IT professional or a power user can aid a group of decision support specialists. This application for views provides similar benefits to reusable software components. It ensures that critical business analyses always use the same set of rules for filtering data. It also helps to reduce the complexity of the database structure, as well as hiding the original data

Another critical role for views is the computation of results. Views are useful for computing values within a row as well as across row sets. Representative examples of computing within a row include:

- ❑ calculating extended price for an order line item based on quantity, unit price, and discount.
- ❑ developing new product prices based on old prices and a standard margin for increases
- ❑ computing net salary as gross salary less withholdings

Views can consolidate and group data across rows. For example, a view can summarize sales by employee, region, customer, product, and more. Similarly, applications can invoke views to aggregate costs by manufacturing line, shift, plant, and product.

What Views Use

Views are powerful tools for re-arranging the data from one, two, or more tables (or views). Two main tools for re-arranging rows are **joins** and **unions**. Joins can merge pairs of data sources, but we can join multiple data sources within a single SELECT statement. UNION statements append one data source to another to form a new one. We can stack more than two data sources together at one time with multiple UNION statements, although, as with all things connected to the database, care must be taken in the design and implementation. A poorly designed view can end up not performing its task efficiently, particularly if more than one data source is used.

With a join, a view typically merges the rows of two tables on a column that is common to each table. For example, the Orders and [Order Details] tables both have an OrderID column. We can merge these two tables with a join so that Orders appear with their matching [Order Details] rows in a view. We'll have a closer look at this potentially complicated tool in the section *Joins*.

Union statements append the results of one data source to another. The columns in the input data sources should have the same data types or convert (implicitly or explicitly) to the same data type. SQL Server's Books Online describes the rules governing implicit conversion between data types, and we can apply the CAST and CONVERT functions to explicitly convert data types. We will see both of these later. In addition to consistent column data types, the input data sources should have the same number of columns in the same order. A union query in a view is useful for collecting the contact information from customers, suppliers, and employees in one virtual table. This topic will be covered in more depth in its own section, *Unions*.

Types of Views

As we apply SQL Server views to perform the above and other kinds of tasks, we will benefit from a working knowledge of how to construct different kinds of views. In many, but not all cases, we can create views with a built-in Query Designer, but a good knowledge of T-SQL data access syntax will allow us to formulate some views more quickly. Furthermore, even with the graphical Query Designer, we will still sometimes need to write T-SQL statements. Some views, such as views that form a union query between two data sources, cannot be created with Query Designer. Beyond that, we will often find uses for T-SQL data access syntax in stored procedures for which there are no graphical development tools. In light of these issues, this section exposes us to the syntax for several major types of SQL Server views.

The things we'll be looking at in this section are as follows:

- ❑ SELECT
- ❑ Joins
- ❑ Unions
- ❑ Subqueries

In the following subsections, there are a lot of examples of how to specify the underlying parts of a view. We can run these examples in Query Analyzer in SQL Server, or by using Query Designer in Access, which we will see more of later. The next section is where we find out how to choose what the view shows.

Basic SELECT Statements

Most Access, and other, developers will be familiar with the syntax for a T-SQL statement that lists all the rows from a table. We include a sample illustrating this approach to confirm its availability and to establish a frame of reference for more advanced T-SQL statements. The following sample extracts all the columns from all the rows of the `Categories` table of the Northwind database:

```
SELECT *
FROM Categories
```

This T-SQL statement is easy to write, but it returns all the rows and columns in the table specified in the `FROM` clause; this can prove expensive to execute in terms of time when our application actually requires only a subset of the rows or columns in a table. In fact, it's never really a good idea to use `SELECT *` when we know exactly which columns we want. We can restrict the row(s) returned by a `SELECT` statement with a `WHERE` clause. A subsequent sample reveals how to apply this clause.

When it is the case that we don't need all the columns from a table, we can restrict the list of columns returned by a `SELECT` statement by simply naming the specific columns our application requires, instead of using the * operator. The following sample extracts just a pair of columns, and all the rows in them, from the Northwind `Categories` table:

```
SELECT CategoryName, Description
FROM Categories
```

Joins

The join is a very flexible tool with T-SQL. It permits us to specify **inner joins**, **left**, **right**, and **full outer joins**, as well as **cross joins** for merging the records from two or more tables. In addition, we can join the records of a table with themselves in a **self join**. When specifying joins, the normal relationship between the common columns in two tables is equality. We can think of this as a criterion for merging the rows from the two sources. That is, rows from the two tables join to form one row in the view when their common column values are equal.

When a view specifies an inner join, only rows satisfying the join criterion merge to form rows in the resulting view. Left, right, or full outer joins will bring a row from the left, right, or both data sources into a view's return set even when there is no match against a criterion. A cross join forms a Cartesian product return set so that every row in one data source merges with each row in the other. This can often generate very large return sets so we should reserve its use to situations that demand it. In a self join, we can merge the rows from one table with itself. This tool enables a view to report which rows match other rows in the same table.

> *When a cross join returns a Cartesian product return set, it merges each record on the left side of the join with every record on the right side of the join. Therefore, if the left side contains 1,000 records, and the right side has 5000 records, the resulting view returns 5,000,000 records! There may be times when we want this type of result, but they are usually cases where there are only a few rows on the left, right, or both sides of a join.*

SQL Server joins do not require an equality operator for matching records. We also can designate that rows join according to any comparison operator, such as $<$, $<=$, $>$, $>=$, or $<>$. Access developers moving to SQL Server will discover that using operators other than equals adds a new dimension of flexibility to how they can designate the merging of two tables. One common type of join statement is to return all records where one column value is greater than another; for example, a view can display all orders shipped late with a self join of records in the `Orders` table where the ship date is greater than the required date (assuming all orders can have same-day delivery).

The following table briefly summarizes the types of joins mentioned in this section.

Type of Join	Summary
Inner	Combine rows from two tables when rows from each table satisfy a join expression.
Left Outer Join	Include all rows from the left table, and rows from the right that satisfy a join expression.
Right Outer Join	Include all rows from the right table, and rows from the left table that satisfy a join expression.
Full Outer Join	Include all rows from the left and right tables whether or not they satisfy a join expression.
Self Join	A join in which the left and right tables are the same.
Cross Join	Unconditionally match each row in the left table with every row in the right table.

Inner Joins

One of the more common uses for a `SELECT` statement is to join two or more tables. In the most basic representation of this kind of view, we can add `INNER JOIN` and `ON` keywords to the `FROM` clause of a `SELECT` statement when we form a joined view. Recall that this type of view can merge records from two data sources, such as the `Categories` and `Products` tables in the **Northwind** database. The list in our `SELECT` statement should reference columns from both data sources. As the column names in two data sources can be the same, we need to add a prefix that denotes which data source we target with a column name. If we don't, we will generate an **Ambiguous column name** error. One commonly used prefix is the table or view name, or its alias, meaning that the names given in the example are **fully qualified**. The following sample merges the `CategoryName` and `Description` columns from the `Categories` table with the `ProductName` and `Discontinued` columns from the `Products` table:

```
SELECT Categories.CategoryName, Categories.Description,
    Products.ProductName, Products.Discontinued
FROM Categories INNER JOIN Products
    ON Categories.CategoryID = Products.CategoryID
```

In order for SQL Server to perform the join, the two data sources must share at least one column in common. The column in each data source does not have to have the same name, but the data type must be the same in each data source. If it isn't, and we still need to join the tables, then we could use the CAST or CONVERT functions, which, as we saw in a previous chapter, are used to change the data type of a column.

The following screen shows an excerpt from the return set for the preceding sample. From the window's title, we can tell that the view has the name **categories_inner_join_products**. Of course, it is wise to use a consistent naming convention for our objects in an Access project and its linked SQL Server database. SQL Server helps in this regard by not permitting us to assign the same name to two database objects. Notice that the Access project view automatically deciphers the 0 and 1 values in the **Discontinued** column as **False** and **True**. SQL Server performs the translation because of the bit data type specification for the **Discontinued** column. Change the data type with a Convert function in the **Select** column list to **tinyint** to report the numerical value without any translation.

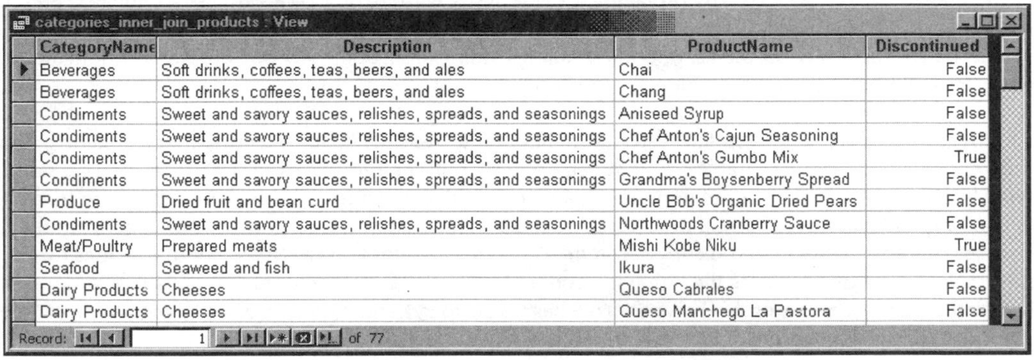

CategoryName	Description	ProductName	Discontinued
Beverages	Soft drinks, coffees, teas, beers, and ales	Chai	False
Beverages	Soft drinks, coffees, teas, beers, and ales	Chang	False
Condiments	Sweet and savory sauces, relishes, spreads, and seasonings	Aniseed Syrup	False
Condiments	Sweet and savory sauces, relishes, spreads, and seasonings	Chef Anton's Cajun Seasoning	False
Condiments	Sweet and savory sauces, relishes, spreads, and seasonings	Chef Anton's Gumbo Mix	True
Condiments	Sweet and savory sauces, relishes, spreads, and seasonings	Grandma's Boysenberry Spread	False
Produce	Dried fruit and bean curd	Uncle Bob's Organic Dried Pears	False
Condiments	Sweet and savory sauces, relishes, spreads, and seasonings	Northwoods Cranberry Sauce	False
Meat/Poultry	Prepared meats	Mishi Kobe Niku	True
Seafood	Seaweed and fish	Ikura	False
Dairy Products	Cheeses	Queso Cabrales	False
Dairy Products	Cheeses	Queso Manchego La Pastora	False

Record: 1 of 77

Counting both current and discontinued products, the data source includes 77 items. This count appears in the status bar for the preceding view.

This view would be more useful to the company if it excluded the discontinued products. We can create this view by appending a WHERE clause to the SELECT statement. The following sample demonstrates the exact phrasing to achieve the objective. The Access project represents the Discontinued column values as True or False, but we must use 0 to select the records that are not discontinued. This is because the data is in a SQL Server database, and the Discontinued column has a bit data type.

```
SELECT Categories.CategoryName, Categories.Description,
    Products.ProductName, Products.Discontinued
FROM Categories INNER JOIN Products
    ON Categories.CategoryID = Products.CategoryID
WHERE (Products.Discontinued = 0)
```

A view based on the preceding T-SQL statement yields a return set that is qualitatively and quantitatively different from the one that includes all products. See an excerpt from the return set for the new view above opposite. Notice that this return set contains just 69 records. The reason that there are fewer records is that this view excludes all the products with a **Discontinued** value of 1. Remember that SQL Server represents True as 1, unlike Access that uses -1. Notice that all the rows in the following screenshot have a **Discontinued** value of **False**.

193

Outer Joins

The OUTER JOIN type of view forces into a view's return set all the records from the data source on the left or right side of the JOIN in the SELECT statement, whether their names or data types match or not. If we need all the records on the left side to be in the return set, then we replace INNER JOIN with LEFT OUTER JOIN. If we need all the records from the right data source to be in the return set, then we replace INNER JOIN with RIGHT OUTER JOIN. By replacing INNER JOIN with FULL OUTER JOIN, we include all records from the data sources on both sides of the JOIN in a SELECT statement. As with the INNER JOIN, any of these alternative joins rely on the list of column names after the SELECT keyword to determine which columns to include from each data source.

The following SELECT statement illustrates the syntax for a LEFT OUTER JOIN that merges records from the Categories and Products tables. This statement forces all the records from the Categories table into the view's return set whether or not they match a record in the Products table. Rows from the Products table can only enter the return set if their CategoryID value matches a CategoryID value from the Categories table. Unmatched records from the Categories table have NULL column values for ProductName. To demonstrate the behavior of the LEFT OUTER JOIN merge, we must first add a new record to the Categories table. This new row has CategoryName and Description values of "New category" and "New product", respectively.

```
SELECT Categories.CategoryName, Categories.Description,
    Products.ProductName
FROM Categories LEFT OUTER JOIN
    Products ON Categories.CategoryID = Products.CategoryID
```

The following excerpt from the return set for the preceding LEFT OUTER JOIN view shows the new record in its final row. Notice two points:

First, there are 78 rows. This is in spite of the fact that there are only 77 products, including the discontinued ones. The forced entry of the new Categories table row creates an extra row in the return set.

Second, the final row has no value for ProductName. This is because the Categories table row with a value of "New category" for CategoryName has no match in the Products table.

Using VBA to Create Extra Columns

The final join sample in this section illustrates the syntax for merging rows from two data sources when the matching values in one column are greater than those in the other. This sample relies on two extra columns in the Orders table. These two new computed columns reveal the days to shipping from the placement of the order and the days between the required date and the shipping of the order.

For your convenience, the following two VBA procedures show how to add these two extra columns to the Orders table and how to remove them. The procedures should reside in the VBA project associated with the Chapter5NorthwindCS Access project.

> *This VBA project has a reference to the Microsoft SQL-DMO Object Library. If you elect to run the procedures from another project, make sure you set a reference to the SQL-DMO library, and don't forget to change the server name. To run these procedures, you'll need to put them in a module attached to the Access project you're working with.*

```
Sub add_2_computed_fields_to_orders()
Dim srv1 As SQLDMO.SQLServer
Dim col1 As SQLDMO.Column

'Connect to server
Set srv1 = New SQLDMO.SQLServer
srv1.Connect "cabxli", "sa", ""

'Add DaysToShip column to Orders
Set col1 = New SQLDMO.Column
col1.Name = "DaysToShip"
col1.DataType = "int"
col1.ComputedText = "DATEDIFF(day, OrderDate, ShippedDate)"
col1.IsComputed = True
srv1.Databases("Chapter5NorthwindCSSQL").Tables("Orders").Columns.Add col1

'Add DaysTilRequired column to Orders
Set col1 = New SQLDMO.Column
col1.Name = "DaysTilRequired"
col1.ComputedText = "DATEDIFF(day, OrderDate, RequiredDate)"
col1.IsComputed = True
```

```
    srv1.Databases("Chapter5NorthwindCSSQL").Tables("Orders").Columns.Add col1

End Sub


Sub drop_computed_fields_from_orders()
Dim srv1 As SQLDMO.SQLServer
Dim col1 As SQLDMO.Column

'Connect to server
Set srv1 = New SQLDMO.SQLServer
srv1.Connect "cabxli", "sa", ""

srv1.Databases("Chapter5NorthwindCSSQL").Tables("Orders"). _
    Columns("DaysToShip").Remove
srv1.Databases("Chapter5NorthwindCSSQL").Tables("Orders"). _
    Columns("DaysTilRequired").Remove

End Sub
```

Using SELECT to get the Records we want

The goal of most businesses will be to make the days to ship less than the days until a customer requires an order. However, things can happen that defeat the achievement of this goal. A continuing audit of operations can select those orders where the days to ship is greater than the days until a customer needs the order. The following T-SQL illustrates how to create a return set with just the desired records.

```
SELECT Orders.OrderID, Orders.OrderDate, Orders.RequiredDate,
    Orders.ShippedDate, Orders.DaysToShip,
    Orders1.DaysTilRequired,
    Orders.DaysToShip - Orders.DaysTilRequired AS DaysPastDue
FROM Orders INNER JOIN Orders Orders1
    ON Orders.OrderID = Orders1.OrderID AND
    Orders.DaysToShip > Orders1.DaysTilRequired
```

This SELECT statement performs a **self join** of the Orders table. The view requires two editions of the table that it calls Orders and Orders1. It is easy to create a second edition of the Orders table by using a synonym. We can create a synonym by placing the synonym's name immediately after the standard name for the data source in the FROM clause of a SELECT statement. Orders1 is a synonym for Orders in the preceding sample. In this case, the INNER JOIN clause nests within the FROM clause, and the synonym appears on the right side of the INNER JOIN clause. The list for the SELECT statement closes with a computed result that shows the difference between days to ship and days until required. The more positive this difference, the more the circumstances surrounding the order's shipment merit investigation.

The INNER JOIN merges rows from the Orders and Orders1 editions of the Orders table when they meet a pair of criteria.

❑ First, the OrderID row values in both editions must be equal. Without this requirement, our view would return a cross join return set.

❑ Second, the DaysToShip column value must be greater than the DaysTilRequired column values. This restricts the return set to those that we want to audit.

The following screenshot shows an excerpt from the preceding SELECT statement that is sorted in descending order by the difference between the DaysToShip and DaysTilRequired columns. Recall that we can sort a view's return set in ascending or descending order with the toolbar buttons in its Datasheet view. This is one way to compensate for the inability to include an ORDER BY clause in the view's T-SQL statement.

OrderID	OrderDate	RequiredDate	ShippedDate	DaysToShip	DaysTilRequir	DaysPastDue
10777	12/15/97	12/29/97	1/21/98	37	14	23
10726	11/3/97	11/17/97	12/5/97	32	14	18
10423	1/23/97	2/6/97	2/24/97	32	14	18
10970	3/24/98	4/7/98	4/24/98	31	14	17
10515	4/23/97	5/7/97	5/23/97	30	14	16
10827	1/12/98	1/26/98	2/6/98	25	14	11
10663	9/10/97	9/24/97	10/3/97	23	14	9
10660	9/8/97	10/6/97	10/15/97	37	28	9
10828	1/13/98	1/27/98	2/4/98	22	14	8
10593	7/9/97	8/6/97	8/13/97	35	28	7
10924	3/4/98	4/1/98	4/8/98	35	28	7

Record: 1 of 37

Unions

A UNION statement is useful for combining identical types of data from two or more sources. For example, we can combine the contact information columns from the Customers and the Suppliers tables. This type of view gives a firm one source to search for either customer or supplier contact data. By default, the UNION statement excludes any duplicate records in its return set. If we wish to retain duplicate rows, we follow the UNION with the ALL keyword.

While a join can merge two data sources, a union can append one set of results to the end of another. Both joins and unions can combine more than two data sources in a single T-SQL statement. Views based on a join can draw different fields from each data source. Views that draw their return set from a UNION statement require that all matching columns from each data source in the combined set be of the same data type. The union of the two data sources is unconditional for all rows in the data source with one exception: by using a WHERE clause for any contributing data source, we can selectively designate rows for inclusion in the union's return set. A join will incorporate rows in a view's return set only if they satisfy any expressions in the JOIN clause.

Views based on joins can be updateable, but views based on unions are not updateable in SQL Server 7.0 or MSDE. SQL Server 2000 enables direct updates as well as updates based on the INSTEAD OF triggers for views based on UNION statements. For views based on other query statements, our applications can perform insert, update, and delete operations in any version so long as SQL Server can unambiguously perform the operation.

Chapter 6 drills down on triggers and you will find a definition for INSTEAD OF triggers there.

The following shows the syntax for merging the Employees table with itself. As the UNION keyword excludes duplicates by default, the view's return set shows each employee just once. If we follow UNION by ALL, the view's return set displays each employee's name twice. Furthermore, it concatenates the second list of employee names to the end of the first list.

```
SELECT FirstName, LastName
FROM Employees e1
UNION
SELECT FirstName, LastName
FROM Employees e2
```

197

The following screenshots show the difference made by using the `ALL` keyword. The one on the left was generated without the `ALL` keyword, so any duplicated fields are missing. The one on the right, however, was generated using the `ALL` keyword, so each name appears twice. You may notice that there is no blank row to add new records in either return set; this is because a `UNION` query's return set is not updateable when the query runs against a SQL Server 7.0 database server (it is updateable when run against SQL Server 2000).

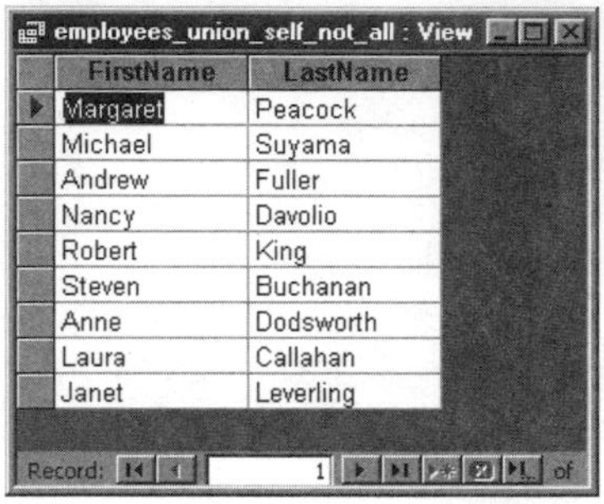

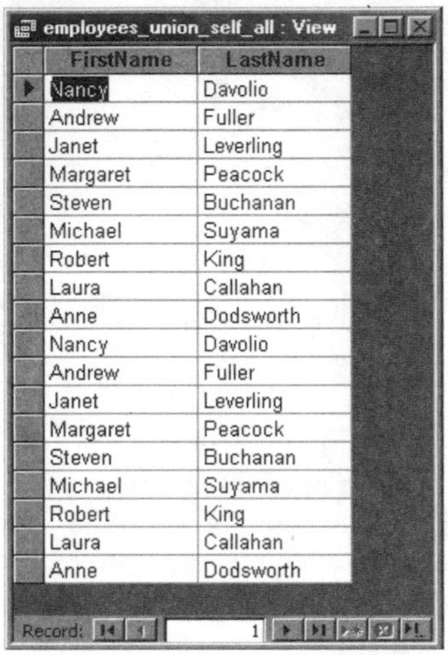

The preceding query is useful for revealing the behavior of the `UNION` keyword, but we are likely to use the `UNION` keyword with other types of queries besides self joins. The following sample illustrates a more normal case. It appends supplier contact information to the end of customer contact information. Although we cannot update the contact data from the view based on the `UNION` keyword (with SQL Server 7.0), the union query will always return the most recent contact data from both data sources whenever we open it.

```
SELECT CompanyName, ContactName, Phone
FROM Customers
UNION
SELECT CompanyName, ContactName, Phone
FROM Suppliers
```

For a better understanding of how unions develop return sets, the next screenshot presents an excerpt from the return set for the preceding view. Notice it has three columns; these correspond to the `SELECT` column list arguments. The status bar shows that the return set contains 120 rows; this is the sum of 91 rows from the `Customers` table and 29 rows from the `Suppliers` table. The first three rows in the excerpt are from the `Suppliers` table; the remaining rows are from the `Customers` table. This sample, along with all the other samples in this chapter, is available in the chapter's sample database. We can therefore examine the two input data sources relative to the full return set to heighten our understanding of any view throughout the chapter.

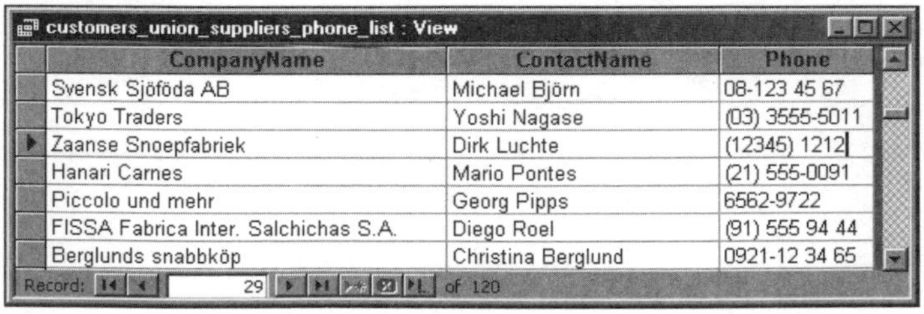

Subqueries

A **subquery** in a view is a SELECT statement nested inside of another SELECT statement. In essence, the return set from one SELECT statement sets a condition for the return set from another SELECT statement. It will often be true that we can replace a subquery with a join. Since join statements are more popular, our query statement for a view will generally be easier to read when we formulate it with a join instead of a subquery. On the other hand, subqueries sometimes express themselves more naturally with the nested SELECT statement syntax.

The following example finds all rows in the Customers table with a country that matches the country for the employee whose last name is Davolio. The WHERE clause in the outer SELECT statement depends on another inner SELECT statement. The outer SELECT statement depends on the Customers table, but the inner statement depends on the Employees table. The return set for the inner SELECT statement can return one or more country names, which is why, instead of =, we use the IN statement. In the case of the Northwind database, the return set is USA.

```
SELECT CompanyName, ContactName, City, Phone
FROM Customers c
WHERE (Country IN
        (SELECT Country
         FROM Employees
         WHERE LastName = 'Davolio'))
```

We can replace the preceding view based on a subquery with another query that draws on an inner join. As pointed out in the discussion of the subquery, the view depends on two tables – Customers and Employees. The two tables must join on their Country columns and the SELECT against the Employees table requires a WHERE clause that specifies a last name of Davolio. Since SQL Server performs these two formulations equally well, there is no performance penalty for the subquery. If you find views easily stated with subqueries, and that style of expression is comfortable then you can use it interchangeably with the alternative inner join formulation.

```
SELECT Customers.CompanyName, Customers.ContactName,
    Customers.City, Customers.Phone
FROM Customers INNER JOIN
    Employees ON
    Customers.Country = Employees.Country
WHERE (Employees.LastName = 'Davolio')
```

Correlated Subqueries

A **correlated subquery** is slightly more sophisticated than a basic subquery, such as the one finding customers from the same country as Davolio. The basic subquery evaluates its inner SELECT statement once and then computes its outer SELECT statement once as well. With a correlated subquery, the inner subquery must be repeatedly executed – once for each possible row in the return set for the outer SELECT statement.

The following view based on a correlated subquery shows just those products whose unit selling price is greater than the average for their category. As we can see, it is necessary to recalculate the inner SELECT statement for each possible row in the outer SELECT statement to determine if the current product in the outer query is greater than the average price for its category. Since the category is not the same for all products, it is necessary to recompute the inner SELECT statement to assess when a product's price exceeds its category's average price. This type of query could take a long time with a large data set.

```
SELECT CategoryID, ProductName
FROM Products p1
```

```
WHERE (UnitPrice >
          (SELECT AVG(p2.UnitPrice)
          FROM Products p2
          WHERE p1.CategoryID = p2.CategoryID))
```

It is possible to represent the above view with a correlated subquery as the join of two tables or a table and a view. We need one data source with the product prices – the `Product` table provides this role. The second data source must have average category prices. All we need is a basic `SELECT` query that computes average price by `CategoryID`. The following T-SQL expression defines a view named `products_average`:

```
SELECT CategoryID, AVG(UnitPrice) AS AveragePrice
FROM Products
GROUP BY CategoryID
```

By formulating an inner join of the `Products` table with the `products_average` view, we can specify a query that eliminates the need for a correlated subquery. The following sample illustrates the T-SQL for the alternative view statement without the correlated subquery:

```
SELECT Products.CategoryID, Products.ProductName,
    Products.UnitPrice,
    products_average.AveragePrice AS [AvgPrice/Product]
FROM Products INNER JOIN
    products_average ON
    Products.CategoryID = products_average.CategoryID AND
    Products.UnitPrice > products_average.AveragePrice
```

In this last pair of samples, the case for the subquery formulation of the view is more compelling since the alternative requires the creation of a new query. To replace the subquery with an inner join, it is necessary to devise a new query and then join that with an existing table. However, the subquery does require the computation of the average category price for each row in the outer `SELECT` statement while the join approach computes the average just once for each category. For a database the size of the Northwind, the difference is inconsequential. For a `Products` table much larger than the one in the Northwind database, other optimizations may well yield superior speed gains by avoiding the correlated subquery.

Access developers do not commonly build solutions with subqueries or correlated subqueries; instead, the typical Access database file solution nests queries within one another. However, the SQL Server literature does not take this approach. If you are an Access developer migrating from Jet to SQL Server, you will open up new opportunities for growth by gaining a basic understanding of subqueries and correlated subqueries.

Using the OPENROWSET Keyword in Views

With the help of the `OPENROWSET` keyword and the Microsoft Distributed Transaction Coordinator (MSDTC) service, views can query OLE DB data sources from homogeneous and heterogeneous data sources on the same or remote computers. The `OPENROWSET` keyword and its parameters operate in the `FROM` clause of a `SELECT` query. When an OLE DB provider permits it, we can use the `OPENROWSET` data source in `INSERT`, `UPDATE`, and `DELETE` statements. The discussion of the `OPENROWSET` keyword here extends beyond views to stored procedures.

The `OPENROWSET` statement will not work unless we have the MSDTC service running on every computer managing a data source associated with the query. For example, if the cabxli computer links a data source on the cab2200 computer, then the MSDTC service needs to be running on the both cabxli and cab2200 computers. We can start the service from SQL Server Service Manager dialog, whose icon appears in the lower right corner of a status bar of a computer running SQL Server or MSDE. The following figure shows the SQL Server Service Manager dialog with the MSDTC service selected in the Services drop-down list box. If the MSDTC service does not show the green arrowhead, then click the Start/Continue button to launch it on a computer participating in an OPENROWSET statement.

The following view illustrates the syntax for invoking OPENROWSET to get data from the cab2200 computer. Notice that it contains the basic elements of a connection string and a data source specification. The connection string content designates the SQLOLEDB provider, which is the OLE DB provider for SQL Server. The connection string also includes the target computer's name as well as a login and password (namely, sa with a blank password). The SQL string in the OPENROWSET argument list requests all columns in all rows from the Customers table in the Northwind database on the SQL Server named cab2200.

```
SELECT CustomerID, CompanyName, ContactName, Address, City, Region,
    PostalCode, Country
FROM OPENROWSET('SQLOLEDB','cab2200';'sa';'',
    'SELECT * FROM Northwind.dbo.customers')
```

The OPENROWSET keyword is very flexible. We can use this keyword to point a SQL Server view at a database object in any ODBC data source. Access developers initially migrating to SQL Server may be especially interested in it for the ease with which they can query a table in a legacy Access database file. The following sample demonstrates the syntax for returning all the rows from the Orders table in the Northwind Access database file on the current computer. You'll need to change the path if Access was installed somewhere else.

```
SELECT *
FROM OPENROWSET('Microsoft.Jet.OLEDB.4.0',
 'C:\Program Files\Microsoft Office\Office\Samples\northwind.mdb';'admin';'',
 'SELECT * FROM Orders')
```

Using the Views Collection

The Views collection on the Access 2000 Objects bar exposes any views in the database connected to an Access project. When we click Views on the Objects bar, the Database window shows the names of any existing views in the SQL Server database behind a project. We can double-click any view name to open the view in Datasheet View, which shows the virtual table specified by the SQL for that view. We can use the default Table Datasheet toolbar to manipulate the view's return set.

If we select a view and then click the Design icon on the Database window, the Design view of the query behind the view appears in up to three Query Designer panes – the Diagram, the Grid, and the SQL panes. We can use these panes to look at or modify the query behind a view.

We can also create a new view by clicking the New icon on the Database window with the Views collection selected. This opens a blank version of the Query Designer, which we can use to populate the new view with data sources. Access 2000 offers developers graphical and text-based approaches for specifying the query associated with a view.

> *Access 2000 projects do not support the T-SQL CREATE VIEW or ALTER VIEW statements in the SQL pane of the Query Designer. Use the New icon on the Database window instead of the CREATE VIEW statement to make a new view. Open an existing view from the Database window in Design view to modify it instead of using the ALTER VIEW statement. The latter part of this chapter illustrates programmatic means of creating views with the CREATE VIEW statement.*

> *Once you have a view created, you can use its Properties dialog to control selected features. One route for opening the Properties dialog is to right-click anywhere in a Query Designer layout for a view and then choose Properties. You can control selected features from the Properties dialog, which include encrypting a view and selecting only unique rows with the DISTINCT keyword.*

We can right-click any view in the Database window to open a context-sensitive menu that allows us to perform the CREATE VIEW and ALTER VIEW functions, as well as other tasks such as renaming, printing, copying, exporting, and deleting. The following screen shows the full context-sensitive menu for any view in the Database window. Here, clicking on the Print menu item prints the return set from the categories_inner_join_products view.

This section covers three important topics:

- ❑ The Three Query Designer Panes
- ❑ Query Designer Samples
- ❑ Manipulating Views in Datasheet View

The Three Query Designer Panes

There are three panes in the Query Designer, the graphical tool Access provides for creating views. The three Query Designer panes enable us to populate and view the data sources behind a view as well as examine the SQL logic defining the view. These panes are the **Diagram** pane, the **Grid** pane, and the **SQL** pane.

The following screen shows the Query Designer in action. It also shows the syntax for the first SELECT statement presented in this chapter, this time being used in a view. The view displays the CategoryName and Description columns from the Northwind Categories table.

The Diagram pane, located at the top of the Query Designer window, reveals a box depicting the Categories table. Check marks next to two of the column names denote those that will participate in the definition of the view.

Below the Diagram pane, the Grid pane appears. This pane displays the two column names and their source – namely, the Categories table. In addition, it indicates that the view will output both columns. If the output column in the Grid pane is checked, the corresponding column can participate in the view's definition. However, the column does not appear when a user opens the view.

The bottom SQL pane appears optionally. This pane shows the SQL text behind the graphical views in the two preceding panes. We can enter text directly into this pane, and Access will automatically populate the two graphical panes. The SQL icon on the View Design toolbar allows us to toggle the visibility of the SQL pane.

Developers can use the Design View toolbar to examine the contents and help design a view. Reviewing the functionality of View Design toolbar icons conveys some of the functionality that the Query Designer affords:

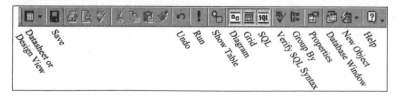

In summary:

- ❏ The View icon allows switching between design and datasheet portrayals of a view.

- ❏ The Save icon is a shortcut for saving a view's design with its current name. We cannot examine the datasheet associated with a view until we save any changes to it.

- ❏ The Undo icon is used to remove a design change.

- ❏ The Run button executes the view, which lets a developer view the datasheet created by the view just run.

- ❏ The Show Table button opens a dialog that allows a developer to choose from any table or view in the database to which an Access project connects. Selected tables and views act as data sources for the current view.

- ❏ The Diagram, Grid, and SQL buttons are toggle buttons that control the visibility of corresponding panes. Notice that the SQL pane does not show by default.

- ❏ The Verify SQL Syntax button checks the syntax in the SQL pane.

- ❏ The Group By button is used to control whether a view aggregates its return set for some columns by one or more other columns. The next section gives a couple of examples illustrating the operation of this control.

- ❏ The Properties button opens a dialog that allows us to specify selected view properties, such as whether we want it encrypted.

- ❏ The Database Window button is used to immediately open the Database window.

- ❏ The New Object button is a drop-down list that lets us choose from a selection of objects. For example, we can use this button to bind a form to a view. We discuss these buttons in the chapters covering forms, reports, and data access pages.

- ❏ Finally, the Help button can open the Help interface, such as the Office Assistant or Answer Wizard.

Query Designer Samples

This section illustrates how to design views with the Query Designer. As we review the examples in this section, we will learn how to manipulate the Query Designer. All developers initially migrating to SQL Server are likely to use the Query Designer because of its flexibility and ease of use, and because it is so similar to the Query designer Access uses for queries. Therefore, gaining a familiarity with this tool for typical kinds of views can accelerate our productivity with SQL Server. In addition to demonstrating techniques for simple SELECT statements, joins, and computations, this section drills down on how to work with dates and string variables. The examples in this section also enhance our understanding of how to make transformations between data types.

In this section, we will build up our knowledge of manipulating views in Query Designer through five subsections. These are:

- ❏ A Simple Select Statement
- ❏ Joining Data Sources
- ❏ Working with Dates

❑ Working with String Columns

❑ Computing Within and Across Records

A Simple Select Statement

Creating a SELECT statement query is a simple way to gain some hands-on familiarity with the Query Designer.

Start by highlighting Views in the Object bar of the Database window. Next, click New: this opens the Query Designer with the Diagram and Grid panes. Click the SQL toolbar button to expose that pane as well.

Next, click the Show Table button. This opens a dialog with a tree interface for exposing the table and view names in the Database collection for the Access project. These are the data sources that we can include graphically in our view. We can designate additional data sources programmatically (for example, via the OPENROWSET keyword).

After highlighting a data source in the Show Table dialog, drag it into the Diagram pane. The first time we do this, it will populate the FROM clause in the SQL pane with the name of the data source. On the second and subsequent times that we add data sources, the Diagram pane will attempt to join the tables and specify an Inner join in the SQL pane. If the Query Designer cannot detect one or more common columns between the data sources, then Access forms a cross join between the data sources.

By clicking check boxes for the table boxes in the Diagram pane, we can add individual columns to the SELECT list. If we click the * (All Columns) check box, our view will extract all columns from a data source. If the application adds new columns after the creation of the view, the view automatically selects those as well. In addition, if an application drops columns from a data source, the * (All Columns) selection adjusts automatically. While this feature set can reduce the possibility of errors in some cases, it can be expensive in performance and speed terms if our application needs only a small subset of columns from the data source and the data source contains many rows.

The following screen depicts a simple SELECT query based on the Shippers table from the Northwind database. Start to construct the sample by dragging the Shippers table from the Show Table dialog to the Diagram pane. Next, click the ShipperID and CompanyName check boxes. Access 2000 automatically denotes both columns in the Grid pane as coming from the Shippers table. If we want a column's name to appear with a column heading other than the column's name, assign an alias in the Grid pane. We can alternatively insert an AS after the column name in the SQL pane's SELECT list and enter an alias name. No matter in which pane we make the alias assignment, Access automatically updates the alias in the other pane as soon as the cursor leaves the pane in which we make the assignment or update.

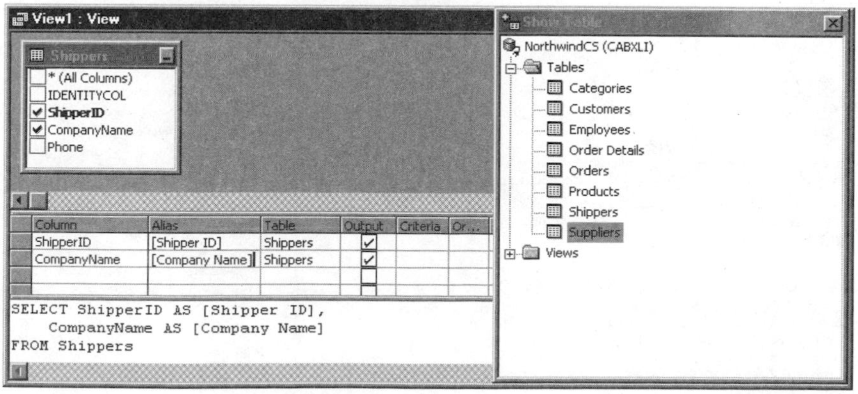

We must assign a permanent name to query settings before opening the virtual table for the view. Save the preceding view, giving the view a name that reflects its content. Access will automatically add a unit to the number following View (View1, View2, etc.) for each successive view that we save unless we name it ourselves.

Naming the views ourselves gives meaning to the views, and means that somebody else looking at them later will know exactly what they contain.

There are many naming conventions, and we can pick one that meets the needs of our development assignments and organization. Here we are using a convention whereby we assign a prefix, such as vw_, to the name of the original data source. By this convention, the name for the above view will be vw_Shippers. Some developers prefer long names that clearly convey the content or purpose of a database object and place a lower priority on the prefixes. There is nothing in SQL Server that forces the use of prefixes. However, the database engine does block us from using the same name to refer to two different database objects, such as two views or a table and a view, within the same database.

Joining Data Sources

One common use for a view like vw_Shippers is as a lookup table. It allows another view to reference the lookup table and display the converted value for a lookup field instead of the coded value. However, the second view will know nothing about the coded or uncoded values – it will only know that the particular field returned from the view is a piece of text. Access has built-in lookup fields when working with Jet databases, but SQL Server requires developers to explicitly create these lookup tables.

The next screen depicts an inner join of the Orders table with the vw_Shippers view. After dragging both data sources to the Diagram pane, Access does not automatically join the Orders table with the vw_Shippers view. However, we can drag from the ShipVia column to the [Shipper ID] column to form the join that we need to decode the ShipVia column values. Without this join, the view presents ShipVia column values as numbers that may be less meaningful to users of the view than the [Company Name] column for each shipper from vw_Shippers.

One distinct advantage of the Query Designer is its ability to generate SQL statements – however, the statements it produces will not be optimal (but the discussion of optimization techniques is outside the scope of this book). Notice from the SQL pane that it forms the syntax for an inner join between the Orders table and the vw_Shippers view. When the column names are unique, SQL Server does not require table or view qualifiers for the columns. For our own custom SQL scripts, we can optionally leave out the qualifier for uniquely named objects, unlike those generated by Query Designer where the qualifier is always present. However, the qualifier prefix denoting a source improves the clarity of the SQL text.

The following screen drives home the clarity that a lookup table can bring to a view's return set. Notice from the window title for the return set that that the view's name is vw_Orders_inner_join_vw_Shippers. It was sorted by Order ID in the Datasheet view to show a mix of shippers in the return set excerpt. Notice that shipping firm names appear instead of ShipperID codes, but the return set represents customer company names with cryptic CustomerID codes.

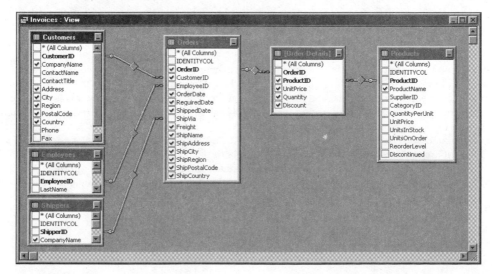

Query Designer Diagram Pane

The compact way in which the Diagram pane can graphically represent SQL statements is one reason why even ardent T-SQL coders may want to consider using this pane when developing views. It is a quick and easy way to produce the SQL for a new view and test it, before modifying it later. When performing multiple joins between more than two tables or views, this succinctness of the graphical tool is particularly evident. The NorthwindCS database features the Invoices view that pulls together fields from six tables (see the following screenshot). The Orders and [Order Details] tables serve as core elements of the views with the Products, Employees, and Shippers tables providing lookup functions. The Customers table serves in a dual capacity. First, it decodes the CustomerID column values in the Orders table. Second, the Customers table contributes several columns of its own, such as Address and City, to the return set from Invoices.

· The power of the Diagram pane is evident when we contrast its graphical representation of the Invoices view (see above) with the SQL pane statement representation below. It is easy to imagine how difficult it would be to understand what was going on by just looking at the SQL statement, and also how difficult it would be to correct errors directly in the code. With a graphical representation, we can see and instantly understand what is happening, and Access converts these views to sources for Access forms, reports, and data access pages, taking the burden of development from us.

```
SELECT Orders.ShipName, Orders.ShipAddress, Orders.ShipCity,
    Orders.ShipRegion, Orders.ShipPostalCode,
    Orders.ShipCountry, Orders.CustomerID,
    Customers.CompanyName AS CustomerName,
    Customers.Address, Customers.City, Customers.Region,
    Customers.PostalCode, Customers.Country,
    Employees.FirstName + ' ' + Employees.LastName AS Salesperson,
    Orders.OrderID, Orders.OrderDate, Orders.RequiredDate,
    Orders.ShippedDate,
    Shippers.CompanyName AS ShipperName,
    [Order Details].ProductID, Products.ProductName,
    [Order Details].UnitPrice, [Order Details].Quantity,
    [Order Details].Discount, CONVERT(money,
    [Order Details].UnitPrice * [Order Details].Quantity * (1 - [Order
Details].Discount)
    / 100) * 100 AS ExtendedPrice, Orders.Freight
FROM Shippers INNER JOIN
    Products INNER JOIN
    Employees INNER JOIN
    Customers INNER JOIN
    Orders ON Customers.CustomerID = Orders.CustomerID ON
    Employees.EmployeeID = Orders.EmployeeID INNER JOIN
    [Order Details] ON
    Orders.OrderID = [Order Details].OrderID ON
    Products.ProductID = [Order Details].ProductID ON
    Shippers.ShipperID = Orders.ShipVia
```

Working with Dates

One of the classic problem areas for specifying queries involves denoting dates and setting criteria for them. When working with dates, it is important to gain a basic degree of familiarity with SQL Server date and time functions. In addition, we will want to learn about the CONVERT function for working with dates.

There are two important things to understand when working with columns representing datetime data types. One of these is understanding that datetime data is both a date *and* a time. The other is to grasp the differences between locale formats, and knowing our server locale setting and how this impacts on the storage and return of dates. It is also worth noting that using dates too often in a view can reduce its efficiency.

We may recall that SQL Server offers two data types, datetime and smalldatetime, both of which are used for containing dates and times. This chapter refers to datetime values for both datetime and smalldatetime data types. SQL Server represents dates and times internally as numbers with days on the left of the decimal point and fractions of a day on the right of the decimal. The same general principles, but not the specific details, apply to Date/Time values in Access database files. See Chapter 3 for more details on SQL Server versus Access datetime and smalldatetime data types.

In the following subsections, we will look more closely at working with dates in SQL Server:

- ❏ Parts and Styles of Dates
- ❏ Using DATEPART
- ❏ Using Different Date Formats

Parts and Styles of Dates

As SQL Server represents dates and times in units not meant for casual users, we can generally write clearer expressions and code when using date and time functions. There are three T-SQL functions we use to make dealing with datetime data easier:

- ❏ DATEPART
- ❏ DATEADD
- ❏ DATEDIFF

The DATEPART function is used to denote any date or time unit in a datetime value. The general format for the DATEPART function is

```
DATEPART(datepart, datetime)
```

The datetime argument is the value representing a date or time. The datepart argument indicates which date or time unit to extract from a datetime value. The following table indicates the date and time units along with the abbreviations to reference them in the DATEPART function:

Date part name	Date part abbreviation
Year	yy, yyyy
Quarter	qq, q
Month	mm, m
Day of year	dy, y
Day	dd, d
Week	wk, ww
Weekday	dw
Hour	hh
Minute	mi, n
Second	ss, s
Millisecond	ms

The DATEADD function enables us to write expressions that add specific date and time parts to a datetime value. Our expressions using the DATEADD function can reference the same date parts as the DATEPART function. This allows us to designate a date a precise number of months into the future without having to account for the number of days in each month.

The DATEDIFF function is provided to compute the difference between two datetime values. This function is particularly convenient for timing the duration of tasks. Save the value of the GETDATE function at the beginning and end of a task. Then, use the DATEDIFF function to express the difference between the two datetime values as a date part. We have the full range of options as for the DATEPART function with the exception of the Weekday part.

Other functions for representing datetime values include DATENAME, DAY, MONTH, and YEAR; while the DATENAME function returns a character string, the DAY, MONTH, and YEAR functions return integers. For the maximum generality with international applications, we should represent dates with numeric values and functions. Date names, such as day and month names, can change from one language to the next. However, the second month of the year has an integer value of 2 in languages with different names for representing the second month of the year. The same general principle applies to the days of the week. When international standards are not an issue with an application, representing dates as character strings often has intuitive appeal because we work in familiar formats and we see what we get.

With the CONVERT function and a collection of built-in style parameters, we can transform numerical datetime values to character strings. These built-in styles represent dates and times with two and four character fields for the year, with and without date or time elements, and with and without milliseconds in the time specification. The styles allow us to readily express SQL Server datetime values in any of several standard formats designated by different countries and worldwide organizations. The general format for using the CONVERT function with a datetime value is:

CONVERT(char or varchar, datetimevalue, styleparameter)

The following table presents the style parameters for formatting datetime values as characters:

Style parameters for two–digit years (yy)	Style parameters for four-digit years (yyyy)	Standard format	Character representation**
-	0 or 100 (*)	Default	mon dd yyyy hh:miam (or pm)
1	101	USA	mm/dd/yy
2	102	ANSI	yy.mm.dd
3	103	British/French	dd/mm/yy
4	104	German	dd.mm.yy
5	105	Italian	dd-mm-yy
6	106	-	dd mon yy
7	107	-	mon dd yy
8	108	-	hh:mm:ss
-	9 or 109 (*)	Default + milliseconds	mon dd yyyy hh:mi:ss:mmmam (or pm)
10	110	USA	mm-dd-yy
11	111	Japan	yy/mm/dd

Style parameters for two–digit years (yy)	Style parameters for four-digit years (yyyy)	Standard format	Character representation**
12	112	ISO	yymmdd
-	13 or 113 (*)	European Default + milliseconds	dd mon yyyy hh:mi:ss:mmm(24h)
14	114	-	hh:mi:ss:mmm(24h)
-	20 or 120 (*)	ODBC canonical	yyyy-mm-dd hh:mi:ss(24h)
-	21 or 121 (*)	ODBC canonical + milliseconds	yyyy-mm-dd hh:mi:ss:mmm(24h)

* The styles 0 or 100, 9 or 109, 13 or 113, 20 or 120, and 21 or 121 always return a four-digit year.

** Year format depends on style code; 1 returns mm/dd/yy, but 101 returns mm/dd/yyyy.

Using DATEPART

The following Query Designer representation portrays the layout for selecting on a year, without displaying that year. However, the return set does display the quarter in which an order's date occurs. The query depicts a view named datepart_sample. The view's return set includes just those orders with an order date in 1998. A DATEPART function with a yyyy datepart argument designates that a column based on the OrderDate field will return a four-digit integer for the column value's year. The =1998 in the matching Criteria column on the Grid pane extracts only those rows with a year value of 1998. This criteria column helps to select records, but it does not show in the return set since its Output check box is empty. Another DATEPART function returns a one-digit integer denoting the quarter for the OrderDate values that satisfy the criterion.

The screenshot to the right offers an excerpt from the return set for the datepart_sample view. The excerpt captures the transition from rows with a Quarter column value of 1 to those with a value of 2. Notice also that there are just 270 records in the return set although the full Orders table contains 830 records. The criterion restricts entries in the return set to those with an OrderDate value in 1998.

OrderID	CompanyName	Quarter
10984	Save-a-lot Markets	1
10985	Hungry Owl All-Night Grocers	1
10986	Océano Atlántico Ltda.	1
10987	Eastern Connection	1
10988	Rattlesnake Canyon Grocery	1
10989	Que Delícia	1
10990	Ernst Handel	2
10991	QUICK-Stop	2
10992	The Big Cheese	2
10993	Folk och få HB	2
10994	Vaffeljernet	2
10995	Pericles Comidas clásicas	2

Record: 1 of 270

Using Different Date Formats

The next Query Designer instance demonstrates strategies for presenting dates with the CONVERT function. It also shows how to compute the difference between two dates with the DATEDIFF function. In light of its function, this view has the name convert_datediff_sample.

The view presents two untransformed columns from the Orders table – OrderID and OrderDate. The next three columns in the view use the CONVERT function to express the OrderDate in different formats. These give us some feel for the range of options available with the built-in style parameters for datetime values.

The column with an alias of [USA date (yy)] represents the OrderDate column in a USA style format with a two-digit field for representing the year. The next column also uses a USA style format, but it represents the year with a four-digit field. The difference between the two specifications is in the style parameter. When the parameter is 1, SQL Server returns datetime values with a two-digit year format. When the parameter is 101, SQL Server expresses the year for a datetime value with a four-digit number.

Column	Alias	Table	Output	Criteria	Or...
OrderID		Orders	✓		
OrderDate		Orders	✓		
CONVERT (char, OrderDate, 1)	[USA date (yy)]		✓		
CONVERT (char, OrderDate, 101)	[USA date (yyyy)]		✓		
CONVERT (char, OrderDate, 9)	[DefaultDate + milliseconds]		✓		
SUBSTRING(CONVERT (char, OrderDate, 9), 22, 3)	[Millisecond part of date]		✓		
DATEDIFF(ms, OrderDate, OrderDate + .0416667)	[Difference in milliseconds]				

```
SELECT OrderID, OrderDate, CONVERT(char, OrderDate, 1)
    AS [USA date (yy)], CONVERT(char, OrderDate, 101)
    AS [USA date (yyyy)], CONVERT(char, OrderDate, 9)
    AS [DefaultDate + milliseconds], SUBSTRING(CONVERT(char,
    OrderDate, 9), 22, 3) AS [Millisecond part of date],
    DATEDIFF(ms, OrderDate, OrderDate + .0416667)
    AS [Difference in milliseconds]
FROM Orders
```

The column with an alias of [DefaultDate + milliseconds] depicts datetime values with both date and time elements. The sample database denotes all times as 12:00 AM. In a typical database, a column of datetime values is likely to have entries with a wide range of different times. The CONVERT function for the column denotes the dates with month, day, and year fields followed by hour, minute, second, and millisecond fields. Since the hours field resets after 12, a suffix marks the time as AM or PM.

The column with an alias of [Millisecond part of date] builds on the preceding column. This column uses the SQL Server SUBSTRING function to extract the millisecond field from the column with the [DefaultDate + milliseconds] alias. The column based on the SUBSTRING function extracts 3 characters from the preceding column starting with the 22nd character. It is the 22nd and not the 21st character since there are always two characters for the day number, even for days numbered below 10. For numbers below 10, the first of the two characters is always a space.

The last column computes the difference between two dates, namely OrderDate and .0416667 more than OrderDate. Recall that SQL Server datetime values represent time values as quantities to the right of the decimal point. The quantity .0416667 is equal to 1 divided by 24. Therefore, the second datetime value in the DATEDIFF function is .0416667 time units ahead of the first one. The DATEDIFF function converts this to 3,600,000 milliseconds based on the product of 60 minutes times 60 seconds times 1000 milliseconds.

The next screenshot illustrates an excerpt of the return set from the convert_datediff_sample. Notice that the first two columns appear right-justified. This signifies their internal representation as numbers. The next four columns represent dates with characters. These columns are left-justified to signify their status as character strings. The last column is a right-justified numeric field. Its value is always 3,600,000 – the number of milliseconds in one hour.

Working with String Columns

Typical string columns have data types such as varchar and nvarchar. Matching these types of columns is typically easier than matching datetime columns, but it may still be worth reviewing a few techniques. Sometimes we will simply list the precise string values from these columns that are to appear in a view. If a view searches for multiple criterion values, these can appear in multiple criteria columns. Alternatively, we can use the IN keyword in a single column. Access developers switching to SQL Server will have to learn a couple of new wildcard parameters for pattern matching. This section recalls these for us as it reviews pattern matching more generally. The topics covered in this section are:

- ❑ Matching one of Multiple Strings
- ❑ Using LIKE with % Wildcard and [ ]
- ❑ Using LIKE with ^ and _ Wildcards

Matching one of Multiple Strings

Perhaps the most intuitive way to search for records that match multiple string criteria is to place each criterion value in a separate column within the Query Designer. The next view we'll take a look at searches for rows in the Orders table with ShipCountry column values that match Argentina, Brazil, or Venezuela. All we have to do is type the search criterion into each column. Access automatically designates these as

Unicode characters with an N prefix if the data type has Unicode formatting, such as nchar and nvarchar data types. If the data type for a column does not have Unicode formatting, then Access doesn't use the N. Instead, it just places the string in single quotes and precedes the criterion with an = sign.

Under special circumstances, we can use double quotes to delimit string criterion values. However, it is best to use single quote marks whenever possible to delimit string values. If our situation demands the use of double quotes, instead of single quote marks to delimit strings, we should either learn about setting the QUOTED_IDENTIFIER value, or repeat the single quote (' followed immediately by ', which gives us " rather than "). This is not the standard, and it is not explored further: we can learn more about the topic by searching for SET QUOTED_IDENTIFIER in Books Online.

Since Access and VBA developers are used to delimiting strings with double quotes, the use of single quotes with SQL Server is a little unusual. In addition, we must still use double quotes in certain VBA contexts even when dealing with SQL Server. Samples later in this chapter, in the Enumerating Views *section, illustrate VBA contexts in which the use of double quotes is appropriate for delimiting strings.*

The following screenshot depicts the view we mentioned a little earlier, in Query Designer. In addition to automatically formatting the string criterion values, Access automatically builds the corresponding SQL string for the query behind the mulitple_search_criteria_sample view. While using the graphical Query Designer is often faster than entering code for the first build of a query, it can sometimes be more expeditious to copy SQL code from another similar query. This is particularly true when developing a slight variation of the original view. Copying the SQL text from the original to the blank **SQL** pane of a new query eliminates the need to manually add data sources, specify joins, and enter multiple criterion values again.

We can shorten the syntax for specifying multiple criteria with the IN keyword. This keyword works for string and numeric criteria. The next screenshot presents another instance of the Query Designer for the multiple_search_with_IN_keyword_sample view. This example illustrates the use of the IN keyword. It shows an alternative means of stating the query behind the preceding view. To apply this keyword, we must type it into the first **Criteria** column followed by an opening parenthesis and the list of string criteria values, separated with commas. The IN clause is terminated by closing the parentheses. Access will automatically enclose our string constants with single quotes and N prefixes, if appropriate.

Both of the two preceding views yield the same return set. They extract all records from the Orders table in the **Northwind** database with the **ShipCountry** column equal to Brazil, Argentina, or Venezuela. The order of the constants within the IN clause and the criteria is immaterial as the records are returned in the order they are in the database.

The following excerpt from the return set for the multiple_search_with_IN_keyword_sample view shows the last five records. This excerpt contains rows that match each of the three criteria (Venezuela, Brazil, and Argentina).

Using LIKE with % Wildcard and []

Before we start showing how SQL Server deals with wildcards, a brief warning note:

*Using the LIKE function, developers can specify open-ended criteria for columns with character data. SQL Server offers four wildcard parameters that enable developers to specify these open-ended criteria. Access developers migrating from Jet to SQL Server will need to learn that % replaces * and _ replaces ?. Access developers can still use the square brackets ([]) to denote any collection of characters as part of a search string. However, when developing with SQL Server, use a leading caret (^) to denote not any of the characters within a pair of brackets instead of an exclamation (!). This information is summarised below:*

Access wildcard symbol	SQL Server wildcard symbol
*	%
?	_
!	^

The following screen displays a pair of Query Designer instances that illustrate different uses of pattern matching to select open-ended row sets from the `Orders` table. The instance on the left extracts all customers from the `Orders` table with a **CustomerID** column that begins with B. The query on the right is more selective. To enter the return set for that query, a record must both begin with B and have one of its next two letters be either L or O.

To enter either criterion, we type `LIKE` followed by the character string representing the search criterion. Access automatically delimits the `LIKE` function argument with single quotes. In addition, it assigns a prefix of `N` if the column has a data type formatted with Unicode characters.

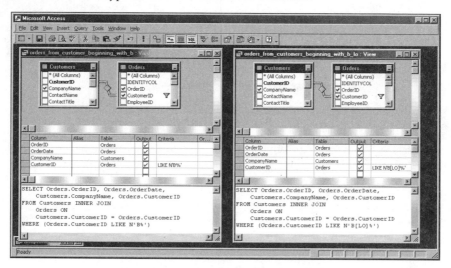

The two queries produce contrasting return sets that appear in the next screenshot. The one on the left shows 80 rows in its bottom window border matching the criterion of any **CustomerID** beginning with B.

Unsurprisingly, the more restrictive criterion based on a starting character of B followed by either L or O returns just 52 rows. Notice also that the return set on the left includes rows with a second character other than L or O. This is not true for return set on the right.

Using LIKE with ^ and _ Wildcards

The next pair of wildcard parameter examples illustrate the use of the ^ and _ operators. The Query Designer instance on the left of the following screen specifies a view that returns records beginning with a B and followed by any character except E or S. The only CustomerIDs in the Orders table, in this particular case, that begin with B are BERGS, BLAUS, BLONP, BOLID, BONAP, BOTTM, and BSBEV. Therefore, requiring the second character in CustomerID to be not either E or S has the same effect as designating the second character to be either L or O.

The Query Designer instance on the right specifies that its return set members shall all have a CustomerID column beginning with B and ending with P. The middle three characters can be any character, but there can only be three characters between B and P. Notice that the _ character represents an individual blank character. For obvious reasons the number of blanks and characters must match exactly to the data in the datasource.

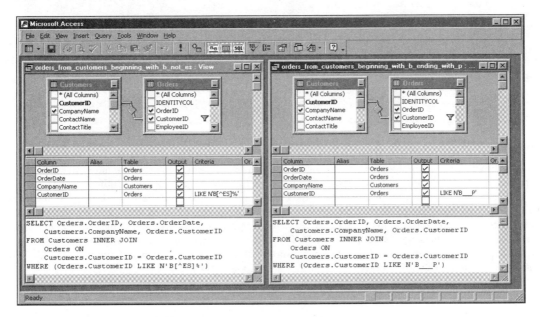

These two queries generate different return sets that appear in the following screen overleaf. The return set on the left corresponds to the preceding left Query Designer instance. Notice that it contains 52 rows. This matches the number returned by the query with a CustomerID criterion of LIKE N'B[LO]%'. In addition, the actual rows from the query with a criterion LIKE N'B[^ES]%' match those from the query with a criterion of LIKE N'B[LO]%'. Don't expect this to always be the case, though – this is just a quirk of this database.

The view based on a query with a CustomerID criterion of LIKE N'B___P' returns the smallest return set of any of the wildcard queries. This return set contains only those rows from the Orders table with a CustomerID column value beginning with B and ending with P.

OrderID	OrderDate	CompanyNam	CustomerID
10265	7/25/96	Blondel père et	BLONP
10297	9/4/96	Blondel père et	BLONP
10326	10/10/96	Bólido Comidas	BOLID
10331	10/16/96	Bon app'	BONAP
10340	10/29/96	Bon app'	BONAP
10360	11/22/96	Blondel père et	BLONP
10362	11/25/96	Bon app'	BONAP
10389	12/20/96	Bottom-Dollar M	BOTTM
10410	1/10/97	Bottom-Dollar M	BOTTM
10411	1/10/97	Bottom-Dollar M	BOTTM
10431	1/30/97	Bottom-Dollar M	BOTTM
10436	2/5/97	Blondel père et	BLONP
10449	2/18/97	Blondel père et	BLONP
10470	3/11/97	Bon app'	BONAP
10492	4/1/97	Bottom-Dollar M	BOTTM
10501	4/9/97	Blauer See Deli	BLAUS
10509	4/17/97	Blauer See Deli	BLAUS
10511	4/18/97	Bon app'	BONAP
10525	5/2/97	Bon app'	BONAP

OrderID	OrderDate	CompanyNam	CustomerID
10265	7/25/96	Blondel père et	BLONP
10297	9/4/96	Blondel père et	BLONP
10331	10/16/96	Bon app'	BONAP
10340	10/29/96	Bon app'	BONAP
10360	11/22/96	Blondel père et	BLONP
10362	11/25/96	Bon app'	BONAP
10436	2/5/97	Blondel père et	BLONP
10449	2/18/97	Blondel père et	BLONP
10470	3/11/97	Bon app'	BONAP
10511	4/18/97	Bon app'	BONAP
10525	5/2/97	Bon app'	BONAP
10559	6/5/97	Blondel père et	BLONP
10566	6/12/97	Blondel père et	BLONP
10932	3/6/98	Bon app'	BONAP
10940	3/11/98	Bon app'	BONAP
11076	5/6/98	Bon app'	BONAP
10584	6/30/97	Blondel père et	BLONP
10628	8/12/97	Blondel père et	BLONP
10663	9/10/97	Bon app'	BONAP

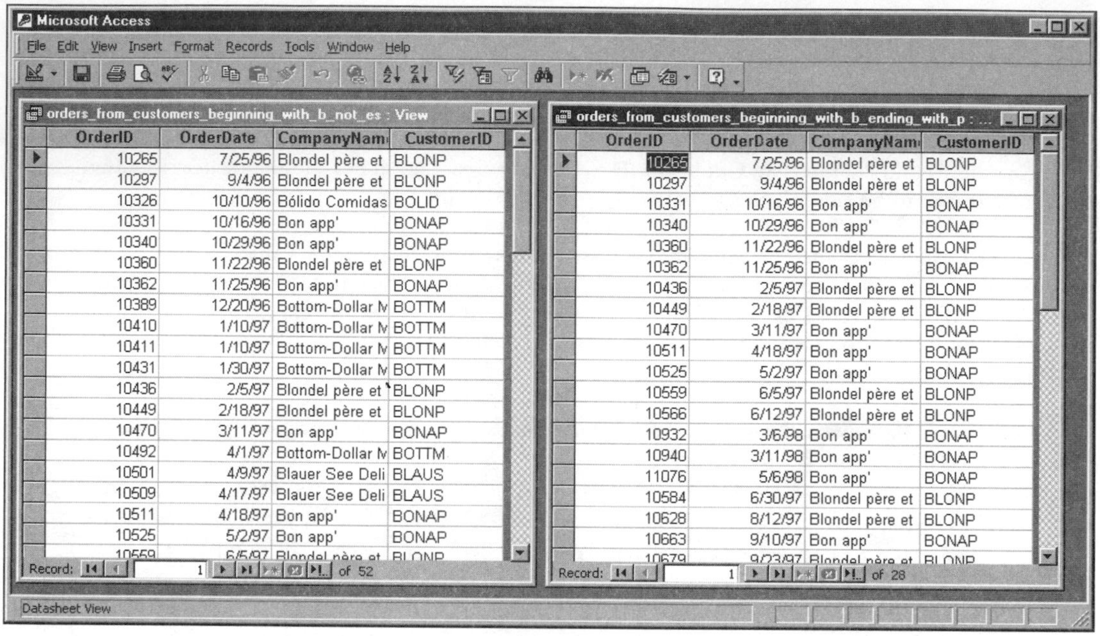

Computing Within and Across records

One of the most common applications for views is to compute results. Through the query behind a view, an application can compute results based on other columns in the same row, across all the rows in a table, or various groupings of the rows in a table. The data source for these computations can be as flexible as the inputs to the queries behind views. Our applications can use various kinds of joins, and we can even combine the results of other computations from other views. Our computations can include basic arithmetic and string computations as well as aggregate functions, built-in functions, and custom functions. Since we can build these views with the graphical Query Designer, Access offers a rich computational environment for SQL Server data with an easy-to-manage user interface.

Using that interface, we will look at the following topics in this section:

- Computing from Existing Columns
- Computing Aggregate Values
- Computing Aggregate Values Across More Than One Dimension

Computing from Existing Columns

When working with financial data, it is often useful to compute new values based on the existing columns in a table. For example, our application can compute extended price as the product of quantity times price times a function of any discounts from the list price. The following Query Designer instance shows such a calculation for the `[Order Details]` table in the Northwind database. If any of the inputs to extended price does not have a monetary or numeric data type, we may want to invoke to the `CONVERT` or `CAST` function. Either function can transform the return value from the extended price expression to a `money` or `smallmoney` data type. The following screenshot for the extended_price_by_order_with_convert view shows how to configure Query Designer for this task.

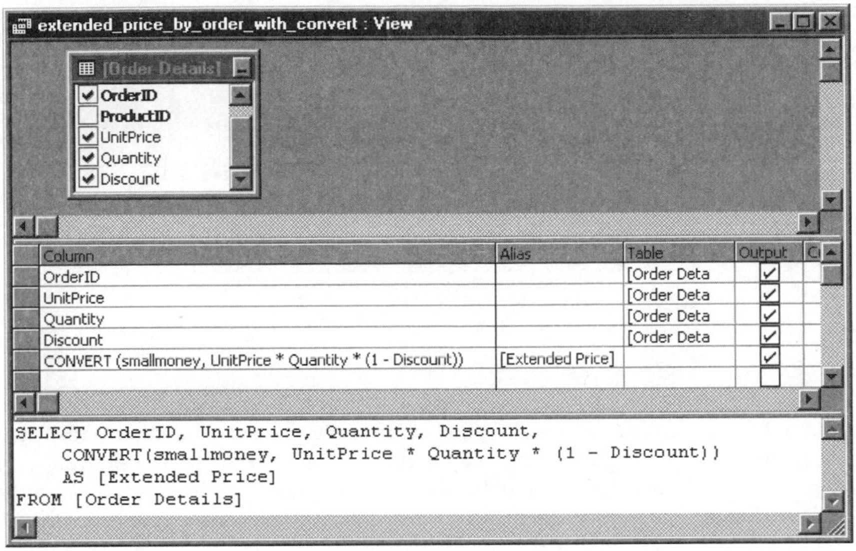

```
SELECT OrderID, UnitPrice, Quantity, Discount,
    CONVERT(smallmoney, UnitPrice * Quantity * (1 - Discount))
    AS [Extended Price]
FROM [Order Details]
```

Notice that we do not need to show the inputs to include them in a computation, although they are in this example to enable us to verify results. This example returns the extended price expression as a smallmoney data type, which was achieved by using the CONVERT function we saw earlier.

The following screen presents an excerpt from the extended_price_by_order_with_convert view. We can use this view to verify that the operation of the formula and the CONVERT function was successful. While the UnitPrice column has a money data type, the two other inputs to extended price have non-monetary data types, so the built-in SQL Server conversion, therefore, does not return a money data type. The CONVERT function transforms this format to a smallmoney data type.

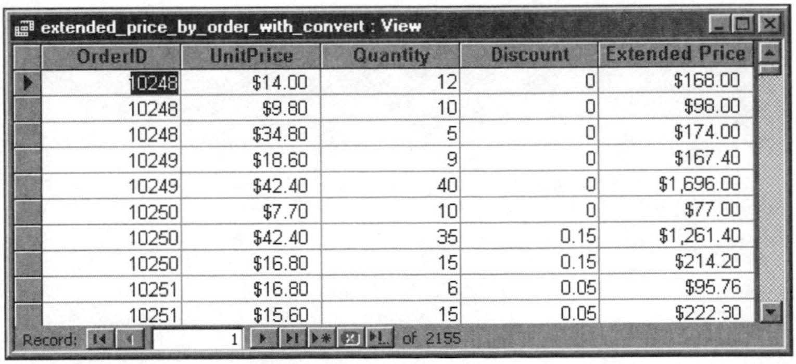

The following screenshot depicts an alternative formulation of a view that uses the CAST function instead of the CONVERT function to transform the result from the extended price expression to a smallmoney data type. This alternative demonstrates that we can compute a result on values that do not show in the view, because the view does not directly present the Quantity, UnitPrice, and Discount columns.

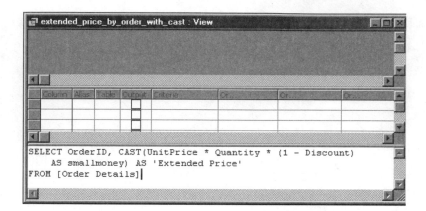

One especially interesting point about this alternative view using the CAST function is that the **Diagram** and **Grid** panes are empty. This is a requirement since the Access Query Designer does not support the use of these panes with a CAST function. When invoking the CAST function to define a view, we must type the T-SQL directly into the **SQL** pane. Note also that the CAST function has a different syntax from the CONVERT function. It represents an expression or value as a data type. In the example, the AS keyword separates the **extended price** expression from its assigned data type – namely, smallmoney. Another application of the AS keyword after the CAST function defines a meaningful alias name for the column. The return set from the view using the CAST function is identical to that from the one relying on the CONVERT function, except for the excluded **Quantity**, **UnitPrice**, and **Discount** columns, which is why we won't be looking at it here.

Computing Aggregate Values

The count_of_orders view in the next screenshot illustrates how to configure Query Designer to count unique occurrences of a value in a table's column. This example counts the OrderID values in the [Order Details] table by applying the aggregate COUNT function to the OrderID column. Since this is an aggregate function and the view defines no groups, the return set consists of a single number – the number of Orders in the Northwind database. (Open the view for yourself to see this, but for easy reference, this quantity is 830.)

Views computing aggregate values start by including a table in their Diagram pane. This example inserts the [Order Details] table in the pane. Next, we select one or more columns for the Grid pane. We will compute our aggregate functions on these columns. It is convenient to select the Group By control on the View Design toolbar when graphically defining views with aggregate functions. The Access window in the above screenshot shows this control invoked with the cursor on it, revealing the ToolTip which names the button. Selecting this control inserts a new column in the Grid pane. This new column has the heading Group By. The rows in the Group By column are drop-down list controls from which we can select an aggregate function. The screen shows the result of selecting the COUNT function.

The preceding example produced a single scalar value. This kind of aggregate scalar quantity can often be extremely useful in decision support and financial analyses. For example, if an analysis had the total of the extended prices for all orders, an application could divide the total revenue quantity by the total count to generate the average revenue per order. If an application had revenue by product and category, then it could calculate percent of total revenue by product and category.

The following T-SQL statement computes the total revenue across all products. We can create the T-SQL graphically by following the guidelines for generating the extended price per line item and also the aggregate across all rows in a table.

```
SELECT SUM(CONVERT(smallmoney,Quantity * UnitPrice * (1 - Discount)))
    AS [Extended Price Sum]
FROM [Order Details]
```

The name of the sample view with the preceding query is sum_of_extended_price. By combining this view with the count_of_orders view with a cross join, we have the quantities to compute the overall average extended price per order. The following screenshot shows the Query Designer layout to implement the calculation. The name for the view performing the computation is overall_average_price. We can duplicate this layout by adding both previously existing views to a new view. Then, we can create a new column that divides the overall extended price by the count of all orders. It is good practice to qualify the scalar values from the two previous views with the query behind each view, just like with other database objects. Therefore, the example expresses total revenue as sum_of_extended_price.[Extended Price Sum].

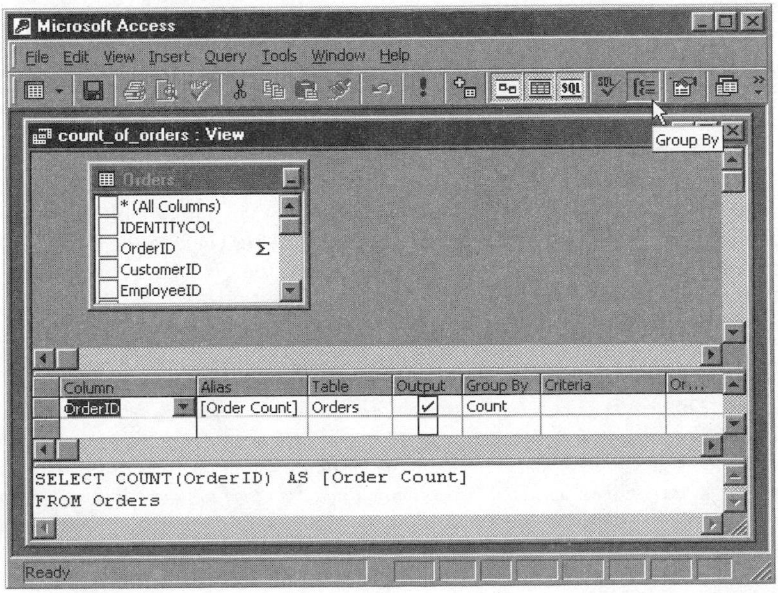

The overall_average_price generates a single row with three columns. These columns appear in the following screenshot. The first two columns present the inputs to the [Overall Average Price] column. The third column reports the result of dividing total revenue by the number of orders.

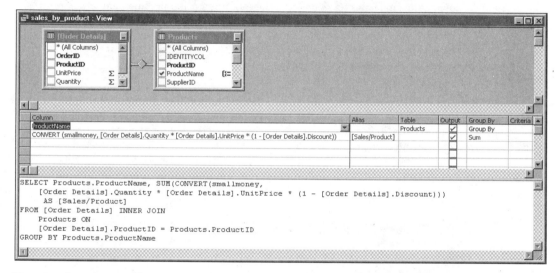

	Order Count	Extended Price Sum	Overall Average Price
▶	830	$1,265,793.04	$1,525.05

The value of aggregate computations grows substantially as we calculate the aggregates for groups of rows. The more members there are in one or more groups, the more information our application generates with its aggregate functions, which can slow down our application. For example, while it is useful to have the overall extended price across all products, it is more informative to have the sales by product for each product in the Northwind database. The following screen illustrates the Query Designer layout for computing sales per product in a view called sales_by_product.

The view draws on two data sources – the [Order Details] and Products tables from the Northwind database. The query for the view performs an inner join between these two tables. We can click the ProductName check box in the Products table to include that field in the view. Either before or after this step, we must select the Group By tool on the View Design toolbar. This enables the view to aggregate extended price for all the line items that reference a product. After clicking the Group By tool, enter the expression for extended price in the second column. Complete the Query Designer settings by making sure that the Group By rows in the Grid pane are Group By for ProductName and Sum for the extended price expression. That's all there is to it!

We will have to type the name of the Sum function into the Group By column for the Sale/Product row in the View Designer. This is because the drop-down box does not include the Sum function when we develop the example as described. The problem relates to the expression for the revenue of a line item; if we use money, instead of smallmoney, as the data type for the converted revenue per line item, Sum does appear in the drop-down box. Microsoft just didn't get around to testing the drop-down aggregate function list with the smallmoney data type. Recall that this is not a problem because we can type Sum into the Group By column for the Sales/Product row. The aggregation results are the same whether we convert to money or smallmoney.

The following screenshot presents an excerpt from the contents of the **sales_by_product** view. Notice that the items occur in no particular order. The view does not sort its rows by the values in the **ProductName** or **Sales/Product** columns. Recall that we cannot pre-specify a sort order for a view. However, it is easy for users to manually sort a view's return set, and developers can programmatically control the sort order for views in Access reports, forms, and data access pages.

Computing Aggregate Values Across More Than One Dimension

When computing aggregates across more than one dimension, we have a couple of different options:

- ❏ First, we can nest groups within one another, and then compute subtotals and grand totals based on the aggregates for the groups.

- ❏ Second, we can compute aggregates for each collection of group members, and then join the groups.

This latter approach has the virtue of controlling rounding error when we have to perform our aggregates with real or float data types. While we can never eliminate rounding errors when working with real and float data types, aggregating across the same members ensures that the rounding error does not change between calculations.

The next example creates two individual views and combines the results from each of these views in a third one that generates the final results. The **sales_by_product_with_Category** view groups revenue by product name, and the **sales_by_categoryID** view groups sales by category name. In order to combine the results of multiple views that perform aggregate calculations, we need to ensure the possibility of properly joining all aggregates. One strategy for accomplishing this goal is to include fields that permit inner joins between views. For example, if we wanted to nest the results from a view containing sales by product within another view calculating sales by category, then we could update the preceding sample to include a **CategoryID** column.

The following T-SQL sample illustrates the application of this approach for a view named **sales_by_product_with_CategoryID**. It adds the `Categories` table to the query computing sales by category. This requires adding the `Categories` table as a data source by inner joining it to the `Products` table. The new **CategoryID** column in a view computing sales by product enables the merging of product sales with category sales.

```
SELECT Categories.CategoryID, Products.ProductName,
   SUM(CONVERT(smallmoney,
   [Order Details].Quantity * [Order Details].UnitPrice * (1 - [Order
Details].Discount)))
   AS [Sales/Product]
FROM [Order Details] INNER JOIN
   Products ON
   [Order Details].ProductID = Products.ProductID INNER JOIN
   Categories ON
   Products.CategoryID = Categories.CategoryID
GROUP BY Categories.CategoryID, Products.ProductName
```

The sales_by_category view has just three columns – one with CategoryID, another with CategoryName, and a third for aggregating extended price by category. The query behind this view requires three Northwind database tables. These are [Order Details], Products, and Categories.

The following T-SQL script presents the detailed logic behind the view. Notice especially the CategoryID column from the Categories table in both views. This permits an application to merge the sales_by_category view rows into the sales_by_product_with_CategoryID view.

```
SELECT Categories.CategoryID, Categories.CategoryName,
    SUM(CONVERT(smallmoney,
    [Order Details].Quantity * [Order Details].UnitPrice * (1 - [Order
Details].Discount)))
    AS [Sales/Category]
FROM [Order Details] INNER JOIN
    Products ON
    [Order Details].ProductID = Products.ProductID INNER JOIN
    Categories ON
    Products.CategoryID = Categories.CategoryID
GROUP BY Categories.CategoryID, Categories.CategoryName
```

The following screenshot shows the Query Designer layout for merging the sales_by_category and sales_by_product_with_CategoryID views. As we can see from the Diagram pane, the query performs an inner join between these two views. The merge positions the matching category sales for each product with sales from the Products table. In addition, the query performs a cross join of the resulting merge with the sum_of_extended_price view. This cross join adds total revenue to each row in the combined view named sales_by_product_within_category_and_overall.

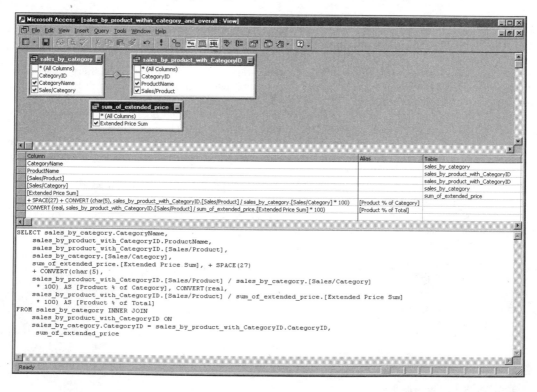

Each row in the sales_by_product_within_category_and_overall view contains product sales, corresponding category sales, and overall sales. The combined view uses these quantities to compute each product's percent of its category sales and the overall sales. The view formats the percentages using two different approaches. Since there is no "correct" approach for all situations, the chapter purposefully exposes two different ways of displaying the percentages. We can choose either one in our applications or blend the two to fit our unique requirements.

The first approach reports product sales as a percent of category sales in a character format. It uses the CONVERT function to transform the ratio of product to category sales times 100 as a five-character field. The preceding SPACE function moves the character field to the right in the column so that it is not left-justified. When computing product sales as a percent of total sales, the view expresses the ratio of product to total sales times 100 as a real data type. This displays the percentage with up to two decimals places. If the second place is 0, then it does not show in the view's return set.

An excerpt from the sales_by_product_within_category_and_overall view appears below. This view uses a Courier New font in a 10-point size to align the characters in the product percent of category sales. A more typical proportional font would not give the column a right-aligned appearance. The Font dialog is available from the Format | Font command. In order to show all the column headings, the ProductName column was purposefully left narrower than necessary to show the full name for longest product title so that there was sufficient space to show all the column headers.

Manipulating Views in Datasheet View

By now, it should be obvious that we have many options for manipulating a view when it is in a datasheet. There are three general classes of changes:

First, we can change the formatting controlling the appearance of the data. The preceding example illustrates this when it selects a new font for the view's display. These changes do not persist between Datasheet View sessions.

Second, users can rearrange data. For example, a view's Datasheet View enables users to sort or filter the rows in a view. A couple of preceding examples presented a view's return set after sorting it on a column in Datasheet View. Like the formatting changes, these new sort orders are not persistent.

Third, when updating is permissible, we can add, update, and delete records from a view in its Datasheet view. These alterations modify the tables that underlie a view's query. Therefore, these data modifications persist.

There are three primary interfaces for modifying the formatting, appearance, and data in a view.

- ❑ First, we can use the Datasheet View toolbar. This toolbar offers controls for some of the most common tasks that we are likely to undertake with a view.

- ❑ Second, we can use the Datasheet view menu. This includes the commands on the toolbar, and it adds more options.

- ❑ Third, when making changes to the cell values in a view's datasheet, we can just type a new value into it or edit the current value in a cell. This approach doesn't work for aggregate functions.

The following screenshot displays the Datasheet View toolbar with captions depicting functions available through three primary interfaces for modifying the the toolbar. Some of these, such as Help and New Object, duplicate those from the Design View toolbar. In addition, other controls represent typical Windows functions, such as Cut and Undo. This subset of controls operates normally. Access 2000 doesn't enable them unless they are available. For example, if the data in a view is not updateable, then the Cut button will not be available, as in this screenshot.

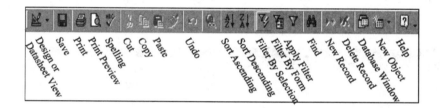

While Access reports make an excellent vehicle for formatting a view's contents, we can directly print the contents of a view. The Print and Print Preview toolbar controls facilitate the printing of a view's return set. The Spelling, Cut, Copy, Paste, New Record, and Delete Record controls are conditionally available. In order for these to work, the query underlying a view must be updateable. A query is always updateable when it relies on a single table with a primary key. We can generally edit data based on an inner join with a one-to-many relationship between a pair of tables. However, we cannot update computed columns, columns based on an image data type, or data locked by another user. We can never modify the data in an aggregate query. In addition, Access does not permit the editing of views based on a SELECT statement with the DISTINCT keyword. Generally, SQL Server must be able to identify unambiguously the value to update in order for a view to be updateable.

The Undo button does what it says. SQL Server does not permit us to undo all actions in the Datasheet View. Access fails to enable the Undo toolbar button in these cases; for example, if we update a column value in a view, we cannot undo it later with the Undo button.

The Sort Ascending and Sort Descending controls permit a user to re-arrange the rows in a view's return set based on a single column. As previously mentioned, this is one simple workaround for the fact that queries for views do not permit the ORDER BY clause.

We can filter a return set with the three buttons after the sort controls. These three buttons work exactly like the corresponding buttons for the Datasheet view of a SELECT query in an Access database file. Filtering a return set does not alter the data in the return set but merely the way a view presents its return set. Using the Filter By Selection control, we can examine just return set rows that match the currently selected value. Invoke the Filter By Form control to specify more advanced filter criteria. After a filter is in effect, the Apply

Filter control changes to a **Remove Filter** control, as seen right. If a user chooses **Remove Filter**, it is possible to re-initiate the filter for the last selected value by choosing **Apply Filter**.

The **Find** control enables a developer to search the records in a column for a specific value. Additionally, we can designate wildcards so that we match more than one specific value. After moving to the first match in a column, users can choose **Find Next** on the Find dialog until they identify a desired record or there are no more matches. The **Find and Replace** dialog that opens when a user chooses the **Find** control offers several other options. Developers can duplicate this functionality programmatically.

Programmatically Manipulating Views with ADO

Many Access developers will discover that the power of SQL Server views grows as we manipulate them programmatically. We can perform many kinds of tasks with views, from printing return sets to creating new views. In fact, we can create some views programmatically that are not possible through the Access user interface. This section explores manipulating views with ADO. The next section examines SQL-DMO routines for programmatically processing views. Subsequent chapters will show how to use views with Access objects, such as forms, reports, and data access pages.

In this section, we deal with three basic themes:

❑ Creating Views Programmatically with ADO

❑ Printing a View's Return Set

❑ Enumerating Views and Showing their Text

Creating Views Programmatically with ADO

In addition to collecting the output from a view and enumerating the views in a database, ADO enables our applications to create views programmatically. While we are creating new views, we can delete older, obsolete views with the same name. In addition, we can take advantage of a new view type introduced with SQL Server 2000 that is not available through the Access user interface for working with views. This new type of view targets applications that work with large recordsets containing many rows where the structure of the underlying tables or views stays the same over time.

You may be wondering – why bother creating views programmatically when it is so easy to create them graphically with the Query Designer? There are several good answers to this question. One of these is that it is generally easier to edit a view that we are applying to multiple data sources than to manually re-create it for each source. Furthermore, having our views in a VBA module can simplify maintenance of our views over time. For example, if we inadvertently delete a view, it is easy to re-create when we already have it in code. Our VBA procedure for creating the view acts like a backup for the view.

There are two things to look at in this section:

❑ Creating a View with ADO

❑ Indexed Views with SQL Server 2000

Creating a View with ADO

Before launching into a sample that demonstrates what we need to create views programmatically, a couple of issues may be worth mentioning. As our application attempts to create a view, it can fail if a view with that name already exists. Happily, we can trap the error, and delete or archive the old view.

After programmatically creating a view, the Database window does not automatically update to show it. This is actually a typical occurrence with other objects, such as forms, that we programmatically create with Access. Microsoft provides the RefreshDatabaseWindow method for the Access Application object to force an update of the Database window. Unfortunately, the method does not work for views that we create programmatically. You or your users must choose View | Refresh (or press F5) from the Database window menu if you want to display in the Database window a freshly created view under programmatic control. Whether or not the views show in the Database window, they are still a database objects. Therefore, this failure of the RefreshDatabaseWindow method is mostly an inconvenience.

The following procedure, commands_can_make_views, illustrates the syntax for creating a view programmatically with ADO. In addition to the background considerations in the preceding paragraph, all we need is an ADO Command object, the right T-SQL syntax for our view, and a VBA module attached to our project.

If you are still getting comfortable with T-SQL, the preceding samples that printed out T-SQL scripts may prove to be a valuable resource as you transition into designing your views without the aid of a graphical query tool.

```
Sub commands_can_make_views()
On Error GoTo commands_trap
Dim cmd1 As ADODB.Command
Dim str1 As String

'Procedure runs, but DB window does not update
'until you Refresh it manually

'Run CREATE VIEW statement with a
'a CommandType of adCmdText
Set cmd1 = New ADODB.Command
With cmd1
    .ActiveConnection = CurrentProject.Connection
commands_start_again:
    str1 = "CREATE VIEW foo " & "AS SELECT * FROM Categories"
    .CommandText = str1
    .CommandType = adCmdText
    .Execute
End With

commands_exit:
Set cmd1 = Nothing
Exit Sub

commands_trap:
If Err.Number = -2147217900 Then
'traps for object with that name existing already with ADO
```

```
        str1 = "DROP VIEW foo"
    With cmd1
        .CommandText = str1
        .Execute
    End With
    Resume commands_start_again
Else
    Debug.Print Err.Number, Err.Description
    Resume commands_exit
End If

End Sub
```

The script for the view in the **commands_can_make_views** procedure is simple by design so as not to distract from the process of creating a view with ADO; notice that our script must start with CREATE VIEW followed by a view name and the AS keyword. Then, we just insert the same text that appears in the SQL window of a Query Designer. After creating the view's SQL text in a string variable, assign that variable to the CommandText property of a command, and set the command's CommandType property to adCmdText. Finally, execute the command. If all goes well at this point, the procedure clears memory for the Command object immediately before invoking an Exit Sub command. Every program is susceptible to run-time failures. In this instance, the procedure can fail if the view, **foo**, already exists in a database. The logic recovers from this particular run-time error by dropping the old version of **foo** and trying to re-run the original script for creating the view. In the case of other run-time errors, the procedure echoes the error number and description to the **Immediate** window before exiting the procedure.

The case for applying this capability to create views programmatically is particularly compelling when working with **indexed views** in Access 2000. SQL Server 2000 introduced this view type after the introduction of Access 2000. Therefore, Access offers no graphical tool for creating indexed views, but we can create them programmatically.

> *Indexed views are a new exciting topic introduced with SQL Server 2000. Their discussion here is in order to use them as a vehicle for demonstrating the value of defining views programmatically. If your needs dictate the use of indexed views, you should fully explore this topic in Books Online; however, as I was writing this book, Microsoft decided to restrict the use of indexed views to the Enterprise Edition of SQL Server 2000, so if you will not be using such an edition, consider skipping the next section on the topic.*

Indexed Views in SQL Server 2000

Before illustrating how to use indexed views, let's pause to give some background on what indexed views are and when we should apply them. An index is a short-cut for finding some content in a source. An index in a view serves this role admirably. Instead of having to leaf through every page of a book until we find some content on a topic, we can jump directly to that page from the index. Indexes are popular tools for speeding searches against tables, but SQL Server 2000 is the first version to use indexes to speed retrieval from a view. Our application must specify a unique, clustered index for the view. Instead of querying a view's underlying data sources or another un-indexed view, our applications should apply indexed views whenever they can enhance performance.

Once we create an indexed view, we cannot change it without diminishing the effectiveness of the index. Even more significantly, we cannot alter the design of the data sources for a view. There is, of course, nothing to stop us recreating the view, but this might take some time, especially because of the need to construct the indexes for the view.

Due to these disadvantages, we should clearly appreciate the circumstances under which indexed views enhance performance. There are three general conditions:

❑   First, the data sources underlying the views should contain very large row sets.

❑   Second, the query defining the view should contain simple aggregate functions, such as SUM and COUNT. Complex aggregate functions, such as STDEV, VARIANCE, and AVG cannot participate in the definition of an indexed view. The T-SQL interpreter does not create an indexed view when we use one of these complex aggregate functions.

❑   Third, indexed views deliver performance gains by enabling the processing of smaller row sets than their underlying data sources. Unless an indexed view does substantially reduce the number of rows requiring processing, we should abandon it.

As we prepare an application to take advantage of indexed views, we will typically use two different VBA procedures. The first one will create the indexed view. We run this one once, or whenever we have to refresh the view because of the need to change the structure of its underlying data sources. We use a second VBA procedure to run a query against the indexed view. Actually, we can (and should) have more than one other VBA procedure to run against the indexed view. The more queries we run against it, the more performance enhancement it can give to an application.

Since indexed views are new technology from Microsoft, you will have to experiment to determine those situations where you get a significant payback. With performance evaluations, you can determine if the improved time to get results is worth the special restrictions that indexed views impose on an application.

Defining an Indexed View

The following sample illustrates the syntax for defining an indexed view. (Lubor Kollar, the Microsoft Program Manager for Indexed Views, provided the T-SQL code.)

You can only run the following sample if you are connected to a SQL Server running the Enterprise Edition of SQL Server 2000.

We actually have to execute a Command object twice to create one indexed view. We add the view, named Vdiscount1 in this case, to the database the first time that we execute the command. We define the index, named VdiscountInd, for the view when we execute the command a second time.

The view in this sample makes it possible to compute the aggregate amount discounted to customers by product. Notice that the view delivers two values for computing this amount, SumPrice and SumDiscountPrice, aggregated to the ProductID level. The original data enables this computation at the level of individual line items from the [Order Details] table. As the number of line items grows relative to the number of products, the benefits from indexed views will grow. In fact, we have to work with very large databases before indexed views start to deliver benefits. This may be why Microsoft restricts its availability to the Enterprise Edition of SQL Server 2000. One indication of the database size issue is that the Northwind database does not have a rowset with enough rows to demonstrate the performance advantage of indexed views.

```
Sub make_an_indexed_view()
Dim cmd1 As ADODB.Command

'Instantiate a Command object
```

```
    Set cmd1 = New ADODB.Command

    'Re-use the object for two purposes
    'First, create a view with it
    'Second, create an index for the view
    With cmd1
        .ActiveConnection = CurrentProject.Connection
        .CommandType = adCmdText
        .CommandText = "CREATE VIEW Vdiscount1 with SCHEMABINDING " & _
            "AS SELECT SUM(UnitPrice*Quantity) SumPrice, " & _
            "SUM(UnitPrice*Quantity*(1.00-Discount)) SumDiscountPrice, " & _
            "COUNT_BIG(*)Count, ProductID FROM dbo.[order details] group By ProductID"
        .Execute

    cmd1.CommandText = "SET ARITHABORT ON " & _
        "CREATE UNIQUE CLUSTERED INDEX VdiscountInd on Vdiscount1 (ProductID)"
    cmd1.Execute
    End With

    'Cleanup
    Set cmd1 = Nothing

End Sub
```

Running a Query Based on an Indexed View

The next VBA procedure demonstrates a sample that returns the five products with the largest rebates. The query in this VBA procedure takes advantage of the **Vdiscount** indexed view since it computes values based on the aggregations in the view, namely **SumPrice** and **SumDicountPrice** at the level of aggregation in the view, namely **ProductID**. Our application can run this procedure many times, but it should run the first procedure, **make_an_indexed_view**, just once to define the indexed view.

```
Sub run_query_based_on_indexed_view()
Dim cmd1 As ADODB.Command
Dim rst1 As ADODB.Recordset

'Instantiate a Command object
Set cmd1 = New ADODB.Command

With cmd1
    .ActiveConnection = CurrentProject.Connection
    .CommandType = adCmdText
    .CommandText = "SELECT TOP 5 ProductID, (SumPrice - SumDiscountPrice) " & _
        "Rebate FROM [VDiscount1] ORDER BY Rebate DESC"
    .Execute
End With

'Assign the return set from the query to
'a Recordset object for printing
Set rst1 = New ADODB.Recordset
rst1.Open cmd1
Debug.Print rst1.GetString

'Cleanup
rst1.Close
Set rst1 = Nothing
Set cmd1 = Nothing

End Sub
```

Printing A View's Return Set

There are many uses for views in an Access application. Often, we will just want to gain access to a view so that we can display its contents. This section shows a couple of approaches to this task. Both print view return sets in the Immediate window of the Visual Basic Editor (VBE) environment, but they take different approaches to the task that trade control for simplicity. In general, our custom applications will not print view return sets in the Immediate window. However, the data access skills this task teaches will help us work with view return sets in any environment, such as with Access forms and reports. Subsequent chapters will explore how to use tables and views with these other Access objects.

Printing a Return Set Using Command and Recordset Objects

The first approach relies on a pair of ADO objects that combine to report the return set from a view. This approach for capturing a return set uses the ADO Command object to execute the T-SQL behind a view. Then, the command passes its contents on to a Recordset object. The Command object offers no way to interact with the data that it captures. You might wonder why bother with a command when all it does is pass data to a recordset. While this may be true for views, the Command object is more flexible than the Recordset object for executing T-SQL statements. We will find the Command object useful for maintaining a database's contents as well as updating its structure.

Recordsets can couple very tightly with Command objects; this makes it easy to pass the data from a Command object to a recordset. Once the data are in a recordset, our application can manipulate it in any of several ways. We can exclude certain columns or rows from a view's return set. We can readily perform this operation selectively so that a column does appear for some rows but not others. While this task is also possible with a T-SQL query statement, many Access developers will be more familiar with ADO than T-SQL so tailoring a canned view is just easier and faster to develop with ADO than T-SQL.

The following VBA procedure, printview, performs three major tasks. First, it uses a Command object to connect to a view (the list_all_in_categories view is the first view in the chapter, which returns all columns from the Categories table), which it then runs. Second, it passes the return set from the view to a Recordset object, which processes the columns to remove the Bitmap Image column. This second step ends with the printing of the data collected from the return set in the Immediate window. Finally, the procedure cleans up the objects it has used.

```
Sub printview()
Dim cmd1 As ADODB.Command
Dim rst1 As ADODB.Recordset
Dim fld1 As ADODB.Field
Dim str1 As String

'Create a Command object that points at view
'and invoke the Execute method for the command
Set cmd1 = New ADODB.Command
With cmd1
    .ActiveConnection = CurrentProject.Connection
    .CommandText = "list_all_in_categories"
    .CommandType = adCmdTable
    .Execute
End With

'Create a Recordset object that points to
'a return set from cmd1
Set rst1 = New ADODB.Recordset
rst1.Open cmd1
```

```
'Loop through rows in recordset
Do Until rst1.EOF
'Pass through columns in a row
    For Each fld1 In rst1.Fields
        If rst1.Fields(fld1.Name).Type <> adLongVarBinary Then
            str1 = str1 & rst1.Fields(fld1.Name) & "; "
        End If
    Next
'Clean up end of row and move to next one
    str1 = Left(str1, Len(str1) - 2)
    str1 = str1 & vbCrLf
    rst1.MoveNext
Loop

'Print out return set of numeric and text fields
Debug.Print str1

'Clean up objects
Set cmd1 = Nothing
Set fld1 = Nothing
rst1.Close
Set rst1 = Nothing

End Sub
```

The initial four `Dim` statements reserve memory for objects and variables local to the procedure. In addition to `Command` and `Recordset` objects, the procedure also relies on a `Field` object. This additional object is convenient when we want to manipulate individually the columns from a return set. Since ADODB is the default data access library for Access 2000, we do not have to do anything special to have these objects available for declaration.

> *Be very careful, however. Users who enter the Visual Basic Editor environment can disable the ADODB library. When this happens, the declarations fail. Do **not** let users enter the VBE environment. Chapter 12 demonstrates how to secure entry to the VBE environment. It also shows how to set programmatically a reference to a library.*

After declaring the `cmd1` Command object, the procedure instantiates it with the `New` keyword. We can declare and instantiate objects in one step, but it is cleaner to only instantiate objects when our application specifically requires them. The procedure assigns `ActiveConnection`, `CommandText`, and `CommandType` properties inside a `With...End` statement. The `CommandText` property points the command at the list_all_in_categories view; this view must reside in whatever data source our code specifies for the `ActiveConnection` property. The `CommandType` setting of `adCmdTable` tells the ADO interpreter to respond to the view as a table (recall that a view is a *virtual* table). The procedure generates a return set from the view by invoking the `Execute` method.

After our application creates the return set from the view, it passes the return set to a `Recordset` object. Our code can accomplish this as easily as invoking the `Open` method for a `Recordset` object with the command as a parameter. A nested pair of loops extracts data from the recordset. The outer loop goes through the rows in the recordset. The inner loop passes through the columns within each row. The sample code retains all rows except those with an `adLongVarBinary` type. This removes the **Bitmap Image** column from the return set. We can use this general formulation for much more advanced tasks. For example, we can conditionally retain column values based on any criteria that we can program with the VBA, Access, and ADO libraries.

Before closing, the procedure cleans up. This requires releasing the memory reserved for the `fld1`, `cmd1`, and `rst1` objects.

Printing a Return Set Using Only the Recordset Object

The above approach has the benefit of being very flexible. It is flexible because we actually pass through each column within each row. This enables our code to perform any filtering or cleaning operations that an application may require. In spite of its flexibility, it is not brief. If all we want to do is print a return set in the Immediate window, we can accomplish it with a lot fewer lines of code. The following VBA procedure, printview2, demonstrates one attempt at attacking the problem more directly. This second approach works exclusively with the Recordset object, and it does not loop through either rows or columns. Yet, it displays a view's return set with the same general format as the preceding sample.

```
Sub printview2()
Dim rst1 As ADODB.Recordset
Dim str1 As String

'Open a Recordset object based on a view
Set rst1 = New ADODB.Recordset
rst1.Open "list_all_in_categories", CurrentProject.Connection, , , adCmdTable

'Use the GetString method to abbreviate printing
str1 = " eol " & vbCrLf
Debug.Print rst1.GetString(adClipString, , " --> ", str1)

'Clean up objects
rst1.Close
Set rst1 = Nothing

End Sub
```

This procedure capitalizes on the ability of the Recordset object to open a view directly. The decision to omit the Command object makes most sense when our application is simply generating a return set from a view. If our aim was to create or modify a database object, then we can omit the Recordset object in favor of the Command object.

After creating a return set in rst1 based on the list_all_in_categories view, the procedure displays the recordset's contents by invoking the GetString method. This is the second major step for saving lines of code. This method prints all rows as a string. Since it is not possible to represent the Bitmap Image column as a string, it does not appear in the return set.

The GetString method can take as many as five arguments. The preceding sample demonstrates the use of three of these. The first parameter can be adClipString or NULL. The Access Help file asserts that a setting of adClipString for the first parameter enables the third, fourth, and fifth parameters – expressions for row delimiters, column delimiters, and values – to represent NULL values. My personal experimentation confirms that these parameters are operational whether the first parameter is adClipString or NULL.

In any event, the second parameter allows our code to designate the returning of just the first so many rows. When we do not specify a number of rows to return, as in the sample, the GetString method passes back all the rows in its record source.

The third and fourth parameters are column and row delimiters, respectively. In the sample, the column delimiter is a character sequence representing an arrow with leading and trailing spaces. The row delimiter is a concatenation of two character constants. Since the GetString method does not support computed parameter values, the procedure saves the concatenated sequence in the str1 string variable, and then uses that variable as the row delimiter parameter.

The last parameter can specify an expression for representing NULL values. When an application does not specify the fifth parameter, it defaults to a zero-length string.

The following screenshot makes it easy for us to contrast the output from the `printview` and `printview2` procedures. The top return set is from `printview` and the bottom one is from `printview2`. Despite different delimiters for columns and rows, the general format is the same. The column values are identical. Since either approach enables the setting of row and column delimiters, we could force them to have an identical appearance.

```
Immediate                                                                        ▣
  1; Beverages; Soft drinks, coffees, teas, beers, and ales                      ▲
  2; Condiments; Sweet and savory sauces, relishes, spreads, and seasonings
  3; Confections; Desserts, candies, and sweet breads
  4; Dairy Products; Cheeses|
  5; Grains/Cereals; Breads, crackers, pasta, and cereal
  6; Meat/Poultry; Prepared meats
  7; Produce; Dried fruit and bean curd
  8; Seafood; Seaweed and fish
  9; New category; New product

  1 --> Beverages --> Soft drinks, coffees, teas, beers, and ales -->  eol
  2 --> Condiments --> Sweet and savory sauces, relishes, spreads, and seasonings -->  eol
  3 --> Confections --> Desserts, candies, and sweet breads -->  eol
  4 --> Dairy Products --> Cheeses -->  eol
  5 --> Grains/Cereals --> Breads, crackers, pasta, and cereal -->  eol
  6 --> Meat/Poultry --> Prepared meats -->  eol
  7 --> Produce --> Dried fruit and bean curd -->  eol
  8 --> Seafood --> Seaweed and fish -->  eol
  9 --> New category --> New product -->  eol                                    ▼
◄ ▏                                                                            ▶▕
```

Enumerating Views and Showing Their Text

Many Access applications have large collections of queries. As Access developers transition from building solutions with Jet to SQL Server, they are likely to rely heavily on views – particularly with their initial solutions. This is because the Query Designer facilitates building queries graphically, and it is relatively simple to design T-SQL statements that deliver segments of data from a SQL Server database. As the collection of views in an application grows, developers will need efficient means of managing them. This section presents three approaches to tracking and examining the design of the views in an application.

While the Database window will give us an inventory of the view names in a database, we must have an Access project open that connects to that database. In addition, the Database window display may not be optimal for every need that we have. SQL Server has many system stored procedures that provide meta-data about its databases. For example, in Chapter 6 we demonstrate the behavior of such system stored procedures as `sp_tables`, `sp_columns`, and `sp_helpconstraint`.

> *When you run system stored procedures, or reference any database object, you can encounter security issues if your user ID does not have the proper security clearance. In an effort to make the presentation of SQL Server topics easy for Access developers switching to SQL Server, we defer a presentation of security issues until Appendix A. All other material in the book assumes a developer opens database connections with an "sa" login.*

The `sp_tables` system stored procedure can yield useful information about the views in a database. A view is a type of table, and the return set from `sp_tables` includes a column that lets us select just the views in a database. We can further filter the views by their owners. Filtering by owner enables an application to track views by their creator. In addition to user-created views, the `sp_tables` stored procedure also includes system views in its unfiltered output. System-generated views generally have an owner qualifier of INFORMATION_SCHEMA. In addition, three more system views, namely **sysalternates**, **sysconstraints**, and **syssegments**, have an owner qualifier of **dbo**. If we want a list of views from `sp_tables` restricted to those created by users, exclude the system views owned by **dbo**.

In this section, we split the task of enumerating views and showing their text into three subsections:

❑   Enumerating Views

❑   Enumerating Views and Showing Their Text

❑   Outputting to a Text File

Enumerating Views

The following procedure enumerates all the user-created views with an owner qualifier of **dbo** in the database associated with the current project. The procedure filters its return set to include just those created by members of the **sysadmin** group, but not **sysalternatives**, **sysconstraints**, and **syssegments**. When members in this group create an object, it has a **dbo** owner qualifier. Since **sa** is a default member of the **sysadmin** group, any view created with the **sa** login has a **dbo** owner qualifier. The `sp_tables` stored procedure permits us to filter on owner qualifier in the **TABLE_OWNER** column of its return set.

> *Notice that the following code sample uses double quote marks to delimit strings: this is standard practice for VBA developers. SQL Server administrators and developers will be used to a QUOTED IDENTIFIER setting: this setting applies exclusively to SQL Server. It does not affect how you specify strings for VBA when working with ADO objects. Instead, you use the standard practice of delimiting strings with double quote marks as in the following code sample.*

```
Sub enumerate_views_ado()
Dim rst1 As ADODB.Recordset

'Run system stored procedure to return all
'tables associated with the database behind
'the current project
Set rst1 = New ADODB.Recordset
rst1.Open "sp_tables", CurrentProject.Connection, , , adCmdStoredProc

'Loop through system stored procedure return set
'enumerate views with dbo owner qualifier
'and no system names
Do Until rst1.EOF
    If rst1("TABLE_TYPE") = "VIEW" And _
        rst1("TABLE_OWNER") = "dbo" And _
        rst1("TABLE_NAME") <> "sysalternates" And _
        rst1("TABLE_NAME") <> "sysconstraints" And _
        rst1("TABLE_NAME") <> "syssegments" Then
        Debug.Print rst1("TABLE_NAME")
    End If
    rst1.MoveNext
Loop

'Clean up objects
rst1.Close
Set rst1 = Nothing

End Sub
```

The procedure uses a `Recordset` object to capture the return set from `sp_tables`. Notice the `Open` method explicitly specifies an `Options` parameter of `adCmdStoredProc`. This saves the ADO interpreter the trouble of detecting the kind of source parameter our application sends it. Inside a `Do` loop, the sample filters the `sp_tables` return set on three criteria. First, it selects rows with a TABLE_TYPE column value of VIEW. Second, it restricts itself to views with a dbo owner qualifier. Third, it excludes any of the three system views with an owner qualifier of dbo.

Enumerating Views and Their Text

With the assistance of the `sp_helptext` system stored procedure, we can extend the design of the preceding VBA procedure to enumerate not only view names but also the T-SQL statements underlying views. This additional information can precisely define the output that a view will generate. One approach to enumerating view names with their matching T-SQL scripts uses two VBA procedures. The first enumerates the views and formats the overall output for a view, but it does not actually print a view's script. Instead, it passes a view name to the second procedure which determines the text for a view and prints it. When the second procedure returns control to the first procedure, it finishes formatting the output from the current view and loops back to start processing a new view.

```
Sub enumerate_views_and_text()
Dim rst1 As ADODB.Recordset

'Run system stored procedure to return all
'tables associated with the database behind
'the current project
Set rst1 = New ADODB.Recordset
rst1.Open "sp_tables", CurrentProject.Connection, , , adCmdStoredProc

'Loop through system stored procedure return set
'enumerate views with dbo owner qualifier
'and no system names
Do Until rst1.EOF
    If rst1("TABLE_TYPE") = "VIEW" And _
        rst1("TABLE_OWNER") = "dbo" And _
        rst1("TABLE_NAME") <> "sysalternates" And _
        rst1("TABLE_NAME") <> "sysconstraints" And _
        rst1("TABLE_NAME") <> "syssegments" Then
        Debug.Print String(25, "=")
        Debug.Print rst1("TABLE_NAME") & " has the following text: " & vbCrLf
        list_view_text rst1("TABLE_NAME")
        Debug.Print String(25, "=")
        Debug.Print vbCrLf & vbCrLf
    End If
    rst1.MoveNext
Loop

'Clean up objects
rst1.Close
Set rst1 = Nothing

End Sub

Sub list_view_text(view_name As String)
Dim rst1 As New ADODB.Recordset
Dim str1 As String

str1 = "sp_helptext " & "[" & view_name & "]"
rst1.Open str1, CurrentProject.Connection
Debug.Print rst1.GetString

End Sub
```

The `enumerate_views_and_text` procedure starts by filtering the `sp_tables` output in an identical fashion to the preceding two views. We can include other owners or different owners to get more or fewer user-created views in our return set.

```
Sub enumerate_views_and_text()
Dim rst1 As ADODB.Recordset

'Run system stored procedure to return all
'tables associated with the database behind
'the current project
Set rst1 = New ADODB.Recordset
rst1.Open "sp_tables", CurrentProject.Connection, , , adCmdStoredProc

'Loop through system stored procedure return set
'enumerate views with dbo owner qualifier
'and no system names
Do Until rst1.EOF
    If rst1("TABLE_TYPE") = "VIEW" And _
        rst1("TABLE_OWNER") = "dbo" And _
        rst1("TABLE_NAME") <> "sysalternates" And _
        rst1("TABLE_NAME") <> "sysconstraints" And _
        rst1("TABLE_NAME") <> "syssegments" Then
```

After finding a row in the `sp_tables` return set that matches its criteria, the procedure prints a couple of formatting lines for delimiting and identifying the output from a view.

```
Debug.Print String(25, "=")
Debug.Print rst1("TABLE_NAME") & " has the following text: " & vbCrLf
```

Next, it passes the view's name to the `list_view_text` procedure.

```
list_view_text rst1("TABLE_NAME")
```

This nested procedure appends the view name as an argument to the `sp_helptext` system stored procedure and opens a recordset to capture the text for that view. Invoking the `GetString` method on the recordset with the text for a view enables a `Debug.Print` statement to send the view's text to the **Immediate** window.

```
Sub list_view_text(view_name As String)
Dim rst1 As New ADODB.Recordset
Dim str1 As String

str1 = "sp_helptext " & "[" & view_name & "]"
rst1.Open str1, CurrentProject.Connection
Debug.Print rst1.GetString

End Sub
```

Notice that we have had to surround the `view_name` with square brackets – [and] – when we use `sp_helptext`. This is because some table names may contain spaces, and `sp_helptext` does not accept a `view_name` with embedded spaces if it is passed without being enclosed in these brackets.

After `list_view_text` returns control to `enumerate_views_and_text`, a couple of more lines mark the end of the view's output. This process repeats until no unexamined records remain in the return set from `sp_tables`.

```
        Debug.Print String(25, "=")
        Debug.Print vbCrLf & vbCrLf
    End If
    rst1.MoveNext
Loop

'Clean up objects
rst1.Close
Set rst1 = Nothing

End Sub
```

This sample generates very nicely formatted output in the Immediate window. The following screenshot shows an excerpt with a couple of views from the database for this chapter. Notice that view scripts begin with CREATE VIEW followed by the name for a view. After the name, the script always includes the AS keyword. In fact, there are other options that we can specify after the view's name and before AS: one of these is WITH ENCRYPTION. This term encrypts the text of a view statement so that others cannot view our T-SQL code for the view. We can also encrypt a view from the Access Query Designer by clicking the Properties button on the View Design toolbar and selecting the Encrypt view check box. Before encrypting a view by either route, we should have a backup of its script if we anticipate the need to revise it in the future. This weakness is characteristic of encrypting technologies.

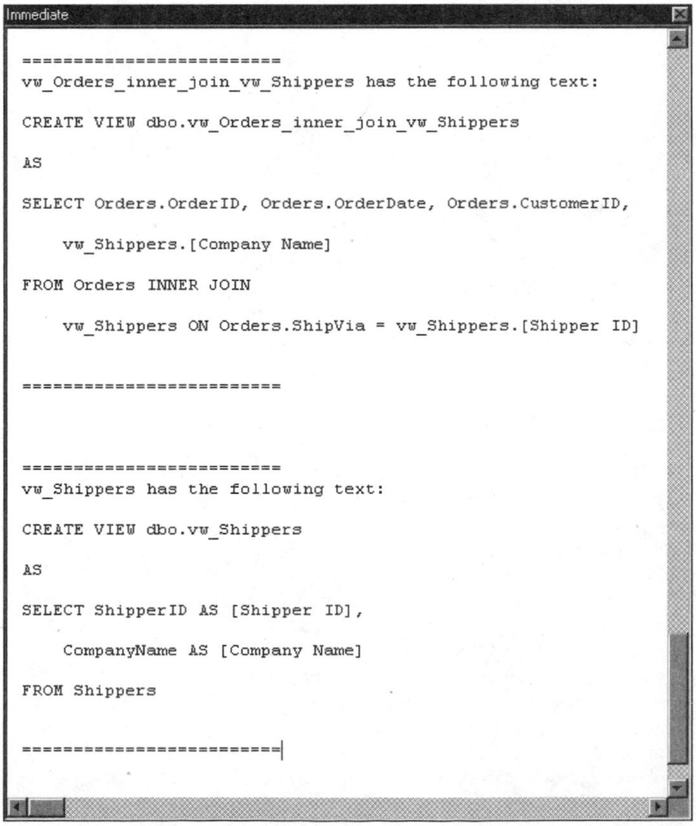

Outputting to a Text File

While the above sample can generate some nicely formatted results, it has one critical weakness: an application can only print a couple of hundred lines in the Immediate window before Access starts scrolling off early output to make room for later output. That's because this window permits the viewing of only about 200 lines. If we have many views in an application, the preceding sample will almost surely fail to show scripts for all views.

One workaround is to print the output to a file – this makes the output more widely available in any event. The next sample application reveals how to print view names and scripts to a text file. This means that anyone who can open a text file, with a package as common as Notepad, can examine the output. Using a text file eliminates the 200-line barrier.

One way to print to a text file with Access is to use a `File System` object. To create an instance of the `File System` object we invoke the `CreateObject` function of VBA with a `ProgID` of `Scripting.FileSystemObject`. The `File System` object's `CreateTextFile` method creates a `Text Stream` object to which an application can write. The `Text Stream` object in a procedure points to a physical file in the file system. The `Write` method for the `Text Stream` object enables an application to insert text into a file. By default, `Text Stream` objects represent characters with an ASCII format. Characters outside the ASCII range of codes appear as squares in the file. Therefore, we exclude these characters from content before inserting a view's script into a `Text Stream` object with the `Write` method. The following sample uses this approach to create a file with the view names and matching text scripts.

```
Sub enumerate_views_and_text2()
Dim rst1 As ADODB.Recordset
Dim str1 As String
Dim rst2 As ADODB.Recordset
Dim str3 As String

'Initialize string and instantiate pointer
str1 = ""
Set rst2 = New ADODB.Recordset

'Run system stored procedure to return all
'tables associated with the database behind
'the current project
Set rst1 = New ADODB.Recordset
rst1.Open "sp_tables", CurrentProject.Connection, , , adCmdStoredProc

'Loop through system stored procedure return set
'store heading for each view
'extract text from view and save in string
'mark end of text for view in string
Do Until rst1.EOF
    If rst1("TABLE_TYPE") = "VIEW" And _
        rst1("TABLE_OWNER") = "dbo" And _
        rst1("TABLE NAME") <> "sysalternates" And _
        rst1("TABLE_NAME") <> "sysconstraints" And _
        rst1("TABLE_NAME") <> "syssegments" Then
        str1 = str1 & String(25, "=") & vbCrLf
        str1 = str1 & rst1("TABLE_NAME") & " has the following text: " & vbCrLf_
        & vbCrLf
        str2 = "sp_helptext " & "[" & rst1("TABLE_NAME") & "]"
        rst2.Open str2, CurrentProject.Connection
```

```
'Replace non-ASCII characters with a single printing cr & lf
    str2 = ""
    str3 = rst2.GetString
    For i = 1 To Len(str3)
        If Not (Asc(Mid(str3, i, 1)) = 10 Or Asc(Mid(str3, i, 1)) = 13) Then
            str2 = str2 & Mid(str3, i, 1)
        Else
            str2 = str2 & vbCrLf
            i = i + 2
        End If
    Next i
    str1 = str1 & str2
    rst2.Close
    str1 = str1 & String(25, "=")
    str1 = str1 & vbCrLf & vbCrLf
    End If
    rst1.MoveNext
Loop

'Write string to a text file
'Update destination for text file on target system
Set fso1 = CreateObject("Scripting.FileSystemObject")
Set tso1 = fso1.CreateTextFile("c:\windows\desktop\testfile.txt", True)
'tso1.WriteLine str1
tso1.Write str1

'Clean up objects
tso1.Close
Set tso1 = Nothing
Set fso1 = Nothing
rst1.Close
Set rst1 = Nothing
Set rst2 = Nothing

End Sub
```

The logic for extracting records from the sp_tables return set is identical to that used in the prior two samples. This sample, the enumerate_views_and_text2 procedure, begins to depart from the prior two samples by collecting the output in the str1 string variable.

```
Sub enumerate_views_and_text2()
Dim rst1 As ADODB.Recordset
Dim str1 As String
Dim rst2 As ADODB.Recordset
Dim str3 As String

'Initialize string and instantiate pointer
str1 = ""
Set rst2 = New ADODB.Recordset

'Run system stored procedure to return all
'tables associated with the database behind
'the current project
Set rst1 = New ADODB.Recordset
rst1.Open "sp_tables", CurrentProject.Connection, , , adCmdStoredProc
```

```
'Loop through system stored procedure return set
'store heading for each view
'extract text from view and save in string
'mark end of text for view in string
Do Until rst1.EOF
    If rst1("TABLE_TYPE") = "VIEW" And _
        rst1("TABLE_OWNER") = "dbo" And _
        rst1("TABLE_NAME") <> "sysalternates" And _
        rst1("TABLE_NAME") <> "sysconstraints" And _
        rst1("TABLE_NAME") <> "syssegments" Then
        str1 = str1 & String(25, "=") & vbCrLf
        str1 = str1 & rst1("TABLE_NAME") & " has the following text: " & vbCrLf_
        & vbCrLf
        str2 = "sp_helptext " & "[" & rst1("TABLE_NAME") & "]"
        rst2.Open str2, CurrentProject.Connection
```

Notice again the use of square brackets around the argument when we use `sp_helptext`.

Before appending a view's script to `str1`, the procedure strips out non-ASCII characters. The non-ASCII characters appeared in the midst of a pair of carriage return/line feed characters. The code removes and replaces this sequence with a single carriage return/line feed sequence. In addition to removing characters that appear as squares in the output, this solution shortens the length of the text file.

```
'Replace non-ASCII characters with a single printing cr & lf
        str2 = ""
        str3 = rst2.GetString
        For i = 1 To Len(str3)
            If Not (Asc(Mid(str3, i, 1)) = 10 Or Asc(Mid(str3, i, 1)) = 13) Then
                str2 = str2 & Mid(str3, i, 1)
            Else
                str2 = str2 & vbCrLf
                i = i + 2
            End If
        Next i
        str1 = str1 & str2
        rst2.Close
        str1 = str1 & String(25, "=")
        str1 = str1 & vbCrLf & vbCrLf
    End If
    rst1.MoveNext
Loop
```

After the code cleans a view's script, it appends the script to `str1`. When the procedure passes through all the records in the return set from `sp_tables`, `str1` contains content in the format of the preceding screenshot, except the lines of T-SQL are single-spaced. Next, the procedure creates a text file and writes `str1` to it.

```
'Write string to a text file
'Update destination for text file on target system
Set fso1 = CreateObject("Scripting.FileSystemObject")
Set tso1 = fso1.CreateTextFile("c:\windows\desktop\testfile.txt", True)
'tso1.WriteLine str1
tso1.Write str1
```

```
'Clean up objects
tso1.Close
Set tso1 = Nothing
Set fso1 = Nothing
rst1.Close
Set rst1 = Nothing
Set rst2 = Nothing

End Sub
```

Notice the pathname of the text file – here we have sent the file to the desktop, so that we can find it easily in this example. Obviously, this pathname can be changed to somewhere more suitable in a real-world situation.

The following screen presents an excerpt from the text file created by the enumerate_views_and_text2 procedure. Notice the file's name is testfile.txt – the preceding example writes this file to the Windows\Desktop folder on the C: drive. The Notepad excerpt from the file shows the scripts for the same two views generated by enumerate_views_and_text and list_view_text procedures above. Notice the view text is identical. The only difference is a shift from double spacing in the Immediate window to single spacing in Notepad. Again, the main advantage of writing to a text file is that we can capture much longer output streams. For example, the output for all the views in testfile.txt is over 500 lines. Even with single spacing, the Immediate window can show just the last 200 of these.

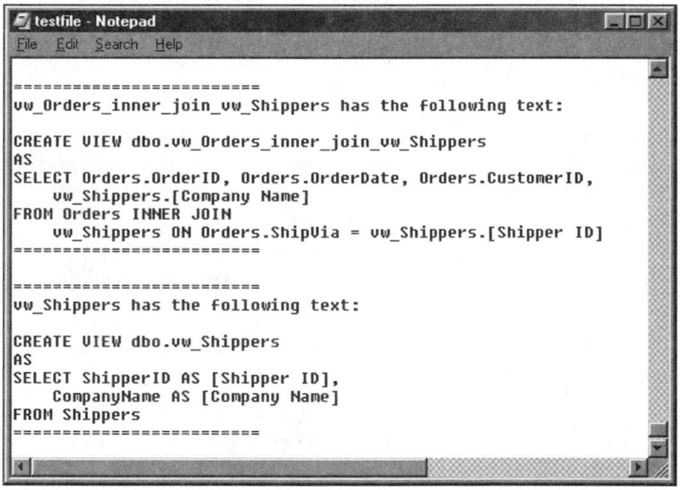

Programmatically Manipulating Views with SQL-DMO

Since SQL-DMO is the object model for SQL Server, it conforms well to typical administrative tasks, such as enumerating and creating objects. SQL-DMO object model is highly hierarchical with a rich tree structure for its objects as opposed to the nearly flat ADO model. In contrast to ADO and T-SQL, SQL-DMO does not readily accommodate data chores such as capturing a view's return set, which we can do with the ADO Recordset object. By learning both SQL-DMO and ADO/T-SQL strengths, we can choose the best approach to each task that we undertake with VBA procedures. This section drills down on performing selected administrative tasks for views with SQL-DMO. It also selectively contrasts SQL-DMO with ADO for performing the same tasks, which we'll look at shortly.

The SQL-DMO model contains a `Views` collection that has as its members the individual views within a database. A database is, in turn, a member of the `Databases` collection. The SQL-DMO `SQLServer` object is the parent object for the `Databases` collection. This object points to a specific SQL Server in the same way that an individual `View` object points at a specific view in a database on a server. The following diagram depicts the graphical relationship of individual views to a `SQLServer` object within the SQL-DMO model.

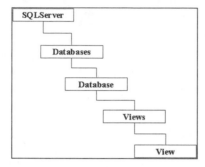

Each of these objects has properties and methods that allow us to manipulate them and the hierarchical elements that it contains. For example, we use the `Connect` method of the `SQLServer` object to point at a particular SQL Server. We can reference individual elements within collections with numeric and literal indexes. For example, `srv1.Databases("foo")` denotes a database named `foo` on the SQL Server at which the `srv1` `SQLServer` object points. If `foo` was the first database in the `Databases` collection on the `srv1` server, we could also refer to it with the following designation: `srv1.Databases (1)`. Since the ordinal position of databases can change with the addition and dropping of databases, we should typically use string designators instead of ordinal designators.

While SQL-DMO is the object model for SQL Server, it is just another library that needs to be referenced when we use it from the VBE window in an Access project. The previous chapter showed how to create a reference manually, and the SQL-DMO appendix demonstrates how to perform the same task programmatically. If we copy an Access `.adp` file from one computer to another, we may need to re-establish the library references. In any event, if there is no reference to the SQL-DMO library in a VBA project that manipulates SQL-DMO object instances, then the procedure will fail.

You can generate the error by failing to set a reference to the Microsoft SQL DMO Object Library. This gains focus in Chapter 1 and Chapter 2.

Having established a reference to the requisite libraries, we need to know what we can do with views. This section shows how to do the following tasks with SQL-DMO:

- ❏ Creating Views using SQL-DMO
- ❏ Enumerating Views using SQL-DMO
- ❏ Listing View Scripts using SQL-DMO

We'll also be comparing ADO and SQL-DMO for listing view scripts, in a section entitled just that: *Comparing ADO and SQL-DMO for Listing View Scripts.*

Creating Views using SQL-DMO

Creating a view requires three elements:

❑ First, we need a view name.

❑ Second, our application must designate a database to contain the view.

❑ Third, a SQL string, or script, is necessary to define the virtual table that the view displays.

Given these elements, it is straightforward to put them together to create a new view with SQL-DMO. This chapter's demonstration of the process with SQL-DMO uses two procedures. The first procedure, called `call_make_a_view` specifies the view name, database, and script. It then calls the second procedure, called `make_a_view`, that which these elements together to make the new view or replace any existing version of the view.

```
Sub call_make_a_view()
Dim dbsname As String
Dim vewname As String
Dim vewtext As String

'Assign text arguments
dbsname = "Chapter5NorthwindCSSQL"
vewname = "foo"
vewtext = "CREATE VIEW foo AS SELECT * FROM Categories"

'Call make a view and pass string arguments
make_a_view dbsname, vewname, vewtext

End Sub


Sub make_a_view(dbsname As String, vewname As String, vewtext As String)
On Error GoTo make_a_view_trap
Dim srv1 As SQLDMO.SQLServer
Dim vew1 As SQLDMO.View

'Connect to server
Set srv1 = New SQLDMO.SQLServer
srv1.Connect "cabxli", "sa", ""

'Instantiate view object, set properties,
'and add it to the database's Views collection
Set vew1 = New SQLDMO.View
vew1.Name = vewname
vew1.Text = vewtext
srv1.Databases(dbsname).Views.Add vew1

make_a_view_exit:
Set vew1 = Nothing
srv1.Close
Set srv1 = Nothing
Exit Sub

make_a_view_trap:
If Err.Number = -2147218790 Then
'traps for object already exists with sqldmo
    srv1.Databases(dbsname).Views(vewname).Remove
    Resume
```

```
    Else
        Debug.Print Err.Number, Err.Description
        Resume make_a_view_exit
    End If

    End Sub
```

The second procedure accepts the three elements as string arguments. Initially, it instantiates a SQLServer object and connects it to the cabxli server. The sample will use the server connection when it attempts to save the view that it creates. While the sample hard codes a server name, our adaptation of this procedure can specify the name of the server similarly to the way the procedure designates the database, the view name, or the view script.

The next step is to define a view and append it to the Views collection of the designated database on the cabxli server. Start this process by instantiating a new view object. Next, assign the Name and Text properties. This step assigns the view's name and script.

The sample attempts to conclude the process by invoking the Add method for the Views collection in the database. If no other view exists with the same name as the proposed view, the procedure succeeds in creating the new view, cleans up objects, and exits. If another view already exists with the same name as proposed view, control then passes to an error trap. When Access detects a duplicate view name error, the procedure invokes the Remove method for the old version from the Views collection. Then, it tries again to attach the view. For any other kind of error, the procedure prints the error number and description before exiting.

Enumerating Views using SQL-DMO

The following procedure demonstrates an approach to enumerating the views in a database with the SQL-DMO model. The procedure starts by declaring both SQLServer and View objects. After instantiating the SQLServer object, the procedure connects it to the cabxli server with a login of sa and a blank password. Then, the procedure specifies a For Each...Next loop to help iterate through the members of a Views collection inside a database on the cabxli server.

When designating a particular element in a collection, such as a database in the Databases collection, identify the element by its name or number and the item's owner. If a member of the sysadmin group created the object, then we can designate the owner as dbo. Recall that the sa login is always a member of the sysadmin group. The procedure completes its reference to the Views collection by appending Views to the end of the object of the Each clause:

```
Sub enumerate_views_sqldmo()
Dim srv1 As SQLDMO.SQLServer
Dim vew1 As SQLDMO.View

'Connect to server
Set srv1 = New SQLDMO.SQLServer
srv1.Connect "cabxli", "sa", ""

'Exclude system objects; compare output
'from this sub with enumerate_views_ado
For Each vew1 In srv1.Databases("Chapter5NorthwindCSSQL", dbo).Views
    If vew1.SystemObject = False Then
        Debug.Print vew1.Name
    End If
Next
```

```
'Clean up
Set vew1 = Nothing
srv1.Close
Set srv1 = Nothing

End Sub
```

The `vew1` object represents a new view on each pass through the `For Each...Next` loop. Our code can use this object to examine and designate properties of the current view in the loop. The `SystemObject` property assumes either of the two Boolean values depending on its status as a user-created view. A `False` value denotes a user-created view. As it turns out, this approach to designating user-created views is cleaner than the one in the samples developed using ADO and T-SQL. For example, this procedure excludes automatically the **sysalternates, sysconstraints,** and **syssegments** views. The `Name` property for a `View` object is a string containing the view's name. By referencing this property for views with a `SystemObject` property of `False`, the `For Each...Next` loop can print the names of those views created by users.

Listing View Scripts using SQL-DMO

This section explores the topic of returning the script for a view. It addresses this topic from several different perspectives:

- ❑ First, it presents a very natural and simple technique that relies on SQL-DMO for printing the script of any view in a database.

- ❑ Second, it contrasts this approach with a roughly analogous technique for ADO/T-SQL that we've already looked at.

This section concludes with a comparison of performance time for listing scripts on SQL Server 7.0, SQL Server 2000, and MSDE servers.

Listing View Scripts

The conformance of the SQL-DMO model to SQL Server and the model's hierarchical nature make it exceptionally easy to list the script for a view. All we have to do is designate the database and view names to specify an individual view. Then, we can use the view's `Text` property to return the script for the view.

The simplicity of this process gives developers a lot of freedom in how they craft a solution based on the technique. The following approach uses a pair of procedures to return the script for a view. The first procedure assigns database and view names to string variables. It then passes these string values to a second function procedure that makes a database connection and collects a view's script from the database connection. The function procedure returns the view's script as its value, which is the argument for a `Debug.Print` statement in the procedure that calls it.

```
Sub print_view_text_sqldmo()
Dim dbsname As String
Dim vewname As String

'Assign string arguments
dbsname = "Chapter5NorthwindCSSQL"
vewname = "list_all_in_categories"
```

```
'Invoke function to return view's
'text inside of a Debug.print statement

Debug.Print text_for_view(dbsname, vewname)

End Sub


Function text_for_view(dbsname As String, vewname As String) As String
Dim srv1 As SQLDMO.SQLServer
Dim vew1 As SQLDMO.View

'Connect to server
Set srv1 = New SQLDMO.SQLServer
srv1.Connect "cabxli", "sa", ""

'Instantiate view object instance, point it
'at a view, return script as function value
Set vew1 = New SQLDMO.View
Set vew1 = srv1.Databases(dbsname, dbo). Views(vewname, dbo)
text_for_view = vew1.Text

'Clean up
Set vew1 = Nothing
srv1.Close
Set srv1 = Nothing

End Function
```

Comparing ADO and SQL-DMO for Listing View Scripts

If SQL-DMO makes this task easy, then just how much harder is it with ADO and T-SQL? The answer depends on our perspective. At the beginning, let's agree that this task is easy no matter how we do it, but the ADO and T-SQL approach is inherently less obvious to someone who is not conversant with T-SQL.

The trick to making the process work with T-SQL is to understand the steps contained within the process:

❑ The sp_helptext system stored procedure can return the script for a view.

❑ Then, we can run a stored procedure with an ADO Command object.

❑ Next, we need to designate that Command object as the source for an Open method of a Recordset object.

❑ Finally, we use the return from the GetString method for the Recordset object as the argument for a Debug.Print statement.

We can shave steps from this process, but if our application uses the ADO approach, then it will always have to deal with both T-SQL and ADO. Some developers can reasonably argue that this is inherently more complicated than dealing with a single object model, namely SQL-DMO, for the same task.

In any event, the following pair of procedures presents some code for printing a single view's script with ADO and T-SQL. Rather than make this approach conform as much as possible to the SQL-DMO approach, this sample reuses the list_view_text procedure from an earlier code sample that listed all the views in a database. This sample reuses the previously developed sample to remind us of the value of reusing code. The outcome from reusing the previously developed procedure is the same as designing a new procedure to conform more closely to the SQL-DMO approach.

```
Sub print_view_text_ado()
Dim vewname As String

'Assign string argument and pass it
'to the sub for printing view text
vewname = "list_all_in_categories"
list_view_text vewname

End Sub
```

```
Sub list_view_text(view_name As String)
Dim rst1 As New ADODB.Recordset
Dim str1 As String

str1 = "sp_helptext " & view_name
rst1.Open str1, CurrentProject.Connection
Debug.Print rst1.GetString

End Sub
```

Another reasonable way to contrast the ADO and SQL-DMO approaches is in terms of output and performance. Again, the comparison depends on some other issues. One significant point is that ADO can use an existing Access project connection to a data source. SQL-DMO cannot share an Access project's connection to its underlying database. The comparison can force a new connection with the ADO and SQL-DMO approaches. However, it will always be true that the ADO approach can take advantage of an Access project connection if there is one (and there will be one much of the time). The following VBA procedure illustrates one way to compare ADO and SQL-DMO for printing view scripts. As you can see, it calls the procedures that we just reviewed. However, it also calls the timer before and after calling each proceedure with SQL-DMO and ADO.

```
Sub compare_print_view_text_times()

Debug.Print "Start SQL-DMO at: " & Now()
print_view_text_sqldmo
Debug.Print "End SQL-DMO at: " & Now()
Debug.Print vbCrLf & vbCrLf
Debug.Print "Start ADO at: " & Now()
print_view_text_ado
Debug.Print "End ADO at: " & Now()

End Sub
```

The performance outcomes vary depending on the system on which the comparison runs. For example, the Immediate window overleaf is from running the compare_print_view_text_times procedure on a Windows 98 computer running a MSDE server. Notice that it takes about 4 seconds to complete the task with SQL-DMO, but ADO completes the task within a second. This screen results from running the procedure immediately after loading the Access project file and confirming its database connection. Rerunning the comparison procedure does not significantly reduce the spread between the SQL-DMO and ADO approaches.

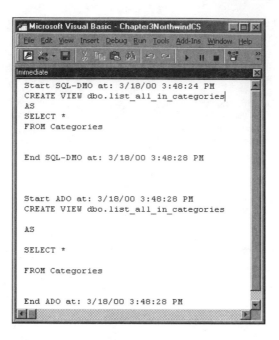

After running the same comparison on another computer running SQL Server 7.0 on Windows NT 4, the ADO speed advantage diminished significantly. This time there was a spread of about one second between the ADO and SQL-DMO approaches. The ADO advantage diminished slightly from the initial spread after repeated runs of the comparison.

The final speed test was on a computer running SQL Server 2000 on Windows 2000 Server. Microsoft claims that it improved the performance of SQL Server 2000 and SQL-DMO on Windows 2000. True to this assertion, there was no difference between ADO and SQL-DMO in this last test environment. This confirms Microsoft's claim, and the strategies Microsoft encourages developers to take. SQL-DMO ran best on the system with the latest operating system and database server. We should also note that the output from SQL-DMO is cleaner with single spacing. In addition, it includes only ASCII characters. This makes the SQL-DMO output more suitable for printing to a text file with the File `System` object than the ADO output.

Summary

Views, like tables, are an essential topic for database developers and users. Seeking to serve diverse audiences, this chapter provides coverage of views at multiple levels. The one common theme is that we learn about SQL Server views from the perspective of an Access project. This background empowers both experienced and beginner SQL Server analysts to build solutions rapidly. On one level, the chapter introduces techniques for creating and using views programmatically. On another level, we learn how to build views graphically. Many advanced and intermediate developers will opt for the programmatic routes. However, these analysts may find the graphical approaches helpful for prototyping strategies when they are not exactly sure what syntax or combination of data sources to use for getting to a specified result.

High-end power users responsible for one or more departmental databases will likely find the graphical tool a more natural approach. However, this audience should also learn about the programmatic techniques because they can reduce database administration burdens and lead to more consistent results. This chapter is rich in examples on how to use the graphical approach. Practically every query discussed for the graphical approach includes at least one sample screen showing how to specify the query for the view. In addition, many query example discussions reference an additional screen depicting excerpts from the return set. Commentary on background techniques precedes all code samples. In addition, there are frequently nearly line-by-line descriptions of how the code samples work. All of these factors combine to make this a chapter in which we have learned a lot about views and how to manippulate them.

So, now that we have a grounding on Views, we can move onto the next topic, which is *Stored Procedures*.

Using Stored Procedures

Stored procedures are the main technology for programmatically controlling access to data within SQL Server. Even if you never intend to program a single stored procedure you will probably be unable to avoid them completely – they are just too useful. It is therefore important to understand how they function and what some of the implications of using and creating stored procedures are.

This chapter begins by describing how to use the simpler system stored procedures that come as part of the SQL Server package, and gives some useful examples such as how to attach and detach databases from a server. Attaching and detaching databases to and from servers are very common tasks, about which many developers have limited knowledge.

The chapter then covers how to create and maintain your own, user-defined stored procedures. As all stored procedures are written in T-SQL (Transact-SQL) the chapter guides you through a review of the language with the emphasis on learning by example. It should be noted however that this will serve only as an introduction to the rich and complex subject that is T-SQL. Even programmers who specialize in this language can take years to uncover all of its intricacies.

After the basic T-SQL statements for selecting and maintaining data, the chapter then moves on to variables and parameters, control-of-flow statements (IF...ELSE statements, CASE functions, and WHILE loops) and using input/output parameters. This section also identifies obstacles to using certain T-SQL statements in Access projects, as well as workarounds. One type of workaround is as simple as using Query Analyzer, and you will discover samples demonstrating this (for example, with a SQL Server 2000 innovation that does not run from Access 2000).

This chapter then looks at how to process stored procedures with VBA and ADO. One of the workarounds to Access 2000 problems with selected T-SQL statements is to program solutions with VBA and ADO.

We've deferred the discussion of triggers until this chapter so that you would have enough T-SQL to learn how to put them to proper use. One trigger sample reveals how to program cascading updates (which is the only way to implement this feature prior to SQL Server 2000).

Finally, the chapter closes with an introduction to user-defined functions – a SQL Server 2000 innovation that offers functionality similar to that of stored procedures.

So, here are all the topics we'll be looking at again:

❑ System Stored Procedures

❑ Used-Defined Stored Procedures

❑ Using VBA and ADO with Stored Procedures

❑ Working with Triggers

❑ User-Defined Functions

Sample Database for this Chapter

The sample database for this chapter is an updated version of the NorthwindCS sample database, the database that ships with Access 2000. The updated version can be found on the Wrox web site. The instructions for downloading and installing this database can be found in Appendix C. The version for the book primarily adds custom stored procedures that help to illustrate the behavior of stored procedures in Access projects. The database's name is Chapter6NorthwindCS. The associated Access project's name is Chapter6NorthwindCS.adp. Several other related code collections exist in Query Analyzer script files (.sql).

What is a Stored Procedure?

All stored procedures begin their life as a collection of T-SQL statements. They are then compiled and, assuming that the compiler agrees with the programmer that the code is syntactically correct, stored as part of a database. Because stored procedures are stored on the server and are pre-compiled they run much faster than T-SQL statements sent on an adhoc basis (statements submitted through the CommandText property of an ADO Command object, for example, or the same statements run from Query Analyzer).

Microsoft has included a large number of built-in, system stored procedures, which we can use as they are or as part of our own, user-defined, procedures. They also serve as useful examples of T-SQL code, which you can use as an aid to learning the language or to help write your own code.

There are various methods for creating user-defined stored procedures but unlike views and database diagrams, stored procedures have no graphical interface. We must always write stored procedures one line at a time using some form of text editor.

T-SQL is a very rich programming environment for SQL Server. Despite the fact that T-SQL has many ways to accomplish tasks, a short list of commands can perform your core database development and management chores. The samples in this chapter demonstrate these statements.

T-SQL may lack some of the fine points common in other programming languages but as it is based on SQL-92 (also known as ANSI-SQL) it is a highly transportable language. Many of the skills and technologies learned here are directly applicable to other Relational Database Management Systems (RDBMSs). It is therefore possible to program solutions that are transportable from one back-end server to another (one running SQL Server and the other running Oracle, say). Note that although this has appeal for large commercial applications that must run with multiple back-end database servers, it is not particularly appropriate for a typical custom Access application that will only run against a SQL Server back-end server. This is because code optimized to run on multiple servers cannot easily take advantage of the unique strengths of SQL Server.

Previously, in Chapter 3, we used Access stored procedure templates as a means of working with T-SQL in Access projects; here we'll revisit them for the purpose of building stored procedures.

Access Project Stored Procedure Templates

An Access project permits us to create new stored procedures using a stored procedure template. Open a new template by highlighting **Stored Procedures** in the **Database** window's **Objects** bar. Then, click **New**. This opens a window like the one that appears below:

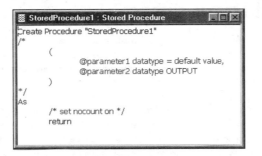

The top line reads **Create Procedure** in blue to show that these words are reserved T-SQL keywords. It is followed by an automatically generated name for the procedure, **StoredProcedure1** in the screen shot above. We can change this name by physically typing over it, or we can choose **File | Save As** and give it a new name in the **Save As** dialog.

> *Create Procedure and Alter Procedure are special SQL commands that initialize the definition of a new stored procedure or modify an existing one. They are described more fully further on when we get to user-defined procedures.*

Immediately after the **Create Procedure** statement is a set of lines delimited by multi-line comment markers /* and */, which are conveniently colored green. SQL Server interprets everything between these two lines as comments. These particular comments remind us of the format for declaring parameters in a stored procedure. A later section in this chapter drills down on that topic.

The **As** keyword follows the comment. Stored procedures always require this keyword. The commented line after **As** in the template can instruct SQL Server not to report the number of rows affected by a stored procedure. In the real world most programmers include this command as a matter of course as the count is rarely required other than for debugging purposes. The default is for SQL Server to report the number of lines affected.

The last line transfers control out of the stored procedure (this can be back to another procedure that called it).

> *Code samples from Books Online and other popular documentation sources routinely type keywords in capital letters. Nevertheless, the Access project stored procedure template deviates from this "all caps" convention. For example, it displays* Create Procedure *and* As *in proper or Title case. In an effort to equip you to use Books Online as well as the documentation in Access Help for stored procedures, this book systematically types all T-SQL keywords in caps, with one significant exception. The exception is that whenever it shows code from an actual stored procedure template, the case for keywords reflects the case as the template displays it.*

Always be careful how you edit the code in a stored procedure template. The Edit menu does not support an Undo command. Therefore, if you get a version of a stored procedure that has some basic functionality, but not all that you want in it, you should consider saving your modified procedure under a new name. You can then make further edits on this new copy as required without destroying the original code. Remember that other procedures you may have written or indeed other programmer's code may rely on the functionality of the old version. Following this practice avoids breaking existing code.

System Stored Procedures

System stored procedures perform a variety of administrative tasks. The System Stored Procedures page of Books Online describes over 400 system stored procedures in twelve major categories. These vary from the barely useful to the absolutely essential. Previous chapters have already touched on a few system procedures but this chapter expands on these.

With so many system stored procedures, the objective of this section is not to demonstrate every, or even most, of the procedures. Instead, we seek to illustrate some of what you can achieve and how to accomplish it with a small subset of system stored procedures. This section's goal is to impress you with the ease of use of these handy, built-in procedures so that you feel confident to explore them more fully on your own. As usual Books Online (the System Stored Procedures page) is a great place to go to after here. There is, however, always space for a warning:

> **Don't alter system stored procedures. If you make changes to a system stored procedure, you could find that product upgrades won't work as they are supposed to. If you really need a stored procedure to do something slightly different from the system stored procedure, write it yourself. We'll show you how to create your own stored procedures shortly.**

The sp_tables System Stored Procedure

The screen opposite shows the relationship between the stored procedure template window and Access projects. The screen depicts a Stored Procedure template window nested within the chapter's sample project Database window:

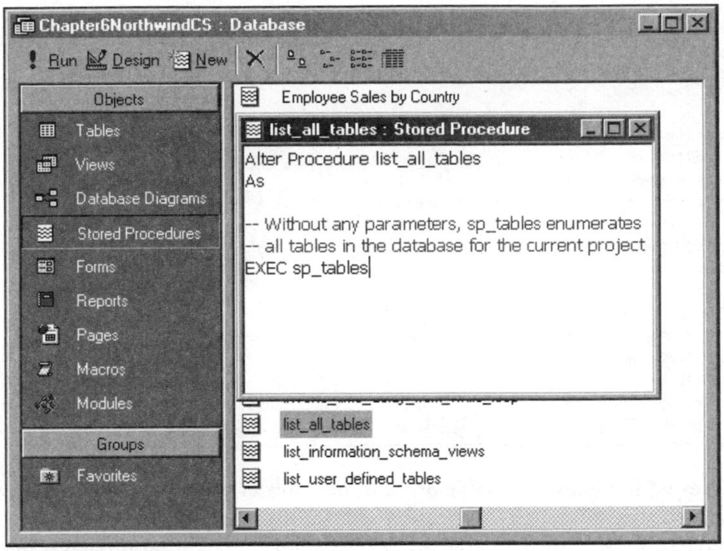

Notice the title bar for the **Stored Procedure** template window matches the selected stored procedure in the **Database** window. Don't worry about the other stored procedures in the **Database** window, we'll show you how to create them shortly. To invoke a system stored procedure from within an Access project stored procedure template simply replace the lines in the template after the **As** keyword with your code to run the system stored procedure. Notice also that the command **Alter Procedure** is used rather than the previous **Create Procedure**. This is the command to modify the existing procedure (**Create Procedure** fails if the procedure already exists). This is explained more fully later on.

The screen above demonstrates the invocation (or "call") for the **sp_tables** system stored procedure. Without any parameters this system stored procedure returns all the objects in a database that can appear in the FROM clause of a SELECT statement. In addition to user-defined tables, this includes user-defined views, INFORMATION_SCHEMA views, and system tables for SQL Server databases.

To run **sp_tables** from within an Access stored procedure you need to embed it in an **EXECUTE** statement, or the shorter **EXEC** statement. Notice the two lines before the one beginning with **EXEC**? These are comment lines, and appear in green. With T-SQL, you can make any single line a comment line by preceding it with two dashes (--). This even works for character sequences within a line – for example, a comment to the right of some code.

The preceding sample is particularly simple. It generates a list of all the tables and views in the database associated with an Access project. For each table or view in a database, it returns five columns of data. As you can see from the next screenshot, these are the table qualifier, which will always be the database name in SQL Server, the table owner, the table name, the table type (for example, system table, table, or view), and a remarks column. SQL Server always leaves this last column null.

If you are only interested in a particular table or view, or a subset of the tables or views, this example for **sp_tables** will give you way too much information as it stands. Chapter 5 shows how to use ADO objects in a VBA procedure to extract a subset from the **sp_tables** return set. This approach is better for developers who feel comfortable with VBA. Chapter 3 presents another sample that extracts information for a particular table. So long as you know the name of the table about which you seek information, this technique is easy. You just follow **sp_tables** with the table's name in single quotes.

Alternatively, the **sp_tables** system stored procedure can take up to four parameters to help you tailor a return set of tables and views to your precise needs.

Parameters for sp_tables

The arguments must be given in the following order after `sp_tables`: `@table_name`, `@table_owner`, `@table_qualifier`, and `@table_type`. Books Online erroneously names them as `@name`, `@owner`, `@qualifier`, and `@type`. You can use wildcards to formulate criteria for subsets of views and tables that your application targets. For example, specifying `'c%'` as the value for `@table_name` would cause **sp_tables** to return all user-defined tables that have names beginning with the letter 'c'. In the case of the **Chapter6NorthwindCS** database, these are **Categories** and **Customers**.

You do not always have to give values for every parameter. For example, you can name a particular table or view without denoting criteria for `@table_owner`, `@table_qualifier`, and `@table_type`. In order to designate any parameter after the first one, you must assign values to all preceding parameters or mark the values as empty by using a comma:

```
sp_tables 'c%',,"'VIEW'".
```

It is also possible to qualify each value with the name of the parameter it belongs to using the syntax `@table_type="VIEW"`, `@table_name='c%'`. Using this method it is possible to omit any values you choose although it is always good practice to present them in the same order.

The `@table_name` and `@table_owner` parameters must appear in single quotes. The `@table_qualifier` for a SQL Server database must always be the name of the database to which your Access project links. This name does not need to appear in quotes. The `@table_type` parameter value (or values – you can specify more than one type of object to be returned) must be in single quotes and that expression must appear within double quotes. For example, `"'VIEW'"` indicates **sp_tables** should return all views in the current database. The arguments are not case sensitive, so you can attain the same results with `"'view'"`. This behavior is consistent with the SQL Server default installation settings. Of course, you can change those settings so that SQL Server is case sensitive.

The following three stored procedure samples illustrate some of the things you can do with sp_tables. In each case, there is a screenshot showing the results, which you can compare with the results for the simple use of sp_tables.

Using sp_tables

The first of these stored procedures demonstrates the syntax for returning all the tables in the current project with the sp_tables command. It uses the % wildcard for the @name and @owner parameters. You will probably remember from our recent discussion on views that the % wildcard means 'any'. You can also use the _ wildcard to represent any single character, and use square brackets ([]) to denote any collection of characters as part of the string, using a leading caret (^) to denote not any of the characters in the square brackets. The @table_qualifier parameter designates the name of the sample database for this chapter. Any other value for this parameter causes the invocation of the stored procedure to fail. By entering `"'table'"` as the value for the last parameter, the stored procedure instructs SQL Server to return just user-defined tables. The two initial wildcard parameters specify that those tables can have any name and owner.

```
Alter Procedure "list_user_defined_tables"
As

--The sp_tables system stored procedure takes as many as
--four parameters. These are:
--    the table name,
--    the table owner,
--    the database name
--    the table type
--
--You can use wildcards, such as _ and %, for selected
--parameters, but not for the database name
--
--The table type parameter must appear in single quotes with
--an outer wrapping of double quotes
EXEC sp_tables '%','%',Chapter6NorthwindCS,"'table'"

return
```

TABLE_QUALIFIER	TABLE_OWNER	TABLE_NAME	TABLE_TYPE	REMARKS
Chapter6NorthwindCS	dbo	Categories	TABLE	
Chapter6NorthwindCS	dbo	CustomerCustomerDemo	TABLE	
Chapter6NorthwindCS	dbo	CustomerDemographics	TABLE	
Chapter6NorthwindCS	dbo	Customers	TABLE	
Chapter6NorthwindCS	dbo	dtproperties	TABLE	
Chapter6NorthwindCS	dbo	Employees	TABLE	
Chapter6NorthwindCS	dbo	EmployeeTerritories	TABLE	
Chapter6NorthwindCS	dbo	Order Details	TABLE	
Chapter6NorthwindCS	dbo	Orders	TABLE	
Chapter6NorthwindCS	dbo	Products	TABLE	
Chapter6NorthwindCS	dbo	Region	TABLE	
Chapter6NorthwindCS	dbo	Shippers	TABLE	
Chapter6NorthwindCS	dbo	Suppliers	TABLE	
Chapter6NorthwindCS	dbo	Territories	TABLE	

list_user_defined_tables : Stored Procedure

Record: 1 of 14

The following code sample illustrates the syntax for reporting information about all the views in the sample database owned by INFORMATION_SCHEMA. Recall that these views give meta-data about the contents of a database. The last parameter designates a return set comprised entirely of views and the second parameter indicates the owner for all views in the return set.

```
Alter Procedure "list_information_schema_views"
As
EXEC sp_tables '%','INFORMATION_SCHEMA',Chapter6NorthwindCS,"'view'"

return
```

Using '%' as the second parameter would cause the stored procedure to return all views from Chapter6NorthwindCS with any owner.

TABLE_QUALIFIER	TABLE_OWNER	TABLE_NAME	TABLE_TYPE	REMARKS
Chapter6NorthwindCS	INFORMATION_SCHEMA	CHECK_CONSTRAINTS	VIEW	
Chapter6NorthwindCS	INFORMATION_SCHEMA	COLUMN_DOMAIN_USAGE	VIEW	
Chapter6NorthwindCS	INFORMATION_SCHEMA	COLUMN_PRIVILEGES	VIEW	
Chapter6NorthwindCS	INFORMATION_SCHEMA	COLUMNS	VIEW	
Chapter6NorthwindCS	INFORMATION_SCHEMA	CONSTRAINT_COLUMN_USAGE	VIEW	
Chapter6NorthwindCS	INFORMATION_SCHEMA	CONSTRAINT_TABLE_USAGE	VIEW	
Chapter6NorthwindCS	INFORMATION_SCHEMA	DOMAIN_CONSTRAINTS	VIEW	
Chapter6NorthwindCS	INFORMATION_SCHEMA	DOMAINS	VIEW	
Chapter6NorthwindCS	INFORMATION_SCHEMA	KEY_COLUMN_USAGE	VIEW	
Chapter6NorthwindCS	INFORMATION_SCHEMA	REFERENTIAL_CONSTRAINTS	VIEW	
Chapter6NorthwindCS	INFORMATION_SCHEMA	SCHEMATA	VIEW	
Chapter6NorthwindCS	INFORMATION_SCHEMA	TABLE_CONSTRAINTS	VIEW	
Chapter6NorthwindCS	INFORMATION_SCHEMA	TABLE_PRIVILEGES	VIEW	
Chapter6NorthwindCS	INFORMATION_SCHEMA	TABLES	VIEW	
Chapter6NorthwindCS	INFORMATION_SCHEMA	VIEW_COLUMN_USAGE	VIEW	
Chapter6NorthwindCS	INFORMATION_SCHEMA	VIEW_TABLE_USAGE	VIEW	
Chapter6NorthwindCS	INFORMATION_SCHEMA	VIEWS	VIEW	

Record: 1 of 17

You can readily create stored procedures that provide multiple return sets of meta-data about the objects in a database with the **sp_tables** system stored procedure. The following sample creates three return sets about the views in the **Chapter6NorthwindCS** database. The first one enumerates all views with an owner of **dbo**. The second return set lists the views owned by INFORMATION_SCHEMA. The third return set includes all views with any owner. When you run this procedure from an Access project, it displays just the first return set. You must run a VBA procedure with ADO objects to present all three return sets. A subsequent section in this chapter will demonstrate how to accomplish this task.

```
Alter Procedure "create_multiple_return_sets_from_sp_tables"
As

--This sample returns three different return sets with meta data
--about views in the Chapter6NorthwindCS database
EXEC sp_tables '%','dbo',Chapter6NorthwindCS,"'view'"
EXEC sp_tables '%','INFORMATION_SCHEMA',Chapter6NorthwindCS,"'view'"
EXEC sp_tables '%', '%',Chapter6NorthwindCS,"'view'"

Return
```

TABLE_QUALIFIER	TABLE_OWNER	TABLE_NAME	TABLE_TYPE	REMARKS
Chapter6NorthwindCS	dbo	Alphabetical list of products	VIEW	
Chapter6NorthwindCS	dbo	Category Sales for 1997	VIEW	
Chapter6NorthwindCS	dbo	convert_datediff_sample	VIEW	
Chapter6NorthwindCS	dbo	Current Product List	VIEW	
Chapter6NorthwindCS	dbo	Customer and Suppliers by City	VIEW	
Chapter6NorthwindCS	dbo	Invoices	VIEW	
Chapter6NorthwindCS	dbo	Order Details Extended	VIEW	
Chapter6NorthwindCS	dbo	Order Subtotals	VIEW	
Chapter6NorthwindCS	dbo	Orders Qry	VIEW	
Chapter6NorthwindCS	dbo	Product Sales for 1997	VIEW	
Chapter6NorthwindCS	dbo	Products Above Average Price	VIEW	
Chapter6NorthwindCS	dbo	Products by Category	VIEW	
Chapter6NorthwindCS	dbo	Quarterly Orders	VIEW	
Chapter6NorthwindCS	dbo	Sales by Category	VIEW	
Chapter6NorthwindCS	dbo	Sales Totals by Amount	VIEW	
Chapter6NorthwindCS	dbo	Summary of Sales by Quarter	VIEW	
Chapter6NorthwindCS	dbo	Summary of Sales by Year	VIEW	
Chapter6NorthwindCS	dbo	sysalternates	VIEW	
Chapter6NorthwindCS	dbo	sysconstraints	VIEW	
Chapter6NorthwindCS	dbo	syssegments	VIEW	

Record: 1 of 20

System Stored Procedures for Attaching and Detaching Databases

As we've already seen from Chapter 2, you can attach and detach databases to and from your SQL Server (or MSDE). Previously, we showed you how to do this for the sample databases you can download. However, as you will see and have probably guessed already, there are other uses for this capability.

The system stored procedure sp_attach_db and it's sister procedure sp_detach_db let you attach or detach database files to or from a server with a single command. When you need to attach some database files in a hurry, this system stored procedure is one you need to know. Many situations call for attaching and detaching databases. Here are three more situations, to illustrate the benefits of this capability.

First, developers frequently work on a database on more than one server. When there is no network connection between the computers, you have to manually detach a database from its server, physically transport the data to the other computer and then re-attach it to the new server.

Second, attaching a database is a cheap and easy way to deploy a SQL Server application based on an Access project. This scenario calls for shipping a client community both the database and .adp files for an application. A local administrator can run a stored procedure to attach the database to the local server and then e-mail, or otherwise distribute, the .adp file to registered users.

Third, attaching databases is one way to recover your databases as you recover from a major system crash. If a crash requires re-installing SQL Server or MSDE, you will create new system files, and those system files will no nothing about your old data. However, you can run a system stored procedure and instantly recover those files so long as they are not damaged. This is useful because it is unlikely that any tape backup you may have will be totally up-to-date. Re-attaching the databases means you may only lose the changes made when the system crashed.

User-Defined Stored Procedures

We have already seen how to create simple user-defined stored procedures (we will just refer to them as procedures from now on to save time) using the Access project Stored Procedure Template earlier in this chapter in order to invoke System Stored Procedures. We will now build on this knowledge to help create more complex procedures with almost any functionality we desire.

Generally speaking there are six broad classes of functionality that procedures can provide:

❑ First, you can run system stored procedures. We have already covered these earlier in the chapter.

❑ Second, you can perform select queries, such as those in views. One critical distinction between a view and a stored procedure is that stored procedures permit the inclusion of an ORDER BY clause in SELECT statements.

❑ Third, stored procedures process INSERT, UPDATE, and DELETE statements to enable tables to be modified.

❑ Fourth, stored procedures can accept parameters. This enables an application to vary the behavior of a stored procedure at run time. In addition, stored procedures can pass back parameter values and/or a return value. This allows procedures to be "nested" (procedures can call other procedures that can call other procedures, that can … etc.) with information being passed between the various levels as required.

❑ Fifth, your applications can process local and global variables that store data to help select, insert, update, and delete records as well as manipulate input and output parameters.

❑ Sixth, you can code stored procedures with control-of-flow statements, such as IF...ELSE and WHILE loops, to allow the conditional execution of statements and/or designate the order of execution.

We've come across many of these SQL statements before, when we looked at tables and views. Here we'll briefly consolidate our knowledge before building on it and digging deeper into the language.

SELECT

SELECT queries are the workhorse of database management systems. You can use these queries to return raw data to an application or to pre-process data through filters, grouping, or computations. Chapter 5 gave detailed coverage of SELECT query syntax and ways of manipulating views with T-SQL. Procedures can also run SELECT queries. One important advantage is that procedures allow the ORDER BY clause. This feature permits a query to pass back a return set in a specific order. Beyond that, stored procedures have other, important advantages over simple Views. They can even pass back multiple return sets (or **recordsets**) with differing rows if required. Multiple return sets are covered later in the section about using VBA. First a very basic example:

```
Alter Procedure "categories_products"
As


--A list of categories
SELECT * FROM Categories


Return
```

This doesn't do anything very exiting, it just returns the contents of the **Categories** table. Let's spice it up a bit with a JOIN:

```
Alter Procedure "categories_products_join"
As

SELECT Categories.CategoryName, Products.ProductName,
    Products.QuantityPerUnit, Products.UnitPrice
FROM Categories INNER JOIN
    Products ON Categories.CategoryID = Products.CategoryID

Return
```

Note that because a column named **CategoryID** appears in both the **Categories** table and the **Products** table, it is necessary to precede each row reference with the table name so it is clear which is which. The following screen shows the Recordset that is returned. Notice that the rows contain a combination of products from several different categories. The data are not sorted on any column.

CategoryName	ProductName	QuantityPerUnit	UnitPrice
Beverages	Chai	10 boxes x 20 bags	$18.00
Beverages	Chang	24 - 12 oz bottles	$19.00
Condiments	Aniseed Syrup	12 - 550 ml bottles	$10.00
Condiments	Chef Anton's Cajun Seasoning	48 - 6 oz jars	$22.00
Condiments	Chef Anton's Gumbo Mix	36 boxes	$21.35
Condiments	Grandma's Boysenberry Spread	12 - 8 oz jars	$25.00
Produce	Uncle Bob's Organic Dried Pears	12 - 1 lb pkgs.	$30.00
Condiments	Northwoods Cranberry Sauce	12 - 12 oz jars	$40.00
Meat/Poultry	Mishi Kobe Niku	18 - 500 g pkgs.	$97.00
Seafood	Ikura	12 - 200 ml jars	$31.00
Dairy Products	Queso Cabrales	1 kg pkg.	$21.00
Dairy Products	Queso Manchego La Pastora	10 - 500 g pkgs.	$38.00
Seafood	Konbu	2 kg box	$6.00
Produce	Tofu	40 - 100 g pkgs.	$23.25
Condiments	Genen Shouyu	24 - 250 ml bottles	$15.50

categories_products_and_join : Stored Procedure. Record: 15 of 77

Now let's add an ORDER BY clause, to make the results easier to read:

```
Alter Procedure "categories_products_join_order_by_categoryID"
As

SELECT Categories.CategoryName, Products.ProductName,
    Products.QuantityPerUnit, Products.UnitPrice
FROM Categories INNER JOIN
    Products ON Categories.CategoryID = Products.CategoryID
ORDER BY Categories.CategoryName

Return
```

This clause lets you designate a specific order for the return set. In this case the data are sorted by **CategoryID**. Again, we must explicitly specify the table name along with the **CategoryID** column reference in the ORDER BY clause. Using a column of type numeric rather than type string as the specified sort field generates a return set more quickly as the server does not have to compare every character in each row to decide on the ordering. When you have a choice, choose the column with numerical values.

263

> **Recall that you can use the Query Designer to build graphical T-SQL `SELECT` query statements. Then, you can cut and paste the T-SQL from the SQL window in View Query Designer to the space after the `AS` clause of a stored procedure template. If your application requires an `ORDER BY` clause, insert one after the pasted code from the View Query Designer's SQL window.**

The following screen presents the results returned using the `ORDER BY` clause. Notice that this time the `Recordset` appears in ascending alphabetical order by the CategoryName column. There is no specific indicator in the `ORDER BY` clause which way to sort, but the implicit order (unless an index in SQL Server designates otherwise) is ascending. If you prefer, follow a column name with `ASC` in the `ORDER BY` clause to declare explicitly an ascending sort order. When you want to make a return set appear in descending order, replace `ASC` with `DESC`.

categories_products_join_order_by_categoryID : Stored Procedure

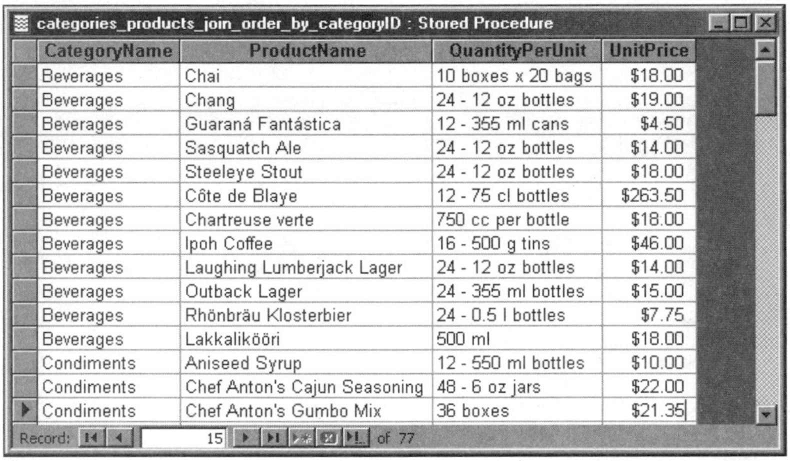

CategoryName	ProductName	QuantityPerUnit	UnitPrice
Beverages	Chai	10 boxes x 20 bags	$18.00
Beverages	Chang	24 - 12 oz bottles	$19.00
Beverages	Guaraná Fantástica	12 - 355 ml cans	$4.50
Beverages	Sasquatch Ale	24 - 12 oz bottles	$14.00
Beverages	Steeleye Stout	24 - 12 oz bottles	$18.00
Beverages	Côte de Blaye	12 - 75 cl bottles	$263.50
Beverages	Chartreuse verte	750 cc per bottle	$18.00
Beverages	Ipoh Coffee	16 - 500 g tins	$46.00
Beverages	Laughing Lumberjack Lager	24 - 12 oz bottles	$14.00
Beverages	Outback Lager	24 - 355 ml bottles	$15.00
Beverages	Rhönbräu Klosterbier	24 - 0.5 l bottles	$7.75
Beverages	Lakkalikööri	500 ml	$18.00
Condiments	Aniseed Syrup	12 - 550 ml bottles	$10.00
Condiments	Chef Anton's Cajun Seasoning	48 - 6 oz jars	$22.00
Condiments	Chef Anton's Gumbo Mix	36 boxes	$21.35

Record: 15 of 77

You can designate multiple columns in an `ORDER BY` clause. The return set from the stored procedure appears sorted according to the sequence of columns in the `ORDER BY` clause. The following stored procedure contains a pair of columns in the `ORDER BY` clause of its `SELECT` query. Although Categories.CategoryName will be ordered ascending by default it is good practice to explicitly specify `ASC` to avoid confusion with the UnitPrice column following for which we have specified a `DESC` order.

```
Alter Procedure categories_products_join_order_by_categoryID_unitprice_desc
As

SELECT Categories.CategoryName, Products.ProductName,
    Products.QuantityPerUnit, Products.UnitPrice
FROM Categories INNER JOIN
    Products ON Categories.CategoryID = Products.CategoryID
ORDER BY Categories.CategoryName Asc, UnitPrice Desc

Return
```

The following screen illustrates the return set:

CategoryName	ProductName	QuantityPerUnit	UnitPrice
Beverages	Côte de Blaye	12 - 75 cl bottles	$263.50
Beverages	Ipoh Coffee	16 - 500 g tins	$46.00
Beverages	Chang	24 - 12 oz bottles	$19.00
Beverages	Chai	10 boxes x 20 bags	$18.00
Beverages	Steeleye Stout	24 - 12 oz bottles	$18.00
Beverages	Chartreuse verte	750 cc per bottle	$18.00
Beverages	Lakkalikööri	500 ml	$18.00
Beverages	Outback Lager	24 - 355 ml bottles	$15.00
Beverages	Sasquatch Ale	24 - 12 oz bottles	$14.00
Beverages	Laughing Lumberjack Lager	24 - 12 oz bottles	$14.00
Beverages	Rhönbräu Klosterbier	24 - 0.5 l bottles	$7.75
Beverages	Guaraná Fantástica	12 - 355 ml cans	$4.50
Condiments	Vegie-spread	15 - 625 g jars	$43.90
Condiments	Northwoods Cranberry Sauce	12 - 12 oz jars	$40.00
Condiments	Sirop d'érable	24 - 500 ml bottles	$28.50

Record: 15 of 77

Working with Ascending and Descending Indexes

SQL Server 2000 updated the CREATE INDEX statement to permit the designation of a sort order for an index. This feature can speed sorts with multiple indexes where the order for the indexes is different, and the data source for the sort is very large. If your application regularly sorts a large data source with multiple columns in different directions, this feature can dramatically speed up the availability of return sets. If your application sorts only on single columns, there is no particular advantage to the feature. This is because SQL Server sorts equally fast in either direction for an index based on a single column.

It takes two steps to take advantage of ascending and descending indexes. The first step to taking advantage of this new feature is to create an index on two or more columns. Set the sort order for at least one column to ASC and the sort order for one or more other columns to DESC. The second step is to run a stored procedure, such as the one in the preceding sample. This stored procedure uses the ASC setting for the first column and DESC for the second column. Because the sort orders for the columns vary, this query can take advantage of ascending and descending indexes.

This technology offers a barrier for Access 2000 developers. They cannot build or edit the ascending and descending indexes from inside an Access 2000 stored procedure template for SQL Server. One solution is to write a script that runs in Query Analyzer for creating the indexes. Once a script exists that creates a stored procedure for generating two or more indexes, you can run the stored procedure from the Database window in an Access project but in order to modify it you would need to return to the Query Analyzer (using Alter Procedure).

The following script is for use in Query Analyzer. It creates an index in the Products table for a local Northwind database version. The first statement establishes a reference to that database. Next, it drops the old versions of the index and stored procedure for creating the index if either already exists. Next, it starts a stored procedure that uses the CREATE INDEX statement to prepare a non-clustered index with an ascending order for the CategoryID columns and a descending order for the UnitPrice column. The stored procedure closes by printing the current list of indexes for the products table. This offers a means to verify the proper operation of the script. The list of indexes should include the one that we just attempted to correct.

```
USE Northwind
IF EXISTS (SELECT name FROM sysindexes
    WHERE name = 'CatID_up_unitprice_down')
    DROP INDEX products.CatID_up_unitprice_down
IF EXISTS (SELECT name FROM sysobjects
    WHERE name = 'create_categoryID_asc_unitprice_desc_indx'
    AND type = 'P')
    DROP PROCEDURE create_categoryID_asc_unitprice_desc_indx
GO

CREATE PROCEDURE create_categoryID_asc_unitprice_desc_indx
As

--Create an index with an ascending order for CategoryID
--and a descending order for UnitPrice
--Requires SQL Server 2000
--Do not edit stored procedure template in Access 2000
CREATE NONCLUSTERED INDEX CatID_up_unitprice_down
    ON Products (CategoryID, UnitPrice DESC)

--Print help for indexes belonging to the Products table
EXEC sp_helpindex 'Products'
GO
```

The preceding Query Analyzer script generates a stored procedure named
create_categoryID_asc_unitprice_desc_indx. If you open an Access project on a local version of the
Northwind database, it will include the stored procedure created by the script. The following script shows the
resulting translation of the original script for the stored procedure. Notice the version inside the Access
project removes the USE and GO statements as well as the two IF EXISTS statements. In addition, the
CREATE PROCEDURE statement changes to ALTER PROCEDURE. Critically, the CREATE INDEX statement
remains the same.

While you can examine the stored procedure in an Access 2000 project stored procedure template, any edits
to the script in the template will cause the removal of the ASC and DESC sort order settings for the column
indexes. You will not notice the removal of the sort order settings until you actually open and save the
procedure. To recover from this loss of sort order settings for indexes, you must return to Query Analyzer
and perform edits from there.

```
Alter PROCEDURE create_categoryID_asc_unitprice_desc_indx
As

--Create an index with an ascending order for CategoryID
--and a descending order for UnitPrice
--Requires SQL Server 2000
--Do not edit stored procedure template in Access 2000
CREATE NONCLUSTERED INDEX CatID_up_unitprice_down
    ON Products (CategoryID, UnitPrice DESC)
--Print help for indexes belonging to the Products table
EXEC sp_helpindex 'Products'
```

The following screenshot presents the enumeration of indexes for the Products table created by running the
sp_helpindex system stored procedure from the create_categoryID_asc_unitprice_desc_indx procedure.
Notice that the last index has the name CatID_up_unitprice_down. Furthermore, the UnitPrice element in
the index has a minus sign after it to denote a descending order. The CategoryID element in the index is
implicitly ascending.

INSERT, UPDATE, DELETE, and TRUNCATE

We have already seen these statements in Chapter 3. However, we will quickly cover the basics here again to consolidate what we already know, as these are important statements that we will use over and over again. Feel free to skip this section, if you wish.

The INSERT, UPDATE, DELETE, and TRUNCATE T-SQL statements allow you to modify the information in a database. This section illustrates the use of these statements with selected samples that demonstrate core database maintenance functions.

The INSERT statement adds data to a table. You can use this command with the CREATE TABLE statement to define a table and then populate it with values. Additionally, you can add records individually or as a set from another table. The other table can be in the same SQL Server database, on another computer, or even in another database package, such as Access.

The UPDATE statement permits you to change the values in a table. You can assign changes globally across all the records in a table or any subset that you define using the FROM clause. You can also use INNER JOIN and WHERE clauses, and sub-queries to restrict the range of records to which an UPDATE applies.

The DELETE statement removes one or more records from a table. As with the UPDATE statement you can define a subset of records to delete using the FROM clause, various joins, and sub-queries.

The TRUNCATE statement removes all records from a table and can be used as a faster alternative to DELETE.

INSERT

The INSERT statement can have up to three parts.

❑   First, you must specify a target table to accept the new values. You can optionally include the INTO keyword between INSERT and the table name.

❑   Second, you can optionally designate a list of columns into which to INSERT values. If you do not include a column list, the INSERT statement assigns values to the table's columns in the order than they appear in the table, excluding any column with an IDENTITY property setting. It is considered very bad practice not to include a column list, however, as any changes to the structure of the table will cause errors (or even worse, values to be inserted into incorrect columns).

❑ The third part (a VALUES list, or a substitute such as a SELECT statement to reference rows from another table or view) designates the specific values to add to columns in the new record. Including a column list also allows the compiler to check that you have included the correct number of values and that they are of the correct types.

The following stored procedure script demonstrates how to use the three parts of the INSERT statement. It also optionally removes the **my_employees** table from a database and adds a new empty version of the table. The table has five columns. The first of these is an IDENTITY column with a seed value of 0 and increment of 2. The IDENTITY column performs a function similar to an autonumber column in a traditional Access database file in that values are guaranteed to be unique within that column. This sample demonstrates some of its special flexibility. Recall that autonumber columns always start with 1 and increment by 1. The remaining four columns are variable length columns for holding string data. They have a VARCHAR data type declaration.

```
Alter Procedure insert_into_my_employees
As

--Drop previous version of my_employees, if it exists
IF EXISTS(SELECT name FROM sysobjects WHERE name='my_employees')
    DROP TABLE my_employees

--Create a new version of my_employees table
CREATE TABLE my_employees
(
employeeID int IDENTITY(0,2) NOT NULL Primary Key,
firstname VARCHAR(10),
lastname VARCHAR (20),
homephone VARCHAR (24),
source VARCHAR (20)
)

--Use a column list to explicitly state which values go with which columns
INSERT my_employees (firstname, lastname, homephone, source)
    VALUES('Tom', 'Jones', '123.456.7890', 'input value')
INSERT my_employees (firstname, lastname, homephone, source)
    VALUES('Terry', 'Johnson', '123.987.7890', 'input value')
INSERT my_employees (firstname, lastname, homephone, source)
    VALUES('Tony', 'Hinton', '123.456.8765', 'input value')

--Use column list to give values in a different order
INSERT my_employees (homephone, source, lastname, firstname)
    VALUES('123.345.1234', 'input value', 'Binton', 'Tomie')

Return
```

After creating a new version of the **my_employees** table, the procedure invokes an INSERT statement to add the first record to the table. This statement lists the columns into which to add values. Since they appear in the same order as in the table, the column list is not strictly necessary but it is good practice to include one. If the elements of the VALUES list that appears next had values in a different order from the one in the CREATE TABLE statement, then the column list would definitely be required to map VALUE list items to matching table columns. The remaining three INSERT statements add three more rows to the **my_employees** table.

The insert_into_my_employees stored procedure creates a my_employees table with five columns and four rows. This table appears in the following screenshot. To see this for yourself you need to go to Tables in the Database window and press *F5* to refresh the table list (or choose View I Refresh) so that we can see the new table. Then you can open it to see the newly inserted data. No matter how many times you run the procedure or what other procedures you run that affect the my_employees table, the stored procedure will always create the same result that appears below. This is because the stored procedure removes any prior version of the table and adds values to an empty version of the table.

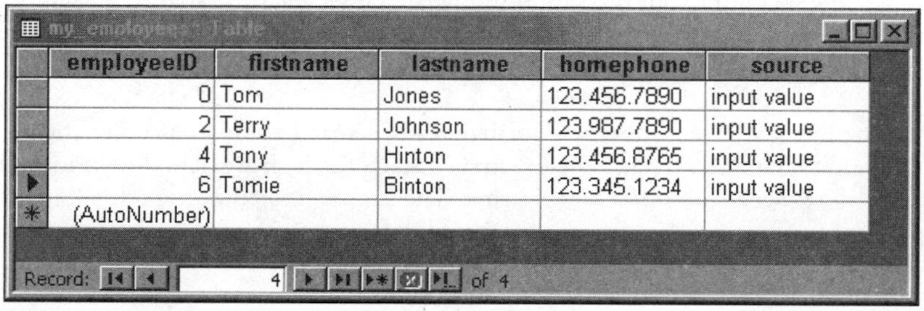

As you can see, the insert_into_my_employees stored procedure actually obliterates not only any prior table values, but also the table as an object in the database. Before taking such a drastic action in an operational system, you may care to archive the values to another table.

The following stored procedure script reveals how to use the INSERT statement to help accomplish this task. It copies four columns of the my_employees table to the my_employees_2 table. The sample, which doesn't copy the employeeID values, is easily adaptable to transfer all the columns. The INSERT statement in this sample uses a SELECT statement instead of a VALUES list to specify the values to INSERT into a table. Otherwise, its syntax is similar to the original sample.

```
Alter Procedure "insert_into_my_employees_2_from_my_employees"
As


--Conditionally drop a table, before creating a new version of it
IF EXISTS(SELECT table_name FROM INFORMATION_SCHEMA.TABLES
    WHERE table_name='my_employees_2')
    DROP TABLE my_employees_2

CREATE TABLE my_employees_2
(
employeeID int IDENTITY(0,2) NOT NULL Primary Key,
firstname varchar(10),
lastname varchar(20),
homephone varchar(24)
)

--Select just a subset of my_employees column values
--for my_employees_2
INSERT my_employees_2
SELECT firstname,lastname, homephone FROM my_employees

Return
```

In the real world you would probably only want to use INSERT like this to archive part of a table (all rows with dates older than 3 months, say).

Collecting Information using SELECT

We can use the techniques we've just looked at to build a table that collects information from multiple sources. For example, our application could use the INSERT statement to append rows to the my_employees tables based on the records in the Customers table. These new records add to those already in the table from the prior sample that created the table and added four rows.

One barrier to this appending operation is that the contactname field from the Customers table has first and last names in a single column, but the my_employees table assigns first and last names to separate columns. By applying a mix of SQL Server string functions, a new sample extracts values for the first and last names so they can be appended to separate columns in the my_employees table.

The PATINDEX function searches for the first occurrence of a string value in another string. The PATINDEX function starts counting characters from 1 for the first character in a string. The function returns a value of 0 when it does not find a search string in a target string. The sample uses the PATINDEX function's return value to find the position of the space separating the first and last names in the contactname column of the Customers table.

The LEFT function extracts a given number of characters from the left end of a string. The next sample uses LEFT to extract one less character than the value of the position of the blank separating the first and last names (one less in order to ignore the space character itself). It captures the last name as the difference between the total length of the string in the contactname column minus the return value from PATINDEX. The LEN function counts the total characters in a string.

The following script shows the code in the sample that appends records from the Customers table to the my_employees table. The core of the script is the INSERT statement. Notice the script depends on a SELECT statement to designate the values to append to the columns. It is not essential to rename columns so that they match, but their data specifications must match those in the table into which you are attempting to INSERT values. For example, you cannot INSERT a string with 11 characters into a column that is set to hold strings of up to 10 characters – you should always make sure that the target table will be able to accept the source data or you may end up with unexpected results! Notice that the last column in the SELECT statement specifies the source for the records that it adds to the my_employees table.

```
Alter Procedure insert_into_my_employees_from_customers
As


--Notice the use of string functions to extract first and last names
--from the contactname column values
INSERT my_employees
SELECT left(contactname, PATINDEX('% %',contactname)-1) AS 'firstname',
    right(contactname, len(contactname)-PATINDEX('% %',contactname))
    AS 'lastname', phone, 'from customers'
FROM customers


Return
```

The following screenshot shows an excerpt from the my_employees table after the appending of the records from customers. The status bar shows 95 records in the table. This results from the initial four records that created the my_employees table, and the 91 more records from the customers tables that the immediately preceding sample appended. The source column denotes the origin for each row. The first four rows have input value in the source column since an INSERT statement added them. The remaining records have from customers in the source column because another INSERT statement appended these records from that table.

INSERT statements are not limited to working with tables from the current database. For example, you can add records to a table in the current database from another database on a different SQL Server. Access stored procedure templates do not permit the processing of distributed queries against other SQL Server data sources, and views only permit SELECT queries for SQL Server data sources from another server. Therefore, you must run INSERT statements in Query Analyzer if they draw data from another SQL Server.

UPDATE

The UPDATE statement permits you to revise existing records in a database. In order for this statement to work, you must unambiguously identify the source. Failing to do so will cause an UPDATE statement to fail so that none of the other UPDATE statements occur.

The UPDATE statement can have up to three parts. The first two of these are mandatory and the third is optional. The statement starts unsurprisingly with the keyword UPDATE followed by the name of the source table that you are going to UPDATE. The second part (most programmers list it on a separate line for clarity) begins with the SET keyword followed by an expression that assigns a new value to a column in the data source identified by the UPDATE keyword.

The third part (also traditionally given on a new line) designates a subset of records for which to apply the UPDATE. If you want your UPDATE to apply to all the records in a data source, then simply exclude this optional part of the UPDATE statement. Otherwise, build WHERE clause arguments that target just the records to which you want to apply the expression following the SET keyword.

```
Alter Procedure update_employees
As

UPDATE my_employees
    SET source = 'NA'

Return
```

The procedure below modifies the source column to read NA. As it has no WHERE clause it will affect all records in the my_employees table.

The next procedure above modifies the source column to read customers but only for those records that have from customers as their current source. This procedure won't have any impact on the table if run after the preceding one.

```
Alter Procedure update_employees
As
```

```
UPDATE my_employees
   SET source = 'customers'
   WHERE source = 'from customers'

Return
```

Notice that if you run this procedure twice in a row then the second run will not modify any records as there will be none remaining with source set to from customers. This is a simple observation but one that, if missed, can cause much confusion!

Single Records

A very common requirement is for a **singleton update**, that is an update of a single record. Obviously, in order to accomplish this you need to be able to uniquely specify the record concerned in the WHERE clause. Here we use a combination of the firstname and lastname columns.

```
Alter Procedure update_employees
As

UPDATE my_employees
   SET source = 'VIP customer'
   WHERE firstname = 'Tony' AND lastname = 'Hinton'

Return
```

Successfully applying UPDATE statements involves mastery of operators, functions, and WHERE clause logic. The operators and functions are important for specifying the expression that follows SET. Your advanced understanding of WHERE clause logic is important for properly restricting the application of the expression to just the records that you want. Unlike with Access database file applications, there is no built-in, graphical way with Access projects to determine to which records an expression will apply. Unfortunately it is all too easy to get the subset wrong and to update no records at all (or worse update the wrong records). A good technique to help avoid this is to first build a SELECT statement using Query Analyzer that targets the same subset. It is then easy to run this and check that your selection logic is correct without affecting any records. When you are happy with it simply paste the code into your UPDATE statement.

The following procedure applies a 10 percent price increase just for seafood products. The FROM and WHERE clauses identify the subset of records for which to apply the price expression. The INNER JOIN clause merges the Categories and Products tables. This is necessary to give individual rows in the Products table a handle that enables the selection of just seafood products. The WHERE clause grabs hold of the handle and restricts the application of the expression to just seafood products. The sample uses the categoryname column to improve readability. In a practical application for a reasonably large table, the categoryID column will be superior since it contains numeric instead of string values, which we told you earlier makes it easier and faster for SQL Server to sort.

```
Alter Procedure raise_seafood_prices_10_percent
As

--Raise just seafood prices by 10 percent
UPDATE products
SET unitprice = unitprice*1.1
FROM categories INNER JOIN
   products ON categories.categoryID = products.categoryID
```

```
WHERE products.categoryname='seafood'

Return
```

DELETE

The DELETE statement is used to remove records. The issues for applying the DELETE statement are even simpler than for UPDATE statements. This is because there is no SET clause with DELETE statements as the statement works only on whole records. You can DELETE either all or a subset of the records in a data source. Just as with the UPDATE statement, you must explicitly identify to which rows your DELETE command applies. Also, if you do not include a WHERE clause, the statement applies to all the records in a data source.

To DELETE all the records from the my_employees table, all you need is the following line of code in a stored procedure template:

```
DELETE my_employees
```

If you want to remove a subset of the records in a data source, add a WHERE clause to the DELETE statement. This works in exactly the same way as it does for the UPDATE statement and the same comments and suggestions for getting the selection correct apply.

The following example shows how to delete all those employees that have their source column set to customers.

```
DELETE my_employees
WHERE source = 'customers'
```

TRUNCATE

The TRUNCATE statement can be used as an alternative to the DELETE statement but works in a slightly different way:

❑ TRUNCATE will only delete **all** records. It is not possible to selectively delete with TRUNCATE.

❑ TRUNCATE operations are not logged and cannot therefore be rolled back as part of a transaction.

❑ TRUNCATE operations always reset the identity seed of any identity columns in the table.

Because of these differences TRUNCATE operations can complete dramatically more quickly than DELETE operations.

To TRUNCATE all the records from the my_employees table, all you need is the following line of code in a stored procedure template:

```
TRUNCATE TABLE my_employees
```

There is one further option to remove data from a database. That is to DROP the table. This does substantially more than remove the records from a table, of course. It physically removes the table and its definition from the database. Many of the previous examples illustrate how to drop a table before creating a new version.

Local Variables, Global Variables, and Parameters

Local variables, global variables, and parameters are three groups of variables that can contain values. A variable is a storage bin that is not part of a table. Local variables, global variables, and parameters hold just one value at a time. They hold a scalar value, but not a collection of values, such as a table. However, the contents of variables and parameters do have data types. You can use variable and parameter values to control the operation of a T-SQL application. Local variables, global variables, and parameters have different areas of focus and relevance with T-SQL. You can easily find a need for two or three of these together within a single stored procedure.

Local Variables

Local variables earn their title by having a scope restricted to a single stored procedure and to a single instance of that procedure. That is, they exist only while the particular procedure is running and cannot be used by any other procedure. It also means that separate instances of the procedure (perhaps running for two different users) have their own, separate variables.

When the execution of an application leaves a stored procedure by returning to a calling procedure, then that procedure's local variables are destroyed and cease to exist. The next time the procedure is run, new local variables will be created.

When the execution of an application leaves a stored procedure by calling a sub-procedure, then that procedure's local variables **lose scope** (they can no longer be viewed or used) until control returns to the procedure when the sub-procedure completes.

Before you can use a local variable you must first declare it. This involves assigning it a name and data type. You need both to complete the declaration. The names for local variables must always begin with an @ sign and follow normal SQL naming conventions. It is always a good idea to give variables meaningful names.

Once the variable is declared you may assign it a value using either a SET statement or a SELECT statement. Before you assign a value to a variable in a procedure, it has a NULL value. The variable can have new values assigned to it whenever required.

You can retrieve local variable values with SELECT statements, use them to specify criteria in WHERE clauses, and use them as inputs for built-in functions within a procedure.

Using Local Variables

The assign_local_variable_value procedure below illustrates the three steps to applying local variables with a very simple application. The application verifies that local variables are null before the assignment of a specific value to them. It begins by declaring three local variables. @a_letter is the name of the central local variable. All three variables have a CHAR data type with a length of 1 character or byte. The @before and @after local variables monitor the contents of @a_letter before and after the assignment of the letter a to it. The second portion of the stored procedure illustrates the syntax for using the SET statement with local variables. First, the procedure assigns the NULL value in @a_letter to @before. Next, the procedure gives @a_letter the value a. The stored procedure then assigns the new value for @a_letter to @after. Third, a SELECT statement displays the value of the @before and @after local variables at the conclusion of the procedure.

```
Alter Procedure assign_local_variable_value
As
```

```
--Declare local variables
DECLARE @a_letter CHAR(1)
DECLARE @before CHAR(1)
DECLARE @after CHAR(1)

--Assign values to preserve initial @a_letter value
SET @before = @a_letter
SET @a_letter = 'a'
SET @after = @a_letter

--Display before and after assignment values for @a_letter
SELECT @before AS 'Before', @after AS 'After'

Return
```

The following screen shows the return set that the stored procedure presents. Notice that the **Before** column, which displays the value of the @before local variable, is blank. This represents the NULL value it has. Recall that @before reflects the value of @a_letter before the assignment of a value. The **After** column, which reflects the value of @after, returns the single letter **a**. This shows the value of @a_letter after the assignment of that letter to it.

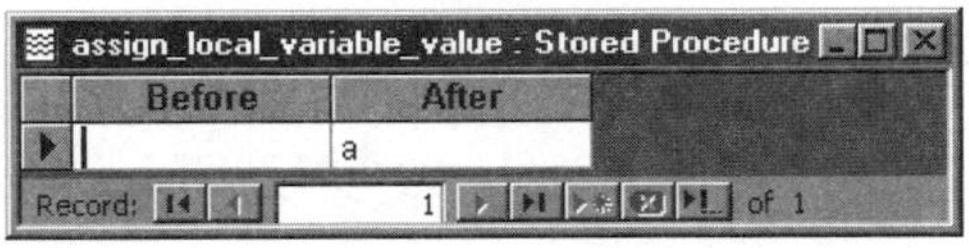

UNICODE character representations are growing in popularity throughout the Microsoft product line (and elsewhere) as an alternative to ASCII character representations. With this in mind, it might help to have a decoder of the numeric codes for UNICODE character representations. The following procedure script demonstrates one approach to this task with local variables.

This procedure contrasts with the previous sample by revealing how to use a SELECT statement, instead of a SET statement, to assign values to a local variable. As you can see, the difference is just a matter of switching the SELECT keyword for the SET keyword. This procedure further varies from the initial sample in that it is more computationally intensive. This procedure presents the UNICODE characters for three code values.

The procedure sets the starting code number and a step value for moving forward to the next two numbers. These three values serve as arguments for the built-in UNICODE and NCHAR functions. The NCHAR function returns the UNICODE character corresponding to a numeric value in the range from 0 through 65,535. This range of values represents the possible values that two bytes can denote. The UNICODE function returns the integer value corresponding to the first character in a string it is given. In this case, it is given the return value of the NCHAR function.

```
Alter Procedure unicode_decoder_with_select_assignment
As

--Declare local variables with data type
DECLARE @my_code_number INT
DECLARE @start_number INT
DECLARE @step_number INT

--Assign values to local variables
```

```
SELECT @start_number = 97
SELECT @step_number = 4
SELECT @my_code_number = @start_number

--Run SELECT statement that returns values based on local variables
SELECT UNICODE(NCHAR(@my_code_number)) AS 'Input1',
   NCHAR(@my_code_number) AS 'Output1',
   UNICODE(NCHAR(@my_code_number+@step_number)) AS 'Input2',
   NCHAR(@my_code_number+@step_number) AS 'Output2',
   UNICODE(NCHAR(@my_code_number+(2*@step_number))) AS 'Input3',
   NCHAR(@my_code_number+(2*@step_number)) AS 'Output3'

Return
```

The following screen depicts the output generated by the preceding stored procedure script:

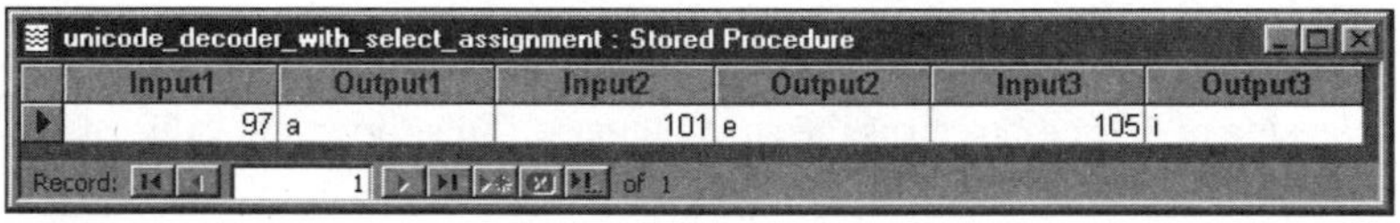

It shows the UNICODE character representations corresponding to code values of 97, 101, and 105. These correspond to the lower case letters of a, e, and i. Notice that the procedure is able to reveal the range of characters that correspond to the different ranges of numeric values. Change the @start_number value from 97 to 65 to return the same letters in upper case.

Use the unicode_decoder_with_select_assignment stored procedure to explore the whole UNICODE character range and identify values for characters local to a particular country or set of countries. Its international character sets is what makes UNICODE representations so popular. This chapter revisits this topic at several points to offer different approaches to this task.

Returning Database Objects

While this chapter was being written, the need arose to identify the most recent stored procedures. The most_recent_5_objects procedure below offers that capability for stored procedures and several other kinds of database objects. Furthermore, you can easily change both the number of objects it returns and the types of arguments that it returns. The procedure additionally illustrates a limitation of local variables.

> **You cannot use a local variable to denote a T-SQL keyword. Local variables are strictly for representing values in expressions.**

The following procedure relies on one local variable to specify the type of database object about which it reports. Assign @object_type a value of p to list the five most recent stored procedures. You can use the stored procedure to report the five most recently selected views, user-defined tables, primary keys, constraints, and foreign keys.

The TOP clause in the SELECT statement designates how many objects to report. The ORDER BY clause designates the return of those objects in descending order by crdate (creation date). The procedure contains a commented line that can report the top 15 objects. While it might seem that specifying the number is an ideal application for a local variable, that is not so. The quantity after the TOP keyword acts like a T-SQL keyword. Therefore, you cannot use a local variable to designate how many top records to display with the

SELECT statement. It is possible to write a procedure that uses ALTER PROCEDURE to modify an existing procedure so that it does and then calls this new procedure (a form of self modifying code) but a full discussion of this advanced (and potentially risky) technique is beyond the scope of this book.

Near the end of the procedure is a reminder that local variables cannot replace keywords. However, you can use local variables with IF...ELSE statements to determine which of two T-SQL statements with different keywords executes. IF...ELSE statements are explained later on in the section *Control-of-Flow Statements*.

```
Alter Procedure most_recent_5_objects
As


--Declare local variables
DECLARE @which_way VARCHAR(4)
DECLARE @object_type CHAR(1)

SET @object_type = 'P'
--Use these codes for object types
--    P --> Procedures
--    V --> Views
--    U --> User-defined tables
--    K --> Primary Key
--    C --> Constraints
--    F --> Foreign Keys

SET @which_way = 'desc'

SELECT TOP 5' name, crdate
--SELECT TOP 15  name, crdate
FROM sysobjects

--This works because local variables can represent assignment values
WHERE type = @object_type

--This does not work because local variables cannot represent keywords
--ORDER BY crdate @which_way

ORDER BY crdate DESC

Return
```

Global Variables

We use the term **global variable** to denote those variables in SQL Server that have scope across an entire database – not just a specific procedure in which you declare them. Unlike local variables, global variables receive assignments from SQL Server instead of a user-defined stored procedure. Therefore, you can use global variables to monitor the behavior and status of SQL Server.

The following excerpt from the Index tab of Books Online shows the complete list of global variables. Notice the search is for @ @ . This is because global variables always start with this prefix.

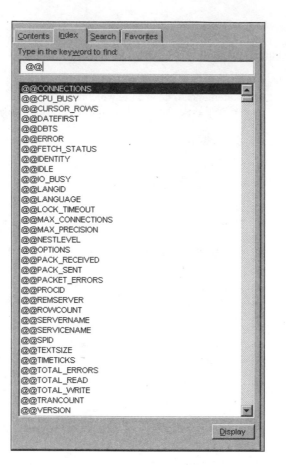

This chapter will not attempt to cover every single global variable in detail. A few are presented below. Books Online has a description for all global variables for use with SQL Server.

@@SERVERNAME

The @@SERVERNAME global variable returns the precise name by which you can refer to a local SQL Server.

@@VERSION

If you need to conditionally execute code based on the version of SQL Server on which your application runs, the @@VERSION can help. This global variable reports the version number, its date, and the processor type.

@@IDENTITY

This variable tracks the last inserted value in a database. It is not just for one user or one table, but it reports for the whole database. Therefore, if you want to make sure that you are capturing the result for an INSERT to a specific table, you may want to wrap the operation in a transaction. This enables SQL Server to assign or display its global value before @@IDENTITY becomes available for other purposes. For simplicity and continuity, this chapter does not demonstrate use of transactions with the @@IDENTITY global variable. We'll briefly touch on transactions later in the chapter.

Applications very often need to know the IDENTITY value for the last record entered in a database. When you have related tables, such as Orders and [Order Details] tables, your application will need to know the Orders primary key if it is to INSERT one or more related records into the [Order Details] table. If the Orders table uses a column with an IDENTITY setting as its primary key, then your application needs to know the IDENTITY value for an order to assign the proper value to the foreign key column in the [Order Details] table.

The following scripts show three different contexts for reporting the last inserted IDENTITY value. These scripts are designed to run from Query Analyzer, although Access stored procedure templates will return the @@IDENTITY value after the operation of an INSERT statement only if you include the SET NOCOUNT ON statement. This statement, as you will remember, comes after the AS keyword. However, the following scripts still highlight three possible uses for @@IDENTITY.

The first code sample creates a new table, adds four records, and prints the value of @@IDENTITY after the last INSERT. Since the IDENTITY property in the CREATE TABLE statement has a seed value of 0 with a step value of 2, the return value will always be 6. For the purposes of a later example, which also provides another way around the return value problem, put these commands in a stored procedure template and call the procedure return_last_changed_identity_value. Don't include the SET NOCOUNT ON statement, as this would defeat the point of the workaround, although the later example does have other uses as well.

```
--Create a new table, insert some values, return the
--IDENTITY value for the last record input
IF EXISTS(SELECT name FROM sysobjects WHERE name='my_employees')
    DROP TABLE my_employees
CREATE TABLE my_employees
(
employeeID int IDENTITY(0,2) NOT NULL Primary Key,
firstname varchar(10),
lastname varchar(20),
homephone varchar(24),
source varchar(20)
)
INSERT my_employees VALUES('Tom','Jones','123.456.7890','input value')
INSERT my_employees VALUES('Terry','Johnson','123.987.7890','input value')
INSERT my_employees VALUES('Tony','Hinton','123.456.8765','input value')
INSERT my_employees VALUES('Tomie','Binton','123.345.1234','input value')
SELECT @@IDENTITY AS 'Last IDENTITY value'
```

The second code sample assigns a new seed value, namely 998, for the my_employees.employeeID column with the DBCC CHECKIDENT statement. This statement assigns a seed value that the next INSERT statement will UPDATE. The following INSERT statement therefore creates a new row in the my_employees table with an employeeID column value of 1000. The final SELECT statement will, therefore, always report a value of 1000. You should be careful when assigning new seed values for identity columns – only do this if you are sure the new value won't conflict with an existing one. Again, for the later example, place this code into a stored procedure template and call the procedure reseed_identity_to_998_before_insert_to_my_employees.

```
--Reseed IDENTITY before inserting a new value and returning
--its IDENTITY value
DBCC CHECKIDENT(my_employees,RESEED,998)
INSERT my_employees VALUES('Brittany','Binton','123.345.1234','input value')
SELECT @@IDENTITY AS 'Last IDENTITY value'
```

The third code sample demonstrates how to write a specific value into a column with an IDENTITY property setting. This is not normally possible because SQL Server automatically assigns values to columns with an IDENTITY property. However, by invoking the SET INDENTITY_INSERT statement with an ON setting, you can suspend the rule denying access to the IDENTITY column of a table. This feature is particularly convenient when you need to DELETE a record that you subsequently want to replace with a new one.

The third code sample shows how to DELETE the my_employees record with an employeeID value of 4, and then restore that specific employeeID value with a new, replacement row. The replacement record has an updated source column setting. The concluding SELECT statement reports 4 since it was the last record updated by the code. Again, be very careful when altering data in a table with an IDENTITY column. If you specify the wrong IDENTITY to replace, you could duplicate an existing value. For this final section of code, call the stored procedure you save it in delete_record_restore_with_same_identity_value.

```
--Delete a record and insert another record with the same
--IDENTITY value in its place
DELETE my_employees
WHERE employeeID=4
SET IDENTITY_INSERT my_employees ON
INSERT my_employees (employeeID,firstname,lastname,homephone,source)
    VALUES(4,'Tony','Hinton','123.456.8765','new input value')
SET IDENTITY_INSERT my_employees OFF
SELECT @@IDENTITY AS 'Last IDENTITY value'
```

The last of these three sections of code, when run in Query Analyzer, produces the results that can be seen in this screenshot. The code in this shot was run on a SQL Server 2000 server named RLYEH.

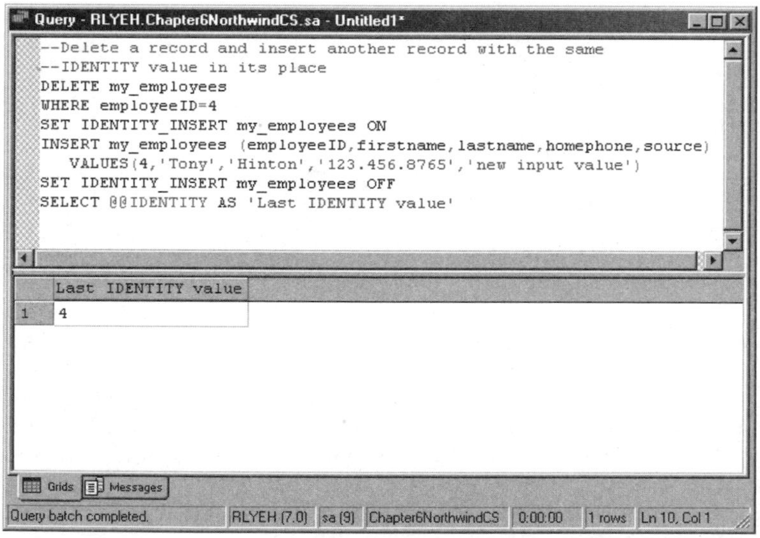

Attempting to run any of the three preceding scripts without the SET NOCOUNT ON statement within an Access project stored procedure template does not produce the requested information about the IDENTITY value for the last INSERT. Instead, Access simply reports that the stored procedure executed and did not return any records, although it does update the table. The following screenshot depicts the result of running the first code segment from the preceding code examples:

You can use Books Online to get started learning about other global variables. For example, the @@ROWCOUNT global variable returns the number of records affected by the last statement. You can use this to track whether an UPDATE statement affected any records, and if so how many. The @@DBTS variable reports the global timestamp value across an entire database. You can use this value to track the sequence of INSERT and UPDATE statement use throughout a database.

Return Values

Return values allow your procedures to pass information back to the procedures that called them in a similar way to the way functions do. They are often used in conjunction with input and output parameters (discussed in the next section).

The first procedure below calls a second and displays the results returned by it using a SELECT statement.

```
Alter Procedure invoke_get_sales
As

--Declare local variables
DECLARE @returned_sales int

--Execute procedure with return value
EXEC @returned_sales = get_sales

--Display the value returned from the second procedure
SELECT @returned_sales AS 'Sales'

Return
```

And now the second, which is to be called by the first. It calculates the sales and returns them to the calling procedure:

```
Alter PROCEDURE get_sales
@sales int
As

--Select sales for fixed category name
SELECT @sales = categorysales
    FROM [Category Sales for 1997]
    WHERE categoryname = 'seafood'

Return Sales
```

Parameters

By using parameters, you can set values to control the behavior of your stored procedure at run time. This is a very powerful feature for enabling user interactivity in your applications and allowing your procedures to make use of the same sub-procedure in many different situations rather than having to write specific code for each one (this is also known as "code reuse").

SQL Server supports two main types of parameter – input and output. With an input parameter, you can pass values into a stored procedure to determine its return set. An output parameter passes values from a stored procedure back to a calling procedure. With a combination of input and output parameters, you can instruct SQL Server to compute a result for a value specified by an input parameter, and then pass the computed value back to the calling routine with an output parameter. Output parameters are scalar values unlike return sets (discussed previously), which are sets of values. You can also use input parameters to specify the column values for a new record that an INSERT statement injects into a table.

Just like local variables, parameter names must begin with an @ sign. In addition, you can use parameters as terms in expressions in the same way as local variables, and you cannot use them as replacements for SQL Server keywords. However, parameters are not declared in the same way as local variables – they are always listed *before* the AS statement and not after. Parameters do have a data type property just like local variables. In addition, you may use parameters and local variables together.

Using Parameters to SELECT Data

The following pair of procedures demonstrates the syntax and behavior of parameters when one procedure calls another. The first procedure calls the second, supplying it with an input parameter. This input parameter is used to make a SELECT statement against the Category Sales for 1997 view, the results of which are returned to the first procedure to be displayed.

The first procedure, invoke_get_category_sales, calls the second one, get_category_sales. Local variables serve two roles in the first procedure. First, a local variable, @category_name, stores the category value to pass on to the second procedure. The value of this local variable is transferred into the input parameter for the second procedure. Second, the value of the output parameter for the second procedure is transferred into the @returned_sales local variable of the first procedure.

The first procedure then goes on to use both of its local variables in a SELECT statement to display the results.

A procedure requires special syntax for its EXEC statement when it is to receive a value back from the procedure it is calling via an output parameter. The procedure must assign the named output parameter to a local variable as part of the EXEC statement. In addition, the calling procedure must designate the parameter as an output parameter using the OUTPUT clause.

Here is the first procedure:

```
Alter Procedure invoke_get_category_sales
As

--Declare local variables
DECLARE @returned_sales int, @category_name varchar(15)

--Assign a value to the variable we are about to send to the second procedure
SET @category_name='meat/poultry'

--Execute procedure with parameters
EXEC get_category_sales
    @category_name, @category_sales = @returned_sales OUTPUT

--Display the value sent to second procedure and the value returned from it
SELECT @category_name AS 'Category', @returned_sales AS 'Sales'

Return
```

And now the second, which is to be called by the first:

```
Alter Procedure get_category_sales

--First parameter is an input parameter (default), and
--the second parameter is an output parameter
@category_name varchar(15),
@category_sales int OUTPUT
As

--Select sales for input category name
SELECT @category_sales = categorysales
    FROM [Category Sales for 1997]
    WHERE categoryname = @category_name

Return
```

In this second procedure there is no need for local variables and so none are declared. The procedure demonstrates how to declare and handle input and output parameters by declaring them after the Alter Procedure line and before the As keyword.

In addition to a data type, you see that output parameters require the OUTPUT keyword. You can also define default values for parameters. You can use the INPUT keyword to denote input parameters but this is optional and commonly ignored.

The @category_name input parameter serves a role in the WHERE clause expression of a SELECT statement. That statement computes the value of the procedure's output parameter in its SELECT clause. Since the data source name contains embedded blanks, the procedure encloses it in brackets.

The following screenshot depicts the SELECT statement output from the first procedure in the preceding code sample:

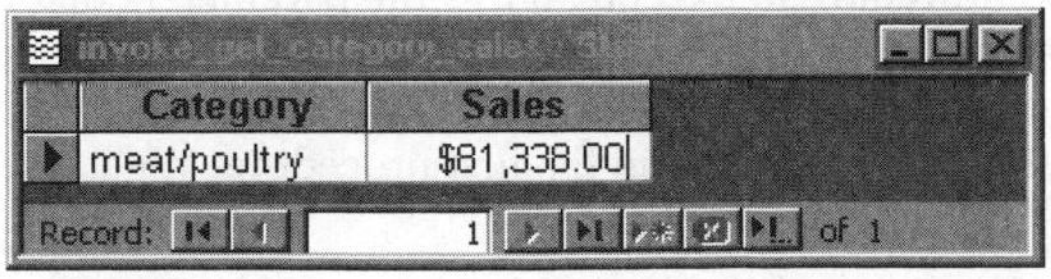

The SELECT statement displays two local variables. The first of these is a local variable set locally. The second is a local variable set according to the value of an output parameter from the called procedure. Users can obtain different results by specifying other category names.

Later in this chapter, we will show programmatic ways of specifying the input for a stored procedure so users can set input parameters at run time. In addition, the next chapter will drill down into this topic further by showing you how to work with SQL Server Stored Procedures from Access Forms.

Using Parameters to INSERT Data

The next pair of procedures demonstrates the behavior of parameters with an application that will INSERT new records into a table. The first procedure passes column values as parameters for a new record that the second procedure will INSERT into a table. The table is the familiar my_employees table. The passed parameters are for firstname, lastname, homephone, and source columns. The first procedure also attempts to accept an output parameter, but this fails.

```
Alter Procedure invoke_insert_into_my_employees_from_parameters
As
DECLARE @my_ident INT, @my_string varchar(3)

EXEC insert_into_my_employees_from_parameters
    'Rick',
    'Dobson',
    '502.426.9294',
    'from parameters',
    @employeeID = @my_ident OUTPUT

--SELECT statement after INSERT statement or call to
--a procedure that runs an INSERT statement does not
--return a value when from a stored procedure template
SELECT @my_ident

Return
```

Here is the second procedure, which makes the INSERT:

```
Alter Procedure insert_into_my_employees_from_parameters
@firstname varchar(10),
@lastname varchar(20),
@homephone varchar(24),
@source varchar(20) = 'from input parameters',
@employeeID INT OUTPUT
As
INSERT my_employees VALUES(@firstname, @lastname, @homephone, @source)
SELECT @employeeID = @@IDENTITY

Return
```

The design of the first procedure is very straightforward. It runs an EXEC statement to call the second procedure. After naming the procedure to execute, it lists the parameters that it passes to the second procedure. The SELECT statement at the close of the first procedure does not operate because the calling procedure does not pass back an output parameter value. This can be rectified by including the SET NOCOUNT ON statement after the As statement in the first procedure. We'll also show you how to work around this problem using VBA later in this chapter.

The second procedure follows the same general layout presented previously for a procedure with parameters. One important distinction is that this sample assigns a default value to @source parameter. Notice that all you need to do is trail the parameter declaration with an equal sign (=) and the default value. If the calling procedure does not assign a value to this parameter, then the procedure uses the default value. If there is a chance that users will not be specifying the value for a parameter, you should consider assigning a default value to avoid a failure based on a missing value. The INSERT statement shows how to use the passed parameters. The syntax is simple, but the impact is great. Users running Access forms can pass values to these parameters as they invoke the procedure. This makes it easy to add records to a SQL Server database from an Access form. We drill down on this topic later in this chapter as well as in the next chapter. Here is the result of running this pair of procedures after the three procedures shown for Query Analyzer have been run in Access stored procedure templates. The returned value is 1002 because the last entry in my_employees had been changed to have an empoyeeID value of 1000.

So why use output parameters instead of return values? I hear you say. Well, a procedure can only have a single return value or set while it may have a multitude of output parameters.

> *It is common practice in commercial applications, where a procedure often needs to return many values and therefore output parameters are required, to use the return value to tell the calling procedure whether its operation was successful or not by returning a Boolean value.*

Control-of-Flow Statements

T-SQL includes a basic set of statements to control program flow by conditional execution and looping. This section drills down on a subset of these statements with samples that illustrate basic T-SQL programming techniques appropriate for Access projects.

For example, the discussion in this section explicitly covers the ELSE clause, RETURN values, and BEGIN...END blocks, which often appear with IF statements when an application needs to execute conditionally two or more lines of T-SQL. You will also learn about the CASE statement in a couple of different varieties. The examination of control-of-flow statements concludes with samples using WHILE loops. One of these references the WAITFOR statement, which can delay the execution of statements until a fixed time or for an interval. This section highlights minor differences in the operation of this statement between Query Analyzer and Access projects.

Several of the samples in this section deal with a view named my_extended_prices. This view draws on the Orders, [Order Details], and Products tables to compute extended price for each line item in the sample database for the chapter. Including the Products table offers the capability to label each row with a product's name instead of a numeric value denoting that name. This improves the readability of sample output. The view computes its extended_price column as a function of the Unitprice, Quantity, and Discount columns from the [Order Details] table. The following T-SQL expression shows the code underlying the view, and the screenshot beyond that presents an excerpt from the virtual table that the my_extended_prices view computes. This T-SQL expression belongs on the SQL pane of a new View, which you will remember from Chapter 5.

```
SELECT Orders.OrderID, Products.ProductName,
    [Order Details].UnitPrice, [Order Details].Quantity,
```

```
        [Order Details].Discount, CONVERT(money,
        [Order Details].UnitPrice * [Order Details].Quantity *
     (1 - [Order Details].Discount))
        AS Extended_Price
  FROM Orders INNER JOIN
     [Order Details] ON
     Orders.OrderID = [Order Details].OrderID INNER JOIN
     Products ON [Order Details].ProductID = Products.ProductID
```

orderid	productname	unitprice	quantity	discount	Extended_Pric
10249	Tofu	$18.60	9	0	$167.40
10249	Manjimup Dried	$42.40	40	0	$1,696.00
10251	Gustaf's Knäcke	$16.80	6	0.05	$95.76
10251	Ravioli Angelo	$15.60	15	0.05	$222.30
10251	Louisiana Fiery	$16.80	20	0	$336.00
10258	Chang	$15.20	50	0.2	$608.00
10258	Chef Anton's Gu	$17.00	65	0.2	$884.00
10258	Mascarpone Fa	$25.60	6	0.2	$122.88
10260	Jack's New Eng	$7.70	16	0.25	$92.40
10260	Ravioli Angelo	$15.60	50	0	$780.00
10260	Tarte au sucre	$39.40	15	0.25	$443.25
10260	Outback Lager	$12.00	21	0.25	$189.00

Record: 12 of 2155

Using IF...ELSE Statements

IF...ELSE statements in T-SQL work more or less like their counterparts in VBA with the major exception that in T-SQL they provide for the conditional execution of just *one* line of code after the IF and ELSE clauses. If you need to execute more than one line of code conditionally, then you must group your statements in a BEGIN...END block. You can apply a BEGIN...END block to statements following either the IF clause or the ELSE clause, or both. Many programmers always use BEGIN...END blocks even with single statements as this makes everything crystal clear – it's up to you.

Several preceding samples demonstrated the use of the EXISTS keyword with an IF statement to determine if a table or other database object already existed. Since these statements execute a single DROP statement when the IF condition is true, they do not require BEGIN...END blocks. Another difference that VBA developers will readily notice is the absence of the THEN keyword following the expression for the condition in an IF clause. As with VBA, developers can nest IF...ELSE statements (place one IF...ELSE inside another), but you may often find the CASE fonction more suitable for situations where you can use a nested IF...ELSE statement. We'll look at use of the CASE fonction later.

The following pair of stored procedures demonstrates the basics of the IF...ELSE statement. The second procedure, are_product_order_prices_higher, draws on the my_extended_prices view. This procedure has a single parameter that the first procedure, invoke_are_product_order_prices_higher, passes to it when it runs an EXEC statement to call are_product_order_prices_higher.

```
Alter Procedure "invoke_are_product_order_prices_higher"
As

EXEC are_product_order_prices_higher
   @in_product='Tofu'
```

```
EXEC are_product_order_prices_higher
    @in_product='Uncle Bob''s Organic Dried Pears'

Return
```

Notice that this first procedure has just two EXEC statements. The parameter passed in the EXEC statements is one of two products. You will have to comment out the first EXEC statement if you want the second one to run. Tofu has an average extended price that is less than the overall average of all extended prices. Uncle Bob's Organic Dried Pears has an average extended price that is greater than the overall average. Because the product names are string constants, they appear in single quotes. To represent the apostrophe in Bob's, the first stored procedure denotes it with two single quotes. This is a standard T-SQL convention.

```
Alter Procedure "are_product_order_prices_higher"
@in_product VARCHAR(40)
As

DECLARE @strMsg VARCHAR(100)

IF (SELECT AVG(extended_price) FROM my_extended_prices
    WHERE productname = @in_product) >
    (SELECT AVG(extended_price) FROM my_extended_prices)
--Begin and End block markers are necessary because IF clause has more than
--one line to run
    BEGIN
        SET @strMsg = @in_product + ' has a higher order price than average.'
--User-defined error number can be from 13000 to 2147483647
        RAISERROR 13000 @strMsg
    END
ELSE
    SELECT @in_product AS 'Product',
        'does not have a higher order price than average.' AS 'Relative Price'

Return
```

This second stored procedure accepts a product name and determines if its extended price is greater than the overall average extended price for all items. If the result is that the product has a higher than average price, a message box is displayed stating this. For those products which do not have a higher than average order price, a SELECT statement displays this information. There is no compelling reason for using two different feedback techniques other than to demonstrate that it is possible.

An IF...ELSE statement conditionally executes one of its clauses to present the message that is appropriate for the product name passed to the stored procedure. The Boolean expression for the IF statement is TRUE or FALSE depending on the product name passed to the procedure, and whether it denotes a product that has a higher than average extended price.

If the SELECT statement condition is TRUE the IF clause runs a BEGIN...END block. This sample has two lines, the first of which computes a string expression, including the product's name. The second line uses the RAISERROR statement to present the string in a message box instead of using a PRINT statement as is common with Query Analyzer. When the number after the RAISERROR keyword is between 13000 and 2147483647 the statement displays the string constant given after the number. Error numbers before 13000 are reserved for use by Microsoft. The screenshot overleaf depicts the message box that appears when a product has a higher extended price than average:

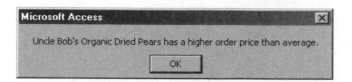

The ELSE clause does not need a BEGIN...END block since it conditionally executes a single line with a SELECT statement. The results of the ELSE clause being executed are shown in the next screenshot.

Product	Relative Price
Tofu	does not have a higher order price than average.

Using the RAISERROR statement is a "quick and dirty" technique to use with Access project stored procedure templates to give the functionality of the VBA PRINT statement that is not directly available to us in Access. It is not recommended that you use this technique as your main method for displaying information to the user. Since the RAISERROR statement does not take an expression, you must first compute a string expression that you save to a local variable. Then, use that variable as an argument for RAISERROR. An alternative to this technique that does not involve any error handling would be to simply use a SELECT statement to display the message.

The RETURN Statement

The RETURN statement is not strictly a control-of-flow statement, but it finds use often with control-of-flow statements. The RETURN statement performs two functions. First, it unconditionally terminates a stored procedure or a script running in Query Analyzer. Second, it can pass back an integer value to another stored procedure or to a VBA application. These two capabilities together enable a calling routine to understand what happened inside a stored procedure without requiring an output parameter.

Handling return values was discussed earlier in this chapter. The calling procedure can use the return value in SELECT statements, IF...ELSE statements, or arguments for RAISERROR statements that report what happened inside the called procedure.

The following pair of stored procedures illustrates the use of the RETURN statement in this context. In this sample, the called procedure, **are_product_order_prices_higher_with_return**, simply passes back a return value of 0 or 1. The return value depends on whether a product's average line item order price is greater than the overall average line item order price. The calling procedure presents one of two messages in a message box based on the return value.

```
Alter Procedure invoke_are_product_order_prices_higher_with_return
As

DECLARE @ReturnStatus INT
DECLARE @local_in_product VARCHAR(40)
DECLARE @strMsg VARCHAR(100)

--SET @local_in_product = 'Tofu'
SET @local_in_product = 'Uncle Bob''s Organic Dried Pears'
EXEC @ReturnStatus = are_product_order_prices_higher_with_return
    @in_product=@local_in_product
```

```
IF @ReturnStatus=1
   SET @strMsg = @local_in_product +
      ' has higher than average order prices.'
ELSE
   SET @strMsg = @local_in_product +
      ' does not have higher than average order prices.'


RAISERROR 13000 @strMsg

Return
```

Here is the second procedure, which passes a return value back to the first procedure.

```
Alter Procedure are_product_order_prices_higher_with_return
@in_product VARCHAR(40)
As

DECLARE @strMsg VARCHAR(100)

IF (SELECT AVG(extended_price) FROM my_extended_prices
   WHERE productname = @in_product) >
   (SELECT AVG(extended_price) FROM my_extended_prices)
   RETURN 1
ELSE
   RETURN 0
```

The called procedure has the simpler logic in this application. It accepts an input parameter that designates a specific product. The SELECT statement serving as the condition expression for an IF...ELSE statement determines the return value. The procedure sets the return value by following the RETURN keyword with either a 0 or a 1.

The calling procedure, invoke_are_product_order_prices_higher_with_return, passes one of two values as the input parameter. These are the same ones as in the preceding sample, with one product having an above average price and the other a below average price. The EXEC statement following the SET statement assigning a value to the input parameter shows the syntax for capturing a return value from the calling procedure. Notice that @ReturnStatus is a local variable. The value returned from the called procedure is assigned to it in the EXEC statement. An IF...ELSE statement invokes one of two string expressions based on the return value. These expressions assign a value to the @strMsg local variable that serves as the string argument for a RAISERROR statement that concludes the calling procedure.

Using CASE Functions

T-SQL offers the CASE function for allowing alternative display output from a SELECT statement based a series of transformations. CASE functions do not alter column values, just their display. CASE function transformations can be of two types:

First, they can replace one constant value with another constant. For example, you could store abbreviations for geographic locations in a database, but use a CASE function to transform the abbreviations to full names when you display record values with a SELECT statement. This is the simplest form of the CASE function.

Second, a CASE function can evaluate a series of Boolean expressions until it finds one that is true. When it does find one, the function can execute a THEN clause that maps a variable to an associated value. This second type of CASE function is a **searched** CASE function.

For both types of CASE functions, you will use WHEN...THEN clauses to specify mapping values.

> Consider the order of your WHEN...THEN clauses carefully. A CASE function stops after it finds the first match. If a column value can match two different WHEN...THEN clauses, it appears with the mapped value of the WHEN...THEN clause that it encounters first, and this may not be the one you want! Another common error is to fail to use conditions that cover every eventuality. In this case particular values may not match any of the WHEN...THEN clauses. You can (and should always) have a trailing ELSE clause to catch any column value instances that fail to find a match.

The following code sample shows a CASE function that re-maps those contacttitle column values from the Customers table specified by the SELECT statement. In particular, it re-maps three titles, and it leaves the others as they are. The three changed titles each have a WHEN...THEN clause that corresponds to them. The trailing ELSE clause captures all titles that are not one of the three titles with their own WHEN...THEN clause. Any record with a contacttitle other than Owner, Sales Representative, or Sales Manager, retains its initial contacttitle column value.

```
Alter Procedure remap_contact_titles_with_case
As

--Re-map customer titles
SELECT contactname, contacttitle, new_contacttitle=
    CASE contacttitle
        WHEN 'Owner' THEN 'Entrepreneur'
        WHEN 'Sales Representative' THEN 'Account Executive'
        WHEN 'Sales Manager' THEN 'Manager of Accounts'
        ELSE contacttitle
    END
FROM customers

Return
```

You're not changing the values in the Customers table because the CASE function does not actually alter column values. It merely returns a value for the new_contacttitle field of a SELECT statement. The screen on the right illustrates that point with an excerpt from the return set for the preceding sample stored procedure. Notice that the return set displays the original values for the contacttitle column along with the remapped ones.

contactname	contacttitle	new_contacttitle
Maria Anders	Sales Representative	Account Executive
Ana Trujillo	Owner	Entrepreneur
Antonio Moreno	Owner	Entrepreneur
Thomas Hardy	Sales Representative	Account Executive
Christina Berglund	Order Administrator	Order Administrator
Hanna Moos	Sales Representative	Account Executive
Frédérique Citeaux	Marketing Manager	Marketing Manager
Martín Sommer	Owner	Entrepreneur
Laurence Lebihan	Owner	Entrepreneur
Elizabeth Lincoln	Accounting Manager	Accounting Manager
Victoria Ashworth	Sales Representative	Account Executive
Patricio Simpson	Sales Agent	Sales Agent
Francisco Chang	Marketing Manager	Marketing Manager
Yang Wang	Owner	Entrepreneur
Pedro Afonso	Sales Associate	Sales Associate
Elizabeth Brown	Sales Representative	Account Executive
Sven Ottlieb	Order Administrator	Order Administrator
Janine Labrune	Owner	Entrepreneur
Ann Devon	Sales Agent	Sales Agent
Roland Mendel	Sales Manager	Manager of Accounts

remap_contact_titles_with_case : Stored Procedure

Record: 20 of 91

You can readily combine the re-mapping feature of CASE functions with SQL Server aggregate functions to develop custom aggregations of data in a SQL Server database. The following sample illustrates one approach to tackling this issue. It computes the distribution of extended_price column values across five custom categories. These categories are not in the database, but the CASE function still allows us to compute aggregations based on them. In addition, we can fine-tune the category definitions just by tweaking the code instead of having to rebuild tables with new category definitions.

```
Alter Procedure compute_distribution_for_my_extended_prices_with_case
As

--Categorize individual rows in my_extended_prices with CASE statement
--Include aggregate functions for distribution statistics
SELECT   'Price Categories' =
    CASE
        WHEN extended_price <= 130 THEN '1. Low (<=$130)'
        WHEN extended_price <= 300 THEN '2. Medium-low (<=$300)'
        WHEN extended_price <= 560 THEN '3. Medium-high (<=$560)'
        WHEN extended_price <= 2000 THEN '4. High (<=$2000)'
        WHEN extended_price >2000 THEN '5. Very-high (>$2000)'
        ELSE 'No extended price'
    END,
    COUNT(extended_price) 'Count of items',
    AVG(extended_price) 'Average item price'
FROM my_extended_prices

--Use GROUP BY clause for aggregate functions
--re-use CASE statement for categorizing rows
GROUP BY
    CASE
        WHEN extended_price <= 130 THEN '1. Low (<=$130)'
        WHEN extended_price <= 300 THEN '2. Medium-low (<=$300)'
        WHEN extended_price <= 560 THEN '3. Medium-high (<=$560)'
        WHEN extended_price <= 2000 THEN '4. High (<=$2000)'
        WHEN extended_price >2000 THEN '5. Very-high (>$2000)'
        ELSE 'No extended price'
    END

--Order distribution rows by category labels
ORDER BY 'Price Categories'
```

To use the CASE function with aggregate functions, you must use the same function in both the SELECT and GROUP BY clauses of a SELECT statement. The CASE function in the SELECT clause categorizes each record in a category. The CASE function in the GROUP BY clause aggregates the rows according to the same rule as the categorization in the SELECT clause. Using the two CASE functions, your SELECT statement can display aggregated data according to new categorizations.

The preceding code sample aggregates data with two functions: COUNT and AVG. The SELECT statement specifies three fields for display. The first field is the remapped names for the extended_price column values. The second and third fields are aggregates of count (COUNT) and average (AVG) for the extended_price column values in the categories designated by the CASE function. Notice the remapped values in the first field are numbered. This is to allow an easy way to order the presentation of the results from the aggregated functions. The ORDER BY clause at the bottom of the sample procedure uses these leading numbers in each category to determine how to order rows of aggregate values.

The following screenshot shows the result of the SELECT statement with the CASE functions. The output displays the extended prices in five categories. As analysts, you can readily re-define categories for grouping data as well as add new categories. This CASE function is great for such ad hoc analyses as this. If you plan on doing reports regularly with a large data source, you may want to consider adding columns to a table that you can pre-code to speed performance.

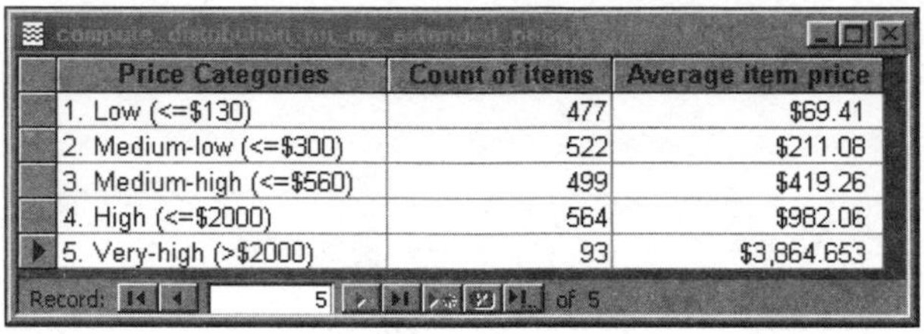

Price Categories	Count of items	Average item price
1. Low (<=$130)	477	$69.41
2. Medium-low (<=$300)	522	$211.08
3. Medium-high (<=$560)	499	$419.26
4. High (<=$2000)	564	$982.06
5. Very-high (>$2000)	93	$3,864.653

Record: 5 of 5

Using WHILE Loops

This section drills down on WHILE loops with two samples. One demonstrates how to pass through a set of UNICODE values to show code values with their matching character representations. You can apply the same technique to any mapping data source. The second example gets into timing issues and contrasts Query Analyzer with Access 2000 stored procedure templates. You may find this sample useful as a starting point for testing the performance of your applications.

The WHILE keyword takes a Boolean expression as its argument. As long as the expression is TRUE, the WHILE loop repeats the next statement. If you follow the WHILE keyword and its argument with a BEGIN...END block, then the loop will repeat the block until the condition turns FALSE. After a condition turns FALSE, controls passes to the first T-SQL line outside the loop's scope. Without a BEGIN...END block, this is the second line after the one containing the WHILE keyword. If you follow the WHILE keyword with a BEGIN...END block, a condition that evaluates to FALSE transfers control to the line after the END keyword.

Passing UNICODE Characters

The following sample shows a very simple application of a WHILE loop. It generates a list of 26 UNICODE values and their corresponding character representations. UNICODE values extend from 0 through to 65,535, which is a 16-bit range. In order to preserve the values for display, the sample saves a range of codes and characters in a table. Then, a user can view the range by opening the table. Because SELECT statements do not always function correctly when run immediately after INSERT statements, we cannot use a T-SQL program to view the table's contents immediately. This is due to client-side cursor caching. A full explanation for this problem and its workarounds is beyond the scope of this book. However, we can use VBA to accomplish this result. This chapter demonstrates that particular technique later on.

```
Alter Procedure loop_through_26_Unicode_codes_and_characters
As

--Create a new version of my_codes table
IF EXISTS(SELECT name FROM sysobjects WHERE name = 'my_codes' and type='U')
    DROP TABLE my_codes
CREATE TABLE my_codes
(
code INT,
character NCHAR(1)
)
```

```
--Local variables for setting limits on iteration through UNICODE codes
DECLARE @my_code_number INT, @start_number INT

--Use @start_number of 65 for English alphabet (upper case)
--Use @start_number of 97 for English alphabet (lower case)
SET @start_number= 97
SET @my_code_number = @start_number

--Loop through 26 sequential codes and characters
WHILE (@my_code_number <=(@start_number+25))
BEGIN
    INSERT    my_codes VALUES(@my_code_number, NCHAR(@my_code_number))
    SET @my_code_number = @my_code_number + 1
END
```

The procedure starts by creating a table to store the UNICODE codes and their character representations. If the table already exists, the procedure drops it. This table is called my_codes.

After preparing a table to store the codes and their representations, the procedure declares a couple of local variables for use with the WHILE loop. The @start_number variable initializes @my_code_number. On each pass through the WHILE loop, the procedure adds a row to the table with a UNICODE value and its representation. After adding the row, the procedure increments @my_code_number by one for the next pass through the loop. The @start_number value is an input to the Boolean expression representing the condition for the WHILE loop. The completed WHILE condition expression permits @my_code_number to grow up to 25 units beyond the @start_number; this is a range of 26 UNICODE values.

The pair of screenshots shows tables generated by the preceding code sample. The screen on the left is the my_codes table with an @start_number setting of 97. It returns the English letters in lower case. The screen on the right depicts lower case letters from various non-English character sets. This character set starts with UNICODE value 224. You can modify the WHILE loop in the preceding sample to save the characters for the whole UNICODE value range, or any subset of it.

code	character		code	character
97	a		224	à
98	b		225	á
99	c		226	â
100	d		227	ã
101	e		228	ä
102	f		229	å
103	g		230	æ
104	h		231	ç
105	i		232	è
106	j		233	é
107	k		234	ê
108	l		235	ë
109	m		236	ì
110	n		237	í
111	o		238	î
112	p		239	ï
113	q		240	ð
114	r		241	ñ
115	s		242	ò
116	t		243	ó
117	u		244	ô
118	v		245	õ
119	w		246	ö
120	x		247	÷
121	y		248	ø
122	z		249	ù

Another potential use for WHILE loops is to run a solution multiple times so that you can test the performance of two or more solutions to the same task.

Performance Testing

The results from this procedure should only be treated as a rough and ready guide to performance. This is because many factors can affect them, such as data caching, other processes running on the same machine, etc. To mitigate this somewhat you should always run your performance tests a large number of times and average the results. Even with this proviso, the example can still provide a useful tool.

The following script from Query Analyzer demonstrates this general approach with a WHILE loop that can call a stored procedure multiple times. The called procedure executes a WAITFOR statement with a delay parameter passed to it by the calling script. The calling script invokes the called procedure just twice – once with a delay parameter of 1 second and then with a delay of 2 seconds. Because the condition for the WHILE loop is always TRUE, the procedure needs to terminate the loop by another method. The combination of an IF...ELSE statement with a BREAK statement meets this requirement. Without this the procedure would simply run forever! The Query Analyzer script uses the DATEDIFF function to compute the difference between the start time just before entering the WHILE loop, and the end time just after the loop completes.

Here is the first procedure to run:

```
CREATE PROCEDURE time_delay @DELAYLENGTH char(9)
As
DECLARE @RETURNINFO         varchar(255)

BEGIN

    WAITFOR DELAY @DELAYLENGTH

    SELECT @RETURNINFO = 'A total time of ' +

                    SUBSTRING(@DELAYLENGTH, 1, 3) +

                    ' hours, ' +

                    SUBSTRING(@DELAYLENGTH, 5, 2) +

                    ' minutes, and ' +

                    SUBSTRING(@DELAYLENGTH, 8, 2) +

                    ' seconds, ' +

                    'has elapsed! Your time is up.'

--Use RAISERROR instead of PRINT for use in Access
--RAISERROR 13000 @RETURNINFO
    PRINT @RETURNINFO
END

GO
```

Follow that up with the following procedure:

```
DECLARE @start_time DATETIME, @end_time DATETIME
DECLARE @my_delay CHAR(9)
```

```
SET @start_time = getdate()
SET @my_delay = '000:00:01'

WHILE 1=1
BEGIN
    EXEC time_delay @my_delay
    IF RIGHT(@my_delay,1)=2
        BREAK
    ELSE
        SET @my_delay= '000:00:02'
END

SET @end_time = getdate()
SELECT 'This While loop terminated after ' +
    CONVERT(VARCHAR(2),DATEDIFF(ss, @start_time, @end_time)) + ' seconds.'
GO
```

The first script, for the stored procedure, performs three tasks:

❑   First, it executes the WAITFOR statement based on its input parameter

❑   Second, it extracts into a string variable the hours, minutes, and seconds for the delay specified by the input parameter

❑   Third, it displays the extracted value

This procedure borrows heavily from a sample in Books Online, but you should understand that this procedure could be any procedure that takes time. The WAITFOR statement clearly takes time to complete.

The second script uses a WHILE loop with a condition argument that is always true, namely 1=1. Since the condition has only constants, there is no way to terminate the loop by altering the condition's value. Therefore, the only way to end the loop is with a BREAK statement. The execution of a BREAK statement immediately transfers control to the first line outside the scope of the loop. The first pass through the loop causes SQL Server to pause for one second, and the second pass lengthens this to two seconds. Assignments of the getdate function to two local variables mark the start and end times of the task. A DATEDIFF function computes the difference between these two datetime values.

The following output from Query Analyzer reveals how it displays results from the scripts. The first two lines are from the first script, and may be on the **Messages** tab of the **Query** window. Each pass through the WHILE loop results in the generation of a new line. The last line is from the second script, and may appear on the **Grids** tab. It reflects the difference in seconds between the start and end times.

A total time of 000 hours, 00 minutes, and 01 seconds, has elapsed! Your time is up.
A total time of 000 hours, 00 minutes, and 02 seconds, has elapsed! Your time is up.

This While loop terminated after 3 seconds.

This WHILE timing application requires some tweaking as you prepare it to run from Access 2000. For instance, the first change you might expect is to replace the PRINT with a RAISERROR statement. This swap means that the procedure will print a message when you run the time_delay stored procedure manually from the Access Database window.

However, if you copy the second script to a stored procedure template, and run time_delay under programmatic control from the stored procedure, the procedure abruptly stops after a single iteration. The RAISERROR statement causes the termination of programmatic control before control passes from time_delay back to the procedure that called it. Commenting out the RAISERROR statement and the PRINT statement in time_delay allows the calling routine to time how long it takes for the WHILE loop to complete. The following stored procedure and screen show a program for timing the duration to pass through a WHILE loop and the result of the program for the delays used from inside an Access 2000 stored procedure template:

```
Alter Procedure invoke_time_delay_from_while_loop
As
DECLARE @start_time DATETIME, @end_time DATETIME
DECLARE @my_delay CHAR(9)

SET @start_time = getdate()
SET @my_delay = '000:00:01'

--This sample demonstrates the behavior of the BREAK keyword
WHILE 1=1
BEGIN
    EXEC time_delay @my_delay
    IF RIGHT(@my_delay,1)=2
       BREAK
    ELSE
       SET @my_delay= '000:00:02'
END

SET @end_time = getdate()

--This line does not work successfully when run from an Access 2000
--stored procedure template unless time_delay does not attempt to print
--or use RAISERROR
SELECT 'This While loop terminated after '
   + CONVERT(VARCHAR(2),DATEDIFF(ss, @start_time, @end_time)) + ' seconds.'

Return
```

I found the stored procedure for using WAITFOR fragile. For example, it was easy to cause a failure with various other combinations of delay values. However, the ability of a WHILE loop to repeatedly perform a sequence of T-SQL statement is highly robust, namely it works consistently for many kinds of statements, such as SELECT, INSERT, and UPDATE.

Aside from demonstrating the capability to time the duration of running a set of statements repeatedly, this sample also points to a peculiar combination between the two stored procedures. Attempting to print a message in the time_delay stored procedure with either PRINT or RAISERROR defeats the ability of the invoke_time_delay_from_while_loop stored procedure to report the duration for running its two delays. Later in this chapter, we show a workaround with the help of VBA.

Using VBA and ADO with Stored Procedures

We looked at using VBA and ADO to create and manage tables in Chapter 3. Here we will consolidate that knowledge.

Developers can manipulate stored procedures in many ways with ADO. This section drills down on several topics.

First, you learn multiple techniques for capturing the return set from a stored procedure. These different techniques complement one another and appeal to developers with their own unique programming styles. In addition, one of the samples shows how to extract more than one `Recordset` from a stored procedure's return set.

Next, the focus shifts to using parameters and return values with stored procedures. By using input parameters, you can vary the behavior of a stored procedure at run time. With output parameters and return values, you can capture scalar output from a procedure without having to use a `SELECT` statement.

The third major topic in this section deals with workarounds to using stored procedures from the Access 2000 user interface. Three VBA procedures present solutions to problems presented earlier in this chapter:

- ❑   Retrieving Return Sets
- ❑   Working with Parameters and Return Values
- ❑   VBA Workarounds for User Interface Issues

Retrieving Return Sets

A particularly simple technique for capturing a return set from a stored procedure is to open an ADO `Recordset` object on the stored procedure. You need to specify just three parameters for the `Open` method.

- ❑   First, designate the stored procedure name as the source for the `Recordset`.
- ❑   Second, designate a connection object. If you are working with a stored procedure in the current Access project, use `CurrentProject.Connection`.
- ❑   Third, the options parameter should be `adCmdStoredProc` to tell the ADO interpreter that it is working with a stored procedure. It is not strictly necessary to designate this setting, but Microsoft claims that it makes the data collection phase for the `Recordset` go faster since the ADO interpreter does not have to determine what kind of data source it references.

Reporting a Return Set with Nested Loops

After opening a `Recordset`, you have the normal range of options. For example, your applications can determine the size of a `Recordset` with the `RecordCount` property for the `Recordset` object and the `Count` property for the hierarchical `Fields` collection object. A `Do` loop with a condition `until EOF` allows your code to successively iterate through the rows of a `Recordset` until you pass the last row. You should be aware that all `Recordset` objects consume resources on both client and server machines. Therefore, you should always close the object as soon as you have no more need for it. You can do this by closing it and setting the `Recordset` equal to `Nothing` before exiting a VBA procedure that uses a `Recordset` object.

The following VBA procedure demonstrates these issues in action. It loops through each row's columns in a `Recordset`. The goal is to print the contents of the **categories_products_join_order_by_categoryID** stored procedure in the VBE **Immediate** window of an Access project. An earlier section (*SELECT,* in this chapter) discussed this stored procedure. The output starts by reporting the number of rows and columns in the `Recordset`. Next, it relies on two nested loops. The outer loop passes through successive rows in the `Recordset`, while the inner loop moves across the columns within a row. Finally, the procedure terminates by closing the `Recordset` object and setting it equal to `Nothing`. This frees the resource and avoids memory leaks.

The following procedure actually overflows the **Immediate** *window. You can copy the full and complete contents to a text file with techniques demonstrated in Chapter 5. Another option is to filter the output before printing it. This is easy since the procedure's nested loops pass through every column value within each row of the Recordset.*

```
Sub print_a_return_set()

'Based on Looping through recordset

Dim rst1 As ADODB.Recordset
Dim strspr1 As String
Dim intCols As Integer
Dim intRows As Integer
Dim fld1 As ADODB.Field

'Instantiate recordset and open it for the
'return set from stored procedure named in strspr1
Set rst1 = New ADODB.Recordset
strspr1 = "categories_products_join_order_by_categoryID"
rst1.Open strspr1, CurrentProject.Connection, , , adCmdStoredProc

'Print out the number of rows and columns in the recordset
'storing the return set from the stored procedure
Debug.Print "Results for: " & strspr1 & vbCrLf
intRows = rst1.RecordCount
Debug.Print "The number of rows are: " & cstr(intRows)
intCols = rst1.Fields.Count
Debug.Print "The number of fields in the recordset are: " & cstr(intCols)
Debug.Print String(15, "-") & vbCrLf

'Print field names and values for recordset rows
Do Until rst1.EOF
    For Each fld1 In rst1.Fields
        Debug.Print fld1.Name & ":" & String(17 - Len(fld1.Name), " ") _
        & fld1.Value
    Next
    Debug.Print String(15, "-") & "  end of row  " & String(15, "-")
    rst1.MoveNext
Loop

'Cleanup recordset resources
rst1.Close
Set rst1 = Nothing

End Sub
```

Reporting a Return Set with the GetString Method

The `GetString` method offers an alternative means of reporting the contents of a stored procedure's return set. Since the `GetString` method belongs to the `Recordset` object, your use of it starts similarly to the nested looping sample described previously. In fact, the `Open` method statement is identical for both sample procedures. After opening a `Recordset`, your application has available the full range of `Recordset` properties and methods. Therefore, this second sample uses the same code as the preceding sample to report the number of rows and columns in the `Recordset`.

This second sample for printing a return set deviates from the earlier one in that it contains no loops at all. Instead, the `GetString` method passes the complete `Recordset` to `Debug.Print`. The `debug.Print rst1.GetString` statement prints the `Recordset` with rows going down the side and columns going across the **Immediate** window. You cannot filter the columns of a `Recordset` as is possible with the preceding sample, and you can filter rows only by selecting the first so many records or by modifying the underlying `SELECT` statement in the stored procedure.

The sample below extracts all the rows from the `rst1 Recordset` object. The `rst1` pointer draws its data from the **categories_products_join_order_by_categoryID** stored procedure. The invocation of the `GetString` method accepts default settings for all five parameters, except for the column delimiter. This is the third parameter, which the procedure sets to `"-->"`. In order to designate the third parameter, you have to leave place markers for the first two parameters with commas. The first parameter is a constant representing a format for the `Recordset` data. Its default value is the only permissible setting. The second parameter can specify a number of rows to extract from the stored procedure's return set. If you assign a value to this parameter, it will extract only that many rows from the beginning of the `Recordset`. The fourth parameter is a row delimiter. Its default value is the carriage return character. The final parameter can change the default convention of representing `Null` values with an empty string to any other expression the `GetString` function denotes in its fifth parameter.

```
Sub print_a_return_set_2()

'Based on GetString function

Dim rst1 As ADODB.Recordset
Dim strspr1 As String
Dim intCols As Integer
Dim intRows As Integer

'Instantiate recordset and open it for the
'return set from stored procedure named in strspr1
Set rst1 = New ADODB.Recordset
strspr1 = "categories_products_join_order_by_categoryID"
rst1.Open strspr1, CurrentProject.Connection, , , adCmdStoredProc

'Print out the number of rows and columns in the recordset
'storing the return set from the stored procedure
Debug.Print "Results for: " & strspr1 & vbCrLf
intRows = rst1.RecordCount
Debug.Print "The number of rows are: " & cstr(intRows)
intCols = rst1.Fields.Count
Debug.Print "The number of fields in the recordset are: " & cstr(intCols)
Debug.Print String(15, "-") & vbCrLf

'Invoke recordset GetString method
Debug.Print rst1.GetString(, , " --> ")
```

```
'Cleanup recordset resources
rst1.Close
Set rst1 = Nothing

End Sub
```

Reporting a Return Set with the GetRows Method

The GetRows method copies the contents of a Recordset into an array in memory. When the Recordset derives its values from a stored procedure's return set, this method gives you an opportunity to represent a return set in memory in a structure that is familiar to many experienced developers. Beware that the array has its indices the opposite way round to the way you might expect, so Recordset rows appear as columns in the array and Recordset columns appear as rows in the array.

The GetRows method can take up to three parameters. First, you can specify how many data rows to extract from the Recordset to the array. Second, you can specify a starting location for extracting rows. This second parameter permits three possibilities: from the beginning, from the current record, or from the last record. Third, you can specify a subset of rows to extract. If you do not designate these parameters as in the following sample, the method extracts all rows and columns from a Recordset.

The following sample highlights another benefit of the GetRows method. After you copy the Recordset values to memory, you can close the Recordset object and set it to Nothing. This is because you have a copy of the Recordset values in memory. Recalling the values from memory is very fast, and it will save the resources allocated to the Recordset object. In web applications, these benefits can be particularly noteworthy.

You should only attempt to use these techniques with relatively small recordsets, as VBA arrays must always be held in main memory as a whole when they are used. Obviously this limits the number of records that can be copied to an array without getting the dreaded "out of memory" error.

```
Sub print_a_return_set_3()

'Based on GetRows function

Dim rst1 As ADODB.Recordset
Dim strspr1 As String
Dim ary1 As Variant
Dim intCols As Integer
Dim intRows As Integer
Dim ary2(3) As Integer
Dim i As Integer, j As Integer

'Instantiate recordset and open it for the
'return set from stored procedure named in strspr1
Set rst1 = New ADODB.Recordset
strspr1 = "categories_products_join_order_by_categoryID"
rst1.Open strspr1, CurrentProject.Connection, , , adCmdStoredProc

'Copy recordset to variant for array with
'    recordset rows as columns in array and
'    recordset columns as rows in array
ary1 = rst1.GetRows

'Cleanup recordset resources here
rst1.Close
Set rst1 = Nothing
```

```
'Print out the number of rows and columns in the recordset
'storing the return set from the stored procedure
Debug.Print "Results for: " & strspr1 & vbCrLf
intRows = UBound(ary1, 2) + 1
Debug.Print "The number of rows are: " & cstr(intRows)
intCols = UBound(ary1, 1) + 1
Debug.Print "The number of fields in the recordset are: " & cstr(intCols)
Debug.Print String(15, "-") & vbCrLf

'Compute maximum string length in the first
'three columns of the return set
intmax = 0
For i = 0 To 2
    For j = 0 To intRows - 1
        If intmax < Len(ary1(i, j)) Then
            intmax = Len(ary1(i, j))
        End If
    Next j
    ary2(i) = intmax
    intmax = 0
Next i

'Printing out the return set in left-aligned columns
For intRecord = 0 To intRows - 1
    Debug.Print "   " & _
        ary1(0, intRecord) & _
        String(ary2(0) - Len(ary1(0, intRecord)) + 2, " ") & _
        ary1(1, intRecord) & _
        String(ary2(1) - Len(ary1(1, intRecord)) + 2, " ") & _
        ary1(2, intRecord) & _
        String(ary2(2) - Len(ary1(2, intRecord)) + 2, " ") & _
        ary1(3, intRecord)
Next intRecord

End Sub
```

After you close a `Recordset` object, your application can use the internal array copy of the `Recordset` values to provide the same information as the `Recordset`. For example, to compute the number of records in the initial `Recordset`, compute the upper subscript bound plus one for the columns of the array. You need to add one to the upper subscript bound because VBA subscript bounds are zero-based by default (subscripts start at 0 and not 1 or some other number). If your base is different, then change the expression accordingly. Similarly, your application can compute the number of columns in the initial `Recordset` as the upper subscript bound plus one for the number of rows in the array holding the `Recordset`'s values. The final loop in the preceding code sample shows one approach to printing values from an array. It concatenates the values in an array column for a `Recordset` row. Spaces left align the columns.

The following screenshot presents an excerpt from the Immediate window output for the print_a_return_set_3 VBA procedure. It starts by reporting the number of rows and columns in the `Recordset`, although the `Recordset` is not available at the time that it prints the values. Notice the left alignment of columns. Individual products appear down the window although the array stores them as columns. Your code must make the transformation. The sample reveals how to do this. Having programmatic access to all the `Recordset` values enables your code to filter values to match the specific needs of special tasks.

```
Immediate                                                                    [x]
Results for: categories_products_join_order_by_categoryID

The number of rows are: 77
The number of fields in the recordset are: 4
---------------


    Beverages       Guaraná Fantástica              12 - 355 ml cans       4.5
    Beverages       Rhönbräu Klosterbier            24 - 0.5 l bottles     7.75
    Beverages       Sasquatch Ale                   24 - 12 oz bottles     14
    Beverages       Laughing Lumberjack Lager       24 - 12 oz bottles     14
    Beverages       Outback Lager                   24 - 355 ml bottles    15
    Beverages       Chai                            10 boxes x 20 bags     18
    Beverages       Steeleye Stout                  24 - 12 oz bottles     18
    Beverages       Chartreuse verte                750 cc per bottle      18
    Beverages       Lakkalikööri                    500 ml                 18
    Beverages       Chang                           24 - 12 oz bottles     19
    Beverages       Ipoh Coffee                     16 - 500 g tins        46
    Beverages       Côte de Blaye                   12 - 75 cl bottles     263.5
    Condiments      Aniseed Syrup                   12 - 550 ml bottles    10
    Condiments      Original Frankfurter grüne Soße 12 boxes               13
    Condiments      Genen Shouyu                    24 - 250 ml bottles    15.5
```

Reporting a Return Set with Multiple Recordsets

When working with stored procedures, it is easy to have return sets with multiple Recordsets – either from user-defined stored procedures with multiple SELECT statements or from system stored procedures that create more than one Recordset in their return set. Query Analyzer makes it no problem to access these Recordsets. Each Recordset resides on a separate tab in Query Analyzer's Results window. Just click a tab to view the Recordset on it. When you run a stored procedure from an Access project template using the Access 2000 user interface, Access 2000 passes back just the first Recordset – no matter how many Recordsets are in the procedure's return set. However, if you run the same stored procedure from a VBA procedure, you can extract all the Recordsets associated with a stored procedure's return set. The secret is the NextRecordset method of the Recordset returned.

The following shows a stored procedure that includes three SELECT statements. Each of these statements has a different Recordset associated with it. However, if you run the stored procedure from the Access 2000 user interface, it only returns the Recordset associated with the first SELECT statement.

```
Alter Procedure categories_products_and_join
As


--A list of categories
SELECT * FROM Categories


--A list of products
SELECT* FROM Products


--A list of products within categories
SELECT Categories.CategoryName, Products.ProductName,
    Products.QuantityPerUnit, Products.UnitPrice
FROM Categories INNER JOIN
    Products ON Categories.CategoryID = Products.CategoryID
```

The print_categories_products_and_join VBA procedure below illustrates the syntax for retrieving multiple Recordsets from a single return set with the NextRecordset method. After opening a Recordset based on the categories_products_and_join stored procedure, VBA has immediate access to the Recordset that corresponds to SELECT * FROM Categories. The inner nested Do...Loop iterates through the records and prints the first two columns to the Immediate window.

After exhausting the records in the first Recordset within the inner Do loop, the procedure prints a marker for the end of the Recordset in the outer Do loop. Then, it invokes the NextRecordset method for rst1. If there is another Recordset in the return set, this makes it available. If not, this sets rst1 to Nothing. Before entering the inner loop to print the records of the new Recordset, the procedure prints in the Immediate window the record count for the new Recordset from the outer Do...Loop.

Once the procedure enumerates the members of the last Recordset in the return set, the application of the NextRecordset method sets rst1 to Nothing. The outer Do...Loop detects this and relinquishes control so the procedure can terminate.

```
Sub print_categories_products_and_join()

'Demonstrates using the NextRecordset method to extract multiple
'recordsets from a stored procedure's return set

Dim strspr1 As String
Dim rst1 As ADODB.Recordset

'Instantiate recordset and open it for the
'return set from stored procedure named in strspr1
Set rst1 = New ADODB.Recordset
strspr1 = "categories_products_and_join"
rst1.Open strspr1, CurrentProject.Connection, , , adCmdStoredProc

'Loop through recordset object until it is nothing
Do Until rst1 Is Nothing
    Debug.Print "Record count = " & rst1.RecordCount, _
        "Number of fields = " & rst1.Fields.Count
    Do Until rst1.EOF
        Debug.Print rst1(0) & String(15 - Len(rst1(0)), " ") & rst1(1)
        rst1.MoveNext
    Loop
'After printing records for a recordset, print end-of-recordset
'marker and advance to the next recordset
    Debug.Print String(10, "-") & " end of recordset " & _
        String(10, "-") & vbCrLf
    Set rst1 = rst1.NextRecordset
Loop

'Cleanup recordset resources
rst1.Close
Set rst1 = Nothing

End Sub
```

The following screenshot shows an excerpt from the output generated by the preceding VBA procedure:

```
Record count = 8
1              Beverages
2              Condiments
3              Confections
4              Dairy Products
5              Grains/Cereals
6              Meat/Poultry
7              Produce
8              Seafood
---------- end of recordset ----------

Record count = 77
1              Chai
2              Chang
3              Aniseed Syrup
4              Chef Anton's Cajun Seasoning
5              Chef Anton's Gumbo Mix
6              Grandma's Boysenberry Spread
7              Uncle Bob's Organic Dried Pears
8              Northwoods Cranberry Sauce
9              Mishi Kobe Niku
10             Ikura
11             Queso Cabrales
12             Queso Manchego La Pastora
13             Konbu
14             Tofu
```

Working with Parameters and Return Values

You can use parameters to work closely with stored procedures from an Access project. By assigning values to input parameters, you can vary the behavior of a stored procedure. For example, you can change values in a criterion to cause SQL server to return different values. Input parameters can also enable a VBA procedure to designate different values for insertion into a SQL Server table. By reading output parameters returned by a stored procedure, you can interpret what happened in a stored procedure. Output parameters can pass back scalar values in a wide mix of SQL Server data types.

The RETURN value from a stored procedure acts like an output parameter in some ways. It passes back a value that allows a VBA procedure to know what happened inside a stored procedure. Two restrictions make RETURN values unique. First, they can assume only integer values, not strings or floating point numbers as with output parameters. Second, the syntax for recovering a RETURN value is different from that for recovering an output parameter.

Putting input and output parameters to work in a stored procedure is a multi-step process. You must initially declare your parameter pointers with DIM statements in your VBA code. Before you can instantiate a parameter, you must have a Command object that references it. The Parameters collection is a hierarchical object of the Command object.

Individual parameters are instantiated with the CreateParameter method of a Command object. You will typically specify the parameter's name, data type, and direction. If the data type denotes a string variable, such as char, then you must designate a length for the string in the CreateParameter method. You can also designate a value for the parameter with the CreateParameter method, although setting a value for a parameter after instantiating it can prove to be more flexible. After instantiating the parameters for a command, you must append them to the `Parameters` collection for that command. If you do not assign a value to the input parameter with the invocation of the `CreateParameter` method, then you must assign values before executing the command. Parameters with default value settings in a stored procedure do not require assignments in the calling VBA procedure if you wish to use the default values.

Assigning Input Parameters

The following stored procedure script, which we've seen before, adds a record to the my_employees table with `INSERT`. The insert_into_my_employees_from_parameters2 procedure differs slightly from the earlier version we examined in that it doesn't have a `RETURN` statement at the end. We demonstrated earlier in this chapter the operation of this procedure from another stored procedure through the Access 2000 user interface. Last time, it inserted the new record, but it did not pass back the output parameter `@employeeID`. With an output parameter declaration in a VBA procedure, you can recover the value of `@employeeID` after the `INSERT` statement. This capability is critical for some operations because it can allow an application to discover the primary key for a record based on an `IDENTITY` value. Your application may need this value to `INSERT` related records in other tables.

```
Alter Procedure insert_into_my_employees_from_parameters2
@firstname varchar(10),
@lastname varchar(20),
@homephone varchar(24),
@source varchar(20) = 'from input parameters',
@employeeID INT OUTPUT
As
INSERT my_employees VALUES(@firstname, @lastname, @homephone, @source)
SELECT @employeeID = @@IDENTITY
```

The following VBA procedure shows the syntax for assigning values to input parameters and recovering the value of output parameters for a stored procedure. It begins with a series of `DIM` statements for a `Command` object and parameters. The `Command` object must reference a stored procedure or other data source specification that requires the parameters.

Before you can instantiate the individual parameters, you need to instantiate a `Command` that points to a stored procedure designating the parameters. The VBA procedure shows the syntax for instantiating parameters with `varchar` and `integer` data types. You have to specify a size for the `varchar` data types. This should match the parameter declaration in the stored procedure. You can use the `Command.Parameters.Refresh` method to get a listing of all parameters, types, and sizes for a given stored procedure. This is especially useful for debugging.

After instantiating the parameters, the procedure assigns values to all input parameters, and it appends the parameters individually to the `Parameters` collection for cmd1, the `Command` object pointing at the stored procedure.

```
Sub working_with_input_output_parameters()

Dim cmd1 As ADODB.Command
Dim prm1 As ADODB.Parameter
Dim prm2 As ADODB.Parameter
Dim prm3 As ADODB.Parameter
Dim prm4 As ADODB.Parameter
Dim prm5 As ADODB.Parameter
Dim rst1 As ADODB.Recordset
Dim fld1 As ADODB.Field
Dim strOut As String
```

```
'Instantiate and assign properties to
'Command object
Set cmd1 = New ADODB.Command
cmd1.ActiveConnection = CurrentProject.Connection
cmd1.CommandType = adCmdStoredProc
cmd1.CommandText = "insert_into_my_employees_from_parameters"

'Create input/output parameters for cmd1
Set prm1 = cmd1.CreateParameter ("@firstname", adVarChar, adParamInput, 10)
Set prm2 = cmd1.CreateParameter("@lastname", adVarChar, adParamInput, 20)
Set prm3 = cmd1.CreateParameter("@homephone", adVarChar, adParamInput, 24)
Set prm4 = cmd1.CreateParameter("@source", adVarChar, adParamInput, 20)
Set prm5 = cmd1.CreateParameter("employeeID", adInteger, adParamOutput)

'Append and assign values to parameters
cmd1.Parameters.Append prm1
prm1.Value = "Rick"
cmd1.Parameters.Append prm2
prm2.Value = "Dobson"
cmd1.Parameters.Append prm3
prm3.Value = "502.123.4567"
cmd1.Parameters.Append prm4
prm4.Value = "from input parameter"
cmd1.Parameters.Append prm5

'Run command
cmd1.Execute

'Use output parameter in SELECT statement formulation as
'criterion and open recordset based on the statement
Set rst1 = New ADODB.Recordset
strSQL = "SELECT * FROM my_employees WHERE employeeID = " & _
    cmd1("employeeID")
rst1.Open strSQL, CurrentProject.Connection, , , adCmdText

'Print return set from SELECT statement
For Each fld1 In rst1.Fields
    strOut = strOut & rst1.Fields(fld1.Name).Value & " --> "
Next
Debug.Print strOut

'Cleanup recordset resources
Set prm1 = Nothing
Set prm2 = Nothing
Set prm3 = Nothing
Set prm4 = Nothing
Set prm5 = Nothing
Set cmd1 = Nothing

'Cleanup recordset resources
rst1.Close
Set rst1 = Nothing

End Sub
```

You can retrieve an output parameter directly from the Command object by specifying the identifier for the parameter in quotes. This will be the output parameter declaration in the stored procedure, excluding the @ prefix. The preceding sample demonstrates this syntax with the identifier for cmd1 in the specification of a SQL string to echo the inserted record. Before exiting a procedure that references parameters for a Command object, you should clean up your resources by setting the Command object and the Parameters collection members to Nothing.

VBA procedures that take advantage of ADO must treat RETURN values like parameters. The CreateParameter method for Command objects has a direction parameter that explicitly references RETURN values. Beyond that, you must adhere to one other rule. Always create the RETURN 'parameter' object, and append Parameters to the collection, before any other real parameters for a Command.

Prompting the User for Input Parameters

The following stored procedure passes back a RETURN value based on the value a calling procedure assigns to an input parameter. The RETURN value receives a value of either 0 or 1 depending on the average price for the product named in the input parameter relative to the overall average price. An earlier sample in this chapter demonstrated how to process the RETURN value by invoking another stored procedure through the user interface.

```
Alter Procedure are_product_order_prices_higher_with_return
@in_product VARCHAR(40)
As

DECLARE @strMsg VARCHAR(100)

IF (SELECT AVG(extended_price) FROM my_extended_prices
    WHERE productname = @in_product) >
    (SELECT AVG(extended_price) FROM my_extended_prices)
    RETURN 1
ELSE
    RETURN 0
```

You can operate the preceding stored procedure with a VBA procedure in the style of the one that appears next. This procedure builds on the techniques already demonstrated as it adds a couple of new ones. The syntax for instantiating a RETURN value explicitly references the type of object in its direction parameter, namely adParamReturnValue.

The procedure assigns the input parameter at run time with an InputBox function. This function presents a dialog that allows a user to type in a product name for the input parameter. To help you test the sample, there are a couple of product names in the comments to the program listing. You can cut and paste these into the InputBox dialog to demonstrate the behavior of the procedure with two products – one with an above average price and the other with a below average price.

```
Sub working_with_an_input_parameter_and_return_value()
Dim cmd1 As ADODB.Command
Dim prm1 As ADODB.Parameter
Dim prm2 As ADODB.Parameter
Dim strMsg As String

'Instantiate and assign properties to
'Command object
Set cmd1 = New ADODB.Command
cmd1.ActiveConnection = CurrentProject.Connection
cmd1.CommandType = adCmdStoredProc
cmd1.CommandText = "are_product_order_prices_higher_with_return"

'Create Parameter objects for return value and input parameter
'The return value must always be the first parameter, and the other
'parameters must follow in the order of their specification in
'the stored procedure with parameters
Set prm1 = cmd1.CreateParameter("RETURN", adInteger, adParamReturnValue)
Set prm2 = cmd1.CreateParameter("@in_product", adVarChar, adParamInput, 40)
```

```
'Append RETURN value and input parameter
'Specify input parameter for product
'Two legitimate product names for prompt are
'    Tofu
'    Uncle Bob's Organic Dried Pears
'Notice that you do not require double single quotes from VBA
cmd1.Parameters.Append prm1
cmd1.Parameters.Append prm2
prm2.Value = Trim(InputBox("Enter product name:"))

'Run command
cmd1.Execute

'Present one of two message boxes based on return value
strMsg = prm2.Value
If cmd1("RETURN") = 1 Then
    strMsg = strMsg & " has higher than average order prices."
Else
    strMsg = strMsg & " does not have higher than average order prices."
End If
    MsgBox strMsg

'Cleanup recordset resources
Set prm1 = Nothing
Set prm2 = Nothing
Set cmd1 = Nothing

End Sub
```

After the procedure executes the command, the RETURN value is available with the same syntax as any output parameter. Reference the RETURN value by including its name as an identifier for the Command object. The VBA procedure uses the RETURN value to determine which of two message boxes to print. The following screen shot shows the outcome when a user inputs Tofu as a product name to the InputBox dialog.

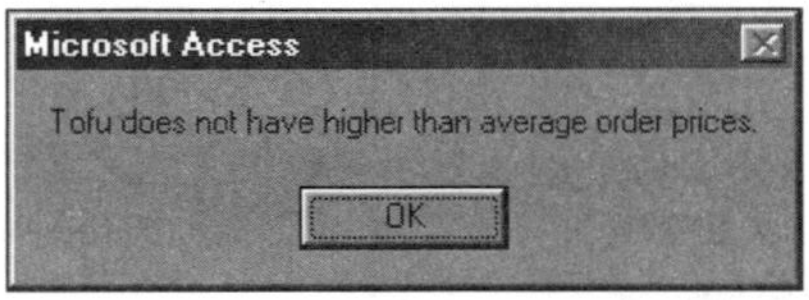

VBA Workarounds for User Interface Issues

In this section, we look at two things. First, we start off with a look at retrieving IDENTITY values, and then we move on to look at timing loops.

The Identity Crisis

As we have seen there are problems retrieving IDENTITY values immediately after an INSERT statement. Previous discussions of this problem presented two workarounds to this problem. One of these discussions demonstrated how to use parameters to resolve the problem. This works, but some developers might consider using parameters more complicated than necessary to solve the problem. Another resolution discussed previously involves manually running a second stored procedure with the statement SELECT @@IDENTITY. This generates the desired result, but it is manual and tedious and may give incorrect results if other users are adding records at the same time. VBA offers an enhancement of the manual solution by coupling the invocation of the separate INSERT and SELECT stored procedures.

The following VBA procedure reveals one approach that programmatically couples the INSERT and SELECT stored procedures. In fact, it confirms the robustness of the coupling by repeating it for three slightly different INSERT samples demonstrated previously in this chapter. These are the examples that we used Query Analyzer for, and asked you to save as stored procedures in your Access Project.

The first INSERT creates a new table and adds four rows starting with an IDENTITY value of 0 and an increment of 2. At the end of the first stored procedure, the @@IDENTITY value should therefore be 6. The next INSERT example reseeds the start value of IDENTITY to 998 before the insertion of a record. After the INSERT statement, the IDENTITY value increments to 1000. The final INSERT statement follows a DELETE statement that removes the record with an IDENTITY value of 4 and then adds a new record with a value of four. The sample below uses a single Recordset object, rst1, to run all stored procedures.

Notice that you do not strictly need a Command object that does not return records. However, after running the second Open method to return the @@IDENTITY value, the application needs to close rst1 before executing another Open method.

```
Sub getting_identity_values_automatically()

'The Access UI does not allow you to retrieve an identity
'value programmatically after an INSERT; this procedure
'offers a workaround in VBA

Dim rst1 As ADODB.Recordset

Set rst1 = New ADODB.Recordset

'Open recordset with stored procedure that inserts 4 rows
'starting with an IDENTITY seed and increment of 0 and 2
'Print IDENTITY value for last inserted record
rst1.Open "insert_into_my_employees", _
    CurrentProject.Connection, , , adCmdStoredProc
rst1.Open "return_last_changed_identity_value", _
    CurrentProject.Connection, , , adCmdStoredProc
Debug.Print "IDENTITY value of the last inserted record is: " & rst1(0)
rst1.Close

'Open recordset again and add a new record with a reseeded
'IDENTITY value of 998 before increment
'Print IDENTITY value for last inserted record
rst1.Open "reseed_identity_to_998_before_insert_to_my_employees", _
    CurrentProject.Connection, , , adCmdStoredProc
Debug.Print "IDENTITY value of the last inserted record is: " & rst1(0)
rst1.Close

'Delete a record and restore and restore the record with new
'values, but the same IDENTITY value (4)
'Print IDENTITY value for last inserted record
rst1.Open "delete_record_restore_with_same_identity_value", _
    CurrentProject.Connection, , , adCmdStoredProc
Debug.Print "IDENTITY value of the last inserted record is: " & rst1(0)
rst1.Close

'Cleanup recordset resources
Set rst1 = Nothing

End Sub
```

Note that there is no need to close the recordset during the cleanup as this has already been done earlier. The next screenshot illustrates the output from the preceding procedure. As you can see, it generates three lines with values of 6, 1000, and 4. These are the IDENTITY values that should appear after the running of the three INSERT operations.

```
Immediate                                          [x]
IDENTITY value of the last inserted record is: 6
IDENTITY value of the last inserted record is: 1000
IDENTITY value of the last inserted record is: 4
```

Timing Loops

A previous sample demonstrated the use of a WHILE loop for repeatedly running a set of T-SQL instructions. The WHILE loop in one stored procedure, invoke_time_delay_from_while_loop, called a second stored procedure, time_delay, until the condition for an IF statement directed control to a BREAK statement that terminated the loop. The time_delay stored procedure included a WAITFOR statement with a DELAY parameter, and it printed its delay setting, which was passed as a parameter from the invoke_time_delay_from_while_loop stored procedure. The sample ran successfully from Query Analyzer.

However, when run from an Access project stored procedure template, it was necessary to modify the time_delay stored procedure. In particular, we had to comment out a PRINT statement in the time_delay stored procedure in order to display the duration for running the WHILE loop in the invoke_time_delay_from_while_loop stored procedure. This unfortunate outcome requires two versions of the stored procedure with the WAITFOR statement. However, VBA offers a workaround!

The main gist of the VBA workaround is to time the duration with VBA statements instead of relying on T-SQL statements. This eliminates any interdependencies between the stored procedures and their statements on the ability to time the duration for running the WHILE loop. The screenshot opposite shows the code for the VBA procedure and the result that it generates in the Immediate window. Notice that it stores the current time on the client just before starting and just after regaining control from the stored procedure. Then, it uses the VBA DateDiff function to compute the duration as the difference between the two stored times.

```
Microsoft Visual Basic - Chapter6NorthwindCS - [Module9 [Code]]
File Edit View Insert Debug Run Tools Add-Ins Window Help

(General)                              timing_a_loop_with_a_waitfor_delay

Option Compare Database

Sub timing_a_loop_with_a_waitfor_delay()

'The invoke_time_delay_from_while_loop stored
'procedure does not display values with a SELECT
'statement; this procedure offers a VBA workaround
'to compute performance time

Dim cmd1 As ADODB.Command
Dim start_time As Date
Dim end_time As Date

Set cmd1 = New ADODB.Command

start_time = Now()
cmd1.ActiveConnection = CurrentProject.Connection
cmd1.CommandType = adCmdStoredProc
cmd1.CommandText = "invoke_time_delay_from_while_loop"
cmd1.Execute
end_time = Now()

Debug.Print "Duration for running " & _
    """invoke_time_delay_from_while_loop""" is " & _
    DateDiff("s", start_time, end_time) & "."

End Sub
```

```
Immediate
Duration for running "invoke_time_delay_from_while_loop" is 3.
```

The invoke_time_delay_from_while_loop stored procedure passes two parameters to the time_delay stored procedure. These call for delays of 2 seconds and 1 second, respectively. The VBA procedure reports a total delay of 3 seconds. The major point of this demonstration is that you can run a process in SQL Server, but time its duration with VBA instructions. For the Access developer who is more comfortable with VBA than T-SQL, this approach may have merit.

Even with these modifications you should still treat the results given by this tool as a rough guide only. Only a sophisticated profiling tool (such as the one that ships with SQL Server) will give you truly accurate timings and it would take another whole chapter to explain how to use *that* properly!

Working with Triggers

Traditional **triggers** are like code behind a form in that they attach to a specific table much like an event procedure attaches to a specific form or control on a form. They are written in T-SQL and are treated in very much the same way as stored procedures.

A trigger intercepts a data operation after the user submits the requested data operation, but before SQL Server actually commits the operation to the database. This allows your trigger code to perform any number of checks or any processing required, or even to cancel the operation altogether.

It is possible to replicate the action of triggers by adding code to your stored procedures provided that access to your data is forced through these procedures and is not allowed by any other method. In addition you would be forced to remember to use this code whenever you wrote a new procedure that accessed the data. For these reasons triggers have become extremely popular – they can protect data regardless of access method or the quality of procedure programming. On the downside, they are more difficult to maintain than simple stored procedures and can become complex and confusing in situations where any form of cascading is implemented.

You can set triggers to fire for INSERT, UPDATE, or DELETE statements. With the FOR clause of a CREATE TRIGGER statement, your applications can designate that a trigger fires for any combination of these statements. In addition, users adding new rows, updating values in rows, or deleting rows from tables directly can invoke triggers. TRUNCATE TABLE and DROP TABLE statements do not fire DELETE triggers. In fact, a DROP TABLE statement wipes out any triggers along with table. If you later re-create the table, you must also independently recreate the triggers.

At the point the trigger intercepts the operation it is tied to, SQL Server offers two special temporary tables. The **Inserted** table contains any new rows for a table. The **Deleted** table contains any rows for removal from a table. INSERT statements and actions create an Inserted table. DELETE statements and actions create a Deleted table. UPDATE statements and actions create both Inserted and Deleted tables. The new row values appear in the Inserted table, and the old row values are in the Deleted table. These special tables exist only for the scope of an event and are destroyed once all relevant triggers have completed and the data modifications have been committed to the database.

Starting with SQL Server 2000, your applications can include INSTEAD OF triggers. This new trigger type fires instead of the usual trigger. You can have multiple normal triggers for each type of triggering action, but SQL Server permits just one INSTEAD OF trigger for each INSERT, UPDATE or DELETE action. In addition, INSTEAD OF triggers fire for views as well as tables, but traditional triggers fire for tables only. Microsoft re-named the older triggers AFTER triggers in its Books Online. In coordination with this new naming convention, you can designate for which operations the older triggers fire with the FOR or AFTER clauses. Use the new INSTEAD OF clause to replace either when you create one of the new triggers.

This section introduces you to triggers by covering AFTER triggers in four areas. First, you learn the basic syntax for writing triggers in Query Analyzer and the Access 2000 interface for managing triggers. Because of the danger of loss when an application drops a table, developing and saving triggers with Query Analyzer can be particularly advantageous.

Second, this section builds your initial understanding of triggers with samples for archiving rows to one table as you DELETE them from another.

Third, you will learn how to maintain a **summary** table as you add rows to and DELETE rows from a table.

Finally, you will learn how to program referential integrity as well as cascading updates and deletes. Chapters 3 and 4 present SQL Server 2000 innovations for these topics from coding and interface perspectives. Developers building solutions with SQL Server 7, or the MSDE version compatible with must it, rely on triggers for building cascading updates and deletes into their solutions. This section closes with trigger samples for referential integrity with cascading updates.

Getting Started with Syntax and Interface Issues

The CREATE TRIGGER statement starts by giving you a chance to assign a name to your trigger. Next, you must specify an ON clause to designate which table it references. Recall that AFTER triggers apply exclusively to individual tables. However, you can run CREATE TRIGGER statements for two or more tables that are identical, except for the ON clause. The FOR clause enables you to specify when a trigger fires. You can specify any combination of INSERT, UPDATE, and DELETE. Next, the AS keyword acts as a delimiter for the start of any custom T-SQL code that you want in your trigger. This code can generally follow the T-SQL conventions for stored procedures. For example, you can run conditional statements and local variables, but you cannot pass parameters to or retrieve return values from a trigger. See Books Online for a detailed listing of the T-SQL statements that do not run from triggers.

The following sample demonstrates the syntax in the context of an example that prevents users from inserting, updating, or deleting records from a table. Since users can open the table, this trigger essentially enforces a read-only rule for the table. While this is not, in itself, particularly useful (as you can easily achieve the same thing using permissions) it gives us the building blocks for more complex processing later on.

```
CREATE TRIGGER my_employees_unconditional_rollback
ON dbo.my_employees
FOR Insert, Update, Delete
As
ROLLBACK TRAN
RAISERROR 50000 'You can''t touch me.'
```

The trigger's name is my_employees_unconditional_rollback. The ON clause indicates that it applies to a table named my_employees, the one from the sample database for this chapter. The FOR clause designates the types of actions that cause the trigger to fire. The trigger has just two lines of code.

First, it specifies a rollback of the current transaction. Transactions, in simple terms, allow us to group together a number of operations and to be able to automatically undo them with a single command (the rollback statement). Since a trigger intercepts a data operation before it fires, this is straightforward and fast. While we don't cover transactions explicitly in this book, we have a small aside at the end of this section discussing them.

Second, it prints a message reminding the user that the my_employees table is not for editing. When run from an Access project, the RAISERROR statement presents a message box.

You can drop a trigger just like any other database object. With a SELECT statement against the **sysobjects** table, you can determine if a trigger exists in a database. Use the DROP statement with a TRIGGER argument and the name of the trigger you want to remove. The following sample for Query Analyzer shows how to remove programmatically an existing trigger:

```
USE chapter5northwindCS
IF EXISTS (SELECT name FROM sysobjects
    WHERE name = 'my_employees_unconditional_rollback'
    AND type='tr')
    DROP TRIGGER my_employees_unconditional_rollback
GO
```

As mentioned above, it is often preferable to manage triggers from Query Analyzer. This gives you a chance to store them with more persistence than the Access user interface offers. This is because you can save your triggers in a file, such as triggers.sql, which is part of the download for this chapter. If you drop a table, you can easily re-create a trigger for a new version of a table just by re-running the CREATE TRIGGER statement from Query Analyzer. You can duplicate these sample triggers, by selecting their CREATE TRIGGER statement in triggers.sql and clicking the **Execute Query** toolbar control in Query Analyzer. You may also need to run some T-SQL to drop the triggers if they already exist.

If you right-click a table name in the Access 2000 Database window, the context-sensitive menu offers a **Triggers** command. Clicking the command pops up a dialog, such as the one in the Database window below. Command button controls on the popup dialog readily expose the ability to create a **New** trigger, **Delete** or **Edit** an existing one, or **Close** the dialog. A drop-down combo box control lets you select any existing trigger for the selected table. After designating a trigger, you delete it or open it for editing.

Clicking the **New** button creates a starter trigger design based on a standard template with a default name. In addition to specifying a name, the starter design completes the ON clause and presents the format to use as you complete the FOR clause. You can override the default name and modify the initial design for your purposes. If you are using Query Analyzer, or another tool for developing your trigger code, you can alternatively just cut-and-paste your code over the starter design. The Access 2000 stored procedure template does not allow CREATE TRIGGER statements.

The next screenshot illustrates the two trigger code segments presented above within Query Analyzer. To make a trigger active select its code, as in the screen. Then, click the Execute Query button. The screenshot shows the mouse resting on this control. We do not select the USE statement since the DB drop-down box already names the sample database. If that box did not designate the database for which you wanted to create your trigger, the USE statement would be mandatory, although it's always a good idea to use the USE statement.

Another trigger appears below the selected code. If you are going to store multiple triggers within a single query file, then you must always select the precise code that you want to run before clicking the Execute Query button. Issue the File | Save As command to assign an initial name to a collection of triggers from a Save Query dialog. This saves the file with a default .sql extension. After you initially save your trigger container (the .sql file), you can UPDATE it just by clicking from the toolbar the Save Query control like any other Save control.

An Aside – Transactions

Let's consider a very simple banking situation where money is being transferred between two accounts. There will effectively be two parts to the overall operation:

❑ Part A – money is deducted from the first account

❑ Part B – that amount of money deducted from the first account is credited to the second account

We want these two operations to be grouped together in a **transaction** – a unit of work that will either all be executed or none of it will be executed. If only part A was executed, and part B failed, the sum of money being transferred would disappear into nowhere! In a defined transaction if part B fails, then the operation is **rolled back** to its original state by adding the money back to the account and effectively undoing the first stage. To the outside world it would look like nothing had ever happened.

We can say that transactions have **ACID** properties, that is they should be:

❑ **Atomic** – either all or none of the operations in a transactions take place

❑ **Consistent** – the transaction should leave the system in a consistent state (if $500 is removed from one account in a transfer, then $500 should, assuming no bank charges, turn up in the receiving account)

❑ **Isolated** – transactions shouldn't interfere with each other, so multiple transactions can't modify the same data at the same time

❑ **Durable** – once completed, the results of the transaction should be properly retained (the customer should not have to repeat completed transactions if the system suddenly fails)

Detailed coverage of the implementation of transactions lies outside the scope of this book; suffice to say in T-SQL there are four important statements that are used for implementing transactions (some of which we've already come across):

❑ BEGIN – used to set the starting point of a transaction

❑ COMMIT – used to make the transaction durable, permanent

❑ ROLLBACK – used for 'undoing' a set of operations

❑ SAVE – sets a marker facilitating the ability to carry out partial rollbacks

Archiving Data as You Delete It

A previous sample in this chapter demonstrates a way of using a stored procedure to copy records from the my_employees table to a backup table named my_employees_2. The prior sample resides in the insert_into_my_employees_2_from_my_employees stored procedure. The stored procedure creates the my_employees_2 table from scratch as an echo of most of the columns from the my_employees table. Then, the stored procedure executes an INSERT statement that copies all rows from my_employees to my_employees_2. This sample requires manual intervention to create an archive, that is, you have to manually invoke the stored procedure. Wouldn't it be nice if SQL Server would automatically archive a record just before deleting it? The next three samples offer three different approaches to the task.

Before launching into the code, let's examine the design of a stored procedure for creating a new archive table. Just like my_employees_2, this table's first four columns will include an int column with an IDENTITY value that serves as a primary key followed by three varchar columns of varying lengths to store firstname, lastname, and homephone values. In addition, the new archive table has a fifth column named oldemployeeID. This column has an int data type. It can store the value of the EmployeeID column from the original table, my_employees, without any special measures.

The following create_my_employees_3_with_oldemployeeID_column stored procedure shows the column settings for my_employees_3. All three archiving samples use this table as a repository for deleted records from my_employees.

```
Alter Procedure "create_my_employees_3_with_oldemployeeID_column"
As

--Conditionally drop a table, before creating a new version of it
IF EXISTS(SELECT table_name FROM INFORMATION_SCHEMA.TABLES
    WHERE table_name='my_employees_3')
    DROP TABLE my_employees_3

--Create my_employees_3 with first four columns plus one for the
--the employeeID column from my_employees
CREATE TABLE my_employees_3
(
employeeID int IDENTITY(0,2) NOT NULL Primary Key,
firstname varchar(10),
lastname varchar(20),
homephone varchar(24),
oldemployeeID int
)
```

The next script contains the three variations of the archiving sample. All three samples demonstrate the use
of the Deleted table. They copy values from each of the records within it to the my_employees_3 table
before committing the DELETE statement impacts on the my_employees table. You should have only one of
the three following scripts working at a time. You can run the conditional DROP statement with a TRIGGER
parameter from a stored procedure (or just run the script directly from Query Analyzer) to remove an
undesired trigger. For the sake of clarity in the following listing, the three triggers have different names. Each
script conditionally deletes the trigger if it already exists. These samples are available in the triggers.sql
file, part of the download for this chapter.

```
--First data archiving sample
IF EXISTS (SELECT name FROM sysobjects
    WHERE name = 'my_employees_copy_to_my_employees_3'
    AND type='tr')
    DROP TRIGGER my_employees_copy_to_my_employees_3
GO
--Archive data to my_employees_3 as you delete
--them from my_employees
CREATE TRIGGER my_employees_copy_to_my_employees_3
ON dbo.my_employees
FOR Delete
As
INSERT my_employees_3 (firstname, lastname, homephone)
    SELECT firstname, lastname, homephone FROM deleted
GO
```

```
--Second data archiving sample
IF EXISTS (SELECT name FROM sysobjects
    WHERE name = 'my_employees_copy_to_my_employees_3_with_identity_intact'
    AND type='tr')
    DROP TRIGGER my_employees_copy_to_my_employees_3_with_identity_intact
GO
CREATE Trigger my_employees_copy_to_my_employees_3_with_identity_intact
ON dbo.my_employees
FOR Delete
As
SET IDENTITY_INSERT my_employees_3 ON
INSERT my_employees_3 (employeeID, firstname, lastname, homephone)
```

```
    SELECT employeeID, firstname, lastname, homephone FROM deleted
SET IDENTITY_INSERT my_employees_3 OFF

GO
```

```
--Third data archiving sample
IF EXISTS (SELECT name FROM sysobjects
    WHERE name = 'my_employees_copy_to_my_employees_3_with_identity_as_int'
    AND type='tr')
    DROP TRIGGER my_employees_copy_to_my_employees_3_with_identity_as_int
GO
CREATE Trigger my_employees_copy_to_my_employees_3_with_identity_as_int
ON dbo.my_employees
FOR Delete
As
INSERT my_employees_3 (firstname, lastname, homephone, oldemployeeID)
    SELECT firstname, lastname, homephone, employeeID FROM deleted

GO
```

You can create my_employees and populate it with four records with primary key values spaced evenly from 0 through 6 by running the insert_into_my_employees stored procedure. This stored procedure like several of the remainder in this example comes from prior samples in this chapter. After also running the stored procedure to create my_employees_3, you have two tables – one with four rows and the other with none. The following screenshots illustrate the contents of both tables at this point:

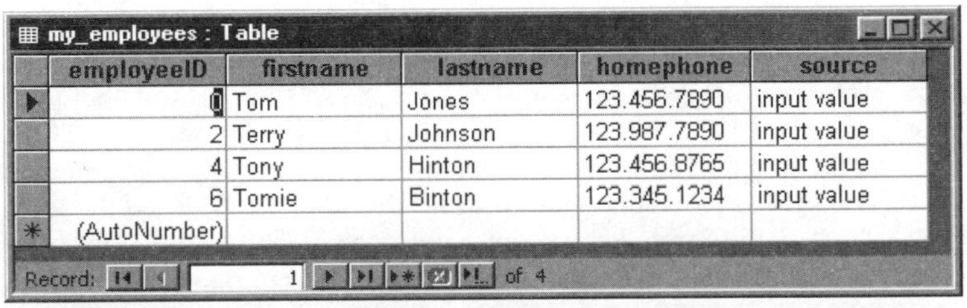

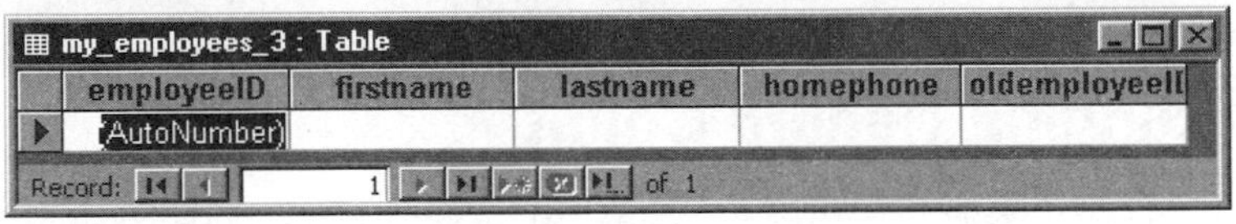

Before proceeding, you should run the script for the first sample. If you are following along exactly, you can just run the CREATE TRIGGER statement from the first script. This adds a new trigger to the my_employees table. You can verify this by right clicking the my_employees table in the Database window and choosing Triggers. This will open a dialog with a combo box that exposes the name of the trigger. Click Close. If you do not have Query Analyzer installed, simply open the triggers.sql file with Notepad. Then, copy the first archiving CREATE TRIGGER sample over the starter design that appears when you click New on the Triggers for Table: my_employees dialog. Save the new trigger and close the trigger window.

Next, run the delete_all_from_my_employees stored procedure. This uses a DELETE statement to remove all rows from my_employees. However, the trigger intercepts the operation of the DELETE statement and copies the firstname, lastname, and homephone column values to the my_employees_3 table before removing the column values from the my_employees table. The following screenshots depict the my_employees and my_employees_3 tables after this operation. Notice the migration of row values from the preceding pair of screen shots. You may need to invoke the View | Refresh command in the Database window to view the new row values. Chapter 3 discusses the reasons for this. You can use *F5* if you don't have View | Refresh.

As it turns out, the employeeID column values of the original four rows in the my_employees table perfectly match the employee_id values of those in the archive table, my_employees_3. This will not necessarily be true. In fact, there is an excellent chance that the employeeID column values will get out of phase over time. In a real production environment, it is more than likely that the employeeID values would be different to the employee_id values. If it is necessary to restore tables from the archive to the original data with the employeeID values intact, this potential for divergence represents a problem. The remaining two archive samples offer two different approaches for resolving this problem.

The second sample copies the employeeID column from the my_employees table to the my_employees_3 table as it creates the archive. It does this by modifying the IDENTITY_INSERT setting. When this setting is ON, your application can write a value into a column with an IDENTITY property. This strategy works, and it has the virtue of storing the archived EmployeeID values in a column with the same name in the original and archival tables. However, the trigger changes and restores the IDENTITY_INSERT setting from its default value with each DELETE. The third sample just copies the original EmployeeID values into a new column named oldemployeeID. This requires storing from a different column name, but it removes the need to constantly flip the IDENTITY_INSERT setting. Many developers prefer this last approach.

Keeping a Running Record Count

One typical use for triggers is to maintain a table of summary values – a kind of mini-data warehouse but without the effort and cost of the real thing! Maintaining up-to-date summary values makes it easy and fast to obtain summary information. Users can simply query a table with a single row of values with one column for every summary number it maintains. As tables grow in size, this approach can deliver a bigger payoff by reducing processing burden. This, in turn, becomes more significant if many users need the summary information.

To demonstrate this capability, we need to perform two preparatory steps before we can create the trigger itself:

First, re-initialize the my_employees table by running the insert_into_my_employees stored procedure. This re-populates the table with four rows, and it wipes out any existing triggers. A former trigger may still appear in the drop-down list of the Triggers for table: my_employees dialog. Choose the View | Refresh command on the Database window to remove any indication of triggers for a former version of the my_employees table.

The second preparatory step involves running a stored procedure to create and populate the summary table. We need to do this because the trigger will only maintain the totals as and when data is modified. We need to start with the summary information already calculated for all existing records. The summary table in the demonstration keeps count of the number of records in the my_employees table. The summary table has two columns. The second of these is a count of the number of rows. The first column contains a label to identify the contents of the second column. After creating the summary table named my_employees_3_summary, the stored procedure counts the rows in the my_employees table and assigns the resulting value to the summary table's second column. The following sample contains the T-SQL for this series of actions:

```
Alter Procedure "create_my_employees_3_summary"
As

--Conditionally drop a table, before creating a new version of it
IF EXISTS(SELECT table_name FROM INFORMATION_SCHEMA.TABLES
    WHERE table_name='my_employees_3_summary')
    DROP TABLE my_employees_3_summary


--Because table does not have a primary key add/edit/update
--is not possible via manual methods - just programmatically
CREATE TABLE my_employees_3_summary
(
count_in_my_employees VARCHAR(100),
my_employees_count INT
)

DECLARE @count INT
SELECT @count = COUNT(*) FROM my_employees
insert my_employees_3_summary VALUES('Count in my_employees = ',@count)
```

The trigger to perform this running tally of the records in my_employees must revise the count when an INSERT statement adds records or a DELETE statement removes records. A TRUNCATE will not reset the totals but this can easily be disallowed by using permissions. These requirements distinguish this trigger from the earlier samples. The first sample fired for INSERT, DELETE, and UPDATE events, but it did not use either the Inserted or Deleted tables. The second series of trigger samples for archiving data fired exclusive for DELETE events.

This trigger differs from the earlier ones in that it processes both the Inserted and the Deleted temporary tables. In the case of the Inserted table, it counts the rows and adds them to the total rows in my_employees. For the Deleted table, it also counts the rows, but this time it subtracts the aggregate function's value from the running total in the my_employees_3_summary table. The following CREATE TRIGGER statement is for the my_employees_count trigger. Assign this trigger to the my_employees table as described previously before proceeding with this demonstration.

```
--Sample trigger to keep a running total of the records in
--the my_employes table as a result of inserts and deletes
CREATE TRIGGER my_employees_count
ON dbo.my_employees
For Insert, Delete
As
DECLARE @count INT
SELECT @count = COUNT(*) FROM inserted
UPDATE my_employees_3_summary
```

```
      SET my_employees_count = my_employees_count + @count
SELECT @count = COUNT(*) FROM deleted
UPDATE my_employees_3_summary
      SET my_employees_count = my_employees_count - @count
```

After the initial creation of the my_employees_summary table, its second column contains a value of 4. Running the insert_into_my_employees_from_customers stored procedure will change this. If you have not modified the initial rows in the customers table, this will add 91 rows to the table. Therefore, the second column of the my_employees_3_summary table grows in value to 95.

Programming Referential Integrity and Cascading Updates

A database is said to have Referential Integrity when all of its references are valid. This is obviously a state we would normally wish all our databases to be in whenever possible. In some commercial applications referential integrity is absolutely essential. You wouldn't want the ambulance dispatcher to try to send out an ambulance that no longer existed because someone correctly deleted the ambulance's record from the "master vehicle" table but forgot to also delete it from the "available" table now would you?

Cascading updates is a way of propagating changes to one table through all other related and/or referenced tables thus preserving referential integrity.

It is generally superior to declare referential integrity than to program it with triggers if at all possible. However, SQL Server 7.0 and the corresponding MSDE server do not support cascading updates and deletes in their current implementations of declarative referential integrity. In addition, you cannot program cascading updates and deletes via triggers if you implement declarative referential integrity. The declarative referential integrity detects a violation of its constraint prior to the trigger for a cascading action gaining control. Therefore, you must program referential integrity with a trigger if you want either cascading updates or deletes via triggers.

The samples in this section depend on two triggers. The first programs referential integrity between the Orders and Customers tables on their CustomerID columns. Referential integrity by itself means that you cannot add a new record or UPDATE an existing record with a foreign key value that does not already exist in the referenced table. In order for this demonstration to work, you must first drop the declarative foreign key reference in the Chapter6NorthwindCS database. Since the foreign key resides in the Orders table, you have to modify that table's design. The following two lines perform this task from Query Analyzer or from within the body of a stored procedure:

```
ALTER TABLE orders
DROP CONSTRAINT fk_orders_customers
```

If you run the following UPDATE statement immediately after dropping the foreign key constraint, it revises the value of CustomerID to a value that is not present in the Customers table. This is possible because you dropped declarative referential integrity without replacing it with programmed referential integrity.

```
UPDATE orders
    SET customerid = 'ALFKZ' WHERE customerid = 'ALFKI'
```

Before proceeding, restore the CustomerID value back to ALFKI from ALFKZ. You can use the following UPDATE statement for that task. It should affect 6 rows if you are using an unmodified version of the Orders table in the Chapter6NorthwindCS database.

```
UPDATE orders
    SET customerid = 'ALFKI' WHERE customerid = 'ALFKZ'
```

Next, you need to assign a trigger to the Orders table that enforces referential integrity. The following CREATE TRIGGER statement can manage referential integrity between the Orders and Customers tables based on the CustomerID column. The trigger extracts the CustomerID value from the Inserted table and saves it in a local variable, namely @cid. An IF statement with a NOT EXISTS operator and a SELECT statement condition determines if @cid is missing from the CustomerID column of the customers table. A missing value signifies a violation of referential integrity. In this case, the trigger rolls back the UPDATE statement and prints a message to alert the user to the difficulty.

```
Create Trigger orders_customers_ri_on_customerid
ON dbo.Orders
FOR Insert, Update
As
DECLARE @cid NCHAR(5)
SELECT @cid = customerid FROM inserted
IF NOT EXISTS(SELECT * FROM customers WHERE customerid = @cid)
BEGIN
    ROLLBACK TRAN
    RAISERROR 50000
        'CustomerID violates RI with Customers.  Operation rolled back.'
END
```

After assigning the preceding trigger to the Orders table, you can re-run the UPDATE statement to change ALFKI values to ALFKZ. Once you assign the trigger, it prints a message if you run it from Query Analyzer or it presents the following message box if you run the UPDATE statement from an Access project stored procedure template. If you try to make this change manually, the operation won't be rolled back until you press the *Escape* key.

A second trigger manages cascading updates. This trigger belongs to the Customers table. The trigger fires just for UPDATE events. If the Deleted table's CustomerID value is in the CustomerID list for the Orders table, then the trigger needs to revise the CustomerID value for those records with the value of CustomerID in the Inserted table. The following script reveals the code for the trigger:

```
Create Trigger customers_customerid_cascade_to_orders
ON dbo.Customers
FOR Update
As
DECLARE @cid_old NCHAR(5), @cid_new NCHAR(5)
SELECT @cid_old = customerid FROM deleted
SELECT @cid_new = customerid FROM inserted
IF EXISTS(SELECT * FROM orders WHERE customerid = @cid_old)
UPDATE orders
        SET customerid = @cid_new
        WHERE customerid = @cid_old
```

With this trigger, your application can make changes to CustomerID values in the Customers table that cascade down to the Orders table. This kind of change is not permissible if you program referential integrity for just the Orders table.

User-Defined Functions

User-defined functions are a SQL Server 2000 innovation. They enable developers to build custom functions that return either a scalar value or a table in response to user input. These are a mixed blessing for Access developers. While the functionality is interesting, you can neither create them nor invoke them from Access 2000 views or stored procedures. If they fit your needs sufficiently anyway, you can still reference user-defined functions in scripts that you build from Query Analyzer. This section briefly introduces the topic and demonstrates the functionality provided by user-defined functions with a pair of samples.

User-defined functions are function subroutines comprised of T-SQL statements. They facilitate the reuse of T-SQL code. A user-defined function works similarly to a function procedure in VBA in that it always returns a value. However, its creation and use follow T-SQL conventions. For example, you make a new user-defined function with a CREATE FUNCTION statement. You can modify an existing user-defined function with an ALTER FUNCTION statement, and you can remove an existing user-defined function with the DROP FUNCTION statement. When you invoke a user-defined function, your code must designate the owner and the function name (for example, dbo.my_function). You cannot just designate the function's name by itself as you can with stored procedures.

Beyond these conventions, a few others are more particular to user-defined functions. First, you must state a data type for the return value. Do this with the RETURNS keyword. It appears on the first line after CREATE FUNCTION. You can declare a function as having a scalar data type or a table data type. You have the full range of scalar types available, except for timestamp, text, ntext, and image.

Second, the body of a user-defined function must appear within a BEGIN...END block. The one exception to this rule is the in-line user-defined function that returns a table. This type of function can serve as a replacement for a view. The AS keyword always precedes the body of a user-defined function whether or not the body contains a BEGIN...END block.

Third, the RETURN keyword must appear as the last line of a user-defined function. This keyword must embrace an expression that computes a result consistent with the data type specified by the RETURNS keyword.

Fourth, you must create a user-defined function before you can invoke it. Its creation persists "as is" until you modify the function with an ALTER FUNCTION statement or delete it with a DROP statement.

The following script demonstrates the syntax for a currency converter function named dollars_to_pounds. The first several lines show how to conditionally drop the function if it already exists. This user-defined function takes two parameters. The first is a number with a float data type, and the second is the @dollars quantity for conversion. The first number is a multiplier for converting US dollars to British pounds. The dollars_to_pounds function passes back its return value as a MONEY data type.

```
--Create dollars_to_pounds function
IF EXISTS (SELECT * FROM sysobjects
    WHERE id = object_id('dollars_to_pounds')
    and xtype = 'FN')
DROP FUNCTION dollars_to_pounds
GO
```

```
CREATE FUNCTION dollars_to_pounds (@dollar_ratio FLOAT,@dollars MONEY)
RETURNS MONEY
As
BEGIN
    RETURN(@dollar_ratio*@dollars)
END
```

The following screenshot depicts a SELECT statement in Query Analyzer with its return set on the Grids tab. The SELECT statement expresses unit prices from the Northwind Products table in both US dollars and British pounds. The SELECT statement also calls on a CAST function to round from the default four places after the decimal to just two places.

> *Do not try to run the SELECT statement with the reference to the user-defined function from either a view or stored procedure in Access 2000. It just does not work. The T-SQL parser in Access 2000 is unfamiliar with the format for creating and invoking user-defined functions. In addition, this sample uses a CAST function. The Access 2000 T-SQL parser does not recognize this function either.*

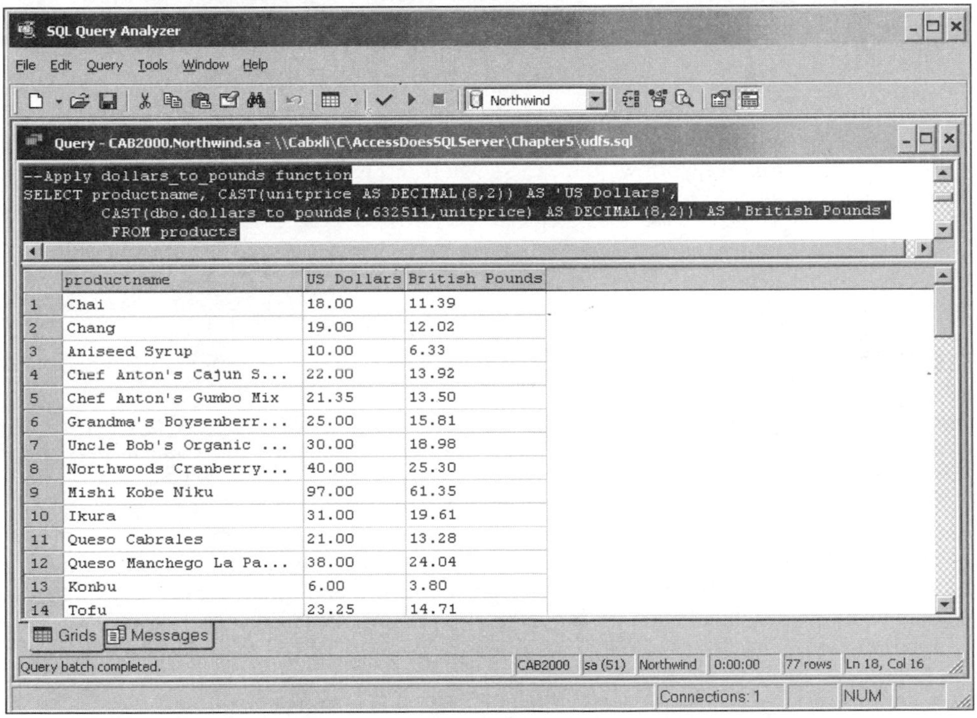

The starts_with user-defined function below returns a table with just those employees whose last name begins with a specified letter. The input parameter designates the letter. The CREATE FUNCTION statement for this user-defined function illustrates the syntax for specifying a user-defined function that returns a table. Notice that you first declare the table in the RETURNS clause of the CREATE TABLE function. This includes a table name with its columns. Next, an INSERT statement references this table, and a SELECT statement defines column values for the table. The RETURN statement after the INSERT statement passes back the rows defined by the SELECT statement.

```
--Create a table inside a function
IF EXISTS (SELECT * FROM sysobjects
    WHERE id = object_id('starts_with')
    and xtype = 'FN')
DROP FUNCTION starts_with
GO
CREATE FUNCTION starts_with (@l as CHAR(1))
RETURNS @fn_table TABLE
(
employeeID int,
firstname varchar(10),
lastname varchar(20),
extension varchar(4)
)
As
BEGIN
    INSERT @fn_table
        SELECT employeeid, firstname, lastname, extension
        FROM employees
        WHERE LEFT(lastname,1) = @l
    RETURN
END
```

The following one-line script invokes the user-defined function to pass back a table with two rows. The rows list the two employees from the Northwind database whose last names begin with 'd' (SQL is not by default case sensitive), namely Davolio and Dodsworth.

```
SELECT * FROM dbo.starts_with ('d')
```

Summary

Stored procedures are pre-compiled collections of T-SQL statements that we can invoke to perform specific tasks. This chapter showed how to use the built-in system stored procedures that come as part of the SQL Server engine package.

We discovered how to program stored procedures with INSERT, UPDATE, and DELETE statements that can manage the contents of a database. We also looked at how to simulate and extend the functionality of views by using stored procedures including multiple SELECT statements and by adding the ORDER BY clause to SELECT statement queries. In addition we learned how to couple stored procedures with VBA code through the use of parameters and RETURN values. This chapter's review of T-SQL control-of-flow statements will help you to program new user-defined stored procedures for custom functionality. The chapter reinforces all these topics with dozens of sample procedures that illustrate syntax and technique.

Using Access Forms with SQL Server

Access forms offer an elegant and highly interactive way to present SQL Server data to application users. If you are an experienced Access developer, this chapter will demonstrate how you can tap your existing knowledge of Access forms to build SQL Server solutions quickly and easily. If you are a SQL Server database administrator, this chapter should give you the essentials for making your database objects accessible from Access forms and for creating a graphical user interface for your SQL Server data.

Over the course of the next few pages we'll be looking at:

❑ Using the AutoForm Wizard to aid rapid application development in creating forms for SQL Server tables, views, and stored procedures. In this section, we'll look at how to customize the forms by exploring selected form properties, and combining forms into main/subforms that conditionally expose SQL Server in a subform based on values in a main form.

❑ Alternative methods of form creation – using the Form Wizard and creating forms by hand.

❑ Working with controls on forms. Here we'll concentrate on using one of the most commonly used Access controls – combo-boxes, and develop a good understanding of the principles of their usage, which can be easily transferred to other controls.

❑ Programmatic form control – creating VBA procedures that specify a form's data source and enable user interaction.

❑ Data presentation in forms – sorting, filtering, finding, and refreshing records.

❑ Miscellaneous advanced topics such as synchronizing forms and working with hyperlinks.

The sample database used for this chapter draws on the SQL Server Northwind database, and is available as downloadable code from www.wrox.com.

Let's begin by using the AutoForm Wizard.

Creating Forms with the AutoForm Wizard

The AutoForm Wizard allows forms to be created against a SQL Server table, view, or stored procedure, with a single click. The forms created have the following features:

❑   There is a text box for each field in the table, return set from the view or stored procedure.

❑   If the data for the underlying data source is editable, then the form can be used for manipulating the data.

❑   The form has built-in buttons for navigation and data entry, along with other buttons to help manage large data sources. One of these extra buttons allows users to cancel a long-running download of data, while retaining the data downloaded to that point. Another button allows users to adjust the maximum number of records that Access will load into the cursor behind the form.

This default limit on record loading into a form is 10,000 records, but if a faster response time (less waiting time) is desired, and not all of the records need to be seen, a smaller limit can be set, using the Max Records property which we will discuss shortly. The form will load faster because it is actually loading fewer records. Conversely, if the Recordset is bigger than 10,000 and there is a need to see all the records, then the limit can be increased (of course, this will cause the form to load slower).

While the AutoForm wizard requires no programming, it gives a great route into providing a basis for developing more sophisticated solutions (like the main/sub combinations we'll see later), and the use of VBA procedures to enhance the form's functionality.

To provide an overview of using the AutoForm Wizard and give us a basis for the rest of the chapter, in this section we're going to cover:

❑   Starting the AutoForm Wizard

❑   Using the AutoForm Wizard with tables

❑   Using the AutoForm Wizard with views

❑   Using the AutoForm Wizard with stored procedures

❑   Specifying Properties

❑   Creating Main/Subforms

Starting the AutoForm Wizard

If you have never used this feature before, you may be a little curious as to how to start the AutoForm Wizard. Our first step in invoking the AutoForm wizard is to select the object on which we will base our new form: to do this, highlight (select) a Table, View, or Stored Procedure from the Objects bar. Next, click the AutoForm tool on the Database toolbar. This tool is actually one in a collection of tools for helping to rapidly automate the creation of Application and Database objects. The toolbar button will expose the last auto tool used. If this was the AutoForm Wizard, then we can just click it. Otherwise, click the arrow next to the button and chose the AutoForm Wizard button from the drop-down button collection. The following screenshot illustrates the drop-down button collection with the AutoForm Wizard menu option highlighted:

Using the AutoForm Wizard with Tables

To create a form based on the Shippers table, we need to highlight the table in the Database window and click the AutoForm Wizard button. After a couple of seconds, we will see a form appear on our screen, such as the following one that appears nested in the Database window with the Shippers table selected:

If we click the Close button on the form, and then click No to the prompt about whether we want to save the form, the form disappears without any way to recover it. Of course, this is not a major problem because it only took one click to get the form in the first place. If we click Yes to the prompt for saving the form, then we can assign the form a name and save it in the Forms collection for the Access project. The default name for the form is the same as the Database object that serves as the form's data source. This chapter adds a prefix of frm to all forms because of the typical conventions for naming Access objects. This is not mandatory, but it is a widely used naming convention and a good practice to get into.

We should name our objects, including forms, according to a convention that makes sense in terms of our project needs and application development environment.

> *Form names can be up to 64 characters long. Names that contain embedded blank spaces do not require any special delimiters, such as leading and trailing brackets ([ ]). Since this book uses a variant of the* Northwind *database, which includes objects with embedded spaces that can serve as data sources for forms, it includes form names with embedded spaces in its samples. In contrast to SQL Server object names that appear with leading and trailing bracket ([ ]) delimiters, form names with embedded spaces do not require any delimiters.*

> *The title for the form window is a caption. By default, Access sets the caption equal to the source for the* Database *object. However, you can override the default setting manually or programmatically. There is no required connection between a form's caption and its name.*

The Navigation Buttons (arrows, record number, etc.) at the bottom of the form let users navigate, and add records to, the `Recordset` behind the form. Users can edit any record by simply clicking in the text box for a field and adding or removing content. Move off the record or click the record selector control (the right arrow just left of the ShipperID label) on the left edge of the form to commit our change. Users can delete the currently selected record by choosing Edit | Delete Record from the Access Menu Bar.

The two controls on the far right edge of the controls have a special meaning for client-server environments, and they are not part of normal forms for Jet databases. The control with an x turns red while Access is downloading the `Recordset` for a form. Users can interrupt the download by clicking the red control. The last control lets a user or developer set an upper limit for the number of records that Access will download for a particular form. This limit is 10,000 by default. We briefly discussed the pros and cons for changing this default in the opening section. Choose Tools | Options from the Database window menu, then select the Advanced tab to expose a text box control for setting an alternative limit that holds across all new forms – we will discuss this further when we look at the Max Records property. Any new values that we enter in the Advanced tab text box affect only new forms. Access does not revise the upper limit setting for existing forms. Access projects, through VBA, enable developers to set these and other form properties programmatically.

> *The setting to control the upper limit of rows downloaded for new forms also applies to all client-server objects, such as tables and views. Therefore, any global limits that we set must be suitable for tables and views, as well as forms.*

We will frequently want to create forms that show pictures. The AutoForm Wizard easily creates forms that show pictures in **bound controls**. A bound control is a control that gets its content from a field in the table or stored procedure that the form is based on. An unbound control is one that does not get its content from a field in a table or stored procedure. Its content is supplied dynamically through code or entered by a user. Since Access projects cache these pictures in a local cursor, they appear much faster than if they had to travel across a remote connection.

Create a form based on the `Categories` table, by highlighting the `Categories` table in the Database window and then clicking on the AutoForm Wizard button. We can change different properties of controls, by clicking on the Design button on the toolbar (or by right-clicking on the form and choosing Design). This is takes us into Access's Design mode where we can make changes to the form.

The Properties dialog displays the properties of the currently selected object. We open this dialog by right clicking on the object we wish to display the properties for, and then selecting Properties from the menu.

The Properties dialog displays the properties of the currently selected object. We open this dialog by right clicking on the object we wish to display the properties for, and then selecting Properties from the menu. This can be the overall form, any of its controls, or sections within a form. We're going to see more of the Properties dialog later, as we use it to set up aspects of our forms. However, we are not so likely to choose form bands or sections. This is more common with reports - the topic for the next chapter. As we click different controls on a form and the overall form, the Properties dialog title changes along with the individual properties on the dialog.

Right-click on the Picture, and then select Properties from the menu. Pictures have a Size Mode property setting. By default, this property has a setting of Clip, which makes the image appear its actual size. At this size, it is entirely possible that the picture will not fill a Bound Object Frame control. Choose either Stretch or Zoom to expand an image so that it fits to the border of its control. Stretch sizes the picture to fit the area within the margins. Zoom sizes the picture to fill either the height or width of the area within the margins. Stretch may distort the picture, but Zoom will not. We can set the Size Mode property manually at design time or programmatically. The following screenshot shows the form we created based on the Categories table. The Bound Object Frame's Size Mode Property setting shows Clip, the default setting.

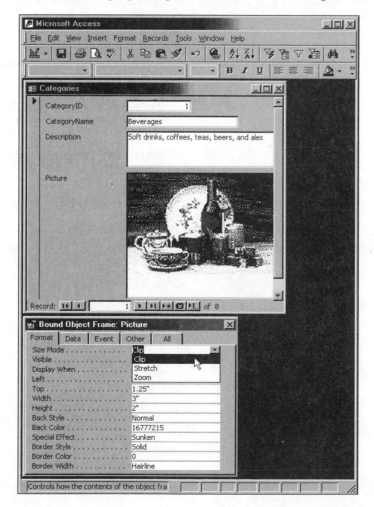

Using the AutoForm Wizard with Views

We can use the AutoForm Wizard to generate forms based on views. Views are great because they allow us to filter rows and columns from an original data source. We can create a form for a view just like for a table, except we start by highlighting a view.

Despite the apparent similarity in the process for generating a form based on either a table or a view, there is at least one possible difference in the result. Some views are not updateable in all or some of their fields. This restriction makes some forms based on views not updateable in the way that forms based on tables are always updateable. In general, we can update all views based on one-to-one and one-to-many relationships. We cannot update views based on aggregate functions, a sub-query, or a SQL statement with DISTINCT. An Access Help screen entitled Determining When Query Results Can Be Updated details all the circumstances under which we can and cannot update the fields in a view.

> *This chapter revisits the update ability of data in a form at several points. Understand that our solutions can always update data if we take the necessary steps. However, this may involve programming solutions based on unbound forms.*

The following form shows the fields in a form with a data source based on a view that returns two rows from the Employees table. To create the form we need to do two things: first we create the view and then we create the form based on the view. To create the view, click on Views from the Database window, then click New. We will be creating the view using SQL code instead of the Designer, so click on the SQL button on the toolbar, then copy the following code into the SQL part of the window, as shown below:

```
SELECT DISTINCT Employees1.FirstName, Employees1.LastName,    Employees1.EmployeeID
FROM Employees INNER JOIN Employees Employees1
ON Employees .ReportsTo=Employees1.EmployeeID
```

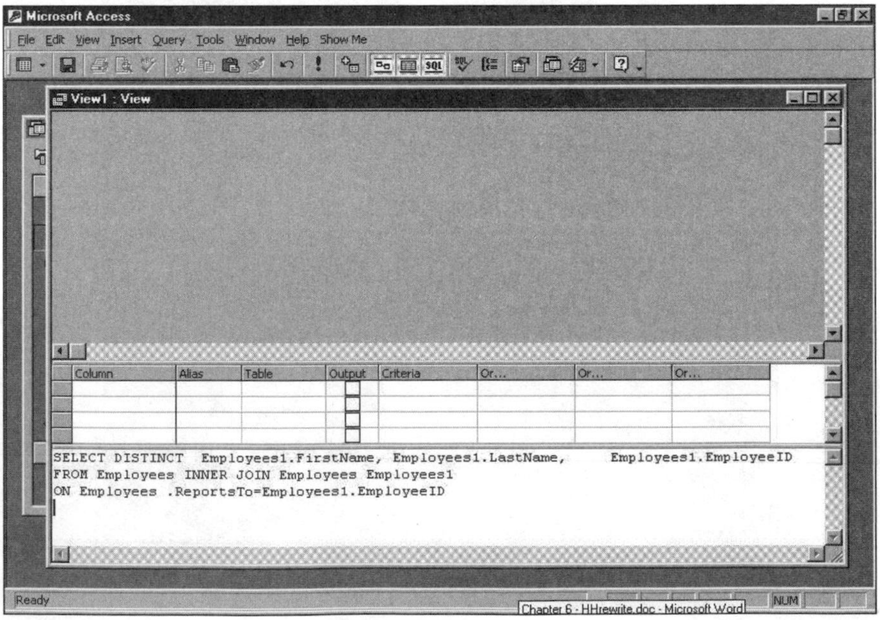

Save the view as **List_Managers**. Now we need to create the form to display the managers. Highlight the **List_Managers** view in the **Database** window and click the **AutoForm Wizard** button. The following form will be created:

Andrew Fuller and Steven Buchanan, are the only two employees in the table with direct reports. We cannot update the records through this form, since its return set comes from a SELECT statement with the DISTINCT keyword. Attempting to update a field generates an error sound and a message in the Access window's status bar stating that: **The recordset is not updateable.** That message applies exclusively to the form and its underlying view. The concluding sample in the chapter presents a similar data source through a form that is updateable. The other approach requires programming solutions for unbound forms. In contrast, the form above requires no programming and just one click.

As you can see, the view joins the **Employees** table with itself, by linking the ReportsTo field from one copy of the table to the EmployeeID field of the other copy. Without the DISTINCT keyword, this query generates eight rows – five identical direct report rows for Andrew Fuller and three more identical rows for Steven Buchanan. There is a separate row for each direct report to each manager. By including the DISTINCT keyword, the return set from the view shows just two rows – one for each manager. Although the DISTINCT keyword eliminates duplicated rows, it has the side effect of making the view not updateable with bound forms.

We can open the SQL statement behind a form based on a view by opening the form in **Design** view, then right-clicking on the form title (**List_Managers**) or anywhere in a gray area, and choosing **Properties**. On the **Form** properties dialog, select the **Data** tab, and click the **Build** button (with the ellipsis) for the **Record Source** property. It is the first property listed on the tab. This opens the **Query Designer** for the view. Click the **SQL** toolbar button to open the SQL window. This exposes the SQL code for the view. We can edit the form's underlying query from the **Query Designer** in any of the standard ways, for example, by adding new fields, performing calculations, or adding criteria. When we close **Query Designer** and save our changes, we can then update the form to include the modifications to the query. If we save our changes, the view will change to reflect the changes made.

We can also click on the Build button for the Record Source property with forms based on tables. This will lead to the opening of Query Designer with a new query based on the table. We can then edit the query as our needs dictate – for example, by excluding selected fields. Saving our changes builds a SQL statement for the Record Source property. When we save our changes to the form, the form will reflect the design of the SQL statement instead of the table. This technique is particularly attractive when we want to restrict the fields that are available to a form.

Using the AutoForm Wizard with Stored Procedures

Stored procedures that have a return set are also candidates for use with the **AutoForm** Wizard. We can edit the underlying data source, if the SELECT statement for the query behind the stored procedure enables this capability. If the stored procedure has input parameters, the form will prompt users to specify the parameters before developing a return set. We can use the **Input Parameters** property of the form to specify parameter values for use whenever the form invokes the stored procedure. By using several different forms with different input parameters, we can build solutions that reduce the burden on users for specifying the input to stored procedures with parameters.

If we have a stored procedure that performs an action, such as inserting or deleting a record, then it is not a suitable candidate for use with the AutoForm Wizard. Since nothing is returned, there is nothing to view on the form. In addition, the AutoForm Wizard does not handle stored procedures with return sets that contain multiple Recordsets. It will only return the first Recordset. Reserve these stored procedures for VBA/ADO coding.

Let us begin by creating a form based on a stored procedure with no input parameters. Then when we move on to our next example, which contains input parameters, we will be able to observe the differences.

However, it is easy for us to create a form with the sample database that uses a stored procedure as its data source and still permits the editing of the form's field values. Highlight the **Top Ten Most Expensive Products** stored procedure (its text appears below). Then, click the **AutoForm Wizard** tool. This creates a new form based on a stored procedure that has no input parameters and lets us modify its records. The SELECT statement for the query within this stored procedure merely returns values for two columns from the Products table. The ORDER BY and ROWCOUNT keywords in the stored procedure do not impact on the ability of users to modify data that appears in the form.

```
Alter procedure [Ten Most Expensive Products]
AS
SET ROWCOUNT 10
SELECT Products.ProductName AS TenMostExpensiveProducts, Products.UnitPrice
FROM Products
ORDER BY Products.UnitPrice DESC
```

This next section uses two forms to demonstrate the impact of setting the **Input Parameters** property. One form – frmSales by Year_without_input_parameters – does not specify the **Input Parameters** property, but the other one – frmSales by Year_with_input_parameters – does. The AutoForm Wizard generates both forms from the **Sales by Year** stored procedure, which has two input parameters. When we run the stored procedure by itself, it pops up two boxes sequentially. The first asks for a beginning date and the second asks for an ending date. The user responds to the dialog boxes by assigning values to the @Beginning_Date and @Ending_Date parameters for the **Sales by Year** stored procedure. We will encounter the pop-up dialogs for parameter values when initially creating a form for the stored procedure with the AutoForm Wizard, and again, when running the resulting form. These dialogs give users the flexibility of specifying different starting and ending dates for the return set. The starting and ending dates range between 07/10/96 and 05/06/98.

First we create the two forms, by selecting the **Sales by Year** stored procedure and click the **AutoForm Wizard** button. Save the form created as frmSales by Year_without_input_parameters. Repeat these steps, but name the second form frmSales by Year_with_input_parameters.

The following screenshot depicts the **Database** window just after we have selected the frmSales by Year_without_input_parameters form and clicked on the **Open** control on the **Database** window. Notice the pop-up dialog – this is the first of two; it requests a beginning date to define elements in its return set. This initial dialog box, and a subsequent one for the ending date, appear every time a user attempts to open the form. For the purposes of this example, feel free to enter any date in these dialog boxes, as long as it is in the range stated above.

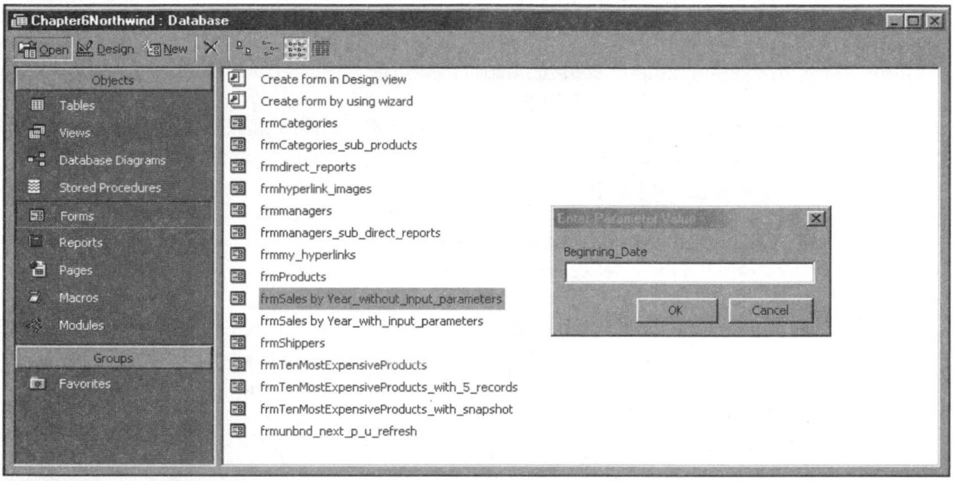

After clicking **OK** on the second dialog box, the form opens with a return set of all the records between the two dates that we specified. As before, we can navigate through the records to prove that this is the case.

When we open the frmSales by Year_with_input_parameters form, we see the same dialog boxes. Again, feel free to enter any date from the above range. After clicking **OK** on the second dialog box, we get the same result as for the previous form. However, what happens if we set the **Input Parameters** property for this form?

The next screen displays the frmSales by Year_with_input_parameters in **Design** view along with the actual **Input Parameters** property setting. The input parameter @Beginning_Date is set to '1/1/97' and the @Ending_Date parameter is set to '12/31/97'. This will bring back all records for the year 1997.

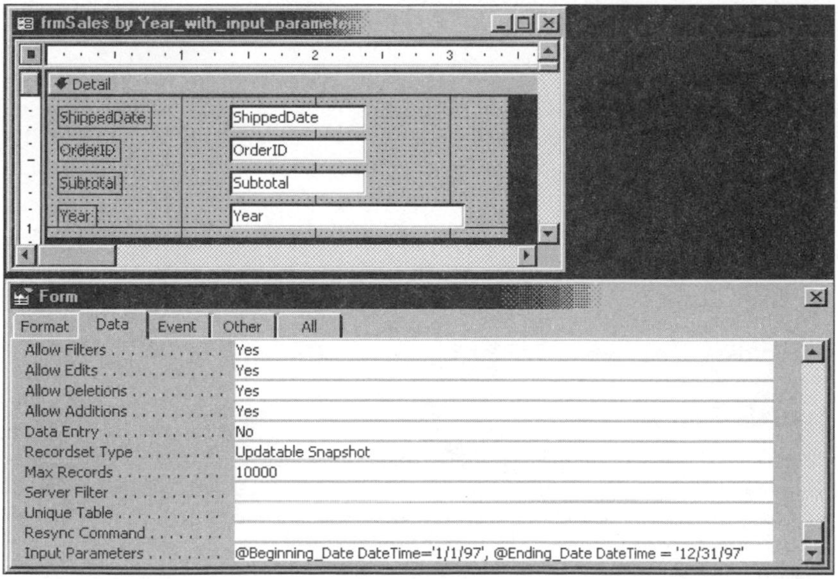

As we can see, the format for specifying parameters is parameter name followed by data type with a trailing equal sign and a parameter value. When the Input Parameters property setting specifies more than one parameter (as in the sample above), delimit the parameter settings with commas.

If we now open the frmSales by Year_with_input_parameters form from the Database window, it immediately opens the form with a return set for 1997, rather than presenting us with the dialog boxes that we saw earlier. This simplifies user input at the cost of making the form's behavior more rigid. Later in the chapter, we will illustrate how to set the Input Parameters Form property programmatically with VBA. This allows us to recover the flexibility lost by the absence of the pop-up dialogs. Using VBA allows us to customize how users enter parameters on Access forms, which allows better error checking and data validation.

By the way, neither of the two forms based on the Sales by Year stored procedure permits editing of the values they display. This is because the SELECT statement inside the stored procedure references a view in its FROM clause that includes an aggregate function. The SQL for the Sales by Year stored procedure is:

```
Alter procedure "Sales by Year"
    @Beginning_Date DateTime, @Ending_Date DateTime AS
SELECT Orders.ShippedDate, Orders.OrderID, "Order Subtotals".Subtotal,
DATENAME(yy,ShippedDate) AS Year
FROM Orders INNER JOIN "Order Subtotals" ON Orders.OrderID = "Order
Subtotals".OrderID
WHERE Orders.ShippedDate Between @Beginning_Date And @Ending_Date
```

Specifying Properties

As we can see from the preceding form samples, properties offer the ability to customize the behavior and appearance of forms. Recall that the Size Mode property for a Bound Object Frame determines the size of an image relative to the size of the control that contains it. The Input Parameters property can suppress the appearance of pop-up dialogs requesting parameter values. This section introduces us to two additional Form properties as it drills down on how to use the Form properties dialog.

We can view and set the Form properties dialog in the three form views - Form view, Design view, and Datasheet view. However, we may find Design view the most convenient one for working with the dialog, since we also have available other design tools, such as the Form Design toolbar and the Toolbox. The Toolbox facilitates the addition of controls to a form, and the Form Design toolbar offers valuable design controls, including one for opening the Form properties dialog.

In this section we'll be looking at:

❑   The Max Records property

❑   The Recordset Type property

The Max Records Property

The Max Records property is an overall form property that is very easy to understand. It sets the maximum number of records that a form makes available. When working with tables that can have a massive number of rows, this is an important property. It avoids a situation where a user attempts to open a form on a data source with hundreds of thousands of rows or more, which will result in an enormous amount of time passing before the form is displayed. Setting the Max Records property to a number like 10,000 will limit the records returned by a form to no more than 10,000. This value is the default setting for a form.

The previous screenshot shows the **Max Records** property for frmSales by Year_with_input_parameters. Notice it resides on the **Data** tab of the **Form** properties dialog. Its default value is 10,000; we can override this value by typing a new value in the cell next to the property name.

The **Max Records** property setting can synchronize with a **Tools | Options** setting on the **Advanced** tab. The setting name is `Default max records` in the **Client-server settings** group. The value for this setting on the **Advanced** tab is the default value for the **Max Records** property of any forms created. As mentioned previously, this control limit applies to the opening of tables and views as well. We can override the global default on the **Advanced** tab by assigning a different value to a specific form. If we change this value it won't affect existing forms, it will only affect new forms.

The following form uses the **Top Ten Most Expensive Products** stored procedure as its record source. Depending on the value we have for the **Max Records** property, we will see a different number of records returned.

If the form's **Max Records** property is just 5, then the form has only 5 rows in the `Recordset` behind it, despite the fact that the form's caption refers to 10 products. Since the `Products` table contains 77 different rows with many more than 10 distinct prices, we can see that the number of records returned by the form is constrained to just 5. If we update the **Max Records** property to, or its current value is, any value of 10 or more, we recover all 10 records in the return set from the **Top Ten Most Expensive Products** stored procedure.

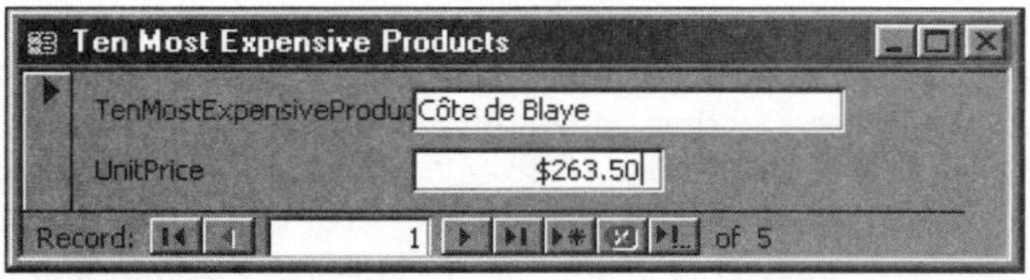

The Recordset Type Property

The **Recordset Type** property allows a developer to specify whether the data on a bound form is available for editing or not. This works hand in hand with the type of `Recordset` the form has. For example, if we are using a `SELECT` with a `GROUP BY` as the `Recordset` (which is not updateable), we can't specify that the data is available for editing via the **Recordset Type** Property. This property pertains to the whole form by specifying a property for the `Recordset` behind a form. With Access projects, there are two possible settings for this property: **Snapshot** and **Updateable Snapshot**. A snapshot is a copy of the `Recordset`. The default setting is **Updateable Snapshot**. Forms created with the **AutoForm Wizard** have this setting. If the data source for the form is updateable, then the form permits it. If the data source is not updateable, then the form doesn't permit updating, even though (by default) the **Recordset Type** property is set to **Updateable Snapshot**. We can change the property setting from its default setting to **Snapshot**. With this property value, a form does not enable the editing of field values, even if the underlying `Recordset` is updateable.

> *There is an alternative set of* **Recordset Type** *property values for Microsoft Access databases. This alternative set (Dynaset, Dynaset (Inconsistent Updates), and Snapshot) does not pertain to the* **Recordset Type** *property for forms in Access projects. The* **Snapshot** *and* **Updateable Snapshot** *options apply to a Microsoft Access project (.adp) and the* **Dynaset, Dynaset (Inconsistent Updates)**, *and* **Snapshot** *options apply to a Microsoft Access Database (.mdb).*

The **Recordset Type** property resides on the **Data** tab of the **Form** properties dialog. A drop-down box next to the property name lets us choose either **Updatable Snapshot** or **Snapshot**. If a user selects

Snapshot then all the fields on the form are read-only. The Snapshot setting also disallows adding new records and deleting existing ones. The controls for permitting the insertion of new records and the deleting of existing ones become disabled when a developer sets this property for a form. The error message for an attempt to edit a field on a form with a Recordset Type setting of Snapshot is Form is read-only because the Unique Table property is not set. This message appears in the status bar of the Access window:

We get this message because the Unique Table property is not set. The Unique Table property can affect whether a form permits the editing of its fields, but it is not relevant in this context since the data can't be updated. A later section in this chapter discusses the Unique Table property.

Another set of form properties can control the ability to add, delete, and edit data on a form. These properties have the names Allow Additions, Allow Deletions, and Allow Edits. They reside on the Data tab of the Form properties dialog. Instead of operating at the Recordset level, these operate at the form level. For example, these properties apply to Access projects with SQL Server data sources as well as to Access database files with Jet data sources. If the three properties have settings of No, then we have behavior that is equivalent to the Snapshot setting for the Recordset Type property. However, we can assign Yes or No to these properties individually to attain more granular control over data updating than is possible with the Recordset Type property. For example, assigning Yes to Allow Edits, but No to Allow Additions and Allow Deletions permits users to edit records without being able to add new records or delete existing ones.

There are times when we'll want to deny editing to just a subset of the fields on a form. The Recordset Type property and the Allow trio of properties are inappropriate for these occasions, since they apply to all fields on a form. However, the Enabled and Locked properties apply to individual controls on a form. These properties appear on the Data tab of a control's properties dialog. With the Enabled property setting, we can disable a form control, so users can view a control's contents without ever being able to select it with either the mouse or the keyboard. The Locked property disallows editing of the contents within a form's field if it is set to True/Yes. Disabled form controls are grayed by default to signify their status:

Enabled Property	Locked Property	Effect on Form Controls
No	No	Control can't get focus; control is grayed out, but data is displayed.
No	Yes	Control can't have the focus; data is displayed normally, but can't be updated or copied.
Yes	No	Control can have the focus; data is displayed normally, and can be updated and copied.
Yes	Yes	Control can have the focus; data is displayed normally, but cannot be updated but can be copied.

These two property settings apply strictly to individual controls on a form. No matter what their settings for individual controls, we can still add new records (some fields may be locked or disabled) and delete existing ones.

Creating Main/SubForms

Because of its versatility, one of the most popular types of forms in larger Access projects is a main/subform. This type of form is actually two forms, bound into one composite form. The main form is an outer form that "contains" the inner subform. The inner form synchronizes with the outer form. For example, with a main/subform duo based on an outer Orders table and an inner table of [Order Details], the inner form will show only those order details that match the current Orderid value in the outer form. This is shown in the form below, which is from the NorthwindCS sample database. The main form is called Orders, and the "inner form" which contains the detailed records is called Orders Subform.

The main and subforms are in a one-to-many relationship. This is typical for main/subform duos. To manage the synchronization between the forms, Access requires a common field (or fields) that both the main and subforms have. The data sources for the two forms do not require the same name for the field. However, the field must at least have the same data type in both data sources. In addition, when we assign the linking fields the same name, Access can automatically recognize them and use them as a basis for linking the forms.

We can use the AutoForm wizard to help construct a main/subform, as shown in the next section, but Access 2000 will not perform the construction with a single click, as it does for Access database files. Instead, we have to construct two main forms with the AutoForm Wizard. Then, we can drag one form from the Database window Forms collection to the other form that we already have open in Design view. We can position the subform on the main form to refine the form's appearance. If the linking fields have the same name on both forms, then we can open the new combined main/subform in Form view. If we wish to retain the original main form, then choose File | Save As and save the new combined form with a different name from the main form. If the main and subforms do not share a common name for the field, or fields, linking the forms, then we need to type the field names into the Link Child Fields and Link Master Fields property text boxes. These boxes appear on the Data tab of the subform control properties dialog. We must look up the field names because Access does not permit us to pick the field name from drop-down lists, as it does with some other property settings.

To illustrate this, we will work through the following example.

Creating a Products Subform within a Categories Main Form

We will demonstrate the process for creating a main/subform with the frmCategories form and a new form named frmProducts. The main form will be frmCategories, and frmProducts will serve as the subform. Notice that these forms are in a one-to-many relationship, because one category can have one or more products within it. Their common field has the name CategoryID.

We can use the AutoForm Wizard to create the initial version for frmProducts. This form lists all the fields for the Products table. After creating frmProducts, we open it in Design view. Then, we open the overall form's properties dialog, and select the Format tab. Click the drop-down list next to the Default View property name and highlight Datasheet, as shown in the following screenshot. Many subforms appear as a Datasheet view within their main form. Click any other property on the dialog to commit our change:

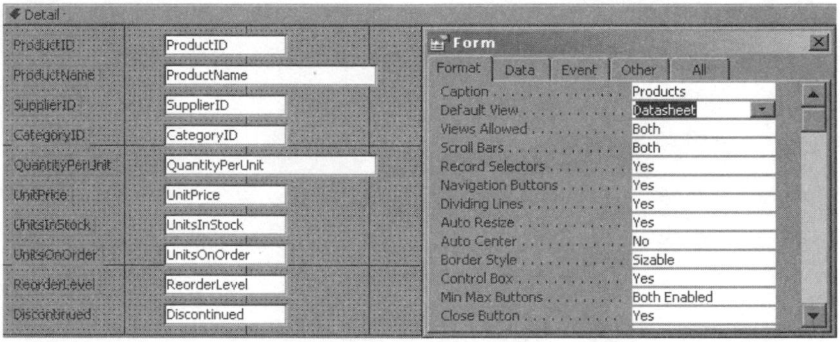

The next step is to insert the subform into the main form. We need to close frmProducts, then open frmCategories in Design view. Next, we highlight frmProducts in the Database window and drag it to frmCategories.

The following screenshot illustrates the frmCategories form open in Design view:

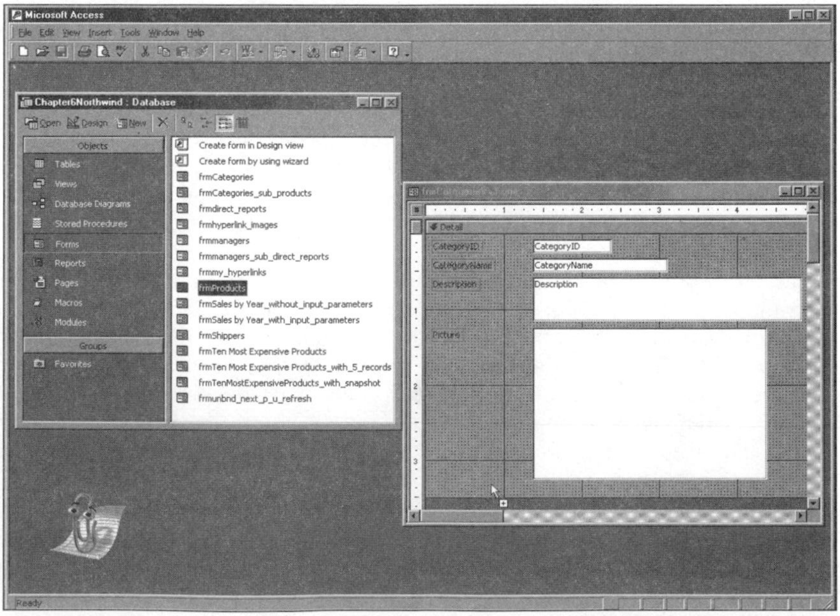

The **Database** window depicts the frmProducts form selected, and the mouse cursor hovers over the lower edge of the frmCategories form. When we release the mouse, the subform control appears on the main form. Aside from the fact that this control has some special properties, and that we can manipulate the subform independently of its membership in the main/subform, the control is just like any other form control. For example, we can drag and resize the control like other form controls. The following screenshot (In **Form** view, not **Design** view) shows our two forms together, although we still need to resize them relative to one another:

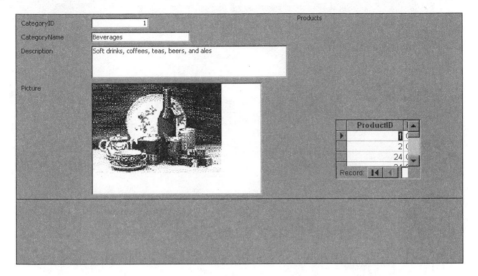

We size and position the subform control as our application requires. We can also set the column widths of its **Datasheet** view by dragging the column headings. We may also have to re-size frmCategories, so that it shows concurrently the fields from frmCategories and frmProducts. Once the layout is appropriate, save the form to preserve our settings. The screenshot in the next section shows our finished form:

After setting properties for the main and subforms, we save the main form with the subform on it. We have two options: save the new main/subform over the original main form, or save our newly designed form with a new name. This example saves the new form as frmCategories_sub_products. By saving the form with a new name, we preserve the initial main form for independent use or for use with other main/subforms.

Let's now look at using our new form.

Using frmCategories_sub_products

The following screen presents the main/subform created by the preceding example. The outer form is derived from frmCategories. This form includes fields for identifying groups of products, but it has no information about individual products; this is the job of the inner form.

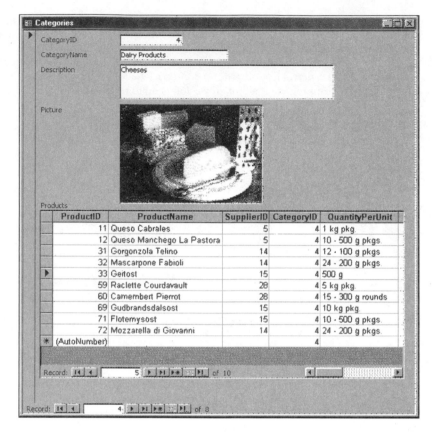

Notice that there are two sets of navigation buttons – one for the main form and the other for the subform. The main form has the fourth record selected: this is for Cheeses. The subform has the fifth record selected, which is for Geitost cheese. The Cheeses category contains 10 products. As we use the outer set of navigation buttons to move between categories, we will notice that the number of products within a category can change. Users can use the scroll bar on the subform to expose more columns of information on the products within a category.

While the subform control is a single control on the main/subform, users can access individual rows of data for the subform, as if they were using the form as a stand-alone form. Nevertheless, the rows in the subform control reflect the currently selected category in the main form. As both the sub and main forms rely on basic SELECT statements for a single table, users can edit the data in the main or subforms. We just type over the contents of a cell in the datasheet in the subform, or a text box in the main form, or press the F2 key to selectively edit or add characters to the currently selected item. After altering the contents of the currently selected item, a pencil appears in the record selector control for that row. Click the pencil to commit the change or press the Escape key to revert to the original value. We can change the contents of the main form the same way, except we need to make sure we are editing the data on the main form.

While the preceding form sample permits editing of records on both the main and subforms, this need not always be true. There is no special warning from Access if a form is not updateable. Furthermore, we create updateable and non-updateable forms in an identical fashion with the AutoForm Wizard. Other samples later in the chapter will explore ways of circumventing the problem of non-updateable forms. In the interim, this section creates a second main/subform sample that does not permit updating in the main form, but does allow it in the subform.

Creating and Using frmManagers_sub_direct_reports

The List_Managers form already presented the employees who have direct reports. Recall that these employees are Andrew Fuller and Steven Buchanan. Users cannot update the fields on the form, because the SELECT statement for the form's data source uses a DISTINCT keyword.

This sample extends the List_Managers form by adding a subform that shows the direct reports to each manager. This second form can depend on a basic SELECT statement from a single table. Any record in the Employees table with a ReportsTo field that is NOT NULL by definition represents an employee who reports to someone else. For example, Steven Buchanan is a manager, but he also reports to Andrew Fuller. Therefore, the ReportsTo field for the row with Steven Buchanan has a ReportsTo field value that matches the Employeeid field value for Andrew Fuller. See the table below to see who reports to whom:

Employee	Manager
Nancy Davolio	Andrew Fuller
Janet Leverling	Andrew Fuller
Margaret Peacock	Andrew Fuller
Steven Buchanan	Andrew Fuller
Laura Callahan	Andrew Fuller
Michael Suyama	Steven Buchanan
Roboert King	Steven Buchanan
Anne Dadsworth	Steven Buchanan

You have probably noticed that all table and field names in this book use consistent capitalization. It is good practice to be consistent on our naming conventions. However, Access and VBA are never case sensitive. In fact, this is the default setting for SQL Server 7.0 and later versions. However, SQL Server can optionally invoke sensitivity to case. We should follow whatever rules are appropriate for our development environment.

The following statement illustrates the T-SQL for a view, named list_direct_reports, that returns all employees from the Employees table who report to another employee. The return set from the query includes Steven Buchanan since he reports to Andrew Fuller. However, Andrew Fuller is missing from the return set because his ReportsTo field is NULL.

```
SELECT FirstName, LastName, Extension, HomePhone, ReportsTo
FROM Employees
WHERE (ReportsTo IS NOT NULL)
```

Run the AutoForm Wizard with the list_direct_reports view as its data source. This creates a form that will serve as a subform in the main form based on the List_Managers form. Name the form with the direct reports as frmdirect_reports.

We then close all forms before starting to create our new main/subform duo. Next, open List_Managers in Design view. Then, we drag and drop frmdirect_reports into the Design view. This creates one form with another nested within it, but it is not a true main/subform. Save this as frmmanagers_sub_direct_reports.

Open this nested combination of forms – we will note that the nested form shows all eight direct reports and the main form shows the two managers. The main form only shows two people because these are the only 'managers' (people who have employees reporting to them). The main and the subforms are not in a one-to-many relationship. This is because the AutoForm Wizard does not recognize the ReportsTo field values from the frmdirect_reports form as matching the Employeeid field values in the List_Managers form.

The following screenshot depicts the completed frmmanagers_sub_direct_reports form with the property values entered in the Link Child Fields and Link Master Fields property settings:

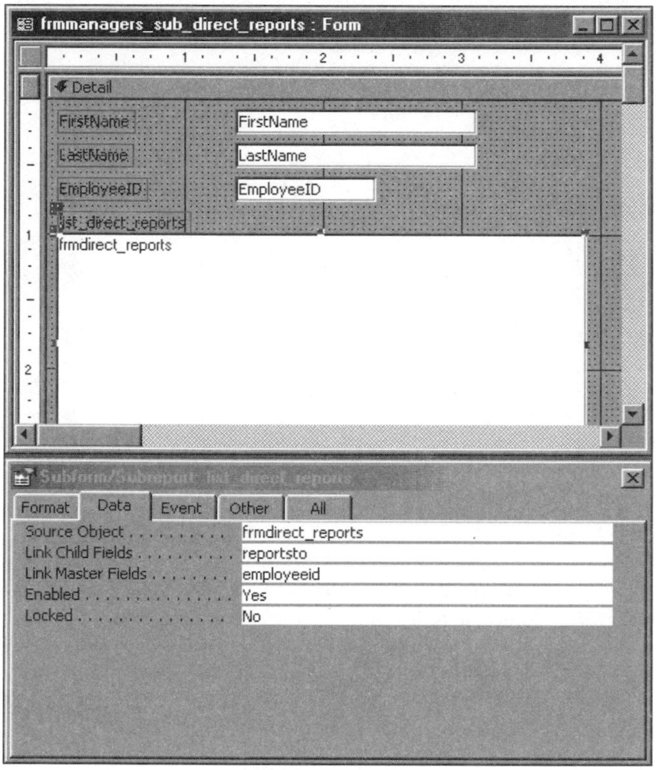

To get to this properties window, go into the Design view for the frmmanagers_sub_direct_reports form, then click on the subform (frmdirect_reports) control, and right-click to bring up the menu. Select Properties from the menu and select the Data tab from the properties dialog. Enter reportsto in the Link Child Fields property and employeeid in the Link Master Fields property. Link Child Field is used to link the subform and the Link Master Fields is used to link the main form.

> *It is good practice to use field names and not control names in the Link Child Fields and Link MasterFields property settings. Using the field names makes it easier to understand what data is being used to link the forms. For example, if we used a control named txtReportsto and we wanted to find out what data was being used to link the forms, we would have to go to the control's (txtReportsto) properties dialog to find out which field was the record source for the control. If we use the field name directly, we don't have to include this additional step. In certain circumstances it is mandatory to use field names. When we use the AutoForm Wizard and do not change the control names, the default field and control names by will typically be the same.*

The following pair of screenshots shows two different records of the frmmanagers_sub_direct_reports form:

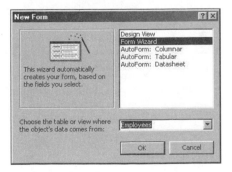

The record on the left shows Steven Buchanan as a direct report to Andrew Fuller. The subform shows Mr. Fuller to have five direct reports. The record on the right shows Michael Suyama as a direct report to Steven Buchanan. The subform indicates that Mr. Buchanan has three direct reports. We can use the navigation button of the subform to progressively display all the direct reports to each manager. We can use the navigation buttons on the main form (the lower set) to progressively display each manager.

Alternative Methods of Form Creation

Apart from the AutoForm Wizard we can create forms either:

- ❑ Via the Form Wizard
- ❑ Manually

Creating Forms using the Form Wizard

There is another wizard that will easily create a form: the Form Wizard functions much like the AutoForm Wizard, except that it allows us to select a few more options, like layout, type of background and style of form (column, tabular etc.). We will walk through creating a form using the Form Wizard instead of the AutoForm Wizard. Click on Forms under Objects on the Database Window. Then Click the New button on the Database window toolbar. This will bring up the New Form dialog box. Select Form Wizard from this dialog and select Employees as the table (see screenshot below). Click on the OK button when you have finished.

The next screen (below) asks us which fields we want to appear on the form. We can select individual fields by highlighting a field and clicking the singe arrow (>) key or we can select all the fields by clicking the double arrow (>>) key. We can remove one field at a time from the selected fields list by highlighting a field and clicking on the singe arrow (<) that points to the left. We can also remove all fields from the selected fields list by clicking on the double arrow (<<) that points to the left. Select all of the fields and click on the Next button when you have finished.

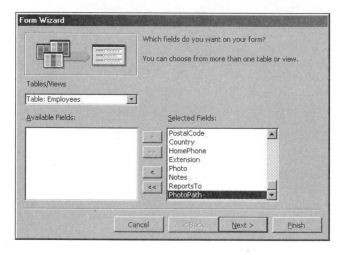

The next screen (below) asks us what layout we want for our form. The choices are: columnar (default), tabular, datasheet, and justified. Choose columnar and click on the Next button.

The next screen asks us to pick a style (for the background) for our form. There are several different ones to choose from: for this example, choose 'Standard' (which is the default) and click the Next Button. The final screen (above opposite) that comes up asks us to name our form and if we want to see our form in Design Mode or Open the form to view or enter Information. Give our form a name (Employees1), select Open the form to view or enter Information and click on the Finish button when you have finished.

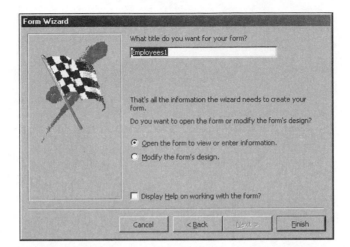

The finished form should look similar to this:

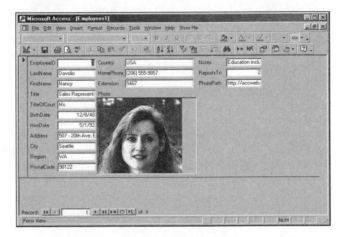

Creating Forms Without a Wizard

The AutoForm Wizard will readily create all the forms presented so far in this chapter, with the exception of the frmhyperlink_images form. While you can edit the form after its creation, there will come a time when you prefer or need a form created without a wizard. This section introduces that topic with forms based on single-table and dual-table data sources.

Creating a Form Based on a Single Table

To create a form without a wizard, we must start with a blank form. One way to do this is to select Forms on the Database window Objects bar, and then click New. With Design View highlighted in the New Form dialog, click OK. This generates a blank form with no data source.

When using a form to display data, the first thing to do is to specify the Record Source property. This is the first property listed on the form's Data tab in its properties dialog, as shown in the next image:

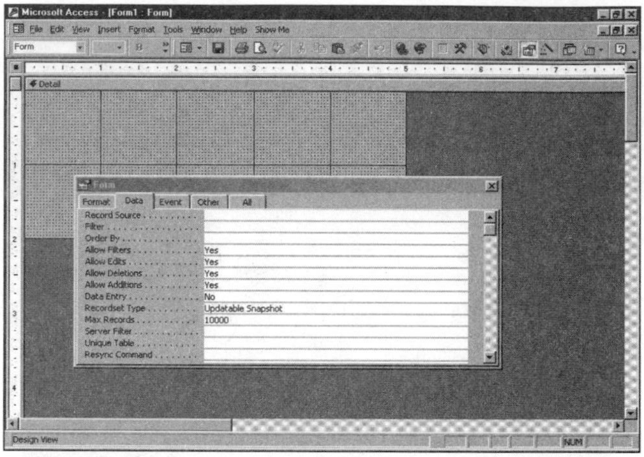

We can open the drop-down box next to the property name and expose all the tables, views, and stored procedures attached to the database for the current project. Selecting one will make the data in a table or the return set from a view or stored procedure available through the form. Another approach is to click the **Build** button next to the `Record Source` property. This opens **Query Designer** with a window title of **SQL Statement** (see Chapter 5 for detailed instructions and examples of how to use **Query Designer**). The tool enables us to build a custom data source for the form. Even if we are working with a single table, this approach can have merit, because it reduces the number of rows and columns that an Access application has to bring to a local cache for the form.

The following screenshot presents the **Query Designer** view of the SQL Statement for the sample form in this section. Notice it relies on a single table – **Products**. Forms based on single tables offer more flexible use than those based on two or more tables: forms based on a single table allow us to add, delete, and modify data, but a form based on several tables may restrict (depending on the type of join used) some data editing. The SQL window shows table name qualifiers in front of the field names. This is not strictly necessary; but it is the best way to reference the field names. A subsequent sample will build on this one, and it will reference another table with a **CategoryID** field of its own. This kind of situation requires table name qualifiers.

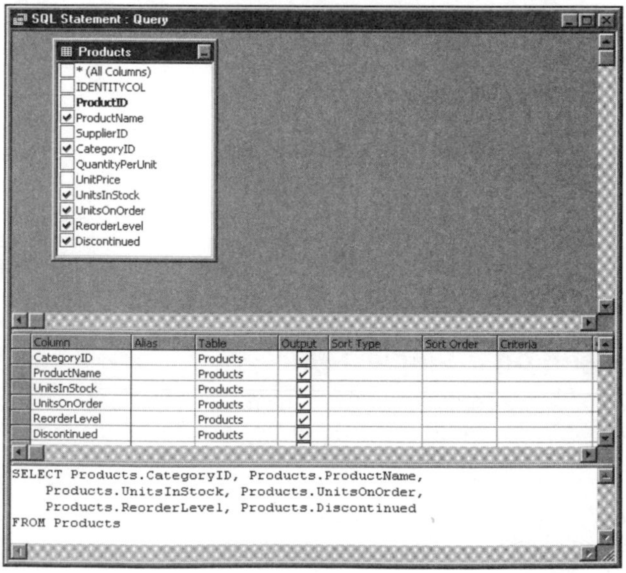

After closing the **SQL Statement** window for a form, we can add fields based on the data source in the query statement to the form. Use the **Field List** control on the **Form Design** toolbar to expose a list of fields that we can drag to our form. By default, the fields will appear as text boxes. We can add other types of controls besides text boxes for displaying data through the **Toolbox** control. We can associate a field with a control by setting the field in the **Control Source** property of the control. After adding controls to a form, we can drag them to their desired positions and sizes. The **Format** menu contains a collection of commands for simplifying the arrangement of controls and labels on a form. To align two or more controls, start by selecting them, then choose **Format | Align**, and click a dimension on which to arrange the selected controls. Our options are top, bottom, left, right, and to grid. We can also use the **Format** command to match controls for size (either vertically or horizontally) as well as to set the spacing between controls on a form. If we use the **Format** commands (**Align**, **Size**, etc.) and select all the controls on a form, we may get strange results.

The form shown below is based on the preceding SQL Statement. Product managers can use the form to survey the inventory position of items and mark in orders for items. As the form has a single table as its data source, users can edit, add, and delete records without restriction.

The form has been laid out such that the six controls are collected into three groups. The top group identifies the product, the next one gives inventory data on the product, and the last group identifies whether the product is available for order. Product managers should not order new supplies of discontinued items and thus we should disable the **UnitsOnOrder** control when the value for the **Discontinued** control is **True**.

Controls can be disabled programmatically by setting a control property or with the aid of the **Format | Conditional Formatting** command on the **Form Design** menu bar. To set the **Conditional Formatting** for this example carry out the following steps:

- ❏ From **Design** view, highlight (select) the **UnitsOnOrder** control.

- ❏ Select the **Format | Conditional Formatting** command on the **Form Design** menu bar. This will bring up the **Conditional Formatting** dialog:

❑   Set the condition that will disable the UnitsOnOrder control when Discontinued is True. Select Expression Is in the Condition 1 dropdown (we are using Expression Is instead of the other two options because we are dealing with the value of a different field – if we were basing the format on the value of this field we would use the Field Value Is option and if we were basing the format on whether or not the field has focus we would use the Field Has Focus option).

❑   Type [Discontinued]=True in the text box next to the Condition 1 dropdown. Then click on the Enabled icon (just to the right of the Font/Fore Color icon). The preview window should show the text as being disabled (see screenshot below).

❑   Click on the OK button.

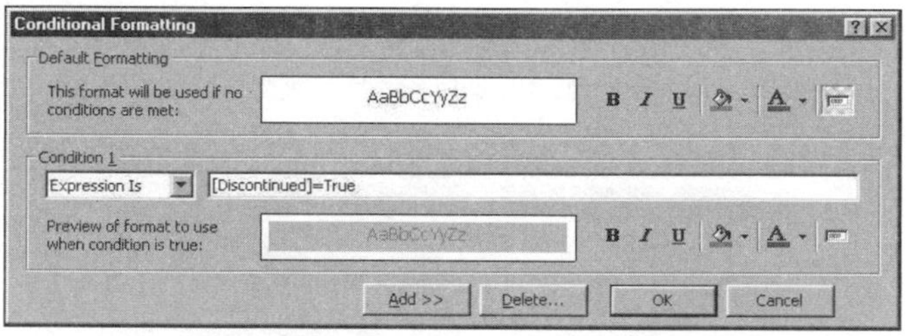

This now means the form will be more user-friendly:

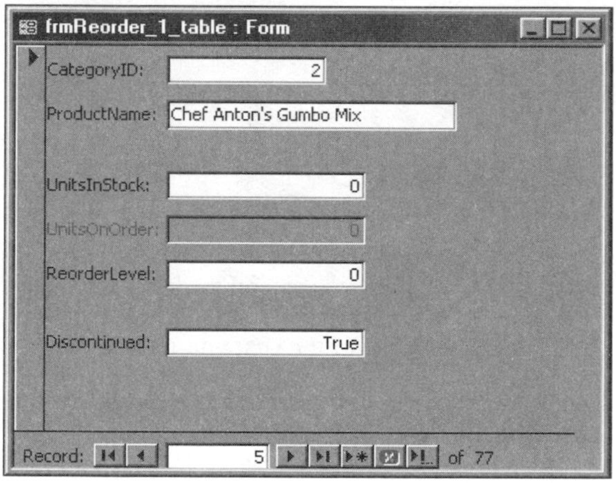

Creating a Form Based on Two or More Tables

There are times when a single table cannot serve the data needs of a form. The following screenshot presents the Query Designer view of the SQL Statement for a sample form based on data from two tables. The field list in the SELECT statement includes a reference to Categories.CategoryName. This reference makes CategoryName available as a field for the form.

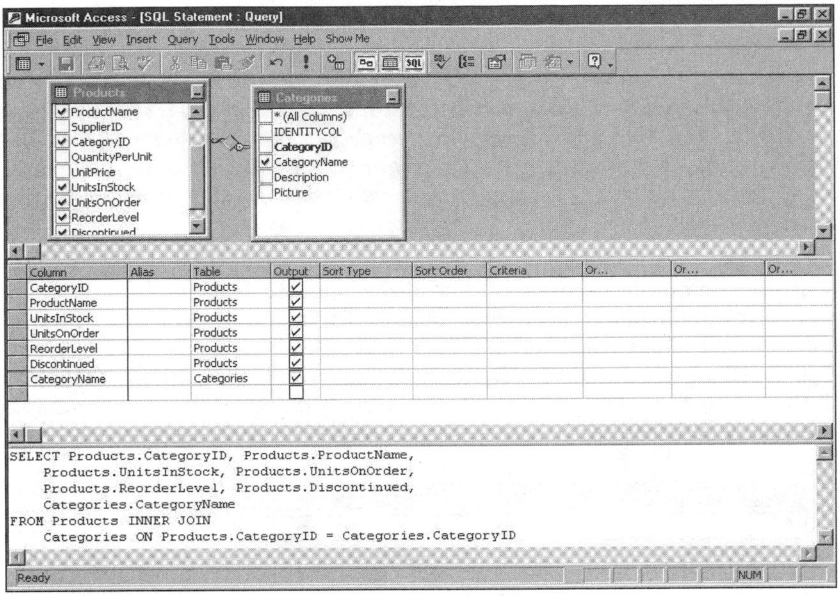

This simple adjustment to the `Record Source` property allows the creation of a new form that includes the **CategoryName** field. See the screenshot below for the look of the new form named **frmReorder_2_tables**. Notice the new field right below **CategoryID**. As uneventful as the design change is, the impact on the behavior of the form is substantial: this simple alteration makes the form read-only and users can no longer update inventory information! Any attempt to edit any field on the form results in a message that says **Form is read-only because the Unique Table property is not set**. This is in spite of the fact that the form relies on a very basic `SELECT` statement without any aggregate functions or other keywords that disable updating in a query statement.

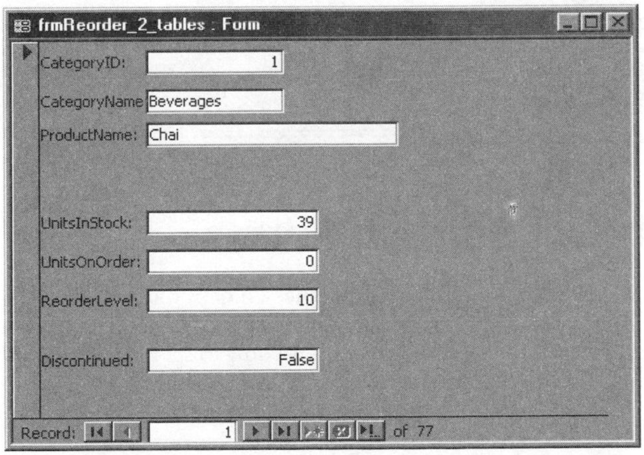

When the data source for a form depends on two or more tables, it will always be read-only unless you specify its `Unique Table` property. You can access the property from the **Data** tab of the form's properties dialog. It is also possible to set the property programmatically. If you want the form to be read/write, then you must name the table that is in a one-to-one relationship with the recordset behind the form. In this case, the form depends on both the **Categories** and **Products** tables, but the records on the form are in a one-to-one relationship with the **Products** table and in a many-to-one relationship with the **Categories** table. Therefore, designate **Products**, as the Unique Table property value to make the form read-write for the fields on the **Products** table. However, the fields from the **Categories** table still cannot be edited.

> *When you want a read-only form, failing to set the Unique Table property is one way of achieving the result. This trick only works when the data source for the form depends on at least two tables. If the form relies on a single table, the Unique Table property does not affect the ability to edit form field values. By the way, forms based on tables in a many-to-many relationship are always read-only, no matter what the setting is for the Unique Table property.*

The following screenshot depicts the **Form properties** dialog immediately after selecting **Products** as the Unique Table property for the frmReorder_with_Unique_Table form. A drop-down list next to the Unique Table property exposes the table names from which you can pick. You can confirm the impact of this selection by attempting to update field values on the frmReorder_2_tables and frmReorder_with_Unique_Table forms. The Record Source property is identical in both cases, but only the one with a Unique Table property setting permits the editing of field values.

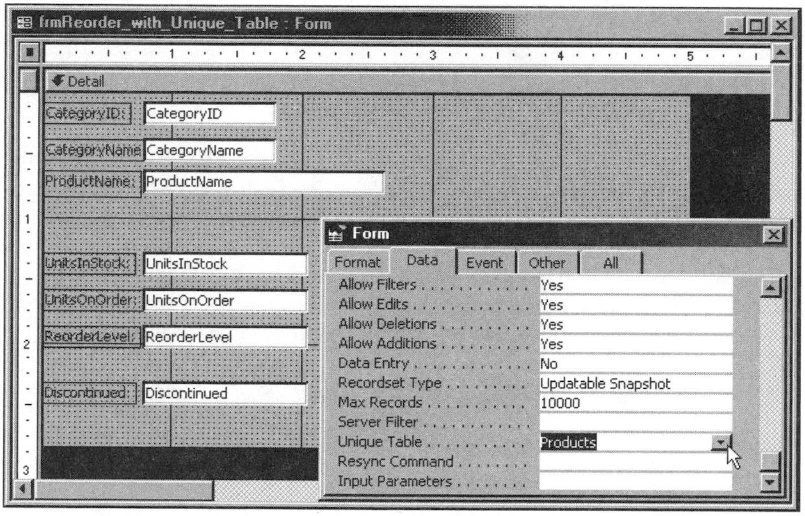

Working with Controls on Forms

Adding the correct controls and properly setting their values unlocks much of the flexibility of forms in SQL Server applications and the programming unlocks the power of a SQL Server application. This section reviews typical controls that we are likely to add to forms and shows how to set their values manually and programmatically. We can use the background to decipher how to set up some of the previous form samples, as well as prepare us for the closing section on advanced topics. This section drills down generally on bound and unbound controls. There is in-depth coverage of how to add combo boxes to forms.

Manipulating Properties for Unbound Controls

Unbound controls do not have a control source that points at a source in a table or the return set from a view or stored procedure. However, whether a control binds to a data source or not, it has properties. By manipulating these properties we can improve the appearance of our forms and enhance their functionality. We see some examples of how to do so in this section.

The `Label` control is the epitome of an unbound control. This is because the `Label` control has no Control Source property to facilitate its binding to a data source. Nevertheless, it does have properties, and we can set these manually at design time and programmatically at run time.

The following screen depicts a form with an edited `Label` control and a new label being added to the form. To start adding a label control, drag the label icon (the one with the 'Aa' just under the icon with the pointer) from the Toolbox and release it where we want it on the form. We can open and close the Toolbox from a control on the Form Design toolbar, which is displayed when we open a form in Design view. The icons on the Toolbox have tool tips that denote the type of control they represent. Once we have a blank label control on the form, start typing a message into the control. The new label appears on a gray background with an 8-point Font Size setting and a Normal setting for its Font Weight property. By pressing the *Enter* key, the form designer completes initial input to the label.

The edited label has four design changes to the initial input:

- ❑ Its font size is 12 points instead of the default 8 points.
- ❑ The weight is bold instead of normal.
- ❑ It has a centered alignment instead of the default left alignment.
- ❑ The background is white instead of the default gray.

These are among the most common design changes that we can make to a label control at design time with the Properties dialog for the control. A fifth design change is the expansion of the label control to the full width of the form. The preceding screenshot shows the Font Size and Font Weight properties on the All tab of the label being entered on the form. You can perform this task through the label's Properties dialog, but it is much easier to just drag the left and right edges by the handles that appear around the border of the label control.

The On Click event, and four more events for labels (On Dbl Click, On Mouse Down, On Mouse Move, and On Mouse Up), give designers the ability to make labels interactive at run time. For example, the label caption in the preceding screenshot instructs the viewer to click the label. When this happens it fires the `Click` event; the implementation appears below. This procedure uses a Static variable declaration to retain the variable's value even after the procedure ends.

The value of a Static variable is maintained for the duration of the Access application. There are two other types of variables: Module-level (the value of the variable is visible to all procedures and functions contained in the module where the variable was declared) variables and Global (the value of the variable is visible to all procedures and functions within all modules) variables. The `bolchanged` variable can be either `True` or `False`. The procedure reads its current value, and then assigns a new caption to the label based on the variable's value. It also toggles the variable's value. This causes the next execution of the procedure to insert the alternative caption for the label. In this fashion, the label caption toggles from one message to the other one as users click the label control.

```
Private Sub lbl_Click()
Static bolchanged As Boolean

If bolchanged = False Then
    lbl.caption = "Click me again to go back to the other message."
    bolchanged = True
Else
    lbl.caption = "Click me to change my message."
    bolchanged = False
End If

End Sub
```

Notice that the preceding screenshot also includes three text box controls; each of these contains a keyword inside it. The keyword Unbound indicates that the text boxes have no links to column values in a record source, such as a table or a return set. The three boxes, along with the four command buttons between the second and third boxes, on the form above provide a basic four-function calculator. The command button and text box templates are on the Toolbox. We drag and position them onto the form just as with a label. We can move the text box and its label together if there is a hand displayed when we click on the controls, or we can move them independently if there is a finger displayed when we click on a control. The text boxes come from the Toolbox with an attached label by default. The command buttons were re-sized to represent square function keys. The caption property for each button denotes a different type of calculation.

Users can type any numbers into the first two boxes and then click one of the command buttons. This performs a calculation based on the entries in the first two boxes and stores the result in the third text box. A `click` event procedure for each button performs a different calculation and stores the result. The following screenshot illustrates the addition function.

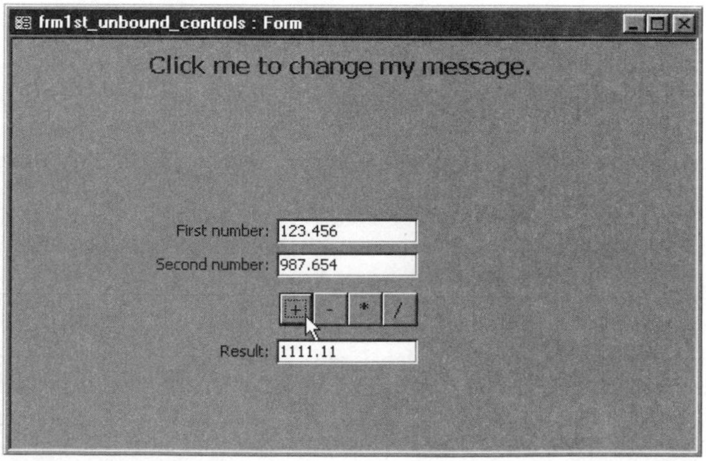

The subsequent VBA event procedures for the buttons show the logic for performing the calculations and storing the result. Notice the application of the CDbl function to the contents of the first two text boxes. This is because they have a string data type that results in uncertain conversion to a numeric data type. Invoking the CDbl function ensures the arithmetic operators perform against 8-byte Double data type values, which are equivalent to SQL Server FLOAT data type values. Storing the result in the third text box automatically converts the result from a numeric to a string data type.

```
Private Sub cmdAdd_Click()
txtResult = CDbl(Me.txtFirstNumber) + CDbl(Me.txtSecondNumber)
End Sub

Private Sub cmdDivide_Click()
txtResult = CDbl(Me.txtFirstNumber) / CDbl(Me.txtSecondNumber)
End Sub

Private Sub cmdMultiply_Click()
txtResult = CDbl(Me.txtFirstNumber) * CDbl(Me.txtSecondNumber)
End Sub

Private Sub cmdSubtract_Click()
txtResult = CDbl(Me.txtFirstNumber) - CDbl(Me.txtSecondNumber)
End Sub
```

Working with Bound Controls

This chapter's discussion of the AutoForm Wizard should convince us that using bound controls is very easy to do. Even if we move away from the AutoForm Wizard, it is still exceptionally easy to work with bound controls. There are two main property settings for bound controls. First, the overall form must denote a data source; we can achieve this with either the Record Source or Recordset properties for the form. The designation of a data source for a form makes accessible a pool of fields available for assignment to individual controls on the form. Second, the Control Source property is a control-level property; use this property to point a control at one of the fields in the form's data source.

The mundane text box is a very suitable control for many types of fields – particularly those with numbers or string values. For fields that can assume a relatively short list of values, such as the employees in a workgroup, a combo box is also attractive. When a field has a relatively short list of numbers representing text strings, then the field is a candidate for representation via an option group control. When we have fields that take Boolean values, they are good candidates for option buttons, check boxes, and toggle button controls. If we have bound images in our forms, then we can use the bound object frame control to display them on forms. Another control that handles unbound images is the image control. This control can take the path and file names for images bound in a table and display them without tying the original image file in the table, thereby yielding faster loading data sources. One good rule of thumb is to add all fields to forms with a text box (unless that is clearly inappropriate, as for a field containing images). Then, right-click the control and choose the Change To menu item to see what alternative control types Access recommends. If you see one you like, highlight it, and Access will automatically convert the text box to the alternate control.

For our next example, create a new form and name it frmbound_txtboxes_optgroup. Select the Employees table as the record source for the form. Add two textboxes to the form: one should have a label of Firstname with the Control Source of FirstName and the other textbox should have a label of Lastname with the Control Source of LastName. Make sure that the wizard button is ON in the Toolbox. Click on the Option Group Control and the Option Group Wizard will come up. The first screen will ask us for the labels we want on the Option Buttons; we want two. Type one in for Andrew Fuller and one in for Steven Buchanan (see scrennshot overleaf). Click on the Next button when you have finished.

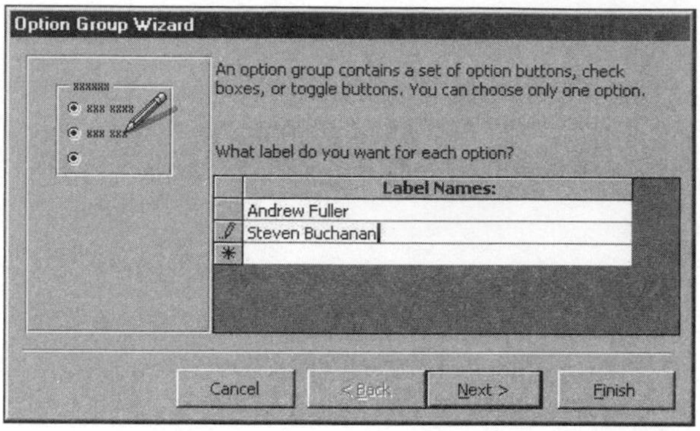

The next screen will prompt us for which Option Button will be our default. Select **Andrew Fuller** and click on the **Next** button. The next dialog will prompt us for what values we want assigned to each choice. These are the values that will be stored in the **Reportsto** field and MUST match the **EmployeeID** for each manager. Assign a value of 2 for Andrew Fuller (this is his **EmployeeID**) and a value of 5 for Steven Buchanan (see screenshot below). Recall that this is a numeric field. When we use a bound option group control, it is imperative that the underlying field contains numeric values – preferably a small collection representing strings that display well in an option group control. If our collection of field values is not a set of numbers, consider an alternative control, such as a combo box. Designers normally place check boxes or option buttons inside an option group control. These behave as a member of the overall control rather than as individual controls when they are in an option group. Click on the Next button when you have finished.

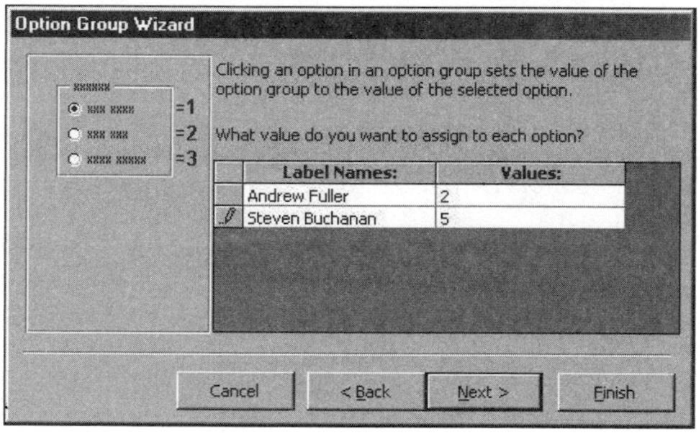

The next dialog asks us if we want to **Save the value for later use** or **Store the value in this field**. We want to store the value in the **ReportsTo** field, so click on the **Store value in this field** option button and choose **ReportsTo** from the dropdown list. This sets the `Control Source` property, which is our vehicle for linking a bound control to a field.

Click on the **Next** button. On the next dialog, choose **Option Buttons** as the type of controls we want. Click on the **Next** button again and this will bring up the last dialog, which asks us what we want the caption to be for the option group. Type in **Managers** as the caption and click on the **Finish** button.

The following screen shows how the final form will look. As users navigate between records, the values change to reflect the content of the current record. The **FirstName** and **LastName** fields appear in the text boxes, and the option group control decodes the numeric value in the **ReportsTo** field to one of the two manager names. Unless you block the capability through any of the techniques described earlier in this chapter, users can instantly update the field values. The screen below shows Andrew Fuller as the manager for Steven Buchanan.

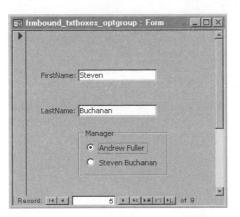

The next screenshot illustrates the functionality available from the ChangeTo menu item. Recall that this item is on the context-sensitive menu for a text box control in Design view. The shot depicts a text box with its control source set to the CategoryName field. However, the context-sensitive menu reveals the designer is about to select the Combo Box item on the ChangeTo menu. This action automatically converts the text box to a combo box. Users can then survey the category name values from any record, and they can re-assign a product to a new category from the combo box. We can even enable users to create new categories on the fly by setting the combo box control's Limit To List property (on the Data tab) to No.

Drilling Down on Unbound Combo Boxes

We already know the basics of how to set up a bound combo box. There are a few other features about combo boxes that are useful to know and will be used often in our development. This section drills down further on combo boxes but focuses explicitly on unbound combo boxes. Just remember that the same development guidelines apply to both unbound and bound combo boxes.

Manually Creating Combo Boxes

After adding the combo box control from the Toolbox to the form, we will need to set several controls that enable it to display data. Use the Row Source Type and Row Source properties to accomplish this goal. There are three types of data sources for a combo box; these are:

- ❑ table/view/stored procedure
- ❑ value list
- ❑ field list

Which selection we make for the Row Source Type property affects the appropriate setting for the Row Source property. If we choose the table/view/stored procedure option, then one of these database object types, or a T-SQL statement, is appropriate for the Row Source property. The return set from the statement should designate one or more columns. As the underlying data source changes through the addition, updating, and deleting of records, so will the items that the combo box displays. Using a value list requires the designation of a semi-colon delimited string constant for the Row Source property. The Column Count property determines how to interpret the string. The Column Count property specifies the number of columns that appear in a combo box. Therefore, a value of 2 will cause two items at a time to appear on a row in the combo box. A field list designation for the Row Source Type property works best with a special user-defined function. This function is highly formatted, and it designates selected other design elements besides the values the combo box displays.

When working with unbound combo boxes, we will typically want to save something about the selected item. The combo box control designates one column from the selected row as the value it saves. We specify which column it saves through the Bound Column property. If our combo box displays three columns on each row, we can have it save the first, second, or third column by entering 1, 2, or 3 for the Bound Column property. The next screenshot shows a combo box and text box control on a form named frmcombo_boxes in Design view. The combo box's name is cboCategories. The Properties dialog exposes selected settings for the combo box, including its Row Source Type, Row Source, and Bound Column properties. It specifies table/view/stored procedure as the Row Source Type property. The T-SQL statement for the Row Source property (see below) designates the CategoryID and CategoryName columns, in that order, from the Categories table as the source for the combo box.

```
SELECT Categories.CategoryID, Categories.CategoryName
FROM Categories
```

The Bound Column property points at the first column from the Row Source so that the cboCategories will save the CategoryID value after a selection from the combo box. The CategoryName is displayed in the combo box. The expression in the text box with an associated label of Text2: points at the combo box (=[cboCategories]). Therefore, the text box reveals the stored value in the combo box.

For the purposes of our example, on the Format tab of the Properties dialog set the Column Count to 2, and the Column Widths to 0; 1 (so the first column has a width of 0 inches and the second 1 inch).

The next screenshot illustrates the Form view of the frmcombo_boxes form immediately after the selection of Seafood. The combo box displays Seafood because the width for the first column is 0 (the combo box displays the contents of the first column with a non-zero width). The text box next to the right of the combo box displays the CategoryID value stored in the combo box. This is 8. If the Bound Column setting for the value intended for display in Text2 were 2 instead of 1, then the text box would display Seafood instead of 8.

Programmatically Populating a Combo Box with a Value List

We should now add another combo box and text box to the bottom of the frmcombo_boxes form. The combo box has a two-column source composed of the ShipperID and CompanyName fields from the Shippers table. We could simply designate a table as the source for the control; however, the next sample uses this control to illustrate how to create a custom value list. This way of populating a combo box has special appeal when the list does not change often. Instead of refreshing the list each time the form opens, the value list remains associated with a combo box until we manually or programmatically revise the list. We can schedule updates to the list on a regular cycle or allow users to request an update of the list on demand.

We delimit our value list string with semi-colons – for example, the list 1;a;2;b;3;c has six elements separated by five semi-colons. If the combo box's Column Count property is 2, then opening the combo box reveals three rows with a pair on each row (namely, 1 and a, 2 and b, and 3 and c). Notice that the Column Count property is integral to how Access interprets the elements in its value list. Therefore, as a minimum, we will need to set the Row Source Type, Row Source, and Column Count properties when assigning a value list. Use the string "Value List" for the Row Source Type property, the semi-colon delimited list as the Row Source property, and an integer designating the number of columns in a row as the Column Count property.

When programmatically (or manually) assigning properties to an unbound combo box, we are especially likely to use two other properties. The first of these is the Bound Column property. This property specifies which column in the selected row an unbound combo box stores. It can be different from the one that a combo box displays as its Text (or Value) property. The property numbers columns sequentially, starting with 1 for the first column. The second property we are likely to use is the Column Widths property. Separate each column width with a semicolon (;). When our first column is an index number that we want to save but not show, set the width for the first column to 0. The column width metric is in either inches or centimeters depending on settings in the Windows Control Panel. Select either U.S. (for inches) or Metric (for centimeters) with the Measurement system control on the Numbers tab of the Regional Settings dialog. Windows 2000 changes the name of the dialog to Regional Options.

The following script shows how to administer the five properties mentioned in the preceding two paragraphs to create a value list for the cbomyvalue_list_combo_box on the frmcombo_boxes form. This is the new combo box we have added to the form. The program reads values from the Shippers table to create a value list for the combo box. After opening a recordset on the Shippers table, the procedure composes a list of ShipperID and CompanyName field values delimited by semi-colons. Using a value list is fundamentally different from assigning the table or a T-SQL string as the source for a combo box, because the value list stores the display for a combo box with the form instead of re-opening a table on the server each time the combo opens. These values persist even when the form is closed. Assigning a value list property can improve the speed and stability of our applications. If the source data for the value list changes frequently, we may need to repopulate the combo box from time to time. The following code would be placed in a module:

```
Sub assign_values_to_combo_box()
Dim rst1 As ADODB.Recordset
Dim str1 As String
Dim obj1 As AccessObject
Dim frmname As String
Dim cboname As String
Dim bolfrm_closed As Boolean

'Make connection to data source for combo box
Set rst1 = New ADODB.Recordset
rst1.ActiveConnection = CurrentProject.Connection
rst1.Open "Shippers", , , , adCmdTableDirect

'Make Value list for combo
Do Until rst1.EOF
    str1 = str1 & rst1("ShipperID") & ";" & rst1("CompanyName") & ";"
    rst1.MoveNext
Loop
str1 = Left(str1, Len(str1) - 1)

'Find form with combo box and assign properties
'Exit sub after setting properties
frmname = "frmcombo_boxes"
cboname = "cbomy_value_list"
For Each obj1 In CurrentProject.AllForms
    If obj1.Name = frmname Then
        If obj1.IsLoaded = False Then bolfrm_closed = True
            DoCmd.OpenForm frmname, acDesign
            Forms(frmname).Controls(cboname).RowSourceType = "Value List"
            Forms(frmname).Controls(cboname).RowSource = str1
            Forms(frmname).Controls(cboname).ColumnCount = 2
            Forms(frmname).Controls(cboname).ColumnWidths = "0;1.5"
```

```
            Forms(frmname).Controls(cboname).BoundColumn = 1
              If bolfrm_closed = True Then
                    DoCmd.Close acForm, frmname, acSaveYes
              Else
              DoCmd.Close acForm, frmname, acSaveYes
              DoCmd.OpenForm frmname
          End If
      Exit Sub
      End If
  Next

  End Sub
```

After composing the value list, the procedure loops through the `AllForms` members to determine if the form is open. The procedure always opens the form in Design view. The identification of the form IsLoaded status is merely to determine whether the form should be open or closed when the procedure exits. Using Design view emulates the manual process for setting these properties and ensures that all the properties are readily available for setting. Next, the procedure assigns the five property values. Just before exiting the sub, the procedure saves its new settings as it closes the form. If the form was initially open, the procedure re-opens the form after saving the settings.

Since the above procedure uses string variables for both the form and control names, we can readily adapt this sample for other combo box controls on different forms; just update the `frmname` and `cboname` values.

Programmatic Form Control

This section looks more deeply at how we can change form settings programmatically, rather than just one particular control on a form. In this section, we will learn a number of things, such as:

- ❑ How to open a form using a stand-alone VBA procedure
- ❑ How to open a form using an event procedure

Programmatically Setting the Record Source Property

We can open forms programmatically, and while we are at it dynamically set their `Record Source` property. This capability enables a single form to serve more than one data source. The feature is attractive for all the reasons that component reuse is a popular topic. High on the list is that we have fewer components, forms in this case, to manage. This section illustrates how to open forms programmatically and set their values dynamically. We start out with a sample that launches a form from a VBA procedure. A second sample reveals how to borrow a part of the sample code and use it to programmatically open one form based on user input from another form.

Opening a Form from a VBA Stand-alone Procedure

We can open any form from a VBA stand-alone procedure. We can also assign the `Record Source` property to any form. When we set the `Record Source` property programmatically, it overrides any design-time setting for the property. This setting will remain during the entire execution of the project unless we reset it programmatically in another event or procedure. Therefore, if a form's `Record Source` property has a setting on its properties dialog, the programmatic setting will override it when we open the form programmatically. This is necessary for a single form to be able to serve multiple data sources. If two different VBA procedures open the same form with different `Record Source` property values, then the form opens with the data that its opening program specifies.

To keep the sample simple, a new form, named frmReorder_without_source, was created. To create this form, make a copy of the frmReorder_2_tables form (from the *Creating a Form Based on Two or More Tables* section) and rename it to frmReorder_without_source . Next go into design mode and delete the Record Source setting (see screenshot below)

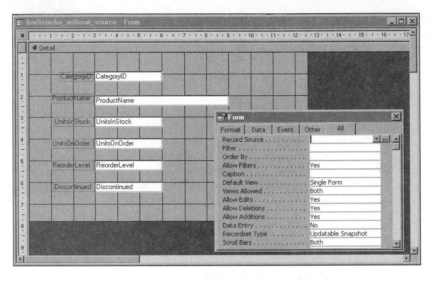

All other property settings and controls are unchanged. Therefore, there is no explicit reference to a CategoryName field (since the first reorder form has no reference to that field). However, the Record Source property can reference multiple tables whether or not the fields from those tables appear on the form. If the Record Source property references more than one table, then the form is read-only unless the Unique Table property points at a table in a one-to-one relationship with the recordset for the form, as we saw earlier.

The following pair of VBA procedures work together to open the frmReorder_without_source form. They use a SQL statement for the Record Source property that references both the Products and Categories tables. The first procedure, invoke_open_form_without_source, sets the form name, caption, and source string. Optionally, depending on what lines we comment out, the first procedure can assign a value for the Unique Table property. This is essential if we want the form to offer readwrite access to its fields. The second procedure, open_form_without_source, opens the form named in its input parameters and then assigns selected properties, including the form's record source. To create the procedures below, hit the *Alt + F11* keys to invoke the VBE window. For this example, close down any other module or class module windows that are opened. From the Project Explorer, right-click to bring up the menu. Select Insert | Module from the menu. This will create a new module, Module1. Copy the following two procedures into the Module1 Code window.

To run the sample, launch the invoke_open_form_without_source procedure from the VBE window. Then, click the View Microsoft Access toolbar button on the standard VBE toolbar. This will expose the form that the VBA procedures opened (see screenshot opposite).

```
Sub invoke_open_form_without_source()
Dim frmname As String, source As String
Dim caption As String, u_table As String

frmname = "frmReorder_without_source"
```

```
source = "SELECT Products.CategoryID, Products.ProductName, " & _
    "Products.UnitsInStock, Products.UnitsOnOrder, " & _
    "Products.ReorderLevel, Products.Discontinued, " & _
    "Categories.CategoryName " & _
    "FROM Products INNER JOIN Categories " & _
    "ON Products.CategoryID = Categories.CategoryID"
caption = "form_without_source"

'does not permit editing
'open_form_without_source frmname, source, caption

'does permit editing
u_table = "products"
open_form_without_source frmname, source, caption, u_table

End Sub


Sub open_form_without_source(frmname As String, _
    source As String, caption As String, Optional u_table As String)
Dim frm1 As Form

DoCmd.Echo False
DoCmd.OpenForm frmname
Set frm1 = Forms(frmname)
frm1.RecordSource = source
frm1.caption = caption

'Optionally specify UniqueTable property value
frm1.UniqueTable = u_table

DoCmd.Echo True
End Sub
```

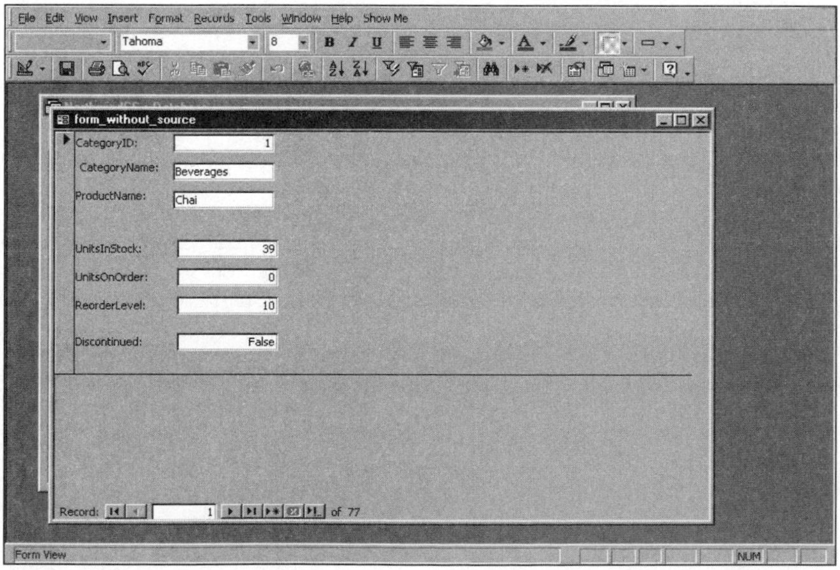

There are four essential steps to the first procedure, `invoke_open_form_without_source`. First, it assigns a string representing the name of the form to open to `frmname`. In the case of the demonstration, this is frmReorder_without_source. However, you can literally use the name of any form that exists in the current project. The trick here is that the form must be consistent with the source that you designate for it. If the source does not include values for the fields that appear on the form (that is, CategoryId, ProductName), then the form will not open with values for those fields.

```
Sub invoke_open_form_without_source()
Dim frmname As String, source As String
Dim caption As String, u_table As String

frmname = "frmReorder_without_source"
```

Second, the first procedure assigns a string denoting a source for the form fields (in this case, Select Products.CategoryId, Products.ProductName...). This can be a name for a table, a name for a view, a SQL statement, or a name for a stored procedure.

```
source = "SELECT Products.CategoryID, Products.ProductName, " & _
    "Products.UnitsInStock, Products.UnitsOnOrder, " & _
    "Products.ReorderLevel, Products.Discontinued, " & _
    "Categories.CategoryName " & _
    "FROM Products INNER JOIN Categories " & _
    "ON Products.CategoryID = Categories.CategoryID"
```

Third, the procedure assigns a string value to a caption variable. This variable's value will be the caption for the form (in this example, frmReorder_without_source) that the second procedure opens.

```
caption = "form_without_source"
```

Fourth, the procedure calls the second procedure, `open_form_without_source`, and includes references to the three parameters (frmname, source, caption).

```
'does not permit editing
'open_form_without_source frmname, source, caption
```

There is one optional task for the first procedure to perform. We didn't have the first procedure perform this task, so the opened form will be read-only (since it depends on two or more tables). As the second procedure accepts this parameter optionally, it is not essential for us to designate a string that denotes the form's `Unique Table` property. The code sample above does assign a string value to a variable that points at a table name for the `Unique Table` property. If you do set this string, it should synchronize with the string assignment for the `Record Source` property. That is, the `Unique Table` parameter should point at the table that is in a one-to-one relationship with the recordset created by the `Record Source` property setting.

The second procedure performs its operations inside a `DoCmd.Echo False` and `DoCmd.Echo True` pair of commands. These instructions eliminate screen jitter while the procedure manipulates the form on the screen.

```
DoCmd.Echo False
...
...
DoCmd.Echo True
```

The first substantive command opens the form in normal view. The `DoCmd.OpenForm` command has several parameters, but it requires just one – the name of the form. For the purposes of this sample demonstration, the default settings are fine. After opening the form, it becomes a member of the `Forms` collection in the current project. The procedure assigns the form to a reference to facilitate setting its properties.

```
DoCmd.OpenForm frmname
Set frm1 = Forms(frmname)
```

The next three lines assign the `Record Source`, `Caption`, and `Unique Table` properties.

```
frm1.RecordSource = source
frm1.caption = caption

'Optionally specify UniqueTable property value
frm1.UniqueTable = u_table
```

Notice that property names appear (in the code above) without a space between properties with two words; this is VBA's convention. Also, VBA is not case sensitive. The second procedure unconditionally assigns a value to the `Unique Table` property. However, if the first procedure does not assign a value to its `u_table` string, then the optional `u_table` string parameter in the second procedure is a zero-length string ("").

Opening a Form from an Event Procedure

The preceding sample runs from inside the **VBE** window of an Access project. We are not likely to have forms open this way except when testing code logic. It is more likely that we will build one form with an event procedure that fires and, in turn, opens another form. Event procedures have two-part names: one for the object to which the event happens, and the other part for the event name.

The next sample illustrates how to use event procedures to open a form as we concurrently set its `Record Source` property. Create a new form (see screenshot overleaf), frmCategoryPicker, with the following objects on it:

❑ **Label:** Caption – text is: "Pick a Category or Ten Best Selling Products to Source the Reorder Form"

❑ **Combo Box:** Label Caption- "Category"; Name: "cboCategoryName"; Row Source – "SELECT CategoryName FROM Categories"

❑ **Option Button:** Label Caption – "Ten Best Selling Products"; Name: -"chkTenBest"

This form offers two different paths for opening the frmReorder_without_source form. Each path has its own control (one is called from a combo box and one from an option button) in the form below. Associated with each control is an event procedure that fires after users do something with the control. In the case of the combo box on the left, an `after_update` event procedure fires when a user makes a choice from the combo box. The user's selection tells the application what group of products to show in the frmReorder_without_source form. In other words, the combo box can open the form with any of eight different groups of products. The option button on the right instructs the application to open the form with the ten best selling products. This is yet another data source for the form, but both of these sources return the same format recordset.

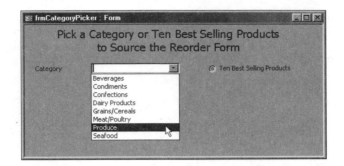

The next thing we need to do is attach the code to the combo box and option button. We should still be in Design mode. Go into the Properties Dialog of the cboCategoryName combo box and click on the Ellipse icon on the AfterUpdate property. This will bring up the following dialog:

Select Code Builder and copy the code for the cboCategoryName_AfterUpdate into the Code window. Close the VBE window when you have finished.

```
Private Sub cboCategoryName_AfterUpdate()
Dim frmname As String, source As String, caption As String

frmname = "frmReorder_without_source"
source = "SELECT Products.CategoryID, Products.ProductName, " & _
    "Products.UnitsInStock, Products.UnitsOnOrder, " & _
    "Products.ReorderLevel, Products.Discontinued " & _
    "FROM Products " & _
    "WHERE Products.CategoryID = " & Me.Controls("cboCategoryName").Value

caption = "Reorder Form for Products in CategoryID " & _
    Me.Controls("cboCategoryName").Value

open_form_without_source frmname, source, caption

End Sub
```

The next thing we need to do is attach the code to the option button. Go into the Properties dialog of the chkTenBest option button and click on the Ellipse icon on the Click property. Select Code Builder from the dialog and copy the chkTenBest_Click code into the Code window. Close the VBE window when you have finished. The second event procedure is a basic click event because clicking the option button selects it. This event procedure merely sets the source string equal to the name of a stored procedure with a return set of the top ten selling products with the associated inventory information. Then, the stored procedure selects the top ten selling products as it merges the associated inventory data.

```
Private Sub chkTenBest_Click()
Dim frmname As String, source As String, caption As String

frmname = "frmReorder_without_source"
source = "Ten Best Selling Products"

caption = "Reorder Form for Ten Best Selling Products"

open_form_without_source frmname, source, caption

End Sub
```

The stored procedure immediately above actually relies on a view named products_by_units_sold, which contains an aggregate function that sums sales quantity by product name. So, the next thing we need to do is to create this view by using the following code:

```
SELECT Products.CategoryID, Products.ProductID,
  Products.ProductName, SUM([Order Details].Quantity)
  AS units_sold
FROM Products INNER JOIN
  [Order Details] ON
  Products.ProductID = [Order Details].ProductID
GROUP BY Products.CategoryID, Products.ProductID,
  Products.ProductName
```

Since the form's records need explicit ordering based on sales quantity, a stored procedure is one candidate for performing the task. The use of the TOP 10 phrase in the SELECT statement restricts the return set to just those products with an entry in the top ten best selling product items. Notice the syntax in the original event procedure requires neither an EXEC keyword nor brackets around the stored procedure's name. As a final step, we alter the stored procedure called Ten Best Selling Products using the following code:

```
alter Procedure [Ten Best Selling Products]
As
SELECT TOP 10 products_by_units_sold.CategoryID,
  products_by_units_sold.ProductName,
  products_by_units_sold.units_sold, Products.UnitsInStock,
  Products.UnitsOnOrder, Products.ReorderLevel,
  Products.Discontinued
FROM products_by_units_sold INNER JOIN
  Products ON
  products_by_units_sold.ProductID = Products.ProductID
ORDER BY products_by_units_sold.units_sold DESC
```

Other means of sorting the records for a form include using a T-SQL statement to specify the data for a form. You do this when you need to specify a custom data source not available from a table, view, or stored procedure. While you cannot include an ORDER BY clause in a view, you can include it in the SQL for a Record Source designed with Query Designer. A sample will demonstrate this later in the chapter.

This example demonstrates forcefully just how easy it is to launch a form and set its Record Source property from another form. Both of these event procedures invoke the open_form_without_source procedure from the preceding example. All the event procedures do is collect information from the controls and pass on parameters to the open_form_without_source procedure. Making a selection from the combo box on the left fires the `after_update` event for the combo box named `cboCategoryName`. This combo box shows a category name, but it stores the matching `CategoryID` value. The `after_update` event procedure uses the value in the combo box to complete the specification of the T-SQL string for the `Record Source` in the frmReorder_without_source form.

Programmatically Setting the Recordset Property

A form's `Recordset` property is like the flip side of the `Record Source` property. Both properties denote the data behind a form, but while the `Record Source` property represents the data as a string, the `Recordset` property represents the data as an ADO `Recordset` object in Access projects. An ADO `Recordset` object is essentially a place for our application to put the data from the record source (a table, say) once we've extracted it. This then allows us to manipulate the data without disturbing the database. Once we've finished, we can empty the `Recordset` back into the source we used, updating the database if necessary.

Despite this difference in substance, they are surprisingly similar in functionality. You can copy the `Record Source` property from one form to a string and then assign that string's value to the `Record Source` property of another form. Similarly, you can copy the `Recordset` property from one form to a `Recordset` object. Then, you can re-assign that `Recordset` object to another form. However, since the `Recordset` object is a collection of records, you can update the records between copying them from one form to another. Another distinction between the `Record Source` and `Recordset` properties is that a `Recordset` object has a **cursor**.

A cursor allows you to pass through the records in the result set of a SQL query one at a time. You can control the updatability of records by the type of the cursor. For example, a forward-only, read-only cursor is not updatable even if you are working with a single table. If you want the data in a form to be updatable, use an appropriate cursor, such as an open keyset cursor with optimistic locking. Despite these distinctions, a `Record Source` property implies a corresponding `Recordset` property and vice versa. This section includes three samples that illustrate how to open forms through their `Recordset` property based on tables, SQL strings, and stored procedures.

Defining the Recordset Property with a Table

The following pair of VBA procedures shows an approach to opening a form based on a table. While this approach relies on the `Recordset` property to achieve this task, an immense amount of similarity exists relative to the `Record Source` samples which points to the **Products** table for the data in a form. To help you appreciate the comparability of the two techniques, the sample form is the same one for each technique, namely frmReOrder_without_source.

Both approaches use two procedures: the first procedure assigns values to parameters for the second procedures which takes those parameters and assigns them to a form's properties. One major distinction is that the following sample for the `Recordset` object passes an object as one of its parameters. Another distinction is that the updatability of the form depends on the settings that you give to the `Recordset` parameter that passes between the procedures. The following code should be placed in a module:

```
Sub invoke_open_form_without_recordset_1()
Dim rst1 As ADODB.Recordset
Dim frmname As String, caption As String

frmname = "frmReOrder_without_source"

'Instantiate and set properties for Recordset object
```

```
'It is critical to set cursortype and locktype for
'for updating if you wish this capability in your form
Set rst1 = New ADODB.Recordset
rst1.ActiveConnection = CurrentProject.Connection
rst1.CursorType = adOpenKeyset
rst1.LockType = adLockOptimistic
rst1.Open "products", , , , adCmdTableDirect

caption = ""

open_form_without_recordset frmname, rst1, _
    caption

Debug.Print Forms(frmname).RecordSource

End Sub
```

This second procedure is going to be used in the next example as well:

```
Sub open_form_without_recordset(frmname As String, _
    rst1 As ADODB.Recordset, caption As String, Optional u_table As String)
Dim frm1 As Form

DoCmd.Echo False
DoCmd.OpenForm frmname
Set frm1 = Forms(frmname)
Set frm1.Recordset = rst1
frm1.caption = caption

'Optionally specify UniqueTable property value
frm1.UniqueTable = u_table

DoCmd.Echo True

End Sub
```

The first procedure, named `invoke_open_form_without_recordset_1`, has a couple of features that merit special attention.

First, the procedure instantiates and opens an ADO `Recordset` object.

```
Set rst1 = New ADODB.Recordset
rst1.ActiveConnection = CurrentProject.Connection
rst1.CursorType = adOpenKeyset
rst1.LockType = adLockOptimistic
rst1.Open "products", , , , adCmdTableDirect
```

In the process, it makes critical property assignments that affect the behavior of the recordset. Specifically, it sets the `CursorType` to `adOpenKeyset` and sets the `LockType` to `adLockOptimistic`. Using these settings means that we can navigate about our `Recordset` and see additions other people make to the data source. The `adLockOptimistic` setting means that the data source is only locked for editing either side of our edit. This object becomes the data source for the form.

Second, after control returns from the second procedure to the first procedure, the first procedure prints the `Record Source` property to the **Immediate** window. This confirms the duality between the `Recordset` and `Record Source` properties (the procedures set the `Recordset` property, but this makes the `Record Source` property available). It also provides an opportunity to examine how `Recordset` property assignments for a form translate into `Record Source` property values. Both the `Recordset` and the `Record Source` values are set to **Products**.

The second procedure is identical to the comparable one for the `Record Source` sample with one exception pertaining to the source of data for the form. This procedure assigns the `Recordset` object `rst1` to the form's `Recordset` property. The comparable sample for the `Record Source` property assigned a string designating a data source to a different property.

Defining the Recordset Property with a T-SQL String

A T-SQL string offers more flexibility than a table in that we can specify any combination of tables and views as the data source for a form. T-SQL strings may be slower to process; therefore we must decide if the advantage is worth any performance penalty. If our application needs to run a query against a large data source or many users run that query often, we should consider using a stored procedure instead of a T-SQL string. Doing so will give us all of the features possible with a T-SQL string, but without the performance hit because stored procedures are pre-compiled and optimized on the server.

The following sample illustrates the syntax for using a T-SQL string as the source for a form. Notice that the procedure uses the same second procedure as in the preceding sample. Once you define the `Recordset`, you assign it to the form in the same way, no matter what the source for the `Recordset` might be. The most significant differences relate to a string variable for defining the T-SQL string statement and the `Options` parameter for the `Recordset.Open` method.

The sample below uses the string variable `str1` to define the string statement for a `Recordset` object. Then, it uses that variable to specify the source for the `Recordset` object's `Open` method.

The `Options` parameter for the string source changes from `adCmdTableDirect` to `adCmdText`. The former setting returns all rows from the table we have named, while the latter indicates that we are not naming a table but passing a T-SQL query string.

There is one other difference between the table and string source samples for defining the `Recordset`: the string sample sets the `u_table` parameter to `Products`. This is not necessary in the case when we are using a single table as the source. In fact, if we do not want to be able to update the data from the form, then it is not even appropriate when our T-SQL string references two or more tables.

```
Sub invoke_open_form_without_recordset_2()
Dim rst1 As ADODB.Recordset
Dim frmname As String, caption As String
Dim u_table As String, str1 as String

frmname = "frmReOrder_without_source"

'Instantiate and set properties for Recordset object
'It is critical to set cursortype and locktype for
'for updating if you wish this capability in your form
Set rst1 = New ADODB.Recordset
rst1.ActiveConnection = CurrentProject.Connection
rst1.CursorType = adOpenKeyset
```

```
        rst1.LockType = adLockOptimistic
        str1 = "SELECT Products.CategoryID, Products.ProductName, " & _
            "Products.UnitsInStock, Products.UnitsOnOrder, " & _
            "Products.ReorderLevel, Products.Discontinued, " & _
            "Categories.CategoryName " & _
            "FROM Products INNER JOIN Categories " & _
            "ON Products.CategoryID = Categories.CategoryID"
        rst1.Open str1, , , , adCmdText

        caption = ""

        'does not permit editing
        'open_form_without_recordset frmname, rst1, caption

        'does permit editing
        u_table = "products"
        open_form_without_recordset frmname, rst1, caption, u_table

        Debug.Print Forms(frmname).RecordSource

        End Sub
```

Defining the Recordset Property with a Stored Procedure

We can also use a stored procedure to define a `Recordset` object that serves as the data source for a form. We can use at least two approaches to this task.

❏   First, we can use a T-SQL string with an `EXEC` statement that references the stored procedure's name. If the name has embedded spaces, we must enclose the name in brackets. Since we are using a string – although it points at a stored procedure – our `Options` parameter for the `Open` method must be `adCmdText`.

❏   Second, we can just enter the name of the stored procedure as the source for the `Recordset` when we invoke the `Open` method. In this case, we are directly referencing a stored procedure. Therefore, the `Options` parameter should be `adCmdStoredProc`.

The following sample gives a specific example for using a stored procedure as the source for a `Recordset` (the example comments out the example using the `EXEC` statement) which, in turn, becomes the data source for a form. The sample demonstrates the syntax for both methods of referencing a stored procedure as the source for a `Recordset`. The sample uses the **Ten Best Selling Products** stored procedure, which we created earlier. Since this procedure relies on a view with an aggregate function, there is no sense to assigning a string for the `Unique Table` property. If the stored procedure did pass back an updateable return set, then our application would have the option of making the form updateable by setting the `Unique Table` property. As usual, we would set it to the table with its rows in a one-to-one relationship with the rows of the `Recordset` behind the form.

```
        Sub invoke_open_form_without_recordset_3()
        Dim rst1 As ADODB.Recordset
        Dim frmname As String, caption As String
        Dim u_table As String

        frmname = "frmReOrder_without_source"
```

```
'Instantiate and set properties for Recordset object
'It is critical to set cursortype and locktype for
'for updating if you wish this capability in your form
Set rst1 = New ADODB.Recordset
rst1.ActiveConnection = CurrentProject.Connection
rst1.CursorType = adOpenKeyset
rst1.LockType = adLockOptimistic

'Stored procedure with embedded spaces must appear in brackets
'Two different formats for invoking a stored procedure
'rst1.Open "EXEC [Ten Best Selling Products]", , , , adCmdText
rst1.Open "[Ten Best Selling Products]", , , , adCmdStoredProc

caption = ""

'Specifying UniqueTable property does not enable
'data editing because query relies on an aggregate function
open_form_without_recordset frmname, rst1, _
    caption, "products"

Debug.Print Forms(frmname).RecordSource
End Sub
```

Sorting, Filtering, Finding, and Refreshing Records with Forms

Forms allow us to manage the way we display SQL Server data through our applications. This section presents a mix of functions that enable us to let forms present data in ways that serve the needs of our applications and enable our applications to interact with its users.

Sorting Records

Up to this point, we've focused on two ways to present data. First, we can present it unsorted with a view. Second, we can present it sorted with a stored procedure. Recall that this is because the ORDER BY clause goes in one but not the other.

The range of options is actually wider than this. For example, the Record Source and Recordset form properties each permit us to sort data. While each of these properties can use stored procedures to sort the data on a form, both can sort the data in a view or table without a stored procedure. This is because both properties allow T-SQL strings that use an ORDER BY clause in the SELECT statement.

In addition, forms in Access projects work with data against a local cache that we can manipulate through the form's Recordset property. The Sort property allows us to specify an order for Recordset rows that determines the order in which they appear for the Find method and variations of the Move method, such as MoveNext.

The following screen shows a form in Datasheet view that takes advantage of an ORDER BY clause in its SELECT statement for its Record Source property. The frmProducts_sorted_by_sales_quantity form relies on the products_by_units_sold view that sums the sales quantity for each product. Since views do not support an ORDER BY clause, if the form just selected the view, the records would appear unsorted in the form. However, this form initializes its records according to a T-SQL statement that includes an `ORDER BY` clause against the units_sold column followed by the `DESC` keyword. Therefore, products appear in descending order by sales quantity. The T-SQL statement for the form's `Record Source` property is as follows:

```
SELECT CategoryID, ProductID, ProductName, units_sold
FROM products_by_units_sold
ORDER BY units_sold DESC
```

CategoryID:	ProductID:	ProductName:	units_sold:
4	60	Camembert Pierrot	1577
4	59	Raclette Courdavault	1496
4	31	Gorgonzola Telino	1397
5	56	Gnocchi di nonna Alice	1263
3	16	Pavlova	1158
1	75	Rhönbräu Klosterbier	1155
1	24	Guaraná Fantástica	1125
8	40	Boston Crab Meat	1103
3	62	Tarte au sucre	1083
4	71	Flotemysost	1057

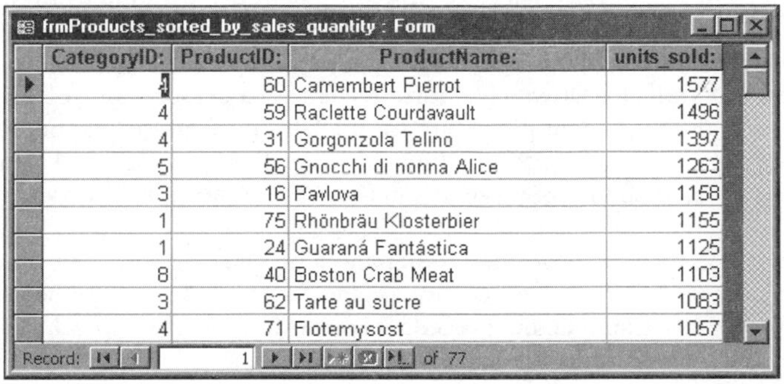

The capability to specify `Record Source` and `Recordset` properties with `ORDER BY` clauses is convenient – especially when we first populate a form with records. However, after initially populating it with records, our application may still need to allow users to sort records in other ways than the initial sort. If we restrict our options to the `Record Source` and `Recordset` properties, our application will require a re-loading of the records from the server to the local cache for the form. However, since the records are already in a local `Recordset` cache, we can enable users to sort the records in that data store.

The next screenshot presents a form, frmProducts_sort_buttons, that takes advantage of this technique. In fact, the form borrows from the preceding sample in that it initially sorts the records in descending order by units_sold based on a T-SQL string for the `Record Source` property. However, we can use this form to re-sort the records in ascending or descending order on any of the four fields that it shows. An option group above a set of buttons allows us to designate a sort direction, and the click of any button below the option group re-sorts the form's records on one of the four columns in the local cache.

Notice that the form has custom navigation buttons instead of the built-in ones. These enable the sample to demonstrate how to control navigation in a form. When you re-sort the records in the local cache behind a form, you must use custom navigation buttons. This is because the built-in navigation buttons do not follow re-sorted orders.

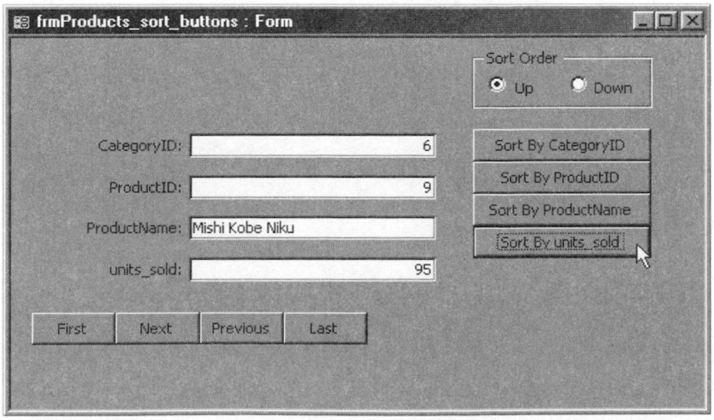

While the form initially loads records in the descending order by units_sold, the form depicts the screen immediately after a click to the Sort By units_sold button with the Up option button selected in the Sort Order group. After re-sorting the records, the application immediately moves to the first record in the re-sorted data cache to confirm the new sort. When the navigation buttons are selected it moves the dataset from one record to the next, or immediately to the first or last record in the local cache, according to the currently active sort order.

The following VBA samples reveal the event procedures for clicks to each of the form's four sort buttons. This VBA code can be viewed from the VBE by selecting frmProducts_sort_buttons from the list of forms. This form will be in the list if you use start the VBE from within the sample access project for this chapter. They all use the same technique. First, they check the value of the option group control above the buttons. This control can assume values of 1 for Up and 2 for Down. The form loads with a default value of 1 for the option group. If the option group control is 1, then the event procedure for the Sort by CategoryID button assigns the Sort property for the form's Recordset to CategoryID (the default order is ascending). This causes Find and variations of the MoveFirst method to access records in ascending CategoryID order.

If the option group control is 2, then the procedure designates a descending sort order based on CategoryID. After assigning a sort variable and order, the procedure applies the MoveFirst method to the form's local cache to confirm the new sort order. For example, the preceding screenshot shows the product with the lowest units_sold value. The event procedures for other buttons follow the same logic as the one for CategoryID: they merely swap the CategoryID column designator with one appropriate for their button. The keyword Me is used in place of the current form name.

```
Private Sub cmdCategoryID_Click()

If optSortOrder = 1 Then
    Me.Recordset.Sort = "CategoryID"
Else
    Me.Recordset.Sort = "CategoryID DESC"
End If
Me.Recordset.MoveFirst

End Sub
```

Next the code for the Sort By ProductID button:

```
Private Sub cmdProductID_Click()

If optSortOrder = 1 Then
    Me.Recordset.Sort = "ProductID"
Else
    Me.Recordset.Sort = "ProductID DESC"
End If
Me.Recordset.MoveFirst

End Sub
```

The code for the Sort By ProductName button:

```
Private Sub cmdProductName_Click()

If optSortOrder = 1 Then
```

```
        Me.Recordset.Sort = "ProductName"
    Else
        Me.Recordset.Sort = "ProductName DESC"
    End If
    Me.Recordset.MoveFirst

    End Sub
```

And finally, the code for the Sort By units_sold button:

```
    Private Sub cmdunits_sold_Click()

    If optSortOrder = 1 Then
        Me.Recordset.Sort = "units_sold"
    Else
        Me.Recordset.Sort = "units_sold DESC"
    End If
    Me.Recordset.MoveFirst

    End Sub
```

The next set of event procedures shows the logic for the four custom navigation buttons on the toolbar. As you can see, they are of two different types. For buttons moving immediately to the first or last record, the procedure can just apply the appropriate method, either `MoveFirst` or `MoveLast`, to the form's `Recordset` object. In the case of buttons that move forward or backward one record, the logic checks to see if the form already displays the first or last record. If so, the procedure presents a message box to that effect and cancels the move.

```
    Private Sub cmdFirst_Click()
    Me.Recordset.MoveFirst
    End Sub
```

The code for the Next button:

```
    Private Sub cmdNext_Click()
    Me.Recordset.MoveNext
    If Me.Recordset.EOF Then
        MsgBox "Already at last record.", vbCritical
        Me.Recordset.MovePrevious
    End If
    End Sub
```

The code for the Previous button:

```
    Private Sub cmdPrevious_Click()
    Me.Recordset.MovePrevious
    If Me.Recordset.BOF Then
        MsgBox "Already at first record.", vbCritical
        Me.Recordset.MoveNext
    End If
    End Sub
```

And finally, the code for the Last button:

```
Private Sub cmdLast_Click()
Me.Recordset.MoveLast
End Sub
```

Filtering Records

Allowing users to filter the records that a form displays is a powerful way of making data available in convenient groups. The classic example is a form for business contacts that duplicates the behavior of an old pushbutton telephone directory. These directories let users push a button to show a page or two of contacts whose last names begin with the same letter of the alphabet. We can readily apply this technique to SQL Server databases. Several different approaches enable this functionality.

For example, we can use ADO-based filtering techniques – just as the previous example relied on ADO-based sorting capabilities. We can also filter with a form's Record Source and Recordset properties. In addition, Access offers two tools explicitly for filtering the records in its forms – one is traditional and the other explicitly filters data on a SQL Server. In SQL Server we can filter the Recordset by adding a WHERE clause to our SELECT statements. This section demonstrates the traditional Access filter technique for filtering records in Access forms.

The following screenshot shows an extension of the frmReorder_1_table form, called frmReorder_filtered_by_CategoryID. The extension includes a button panel that lets us filter the records that the form shows. We can click one of the first eight buttons to restrict the products the form displays to just one of the product categories. The ninth button turns the filter off so that all products are available for browsing. When the form initially opens, it makes all products available for viewing. An Open event procedure ensures this by turning off the filter property. This does the same thing as the All button. The screen below depicts the form after a click to the Beverages filter button and clicking on the built-in Next navigation button twice (to advance to the third record). Notice that we're using the built-in navigation buttons for this form, since we're using filtering instead of sorting. The form grays the UnitsOnOrder control to signify that it is disabled.

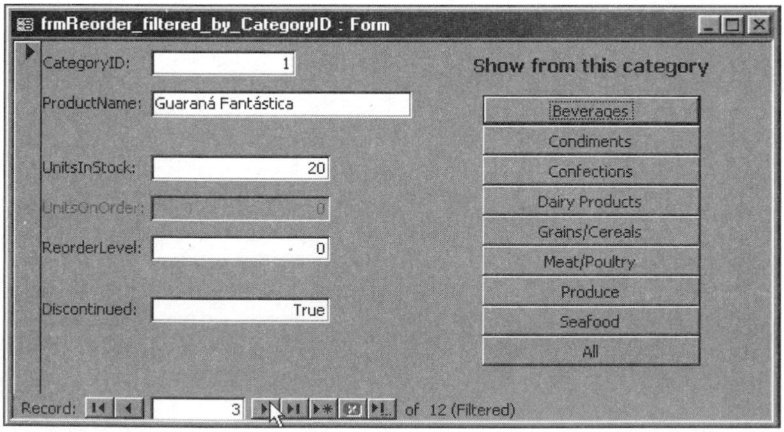

The form's Open event procedure, which appears above opposite, is important for the reliable execution of the filters. As soon as the form opens, it turns off filtering by assigning False to the FilterOn property and saving the form. Without this step, filters would work unreliably or only after manual intervention, such as to remove any existing filter. By setting the form's `FilterOn` property to `False` and saving the form, we programmatically achieve the same result. Also note, that when you click on the All button the `FilterOn` property is set to `False` to achieve the same effect.

```
Private Subform_Open(Cancel As Integer)
'Filter procedures require these on Open
'to work reliably
Me.FilterOn = False
DoCmd.Save acForm, Me.Name
End Sub
```

The next two event procedures show the code behind the filtering buttons and the one that removes any active filtering. The first procedure is the same for each of the filtering buttons, except for two features. First, it assigns a different criterion to the form's `Filter` property. Each event procedure sets the `Filter` property to one of the `CategoryID` values. Second, the event procedure name is different. The second line of the first eight is identical in all event procedures. It turns on the new `Filter` property by setting the `FilterOn` property to `True`. In essence, this last line refreshes, or initially sets for the first filter action, the `Filter` property.

```
Private Sub cmdCategoryID_1_Click()
Me.Filter = "CategoryID=1"
Me.FilterOn = True
End Sub
```

And now the code for the All button:

```
Private Sub cmdShowAll_Click()
Me.FilterOn = False
End Sub
```

The second event procedure temporarily turns off the `Filter` property by setting the form's `FilterOn` property to `False`. We can restore the last active `Filter` by clicking the Apply Filter control on the Form View toolbar, or clicking the appropriate button on the form.

Finding Records and Refreshing Forms

Users can always browse individual records until they find a record of interest. When our applications offer filtering, browsing can be a very natural way to find a record.

First, we can narrow the possibilities with filtering. Second, we search the filtered records sequentially until a match appears. However, sometimes database users just want a means of jumping directly to a record with a specified value. As with sorting and filtering, Access again gives you alternative approaches to the task. First, a `Find` method for ADO `Recordsets` exists that your applications can apply to the ADO `Recordset` associated with a form.

The basic syntax for the `Find` method for `Recordset` objects is as follows:

`Recordsetname.Find strCriteria`

`Recordsetname` is the name of the `Recordset` to search, and `strCriteria` is a SQL `WHERE` clause without the word `WHERE`. For example if you wanted to search the `rstProducts Recordset` for the record where `productName = Tofu`, your code would look like this:

```
rstProducts.Find productName="Tofu"
```

Second, your applications can invoke the DoCmd.FindRecord method. This method duplicates programmatically the functionality provided by the Find button of the Form View toolbar. This chapter's sample for finding records takes the traditional approach because it integrates so tightly with Access forms and because developers can learn about its features by experimenting with the Edit | Find command or the Find button.

Finding a Record

The following form, frmReorder_find_productname, shows another extension of the basic Reorder form. This has the familiar elements on the left and a combo box on the right. The combo box lists the names of all items in the Products table. It has an after_update event procedure associated with it. After a user makes a selection from the comb box, the event procedure fires. This procedure moves the focus to the ProductName field on the left of the form and then invokes the FindRecord method of the DoCmd object with the combo box's value as its sole argument. This causes Access to move the controls on the left to the row with a product name matching the combo box on the right.

The preceding description suggests a very simple event procedure, and the following sample code confirms it. The event procedure takes just two lines. The SetFocus method moves the focus to a field on a form. The FindRecord method locates the first match to the criterion argument in the current column of the datasheet associated with the form. Since the FindRecord method operates on a single column, we must first execute the SetFocus method to the column that our application needs to search, which we do in this example by use of the combo box. So, when the value in the combo box is updated (when we select a line from it), the AfterUpdate event switches the focus to the ProductName box. It then uses the value we've just selected for the combo box as an argument for the FindRecord method, which returns the details of the product we are looking for.

```
Private Sub cboProductName_AfterUpdate()
Me.ProductName.SetFocus
DoCmd.FindRecord cboProductName
End Sub
```

Refreshing

Refreshing is how client-server applications update their `Recordsets` to learn of changes by other users since they last populated a form with data. Finding a record does not obviously relate to refreshing a form until you think about how Access refreshes the local cache for a form: it re-populates the whole cache.

The refreshing process therefore wipes out the current record. If you want to restore that record, you need to save an indicator of the record before the refresh, and then find that record after the refresh. If another user deletes the cache's current record, the `FindRecord` method leaves the current record at the first record in the form's datasheet. The following screenshot illustrates a form with a button for refreshing the data. The purpose here is to show how to refresh the `Recordset` within an event procedure. When the Refresh button is clicked, the information on the left of the form will be refreshed to correspond with the product selected in the drop down box.

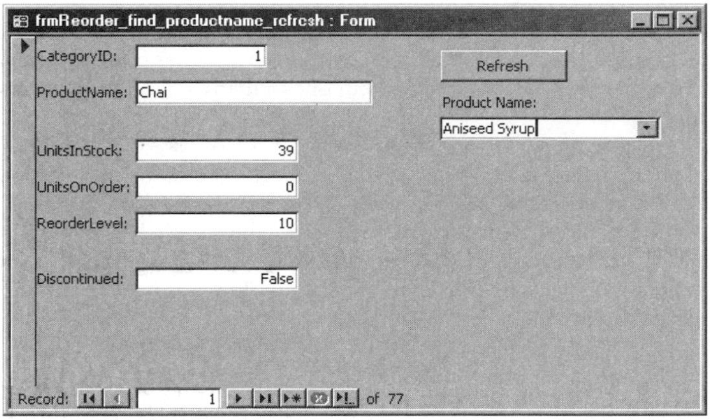

The procedure to perform the refresh and restore the former current record position appears below. It starts by copying the contents of the ProductName field to a string variable. This field is unique for the Products table because no two rows have the same ProductName value. In any event, when we adapt this logic to our tasks, we have to understand that we need a primary key column or a column with a `Unique` constraint.

Next, the procedure re-populates the local cache by invoking the form's `Requery` method. Then, it attempts to restore its former position by switching the focus to the ProductName field.

Then it invokes the `DoCmd.FindRecord` method using the string variable value saved before the `Requery` as a criterion. If the product is still in the datasheet for the form, the `FindRecord` method moves to it. Otherwise, the form's first record retains the focus as if there was no attempt to find a record.

```
Private Sub cmdRefresh_Click()
Dim str1 As String

str1 = Me.ProductName
Me.Requery
Me.ProductName.SetFocus
DoCmd.FindRecord str1

End Sub
```

This allows us to type a product name into the combo box and press Refresh to have the details displayed in the text boxes on the left side of the form.

Miscellaneous Advanced Topics

This chapter closes with a review of four topics addressing advanced form development issues. First, you learn how to resynchronize forms so that you can speed the way users work with one-to-many data behind a form. The second topic to gain focus in this section is setting parameters for stored procedures with Access forms. Two approaches to this topic tackle the problem from the perspectives of easy, fast, and limited versus flexible, but more programmatically demanding. Thirdly we look at a sample that demonstrates how to make unbound data appear on a form as if it were bound data. In the process, you learn how to do data updates from unbound forms that are not possible with bound forms. Finally, we take a look at hyperlinks. Although SQL Server doesn't support hyperlink data types, we can work around this with the `Is Hyperlink` property for text boxes.

Resynchronizing Forms

The `Resync Command`, `Unique Table`, and `Recordset Type` properties of a form can combine to enable a special kind of functionality for forms based on tables with one-to-many joins between them. Microsoft calls this functionality **Resynchronizing** (or resyncing) a form.

Resynchronizing pulls in values from the one- side of the relationship based on a specification of the foreign key value on the many- side of the relationship. For example, a value for the ShipVia column in the Orders table can be used to find the CompanyName and Phone values from the Shippers table. In addition to pulling in values from the one- side of the relationship based on a foreign key value, resynchronization also enables fast, automatic updates to the field values on the one- side for existing records. In this section we examine how this feature works, and describe the steps to enable this capability.

Our discussion of resynchronization depends on the frmshippers_orders form. This form draws its data from a view named shippers_orders that shows all the Orders (from the Orders table) for a Shipper, together with the CompanyName and Phone columns for each Shipper. What the form does is update the information in its CompanyName and Phone fields when we change the information in the ShipVia box. The resynchronization isn't immediate, but when we navigate back to the changed entry we will find it has been updated. Because these updates also change the Orders table, this would be a useful method if a business needed to change its records of what was shipped by which company.

The Resynchronizing Form

The AutoForm Wizard can create the form, but to enable resynchronization some customization is necessary. The amount of customization depends on the data source for our form. As a minimum, we will need to reset the `Unique Table` property. This property must point at the table on the many side of the relationship. This is the Orders table in the context of this example.

The `Recordset Type` property for the form should be set to be an `Updatable Snapshot`. We can select this from a drop-down box on the form's Properties dialog or program it with VBA by assigning the appropriate constant (namely, 4) to the form's `Recordset Type` property. The AutoForm Wizard makes this setting by default, so if we make our form that way we don't have to change it. It is imperative that in our source for the form, the foreign key on the many- side of the relationship designates the entity on the one- side of the relationship. If we use the primary key from the one- side of the entity, then we will not be able to resynchronize our form.

Curiously, the specification of the `Resync Command` property is optional. If we do use it, then we need a special parameterized adaptation of the T-SQL statement for the form's data source. This expression appears at the conclusion of the example.

The following screenshot depicts the Query Designer view of the shippers_orders view. Notice that the view represents the shipper ID for an order with the foreign key in the Orders table (namely, ShipVia) as opposed to the ShippersID field from the Shippers table.

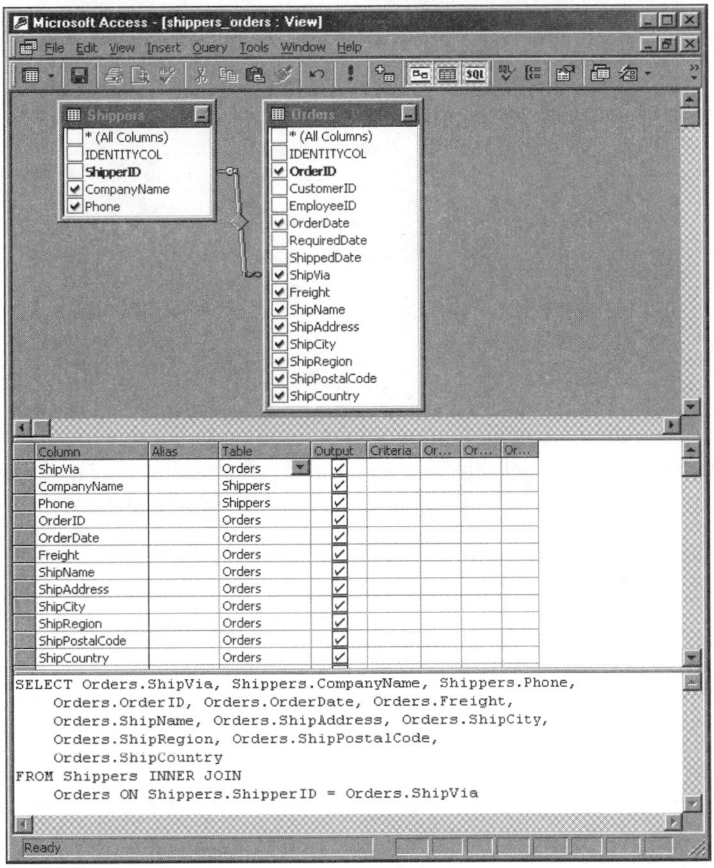

If we want to preserve the ability to add new records via the form, we must use the foreign key on the many side of the relationship. We can update field values on the many side of the relationship without using the foreign key. However, resynchronization facilitates the automatic pulling in of values for the one side as well as enabling the addition and deletion of records. Users just input a foreign key value and click a form's record selector to resync the form. The Resync command goes out and gets all matching values on the one side of the relationship when you are adding a new record. The command also automatically updates control values based on the one side of the relationship when users change the ShipperID for an existing Order. This means by just typing in a new ShipperID for an existing order and clicking the next record navigation button, all the control values for fields on the one side of the relationship update in a matching way.

The frmshippers_orders form overleaf appears immediately after a Resync command automatically added the CompanyName and Phone fields. In addition, the Resync command automatically inserted the next OrderID value based on the Identity property, and it inserted a default value ($0) for the Freight charge. This functionality is truly amazing considering that without updating the form's Unique Table property users cannot even edit a single value. In this operation, users are adding a new record, and Access is automatically completing selected fields. In applications where there is a substantial amount of entry based on joined tables by experienced data input operators, the Resync command shows a lot of promise.

As mentioned previously, it is not necessary to designate the Resync Command property when the data source is a view that defines a one-to-many relationship. The Resync Command property setting should be an edited version of the T-SQL statement for its view. The addition should be a parameter expression with a question mark (?) that identifies the primary key for the table on the many side of the relationship. In this example, the Resync Command property is the following string:

```
SELECT Orders.ShipVia, Shippers.CompanyName, Shippers.Phone,
    Orders.OrderID, Orders.OrderDate, Orders.Freight,
    Orders.ShipName, Orders.ShipAddress, Orders.ShipCity,
    Orders.ShipRegion, Orders.ShipPostalCode,
    Orders.ShipCountry
FROM Shippers INNER JOIN
    Orders ON Shippers.ShipperID = Orders.ShipVia
WHERE Orders.OrderID=?
```

You need either an empty Resync Command property setting or the full T-SQL statement above for resynchronization to work.

Specifying Input Parameters from Form Fields

Another use of Access forms in SQL Server solutions is the specification of parameters for stored procedures. This section illustrates two approaches to this task. Both rely on unbound forms to specify the parameters.

The first approach uses the parameters with the Input Parameters property for a form that is bound to a stored procedure with parameters. An Access form allows SQL Server developers to control the prompt for the parameters and even do some error checking for their specification. However, the use of the Input Parameters properties minimizes the VBA code necessary to launch the stored procedure.

The second approach uses the entries on an unbound form as inputs for a stored procedure that inserts a new record into a table. This sample demonstrates how to use Access forms with the ADO Parameters collection.

Specifying the Input Parameters Property

The first sample extends a prior sample based on the frmSales by Year_with_input_parameters form. Recall that previous sample automatically passed parameters to a stored procedure based on the Input Parameters property for the form. This created a return set from which users could browse, edit, add, and delete records from the form. While the sample is attractive and easy for users, it does not give them a chance to change the parameters. The return set is always the same. In fact, one critical advantage of the technique is that it avoids the need for pop-up prompts from Access requesting parameter values. The built-in prompts do not enable any error checking so applications can readily fail because of faulty or missing input.

By using an unbound form to collect parameters for a stored procedure, an application can perform checks on the parameters to ensure their validity and appropriateness for a stored procedure's data source. After checking the input to unbound text boxes on a form, an event procedure can comprise a string for a second bound form's Input Parameter property. Using the Input Parameters property keeps things simple from a couple of perspectives.

- First, it is faster and easier to define a string than instantiate one or more parameters.
- Second, you can use a bound form to display the return set from the stored procedure.

Bound forms are exceptionally easy to create, and they offer many properties and events to help customize their use. This first sample for using Access forms with SQL Server stored procedure parameters uses the unbound form frmfor_Sales by Year. This form is used to collect data for and invoke a bound form frmSales by Year_with_input_parameters.

The new form, frmfor_Sales by Year, appears below. It consists of a title label that explains its role, a couple of text boxes, and a command button. We can control the text that appears on the form as well as the error checking of the inputs. Our application can write messages back to the form's user. If necessary, we can even write code to abort conditionally the process of calling the second form with a custom explanatory message.

The event procedure behind the command button, which appears overleaf, illustrates some of the possible ways of controlling the processing of the input and the feedback to a user. Recall that the stored procedure behind the frmSales by Year_with_input_parameters form calls for two parameters: a starting date and an ending date for the return set. The On Click event procedure for the command button tackles two typical problems with inputs to the stored procedure behind the form.

- First, it does not allow the input of dates outside the range for which return records are available. These dates are from 7/10/1996 through 5/6/1998.
- Second, it automatically replaces missing data fields with default values.

We can manipulate these default values without going back to the original T-SQL stored procedure code. We could also do the same type of data validation using the Input Mask property on the control.

```
Private Sub cmdsubmit_request_Click()
Dim in_begin As String
Dim in_end As String
Dim frmname As String

'Specify value for beginning date
If IsNull(Me.txtbeginning_date) Or Me.txtbeginning_date > #5/6/1998# Then
    MsgBox "Beginning date is out of data range. Will use default " & _
        "beginning date of 7/10/96.", vbCritical
    in_begin = "7/10/96"
Else
    in_begin = DateValue(Me.txtbeginning_date)
End If

'Specify value for ending date
If IsNull(Me.txtending_date) Or Me.txtending_date < #7/10/1996# Then
    MsgBox "Ending date is out of data range. Will use default " & _
        "ending date of 5/6/98.", vbCritical
    in_end = "5/6/98"
Else
    in_end = DateValue(Me.txtending_date)
End If

'Open an instance of the frmSales by Year_with_input_parameters
'form and set its InputParameters property
'Print property value before and after update
frmname = "frmSales by Year_with_input_parameters"
DoCmd.OpenForm frmname
Debug.Print Forms(frmname).InputParameters
Forms(frmname).InputParameters = "@Beginning_Date DateTime = '" & _
        in_begin & "', @Ending_Date DateTime = '" & in_end & "'"
Debug.Print Forms(frmname).InputParameters

'Close frmfor_Sales by Year form
DoCmd.Close acForm, Me.Name

End Sub
```

The procedure checks, in turn, each of the unbound text boxes. An If...Else statement either retains the value in a text box as the parameter argument or replaces it with a default value if it is either Null or outside the legitimate range of dates.

```
If IsNull(Me.txtbeginning_date) Or Me.txtbeginning_date > #5/6/1998# Then
    MsgBox "Beginning date is out of data range. Will use default " & _
        "beginning date of 7/10/96.", vbCritical
    in_begin = "7/10/96"
Else
    in_begin = DateValue(Me.txtbeginning_date)
End If
```

In the case of a faulty input parameter, the procedure sends a message to the user indicating the action that it takes.

After validating the input parameter values in the in_begin and in_end variables, the event procedure opens the frmSales by Year_with_input_parameters form. This is necessary to gain access to the form's Input Parameters property.

```
frmname = "frmSales by Year_with_input_parameters"
DoCmd.OpenForm frmname
Debug.Print Forms(frmname).InputParameters
Forms(frmname).InputParameters = "@Beginning_Date DateTime = '" & _
      in_begin & "', @Ending_Date DateTime = '" & in_end & "'"
Debug.Print Forms(frmname).InputParameters
```

Then, it assigns a string to the property based on the validated properties in the two VBA variables (namely, in_begin and in_end). The last command in the event procedure closes the frmfor_Sales by Year form.

```
DoCmd.Close acForm, Me.Name
```

This leaves open just the frmSales by Year_with_input_parameters form.

Notice that there are Debug.Print statements in the event procedure both before and after the assignment for the Input Parameters property. The initial Print statement captures the parameter values in the original form, and the second statement reflects the values from the event procedure. No matter how many times users run the event procedure by clicking the command button, the first print statement will always return the values on the original form. This is because the assignment is strictly for the form instance created by the OpenForm method for the DoCmd object.

Passing Values from Access Forms to the ADO Parameters Collection

Using the Input Parameters is fast and easy, but it does not offer the benefits of the ADO Parameters collection. These include strong data typing and the ability to accept output parameters from a stored procedure. The sample to demonstrate this functionality builds on a prior one from Chapter 6. That sample added a record to a custom table based on parameters passed to it. It also returned the identity value in the primary key for the record inserted by the stored procedure. For your convenience and ease of understanding, the two stored procedures from Chapter 6 appear below, to remind you of how they work.

The insert_into_my_employees stored procedure that appears below creates a table called my_employees, and it adds four new records to the table. The table's primary key has an IDENTITY property with a seed of 0 and an increment of 2. Therefore, the four new records have primary key values that range from 0 through 6. This stored procedure is useful for creating the table to which you add a record from the form.

```
Alter Procedure insert_into_my_employees
As

-Drop previous version of my_employees, if it exists
IF EXISTS(SELECT name FROM sysobjects WHERE name='my_employees')
   DROP TABLE my_employees

-Create a new version of my_employees table
CREATE TABLE my_employees
(
employeeID int IDENTITY(0,2) NOT NULL Primary Key,
firstname varchar(10),
lastname varchar(20),
homephone varchar(24),
```

```
source varchar(20)
)

-Use a column list to explicitly state which values go with which columns
INSERT my_employees (firstname,lastname,homephone,source)
        VALUES('Tom','Jones','123.456.7890','input value')

-Optionally, include values only without a column list (when values appear in
column order)
INSERT my_employees VALUES('Terry','Johnson','123.987.7890','input value')
INSERT my_employees VALUES('Tony','Hinton','123.456.8765','input value')
INSERT my_employees VALUES('Tomie','Binton','123.345.1234','input value')
```

The second stored procedure, insert_into_my_employees_from_parameters, accepts four input parameters and returns one output parameter. Run the insert_into_my_employees stored procedure before running this one. This second stored procedure uses an INSERT statement to create a new record in the my_employees table with field values set to the input parameters. The output parameter reflects the primary key value for the inserted record. For your reference, the second stored procedure appears below:

```
Alter Procedure insert_into_my_employees_from_parameters
@firstname varchar(10),
@lastname varchar(20),
@homephone varchar(24),
@source varchar(20) = 'from input parameters',
@employeeID INT OUTPUT
As
INSERT my_employees VALUES(@firstname, @lastname, @homephone, @source)
SELECT @employeeID = @@IDENTITY
```

The key to this sample is the form for collecting the input parameters and the event procedure for passing those values on to the second stored procedure. The unbound form for gathering input parameters appears below. It contains three text boxes for accepting input parameters. The fourth input parameter designates the source. Since the source for the form below will always be an Access form, the form designates *from Access form* as the Control Source property for the fourth text box. The application disables this text box so users cannot type over the control's value. It is popular to want to designate disabled fields with some other formatting besides the default gray-on-gray format in which the fourth text box's label appears. This sample used the Format | Conditional Formatting menu to assign a bold, italic font to the contents of the text box. The new font specifications make the contents easier to read even while the text box maintains the same general look of a standard Access disabled field value.

The final text box is for the display of the output parameter from the insert_into_my_employees_from_ parameters stored procedure. The two command buttons animate the form. The command button labeled Submit passes the form control values on to the stored procedure for insertion into the my_employees table as a new record. The other button, labeled Reset, clears the four text boxes that are not disabled.

The following VBA event procedure passes the values from the form to the stored procedure. Most of this procedure has nothing to do with the form. It just happens to part of an event procedure for a command button on a form. The event procedure's primary focus is creating a `Command` object to point at the stored procedure for inserting a record and defining input and output parameters. Just before executing the `Command` object, it assigns the first four text box values to the input parameters. However, by this point, the event procedure has declared the parameters and instantiated them. Immediately after executing the `Command` object, the event procedure inserts the output parameter from the stored procedure into the last text box on the Access form. As you can see, this requires nothing more than a simple assignment statement.

```vba
Private Sub cmdSubmit_Click()
'working_with_input_output_parameters

Dim cmd1 As ADODB.Command
Dim prm1 As ADODB.Parameter
Dim prm2 As ADODB.Parameter
Dim prm3 As ADODB.Parameter
Dim prm4 As ADODB.Parameter
Dim prm5 As ADODB.Parameter
Dim rst1 As ADODB.Recordset
Dim fld1 As ADODB.Field
Dim strOut As String

'Instantiate and assign properties to
'Command object
Set cmd1 = New ADODB.Command
cmd1.ActiveConnection = CurrentProject.Connection
cmd1.CommandType = adCmdStoredProc
cmd1.CommandText = "insert_into_my_employees_from_parameters"

'Create input/output parameters for cmd1
Set prm1 = cmd1.CreateParameter("@firstname", adVarChar, adParamInput, 10)
Set prm2 = cmd1.CreateParameter("@lastname", adVarChar, adParamInput, 20)
Set prm3 = cmd1.CreateParameter("@homephone", adVarChar, adParamInput, 24)
Set prm4 = cmd1.CreateParameter("@source", adVarChar, adParamInput, 20)
Set prm5 = cmd1.CreateParameter("employeeID", adInteger, adParamOutput)

'Append and assign values to parameters
'The text boxes for this form start their names with
'txt, so txtFirstname is the text box for the
'@firstname parameter. Again, we use Me to refer
'to the current form

cmd1.Parameters.Append prm1
prm1.Value = Me.txtFirstname.Value
cmd1.Parameters.Append prm2
prm2.Value = Me.txtLastname.Value
cmd1.Parameters.Append prm3
prm3.Value = Me.txthomephone.Value
cmd1.Parameters.Append prm4
prm4.Value = Me.txtSource.Value
cmd1.Parameters.Append prm5

'Run command
cmd1.Execute

'Save output parameter from stored procedure in the form
```

```
Forms("frminsertparameters").txtEmployeeID.Value = cmd1("employeeID")

'Cleanup recordset resources
Set prm1 = Nothing
Set prm2 = Nothing
Set prm3 = Nothing
Set prm4 = Nothing
Set prm5 = Nothing
Set cmd1 = Nothing

End Sub
```

The preceding event procedure is very similar to the working_with_input_output_parameters VBA procedure from Chapter 6. However, its use as an event procedure adds significant new customization features. If you look over the earlier chapters, you are likely to find numerous samples that lend themselves to extension and adaptation. Some may not require much more adaptation (for example, error checking on the input) than was necessary in this case.

Here is the relatively simple code for the **Reset** button:

```
Private Sub cmdReset_Click()

Me.Controls("txtfirstname") = NULL
Me.Controls("txtlastname") = NULL
Me.Controls("txthomephone") = NULL
Me.Controls("txtemployeeID") = NULL

End Sub
```

This simply sets the controls to NULL in each case, clearing out any former values they contained.

Navigating, Updating, and Refreshing with Unbound Forms

With some code, unbound forms can exhibit many of the features that characterize bound forms, such as navigating through records and updating their values. When we work with some queries, we can even perform tasks with unbound forms that bound forms do not permit. For example, we cannot update records in a bound form when the T-SQL statement for its source includes the DISTINCT keyword. However, unbound forms allow us to update the table reference in the source for a Recordset object directly. By addressing a data source directly, we can eliminate the restriction resulting from the use of the DISTINCT keyword in the SELECT statement for a form's data source. The following sample for unbound forms illustrates this and other features.

The form design for the final unbound form sample in this chapter appears in the following screenshot. Notice that the form has no record selector. In addition, it is missing the built-in navigation buttons. These items do not function in an unbound form. There is no Record Source property for the form, and the four text boxes do not have Control Source property settings. Users can interact with the form through a series of four buttons that appear below the text box controls. Each button has a custom event procedure that implements its function, and there is a fifth event procedure associated with the form's Open event. This event procedure initially loads values from a data source into the four text box controls.

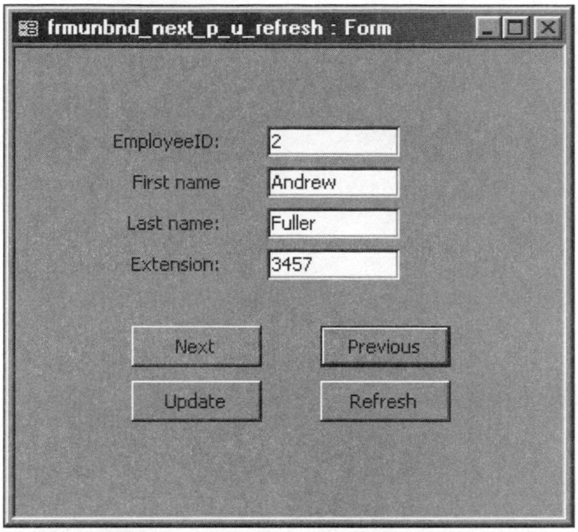

The data source that the `Form_Open` event procedure loads is the **list_managers_extensions** view. The view lists the two employees, Andrew Fuller and Steven Buchanan, who have direct reports to them in the **Employees** table. The T-SQL statement for this view, which appears below, includes a `DISTINCT` keyword; therefore, SQL Server does not allow updates to the view. The statement below shows that the view is a self-join of the **Employees** table with itself. This is a second reason why you cannot directly update the **Employees** table through the view with values from the text boxes on the preceding form. However, the data on which the view is based can be updated using this unbound form example.

```
SELECT DISTINCT
    Employees1.EmployeeID, Employees1.FirstName,
    Employees1.LastName, Employees1.Extension
FROM Employees INNER JOIN
    Employees Employees1 ON
    Employees.ReportsTo = Employees1.EmployeeID
```

The five event procedures that govern the behavior of the unbound form appear below. While together they extend over a couple of pages, not one of the procedures is long or complicated. The main points to making an unbound form work like a bound form are to manage the appearance of values in the form controls from the local cache and update the server from the form. Our code manages the form's local cache and its relationship to the server database.

The `Form_Open` event procedure launches whenever a user opens the form. It creates an ADO `Recordset` object based on the **list_managers_extensions** views. The scope of this ADO `Recordset` variable is good while the form is opened. This `Recordset` acts as the local cache. After opening the `Recordset`, the procedure assigns fields from the first row of the `Recordset` to the form's controls.

```
Private Subform_Open(Cancel As Integer)

Dim rst1 as ADODB.Recordset
Set rst1 = New ADODB.Recordset
rst1.ActiveConnection = CurrentProject.Connection
rst1.source = "list_managers_extensions"
'Because we're setting the recordset from the
```

```
'CurrentProject.Connection, we don't need to specify
'LockType or CursorType
rst1.Open

Me.txtEmployeeID = rst1("employeeID")
Me.txtFirstname = rst1("firstname")
Me.txtLastname = rst1("lastname")
Me.txtExtension = rst1("extension")

End Sub
```

Next we have the code for the **Next** button:

```
Private Sub cmdNext_Click()

rst1.MoveNext
If Not rst1.EOF Then
    Me.txtEmployeeID = rst1("employeeID")
    Me.txtFirstname = rst1("firstname")
    Me.txtLastname = rst1("lastname")
    Me.txtExtension = rst1("extension")
Else
    MsgBox "Already at end of recordset."
    rst1.MovePrevious
End If
End Sub
```

The **Next** button's `click` event procedure advances the current row in the `Recordset` and assigns the new row to the form's control. If the move to the next record moves to the EOF marker, the procedure backs out of the advance and informs the user. The **Previous** button performs similarly, except it moves in a different direction and checks for a BOF marker.

And now the code for the **Previous** button:

```
Private Sub cmdPrevious_Click()

rst1.MovePrevious
If Not rst1.BOF Then
    Me.txtEmployeeID = rst1("employeeID")
    Me.txtFirstname = rst1("firstname")
    Me.txtLastname = rst1("lastname")
    Me.txtExtension = rst1("extension")
Else
    MsgBox "Already at beginning of recordset."
    rst1.MoveNext
End If
End Sub
```

Here is the code for the **Update** button:

```
Private Sub cmdUpdate_Click()
Dim ctl1 As Control
Dim cmd1 As ADODB.Command
```

```
    Dim prm1 As ADODB.Parameter
    Dim prm2 As ADODB.Parameter
    Dim prm3 As ADODB.Parameter
    Dim prm4 As ADODB.Parameter
    Dim str1 As String

    'Instantiate Command object to run stored procedure that updates
    'a record and do same for its parameters
    Set cmd1 = New ADODB.Command
    cmd1.ActiveConnection = CurrentProject.Connection
    cmd1.CommandType = adCmdStoredProc
    cmd1.CommandText = "update_employees_firstname_lastname_extension"

    Set prm1 = cmd1.CreateParameter("@employeeid", adInteger, adParamInput)
    Set prm2 = cmd1.CreateParameter("@fname", adVarChar, adParamInput, 10)
    Set prm3 = cmd1.CreateParameter("@lname", adVarChar, adParamInput, 20,
    Me.Controls("txtLastname"))
    Set prm4 = cmd1.CreateParameter("@extension", adVarChar, adParamInput, 4,
    Me.Controls("txtExtension"))

    cmd1.Parameters.Append prm1
    prm1.Value = CInt(Me.Controls("txtemployeeID"))
    cmd1.Parameters.Append prm2
    prm2.Value = Me.Controls("txtFirstname")
    cmd1.Parameters.Append prm3
    prm3.Value = Me.Controls("txtLastname")
    cmd1.Parameters.Append prm4
    prm4.Value = Me.Controls("txtExtension")
    cmd1.Execute

    'Requery local recordset against server version and
    'Find updated record
    str1 = "EmployeeID = " & Me.txtEmployeeID
    rst1.Requery
    rst1.Find str1

    'Assign found record in cache to form controls
    Me.txtEmployeeID = rst1("employeeID")
    Me.txtFirstname = rst1("firstname")
    Me.txtLastname = rst1("lastname")
    Me.txtExtension = rst1("extension")

    End Sub
```

The most advanced event procedure is for the **Update** button. This procedure passes the form control's values to a stored procedure that updates the record identified by the `txtemployeeID` control. The event procedure passes the control values to the stored procedure through the ADO parameters collection. The T-SQL for the stored procedure appears below. After the update, the procedure requeries the local `Recordset` against the view to obtain the result of the update in the local cache. Then, it finds the updated record in the cache and assigns its fields to the controls on the form.

```
    Alter Procedure update_employees_firstname_lastname_extension
    @employeeid INT,
    @fname NVARCHAR(10),
```

```
@lname NVARCHAR(20),
@extension NVARCHAR(4)
As
UPDATE employees
    SET firstname = @fname, lastname = @lname, extension = @extension
where employeeid = @employeeid
```

And finally, the code for the **Refresh** button:

```
Private Sub cmdRefresh_Click()
Dim int1 As Integer

int1 = Me.Controls("txtemployeeID")
rst1.Requery
rst1.Find ("employeeID = " & int1)

Me.txtEmployeeID = rst1("employeeID")
Me.txtFirstname = rst1("firstname")
Me.txtLastname = rst1("lastname")
Me.txtExtension = rst1("extension")


End Sub
```

The last event procedure refreshes the `Recordset` to reflect changes by other users since the initial opening of the form, or the last refresh request, whichever is more recent. The `cmdUpdate_Click` and `cmdRefresh_Click` event procedures demonstrate subtly different approaches to tackling the same issue – finding the current record before the requery of the local cache. In the end, both assign the `Recordset` fields to the controls on the form.

Working with Hyperlinks on Forms

SQL Server does not support hyperlink data types like Access database files, but you can work with functioning hyperlinks through the `Is Hyperlink` property for a text box or combo box on a form. If your application can benefit from live hyperlinks right on Access forms, then assign a table of hyperlinks as the data source for a form. The table contains text, which the form interprets as hyperlinks. The data source can be very basic, for example two columns with one for a primary key index and the other for the hyperlinks. We would declare the column of hyperlinks to be any string data type such as `VARCHAR`. We would also need to make sure that our maximum length is long enough to hold our longest hyperlink address.

About Hyperlinks

We can populate the table with hyperlinks manually or programmatically. In fact, we can use both methods to populate the same table. Therefore, if we have a large collection of links in a prior format, we can re-format them and insert them programmatically. Then, we can have users continue to add new hyperlinks individually through the standard Access interface or any custom interface that returns a string in hyperlink format.

Although there is no hyperlink data type in SQL Server, you still need to understand the Access hyperlink data type design because this is the format to enter strings that represent hyperlinks. A value in hyperlink data type format can have up to four parts delimited by hash signs (#). The syntax is displaytext#address#subaddress#screentip.

The first part, `displaytext`, denotes the display text for the hyperlink. This part is typically a meaningful text message that characterizes or explains the hyperlink. If it is present, `displaytext` appears in the text box in lieu of `address` and `subaddress`. There can be as many as two parts to the address. Access refers to these as the `address` and the `subaddress`. These two parts constitute `address` and `subaddress` in the hyperlink data format. The `address` part refers to a standard hyperlink address (like http://www.wrox.com), while the `subaddress` part is used to refer to an object in the current database, or to a bookmark for a site. The `screentip` is a string that appears when users rest a cursor over a hyperlink field value. While you can specify both `address` and `subaddress` in a single hyperlink, you only need to designate one of these parts for the hyperlink value to be valid. Neither `displaytext` nor `screentip` is required, but they can improve the readability of a hyperlink field value. In the next section we show some examples of valid hyperlinks.

Hyperlinks in an Access application are a very flexible construct. They enable transfer of control to a web page on the Internet or to a web page on a local intranet. In addition, hyperlinks can open a file on a LAN or a file on your computer's hard drive. These files can be from other applications, such as Word or Excel. You can also open any object for the current project, including other forms and reports, as well as tables, views, and stored procedures in the database to which a project connects. You can also connect to other databases. The hyperlink format even embraces the notion of addressing an e-mail message to a recipient and specifying a subject, so long as there is an e-mail client present.

Using Hyperlinks with Forms

As mentioned above, we use the `Is Hyperlink` property, set to `Yes`, to designate a text box or combo box as representing hyperlinks. Although we specify the data type as a string for the field representing the hyperlinks, such as `VARCHAR(255)`, the text box will display the string as a live hyperlink that facilitates a transfer of control from the form to a designated hyperlink. This property resides on the Format tab of the Properties dialog for the form control.

The table overleaf, named my_hyperlinks, shows a selection of hyperlinks from the sample database for this chapter. This is a custom table not in the standard Northwind database, and it illustrates some of the options for specifying hyperlinks.

The first link field provides a link to the Microsoft SQL Server site. The first part shows the display text for the hyperlink, and the second part points at the web page to which the hyperlink transfers control. The third part is empty. If there were a bookmark or anchor on the page to which control should transfer, its name would go here. The fourth part is the tip message (SQL Server tip) that appears when the mouse hovers over a control with the first link as its field value.

The second and third links are two resource sites that my practice maintains. They appear in the same format as the SQL Server site. The fourth hyperlink transfers control to the frmShippers form in the sample Access project – `Chapter7Northwind.adp`.

The fifth, sixth, and seventh links transfer control respectively to a table, a stored procedure, and a view for the sample database – `Chapter7Northwind`. Notice that the last two hyperlink fields do not use either `displaytext` or `address` of the hyperlink format. The `subaddress` part starts with a name denoting the object type followed by a space and the name of the object to which the hyperlink transfers control. These links are internal to the current database.

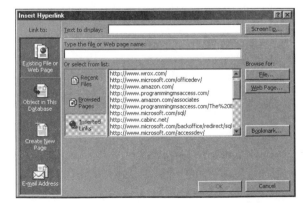

link id	link
1	Microsoft SQL Server site#http://www.microsoft.com/sql/##SQL Server tip
2	ProgrammingMSAccess.com#http://www.programmingmsaccess.com/##ProgrammingMSAccess.com tip
3	Cabinc.net#http://www.cabinc.net/##Cabinc.net tip
4	Shippers AutoForm##Form frmShippers#Shippers AutoForm tip
5	My hyperlinks table##Table my_hyperlinks#my_hyperlinks tip
6	##StoredProcedure Ten Most Expensive Products#Ten tips
7	##View list_managers#my hand entered tip

The following screenshot depicts a form named frmmy_hyperlinks that opens on the my_hyperlinks table. The cursor rests over a field with the first hyperlink in it. Notice that the `screentip` part of the hyperlink field appears below the cursor tip, and the `displaytext` part appears as text. Users can click the hyperlink to transfer control to the Microsoft SQL Server web site. This will launch the browser as a separate application. Once there, a user can return control to the application by clicking the back arrow in the browser. It's that simple. The process is similar when you hyperlink to another Access application object or a database object. If a user clicks the text with the fourth hyperlink showing, control transfers to the frmShippers form. If the web toolbar is not already exposed, Access opens it as control transfers. Then, a user can click the back arrow on the web toolbar to return control to the frmmy_hyperlinks form. The frmShippers form does not close when you transfer control back to frmmy_hyperlinks; users have to perform this task manually. While it is possible to achieve this programmatically, one major thrust of hyperlinks is to eliminate the need for programming simple navigation tasks.

If you click the Insert Hyperlink tool on the Form Design toolbar (in Design view), it opens a dialog for inserting a new hyperlink into the form. The Insert Hyperlink dialog is convenient for entering individual hyperlinks into a form.

From the Link to bar on the dialog's left edge, you can see the dialog facilitates the creation of hyperlinks to existing and new web pages as well as objects in the current database (this includes the Access project as well). You can additionally designate the creation of a new e-mail address to a particular recipient for a specific subject. When the user clicks the hyperlink, it will open the e-mail client (assuming there is an e-mail client installed) with the recipient and subject fields specified in the hyperlink. The layout of the area to the right of the Link to bar changes depending on which icon we choose from the bar. This allows the dialog to customize its fields for whatever purpose we plan to use our new hyperlink field value for.

While the **Insert Hyperlink** dialog is convenient for working with hyperlinks one at a time, it can quickly become tedious if we have a large number of hyperlinks to enter. However, a simple VBA procedure can readily address this task. The procedure below adds hyperlinks for the Microsoft Access Developer site and the Wrox Press site to the **my_hyperlinks** table in the sample database. Recall that a hyperlink in a SQL Server table is nothing more than a string. Therefore, we can programmatically construct hyperlinks in the proper format from any collection of hyperlink addresses.

The following VBA procedure illustrates design elements to consider as we approach this task for our custom collection of links. The overall strategy is to open an ADO `Recordset` object on an existing collection of hyperlinks with a design like the **my_hyperlinks** table. After instantiating and opening the `Recordset`, we can use the `AddNew` and `Update` methods to create more hyperlinks in the table. If we had a large collection of hyperlink addresses, we could read them sequentially from a text file and add them within a loop that continued to read the text file until it has no more address records. See Chapter 5 for sample code for working with text files from within a VBA project.

```
Sub add_two_hyperlinks()
Dim rst1 As ADODB.Recordset
Dim str1 As String
Dim int1 As Integer

'Instantiate Recordset object, assign properties,
'and move to end of recordset
Set rst1 = New ADODB.Recordset
rst1.ActiveConnection = CurrentProject.Connection
rst1.CursorType = adOpenKeyset
rst1.LockType = adLockOptimistic
rst1.Open "my_hyperlinks"
rst1.MoveLast

'Use a clustered primary key for link_id field
'Assign first hyperlink
'get the value of the last entry and add one to it
int1 = rst1("link_id")
str1 = "Microsoft Access Developer site" & _
       "#http://www.microsoft.com/accessdev/##" & _
       "tip for Access Developer site"
rst1.AddNew
rst1("link_id") = int1 + 1
rst1("link") = str1
rst1.Update

'Assign second hyperlink
int1 = int1 + 1
str1 = "Wrox Press" & _
       "#http://www.wrox.com/##" & _
       "tip for Wrox Press site"
rst1.AddNew
rst1("link_id") = int1 + 1
rst1("link") = str1
rst1.Update

'Release recordset resources
rst1.Close
Set rst1 = Nothing

End Sub
```

The sample procedure illustrates another capability in which many developers express an interest. It demonstrates how to manage a custom numeric field that serves as a primary key without relying on the built-in Identity property. In order to control the order of records, we will want to make our primary key clustered with an INT data type. Then, all we have to do is manage the last value in the table. For example, before entering any new hyperlinks we collect the link_id value of the last hyperlink. The sample procedure does this by moving to the last record and assigning the link_id field value to a local integer variable. The procedure then increments that local integer variable by one. Before entering the second record, it again increments the local integer by one. So, we take the value of the last record and add one to it before creating a new record. Unfortunately, this method could fail if there are concurrent inserts to the table. To avoid this problem, you could use a different LockType that will lock the table when you run the application, like adLockPessimistic.

This sample procedure has the benefit of conducting most of its logic in VBA and ADO. If you are comfortable with VBA and ADO versus, say, T-SQL and triggers, then this might be desirable. However, this design is not the fastest way to code the task. In general, we should code as much possible in T-SQL that runs on the server for optimal performance. For example, a trigger might store and retrieve the last primary key value. In addition, we could use a T-SQL INSERT statement instead of the ADO AddNew and Update methods to create new records in the table. However, if our list is relatively small, then programming the task for convenience is probably a better design tradeoff than programming it for speed.

Using Hyperlinks with Images on Forms

One way to add excitement to an application with little or no effort is to add some images to a blank form and then assign hyperlink addresses to them. Access offers hyperlink address and hyperlink subaddress properties for each image on a form. You can assign these from the Properties dialog for the images or with the Insert Hyperlink tool on the Form Design toolbar. The hyperlink properties reside on the Format tab of the Properties dialog for an image. Whichever way we choose to assign the hyperlink properties, it is easy to do. If we assign a hyperlink address to an image on our form, clicking on that image will execute the hyperlink and take us to the corresponding web site. If we assign a hyperlink subaddress, then clicking that image will take us to the corresponding database object or bookmark page.

If we pick our images correctly, this will add color to our application. Frequently, the best choice is the logo image from the site to which the hyperlink directs control. You can use your browser to capture these images from the site, although be careful of copyright issues. We've already looked at how to create a blank form. Once we have a blank form, we can do anything with it, such as add images or specify a data source for it. The Unbound Object Frame control on the Toolbox is appropriate for containing a bitmap image on a form.

The screenshot on the right depicts a form with four images that direct users to four sites on the Internet. A single click of the top image gives control from our application to the Wrox Press site. Users can return to our application by clicking the browser's Back control. Due to the flexibility of hyperlinks, this simple design technique can offer substantial capabilities; for example, you can use an image on a form to start a message for sending new orders from a client to your firm.

Summary

This chapter demonstrates how to use Access forms at many different levels to facilitate application development with SQL Server databases. Early sections emphasize how simple it is to create forms for SQL Server tables, views, and stored procedures. Here we looked at selected features that control how Access exposes SQL Server database objects.

From there we moved on to discover how to combine simple forms into main/subforms that conditionally show values from a SQL Server database in a subform based on the current value of controls in an Access main form. Then the chapter switched focus to building solutions from scratch. Initially, the emphasis was on manual techniques, but then switched to a blend of manual and programmatic techniques for empowering Access forms to expose SQL Server data and permit user interaction with SQL Server data sources. The concluding section drilled down on a mix of advanced development approaches, including resynchronizing a form, passing parameters into and receiving parameters from stored procedures, and using unbound forms with ADO to work with data in ways not possible with bound forms, and live hyperlinks stored in a SQL Server database through Access forms.

Using Access Reports with SQL Server

Access reports have long been a major way of tapping SQL Server data sources. This is because it is easy to create flexible reports with Access. Since Access 2000 offers improved data definition capabilities for SQL Server over earlier Access versions, the value of Access reports is greater than ever. This chapter helps existing Access developers make their knowledge of Access reports pay off with SQL Server data sources, including linked data sources. In addition, SQL Server database administrators and others who need rapid application development tools for disseminating SQL Server data in report format can learn valuable techniques for quickly developing reports that look great.

The chapter starts by introducing the design elements of an Access report. Next, the content shifts to the AutoReport Wizard: we will learn how to customize reports created by the wizard and how to include bound images in Access reports based on SQL Server data sources. The focus then turns to making reports dynamic with stored procedures. This section is especially valuable because it highlights how to allow users to specify report data sources on the fly. The final two sections are for generating reports at a higher level. The penultimate section demonstrates how to work with conditional formats, both through the user interface and programmatically; conditional formats can make important points jump out of standard database reports. Another way to make reports says more is with charts; remember the phrase "a picture is worth a thousand words"? Well, a chart can succinctly convey tens of thousands of numbers! The coverage of this topic shows how to use the Chart Wizard to create charts for SQL Server data sources that work in Access database files as well as Access projects. The chapter also conveys programmatic means of specifying the content for graphs.

So in this chapter we'll be covering:

- ❑ The elements of an Access report
- ❑ Using the AutoReport Wizard

❑ Creating dynamic reports using stored procedures

❑ How to work with conditional formats through the user interface and also programmatically

❑ How to create reports incorporating charts for SQL Server data sources using the Chart Wizard

❑ How to specify the content for graphs programmatically

> This chapter makes use of a sample database, which is an adaptation of the classic **Northwind** database. The corresponding Access project's name is `Chapter8Northwind.adp`. The project file contains sample reports from this chapter. It connects to the adapted version of the **Northwind** database that includes its standard database objects along with custom additions that act as data sources for some of the reports in this chapter. You will also find that for a number of the examples in the chapter, you can utilize the standard **Northwind** database too.

Overview of Access Reports

Fortunately for us, Access reports are similar to forms, in that both can contain bound and unbound controls. Owing to this mutual functionality between forms and reports, this chapter addresses many topics that apply to forms as well.

Report Sections

The Access report writer has long been one of Access' most popular features – particularly for SQL Server development. Design elements of Report objects reflect both data source and report features; for example, reports have sections. A report section is a grouping of information on a report and is graphically represented by a band. The major report sections are:

❑ Report header

❑ Page header

❑ Detail

❑ Page Footer

❑ Report Footer

Understanding these sections can often materially enhance the flexibility of our reports. The power of these sections combined with selected control features removes the need to write code to solve selected problems. For example, basic sorting, grouping, subtotaling and report totaling can be done automatically without writing code. Even when we do have to write code, the sections within a report can drastically simplify the process.

Creating a Basic Report

To get into the report designer and create a basic report, we click on Reports under Objects on the Database Window in Access. Then we click the New button on the Database window Toolbar. This will bring up the New Report dialog box, shown opposite:

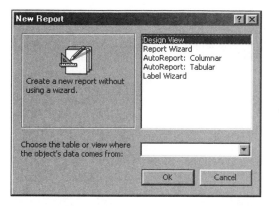

We click **Design View** from this dialog. Once we are in the Report Designer, we can click on the **Toolbox** Icon from the Toolbar or Select **Toolbar** from the **View** Menu. This will bring up the toolbox, which contains all of your report controls. The following screen shot displays an empty report in a design view with five built-in sections showing, along with the Toolbox and the **Data** tab of the report's properties dialog:

The availability of a Toolbox and **properties** dialog bears the similarity with the design environments for forms. In addition, the **Data** tab in the properties dialog displays a **Record Source** property.

The five built-in sections, which we referred to earlier, enable easy management of the different parts of a report. For example, the **Report Header** section occurs once at the beginning of a report and should therefore contain information designed to appear only once, such as a firm's contact information. As the **Report Header** and **Footer** sections occur just once at the beginning and end of a report, we could place logo graphics and other artwork here that we would not want to appear on each page of a report; we could also insert a date to timestamp it.

The **Page Header** and **Page Footer** sections occur once for each page in a report – however, if we don't add any content to them, they will not be printed. We can conveniently position static as well as dynamic content in these sections. Built-in menu commands simplify the addition of a page number in a select choice of formats. You can place unbound controls in the **Page Header** and **Page Footer** sections that compute values based on the contents of a page. The **Page Header** and **Page Footer** properties also make it straightforward to suppress **Page Header** and **Page Footer** content in the **Report Header** and **Report Footer** sections. This can be useful when we only want information appearing at the beginning (Report Header) and end (Report Footer) of the report and do not want any information appearing at the beginning (Page Header) and ending (Page Footer) on each page. The four possible settings for these two properties are:

- All Pages
- Not With Rpt Hdr
- Not With Rpt Ftr
- Not With Rpt Hdr/Ftr.

These properties are set in the properties dialog of the report. Clicking on the Report title band, and then right clicking brings up the reports menu. From the menu, we select **Properties**. The two properties are **Page Header** and **Page Footer**.

The **Detail** section ties tightly to the report's **Record Source** property. This section repeats its content for each row in the data source behind a report. You can use the **Record Source** property to designate a table, view, stored procedure, or T-SQL statement for the data source behind a report. The **Force New Page** property enables us to specify that the **Detail** section starts on a page of its own. This is important in reports where we have multiple detail sections and we want each detail section to be on a page of it's own.

This property is also useful when working with custom report sections; for example, we may need to have the section for each department start at the top of a page.

The **Can Grow** and **Can Shrink** properties allow a **Detail** section to grow or shrink according to the length of the content within a section. This property also applies to individual controls. Setting these properties to `True` for text boxes bound to text and ntext data types can achieve the dynamic positioning and sizing of controls on a report. The following diagram shows a completed report in design view. We could look at our report by highlighting the **Sales by Year** report and then clicking on the **Design Icon** on the **Database Window** Toolbar.

Working with the AutoReport Wizard

The AutoReport Wizard delivers a new report based on a table, much as the AutoForm Wizard does for a form. In both cases, database developers can create their new object with just one click. The AutoReport Wizard creates a new report in a columnar format that mimics the style of forms generated by the AutoForm Wizard. We must select a table, view, or stored procedure with a return set, for example categories in the Northwind database, before clicking the AutoReport Wizard button on the Database Toolbar:

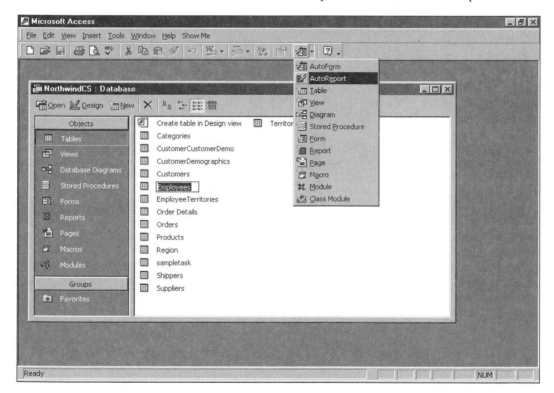

The AutoReport Wizard control has the image of a report with a lightning bolt on its face. The tool is part of a set of controls that occupy the same spot on the Toolbar as the AutoForm Wizard. If the AutoReport Wizard control does not show, select the down arrow to expose all the controls on that position:

Once you invoke the AutoReport Wizard, it appears on top until another control from the drop-down list is selected.

Creating a Columnar Report with Bound Images

The following screen depicts a preview page from a report prepared by the AutoReport Wizard for the Employees table. To generate the report, all we need to do is select the Employees table in the Database window, and then click the AutoReport tool. The Employees table includes a bound image of the employees in .bmp format that appears on the report. Each employee appears on a separate page. This will not always be the case: it depends on the amount of content available for printing. For

403

example, if we were to use the AutoReport Wizard on the Shippers table, its three default records would appear on a single page.

Users can navigate between pages with the controls at the bottom of the Preview window.

Although this automatically generated report makes a great starting point for customized reports. There are a few aspects which we need to iron out. The most obvious one may be that the picture does not fill its control. The control appears like a border around the image, but there is a substantial amount of white space inside the border.

The second issue relates to the clipping of the content in the Notes field. The text box is big enough for most, but not all, fields. This situation will be common with text box controls for text or ntext data type columns, such as the Notes column. Columns with these data types can have values with lengths varying wildly from one record to the next.

The third point is that the ReportsTo text box displays numeric values indicating the EmployeeID value for an employee's manager. For example, values of 2 in the above report page point to Andrew Fuller. Access database, files support lookup data types that automatically convert the number corresponding to a related field. This is not so for Access project reports with SQL Server data sources.

We'll be looking at workarounds for these issues a little later on.

Creating a Report using the Report Wizard

There is also another wizard that will easily create a report. The Report Wizard functions much like the Autoreport Wizard except it allows us to select a few more options such as sorting, grouping and the style of report (columnar, tabular etc.). We will walk through creating the same report as the one above using the Report Wizard instead of the Autoreport Wizard.

We'll start by clicking on Reports under Objects on the Database window. Then we click the New button on the Database window Toolbar. This will bring up the New Report dialog box. We select Report Wizard from this dialog and select Employees as the table. Finally we finish the process by clicking on the OK button.

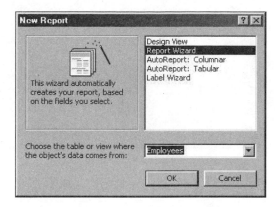

This will bring up a dialog asking us to select the fields from the Employee Table that we want on the report. We want all of the fields, so we click the button with the two arrows (>>) to select all of the fields.

When we're finished, we click on the Next button.

We then encounter a dialog, which asks us to specify any form of grouping that we require on our report. We could group according to any of the fields listed. We don't want to specify any grouping right now so we just click on the Next button. The subsequent dialog that pops up allows us to specify the sort order that we want to impose on the report. In this example, we select Employee ID as the sort order and click on the Next button to finish.

We then see a dialog asking how we wish our report to be layed out. The options provided are columnar, tabular or justified:

❑   Columnar – This puts one field on each line from top to bottom on the report.

❑   Tabular – This puts each field next to each going left to right across the page, in a similar layout to a grid structure.

❑   Justified – This puts fields next to each other from left to right and top to bottom. Long fields are positioned on a line by themselves and short fields share a line with other fields.

For our example, we select Columnar. We can also specify if we want our report to print in Landscape or Portrait format. To finish we click on the Next button.

The next dialog asks us what style (corporate, compact, bold etc.) we want our report to be presented in. In this case, we accept the defalt and click on the Next Button. This generated the final dialog which asks us to supply a name for our report and whether we want to Preview or Modify the report. We assign Employee as the name of our report and select Preview the Report. We then click Finish to preview the report.

The report will look similar to the report we created previously using the AutoReport Wizard. As we can see, the AutoReport Wizard is the simplest method but the Report Wizard does allow us more control over the appearance of our report.

Editing a Report

> Throughout this section, we will be using the **Employees** Report that we made with the AutoReport Wizard.

When we looked at how to create a report using the AutoReport Wizard a little earlier on, we took note of a few aspects of the finished report that we would want to neaten up. We can smooth out these "wrinkles" with some minor editing, for both the report generated by the AutoReport Wizard and the similar report that we have just seen how to create using the Report Wizard.

First, we can change the dimensions of the control for the bound images. Second, we can rearrange controls to free space at the bottom of the report. This, in turn, permits the expansion of the control for the Notes field so that it can display all the Notes values in the Northwind Employees table.

The following screen depicts the new report page for Steven Buchanan:

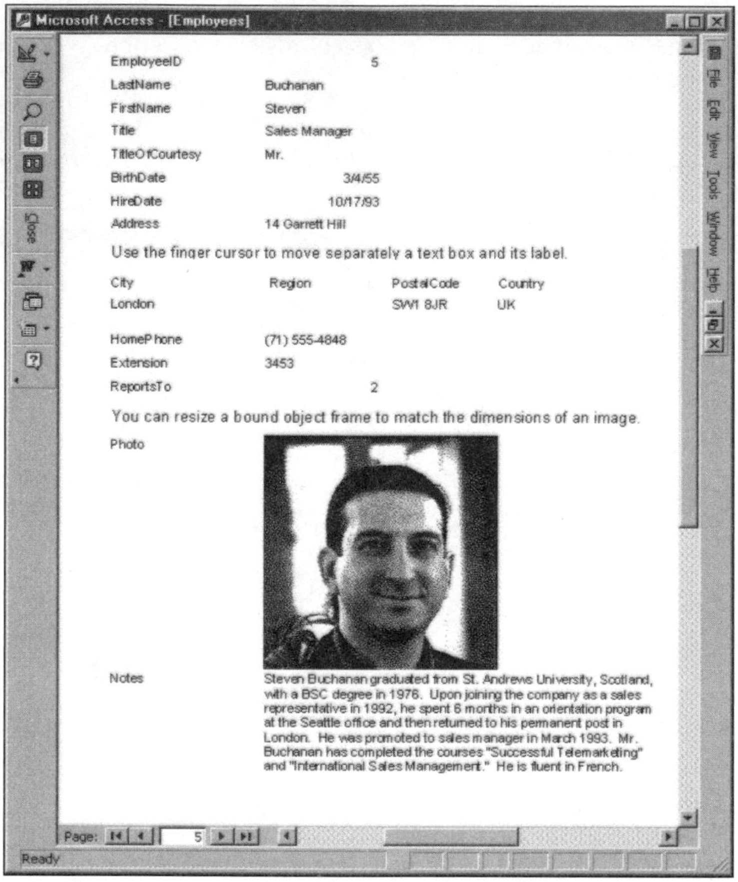

Notice that his image appears without any white space at the right side of the frame containing the picture. In addition, the new version repositions several controls for address fields so that they are horizontal in relation to one another. This second version of the report also moves the two controls below the text box for the Notes column. The new version moves the ReportsTo control above the image, and strikes the other field from the report. Finally, the original version of the Notes control has been dragged to make room for more text. This is one approach to tackling the problem of making a box big enough to hold text and text fields.

The other alternative for changing the position of the controls is to use the Can Grow or Can Shrink properties:

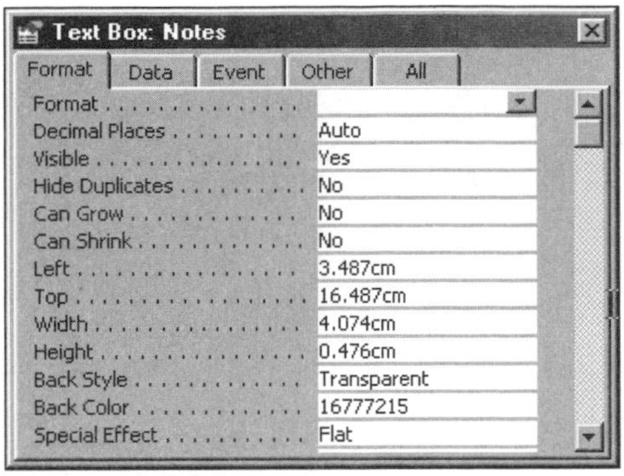

If we change the **Can Grow** property on the **Notes** field (right click on the field to see it's properties) from its default setting of **No** to **Yes**, we enable the control to grow vertically as the content in the field grows. The field will grow automatically so that the default size for the control is acceptable, although that size does not accommodate the content in some of the records.

Just as we do with a form, we edit a report in **Design view** (reports created with the Report Wizard must be saved before they can be edited). And, we enter a report's **Design view** in the same way that we do for a form. From the preview mode, we can click on the **Design** icon on the **Toolbar**. Alternatively, from the **Database window**, we can select **Reports**, highlight the **Employees** report, and click on the **Design** icon on the **Database window** Toolbar.

To move the **City** text box control below its label in the image below, we must position the mouse cursor on the handle at the top left corner of the text box, and drag it below the label. The cursor icon changes to a hand with a finger extending from it. If we were just to try to move the text box normally, we would end up repositioning both the label and its text box jointly. The following screen shot shows the **City** text box it is dragged below its label. We can duplicate the sample report we've just looked at by repeating this process for the **Region**, **PostalCode**, and **Country** text boxes.

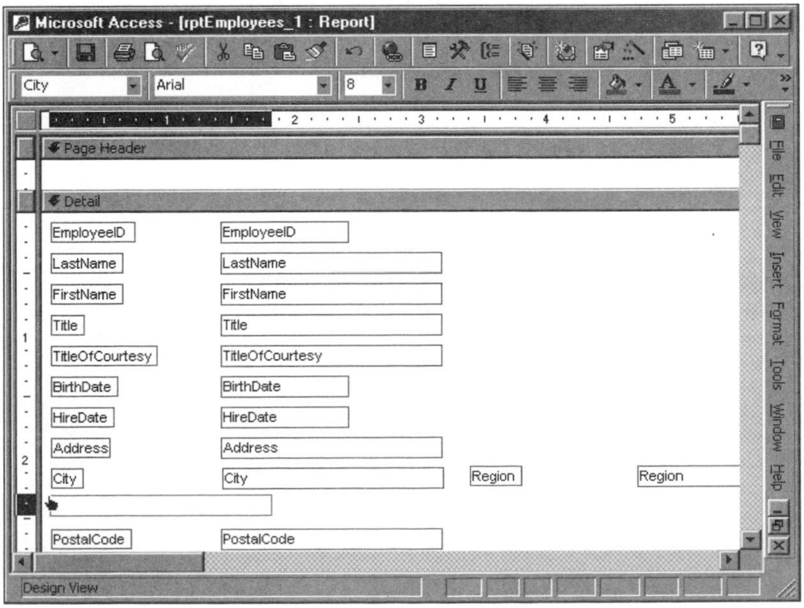

The image depicting employees resides in a Bound Object Frame control. This is the same control used to display the category images in the sample forms for the preceding chapter. If we want to automatically fill the control with the picture, we can change the Size Mode property from Clip to Stretch (just to refresh your memory – right-click on the object and select Properties; the Size Mode property can be found on the Format tab). This, however, has the unfortunate side effect of distorting the image (probably, the employees will not think this is such a great solution).

Another approach is to assign a new value to the Width property for the Bound Object Frame control (again found on the Format tab of the Properties dialog). However, what should the new setting be? We can get the answer by opening the Employees table and double clicking the Bitmap Image label for any row. This opens the image in the Windows Paint program (or whatever program has otherwise been assigned as the default picture editor for the particular machine). We can then choose the Image | Attributes command and display the picture's dimensions in a measure that matches the Regional Settings for the measurement system on the Number tab. For example, if we were using inches, we could click the Inches option button to display the images dimensions in that scale of measurement. We can then change the dimensions in the report to match the images dimensions we obtained from the Employees table. The AutoReport Wizard will always have at least one image dimension right already, so we only have to change the other.

Sorting and Grouping

For small datasets, we can easily sort the records in the data source of an Access report with graphical controls. Since the sorting feature is slow in Access it makes sense to use it only for small datasets; if we have large datasets that need to be sorted, we should consider using a stored procedure to return the dataset "ready-sorted" (using an `Order by` clause) rather than carrying out the sorting in a report.

In addition, we can graphically create our own custom report sections to group data to meet our specific needs. Custom report sections can nest within one another, and we can specify independently, header and footer areas for each custom section – though these are not to be confused with page, or report, headers and footers. Aggregate functions in a report automatically recognize group boundaries. So, unbound text box controls within the header and footer areas of custom sections can perform computations such as the summing, averaging, and counting of the data for the rows within the section in which the control is housed.

The Grouping and Sorting Control

We use the Grouping and Sorting control on the Report Design Toolbar to specify columns for sorting and grouping the records in a report:

The sorting capability allows several different reports to use the same data source (view, stored procedure, table, etc.), but present the data sorted by different criteria. For example, the Shipping Department may need a report showing items by the required date. The Accounting team, however, may need the same data organized by order date.

Another example is when the sort order or sort criteria has to be set at report time (using parameters). For example, a manager may need a report of the employees sorted alphabetically on one occasion, but may need the same report sorted by employment date another time.

With Access reports, one consistent view can serve all requirements, while different personnel can show items on the report in a way that meets their needs The following Sorting and Grouping dialog shows the specification of the RequiredDate column as a sorting criterion:

Rows within the Detail section of the report will appear with the earliest due dates listed first. We could select any column in the data source behind a report as a sort criterion, and we can specify nested sorted orders with the columns at the bottom of the list being sorted before those at the top. We use the drop-down boxes to specify both the columns and their sort order.

The Sorting and Grouping dialog also controls the grouping of records against one or more criteria. We specify a Field/Expression for grouping by selecting it as we would do for sorting. Then, we change the Group Header or Group Footer settings for that column to Yes (the default setting is No). The Group On setting enables us to specify different ways of grouping items. For example, in the case of a datetime column, such as RequiredDate, we can designate Year, Qtr, Month, Week, Day, Hour, or Minute. In the case of a column with string values, we can specify how many prefix characters to evaluate for assigning a record to a group.

The Group Interval setting works in coordination with the Group On setting. A Qtr setting for Group On and a value of 1 for Group Interval instructs Access to group by quarter. However, a value of 1 for the Group Interval setting, with a Group On equal to Prefix Characters for a column of string values, means to group records alphabetically by the first letters in column values. The Keep Together Property is used to keep parts of a group (for example, groupheader detail section, or group footer) together on the same page. The Keep Together setting functions like the Keep Together property, but it applies to a custom section when we set the property from the Sorting and Grouping dialog.

Let's walk through an example to show the affects of changing the sorting and grouping options. We open the Employees Report that we made earlier on in the chapter using the AutoReport Wizard in Design mode. The report was created with EmployeeID as the sort field because EmpoyeeID is the primary key on the field. We are going to change the Sort criteria to display the employees in alphabetical order by name.

We start by selecting Sorting and Grouping from the View menu. This brings up the Sorting and Grouping Dialog. We want to sort the employees in alpahabetical order by name, so the first sort field we want is LastName. We select LastName from the list under Field/Expression on the first line. By default, the Sort Order is Ascending. If we wanted the sort order to be descending we could change it here. Since, we also want to sort by firstname, we want to add another sort field. We select FirstName from the list in line 2:

411

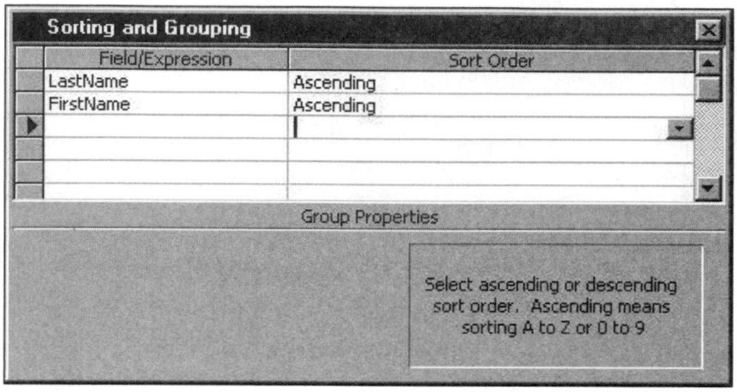

Once we've finished setting the sort order, we can preview the report and go through the records. The records are now in alphabetical order. Steven Buchanan is the first record, Laura Callahan the second...and Michael Suyama the last.

Special Report Capabilities

We can build sub reports within a main report just as we can create sub forms within a main form. A sub report links to its main report by one or more common fields. This type of application is convenient for generating estimates where the records for the prospect's name and contact information appear in the main report, and a sub report formats line item detail, such as quantity and cost. The main report can also contain summary information, such as subtotals, tax, freight, discounts and other factors impacting the final amount for a bid. Chapter 7 looks at how to build main and sub forms. We'll look at how to create a sub report now.

We start by creating a report for the Customers table using the AutoReport Wizard:

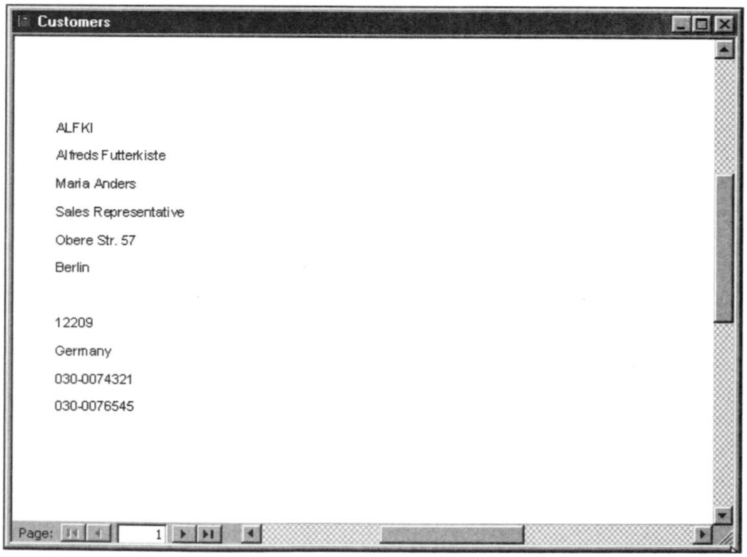

This report shows us customer information for all customers. But what if we also wanted to see the order information for each customer? We can add a sub report to this main report to show each cutomer's order information. First, we go into design mode and ensure the Wizard Icon on the Toolbox is **on** (it's a toggle icon):

Next we click on the SubForm/Report Control on the Toolbar and place it on the detail section of the Customers Report. This will bring up the SubForm Wizard:

We want to use our existing the (Northwind) database, so we accept the default and click on the Next button. The next dialog will ask us what table and fields we want to use. We select the Orders Table and the following fields:

- ❑ CustomerID
- ❑ OrderDate
- ❑ RequiredDate
- ❑ ShippedDate

When we are finished, we click on the Next button.

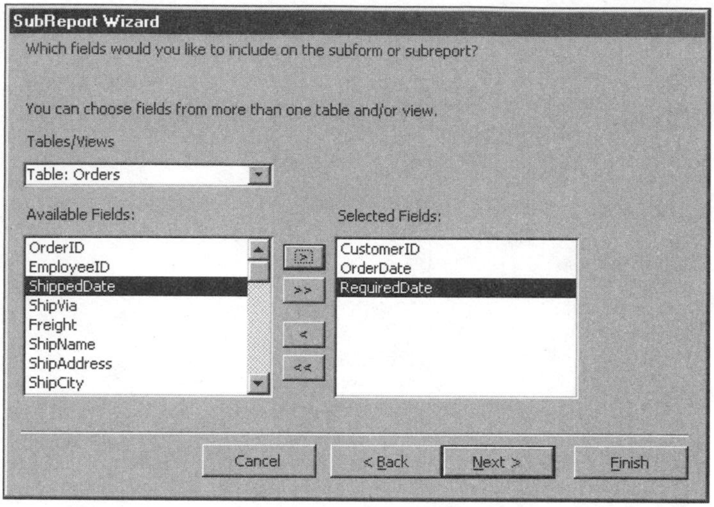

The next screen asks us how the two reports are matched up. We select CustomerID for both the Form/Report fields and the SubForm/SubReport fields:

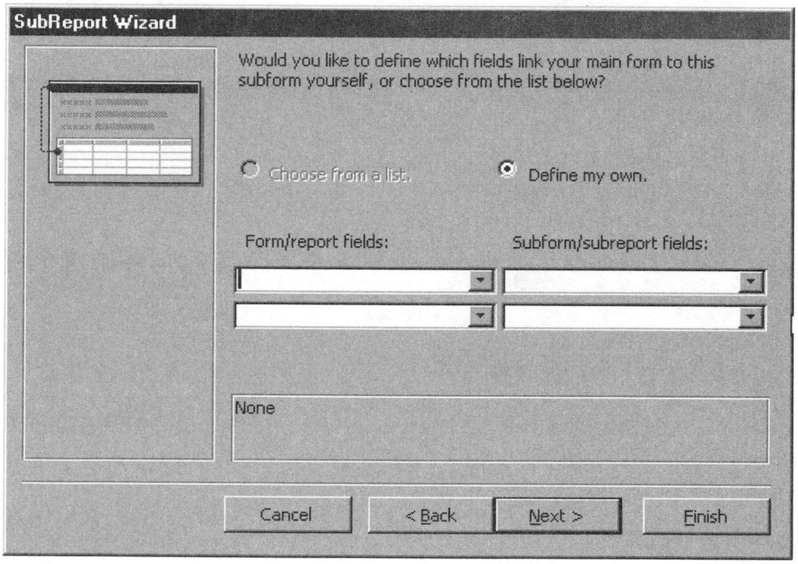

To move on, we click on the Next button. The last screen asks us to supply a name for the subform. After adding a name and, we click the Finish button. Finally we move the subform control to the right of the report and size it so that we can see all of the fields and then we preview the report:

When working with reports we can include multiple summary reports within a main report . This type of report application does not require a link between the report container and the reports that it contains. For example, you may have a summary report that includes three other reports for sales by category, sales by quarter, and sales by employee. No common link exists between these sub reports other than that clients request to view them together.

Adding a Lookup Field to a Report

The numbers appearing in the ReportsTo control on our Employees report result from the fact that the Employees table represents an employee's manager using the manager's EmployeeID value. We can replace this numeric value by using a view as the source for the report. The view can decode the manager's EmployeeID value to the manager's first and last name by self-joining the Employees table with itself. The second copy of the Employees table, which is refered to as Employees1, provides a lookup table capability for the manager's name. The T-SQL for the view is as follows:

```
SELECT Employees.*, Employees1.FirstName AS man_fname,
    Employees1.LastName AS man_lname

FROM Employees INNER JOIN
    Employees Employees1 ON
    Employees.ReportsTo = Employees1.EmployeeID
```

The first thing we need to do is to create a view using the above code. Name the view my_employees.

You can use this view, called my_employees, as the source for a new report. The AutoReport Wizard can generate the first version of the report. Then, we edit the entry in the ReportsTo text box. The trick to solving the decode task on the report is to replace the ReportsTo text box Control Source property with an expression instead of a single field as its source. The expression concatenates the first and last name fields for managers. Make your expression start with an equal sign and refer to the field names in the view that serves as the record source for the form. The exact expression is

```
=[man_fname] & " " & [man_lname]
```

Using this expression will mean that the report will include man_fname and man_lname as fields from the view. We need to remove these two fields from the report so they will not be displayed.

The following screen shot shows the page for Steven Buchanan from the new version of the report. We can see that the manager's name appears instead of a cryptic EmployeeID code.

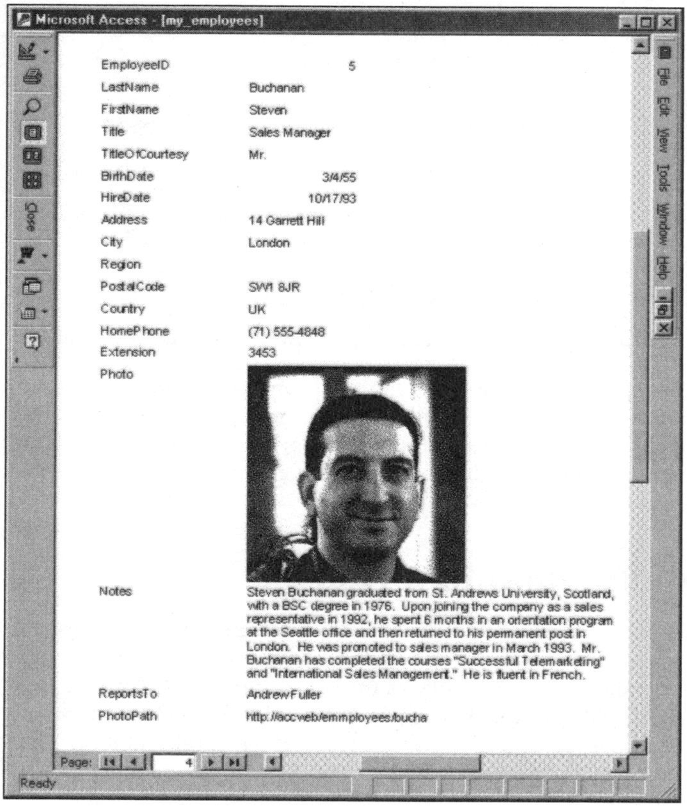

Incidentally, this report version shows the Notes control with two controls after it. In fact, the Notes field has its Can Grow property changed from its default setting of No to Yes. This enables the control to grow vertically as the content in the field grows. The field grows automatically so that the default size for the control is acceptable, although that size does not accommodate the content in some of the records.

Placing Controls in Header and Footer Areas

One of the ways we can improve the appearance of our forms is to take full advantage of all the sections of Access reports. The next sample demonstrates how to use label and text box controls in the Page Header and Page Footer report sections. The same approach works for the header and footer areas in the custom sections that you create for a report.

The following screen shot shows a full-page view of the previous sample embellished with content in its **Page Header** and **Page Footer** sections. The rptmy_employees_2 report content in the two new sections has an oversized font so that it can remain visible even when the rest of the material on the page is too small to read. We can change the size of the font by selecting the text box in **Design** mode and selecting the size of the font we want from the **Formatting Toolbar**.

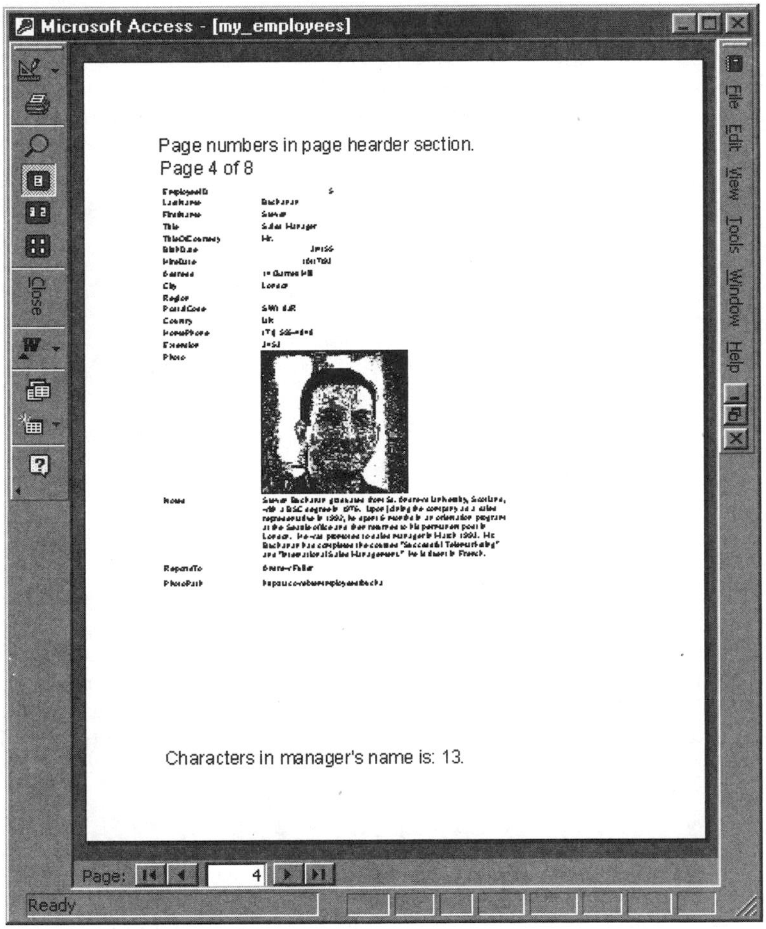

There are two controls in the **Page Header** section. The top line in the section, 'Page numbers in....' shows from a label control. Use the label's **caption** property to insert a string constant denoting the message that the label displays. You cannot use expressions with field values in a label's **caption** value. You would expect that the value of the expression would be displayed but the actual contents in the label caption will be displayed. For example, if you wanted to display a heading "**Employees**" with today's date in a text box you would use "**Employees** " & date() and the heading will bedisplayed as "Employees 08/17/00". If you use the same expression in a label control the heading will be displayed as "**Employees** & date()".

If you need to use string expressions so that a control's value will change depending on column values for the current record of the report's underlying record source, use a text box instead of a label. You can assign the expression to the **Control Source** property for the text box.

The message in the Page Footer section of the preceding report includes the length of the string representing a manager's name. The return value from the Len function is part of an expression with a string constant that identifies the return value from the function. The following line shows the function in the Control Source property. To make this change, we just add the following line to the Control Source property of the text control.

```
="Characters in manager's name is: " & Len([ReportsTo]) & "."
```

One of the most common entries in Page Header and Page Footer sections is a page's number. You can add page numbers to your reports with the Insert | Page Numbers command on the report's Design menubar:

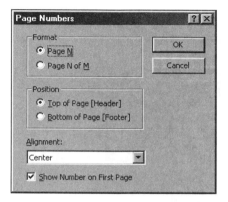

This command opens a dialog that offers a couple of formats for showing page numbers on a report in either the Page Header or Page Footer section. The command inserts the page number as an expression in a text box control. You can even specify the alignment (for example, left, right, or center) of the text box within a section. Even if you have more specialized requirements than the command satisfies, the Insert | Page Numbers command can still generate a good starting point. If you are inexperienced with Access reports, this command will number your pages automatically.

Developing Reports Based on Stored Procedures

While we can invoke stored procedures as sources for reports with the AutoReport Wizard, stored procedures are not available as a source when we want to create a new report any other way. For example, the drop-down list on the New Report dialog that appears after we click New with Reports selected from the Database window does not list stored procedures – just tables and views. However, we can reference a stored procedure from the Record Source property box after a report is open. This section gives us several samples of reports that use stored procedures as a data source. In the process, we will cover some new issues for working with reports.

Creating a Report from a Blank Design View

If you have a stored procedure that passes back a return set, you can create a report for it from a blank report template in Design view.Start by choosing Reports in the Objects bar on the Database window. Then click New. In the New Report dialog, click Design View. Do not choose a data source from the drop-down list on the dialog (recall that the list does not show stored procedures in any event). Then, open a blank report template by clicking OK. Before doing anything else, open the report's properties dialog by clicking the **Properties** tool on the **Report Design** Toolbar. Select the **Data** tab, and click the drop-down arrow in the **Record Source** property box. The arrow opens a list of stored procedures as well as tables and views from the current database connection as potential sources for the report.

The first sample selects the **Ten Most Expensive Products** stored procedure. The Access project template listing for this stored procedure appears below. This stored procedure appears in the original **NorthwindCS** sample project file.

```
Alter procedure "Ten Most Expensive Products" AS
SET ROWCOUNT 10
SELECT Products.ProductName AS TenMostExpensiveProducts, Products.UnitPrice
FROM Products
ORDER BY Products.UnitPrice DESC
```

The SET ROWCOUNT T-SQL statement restricts the output to just 10 records. The ORDER BY clause arranges product records in descending order by price. The SET ROWCOUNT statement assigns a value to the @@ROWCOUNT global variable that restricts all subsequent T-SQL statements to just 10 records until we've reset the variable with a SET ROWCOUNT 0 statement.

You can also write this stored procedure using the SELECT Top 10 syntax. This functions just like the previous example and will only return the top 10 records in the dataset.

```
Alter procedure "Ten Most Expensive Products" AS
SELECT TOP 10 Products.ProductName AS TenMostExpensiveProducts, Products.UnitPrice
FROM Products
ORDER BY Products.UnitPrice DESC
```

After selecting a stored procedure as the data source for a report, we can add fields from its return set. We open the list of fields by clicking the **Field List** control on the report's **Design Toolbar** if it is not already open. Then we drag and drop field names from the expanded control to the report's **Detail** section. The following screen shot illustrates this process for the **Ten Most Expensive Products** stored procedure:

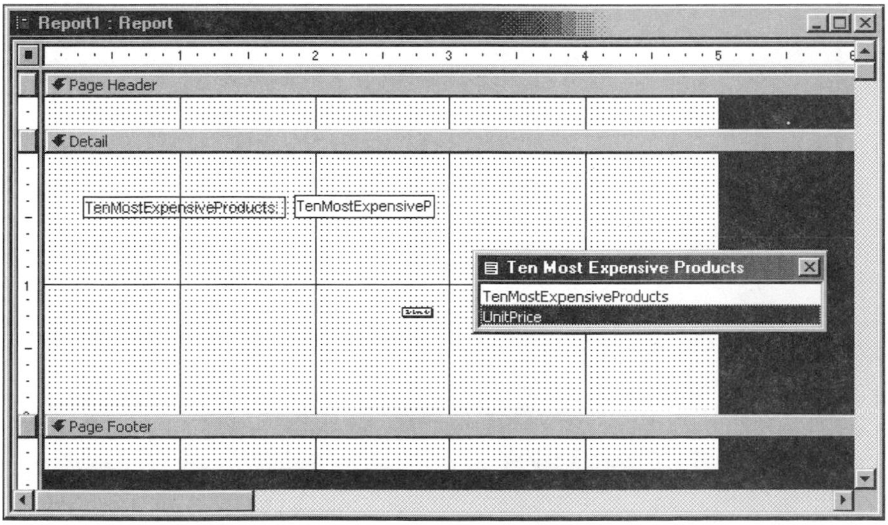

The screen depicts the report as the second field, UnitPrice, is being dragged to the report. The TenMostExpensiveProducts field is already on the report. Once the fields are on the report as text boxes, we click on the Page Header bar, and then cut the label from each text box in the Detail section and paste it into the Page Header section. It is a good idea to position column headings for a tabular report in this section since the headings appear at the top of every page.

The last thing we want to do is reduce the spacing between the lines by shrinking the detail section. The next two screen shots show a finished version of the report layout and its final design with content from the stored procedure:

The Format | Align and Format | Size commands are convenient when we're positioning labels and text boxes on the report relative to one another.

❑ The Format | Align command will align all the controls you have selected.

❑ The Format | Size command will make all of the controls you have selected the same size.

When you use labels in tabular reports, it is common to remove the colon that Access routinely puts at the end of label captions. While the report contents have practically no formatting, the column headings do stand away from the columns that appear below them. A subsequent sample on conditional formats will demonstrate more sophisticated report layout procedures. However, this sample exposes the basics of building a report from scratch, and highlights how to reference a stored procedure as the source for a report.

Using Stored Procedures with Parameters as Record Sources

One significant strength of stored procedures is their ability to take arguments. With arguments, a single stored procedure can deliver many different return sets based on the inputs that users specify for it. The samples in this section illustrate simple ways of tapping into this capability for reports.

The next group of report examples use the Label Wizard. As label reports work so nicely with subsets of data, they make good candidates for illustrating the power of parameters with stored procedures as record sources for reports.

> *The samples in this section are for standard 3-across laser mailing labels. However, the Label Wizard can create report templates for labels with different dimensions and purposes from more than a dozen worldwide manufacturers of sheet and continuous feed labels.*

You can select the Label Wizard from the New Report dialog. The mailing label template was initially created for the whole Customers table from the Northwind database; we're using an adapted version of this database as a sample databases for this chapter. The Customers table was then removed as the Record Source property for the report and replaced with a stored procedure that returns just a subset of the Customer table records based on user input. The mailing label report, named rptcustomer_labels_with_auto_prompt, appears below:

As you can see, it consists of four text boxes stacked on top of the other. These designate an upper limit of four lines per label. The Can Shrink property for each of the text boxes is set to Yes. This enables a line to disappear without leaving a blank line if there is no data for a line, such as when some members in a return set have a CompanyName field but others do not.

Only a portion of the last field appears in the text box in the Design view below. We must resist the temptation to widen the text box since the Label Wizard precisely calibrates the dimensions of its controls for the manufacturer and stock number that you specify. If the text box clips a portion of the text boxes contents in Print Preview mode, we simply reduce the size of the font so that the material fits within the box.

As we mentioned a little earlier, all the samples in this section rely on a stored procedure that returns a subset of the Customers table. Users can determine which subset it is by setting a country designation. In response to user interaction, the stored procedure returns a recordset with just the customers from a single country. The stored procedure sorts customer contacts by postal code to facilitate reduced-cost processing of mail. The T-SQL for running the stored procedure from an Access project appears below:

```
Alter Procedure customers_in_a_country @country_name NVARCHAR(15)
As
SELECT ContactName, CompanyName, Address, City, Region,
    PostalCode, Country
FROM Customers
WHERE Country = @country_name
ORDER BY PostalCode
```

As the Stored Procedure requires a parameter, the user is queried for this parameter, so invoking the rptcustomer_labels_with_auto_prompt report prompts the dialog that appears below in the Database window:

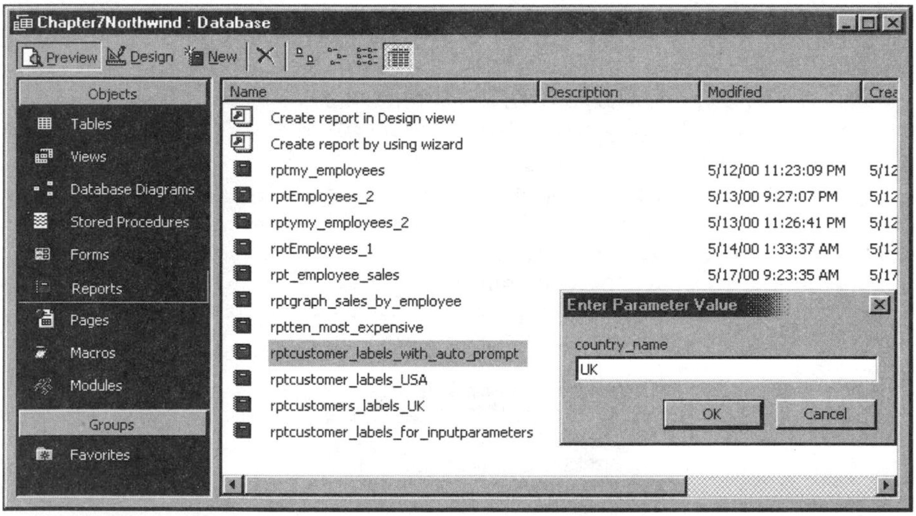

The popup dialog requesting a setting for the country_name parameter can appear in either of two ways:

❑ First, when we want to send the reports output to a printer, double clicking the report's name in the Database window.

❑ Second, when we select the report's name in the Database window and click Preview to open the report in a Print Preview window.

The latter option is particularly advantageous when you want to scan the names on a list before printing them.

422

You can't however edit the list of names like you can with Microsoft Word Merge.

Allowing Access to prompt for a country before running the report offers substantial flexibility, but it is at the cost of possible user input errors. If a user fails to input a proper designation for a country, such as US instead of USA, the program can fail to return the correct return set. The preceding screen shows a couple of reports with names of rptcustomer_labels_USA and rptcustomers_labels_UK. In both cases, the country is pre-set for the procedure using the Input Parameters field. We can invoke these stored procedures easily from a panel of command buttons where each button invokes a different report. We prepare multiple reports like rptcustomers_labels_USA by varying the setting of the Input Parameters property for each report. The Input Parameters property is located on the Data tab of the Properties tab – just as with forms.

See Chapter 7 for a programmatic solution for setting the Input Parameters property.

The following screen shot illustrates the Input Parameters settings for the rptcustomers_labels_USA report:

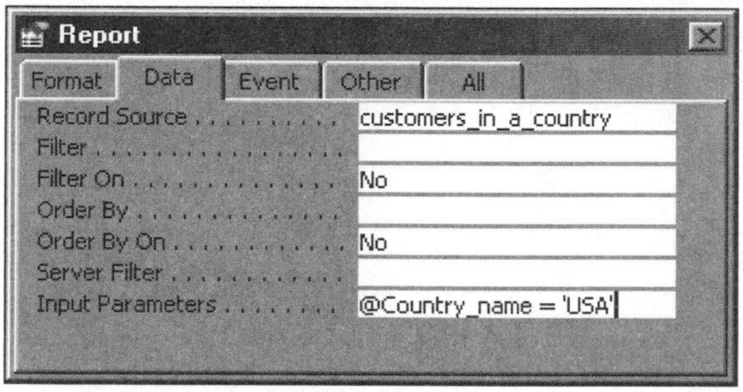

Using a Form to Generate Reports Dynamically

It is common in professional applications to allow users to select a subset of records and preview a report before printing it. This is easy to accomplish using an Access form for a SQL Server data source. The following screen shot depicts a form that permits this capability with three easy steps:

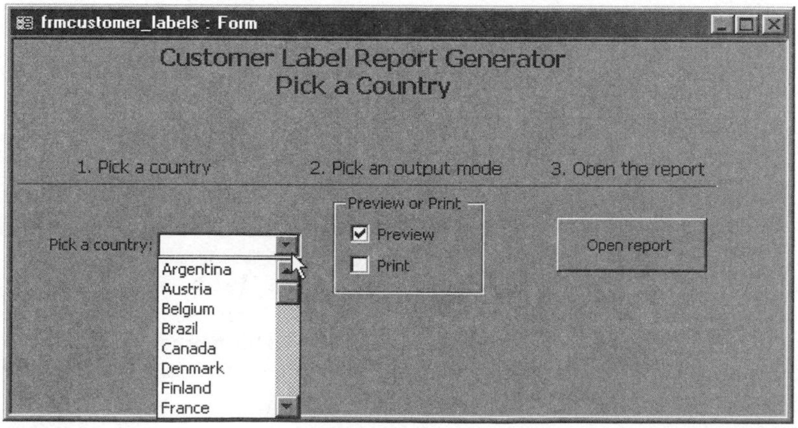

The form actually includes numbered on-screen instructions for how to perform the task. Here, the user is performing the first step. This involves selecting a country name from a combo box.

Chapter 7 describes techniques for programming a combo box so that it always returns the current list of countries in the Customers table.

After selecting the country, the instructions request the user to check an option group control; either a Print Preview window or the printer as an output container for the report. Clicking the command button labeled Open Report generates the report according to the selections made for the combo box and option group controls.

The following VBA procedure shows the code behind the preceding form:

```
Private Sub cmdprint_report_Click()
Dim str1 As String

'Specify name of report
str1 = "rptcustomer_labels_for_inputparameters"

'Suppress screen feedback
DoCmd.Echo False, "I'm preparing the report."

'Open report in Design view and update
'InputParameters property
DoCmd.OpenReport str1, acViewDesign
Reports(str1).InputParameters = _
    "@Country_name = '" & Me.cbopick_a_country.Value & "'"
    DoCmd.Close acReport, str1, acSaveNo
'Print report or print
If Me.opgpreview_or_print = 1 Then
    DoCmd.OpenReport str1, acViewPreview
Else
    DoCmd.OpenReport str1, acViewNormal

End If

'Restore screen feedback
DoCmd.Echo True

End Sub
```

This event procedure fires when a user clicks Open Report. It collects the input from the form to generate a report dynamically for either the printer or a Print Preview window. The form uses a variation of the preceding report that initially has a blank setting for its Input Parameters property setting. It does not matter what the property setting is for this event procedure since the procedure will change it.

The report opens in Design view and assigns the new Input Parameters property value. This reduces screen jitter as the program opens the report to set a property and does not have to prompt the user for it. After setting the Input Parameters property according to the value of the cbopick_a_country combo box, the procedure reads the value of the option group control. A value of 1 causes the form to appear in Print Preview mode, and a value of 2 sends the report to the printer. Just before terminating, the procedure restores screen updating by invoking the DoCmd Echo method with an argument of True. This is a critical step, since failing to do so will cause users to get no feedback about their behavior after the procedure terminates.

Designing Reports with Conditional Formatting

Microsoft Access has a sequence of events that are handy for formatting reports dynamically at run time. However, with the release of Access 2000, Microsoft introduced a much simpler way to assign formats dynamically to the values in a report. We can access this functionality – called conditional formats – manually and programmatically. This section illustrates both approaches.

Refer to Chapter 7 for a discussion of conditional formatting. The earlier presentation of the topic bears directly on special issues pertaining to forms. Its discussion provides a very brief overview of conditional formatting. This section drills down on the topic as it shows techniques that apply to both reports and forms.

Manually Setting Conditional Formats

The following screen shot for the rpt_employee_sales report illustrates the kind of effects that you can manually format for Access reports. This example shows how to change, dynamically, the formatting of the report output based on a value of a field. The report presents sales by employee for the Northwind sample for the chapter. The sample database for this chapter includes a view called sales_by_employee that aggregates the extended price for all order detail items by the employee who booked the order. The extended price for the Northwind database is Quantity times UnitPrice times one minus Discount.

Since this product assumes a float data type, the T-SQL for the view applies a CONVERT function to format the value to a money data type. We use the CONVERT function to ensure that that the result of the formula:

```
([Order Details].Quantity * [Order Details].UnitPrice * (1 - [Order
Details].Discount)
```

is of type money and not of a float type.

```
SELECT Employees.EmployeeID, Employees.FirstName,
    Employees.LastName, SUM(CONVERT(money,
    [Order Details].Quantity * [Order Details].UnitPrice * (1 - [Order
Details].Discount)))
    AS e_sales
FROM Employees INNER JOIN
    Orders ON
    Employees.EmployeeID = Orders.EmployeeID INNER JOIN
    [Order Details] ON
    Orders.OrderID = [Order Details].OrderID
GROUP BY Employees.EmployeeID, Employees.FirstName,
    Employees.LastName
```

Employees with a below average sales number appear in red. Employees with sales above average appear in green, but the sales for the top employee show in bold, italic green against a black background:

425

If the numbers change, so does the formatting. In this sense, the formatting is conditional on the sales values at run time. You can assign formats to a control in Design view with a simple menu command and dialog. We describe how to do this in detail below. Access then dynamically assigns the formats based on expressions that the dialog helps you to write. You do not have to code event procedures, but you get the benefits of events procedures in your applications for formatting the values in reports.

One especially easy way to start understanding conditional formats is to view the Conditional Formatting dialog. An instance of this dialog appears below for employee sales values in the preceding report, rpt_employee_sales. To open the dialog, we must first select either a text box or a combo box. We'll select one that has e_sales as its control source. Then, we choose Format | Conditional Formatting from the Report Design menubar. We can add up to three conditional formats to any control. In addition, a fourth default format applies when none of the conditions for one of the conditional formats is true.

Conditional formatting refers to both reports and forms.

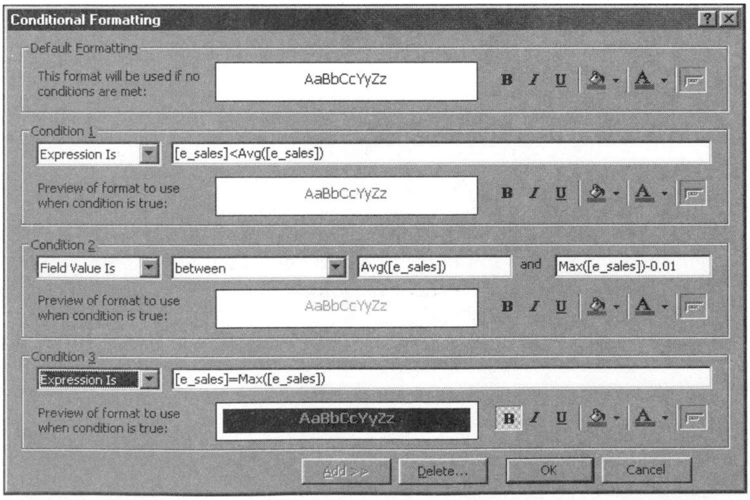

We can assign conditional formats to a control, such as the one displaying sales by employees, with either an expression or a range of values for the control. When we use an expression, we have the option of setting the formatting for one control based on the values of one or more of the other controls. We can also designate a wide range of operators. One advantage of doing this is that we can compare against the average of e_sales even though the average expression is not specified in the record source. Some developers may just find it more natural to write expressions in the free form permitted with the Expression Is selection from the first combo box for a condition. Condition 1 assigns red to all text box values less than the average sales for employees. Condition 3 formats the text box value that is the largest for any employee to bold, italic green with a black background.

When we use a range of values for a control, we are more limited in what we can accomplish, but Access helps us to write the expression. Since the whole purpose of this feature is to simplify the assignment of conditional formatting, this is a worthwhile trade-off when the limitations let us express the condition that we need for a format. Condition 2 demonstrates the layout for specifying a range of values as a condition. First, we select Field Value Is from the initial combo box for a condition. Second, we designate an operator. The sample dialog above chooses the between operator. The other 7 are:

- ❑   not between
- ❑   equal to
- ❑   not equal to
- ❑   greater than
- ❑   less than
- ❑   greater than or equal to
- ❑   less than or equal to

With the exception of the between and not between operators, all operators take just one expression. For example, if a date field is less than today then make it red, but leave it with the default format otherwise.

When we're using more than one conditional format, it is important that our conditions do not overlap. The system uses the first matching expression found on overlap. The range of values for Condition 2 in the preceding dialog illustrates a respect for this principle of non-overlapping conditions. The upper value extends to within one cent of the maximum sales value for any employee. Letting Condition 2 extend all the way up to the maximum sales value for any employee causes it to overlap with Condition 3. When there is overlap in this instance, Condition 2 wins for the employee with the maximum sales, so, that employee's sales do not stand out from the rest of the employees with above average sales.

Programmatically Working with Conditional Formats

One of the biggest advantages of conditional formats is that they allow copying of conditional formats between reports. Sometimes it makes sense to program conditional formats. For example, if you developed a great set of formats for one report that you want to apply to one or more other reports, programming the solution ensures a consistent copy of formats from one report to others. Similarly, if you need to remove the formats from one or more reports, programming can make fast work of the task (and it is very straight forward). The next two code samples demonstrate ways of tackling each of these tasks.

To demonstrate the potential to apply conditional formats programmatically, we created a copy of the rpt_employee_sales report with the name rpt_employee_sales_2. The copy has the same record source and control layout as the original report, but the copy contains no conditional formats. The following VBA procedure that is in Module1 demonstrates the syntax for copying the conditional formats from the original report to the copy that had its conditional formats removed:

```vba
'Manually or programmatically close any open reports before running

Sub copy_format_conditions()
Dim rpt1 As Report
Dim rpt2 As Report
Dim ctl1 As Control
Dim ctl2 As Control
Dim fcn1 As FormatCondition
Dim fcn2 As FormatCondition

    'Assign rpt1 and rpt2 pointers; assumes no other reports open
    DoCmd.OpenReport "rpt_employee_sales", acViewDesign
    Set rpt1 = Reports(Reports(0).Name)
    DoCmd.OpenReport "rpt_employees_sales_2", acViewDesign
    Set rpt2 = Reports(Reports(1).Name)

    'Loop through controls in rpt1 to find text boxes
    For Each ctl1 In rpt1.Controls
        If TypeOf ctl1 Is TextBox Then
            If rpt1.Controls(ctl1.Name).FormatConditions.Count > 0 Then
    'If you find a text box with format conditions in rpt1 copy them to rpt2
                For Each fcn1 In rpt1.Controls(ctl1.Name).FormatConditions
                    Set fcn2 = rpt2.Controls(ctl1.Name).FormatConditions.Add _
                    (fcn1.Type, fcn1.Operator, fcn1.Expression1, fcn1.Expression2)
                        fcn2.ForeColor = fcn1.ForeColor
                        fcn2.BackColor = fcn1.BackColor
                Next
            End If
        End If
    Next ctl1

    'Close original report with format conditions
    DoCmd.Close acReport, rpt1.Name, acSaveNo

    'Save changes to report with copied format conditions
    DoCmd.Save acReport, rpt2.Name
    DoCmd.Close acReport, rpt2.Name

End Sub
```

The procedure starts by opening both reports in Design view. This is imperative since you cannot manipulate conditional formats except in Design view.

You can always re-open the report later in Normal view for the printer or Print Preview mode for the monitor.

To simplify references to the reports, the procedure assigns the reports to points, namely rpt1 for the original and rpt2 for the copy. Next, the procedure starts a loop that iterates through the controls on the original report with a text box that has at least one conditional format. When the procedure discovers a text box having one or more conditional formats, it adds a FormatCondition object to the second report. Then, it copies the format settings from the FormatCondition object on the original report to the new FormatCondition object on the copied report. Finally, after transferring all the conditional formats, the report closes the original report, saves the changes to the copy, and closes it.

While the above sample works with only a single copied report, the power of the technique multiples as you apply the formats from one report to multiple reports. You can use the AllReports collection to iterate through all the reports that are in the current project. As your application discovers each existing report, it can determine if a report needs the application of the conditional formats from another report and apply them if appropriate. The AllReports collection works for the Reports collection like the AllForms collection works for the Forms collection (see Chapter 7).

The preceding sample requires that just two reports are open. You can manually or programmatically close other reports. If necessary, you can re-open any closed reports after the procedure finishes copying the conditional formats between two reports. Chapter 7 demonstrates how to restore a form that a procedure closes after the main work of the procedure completes. The same technique applies to reports, but you use the AllReports – instead of the AllForms – collection.

Programmatically removing conditional formats is easier than adding them – especially if we want to remove all the conditional formats. The following VBA sample shows how to eliminate the formats just copied to the rpt_employee_sales_2 report:

```
'Manually or programmatically close any open reports before running

Sub remove_format_conditions()
Dim rpt1 As Report
Dim ctl1 As Control


'Assign rpt1; assumes no other reports open
DoCmd.OpenReport "rpt_employees_sales_2", acViewDesign
Set rpt1 = Reports(Reports(0).Name)

'Loop through controls to find a text box with format conditions
For Each ctl1 In rpt1.Controls
    If TypeOf ctl1 Is TextBox Then
        If rpt1.Controls(ctl1.Name).FormatConditions.Count > 0 Then
'If you find one, delete all the conditions
            rpt1.Controls(ctl1.Name).FormatConditions.Delete
        End If
    End If

Next


'Save changes to the report
DoCmd.Save acReport, rpt1.Name
DoCmd.Close acReport, rpt1.Name

End Sub
```

After eliminating the conditional formats, the procedure saves the revised report to lock in the changes.

Inserting A Chart into a Report

One of the more attractive features of Access forms and reports is their ability to present data graphically. Your applications can take advantage of this capability to display the distribution of values and plot the relationships between columns with bar, line, scatter, pie, and a variety of other less common two and three-dimensional chart formats. Since many business analysts find it easier to interpret results from a chart than a table of numbers, the graphing ability is important.

To include a chart in a report, you need to add an unbound OLE Object control to the report. The target computer must also have Microsoft Graph 2000 installed.

> **If you don't have Microsoft Graph 2000 installed, you can install it from the Microsoft Office 2000 installation CD's.**

The Access 2000 documentation describes the availability of a wizard to hold your hand through the process of adding a chart to a report. However, this wizard is only for Access 2000 database files. It does not work with Access projects. The good news is that you can still add a chart to a report in an Access project. However, you must manage the whole process yourself, and there is a peculiar requirement for specifying the Row Source property when you do this. So, this section shows two different approaches for creating a chart for the data in a SQL Server database.

❑   The first approach uses an ODBC connection from an Access database file (namely, one with an .mdb extension). This permits a demonstration of the Chart Wizard. Your application can use the chart directly from the Access database file or you can import the chart with a live link to the data and run it from an Access project.

❑   The second approach develops a chart without a wizard directly within an Access project. This technique relies on a VBA procedure that pre-processes the record source data for easy graphing by the Microsoft Graph 2000 Chart OLE Class. In some ways, the pre-processing program replaces the Chart Wizard for Access projects.

Using the Chart Wizard

We use the Chart Wizard exclusively from Access database files. So, in order to plot SQL Server data, our .mdb file needs to link to the remote data source. To accomplish that, we need to create an ODBC connection to the SQL Server database with the table or view that you wish to link.

> **You'll find detailed steps on how to set up a DSN connection in Appendix D.**

The following screen presents the final ODBC SQL Server setup dialog:

You must make sure that you have a driver version that is compatible with SQL Server 7 or later.

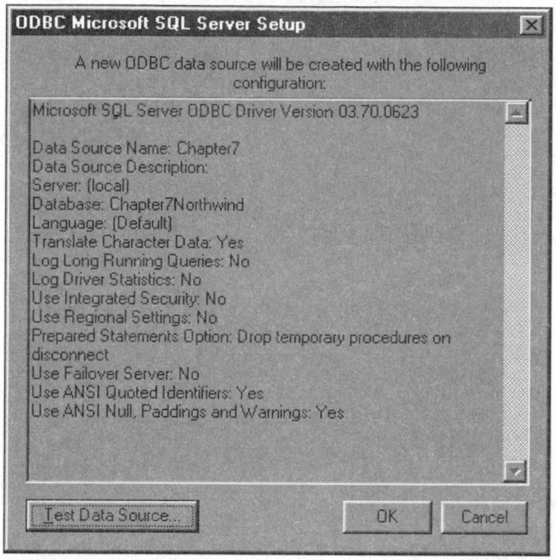

First of all we need to create a standard Access `.mdb` file . We can then select tables in the database window, and from the file menu we Choose File | Get External Data | link tables to create an attached table in the Database window of our Access database file:

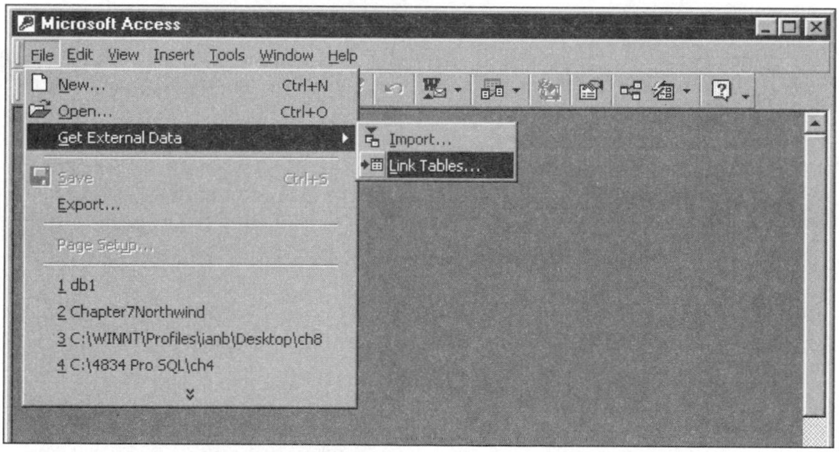

We then have to select ODBC data sources form the drop down list box, so that we can link to the sample database using the DSN we created:

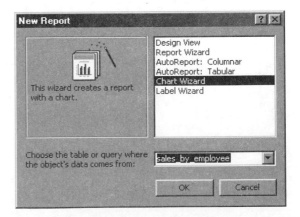

Clicking the Link button produces a dialog in which we simply need to specify our DSN name as well as a server and database.

When Access creates the link, it will name the link after the original data source with a prefix of dbo_. For the purpose of demonstrating the chart wizard we're going to create a n example chart using a view called sales_by_employee, so, attaching the sales_by_employee view creates a link named dbo_sales_by_employee. When we attach the view, Access will prompt us to select a field that uniquely identifies a record. Selecting the primary key field is the obvious choice here. If you don't have one just hit the OK button. We can rename the link to exclude the dbo_ prefix. This does not affect our link to the remote SQL Server data source, but it does permit the objects based on the attached table to work in an Access project without any editing of T-SQL statements designating record sources.

> To rename an attached table name, we right click the link in the Database window. Then, we choose Rename and assign a new name, or highlight the table and press F2 to edit.

After we have the link properly named, we select Reports in the Objects bar and click New on the Database window. This generates the New Reports dialog:

Here we select **Chart Wizard** and select the name of the linked data source from the drop-down list below **Chart Wizard**. We have to designate a data source before Access will let us proceed. Our example in the screenshot uses sales_by_employee as the name of the link.

The Chart Wizard screens offer four major functions. First, we get to pick fields from the data source designated in the **New Report** dialog for inclusion in the chart:

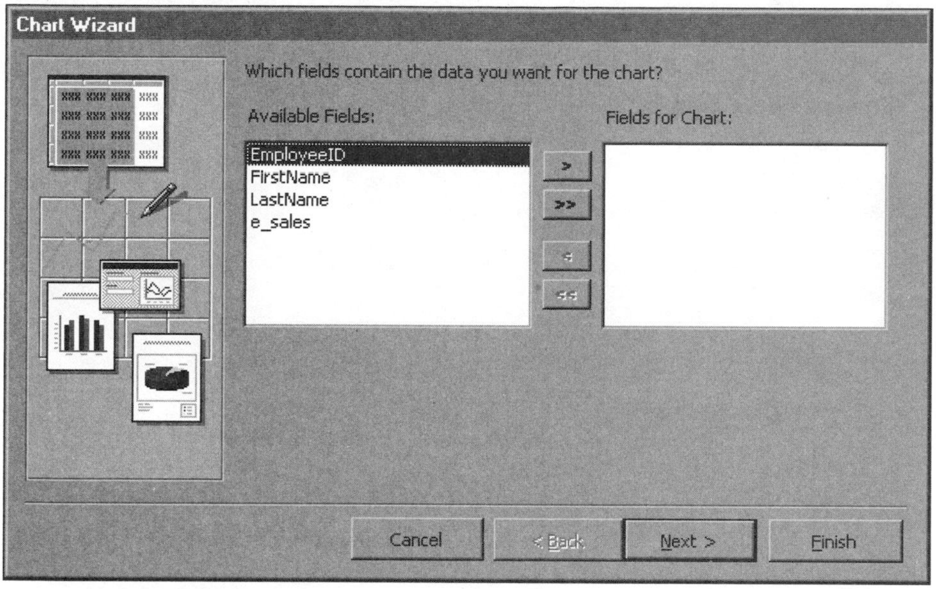

Next, we must select a type of chart. The wizard offers 20 different chart types, including several versions of bar, pie, and line charts as well as some other specialized chart types, such as a bubble chart:

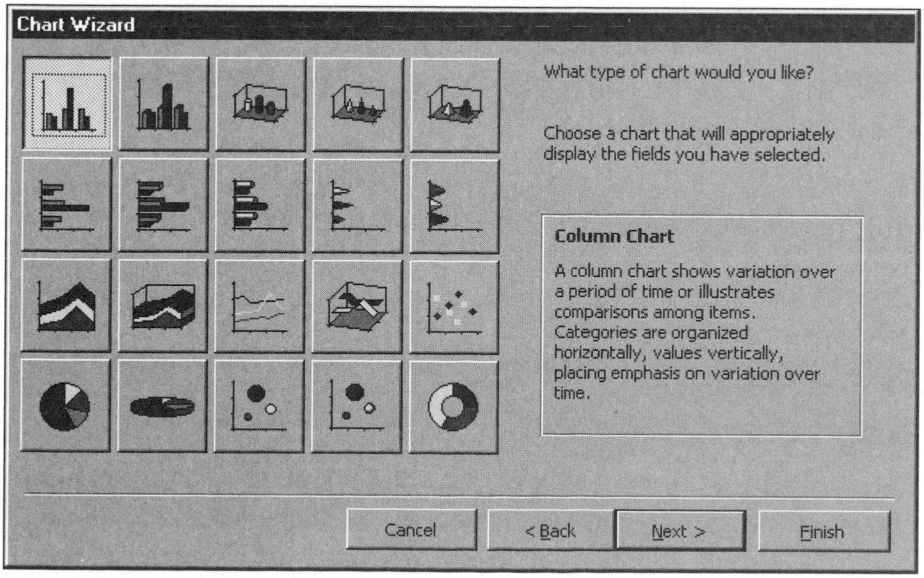

The next wizard screen offers us layout options for our chart. The wizard makes a suggestion based on our earlier choices.

And finally, we can assign a title for our chart. The Chart Wizard will automatically suggest the name of the data source from the New Report dialog:

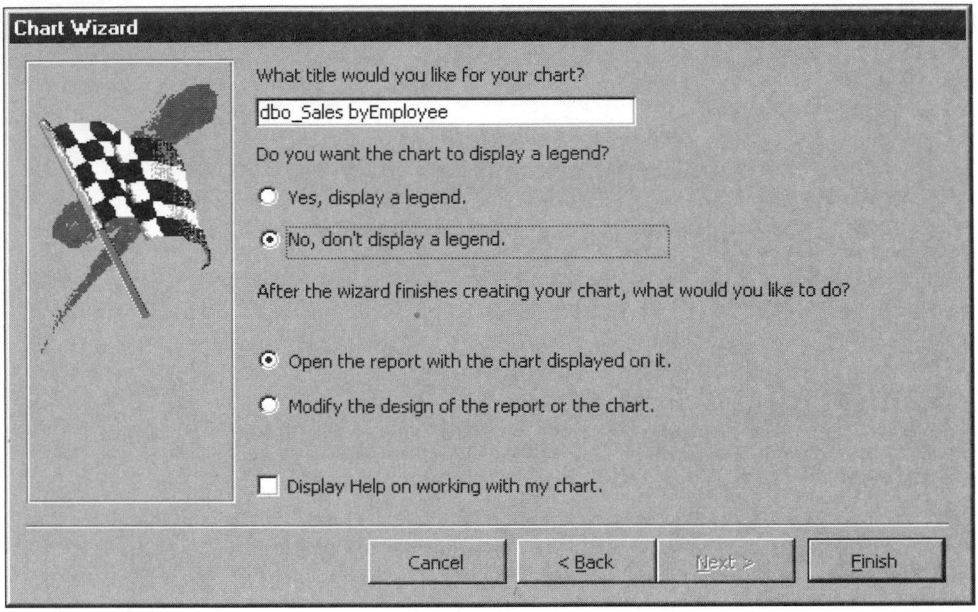

We can override this with a more appropriate title for viewing by end users who may not be familiar with the names that a database applies to tables and views.

After the completion of the wizard screens, Access composes a first draft of our chart on a report page. The report is saved as rptsales_by_employee_live_by_odbc Typically we will need to edit this. However, before doing that, let's regroup and get an appreciation of what the Chart Wizard did.

We do this by switching into Design view. We click the report's properties dialog and then click on the Data tab. By default, the unbound OLE object container for the chart has focus. We click the Data tab to show the SQL statement serving as the source for the chart. It appears as the Row Source property for the unbound OLE object. We can then, double click the center of the graph in the Detail section. This opens a worksheet with **sample data** and exposes the border for the chart within the OLE object.

There are several containers in the chart. The report's Detail section serves as a container for the unbound OLE object. That object, in turn, acts as a container for the chart. All three of these containers have separate boundaries that the following screen shot illustrates. We need to manage these boundaries to get the right look for our chart.

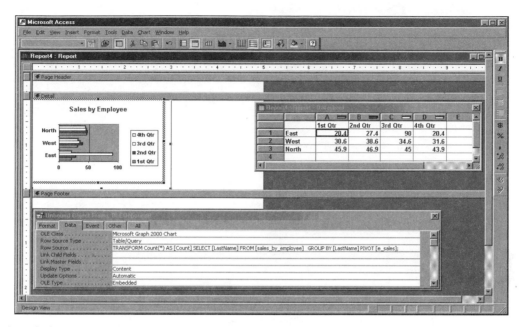

Before doing any chart formatting, we need to ensure the SQL statement in the Row Source property box specifies the data that we want to chart. The wizard tries to group and aggregate our data in ways that may not suit our purposes. For the sample, we merely want to plot aggregated sales for each employee. Since the sales_by_employee view already does the aggregation and grouping, there is no need to do it again. A simple SQL statement like the following is sufficient for the sample:

```
SELECT LastName, e_sales FROM sales_by_employee
```

After fixing the data source, we can change our focus to layout issues. When developing charts for reports we are able to remove the Page Header and Page Footer sections since they do not really contribute to the chart and we can add many of the same elements directly to the charts. The space these sections consume can better serve a larger chart on the report's page. The worksheet will often appear when we double click the chart to edit it. If we click the worksheet's close button We can remove it. Next, we can drag the Detail section until it is large enough for the chart. Then, we can drag the boundaries for the chart's container and the chart itself to about the original size of the Detail section.

With these details out of the way, we are ready to work with the chart. Double clicking the chart converts the menubar and Toolbar so that we have commands for manipulating the chart. For example, the Chart | Type command lets us alter the type of chart for our data. The Chart | Options command permits us to perform such formatting tasks as assigning labels, setting the visibility of axis labels and the legend, and controlling the visibility of tick marks. We can also double click on any part of a chart and right click to bring up a menu command that opens a multi-tabbed dialog of options for that chart element. For example, right clicking the chart's horizontal axis and choosing Format Axis opens a dialog that lets us control such features as the font, number format and orientation of the values along the axis.

> *As you edit a chart to set it in a way an application requires, we will typically go back and forth between Design view and Print Preview mode. In most cases, you never see your real data in Design view (typically, the sample data appear instead). So, to get a look at the effect of formatting changes for your data you must switch to Print Preview mode.*

435

The following screen shot shows an edited version of a chart graphing sales by employee:

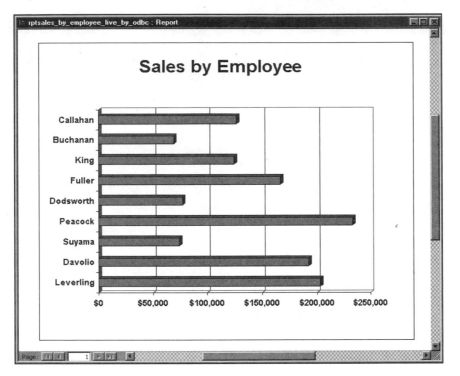

The final version saves space by removing the legend. It is not necessary since the chart plots a single series – sales. The edits reduced the horizontal and vertical axis labels to show all points along both axes. Since the horizontal axis denotes sales dollars, the editing included the application of a currency format with zero places after the decimal for it. Other editing revised the format wall color from menu bar gray to white.

After completing the above tasks, we have a chart that meets our objective. There is just one problem – the chart is in an Access database file, the old-fashioned .mdb type (called chapter8_mdb_for_chart_2.mdb), rather than the new type with enhanced SQL Server compatibility. However, since we took precautions to prepare the chart against an ODBC data source, we can easily import the chart into an Access project and run it from there. This gives us just one file type to distribute for our application.

We actually import the report that houses the chart. The report's name with the chart is rptsales_by_employee_live_by_odbc. The following short VBA script illustrates how to invoke the DoCmd object's TransferDatabase method in an Access project module to import a report from chapter8_mdb_for_chart_2.mdb. This file contains the report that has the chart created with the help of the Chart Wizard. The VBA procedure assigns the same name to the report with the chart in the .mdb and .adp files. As the chart has a live ODBC link to the data, which resides in the database connected to the Access project, we need to import the report just once. The chart it contains will automatically update as the data changes because of its live link to the database.

```
Sub import_chart()
Dim strDBName As String
```

```
Dim strDBPath As String
Dim strDB As String
Dim stroldchartname As String
Dim strnewchartname As String

strDBName = "chapter8_mdb_for_chart_2.mdb"
strDBPath = "c:\AccessDoesSQLServer\Chapter7\"
strDB = strDBPath & strDBName
stroldchartname = "rptsales_by_employee_live_by_odbc"
strnewchartname = "rptsales_by_employee_live_by_odbc"

DoCmd.TransferDatabase acImport, "Microsoft Access", _
                strDB, acReport, stroldchartname, strnewchartname, False
End Sub
```

Creating a Chart without the Chart Wizard

Creating a chart directly in an Access project is a task that we have to undertake without the benefit of the Chart Wizard. Fortunately the process is still fairly straight forward, and it has a lot in common with the approach of using a wizard. The most distinctive aspect of creating a chart directly, is in setting the Row Source property for the unbound OLE object that holds the chart object. Since it easy to get this setting wrong, this section includes a VBA procedure that automatically updates the setting for a report. You can run the program to update the data for the chart in a report.

We begin the process of directly adding the chart to an Access project by opening a blank report in Design view. We don't assign a Record Source property setting to the report. Instead, we add a new Unbound OLE Object to the report. We do this by dragging an Unbound Object Frame control from the toolbox to the report. When we release the control icon, Access opens the Insert Object dialog: control:

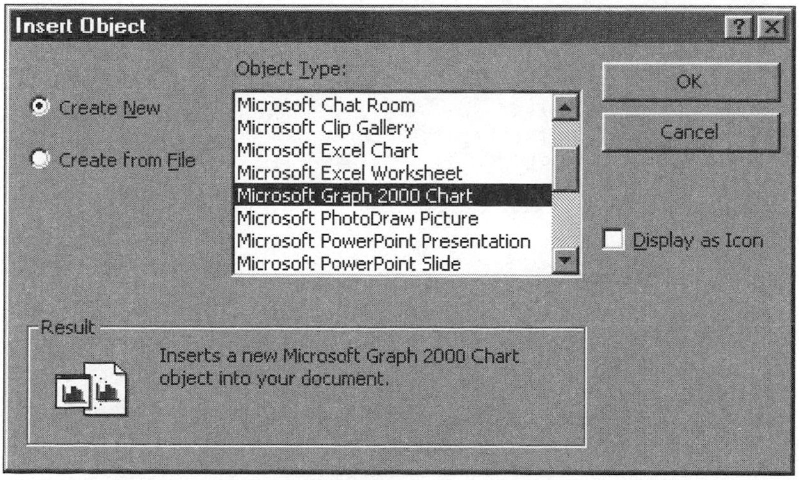

By default, Access selects the Create New option button. We can then highlight Microsoft Graph 2000 Chart in the Object Type list box, and click OK. When we click OK, Access adds an OLE Object control based on the Microsoft Graph 2000 Chart OLE Class to the report. As we did when working with the Chart Wizard, you will probably find it useful to remove the Page Header and Page Footer sections so the report appears with just a Detail section that contains the OLE Object.

The OLE object initially displays a sample data source based on a worksheet (the worksheet also shows unless we explicitly close it). Our first task in creating a chart with the control is to replace the sample data with data from our database. We accomplish this by assigning values to the Row Source Type and Row Source properties. We're using the sales_by_employee view. Settings that work for the Chart Wizard fail when you use them with a chart that you are creating on your own. This is because the Microsoft Graph 2000 Chart OLE Class ignores the first row of the record source that you submit. Therefore, if you submit a table with 9 rows of employee LastName and e_sales fields, it returns a chart with the last eight rows.

There are several means of resolving the "disappearing first row"' problem. One particularly easy approach is to assign values to the Row Source property with the first row containing two blank values (one each for the horizontal and vertical axes). In order for this solution to work, we need to coordinate two other property settings. First, we set the Row Source Type property for the unbound OLE object to "Value List". Second, we set the ColumnCount property to 2. When we create a chart with the Chart Wizard, it uses different settings for these latter two properties, and the Row Source property is typically a SQL statement specifying a recordset.

Since it is very easy, but awkward, to make the settings manually, a VBA procedure is an ideal candidate for making the settings. The following listing shows the code, which can be found in the sample project, to revise the Row Source Type, Row Source, and ColumnCount property settings for an OLE object named OLEUnbound0 in a report named rptsales_by_employee_graph:

```
'Manually or programmatically close any open reports before running

Sub set_for_employee_sales_chart()
Dim rpt1 As Report
Dim rst1 As ADODB.Recordset
Dim str1 As String

'Open report with graph
DoCmd.OpenReport "rptsales_by_employee_graph", acViewDesign
Set rpt1 = Reports(0)

'Open recordset that will serve as the record source for the form
Set rst1 = New ADODB.Recordset
rst1.ActiveConnection = CurrentProject.Connection
rst1.Open "sales_by_employee", , , , adCmdTable

'Put a leading blank row in record source
str1 = ";;"

'Add the rest of the data
Do Until rst1.EOF
    str1 = str1 & rst1("Lastname") & ";" & rst1("e_sales") & ";"
    rst1.MoveNext
Loop

'Assign the data to unbound OLE container for the graph
With rpt1.OLEUnbound0
    .RowSourceType = "Value List"
    .RowSource = str1
    .ColumnCount = 2
End With

'Save the data update
DoCmd.Close acReport, "rptsales_by_employee_graph", acSaveYes

End Sub
```

The procedure refreshes the Row Source property with the most recent values from the sales_by_employee view. The string variable, str1, holds a semi-colon delimited list of values that commences with two semicolons without values between them. These establish the first blank row.

There are a couple of ways in which we can use this procedure. First, we can use it as we initially define a new chart. It is easy to edit the record source providing data to a chart and the name of the report containing a new chart. Second, we can run this procedure whenever we want to update the data in a chart on a report. As the procedure assigns a value list as the Row Source Type property, the chart does not automatically update as the data changes in the record source behind a chart. This behavior is different to the chart created with the Chart Wizard. The chart it created had an ODBC link to its data source. Neither approach is fundamentally better. It is very easy to refresh the data with the VBA procedure when we're using a value list, and we have precise control over when a chart shows displays data.

After we add the control for the Microsoft Graph 2000 Chart OLE Class and get its data source settings right, we format the chart just as if we had created it with the Chart Wizard. When we manually enter a chart, we sometimes need to re-position the OLE control containing the chart. We can do this on the page by dragging the unbound OLE object to a new position, such as the top left corner of the Detail section. We just move the mouse cursor until it appears as a hand with a finger pointing up. Then, we just drag the unbound OLE object to where we want it within the Detail section.

Contrasting the Updating Behavior of Two Charts

We close this chapter by looking at the difference between the updating behavior of the Chart Wizard and locally created Access project charts. The imported Chart Wizard chart resides in a report named rptsales_by_employee_live_by_odbc. The Chapter8Northwind.adp file for this chapter includes another chart created locally using the procedure described in the previous section. The locally created chart resides in a report named rptsales_by_employee_graph. After refreshing the locally created chart, the quantity in the line item for OrderID 11077 for product 77 was also updated from 2 to 10,000. This is the last row in the [Order Details] table. The employee who booked that order is Nancy Davolio.

The following two Print Preview windows show each chart immediately after the data revision. The first one is for rptsales_by_employee_live_by_ odbc. It shows Nancy Davolio as having greater sales than any other employee, which is correct. This is because the line item quantity for one of her orders has been increased as we mentioned just a moment ago.

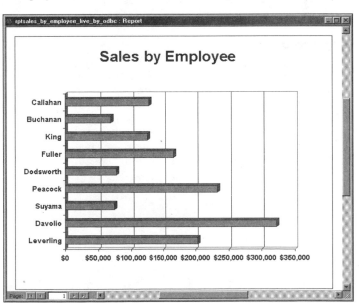

The second report window is for rptsales_by_employee_graph. Davolio is the third leading salesperson behind Peacock and Leverling. This chart does not show the revision to OrderID 11077 because its data source settings were refreshed just before revising the order. If we wanted the locally created chart to reflect the most recent data whenever it opens, we would simply need to launch the preceding VBA procedure just before opening the report. We must do this in a stand-alone procedure instead of an event procedure for the report. This is because event procedures do not permit revisions to the Row Source property for the unbound OLE object.

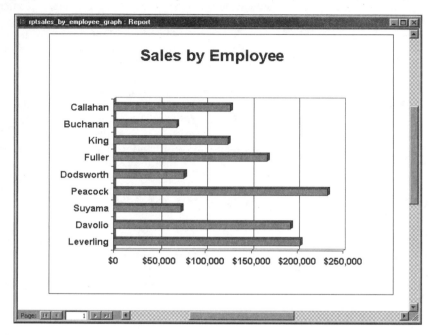

Summary

This chapter covers creating Access reports, using the Report Wizard and , in contrast, the AutoReport Wizard. We also saw how we can edit our report once it has been created, and explored how we can use different property settings to display the information the user needs in the most appropriate presentation format. We looked at sorting and grouping and then moved on to look at conditionally setting formatting options. Finally we examined how we can add chart and graphs to reports. We looked at how we can create charts using a wizard which we can then insert into our report and then we contrasted this technique with the manual creation of charts for reports.

Publishing Datasheets

The web continues to grow in popularity because of the exciting possibilities that the Internet, extranets that serve communities with common interests, and company intranets offer. Organizations are rapidly re-orienting themselves to take advantage of new approaches for serving clients, interacting with their partners, and performing internal communications. Access developers who want to take advantage of these emerging trends require the capability to deliver high-powered database applications that work seamlessly over webs.

This chapter shows how to deliver numbers, words, and pictures over webs from SQL Server with Access. It drills down on providing data via **datasheets** on web pages. A datasheet is a tabular display of an excerpt from a database at any given point in time when the database is run.

The chapter first presents the basics of web development, including setting up and managing web pages, posting data to them, and retrieving data from them. The chapter's coverage of web management centers around using FrontPage, an ideal development tool for the Access developer – to administer, create content, and programmatically manipulate web sites. You will learn both static and dynamic techniques for publishing data from a SQL Server to a web site. We'll also cover manual, wizard-based technologies as well as programmatic means of publishing content. Additionally we'll explore techniques for managing content once it is on a web server. Both the static and programmatic methods covered in this chapter work with any browser that can read HTML.

So we'll be covering six main topics in this chapter:

- ❑ Managing Web pages with FrontPage 2000
- ❑ Creating dynamic reports with the FrontPage Database Wizard
- ❑ Statically publishing datasheets with Access
- ❑ Programmatically manipulating datasheets in FrontPage

❑ Dynamically publishing SQL Server datasheets with Access

❑ Programmatically publishing datasheets with Access

Managing Web Pages with FrontPage 2000

FrontPage 2000, along with Access 2000 and either SQL Server 7 or SQL Server 2000, is particularly convenient for managing web database applications. With FrontPage Server Extensions on your web server, you can create a web folder to hold the files for an individual project. If you require a higher degree of separation between project files, you can create subwebs based on web folders. The subwebs can be quite complex once you begin to delve into them, however, they can be useful at this basic level too.

This chapter assumes you are working with an IIS server for the material that deals with dynamic publishing.

> **To run the examples in this chapter, you will need Microsoft FrontPage 2000, Microsoft FrontPage 2000 Server Extensions and either Microsoft's Personal Web Server or Internet Information Services 4.0 or later installed. You will also need Microsoft Internet Explorer 4.0 or above on you machine.**

More about Web Servers

HTML files *may* be stored anywhere on a machine and can be displayed through a browser, by pointing the browser at the file location (as the browser processes the file). In contrast, Active Server Page (.asp) files, which require processing by the server, *need* to be stored at defined locations. By default, when PWS or IIS is installed, it nominates a folder into which files we wish to access through the server (whether .html or .asp) should be stored. This **root folder** is usually located at c:\inetpub\wwwroot.

> *As we'll see below, although, this is the physical location of the Web pages, when we use the server this will not be the URL displayed in the browser address box.*

Both for aiding our general understanding, and in the case that you're working in a networked environment where the systems administrator may have changed this from the default setting, let's dig into this a bit deeper.

> **For PWS users, the steps below will also be helpful in ensuring that the Web Server on your system is running – if it isn't the pages won't display.**

To find the root folder for your system, and also ensure that the Web Server is running, the precise steps will depend on the operating system you are running:

Windows 95/98

To find the folder of the default Web site select Start | Microsoft Personal Web Server | Personal Web Manager and, if the Web server isn't running click the Start button in the dialog box. The screen will display the default (home) directory:

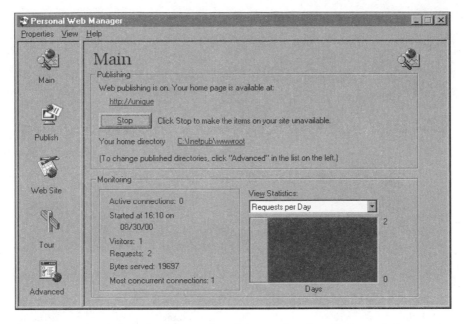

If you wish to change the default directory, select Advanced and work through the screen revealed.

Not only does this screen show the root directory, it also shows the address of the Web server (which here is the local computer name) through which pages saved in the root directory can be accessed.

Windows NT

To find the root in Windows NT, select Start | Programs | Windows NT 4.0 Option Pack | Microsoft Internet Information Server to start the IIS management console. Then expand out the server object, right-click on Default Web Site, select Properties and the root folder can be found on the page revealed by the Home Directory tab in the Local Path box.

Windows 2000

In Windows 2000, again the information is found through the IIS management console. To open this either select Start | Programs | Administrative Tools | Internet Services Manager, or go via the Control Panel (Start | Settings | Control Panel) then select Administrative Tools and Internet Services Manager.

Creating a Subweb

To create a subweb choose File | New | Web. We specify a folder path below the root for the new subweb in the New dialog. For instance, if the root directory on a server is http://cabarmada, then we can designate a subweb as http://cabarmada/adss. FrontPage responds by creating a new subweb that we can populate with web pages and database connections. A blank default.htm page is automatically generated when FrontPage creates the subweb. The following New dialog creates a new subweb with a single blank page:

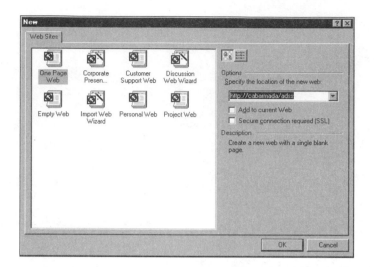

We could open the subweb from FrontPage in the future by opening http://cabarmada/adss.

Until some content is placed in the default page for the site, those who browse the site would not see anything. Instead, they will view the blank default.htm page. We could add some content to the default.htm (for example, "you arrived at my site") to let browsers see some content in their browser.

We have the liberty to add as many additional pages as your application development needs dictate. Except for the way it is addressed, this subweb behaves like a stand-alone web.

Nesting Subwebs

Subwebs can be nested from within one another so they do not necessarily have to nest directly within the root directory of a web site. We can access subwebs with the FrontPage Interface. Choosing File | Recent Webs from the FrontPage menu bar displays a list of recently opened subwebs. Alternatively, selecting File | Open Web, prompts the Open Web dialog, which presents a list of subwebs on the server. The following screenshot presents the Open Web dialog for the cabarmada server:

The Look in: box shows the name of the web server's root folder, cabarmada. Within the root folder, there is the adss subweb that was just created.

When FrontPage creates a new subweb, it automatically creates the _private and images folders. We can also add our own custom folders. Once you've opened a folder within a web, right-clicking within the Folder List window, creates a new folder. The Folder List window appears as the left-hand pane in the screenshot below:

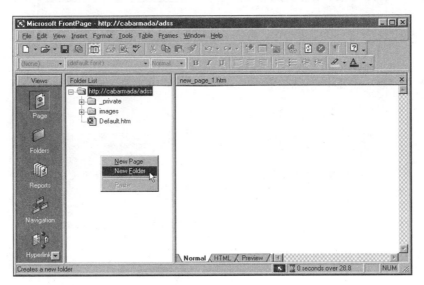

The new folder will appear nested within the folder that was right-clicked upon.

Adding Content to a Subweb

We can open Default.htm and start to populate it with content as easily as typing some text on the page and saving the changes. By double-clicking the page in folder view, it becomes available for editing and we can begin to edit the page from the Normal tab.

One useful way of becoming familiar with FrontPage is to add two pages with hyperlinks that point at one another. By alternately clicking the link on each page, we can easily verify their operation and availability. The Insert Hyperlink tool on the FrontPage toolbar for the Normal tab works in a similar way to the one in Access and the other Office components. We select some text for users to activate the link and then we click the Insert Hyperlink tool:

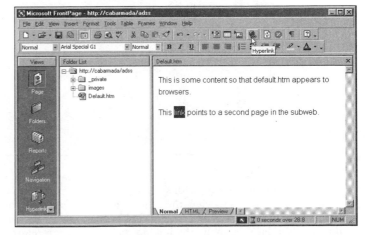

This generates the **Create Hyperlink** dialog. Here, we select the page to which we want the hyperlink to transfer control, and then we click **OK** to close the dialog:

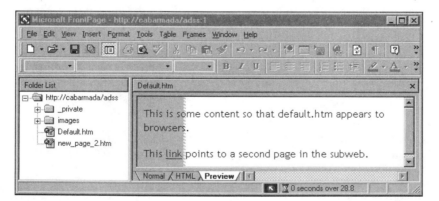

Creating a hyperlink on a web page is like adding a hyperlink label to an Access form. This capability has existed since Access 97, and the process is essentially the same across all the Office components.

Viewing the Web Pages

Next we can view the results of the hyperlinks we created. The following pair of screenshots reveals two different views of http://cabarmada/adss site. The first window shows the default page with the **Preview** tab selected:

This tab will be available if you have Microsoft Internet Explorer 3.0 or later installed on your computer. When working with some web features, such as hyperlinks on two pages that point at one another, this tab lets us view the page as it would appear in the browser. In addition, it also allows us apparently to operate the links. So, clicking the link on the default page lets us view the second page at the site. Similarly, clicking the link on the second page returns the view to the default page.

Not all browsers show web pages in identical formats. When creating web content with Microsoft web authoring techniques, it is best to use Microsoft browsers to view that content. Some Microsoft web technologies, such as data access pages, require Internet Explorer 5, rather than any of the earlier Internet Explorer browsers. Internet sites that strive for large audiences with advanced browser effects will most often detect the browser, and then present a web page optimized for that particular type of browser. Although the techniques demonstrated in this chapter are robust enough to work in many browsers, if you require cross-browser versatility, then you need to test your pages in all the browsers that you must support. This current example works identically in IE 4, IE 5, and Netscape Communicator 4.

The second window displays the site's second page from the Normal tab:

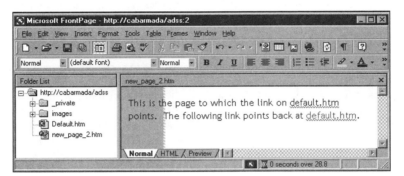

Although when in the Preview tab, it appears that control transfers from one page to the other when we click the links, we are actually still on the page originally displayed in the window's title – in this case default.htm which is in the title bar for the Preview panel in the top screenshot. We could also verify the selection of default.htm by clicking the Normal tab and noticing that default.htm appears on the title bar – even if the Preview tab last displayed another page.

We can edit a page by typing new content and by invoking its menu commands. This page also permits us to develop links, as we've just seen. The links in the previous example are both text, but we can also have hyperlinks associated with images.

Notice that we've added some background designs to our web pages in the screenshots. This screen design is one of more than sixty themes available to web developers with FrontPage 2000. We can select colur schemes and designs in the Themes dialog that opens with the Format | Theme command. When applying a theme through the dialog, we can invoke it for a single page or for all the pages in a site. The Themes dialog also allows us to remove any themes at a site (select No Theme as a theme name).

The HTML tab gives us a chance to examine the HTML behind a web page. This is generally a good way to gain some insights into HTML coding practices. If you are not already proficient at HTML, this represents a way to learn HTML and other web development technologies, such as ASP. Pages with an .asp file extension have a mix of HTML, VBScript or JScript, and ADO programming (when data access is necessary for a page). For example, selecting the HTML tab for either of the two preceding pages will acquaint you with the syntax for hand-coding a hyperlink with the <A> (or Anchor) tag. If you already know HTML and ASP, use the HTML tab to hand-edit pages in ways that the menu does not permit. FrontPage saves web pages without any server-side scripts as files with a .htm file extension.

On Windows 2000 platforms that are running IIS 5, .htm files can now be saved as .asp files for consistency within an application.

Creating Dynamic Reports with the FrontPage Database Wizard

The FrontPage Database Wizard offers much more functionality than the scope of this chapter allows. We're using the Database Wizard here to demonstrate how we can use Access and FrontPage together and to indicate that we can also publish SQL Server data directly from FrontPage without relying on Access. For example, we can use Access to manage a SQL Server database as we've looked at in the early chapters of the book. We can then publish the datasheets to the web from that database with FrontPage. The Database Wizard offers an easy route for publishing data-based web pages because it is graphical. If you are initially learning about publishing data-based web pages based on SQL Server data sources, the Database Wizard can make getting started easy.

The FrontPage Database Wizard offers menu-based simplicity for creating web pages based on SQL Server tables and views, while also allowing the flexibility of being able to construct custom queries with T-SQL.

The Database Wizard is an attractive development tool because it insulates developers from HTML, while still allowing us to make our data available over a web. At the same time, if you're a web developer with limited database experience the Database Wizard will enable you to add data to web pages. After adding a reference to a database on a web page, we can reuse that reference on as many pages as require information from the database. In addition, you can reference multiple data sources from a single web site. The wizard even permits us to mix and match data from multiple databases on the same page.

This section introduces the Database Wizard in the context of publishing datasheets and columnar reports. We will be returning to this wizard in the next chapter when we treat HTML forms on web pages.

We'll start by exploring the FrontPage Database Wizard as a vehicle for publishing data-based web pages. And then progress to a general summary of the steps for publishing data-based pages with the FrontPage Database Wizard. Then, we'll look at three examples of how to work with pages created by the wizard.

Steps for Using the Database Wizard

Before we can actually begin to use the Database Wizard, we need to make sure that we have an established connection to the database from which we wish to publish data. We can define our database connection in either of two ways:

❏ We can specify a **Data Source Name** (DSN) that points at a SQL Server database. The DSN references an ODBC connection to a data source. You can create a DSN for your database in the Windows ODBC Administrator in the Windows Control Panel. A DSN has the benefit of being a relatively mature technology.

❏ We can specify a database by designating the database server name and the database that you want to reference on it. Both approaches with the Database Wizard require that you designate a user ID and password when you specify the connection to the database.

A DSN when used outside of the FrontPage Database Wizard does not strictly require that you pre-specify the user ID and password. However, when you use a DSN with the Database Wizard, you do require the user ID and password. You can do this in the DSN specification or in the steps to building the FrontPage database connection.

You can review how to create a connection to a database in Chapter 2.

 To create a report for a web page with the Database Wizard start by creating a new blank page within a subweb, such as the adss subweb on the web cabarmada server created previously in this chapter. We can accomplish this with the File | New | Page command or just click the New Page tool on the toolbar for the Normal tab in FrontPage.

If you previously selected one theme to appear on all pages, the new page appears with this theme. If you want a different theme for the database report on this web page, invoke the Format | Theme command. Click the Selected page(s) radio button and highlight your new theme. Then, apply your new theme by clicking OK. You can alternatively add other content to the page, such as a page header, graphic images, and any other appropriate content that is not dependent on the database.

> *You do not have to specify the type of web page (for example, .htm or .asp) at the point that you open a page. When you add a database connection to a page with the FrontPage Database Wizard, FrontPage detects the connection at the time that you save the page and automatically specifies an .asp extension.*

This book's discussion of the wizard focuses on using the Database Wizard with SQL Server databases, but it can work with many different kinds of databases. The FrontPage Database Wizard can readily work with SQL Server, Access, Oracle, and any other ODBC-compliant databases. Since the Database Wizard can work from a DSN that points at a database, you have immense flexibility in the source for a database on a web page. On the other hand, you will not be able to run the Database Wizard at all if the web server administrator elects not to make the option available. Not all ISPs, for example, enable the FrontPage Database Wizard. If you control your own web server, the Database Wizard is part of a typical FrontPage install.

Step 1

Once we have a web page, we position our cursor on the page where we want to start our database content. We start the Database Wizard by choosing Insert | Database | Results from the menubar. This opens the first of five steps for using the wizard.

The screen on the left presents the dialog that opens during the first step. When we initially invoke the wizard at a web site, there are no existing databases in the drop-down database control. We add new connections by selecting Use a new database connection and clicking Create. FrontPage numbers our database connections in the order that we make them. For example, this drop-down list shows Database1. This is not a default connection. We have to create it with the process, which we're going to step through now. The Database1 entry, points to the pubs database on a database server called cabarmada.

Database Results Wizard - Step 1 of 5

This five-step wizard creates a database results region that displays information from a database. The wizard can also create a search form on the same page to let site visitors look up specific information.

You can:

○ Use a sample database connection (Northwind)

● Use an existing database connection

Database1

○ Use a new database connection

Create...

Cancel   < Back   Next >   Finish

Clicking Create on the above dialog opens the Web Settings dialog for the Database tab which allows us to create a new connection to a SQL Server database. The following screenshot depicts the Web Settings dialog just before the creation of a database connection named Database2:

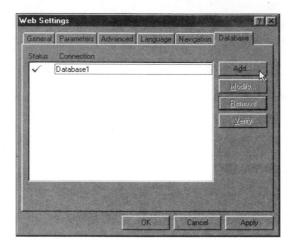

Since the first database connection, Database1, to the pubs database already exists, it appears in the dialog.

We click Add to open the New Database Connection dialog:

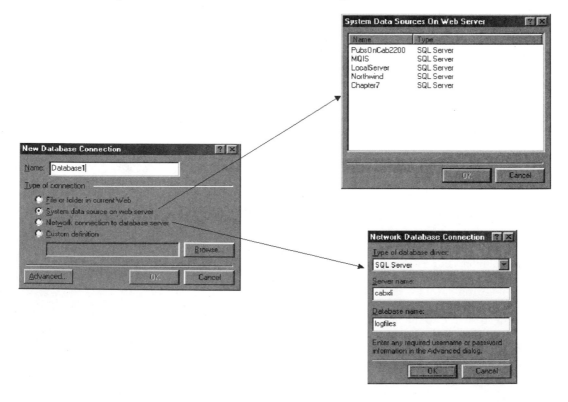

When creating a new connection to a SQL Server database, we typically select either the System data source on web server or the Network connection to database radio button. Selecting the former option and clicking Browse opens a list of data source names (DSNs) that reside on the web server. They are system DSNs so any one connected to the web server can use them. Highlighting one and clicking OK makes the database that the DSN points to the source for the new database connection. Clicking Browse when Network connection to a database server opens the Network Connection dialog allows us to specify a database server name and a database name.

After attempting a database connection by either of the two preceding approaches, we can try to verify our connection by clicking Verify on the Web Settings dialog. This will allow us to spot, and attempt to fix, any errors in a connection before proceeding.

For example, one easy mistake to make, is to fail to designate a user ID and password for the database. This emerges as a potential difficulty after designating server and database names on the Network Database Connection dialog. Since the dialog itself does not offer an opportunity to specify the information, but FrontPage cannot make a connection to the database without the user ID and password, we click Advanced on the New Database Connection dialog to open the Advanced Connection Properties dialog. From here, we can input the user ID and password.

If you cannot return to the Web Settings dialog from within the Database Wizard screens after an error, cancel the wizard and choose Tools | Web Settings from the menubar. Then, select the Database tab. Use Verify to help track down the reason for a faulty connection. If you can detect the failure's cause, click Modify to fix it. Otherwise, you can delete the connection and attempt to specify it later when you have the correct connection string details. There are many reasons that a web page may not have a correct connection to a database. Is the database server down? Is the physical connection to the server broken? Is the login or password wrong? A "yes" to any of these questions is among the factors that can cause a FrontPage database connection to malfunction.

Step 2

The dialog for the second Database Wizard step permits us to designate a table or view as the source for our database web report. For example, if we designate the pubs database in the first step, the wizard automatically suggests the authors table in the second step. We can use a drop-down list to expose and select any other table or view from the database. We can also use this dialog to open another screen that lets us input a T-SQL statement for custom queries and row-returning stored procedures. The screenshot on the right depicts the screen for step 2 of the Database Wizard. It shows the authors table selected as the source for the web page. The mouse cursor rests on the drop-down control that lets us select another table or view as a source for the web page.

Database Results Wizard - Step 2 of 5

Specify the record source that contains the information you want to display. You can select a table or view from the Record Source list, or you can create a custom query using a Structured Query Language (SQL) statement.

Record source:
authors

Custom query
Edit...

Cancel | < Back | Next > | Finish

Step 3

The dialog for the third step offers more graphical aids to insulate those who are new to T-SQL from potential syntax errors. With the dialog for this step, we can specify a subset of fields for inclusion in our report. We can also designate conditions for records participating in a report as well as sort criteria for ordering records. The next image presents the screen for the Database Wizard's third step:

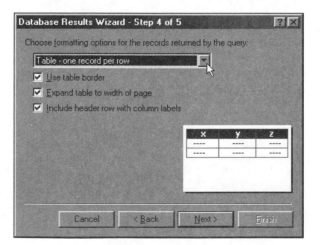

This step controls a grab bag of functions that minimizes the need to use T-SQL to specify a custom query. For example, we can click **Edit List** to specify a subset of columns as we might with a column list argument for a SELECT statement. Clicking **More** opens another dialog that ultimately lets us designate one or more columns as sort criteria in the same way that we can with an ORDER BY clause in a SELECT statement.

Step 4

In the dialog for the fourth step, we can specify how to format our report:

The dialog for this step also reveals that we can use the Database Wizard for specifying the behavior of a drop-down box. The next chapter discusses this functionality. We'll be viewing the tabular and columnar report output styles available later in this chapter.

We can choose any of the output styles from the drop-down box. The mouse cursor rests on the drop-down control in the screenshot. Our selection in this box controls the other controls on the dialog for formatting a data-based web page. For example, when we choose a tabular format, the dialog permits us to specify whether the table has a border and a row of column titles. When we chose a columnar report style for outputting database values (FrontPage calls it a list), our formatting options change. We can specify whether to display labels with database values and whether to use horizontal rule lines to separate records.

Step 5

The fifth dialog is particularly handy for displaying results in a tabular format. We can use this dialog to specify how many records appear on a report page. The default value is 5. If fewer than 5 records exist on the last page, FrontPage shows as many as there are available. For other report pages, the maximum number of records always appears. The cursor in the following screenshot rests in the box specifying the maximum number of rows per web page. We can enter a new number in this box to designate a lesser quantity of rows per page rather than the maximum of 5.

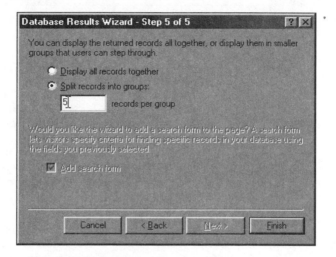

Creating Web Pages with Databases

Now that we've stepped through the stages for using the Database Wizard itself, we'll take a look at it within the context of some web pages and see how it actually publishes the data we choose. The next three sample pages help to illustrate the flexibility of the Database Wizard, with its ability to generate data-based web pages quickly and easily without recourse to advanced level programming skills.

> We'll be using web pages with an `.asp` file extension in this section. Active Server Pages is the technology behind the dynamic server-side publishing of web pages. We do not need to be familiar with the technology in order to publish pages dynamically in this chapter or even this book since FrontPage automatically generates any required ASP script for us. The ASP we encounter in this chapter and Chapter 10, is designed as a demonstration of the potential that ASP can offer for the publication of data. All aspects that we introduce will be explained but the chapters won't attempt to teach you ASP. To learn ASP, try out *Beginning Active Server Pages 3.0*, published by Wrox Press, ISBN 1-861003-38-2.

authors_table.asp

The first example in this section shows the behavior of the `authors_table.asp` page:

Each virtual page in the table has the same heading, "This is my custom title". In order to enliven the data presentation, the page has a Dynamic HTML effect that imposes a wave pattern on words in the page's heading. The image shows the effect in action. The word custom *is falling down into the line containing earlier words in the page's heading. After the word* custom *reaches its resting location, the last word,* title, *which does not yet appear, follows a similar pattern. This wave trajectory repeats whenever a new page loads. We can use the* Format | Dynamic HTML Effects *to assign an effect to a web page heading by referencing an event, such as a page load, to trigger the onset of the effect.*

The screenshot illustrates what appears to be the last page of a set of five web pages displaying the contents of the Authors table from the pubs database. The 5/5 in brackets adjacent to the button panel designates the page as the last. The authors table in the pubs database contains a total of 23 records. Since the published datasheet displays up to 5 records per page by design , the final page that appears here contains just 3 records. Actually, the Database Wizard creates a single web page file with an `.asp` extension that lets users browse any of the five virtual pages.

The button controls in the lower left hand corner below the records provide an interface for users to move back and forth across the five pages for the authors table. These are smart controls. For example, since the page reflects the last one for the authors table, only the buttons for moving to the first record and the previous record appear. The controls that can normally move to the next page and the last page have a dash instead of an icon reflecting that they are currently no longer usuable. On all other pages these buttons show > and >| symbols to reflect that they permit the user to move to the next page and the last page.

It's possible to vary the number of records that appear per web page. For example, changing the page size to 4 records for the current sample would result in 6 virtual pages with 3 records on the last page. So, how did we create this web page?

Creating the Web Page

We can publish a page in this format very easily. From within a subweb (or the root web if we prefer), we create a new page. We do this by clicking the New Page control on the FrontPage toolbar. We then select the Normal tab (if it is not already selected). After positioning the cursor inside the new page where we want to publish the table, we select Insert | Database | Results from the FrontPage menubar.

This opens Step 1 of 5 for the Database Wizard. In the previous section, we learned how to create a database connection within a subweb. A connection can point at any database the web page needs. In our example, the Database1 connection points at the pubs database on the cabarmada database server. We follow the step for creating a new connection as we did before. Then, instead of pointing at the logfiles database on the cabxli server, we reference pubs on the cabarmada server. The following Network Database Connection dialog shows this setting.

Of course you'll need to replace cabarmada *with the name of a your server that has the* pubs *database installed.*

After completing this dialog we will have added a new database connection to our web site. In our example, FrontPage assigns Database3 as the name for the connection since it previously assigned the names Database1 and Database2. The following screen shows the completed step 1 of 5 screen from the Database Wizard. It shows Database3, which points at the database designated in the preceding screen:

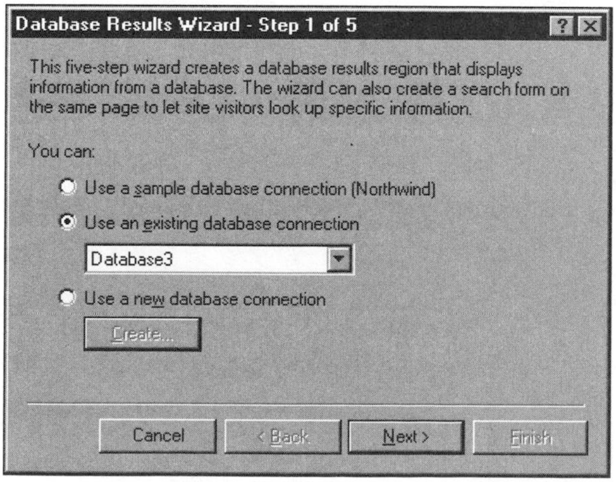

After designating the database connection, we are nearly done for creating the `authors_table.asp` page. We click Next on the screens for steps 1 through 4 and then Finish on the screen for step 5. This creates the new web page, but we cannot view its data from within FrontPage. We need to save the page, and then view the page within a browser. We choose File | Save As to save the page. The following screen displays the web page as it appears in FrontPage and the completed Save As dialog for saving the page:

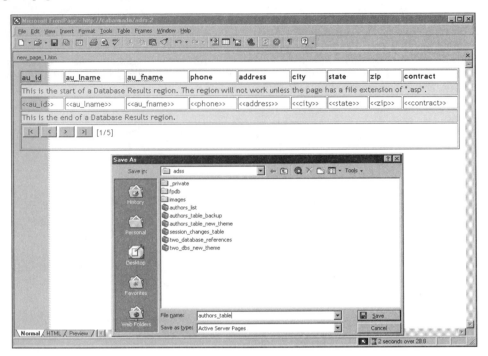

After saving the page, we can view it in either of two ways. First, we can click the Preview in Browser control on the FrontPage toolbar. This can automatically open a browser session or reuse an existing browser session so that it points at the web page created by the FrontPage Database Wizard. Second, we can manually open a new browser session for the page or point an existing browser session at the page's file.

authors_list.asp

Instead of presenting the table in a control that lets users browse through its pages, we can display data with a columnar report format. The wizard implements this format by presenting some HTML text followed by a data field that displays the current value of a field in a record. Users can examine the contents of the list by scrolling through the records. However, all the records in this layout appear on a single web page. The following screen shows `authors_list.asp`, an instance of this columnar format for the authors table:

This web page displays data for **Abraham Bennet** on the first record and **Akiko Yokomoto** on the second record. While we cannot tell from the excerpt with just two author names, the web page (`authors_list.asp`) presents the authors in alphabetical order by their first name. If we scroll down the web page, the third, fourth, and fifth authors are **Albert Ringer, Anne Ringer,** and **Ann Dulles**.

This columnar format with all the data for a record source on a single web page is not good for long lists of data, but it is ideal for data sources with very small return sets. For a data source with just one record, the columnar format is potentially good since the format presents the return set fields as separate paragraphs.

So how did we achieve this page? Well, the Database Wizard makes it easy to create this type of report.

Creating author_list.asp

The `authors_list.asp` example uses the same database connection as the `authors_table.asp`. However, `authors_list.asp` is different in two ways. First, it uses a columnar format for displaying data. Second, it sorts authors by their first name. So, we can use step 1 to point at **Database3** (or whatever database connection you are using to point at the **pubs** database on your local database server). The **Step 2 of 5** screen is identical to the preceding example. It designates the **authors** table in the **pubs** database.

The **Step 3 of 5** Database Wizard screen lets us specify the sort order for the report. To do this we click **More Options**:

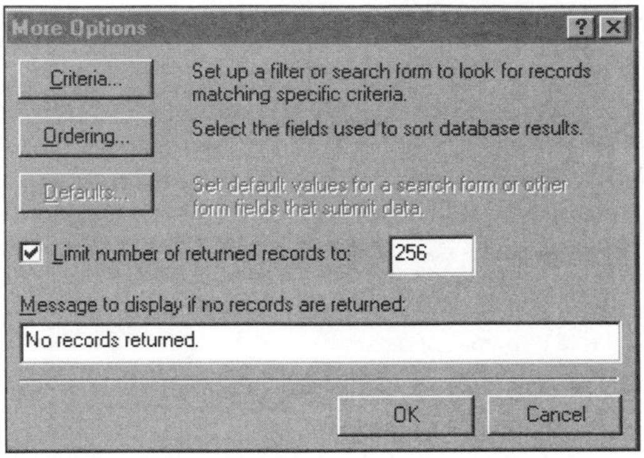

Then we click Ordering to open the Ordering dialog:

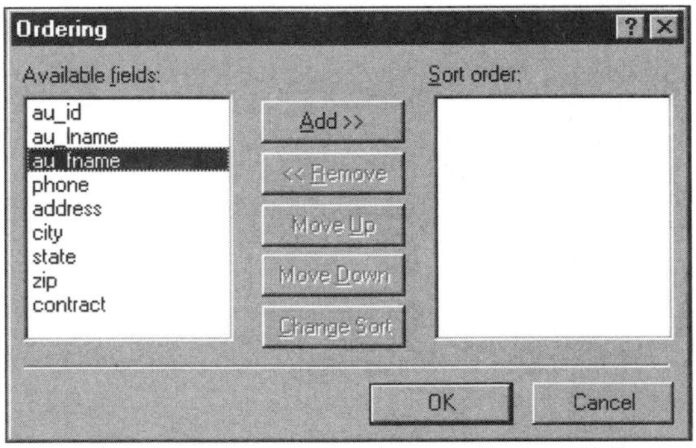

With this, we can select the fields by which to order the web page report. In the screenshot, the au_fname column is selected. Clicking Add transfers the field name from the Available fields box to the Sort order box. The default sort order is ascending. You can toggle this by clicking a field name in the Sort order dialog. An indicator next to the field name in the Sort order box reveals the direction of the sort.

It is in the Step 4 of 5 dialog that you specify a columnar report format:

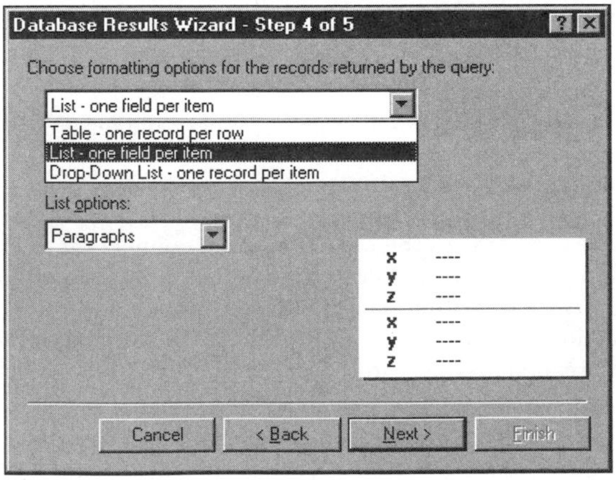

We can designate a columnar format for the web page report by selecting List - one field per item in the top drop-down box on the screen.

After making this selection, we can develop the page with the same steps as the preceding example. Click Next on the Step 4 of 5 screen and Finish on the last screen. The following screen illustrates the layout of the list report in FrontPage:

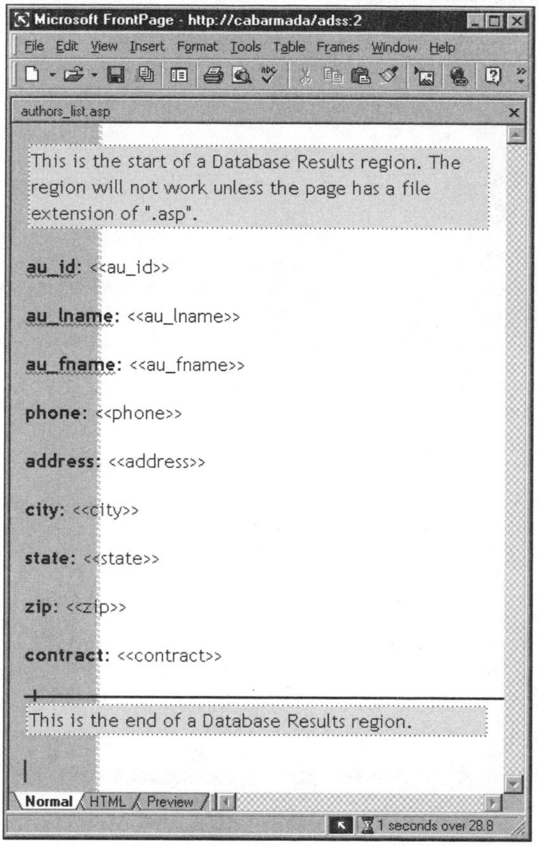

Then, we save the web page with the name `authors_list.asp` so we can view it in a browser.

authors_and_visitors.asp

The `authors_and_visitors.asp` is a web page with data from two separate databases on two different computers. This is easily generated using the Database Wizard. Unlike the preceding web pages in this chapter, the browser's address box shows that this page sits on a web server called cabxli in the adss folder. The web page exposes data from both the cabarmada database server and the cabxli database server. In the image overleaf, we can see the first five records from the authors table for the pubs database on the cabarmada server:

This extract from the database displays data in a tabular format. The bottom of the screen shows the total number of unique visitors from the logfiles database on the cabxli server. The unique visitors result appears in a columnar format.

This web page uses a different theme from the preceding two reports. Since FrontPage enables the creation of custom themes based on over 60 built-in ones, substantial latitude exists for us to customize the format of different reports.

The reports generated by the Database Wizard are dynamic. If the original table changes between two different viewings of a web page that's attached to a database, then the published report changes once the browser cache refreshes to obtain a new page from the web server. For example, if the author Majorie Green was to get married, she might change her last name from Green to Green-Jones. After someone revises her record in the database, the report generated will automatically reflect the revision:

Built-in programming associated with the web page automatically detects the revision to the database whenever a browser refreshes the page from the server. As long as the web page is refreshed, thereby updating the datacache, webmasters do not have to re-publish a page in order for a revision to the database to be displayed. With static publishing, any revisions to the database would not appear on a web page until the webmaster, or someone else, physically re-published the pages. When there are many reports, this can be cumbersome. In addition, this dynamic method requires that both the web server and the database server operate for a page to appear. If there is an unreliable link between the two, the database content on a web page will not appear and an error is likely to be generated.

Creating authors_and_visitors.asp

We begin to construct the sample by creating a subweb on a web server in Frontpage, in this case, the adss subweb on the cabxli web server. Next, we add a new blank page by clicking the New Page control on the FrontPage toolbar.

We can now add the first of the two database connections. Set Database1 to the pubs database on the cabarmada database server. We create the database connection to pubs on cabarmada in exactly the same way as we have done for the prevous examples. After advancing from step 1 of the Database Wizard, we step through the remaining screens to create a table on the page that shows the rows in the authors table. The instructions to accomplish this part are identical to those for the authors_table.asp page.

We then add the line, "From the logfiles database on cabxli."

> Obviously you're database connections will point at different locations on your
> database server, depending where you happen to have them stored.

We're then ready to add the second of the two database connections. In this example we set Database2 to the Logfiles database on the cabxli database server. Having created the connection and verified it, we can advance to the second wizard screen to designate the source for the second database report on the web page. We select the count_of_unique_visitors view as the source. The following screen shows the selection in step 2 of the Database Wizard screen:

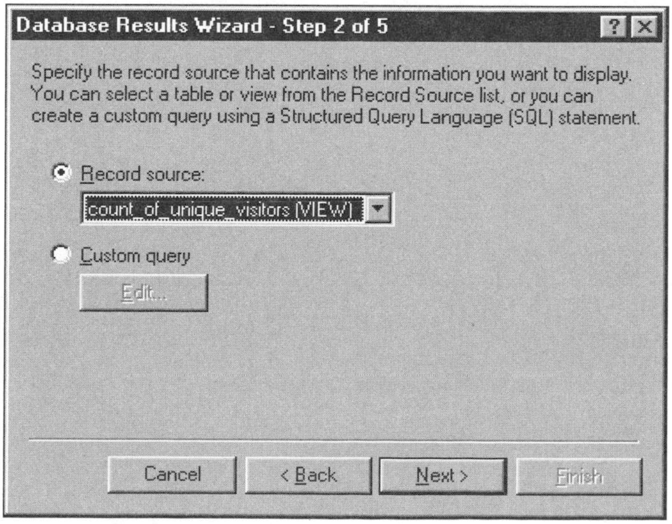

After specifying a record source for the second report, we click **Next** and bring up the third screen. Here we are presented with the field that will be displayed in the second database report:

Progressing from this screen brings up the **Step 4 of 5** dialog, where we can select a list format for the report under consideration:

Clicking **Next**, and accepting the default suggestion on the fifth screen, completes the process. When the wizard closes, we can save the page with the file name of `authors_and_visitors.asp`. FrontPage will automatically assign an `.asp` extension.

Statically Publishing from Access

Static publishing is good for publishing a relatively small number of pages that do not require frequent data updates. When we publish via the FrontPage Database Wizard as described previously, all our reports are automatically dynamic – whether or not that suits our purposes. In addition, the Database Wizard is for reporting content via a web site – not constructing database objects, such as tables and views. Access 2000, on the other hand, has rich development techniques that target SQL Server. While Access 2000 does not integrate as tightly with FrontPage 2000 as SQL Server 2000 does, Access offers particularly strong datasheet publishing capabilities. In this section of the chapter we're going to look at the following:

❑   Statically publishing datasheets from Access

❑   Formatting issues

❑   Statically publishing datasheets with graphic images

We're going to drill down on static datasheet publishing from Access projects. Access can publish datasheets to a web site based on tables, views, the datasheets behind forms, and row-returning stored procedures. One value of approaching the publishing task from Access is that if we do not have the optimal data source for our needs, we can easily create a new database object directly from Access.

Publishing a Datasheet Based on a Table

When we publish statically to a web site from an Access project, we start by selecting one of the objects to publish from the Database window, in this case a table:

After selecting a data source, the next step is to invoke the File | Export command. This opens an Export dialog.

The screenshot on the following page presents the Export dialog for publishing a datasheet based on the authors table in the pubs database:

In order to publish a datasheet statically, we have to select **HTML Documents** from the **Save as type** drop-down control. Next, we designate a folder to receive the published datasheet by selecting from the **Save in** drop-down control. In this case, the adss folder is designated, which serves as a subweb to a web server called cabxli.

If your workstation connects to a web server (or it is the web server), then you could deposit a published datasheet directly into the location from which the web server will distribute it in a web page. If you are ultimately publishing to a remote web server, then create a local folder to hold your published datasheets. Then, upload them from that folder to the appropriate web folder in a subsequent step. FrontPage has built-in support for uploading files from a workstation to a web server through the FrontPage server extensions.

> *Many Internet Service Providers and local intranet web server administrators routinely install these server extensions. Otherwise, they typically support FTP methods for transferring files from a local workstation to a web server. Chapter 7 gives you a brief demonstration of how to use FTP, but you should check with your web server administrator to make sure support is available for the web server you are using.*

Access automatically populates the **File name** text box according to the database object selected as the source for the datasheet; in this example it has automatically selected the title of the table, authors, by default. We can override this if appropriate. Whenever we highlight **HTML Documents** in the **Save as type** control, Access appends an .html extension to the filename when it saves the datasheet as a file.

> *FrontPage on the other hand, routinely creates static files with an .htm extension. In addition, data access pages that you can create from Access 2000 have an .htm extension. These differences are important since browsing for a page with an .htm extension does not return an identically named file with an .html extension.*

Formatting and Display Issues

Three interrelated formatting and display options control how and when our published page displays. By default, the **Save formatted** check box on the **Export** dialog appears initially unchecked. If we leave it this way, your datasheet publishes to the site with default web page formatting for a table. Access does not publish a row of column headers with the default format. In addition, it discards some special formatting with the default setting for the check box. For example, the authors table in the pubs database contains a contract column with True and False values. When we publish without selecting the Save formatted check box, our datasheet shows the underlying 0 and 1 values instead of the converted True and False values that are more meaningful to most web page viewers. We'll take a look at the default format in a moment.

Formatting from Access

If we publish with the check box selected, Access publishes our table so that it has the look of a datasheet as it would usually appear in the Access environment.

Clicking the Save formatted check box, enables the Autostart check box. When we select the Autostart check box, Access automatically opens our published table in a browser window after it publishes our datasheet. This gives us an opportunity to verify that the output meets our requirements. If not, we can change the original source for our datasheet.

The status of the Save formatted check box also impacts on the operation of the Save button. Unsurprisingly, this button stores our datasheet as a file. Two other dialogs can pop up after we click Save. First, if the file already exists in a folder, as is standard in Windows applications, Access will ask if we want to replace the prior version. Second, Access opens the HTML Output Options dialog:

There is just one option when we are statically publishing a datasheet. This option allows us to designate an exisiting web page to serve as a formatting template for our new page. For example, if we have previously assigned a FrontPage theme to the default page at a web site, we can also assign this theme to our published datasheet pages by referencing that default page at the site. There is nothing special about the default.htm file at a site for this task. We could set up several different pages with specific formatting to serve as models for different types of datasheets. For example, we may need a different format for each department in a company: Human Resources, Finance, and Engineering. We could set up a special format for each department, and then reference the appropriate page whenever we publish a datasheet for a department. If we don't want to use any pre-existing special format, we leave the text box blank.

We can then publish the datasheet by clicking OK on the HTML Output Options dialog. This saves the datasheet with the standard Access formatting:

With this format, our web site can have the same look and feel as our LAN-based datasheets. And additionally, as we've just seen, this format requires no manual formatting actions. This benefit can be extremely useful if we have more than one or two datasheets to publish and manage at a web site.

Notice that the table, the browser window, and the file for the web page all bear the name – authors. These are default settings. The browser opens an .html file that we had saved in the adss folder of the wwwroot folder of the Inetpub directory. When you create a subweb in FrontPage, such as adss, below a server's root web, its default location is within the \Inetpub\wwwroot path as indicated in the Address box above.

> *When working with web pages based on static HTML, it is possible to call up a web page using a normal file location as we have done here. This is because a web server is not necessary to render a static page. When working with a dynamic page that relies on server-side code, such as one based on ASP technology, we must reference the page through a web server. This is because the server has to render the page before passing it on to the browser. The format is http://servername/path/filename. With PWS or IIS, you'll find that your web server takes the name of your computer by default.*

We can see that a row of column headers appears in a contrasting style and in addition, the contract column represents its values as True and False although the underlying values are 1 for True and 0 for False. These are the conventional formatting aspects of an opened datasheet in Access. Other than selecting the Save formatted check box, no special options were necessary to attain this formatting.

Manual Formatting

If we do not check the Save as formatted box, the page is just saved without Access style formatting in the location we have specified. If we open the page up in a browser window, it appears with the basic default web page table format:

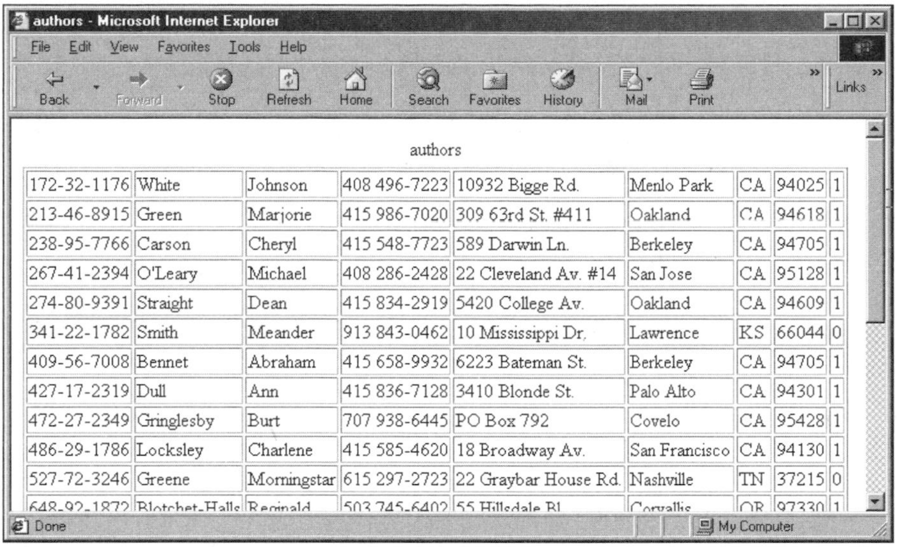

If we have just a few tables to manage, this display may be appropriate especially since we may prefer to format the table's appearance ourselves in FrontPage. Formatting a statically published data-based web page is appropriate when the data is likely to change very infrequently or not at all. This is because we have to repeat all manual formatting steps every time we re-publish the table. Each publication of a table wipes out the formatting for the previous datasheet version.

> *For larger amounts of data, we can format the tables programmatically. We'll be introducing this technique later in the chapter.*

The following screenshot shows our non formatted version of the authors table which we've opened up in FrontPage. If FrontPage is already open at the time that we publish the table, we must refresh the Folder window before it reveals any newly published pages.

> *Do this by selecting any file or folder in the Folder window, then refreshing the display. No matter how you display the file for the web page, you can open it by double-clicking the filename and extension, authors_no_formatting.html, in the Folder window.*

The table's appearance on the **Normal** tab in FrontPage resembles its appearance in the browser that we looked at just a moment ago. The table's title and the file containing the page both have the same name, `authors_no_formatting`. With the web page open in FrontPage, we can begin to customize its formatting.

*There are two general approaches to formatting web pages manually in FrontPage. First, we can edit the table with the menubar commands on the **Normal** tab. This is easy and fast, but it does not expose the full range of standard and dynamic HTML formatting options. Second, we can manually enter HTML code and either VBScript or JavaScript/JScript code in the HTML window. We can program actions to take place when events happen, such as users clicking a button, or a page loading into a browser. While the flexibility is substantially greater in the **HTML** tab than the **Normal** tab, the granular level of the techniques in the **HTML** tab will slow development. Unless this is an everyday task, you will probably keep referencing specific HTML commands before you get it right each time.*

Notice the `schema.ini` file in the **Folder** list. This text-based file is automatically generated by FrontPage and contains the formatting schema specification for the `authors_no_formatting` page. In addition to the page's file name and code page number for the character set, this text file contains the column name, data type, and length, when appropriate, for individual table columns. The meta-data for individual columns appears by column number from left to right. As we add more datasheets with no formatting to the folder, meta-data for those datasheets appends to the end of the `schema.ini` file.

We can also see in the **Folder List,** a file called `global.asa`. You may have seen this before. This is a special file that is automatically created when we develop in FrontPage using the Database Wizard, however we can also create this file ourselves with a little familiarity with web development techniques and creating solutions in a manual environment using Active Server Pages.

As its name suggests, this file is application-level, housing objects and variables that are utilised by the complete application. IIS web server and Personal Web Server both use this file to help manage application start and end actions as well as session start and session end actions. We don't need to worry about `global.asa` in this chapter or even this book since the techniques we're covering here do not require us to edit the file. However, it's helpful to be aware of its existence. Developers who wish to build sophisticated custom web-based solutions, may find a need to work with the `global.asa` file. As we mentioned at the beginning of the section, if you're interested in web development, you can find information on the `global.asa` file in *Beginning Active Server Pages 3.0* by Wrox Press (ISBN 1-861003-38-2).

Published Datasheets Based on Other Database Objects

The general method for statically publishing datasheets based on views, forms, and stored procedures is very similar to the procedure we have just seen for tables. This section will present published datasheets based on these other database objects. In addition to presenting the published datasheets, the section describes special issues relating to the publication and use of the datasheets.

Publishing and Editing a Datasheet for a View

The pubs database comes with one view named titleview. We can publish it the same way that we described for the authors table.

title	au_ord	au_lname	price	ytd_sales	pub_id
The Busy Executive's Database Guide	1	Bennet	$19.99	4095	1389
Fifty Years in Buckingham Palace Kitchens	1	Blotchet-Halls	$11.95	15096	0877
But Is It User Friendly?	1	Carson	$22.95	8780	1389
The Gourmet Microwave	1	DeFrance	$2.99	22246	0877
Silicon Valley Gastronomic Treats	1	del Castillo	$19.99	2032	0877
Secrets of Silicon Valley	1	Dull	$20.00	4095	1389
The Busy Executive's Database Guide	2	Green	$19.99	4095	1389
You Can Combat Computer Stress!	1	Green	$2.99	18722	0736
Sushi, Anyone?	3	Gringlesby	$14.99	4095	0877
Secrets of Silicon Valley	2	Hunter	$20.00	4095	1389
Computer Phobic AND Non-Phobic Individuals: Behavior Variations	1	Karsen	$21.59	375	0877
Net Etiquette	1	Locksley			1389
Emotional Security: A New Algorithm	1	Locksley	$7.99	3336	0736
Cooking with Computers: Surreptitious Balance Sheets	1	MacFeather	$11.95	3876	1389
Computer Phobic AND Non-Phobic Individuals: Behavior Variations	2	MacFeather	$21.59	375	0877
Cooking with Computers: Surreptitious Balance Sheets	2	O'Leary	$11.95	3876	1389
Sushi, Anyone?	2	O'Leary	$14.99	4095	0877
Onions, Leeks, and Garlic: Cooking Secrets of the Mediterranean	1	Panteley	$20.95	375	0877
Is Anger the Enemy?	1	Ringer	$10.95	2045	0736
Life Without Fear	1	Ringer	$7.00	111	0736
The Gourmet Microwave	2	Ringer	$2.99	22246	0877
Is Anger the Enemy?	2	Ringer	$10.95	2045	0736
Straight Talk About Computers	1	Straight	$19.99	4095	1389
Prolonged Data Deprivation: Four Case Studies	1	White	$19.99	4072	0736
Sushi, Anyone?	1	Yokomoto	$14.99	4095	0877

471

The next screen shows an excerpt from the Normal tab of the same datasheet inside FrontPage:

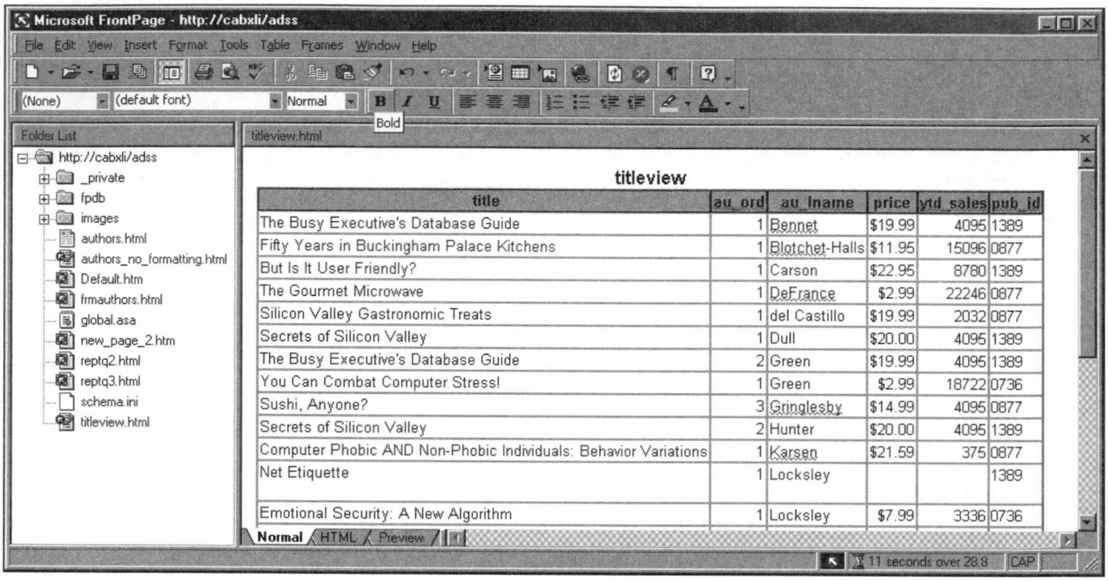

Notice that the Net Etiquette title listing occupies two rows. The entries for all other titles appear on a single row. This problem stems from the HTML conversion. When Access converts the null values for the price and ytd_sales columns for the Net Etiquette title, it inserts a
 HTML tag (the HTML equivalent of a carriage return) to mark the null value for the column value. This tag creates the extra row creating a line break in HTML text. We can remove the blank row by taking out the< BR> tag and replacing it with some text – for example, "0". This approach is useful when you are only working with a couple of pages or have only a minimal knowledge of HTML. We'll be looking at how to make programmatic alterations for larger sets of pages a little later in the chapter.

The following code from the preceding page shows the HTML for the Net Etiquette title row before and after the simple edit described above.

This is the original HTML for Net Etiquette title row:

```
<TR VALIGN=TOP>
<TD BORDERCOLOR=#c0c0c0 ><FONT SIZE=2 FACE="Arial" COLOR=#000000>Net
Etiquette</FONT></TD>
<TD BORDERCOLOR=#c0c0c0 ALIGN=RIGHT><FONT SIZE=2 FACE="Arial"
COLOR=#000000>1</FONT></TD>
<TD BORDERCOLOR=#c0c0c0 ><FONT SIZE=2 FACE="Arial"
COLOR=#000000>Locksley</FONT></TD>
<TD BORDERCOLOR=#c0c0c0 ALIGN=RIGHT><FONT SIZE=2 FACE="Arial"
COLOR=#000000><BR></FONT></TD>
<TD BORDERCOLOR=#c0c0c0 ALIGN=RIGHT><FONT SIZE=2 FACE="Arial"
COLOR=#000000><BR></FONT></TD>
<TD BORDERCOLOR=#c0c0c0 ><FONT SIZE=2 FACE="Arial" COLOR=#000000>1389</FONT></TD>

</TR>
```

And this is the Edited HTML for Net Etiquette title row:

```
<TR VALIGN=TOP>
<TD BORDERCOLOR=#c0c0c0 ><FONT SIZE=2 FACE="Arial" COLOR=#000000>Net
Etiquette</FONT></TD>
<TD BORDERCOLOR=#c0c0c0 ALIGN=RIGHT><FONT SIZE=2 FACE="Arial"
COLOR=#000000>1</FONT></TD>
<TD BORDERCOLOR=#c0c0c0 ><FONT SIZE=2 FACE="Arial"
COLOR=#000000>Locksley</FONT></TD>
<TD BORDERCOLOR=#c0c0c0 ALIGN=RIGHT><FONT SIZE=2 FACE="Arial"
COLOR=#000000>0</FONT></TD>
<TD BORDERCOLOR=#c0c0c0 ALIGN=RIGHT><FONT SIZE=2 FACE="Arial"
COLOR=#000000>0</FONT></TD>
<TD BORDERCOLOR=#c0c0c0 ><FONT SIZE=2 FACE="Arial" COLOR=#000000>1389</FONT></TD>

</TR>
```

We can make the change by opening the HTML tab for the web page with the datasheet. Next, we invoke the Edit | Find command and search for a
tag to locate the first row to edit. Each row begins with a <TR> tag and ends with a </TR> tag. HTML syntax marks the individual column values within a row with <TD> and </TD> tags. Notice the <BR> tags in the fourth and fifth cells for the original version. The edited version shows the replacement of each <BR> tags with 0. We could have replaced the tag with any other text we wanted.

The following screen illustrates the new look of the datasheet on the Normal tab after modifying the code so that all the <BR> tags have been replaced by 0s for the Net Etiquette row. Notice that the Net Etiquette listing now occupies just one row:

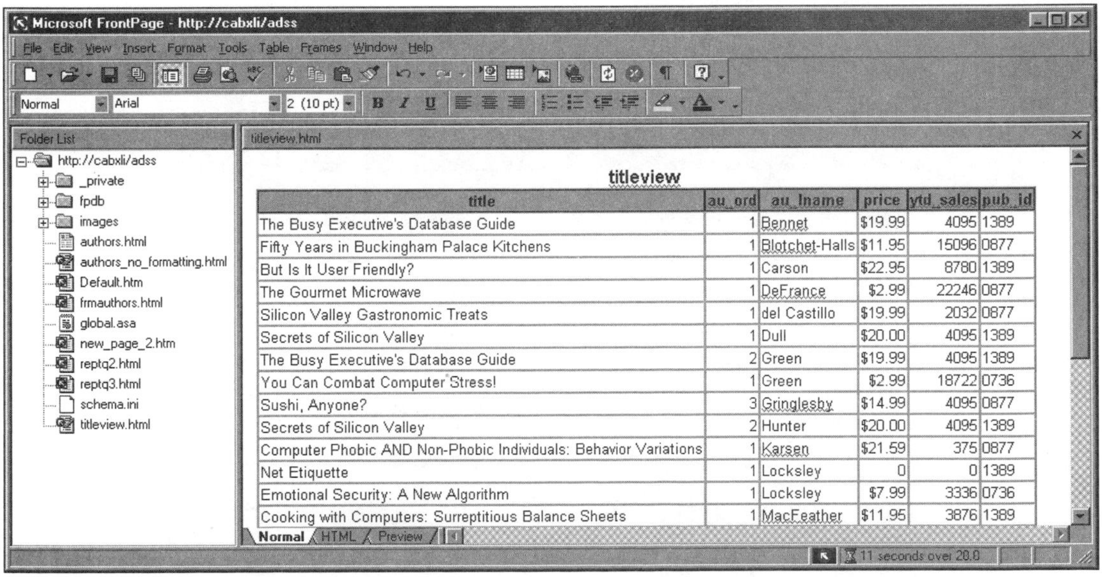

The <BR> tag problem in conversion is not unique to views. The same difficulty manifests itself for published datasheets based on other objects that we can select from the Objects bar of the Access Database window. However, the problem can be resolved in the same way.

Publishing and Editing a Datasheet for a Form

When we select a form to publish, Access actually publishes the datasheet behind the form. With the default font settings, the published datasheet appears in a smaller font than for either a table or a view. This is because Access uses smaller fonts for form fields than for column values for tables and views in Datasheet view. We can resolve the diminished font size issue for datasheets based on forms in either Access or FrontPage.

The following screen shows a pair of forms based on the authors table from the pubs database:

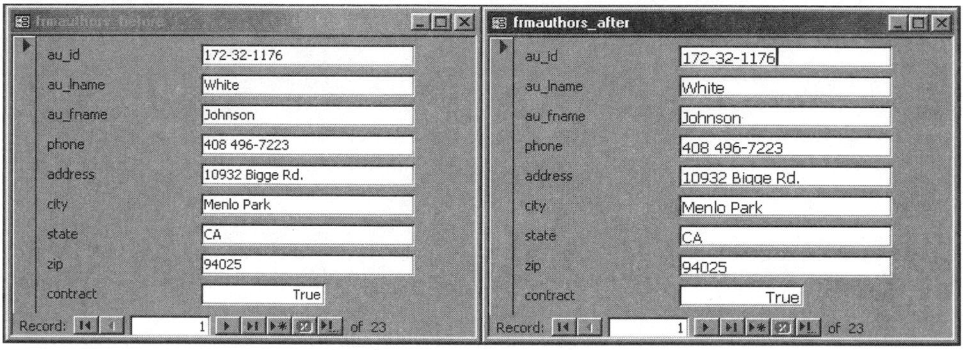

The form on the left with the frmauthors_before caption is the standard output from the AutoForm Wizard. The only change to the output from the AutoForm Wizard is the revision to its caption, frmauthors_before. The form on the right is also from the AutoForm Wizard. In addition to a different custom caption, frmauthors_after, this second form increases the font size for form fields from 8 to 10 points. The default font size in which Access displays datasheets for tables and views is also 10 points. We can alter font size for the fields by selecting all the text boxes in Design view and then updating the Font Size property setting.

See Chapter 7 for instructions on setting properties for Access forms.

The following screens depict the unedited version of the datasheet for each of the preceding forms:

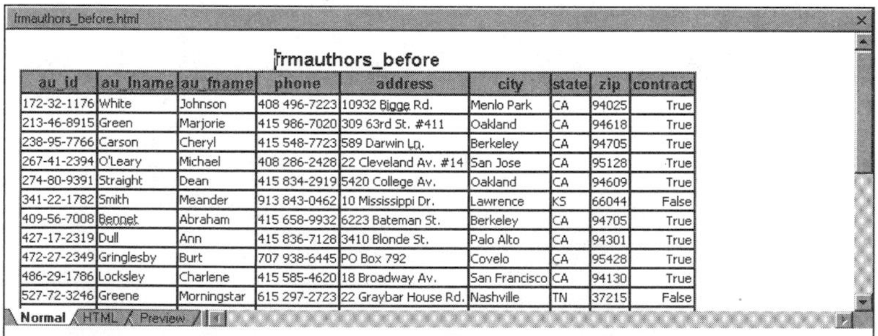

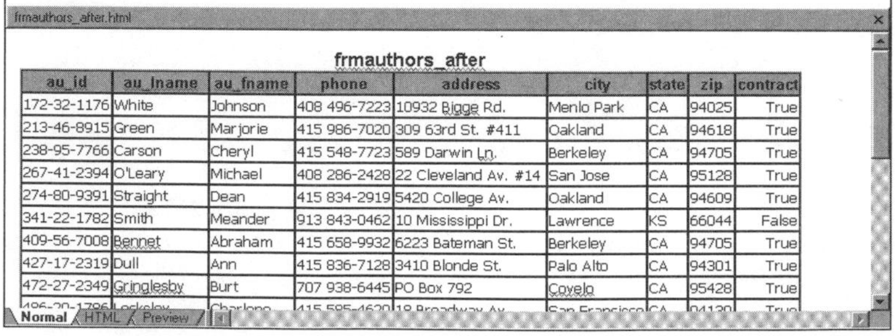

Both screens contain the same number of rows, but they display a different number of rows on their initial screen. This is because the bottom datasheet appears in a larger font size. The File | Export command in Access 2000 preserves the font size setting in the source Access object as it converts the datasheet behind a form for publication on a web site. In this case, the font size setting is for the text boxes on the form.

If it is not appropriate to change the font in Access, we can achieve the same result in FrontPage. If we open the web page with the datasheet based on the form, we can choose Table | Select | Table from the Normal tab menubar. Next, we choose Format | Font and highlight the 10-point size before clicking OK to close the dialog. This achieves the same result as editing the form field fonts to 10 points in the Access project, although this method also changes the sizes of the column headings as well as the data entries.

Publishing and Editing Datasheets for Stored Procedures

We can publish the return sets from stored procedures in three general cases:

❑ The results of a stored procedure that includes a clause, such as the ORDER BY clause, with a single return set. The clause enables you to control the order in which rows appear in a return set.

❑ Stored procedures with parameters. These allow an application to configure output at run time.

❑ Stored procedures that have multiple return sets. This requires special planning with Access from the user interface since this mode of activating a stored procedure returns just the first return set.

Return Sets from Stored Procedures with Clauses

One of the stored procedures that ships with the pubs database is named byroyalty. This stored procedure returns the names of authors that match a parameter value. The return set from the stored procedure is simply a list of author ID values (au_id column values).

This stored procedure has been adapted in a couple of ways for this chapter. The first adaptation of the byroyalty_all stored procedure returns all the authors with a separate row for each book to which they contributed. In addition, this adaptation has more columns than the original version (byroyalty) to generate output that can be more clearly interpreted than a list, which contains only author ID values. Finally, the byroyalty_all stored procedure sorts its records by royalty percentage. The T-SQL for the stored procedure appears below:

```
Alter Procedure byroyalty_all
As
SELECT authors.au_id, authors.au_fname, authors.au_lname,
   titles.title, titleauthor.royaltyper
FROM authors INNER JOIN
   titleauthor ON authors.au_id = titleauthor.au_id INNER JOIN
   titles ON titleauthor.title_id = titles.title_id
ORDER BY titleauthor.royaltyper DESC
```

We can create the new stored procedure by opening up the existing byroyalty stored procedure in design view in Access. We can then add the new T-SQL to the existing code in the template. This is why we use Alter Procedure rather than Create Procedure, as you might otherwise expect.

We publish the returned results of the stored procedure in exactly the same way that we published a table or a view. The screen overleaf shows the browser view of the published datasheet based on the byroyalty_all stored procedure:

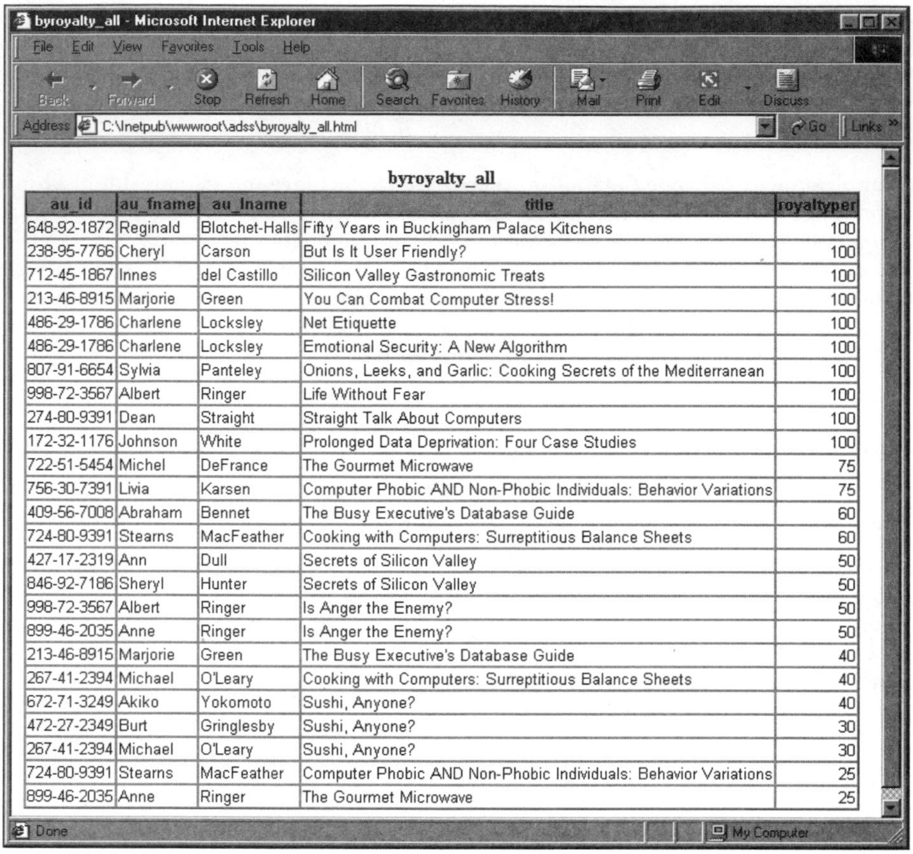

byroyalty_all

au_id	au_fname	au_lname	title	royaltyper
648-92-1872	Reginald	Blotchet-Halls	Fifty Years in Buckingham Palace Kitchens	100
238-95-7766	Cheryl	Carson	But Is It User Friendly?	100
712-45-1867	Innes	del Castillo	Silicon Valley Gastronomic Treats	100
213-46-8915	Marjorie	Green	You Can Combat Computer Stress!	100
486-29-1786	Charlene	Locksley	Net Etiquette	100
486-29-1786	Charlene	Locksley	Emotional Security: A New Algorithm	100
807-91-6654	Sylvia	Panteley	Onions, Leeks, and Garlic: Cooking Secrets of the Mediterranean	100
998-72-3567	Albert	Ringer	Life Without Fear	100
274-80-9391	Dean	Straight	Straight Talk About Computers	100
172-32-1176	Johnson	White	Prolonged Data Deprivation: Four Case Studies	100
722-51-5454	Michel	DeFrance	The Gourmet Microwave	75
756-30-7391	Livia	Karsen	Computer Phobic AND Non-Phobic Individuals: Behavior Variations	75
409-56-7008	Abraham	Bennet	The Busy Executive's Database Guide	60
724-80-9391	Stearns	MacFeather	Cooking with Computers: Surreptitious Balance Sheets	60
427-17-2319	Ann	Dull	Secrets of Silicon Valley	50
846-92-7186	Sheryl	Hunter	Secrets of Silicon Valley	50
998-72-3567	Albert	Ringer	Is Anger the Enemy?	50
899-46-2035	Anne	Ringer	Is Anger the Enemy?	50
213-46-8915	Marjorie	Green	The Busy Executive's Database Guide	40
267-41-2394	Michael	O'Leary	Cooking with Computers: Surreptitious Balance Sheets	40
672-71-3249	Akiko	Yokomoto	Sushi, Anyone?	40
472-27-2349	Burt	Gringlesby	Sushi, Anyone?	30
267-41-2394	Michael	O'Leary	Sushi, Anyone?	30
724-80-9391	Stearns	MacFeather	Computer Phobic AND Non-Phobic Individuals: Behavior Variations	25
899-46-2035	Anne	Ringer	The Gourmet Microwave	25

Notice that it has 25 rows sorted by royaltyper value. One reason for using a stored procedure instead of a view or a table is that you can more precisely control the datasheet. For example, the byroyalty_all stored procedure sorts the rows in a particular order. If we wanted, we could change the sort order for the royaltyper column values or sort by additional or alternative column values.

Return Sets from Stored Procedures with Parameters

A second adaptation of the original byroyalty stored procedure appears below:

```
Alter Procedure byroyalty_some
           @percentage int
As
SELECT authors.au_id, authors.au_fname, authors.au_lname,
  titles.title, titleauthor.royaltyper
FROM authors INNER JOIN
  titleauthor ON authors.au_id = titleauthor.au_id INNER JOIN
  titles ON titleauthor.title_id = titles.title_id
WHERE titleauthor.royaltyper = @percentage
```

This variation references a parameter at run time that permits users to specify which records the byroyalty_some stored procedure returns. When a user invokes the procedure from the Database window, a popup window requests a value for the `@percentage` parameter. The value is utilized by a `WHERE` clause to control which records the stored procedure returns.

The procedure for publishing a stored procedure that requests parameters is nearly identical to that for a stored procedure without parameters. The main difference is that Access will prompt for one or more parameter values as the last step in the process.

So, we begin to publish the datasheet for the results of the byroyalty_some stored procedure by first selecting it in the **Database** window. Next, we choose File I Export and complete the resulting dialog as we do when publishing other database objects. Access automatically selects **Save formatted** on the **Export** dialog, and it disables the check box so that we cannot alter its default selection. This convention departs from the way Access publishes other objects. After clicking **Save**, Access prompts for an output template in the same way as we have seen when publishing tables, views, and forms. As we've seen earlier in this section, we can respond to this prompt dialog either by leaving it blank if we want to use default publishing or by referencing another file at the web site to act as a template.

Just before publishing the datasheet, Access prompts for a parameter value. The following screen illustrates the prompt with an entry of 50:

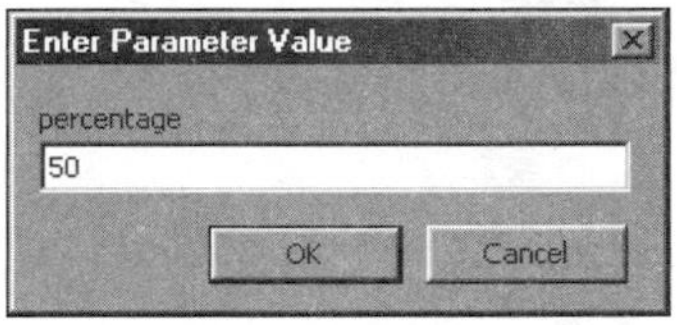

Running the stored procedure with this entry generates a published datasheet with just the four records that have a royaltyper value of 50:

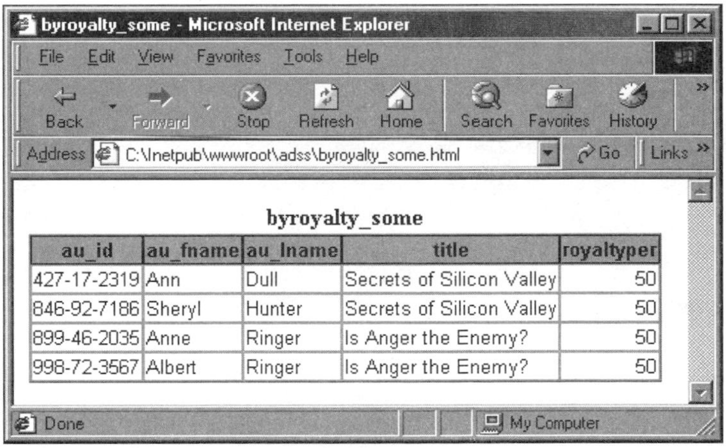

Multiple Return Sets from Stored Procedures

The reptq1 stored procedure also ships with the pubs database. The T-SQL for the procedure below shows that it returns pub_id, title_id, price, and pubdate column values from the titles table for titles that have a non-NULL price value:

```
Alter PROCEDURE reptq1 AS
select pub_id, title_id, price, pubdate
from titles
where price is NOT NULL
order by pub_id
```

477

```
COMPUTE avg(price) BY pub_id
COMPUTE avg(price)
```

The two COMPUTE statements at the end of the stored procedure compute the average price of titles from each publisher and the overall average price.

Three publishers in the pubs database have at least one title with a non-NULL price. This stored procedure generates seven recordsets in its return set. Each of the three publishers has two recordsets, one with a row for each title that has a non-NULL price and a second return set with the average price for titles from that publisher. The seventh recordset contains the overall average price. Unfortunately, Access 2000 returns just the title listing for the first return set when you run it from the Database window.

The following pair of screenshots presents the first two recordsets when you run the reptq1 stored procedure from Query Analyzer. Using Query Analyzer is a fast and easy way to view all the recordsets.

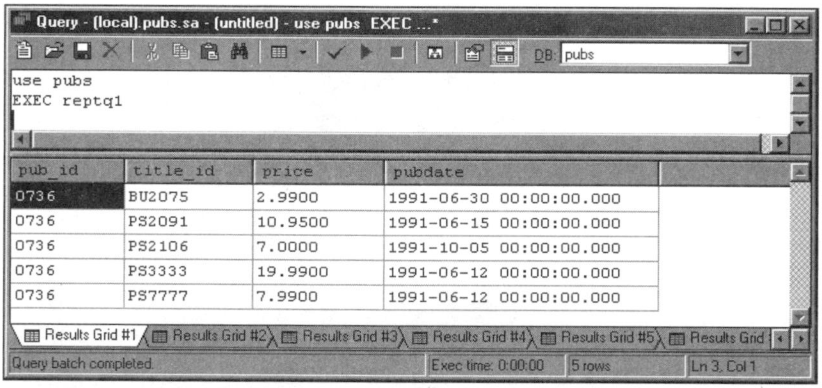

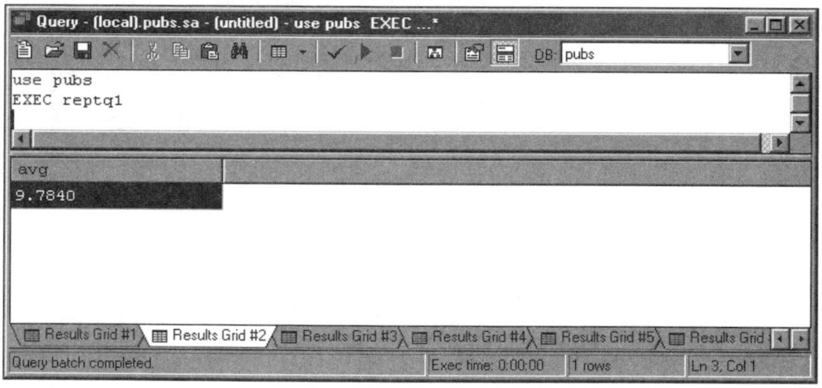

Since Access does not return multiple return sets when we run stored procedures from the Database window, publishing a datasheet based on the reptq1 stored procedure will provide a single datasheet with the values in the first return set. The process for publishing a datasheet based on reptq1 is identical to publishing byroyalty_all, except that we designate a different stored procedure to start the process. The preview browser window for the published datasheet from reptq1 appears next. This is the only datasheet that appears when we publish reptq1 manually. If we publish programmatically, we can extract all the recordsets, and then publish them individually. We'll be taking a look at programmatic publishing later in the chapter.

See Chapter 5 for sample code to extract multiple recordsets from a database object. Then, use the extracted recordsets as the source for objects. For example, we can use the code in Chapter 3 to create new tables for each recordset, and then populate the table with values from the recordset.

Publishing Static Datasheets with Graphic Images

The techniques covered so far in this chapter will help us to generate static and dynamic displays of SQL Server data, but they do not enable the display of images in tables. This section presents two different manual techniques for populating graphic images in a datasheet column. A subsequent section builds on one of these techniques to illustrate how to automate the process with a VBA procedure.

We'll be using the categories table from the Northwind database to illustrate these techniques.

> **You will need to create a new access project to link to the Northwind database in SQL Server.**

The categories table contains images that illustrate the products composing a particular category. These images are not unlike those that might appear in an online product catelogue.

Access does not actually display the graphic images when we first open the categories table. It makes them available when a user clicks on a link in the Picture column which points at the image:

CategoryID	CategoryName	Description	Picture
1	Beverages	Soft drinks, coffees, teas, beers, and ales	Bitmap Image
2	Condiments	Sweet and savory sauces, relishes, spreads, and seasonings	Bitmap Image
3	Confections	Desserts, candies, and sweet breads	Bitmap Image
4	Dairy Products	Cheeses	Bitmap Image
5	Grains/Cereals	Breads, crackers, pasta, and cereal	Bitmap Image
6	Meat/Poultry	Prepared meats	Bitmap Image
7	Produce	Dried fruit and bean curd	Bitmap Image
8	Seafood	Seaweed and fish	Bitmap Image
(AutoNumber)			

This marker called Bitmap Image works like a hyperlink in a web application. When we double-click on any markers, Windows responds by opening the corresponding category image in its default Paint application:

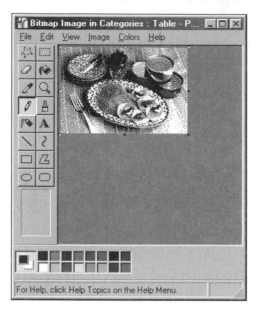

The FrontPage Database Wizard, however, is unable to capture images from the Northwind database or any other SQL Server database. Additionally, the static publishing techniques that worked for the authors table and selected other database objects in the pubs database, which we saw earlier in the chapter, do not work for images either. If we publish the categories table in the Northwind database with the same technique that we used for the authors table in pubs, the published datasheet appears like this:

Categories

CategoryID	CategoryName	Description	Picture
1	Beverages	Soft drinks, coffees, teas, beers, and ales	
2	Condiments	Sweet and savory sauces, relishes, spreads, and seasonings	
3	Confections	Desserts, candies, and sweet breads	
4	Dairy Products	Cheeses	
5	Grains/Cereals	Breads, crackers, pasta, and cereal	
6	Meat/Poultry	Prepared meats	
7	Produce	Dried fruit and bean curd	
8	Seafood	Seaweed and fish	

The first three columns accept values, but the fourth column, which we just looked at in Access with bound image files, is blank when the datasheet is published in the browser.

So how do we get round this problem? Well as we said at the beginning of this section, there are two ways in which we can publish graphics within our datasheet:

❑ By inserting links into the Pictures column which point to the location of the image files

❑ By inserting the image files directly into the table

The choice of which technique to use will depend on the speed at which users connect to a site, the number of bound images in your datasheet, the size of your image files, and the number of users simultaneously hitting your web server.

Well look at each of these methods now starting with how we insert links into our table.

Inserting Links

Before we actually turn our attention to inserting the links, we need to ensure that the necessary images are stored in the right format. Since our published datasheet will work over the web, converting the images to a lighter graphic format, such as a `.j-peg` or `.gif file` type rather than a bitmap image makes the download of images more efficient in the browser.

The simplest way of achieving this is to open the images in Microsoft Paint, by clicking on the links in the categories table, and then save the bitmap graphics in a suitable location. The images folder which is automatically generated when we create a web or a subweb in FrontPage is one obvious place to store them. Once we have the images stored, we can open the files up in a package such as Microsoft PhotoDraw, which ships with most versions of the Office suite, and convert the files to a new type.

> *Microsoft PhotoDraw ships with both the Premium and Developer additions of Microsoft's Office suite. It does not, however, ship with the Professional version. If you do not have Photodraw installed on your machine, you can use any graphics package such as Corel Draw or Paintshop Pro to carry out the conversion.*

With the images stored in an appropriate location in the correct format, we can now set about modifying the page with the datasheet to display the links that will point to them.

We're going to populate the Picture column of the datasheet, which currently appears blank when the page is published in the normal way, with links to the corresponding images. The result will be a page which looks like this:

When the user clicks on a link, the datasheet is replaced in the browser by the image file that the link points to:

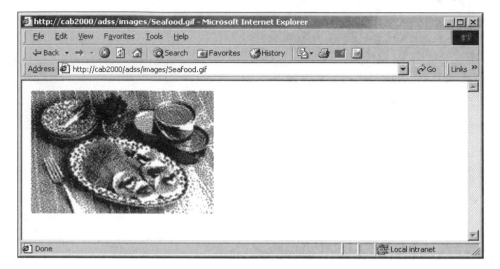

This example, as many of the examples throughout the book, assumes defaults. In this case, the appearance of the .gif *image file in a browser relies on the fact that the user did not change the default association between* .gif, *and other web image files, and your browser.*

So how do we implement these changes? Well modifying the original data sheet created with Access is very straightforward. First of all, after opening the file in FrontPage on the normal tab, we simply type the text for the hyperlinks in the corresponding rows of the Picture column.

Then, we select the text and choose the Hyperlink tool on the FrontPage toolbar:

This throws up the **Create Hyperlink** dialog in which we can point the text at a specific file in the images folder:

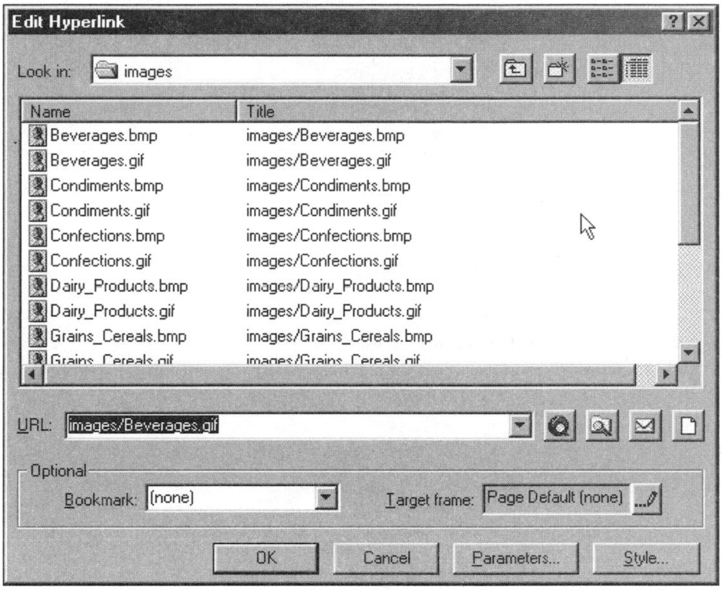

So, once we've repeated this process for each of the fields in the **Picture** column, our links are fully in place, and a user would be able to view the images in the browser.

If we examine the actual HTML code for the **categories** page, `categories.html`, and the modified version, which is named `categories_bound_links.htm`, we can see the alterations that we have made.

The first sample is from the original `Categories.html` datasheet file showing the code for the **Beverages** row in the datasheet. `<TR>` tags delimit rows in the table, and `<TD>` tags delimit cells within rows. The only cell on which we need to focus here is the last one. Notice that it displays the vacant cell with its normal conversion to a `<BR>` tag.

```
<TR VALIGN=TOP>
<TD BORDERCOLOR=#c0c0c0 ALIGN=RIGHT><FONT SIZE=2 FACE="Arial"
COLOR=#000000>1</FONT></TD>
<TD BORDERCOLOR=#c0c0c0 ><FONT SIZE=2 FACE="Arial"
COLOR=#000000>Beverages</FONT></TD>
<TD BORDERCOLOR=#c0c0c0 ><FONT SIZE=2 FACE="Arial" COLOR=#000000>Soft drinks,
coffees, teas, beers, and ales</FONT></TD>
<TD BORDERCOLOR=#c0c0c0 ALIGN=RIGHT><FONT SIZE=2 FACE="Arial"
COLOR=#000000><BR></FONT></TD>

</TR>
```

When we compare this to the second sample from the `Categories_bound_links.htm`, we can see the HTML code for inserting a link in the **Picture** cell. This HTML replaces the `<BR>` tag with an `<A>` tag (A for Anchor) that has an `href` attribute value pointing at the **beverages** image file. The display text that appears in the browser (which we actually typed directly into the page) sits in between the opening and closing `<A>` tags:

```
<TR VALIGN=TOP>
<TD BORDERCOLOR=#c0c0c0 ALIGN=RIGHT><FONT SIZE=2 FACE="Arial"
COLOR=#000000>1</FONT></TD>
<TD BORDERCOLOR=#c0c0c0 ><FONT SIZE=2 FACE="Arial"
COLOR=#000000>Beverages</FONT></TD>
<TD BORDERCOLOR=#c0c0c0 ><FONT SIZE=2 FACE="Arial" COLOR=#000000>Soft drinks,
coffees, teas, beers, and ales</FONT></TD>
```

```
<TD BORDERCOLOR=#c0c0c0 ALIGN=RIGHT><FONT SIZE=2 FACE="Arial" COLOR=#000000><a
href="images/Beverages.gif">Beverages</a></FONT></TD>
```

```
</TR>
```

Inserting the Image File into the Table

As we said at the beginning of this section, there are two methods we can use to display the images from the datasheet and we are not restricted to using links in the page. Instead, we can modify the datasheet so that it displays images directly within the table. The following screen presents an excerpt of a datasheet that has the images embedded within the table:

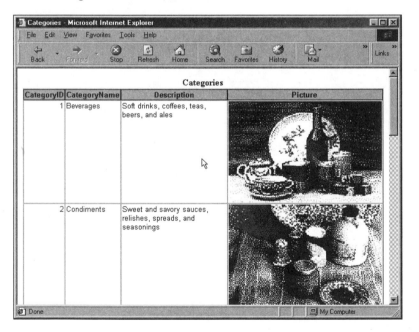

> This file is called `Categories_bound_images.htm` in the sample code download at www.wrox.com.

This method is also easily achieved. We start by positioning the cursor in a cell. Then we simply choose Insert | Picture | From File. This opens the Picture dialog to the images folder from which you can select an image file corresponding to the category row:

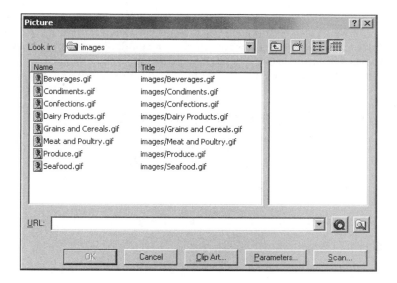

The Picture dialog automatically opens at the images folder for the subweb that the page is stored in. Conveniently, in this example, this is where we have stored our images. If we had stored them elsewhere, we would obviously have to browse to the folder.

We can view the code for the Beverages row of this modified page to see the changes that are made to the HTML by FrontPage when we insert a picture:

```
<TR VALIGN=TOP>
<TD BORDERCOLOR=#c0c0c0 ALIGN=RIGHT><FONT SIZE=2 FACE="Arial"
COLOR=#000000>1</FONT></TD>
<TD BORDERCOLOR=#c0c0c0 ><FONT SIZE=2 FACE="Arial"
COLOR=#000000>Beverages</FONT></TD>
<TD BORDERCOLOR=#c0c0c0 ><FONT SIZE=2 FACE="Arial" COLOR=#000000>Soft drinks,
coffees, teas, beers, and ales</FONT></TD>

<TD BORDERCOLOR=#c0c0c0 ALIGN=RIGHT><FONT SIZE=2 FACE="Arial" COLOR="#000000"><img
border="0" src="http://cab2000/adss/images/Beverages.gif" width="270"
height="184"></FONT></TD>

</TR>
```

The <BR> tag is replaced with an <IMG> tag. HTML uses this tag as a container for graphic images on web pages. The <IMG> tag uses the src attribute to specify the source for the image. The value for the src attribute should be the URL for the image file that we want to display. In this case, cab2000 refers to the web server's name. The "adss/images" is the path to the image file on the server, and Beverages.gif is the name of the image file itself. We can optionally shorten the full URL to a relative URL if the images are stored on the same server or in the same directory as the page itself. So for example, our URL could be shortened to just "images/beverages.gif" because the graphics are located in the images folder within the same subweb.

The width and height attributes for the <IMG> tag specify a frame size for the graphic image in pixels. We can leave these settings unspecified, and the image frame automatically sizes to the dimensions of the image. So essentially, we can use the width and height setting for clipping the image or reserving extra white space on a web page.

485

If we have a relatively small set of images bound to a datasheet that rarely if ever changes, this approach is useful. However, if we wanted to add and revise images on a regular basis or we had many images, we'd probably find that we needed a less work-intensive method. Now that we're familiar with the <IMG> tag and some of its attributes we can have a look at automating this task by programmatically inserting images into cells on the datasheet. We'll be taking a look at how we can perform this task in the second half of the next section.

Programmatically Manipulating Datasheets in FrontPage

For the next examples we will be using VBA and the Visual Basic Editor (VBE) for Microsoft Office. We can open the VBE to enter or edit code by choosing Tools | Macros | Visual Basic Editor *from any of the three tabs in FrontPage. When working with FrontPage, it automatically adds a reference to the libraries for its object models.*

The FrontPage Object Model comprises three smaller object models:

❑ The Application Object Model

❑ The Web Object Model

❑ The Page Object Model

Although the object models are really beyond the scope of the chapter, we should be aware of some of their most useful objects for working with VBA. The object models for FrontPage enable the manipulation of webs, files, and document elements. We can enumerate files within a web as well as elements within a web page. FrontPage has a WebFiles collection that includes all the WebFile objects within a web. Code can get to individual WebFile objects through the RootFolder of the ActiveWeb object. A web is active once it has been opened.

Each WebFile object has a number of properties: a Name, a Title, and a Url property. The Name property, which is the actual filename itself, forms a subset of the Url property. The Url property defines the location of a WebFile. The Title property returns the title for a WebFile object which appears in the browser when a web page is displayed. The good news about FrontPage object models is that they are hierarchical, and we can manipulate them with VBA. This section is going to examine a starter pair of samples that convey the potential of programmatically assigning HTML using VBA.

1. This sample is going to demonstrate code could assign a corporate tag line throughout a set of files composing a company web site.

2. The second example is going to go back to our graphic images example from the previous section and show how we can programmatically insert images for large sets of datasheets.

Revising the Content of a Page

Commercial web site content can readily grow to hundreds or thousands of pages. After you work on this content for a while, it will become time to change it. While some changes will be so specific that they require manual editing, other revisions will be standard and can benefit from a program that applies the changes en masse. Increasing your familiarity with HTML will enable you to make changes to datasheets by programmatically assigning new HTML to pages in one fell swoop.

One common requirement is to add a tag line to every page. For example, if our firm just introduced a new product, it may want to add some text to all the web pages at its site announcing the new product and leading folks to another page for additional details. Acting as a web site developer, we need to add this new promotional text to the end of every single page.

This sample shows how we can use a VBA procedure to add content to all the web pages at a site:

```
Private Sub add_tag_line()
Dim web1 As Web
Dim str1 As String
Dim wbf1 As WebFile
Dim pgw1 As PageWindow

'Define string to append to pages
str1 = "<BR>" & String(25, "-") & "<BR>" & _
  "Brought to you by the good folks from CAB and Wrox"

'Open web
Set web1 = Webs.Open("http://cabxli/adss")
web1.Activate

'Loop through files in web
'and insert text at end of each web page
For Each wbf1 In ActiveWeb.RootFolder.Files
'  Debug.Print wbf1.Url
  If Not (wbf1.Name = "global.asa" Or wbf1.Name = "schema.ini") Then
    wbf1.Edit
    Call ActiveDocument.body.insertAdjacentHTML("BeforeEnd", str1)
    ActivePageWindow.Save
    ActivePageWindow.Close
  End If
Next

'Close active web
ActiveWeb.Close

End Sub
```

The procedure begins by assigning a value to a string variable, str1. This variable holds the HTML content that the procedure is going to add to each page:

```
str1 = "<BR>" & String(25, "-") & "<BR>" & _
  "Brought to you by the good folks from CAB and Wrox"
```

The String function is a built-in VBA function that returns a string a fixed number of times. The & operator concatenates the HTML tags, string functions, and string constant. Although this sample applies the same content to the web pages in a site, it could easily be adapted so that it applies different content to different pages by making the expression for str1 conditional on some other value. For example, you could make the content conditional on the file extension or a title or URL.

> *Although the content will be applied to all the web pages in the site, it won't apply the content to the special files, global.asa and schema.ini.*

After creating the content for insertion into the pages of a site, the procedure opens a site with the Open method for the Webs collection:

```
Set web1 = Webs.Open("http://cabxli/adss")
web1.Activate
```

487

This collection designates the set of all the webs at a server. Next, the procedure invokes the `Activate` method for the opened web site to make sure that it has focus.

The heart of the procedure is a loop that passes through all the `WebFile` objects in the root folder of the active web:

```
For Each wbf1 In ActiveWeb.RootFolder.Files
'   Debug.Print wbf1.Url
    If Not (wbf1.Name = "global.asa" Or wbf1.Name = "schema.ini") Then
        wbf1.Edit
        Call ActiveDocument.body.insertAdjacentHTML("BeforeEnd", str1)
```

Two of these files in our sample site are not appropriate for editing. These are the `global.asa` and `schema.ini` files. You may easily have to adapt this line for other files in your site. Notice the commented line for printing the `Url` property for a file. Remove the comment for help in finding the files that are not appropriate for editing.

The `Edit` method for a `WebFile` object makes its content available for editing. The `insertAdjacentHTML` method actually inserts the new HTML into the currently open document. The method takes two arguments. The first is a positional argument that designates where to insert the new content. There are four possibilities: `BeforeBegin`, `AfterBegin`, `BeforeEnd`, and `AfterEnd`. These apply to whatever HTML element our code invokes the method for. In the sample, this is the body of the web page. This application of the `insertAdjacentHTML` method assigns the new content immediately before the end of the web page. The second argument is the actual HTML for placement in the document.

The invocation of the `Save` and `Close` methods for the `ActivePageWindow` object saves the update to the document and closes page:

```
        ActivePageWindow.Save
        ActivePageWindow.Close
    End If
Next
```

The `For loop` then takes over and goes back for another `WebFile` object if there is one left to open. If not, the procedure concludes by closing the active web.

Programmatically Inserting Images into a Page

This sample is going to enable us to add images to our published categories datasheet programmatically. When we first published this datasheet straight from Access, it failed to include either a link or the actual graphic image in its original Picture column. We now know how to add either the links or the actual graphic images to the datasheet manually. However, re-publishing the datasheet with new data causes the loss of this effort, and in addition, if there are many images to add to a table in one go, programming the insertion of the images into the table will save labor.

The `add_category_image_tags` procedure that follows requires a recently published version of the categories table from the Northwind database. When you publish the table, it will generate a file named `Categories.html` at the site, as we've seen before.

If you have image files stored in another folder besides images, then revise the procedure to reflect their location.

```vb
'Run this procedure after manually or programmatically publishing
'a static version of the Categories table from the Northwind database

Sub add_category_image_tags()
Dim wbf1 As WebFile
Dim pgw1 As PageWindow
Dim myTable As FPHTMLTable
Dim myRow As FPHTMLTableRow
Dim str1 As String
Dim str2 As String

'Get the table in categories.html
Set wbf1 = ActiveWeb.RootFolder.Files("categories.html")
wbf1.Open
Set myTable = ActiveWeb.Application.ActiveDocument.all.tags("TABLE").Item(0)

'Set outerHTML replacement text
For Each myRow In myTable.rows

'Assign the appropriate image filename to str1
  Select Case myRow.cells(0).innerText
    Case "1"
      str1 = "Beverages.gif"
    Case "2"
      str1 = "Condiments.gif"
    Case "3"
      str1 = "Confections.gif"
    Case "4"
      str1 = "Dairy Products.gif"
    Case "5"
      str1 = "Grains and Cereals.gif"
    Case "6"
      str1 = "Meat and Poultry.gif"
    Case "7"
      str1 = "Produce.gif"
    Case "8"
      str1 = "Seafood.gif"
    Case Else
      str1 = ""
  End Select

'If table row is for a category and not a header, then
'update HTML for fourth cell and copy into table
  If myRow.cells(0).innerText <> "CategoryID" Then
    str2 = "<TD BORDERCOLOR=#c0c0c0 ALIGN=RIGHT>" & _
      "<FONT SIZE=2 FACE=" & """" & "Arial" & """" & _
      "COLOR=#000000><img border=" & """" & "0" & """" & _
      "src=" & """" & "images/" & str1 & """" & _
      "width=" & """" & "270" & """" & _
      "height=" & """" & "184" & """" & ">" & _
      "</FONT></TD>"
    myRow.cells(3).outerHTML = str2
  End If
Next
```

```
'Save page revisions and close page
Set pgw1 = ActivePageWindow
pgw1.SaveAs "C:\inetpub\wwwroot\adss\categories.html", True
pgw1.Close

End Sub
```

Again, we'll break down the code and examine it in sections. After opening the file, the procedure will eventually set a pointer to the table on the web page:

```
Set wbf1 = ActiveWeb.RootFolder.Files("categories.html")
wbf1.Open
Set myTable = ActiveWeb.Application.ActiveDocument.all.tags("TABLE").Item(0)
```

Then, it starts a `For` loop to pass through each of the rows in the table:

```
'Set outerHTML replacement text
For Each myRow In myTable.rows

'Assign the appropriate image filename to str1
  Select Case myRow.cells(0).innerText
```

The row of column headers counts as a row like any other row in the table. Therefore, your code needs to account for this non-data row. In addition to that, you must reference table entries by their HTML names. The nomenclature starts with a `Table` object that has a collection of `Row` objects. Each row contains a collection of `cell` objects. The numbering of these `cells` starts with an index of 0.

The main objective of the procedure is to replace the `<BR>` tag and its associated HTML code in the Picture column with some HTML that points at an image. The code starts by assigning an image filename to the `str1` variable. The assignment occurs within a `Select Case` statement:

```
Select Case myRow.cells(0).innerText
    Case "1"
      str1 = "Beverages.gif"
    Case "2"
      str1 = "Condiments.gif"
    Case "3"
      str1 = "Confections.gif"
    Case "4"
      str1 = "Dairy Products.gif"
    Case "5"
      str1 = "Grains and Cereals.gif"
    Case "6"
      str1 = "Meat and Poultry.gif"
    Case "7"
      str1 = "Produce.gif"
    Case "8"
      str1 = "Seafood.gif"
    Case Else
      str1 = ""
  End Select
```

The statement detects the index for the current row in the first column, and it then assigns an image filename to `str1` based on the index value. If there is no index value because it is the first header column or a column value is greater than eight, the `Select Case` statement assigns a zero-length string to `str1`. After the `Select Case` statement, the code examines the value of the first cell in the row:

```
If myRow.cells(0).innerText <> "CategoryID" Then
    str2 = "<TD BORDERCOLOR=#c0c0c0 ALIGN=RIGHT>" & _
       "<FONT SIZE=2 FACE=" & """" & "Arial" & """" & _
       "COLOR=#000000><img border=" & """" & "0" & """" & _
       "src=" & """" & "images/" & str1 & """" & _
       "width=" & """" & "270" & """" & _
       "height=" & """" & "184" & """" & ">" & _
       "</FONT></TD>"
    myRow.cells(3).outerHTML = str2
  End If
Next
```

If its value is not equal to the string `"CategoryID"`, then the procedure creates an expression that represents the HTML code to insert the image file into the Picture column of the datasheet. Otherwise, the procedure just loops around for the next row. The `str2` string expression forms the HTML to insert the image in the fourth or last cell of the current row. This expression depends on the value in `str1`. The loop for any row with a numeric value in its first cell concludes by assigning the expression for `str2` to the fourth cell in the row.

After iterating through all the rows in the table, the procedure saves its updates to `Categories.html` with the `SaveAs` method for the `ActivePageWindow` Object:

```
Set pgw1 = ActivePageWindow
pgw1.SaveAs "C:\inetpub\wwwroot\adss\categories.html", True
pgw1.Close
```

The procedure concludes by closing the `ActivePageWindow` object.

At the conclusion of this procedure, browsers will be able to view images in the categories datasheet. No matter how many times it is necessary to re-publish the Access table, it can always be re-formatted by running a single sub procedure. Furthermore, updates and additions to the collection of images are easy to manage.

Dynamically Publishing SQL Server Datasheets with Access

Access 2000 offers two routes to publishing datasheets dynamically from Access projects. These include ASP and `idc/htx` technologies. In its user interface, Access 2000 refers to publishing datasheets with `idc` and `htx` file types as Microsoft IIS 1-2. Microsoft used to endorse `idc` and `htx` files for publishing databases during the early days of its Microsoft Internet Information Server (IIS). Later versions of IIS shifted toward support for Active Server Pages as the way to provide dynamic server-based content over a web. The release of Windows 2000 included IIS version 5, and it continues to support Active Server Pages as a mature technology for publishing datasheets. Owing to Microsoft's long-standing support for ASP, this section drills down on that technology for dynamically publishing datasheets.

This section covers four topics. These are:

❑   Publishing Dynamic Datasheets with Active Server Pages

❑   Contrasting Active Server Pages Published from Access with the FrontPage Database Wizard

❑   Adding Paging to a Published Datasheet

❑   Specifying Stored Procedure Parameters in ASP

Publishing Dynamic Datasheets with Active Server Pages

This chapter previously showed how to use the Database Wizard in FrontPage to publish datasheets dynamically to the web. This section reviews the procedure for performing the same task from Access. Although both techniques offer .asp files as output, their structure is substantially different. In addition, the extensive development tools for SQL Server from Access make it good to consider Access when rich data development capabilities are important.

Publishing a datasheet dynamically with Access 2000 is not dissimilar to publishing a datasheet statically. However, there are some important factors to bear in mind. Foremost among these is that, just as with the Database Wizard at the beginning of the chapter, we require a mechanism for linking a web page to an underlying data source. Probably the most straightforward way of doing this, as we already know, is via a DSN (data source name) that points at a SQL Server database. You can create a new DSN or reconfigure an existing one with the **ODBC Data Source Administrator** in **Control Panel** in Windows 9x and Windows NT, or the **Administrative Tools** dialog in **Control Panel** on Windows 2000. See Appendix D to review how to make connections to underlying data sources.

> *It is important to understand that the DSN name must work on the web server. Coordinate with your web server administrator to make sure the DSN that you use is available on the web server that houses the ASP web page.*

The example which we're going to look at next publishes the authors table from the pubs database, which sits on a database server called cabarmada, to a web server called cabxli. The cabarmada and cabxli servers are two separate computers. The cabxli web server has a DSN named PubsOnCabarmada that points at pubs on the cabarmada database server. The DSN must exist on the computer that acts as a web server so it is essential that it is specified correctly. The ODBC settings for the DSN that points at the pubs database on the cabarmada database server appear to the right.

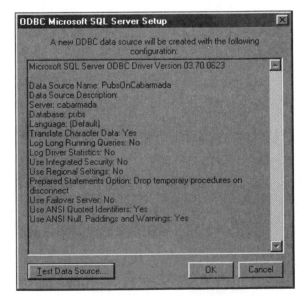

Once we have a DSN, it is very straightforward to publish a dynamic table, view, datasheet behind a form, or return set of a stored procedure without parameters. As we did when with our static publishing, we open an Access project that connects to a SQL Server database. In this example, the cab2200 computer opens an Access project that points at the pubs database on a database server called cabarmada. The following screen shows the Data Link Properties dialog for the Access project:

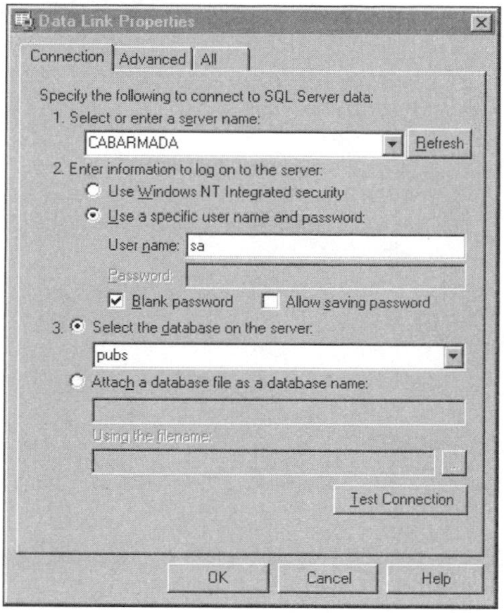

With the Access project open, we then highlight the database object that we wish to publish in the Database window, and then we select File | Export:

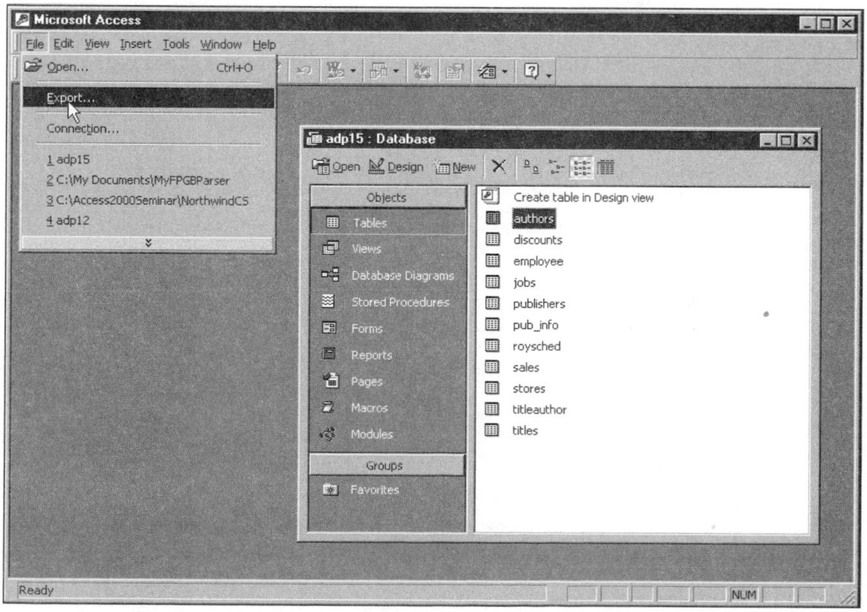

The previous screen shows the authors table selected in the Database window. We can also see the Export menu selection from the File menu of an Access project. We click Export to launch the process of publishing the authors table as an Active Server Page:

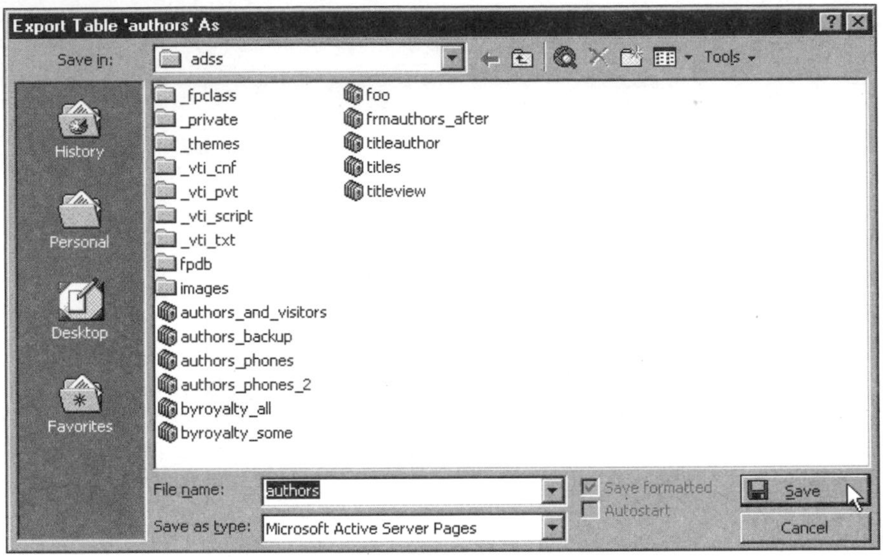

In the Export dialog, we choose Microsoft Active Server Pages from the drop-down Save as type box. Next, we can select a destination folder for the new .asp file in the Save in box. Access automatically inserts the name of the selected object in File name.

If your web server is not locally available, you can save the .asp file in a local folder, and then transport it to a web server later.

Access does not automatically offer the option to preview a published dynamic datasheet, but we can just open the .asp file directly from FrontPage or access it from the server via a browser. Next, we click Save to open the Microsoft Active Server Pages Output Options dialog:

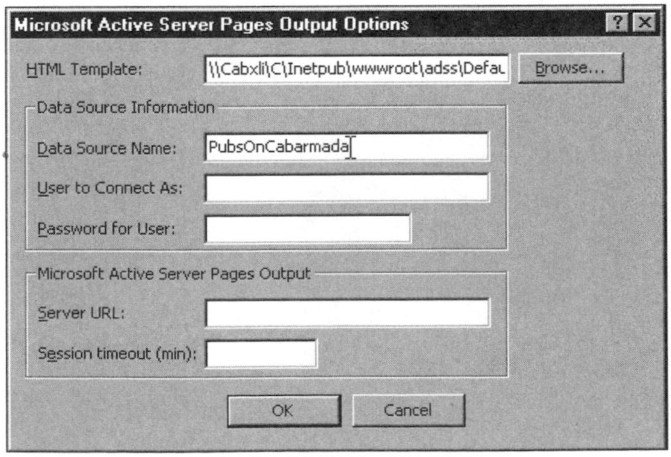

The cursor rests right after the entry of the DSN in the dialog. This is the only box in the process that requires a typed entry.

If we like, we can also use this dialog to designate a web page that acts as a template for formatting the `.asp` file. This works exactly as it does for statically publishing a page. Clicking OK on the Output Options dialog creates the page and saves it in the folder that we designated on the Export dialog.

After that, we are ready to browse the page. The following screenshot shows the browser on the cab2000 computer pointing at the `authors.asp` file on the cabxli server. All the browsing computer requires is a valid HTTP connection to the web server, which in this example is cabxli.

authors

au_id	au_lname	au_fname	phone	address	city	state	zip	contract
409-56-7008	Bennet	Abraham	415 658-9932	6223 Bateman St.	Berkeley	CA	94705	True
648-92-1872	Blotchet-Halls	Reginald	503 745-6402	55 Hillsdale Bl.	Corvallis	OR	97330	True
238-95-7766	Carson	Cheryl	415 548-7723	589 Darwin Ln.	Berkeley	CA	94705	True
722-51-5454	DeFrance	Michel	219 547-9982	3 Balding Pl.	Gary	IN	46403	True
712-45-1867	del Castillo	Innes	615 996-8275	2286 Cram Pl. #86	Ann Arbor	MI	48105	True
427-17-2319	Dull	Ann	415 836-7128	3410 Blonde St.	Palo Alto	CA	94301	True
213-46-8915	Green	Marjorie	415 986-7020	309 63rd St. #411	Oakland	CA	94618	True
527-72-3246	Greene	Morningstar	615 297-2723	22 Graybar House Rd.	Nashville	TN	37215	False
472-27-2349	Gringlesby	Burt	707 938-6445	PO Box 792	Covelo	CA	95428	True
846-92-7186	Hunter	Sheryl	415 836-7128	3410 Blonde St.	Palo Alto	CA	94301	True

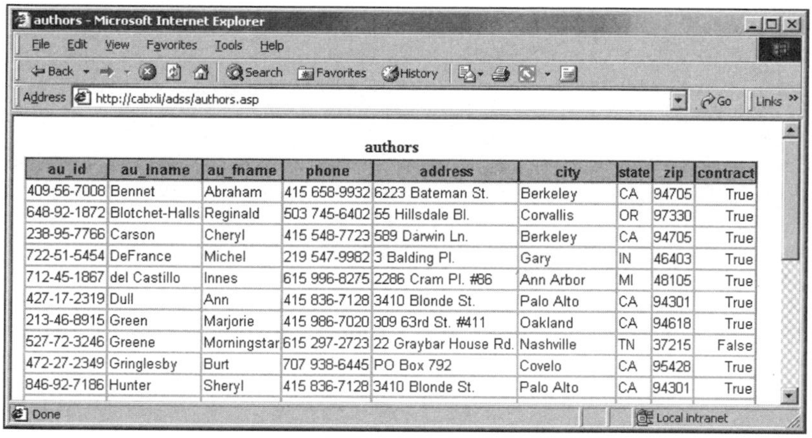

This example demonstrates technically how to have SQL Server share data with anonymous users who approach a web site. Microsoft offers various licensing schemes to support this kind of SQL Server use. Refer to the Microsoft's SQL Server web site (www.microsoft.com/sql/) to find which licensing convention meets your needs.

If anyone changes the contents of the authors table, the next new user to browse or refresh the table will see the change. For example, imagine that a database administrator connects to the pubs database via an Access project on cab2200. This individual can use the project to revise Marjorie Green's last name to Green-Jones. However, the next user to connect to `authors.asp` on the cabxli web server or refresh an existing page will see the new last name for Marjorie Green:

authors

au_id	au_lname	au_fname	phone	address	city	state	zip	contract
409-56-7008	Bennet	Abraham	415 658-9932	6223 Bateman St.	Berkeley	CA	94705	True
648-92-1872	Blotchet-Halls	Reginald	503 745-6402	55 Hillsdale Bl.	Corvallis	OR	97330	True
238-95-7766	Carson	Cheryl	415 548-7723	589 Darwin Ln.	Berkeley	CA	94705	True
722-51-5454	DeFrance	Michel	219 547-9982	3 Balding Pl	Gary	IN	46403	True
712-45-1867	del Castillo	Innes	615 996-8275	2286 Cram Pl. #86	Ann Arbor	MI	48105	True
427-17-2319	Dull	Ann	415 836-7128	3410 Blonde St.	Palo Alto	CA	94301	True
213-46-8915	Green-Jones	Marjorie	415 986-7020	309 63rd St. #411	Oakland	CA	94618	True
527-72-3246	Greene	Morningstar	615 297-2723	22 Graybar House Rd.	Nashville	TN	37215	False
472-27-2349	Gringlesby	Burt	707 938-6445	PO Box 792	Covelo	CA	95428	True
846-92-7186	Hunter	Sheryl	415 836-7128	3410 Blonde St.	Palo Alto	CA	94301	True

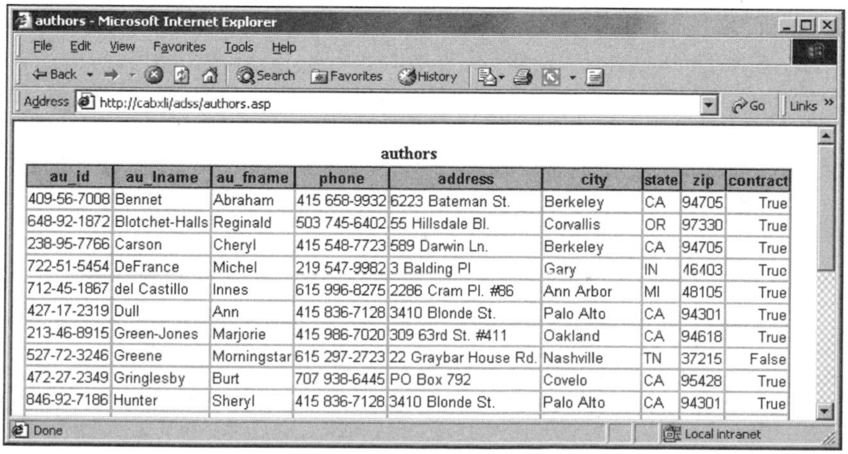

The preceding example specifically illustrated how to publish and use an .asp file based on the authors table in the pubs database. However, the process is essentially the same for views, datasheets behind forms, and row-returning stored procedures with no parameters giving this basic approach broad applicability. A subsequent section illustrates special procedures for publishing .asp files based on stored procedures that require parameters.

Contrasting Active Server Pages Published from Access and the FrontPage Database Wizard

As we've now seen, both the File | Export command in Access and the Database Wizard in FrontPage can generate .asp files. While these files function identically in that they update automatically when alterations are made to the original data source, their structure is radically different. This impacts on your ability to use them as a model for your own custom .asp files.

The Database Wizard is very easy to use, but the code that it generates to support its dynamic datasheets is cryptic. This code does not serve well as a model for your custom development efforts. In addition, the HTML and ASP script consists of value assignments that the code passes to webbots that do the work of making the connection and presenting the result. Unfortunately, FrontPage does not expose the code for the webbots. Therefore, we can see that automated procedures are managing the publication of the datasheet, but we cannot see how FrontPage manages the process. Furthermore, the code that is does expose is very long. This makes it difficult to follow and edit, if necessary, for custom requirements. This limitation forces us to recreate new .asp files instead of enabling us to reuse existing files.

The following is an excerpt from the HTML tab for the .asp file that the Database Wizard creates for the authors table that we just published:

```
<table width="100%" border="1">
 <thead>
  <tr>
   <td><b>au_id</b></td>
   <td><b>au_lname</b></td>
   <td><b>au_fname</b></td>
   <td><b>phone</b></td>
   <td><b>address</b></td>
   <td><b>city</b></td>
   <td><b>state</b></td>
   <td><b>zip</b></td>
   <td><b>contract</b></td>
  </tr>
 </thead>
 <tbody>
  <!--webbot bot="DatabaseRegionStart" startspan
  s-columnnames="au_id,au_lname,au_fname,phone,address,city,state,zip,contract"
  s-columntypes="200,200,200,129,200,200,129,129,11"
  s-dataconnection="Database1" b-tableformat="TRUE" b-menuformat="FALSE"
  s-menuchoice s-menuvalue b-tableborder="TRUE" b-tableexpand="TRUE"
  b-tableheader="TRUE" b-listlabels="TRUE" b-listseparator="TRUE"
  i-ListFormat="0" b-makeform="TRUE" s-recordsource="authors"
  s-displaycolumns="au_id,au_lname,au_fname,phone,address,city,state,zip,contract"
  s-criteria s-order s-sql="SELECT * FROM authors" b-procedure="FALSE"
  clientside SuggestedExt="asp" s-DefaultFields
```

```
   s-NoRecordsFound="No records returned." i-MaxRecords="256" i-GroupSize="5"
   BOTID="0" u-dblib="_fpclass/fpdblib.inc" u-dbrgn1="_fpclass/fpdbrgn1.inc"
   u-dbrgn2="_fpclass/fpdbrgn2.inc" tag="TBODY"
   local_preview="&lt;tr&gt;&lt;td colspan=64 bgcolor=&quot;#FFFF00&quot;
align=&quot;left&quot; width=&quot;100%&quot;&gt;&lt;font
color=&quot;#000000&quot;&gt;Database Results regions will not preview unless this
page is fetched from a Web server with a web browser. The following table row will
repeat once for every record returned by the
query.&lt;/font&gt;&lt;/td&gt;&lt;/tr&gt;"
   preview="<tr><td colspan=64 bgcolor=&quot;#FFFF00&quot; align=&quot;left&quot;
width=&quot;100%&quot;><font color=&quot;#000000&quot;>This is the start of a
Database Results region.</font></td></tr>" --><!--#include
file="_fpclass/fpdblib.inc"-->
<%
fp_sQry="SELECT * FROM authors"
fp_sDefault=""
fp_sNoRecords="<tr><td colspan=9 align=left width=""100%"">No records
returned.</td></tr>"
fp_sDataConn="Database1"
fp_iMaxRecords=256
fp_iCommandType=1
fp_iPageSize=5
fp_fTableFormat=True
fp_fMenuFormat=False
fp_sMenuChoice=""
fp_sMenuValue=""
fp_iDisplayCols=9
fp_fCustomQuery=False
BOTID=0
fp_iRegion=BOTID
%>
<!--#include file="_fpclass/fpdbrgn1.inc"-->
<!--webbot bot="DatabaseRegionStart" i-CheckSum="7685" endspan -->
```

We can clearly see the column headings in the beginning of the `<Table>` element code:

```
<table width="100%" border="1">
 <thead>
  <tr>
   <td><b>au_id</b></td>
   <td><b>au_lname</b></td>
   <td><b>au_fname</b></td>
   <td><b>phone</b></td>
   <td><b>address</b></td>
   <td><b>city</b></td>
   <td><b>state</b></td>
   <td><b>zip</b></td>
   <td><b>contract</b></td>
  </tr>
 </thead>
```

This appears in typical HTML format so that you could use or adapt it if you wanted, but the wizard-generated code soon departs from that model. Notice the reference to a webbot very shortly after the HTML for the column headings. After that, there is a long series of assignment statements. Some of these are in HTML – namely those outside the `<%` and `%>` delimiters. Many other assignment statements are within the preceding delimiters that mark the beginning and end of script within .asp files.

Several other blocks of code populate the remainder of the HTML tab for an .asp file created by the Database Wizard. The wizard organizes these blocks into shorter groups of assignment statements for each column of the resulting table. A webbot reference precedes the assignment statements for each column in the table.

The HTML tab for an .asp file created with the File | Export command in Access is substantially different. One of the most profound differences is that it exposes standard HTML and VBScript. Much of the VBScript relates directly to ADO objects, such as connections and recordsets. Therefore, a VBA developer proficient in ADO can readily interpret the code generated by the File | Export command. In addition, the table itself appears as two parts. The first part prints the column headings. Since Access attempts to emulate the formatting of Access datasheets by default, the formatting of the column heading is lengthy. Nevertheless, it includes nothing more than standard HTML that can be reused when you build your own .asp files from scratch. The second part embeds some HTML code for formatting the columns of database values inside a Do loop that iterates through a recordset until an EOF. Since this is standard programming for VBA developers, the techniques can be readily acquired. This code can be adapted for different tasks because it is typical of the way Access solutions are coded.

The following excerpt is from the script at the beginning of the .asp file generated by the File | Export command for the authors table. Notice that it performs two basic tasks. First, it creates a connection to the database at which the PubsOnCabarmada DSN points. If the connection already exists from earlier in the session, then it reuses the connection instead of re-creating it. Second, the code creates a recordset based on the authors table. If the recordset already exists, then the code again reuses it instead of recreating it.

```
<%
If IsObject(Session("PubsOnCabarmada_conn")) Then
  Set conn = Session("PubsOnCabarmada_conn")
Else
  Set conn = Server.CreateObject("ADODB.Connection")
  conn.open "PubsOnCabarmada","",""
  Set Session("PubsOnCabarmada_conn") = conn
End If
%>
<%
If IsObject(Session("authors_rs")) Then
  Set rs = Session("authors_rs")
Else
  sql = "SELECT * FROM [authors]"
  Set rs = Server.CreateObject("ADODB.Recordset")
  rs.Open sql, conn, 3, 3
  If rs.eof Then
    rs.AddNew
  End If
  Set Session("authors_rs") = rs
End If
%>
```

After reusing an existing recordset or creating a new recordset based on the authors table, the code progresses to create an HTML table. The following excerpt from the page demonstrates that portion of the code within the .asp file.

```
<TABLE BORDER=1 BGCOLOR=#ffffff CELLSPACING=0><FONT FACE="Arial"
COLOR=#000000><CAPTION><B>authors</B></CAPTION></FONT>

<THEAD>
```

```html
<TR>
<TH BGCOLOR=#c0c0c0 BORDERCOLOR=#000000 ><FONT SIZE=2 FACE="Arial"
COLOR=#000000>au_id</FONT></TH>
<TH BGCOLOR=#c0c0c0 BORDERCOLOR=#000000 ><FONT SIZE=2 FACE="Arial"
COLOR=#000000>au_lname</FONT></TH>
<TH BGCOLOR=#c0c0c0 BORDERCOLOR=#000000 ><FONT SIZE=2 FACE="Arial"
COLOR=#000000>au_fname</FONT></TH>
<TH BGCOLOR=#c0c0c0 BORDERCOLOR=#000000 ><FONT SIZE=2 FACE="Arial"
COLOR=#000000>phone</FONT></TH>
<TH BGCOLOR=#c0c0c0 BORDERCOLOR=#000000 ><FONT SIZE=2 FACE="Arial"
COLOR=#000000>address</FONT></TH>
<TH BGCOLOR=#c0c0c0 BORDERCOLOR=#000000 ><FONT SIZE=2 FACE="Arial"
COLOR=#000000>city</FONT></TH>
<TH BGCOLOR=#c0c0c0 BORDERCOLOR=#000000 ><FONT SIZE=2 FACE="Arial"
COLOR=#000000>state</FONT></TH>
<TH BGCOLOR=#c0c0c0 BORDERCOLOR=#000000 ><FONT SIZE=2 FACE="Arial"
COLOR=#000000>zip</FONT></TH>
<TH BGCOLOR=#c0c0c0 BORDERCOLOR=#000000 ><FONT SIZE=2 FACE="Arial"
COLOR=#000000>contract</FONT></TH>

</TR>
</THEAD>
<TBODY>
<%
On Error Resume Next
rs.MoveFirst
do while Not rs.eof
 %>
<TR VALIGN=TOP>
<TD BORDERCOLOR=#c0c0c0 ><FONT SIZE=2 FACE="Arial"
COLOR=#000000><%=Server.HTMLEncode(rs.Fields("au_id").Value)%><BR></FONT></TD>
<TD BORDERCOLOR=#c0c0c0 ><FONT SIZE=2 FACE="Arial"
COLOR=#000000><%=Server.HTMLEncode(rs.Fields("au_lname").Value)%><BR></FONT></TD>
<TD BORDERCOLOR=#c0c0c0 ><FONT SIZE=2 FACE="Arial"
COLOR=#000000><%=Server.HTMLEncode(rs.Fields("au_fname").Value)%><BR></FONT></TD>
<TD BORDERCOLOR=#c0c0c0 ><FONT SIZE=2 FACE="Arial"
COLOR=#000000><%=Server.HTMLEncode(rs.Fields("phone").Value)%><BR></FONT></TD>
<TD BORDERCOLOR=#c0c0c0 ><FONT SIZE=2 FACE="Arial"
COLOR=#000000><%=Server.HTMLEncode(rs.Fields("address").Value)%><BR></FONT></TD>
<TD BORDERCOLOR=#c0c0c0 ><FONT SIZE=2 FACE="Arial"
COLOR=#000000><%=Server.HTMLEncode(rs.Fields("city").Value)%><BR></FONT></TD>
<TD BORDERCOLOR=#c0c0c0 ><FONT SIZE=2 FACE="Arial"
COLOR=#000000><%=Server.HTMLEncode(rs.Fields("state").Value)%><BR></FONT></TD>
<TD BORDERCOLOR=#c0c0c0 ><FONT SIZE=2 FACE="Arial"
COLOR=#000000><%=Server.HTMLEncode(rs.Fields("zip").Value)%><BR></FONT></TD>
<TD BORDERCOLOR=#c0c0c0 ALIGN=RIGHT><FONT SIZE=2 FACE="Arial"
COLOR=#000000><%=Server.HTMLEncode(rs.Fields("contract").Value)%><BR></FONT></TD>

</TR>
<%
rs.MoveNext
loop%>
</TBODY>
<TFOOT></TFOOT>
</TABLE>
```

While this code is reasonably lengthy, it is highly structured. We would need nothing more than this code to generate a datasheet based on the authors table. A standard HTML <TABLE> tag marks the beginning and end of the code. This practice of using standard tags in typical ways extends to the HTML between the beginning and ending <TABLE> tags. A little VBScript extends the HTML.

> *Most HTML tags appear in pairs – one to start the beginning of an element and another to mark its end. You can often control the impact of a tag through attribute settings that occur within it. For example, attribute settings for the <TABLE> tag designate overall border width, background color, and cell spacing. Individual cells within the table can override these general settings. For example, the column header cells marked by <TH> tags have their own distinct border and background colors that helps to set them apart from the remainder of the table.*

A second block of HTML and VBScript combine to present the data-based rows in the datasheet. Inside the HTML formatting tags of this second block of HTML are field names from the data source underlying the datasheet with a beginning delimiter of <% and an ending delimiter of %>. Within these delimiters is a call to the HTMLEncode function for translating standard text values to special HTML codes. Each function call includes a reference to a recordset field. These field names appear in double quotes. The HTML specifying the values of formatting for data-based rows appears within a Do loop. This loop passes through each record within the recordset assigned early in the .asp file.

These two major blocks comprise all the operational code of the .asp file generated by the File | Export command. Furthermore, they perform the whole task of publishing the table in a database to a datasheet on a web page. Subsequent samples, starting with the next one, show how to borrow from and build on the code generated by the File | Export command.

Adding Paging to a Published Datasheet

The sample .asp file presents the data in one table. A very common request from web users is that they should be able to page through the data. The following .asp file extends the preceding sample to enable this functionality.

This section introduces us to the potential of using ASP to create interactive and dynamic pages to display data. It is designed to give us an overview of the possibilities rather than a tutorial in ASP, which is beyond the scope of this chapter. Chapter 10 will provide a familiarization with some initial aspects of ASP, which we can utilize in the publication of data. For a fuller introduction to web development with ASP however, check out *Beginning Active Server Pages 3.0* published by Wrox Press, ISBN 1-861003-38-2.

To add this capability, the following sample in this section makes changes in two areas:

- ❑ It displays the rows from the authors table in blocks of four records at a time.
- ❑ It adds two hyperlinks to the page. These enable a user to signal that they want to move forward or back one page relative to the current page.

Two recordset properties enable us to control paging:

❑ The `PageSize` property specifies the maximum number of records that compose a page. The last page will vary from one record up to the maximum number of records.

❑ The `AbsolutePage` property designates which of the pages in a recordset is current.

As we iterate through the records of a recordset with a `PageSize` property setting, the loop will return just those records for the current page. So we need to set the `AbsolutePage` and `PageSize` properties before launching a loop to pass through a paged recordset.

The sample offers hyperlinks that enable a user to indicate whether they want to page forward or backward. When a user clicks a hyperlink, the code assigns a value to a parameter and calls the current page from the server. Code at the top of the page reads the parameter, which can take any of three different values. The code uses this parameter to compute the `AbsolutePage` property value. One of the parameter values denotes a click of the Next hyperlink. This advances the current page indicator by one. Another parameter value denotes a click of the Previous hyperlink. This subtracts one from the current page indicator. If a user browses to the `.asp` file for the first time in a session, the parameter is a zero-length string because it is not set. This causes the current page indicator to initialize to a value of 1.

The following `.asp` file sample demonstrates specifically how to construct a web page that implements the logic for paging through a recordset as it builds on the preceding sample. New code appears in three areas of the listing. A block of code towards the beginning of the listing determines which link, if any, a user clicks to open the page. In a second block of new code, the new sample replaces the `Do loop` for passing through all the records with a `For...Next` loop that passes through just the number of records on a page.

This second block of code also sets the `AbsolutePage` property before launching the `For` loop to pass through the records for the particular page that a user requests. A final block of code at the end of the listing includes the `Next` and `Previous` hyperlinks embedded in `If...Then` VBScript statements. These statements suppress the visibility of hyperlinks when they do not apply. For example, the Previous hyperlink should not appear when the `.asp` file already shows the first page. The final block of code also indicates which of the pages is current and how many total pages are available from the recordset.

```
<HTML>
<HEAD>
<META HTTP-EQUIV="Content-Type" CONTENT="text/html;charset=windows-1252">
<TITLE>authors</TITLE>
</HEAD>
<BODY>
<%

'Designate a page based on a first call of the page in
'a session or a hyperlink click
  Select Case Request.QueryString("Direction")
    Case ""
      Session("CurrentPage") = 1
    Case "Next"
      Session("CurrentPage") = Session("CurrentPage") + 1
    Case "Previous"
      Session("CurrentPage") = Session("CurrentPage") - 1
  End Select

'Create or reuse a connection
If IsObject(Session("PubsOnCabarmada_conn")) Then
  Set conn = Session("PubsOnCabarmada_conn")
Else
```

```
   Set conn = Server.CreateObject("ADODB.Connection")
   conn.open "PubsOnCabarmada","",""
   Set Session("PubsOnCabarmada_conn") = conn
End If

'Create or reuse recordset
If IsObject(Session("authors_rs")) Then
   Set rs = Session("authors_rs")
Else
   sql = "SELECT * FROM [authors]"
   Set rs = Server.CreateObject("ADODB.Recordset")
   rs.Open sql, conn, 1, 3
   If rs.eof Then
     rs.AddNew
   End If
   Set Session("authors_rs") = rs
End If
%>
<TABLE BORDER=1 BGCOLOR=#ffffff CELLSPACING=0><FONT FACE="Arial"
COLOR=#000000><CAPTION><B>authors</B></CAPTION></FONT>

<!-- Designate column headers -->
<THEAD>
<TR>
<TH BGCOLOR=#c0c0c0 BORDERCOLOR=#000000 ><FONT SIZE=2 FACE="Arial"
COLOR=#000000>au_id</FONT></TH>
<TH BGCOLOR=#c0c0c0 BORDERCOLOR=#000000 ><FONT SIZE=2 FACE="Arial"
COLOR=#000000>au_lname</FONT></TH>
<TH BGCOLOR=#c0c0c0 BORDERCOLOR=#000000 ><FONT SIZE=2 FACE="Arial"
COLOR=#000000>au_fname</FONT></TH>
<TH BGCOLOR=#c0c0c0 BORDERCOLOR=#000000 ><FONT SIZE=2 FACE="Arial"
COLOR=#000000>phone</FONT></TH>
<TH BGCOLOR=#c0c0c0 BORDERCOLOR=#000000 ><FONT SIZE=2 FACE="Arial"
COLOR=#000000>address</FONT></TH>
<TH BGCOLOR=#c0c0c0 BORDERCOLOR=#000000 ><FONT SIZE=2 FACE="Arial"
COLOR=#000000>city</FONT></TH>
<TH BGCOLOR=#c0c0c0 BORDERCOLOR=#000000 ><FONT SIZE=2 FACE="Arial"
COLOR=#000000>state</FONT></TH>
<TH BGCOLOR=#c0c0c0 BORDERCOLOR=#000000 ><FONT SIZE=2 FACE="Arial"
COLOR=#000000>zip</FONT></TH>
<TH BGCOLOR=#c0c0c0 BORDERCOLOR=#000000 ><FONT SIZE=2 FACE="Arial"
COLOR=#000000>contract</FONT></TH>

</TR>
</THEAD>
<TBODY>
<%
On Error Resume Next
'Set parameters for looping by page through recordset
dim i
rs.AbsolutePage = CLng(Session("CurrentPage"))
rs.PageSize = 4
For i= 1 to rs.PageSize
 %>
<TR VALIGN=TOP>
<TD BORDERCOLOR=#c0c0c0 ><FONT SIZE=2 FACE="Arial"
COLOR=#000000><%=Server.HTMLEncode(rs.Fields("au_id").Value)%><BR></FONT></TD>
<TD BORDERCOLOR=#c0c0c0 ><FONT SIZE=2 FACE="Arial"
COLOR=#000000><%=Server.HTMLEncode(rs.Fields("au_lname").Value)%><BR></FONT></TD>
<TD BORDERCOLOR=#c0c0c0 ><FONT SIZE=2 FACE="Arial"
COLOR=#000000><%=Server.HTMLEncode(rs.Fields("au_fname").Value)%><BR></FONT></TD>
<TD BORDERCOLOR=#c0c0c0 ><FONT SIZE=2 FACE="Arial"
```

```
COLOR=#000000><%=Server.HTMLEncode(rs.Fields("phone").Value)%><BR></FONT></TD>
<TD BORDERCOLOR=#c0c0c0 ><FONT SIZE=2 FACE="Arial"
COLOR=#000000><%=Server.HTMLEncode(rs.Fields("address").Value)%><BR></FONT></TD>
<TD BORDERCOLOR=#c0c0c0 ><FONT SIZE=2 FACE="Arial"
COLOR=#000000><%=Server.HTMLEncode(rs.Fields("city").Value)%><BR></FONT></TD>
<TD BORDERCOLOR=#c0c0c0 ><FONT SIZE=2 FACE="Arial"
COLOR=#000000><%=Server.HTMLEncode(rs.Fields("state").Value)%><BR></FONT></TD>
<TD BORDERCOLOR=#c0c0c0 ><FONT SIZE=2 FACE="Arial"
COLOR=#000000><%=Server.HTMLEncode(rs.Fields("zip").Value)%><BR></FONT></TD>
<TD BORDERCOLOR=#c0c0c0 ALIGN=RIGHT><FONT SIZE=2 FACE="Arial"
COLOR=#000000><%=Server.HTMLEncode(rs.Fields("contract").Value)%><BR></FONT></TD>

</TR>
<%
rs.MoveNext
Next%>
</TBODY>
<TFOOT></TFOOT>
</TABLE>

<!-- NEXT HyperLink -->
<%If CLng(Session("CurrentPage")) < rs.PageCount Then %>
<P><A HREF="authors_phones.asp?Direction=Next">Next Page</A></P>
<%End If%>

<!-- PREVIOUS HyperLink -->
<%If CLng(Session("CurrentPage")) > 1 Then %>
<P><A HREF="authors_phones.asp?Direction=Previous">Previous Page</A></P>
<%End If%>

<!-- Print page/page of detail -->
<p><%=Session("CurrentPage")%>/<%=rs.PageCount%>
</p>

</BODY>
</HTML>
```

At the beginning of each of the preceding three code segments as well as selected other code blocks, the .asp file includes a short comment to indicate the functionality provided by lines of code. There are two different types of comment indicators. First, you can insert one or more comment lines in HTML text with the following delimiters.

```
<!-- this is my comment -->
```

Second, you can designate a comment within an ASP script area with a preceding apostrophe. This works just as with VBA. However, you can only use it when you are in an ASP script area delimited by <% and %>.

The code for deciphering which link, if any, a user clicked relies on the QueryString property of the Request object. The Request object is part of the ASP object model. Chapter 10 discusses this in more detail. This chapter selectively applies a few ASP objects for specific tasks. Its QueryString property recovers data passed along with a hyperlink. A Select Case statement reads the value and computes a corresponding one for the CurrentPage Session variable. ASP uses Session objects and variables to keep track of values for as long as a user's session lasts. This is typically from the first page requested by a user in a session through 20 minutes in which there are no page requests.

The code for launching the loop that passes through records will likely be mostly familiar to the VBA developers reading this book. However, the PageSize and AbsolutePage properties may be new.

The page size can be changed by altering the value of the `PageSize` property. This, in turn, modifies the total number of pages from a recordset.

The code at the end of the `.asp` file demonstrates the logic for controlling the visibility of hyperlinks and the syntax for controlling the values that they return to the `QueryString` property. We can create a hyperlink in the normal way with the `<A>` tag. Follow the URL destination for the link with a question mark, the passed parameter value name, and equal sign, and its value. The `If...then` statements suppress a link when it does not apply. This code also shows how to use a `session` variable with a `recordset` property to specify the current page versus the total number of pages in a recordset.

Specifying Stored Procedure Parameters in ASP

When publishing return sets of stored procedures that require parameters, we can only set the parameters programmatically. This is true even if we're assigning a constant to the parameter rather than enabling user-defined values for one or more parameters.

The following code segment demonstrates the syntax for setting the parameter for the byroyalty_some stored procedure discussed earlier in the chapter. This is a custom stored procedure that we added to the pubs database. It returns author and title information for authors earning a specific royalty percentage on a title. The stored procedure requires the user to specify the percentage parameter as a criterion that determines which records are returned. In addition to revealing the syntax for setting parameters, the following ASP code sample demonstrates how to designate constants by their VBScript name rather than their defining value:

```
<!-- Declare language and constants file -->
<%@ LANGUAGE = VBSCRIPT %>
<!-- #include file="adovbs.inc" -->

<!--HTML inserted by FrontPage -->
<html>

<head>
<meta http-equiv="Content-Type" content="text/html; charset=windows-1252">
<meta name="GENERATOR" content="Microsoft FrontPage 4.0">
<meta name="ProgId" content="FrontPage.Editor.Document">
<title>New Page 1</title>
</head>

<body>
<!--Start of custom ASP script -->
<%
'Create connection
'Change the DSN, user ID, and password for your needs
set cnn1 = Server.CreateObject("ADODB.Connection")
cnn1.open "PubsOnCabarmada","sa",""

'Create a command for the stored procedure
set cmd1 = Server.CreateObject("ADODB.Command")
set cmd1.ActiveConnection = cnn1
cmd1.CommandText = "byroyalty_some"
cmd1.CommandType = adCmdStoredProc

'define the stored proc's parameter and value
cmd1.Parameters.Append cmd1.CreateParameter("percentage",adInteger,1)
cmd1.Parameters("percentage") = 50
```

```
'Run stored procedure and assign its return set to a recordset
cmd1.Execute
set rst1 = Server.CreateObject("ADODB.Recordset")
rst1.open cmd1
%>

<!--Borrow HTML formatting code from statically published version of page -->
<TABLE BORDER=1 BGCOLOR=#ffffff CELLSPACING=0><FONT FACE="Arial"
COLOR=#000000><CAPTION><B>byroyalty_some in custom asp</B></CAPTION></FONT>
<THEAD>
<TR>
<TH BGCOLOR=#c0c0c0 BORDERCOLOR=#000000 ><FONT SIZE=2 FACE="Arial"
COLOR=#000000>au_id</FONT></TH>
<TH BGCOLOR=#c0c0c0 BORDERCOLOR=#000000 ><FONT SIZE=2 FACE="Arial"
COLOR=#000000>au_fname</FONT></TH>
<TH BGCOLOR=#c0c0c0 BORDERCOLOR=#000000 ><FONT SIZE=2 FACE="Arial"
COLOR=#000000>au_lname</FONT></TH>
<TH BGCOLOR=#c0c0c0 BORDERCOLOR=#000000 ><FONT SIZE=2 FACE="Arial"
COLOR=#000000>title</FONT></TH>
<TH BGCOLOR=#c0c0c0 BORDERCOLOR=#000000 ><FONT SIZE=2 FACE="Arial"
COLOR=#000000>royaltyper</FONT></TH>

</TR>
</THEAD>
<% Do Until rst1.EOF %>
<TBODY>
<TR VALIGN=TOP>
<TD BORDERCOLOR=#c0c0c0 ><FONT SIZE=2 FACE="Arial" COLOR=#000000><%=
Server.HTMLEncode(rst1.Fields("au_id").Value) %></FONT></TD>
<TD BORDERCOLOR=#c0c0c0 ><FONT SIZE=2 FACE="Arial" COLOR=#000000><%=
Server.HTMLEncode(rst1.Fields("au_fname").Value) %></FONT></TD>
<TD BORDERCOLOR=#c0c0c0 ><FONT SIZE=2 FACE="Arial" COLOR=#000000><%=
Server.HTMLEncode(rst1.Fields("au_lname").Value) %></FONT></TD>
<TD BORDERCOLOR=#c0c0c0 ><FONT SIZE=2 FACE="Arial" COLOR=#000000><%=
rst1.Fields("title").Value %></FONT></TD>
<TD BORDERCOLOR=#c0c0c0 ALIGN=RIGHT><FONT SIZE=2 FACE="Arial" COLOR=#000000><%=
Server.HTMLEncode(rst1.Fields("royaltyper").Value) %></FONT></TD>
</TR>


<%
rst1.MoveNext
Loop
%>
</TBODY>
<TFOOT></TFOOT>
</TABLE>
</BODY>
</HTML>
<%
'Cleanup objects
rst1.close
set rst1 = Nothing
set cmd1 = Nothing
cnn1.close
set cnn1 = Nothing
%>
```

This sample starts with an ASP Directive that explicitly sets the language to VBScript. This allows us to reference the adovbs.inc file. This is a special include file distributed by Microsoft to support

VBScript programming. It is useful to include a reference to this file in ASP applications because doing so permits us to reference VBScript constants by their names rather than their values. This can improve the ease of initially developing and maintaining ASP scripts that use VBScript. For server-side scripting, such as .asp files, use the adovbs.inc that Microsoft distributes from \Program Files\Common Files\System\ado. The include statement at the top of the .asp file references a copy of the adovbs.inc file in the current web folder.

In the context of the preceding .asp file, two constant names appear. These are adCmdStoredProc for designating a CommandType property and adInteger for denoting a data type as an argument in a CreateParameter method.

The main purpose for the preceding sample is to demonstrate the syntax for specifying a parameter for a stored procedure. This occurs in the first block of VBScript within the .asp file. The code initializes a connection based on the PubsOnCabarmada DSN. You must customize this name for your environment.

> *Notice that the sample does not cache the connection for reuse within a session. In a production environment, you will probably want to create a session variable to cache the connection.*

Next, the script creates a Command object, and it assigns the byroyalty_some stored procedure as the CommandText for the command. After creating the Command object, the script invokes the CreateParameter method as an argument for the Append method to the Parameters collection for the Command object. This creates a Parameter object and assigns it to the Parameters collection of the Command object. After this, the code assigns a value to the parameter (namely, 50) so that the stored procedure has sufficient information to create a return set. Then, it stores the return set in a recordset by executing the command object and using it as the source argument for a recordset.

The script moves next to printing the column headings and return set values from the stored procedure. Rather than develop new custom code for this, the sample illustrates how to reuse the code generated by the File | Export command. To reuse the code, copy it into your file. Then, change the column header and field names. That's it!

This indicates how you can expedite your .asp file development through the reuse of code. The .asp file concludes by reclaiming the resources assigned to the objects created within the script.

Programmatically Publishing Datasheets with Access

If you had been wondering about how to publish datasheets to the web based on SQL Server data sources, you should feel comfortable about how it works by this point in the chapter. However, at least one area has not received any coverage. This is how to programmatically publish datasheets. In case you've been wondering, this chapter may have saved the best until the last. That is, programming the publishing of datasheets is remarkably easy. All we need to know is a handful of arguments for a DoCmd method. With this command, you can publish one datasheet repeatedly, multiple datasheets once, or multiple datasheets repeatedly.

Any of these options can save web developers time. Dynamic datasheet publishing is nice, but it can slow the performance of a web server. Every time the server sends out a data-based page, it must refresh its link with the server and re-construct the whole page – whether or not the data has changed. With a statically published datasheet, the server just sends a previously constructed page back to the client. If close-enough updates are acceptable, you can statically re-publish a datasheet once every minute, hour, day, or week. Programmatically re-publishing a datasheet statically can make it behave like a dynamically published datasheet. The main advantage is that the web server can send static pages to browsers faster than dynamic ones.

The `DoCmd` method that we use to publish datasheets is the `OutputTo` method. This same command works for both statically and dynamically published datasheets. While the method does require that we set a handful of arguments, it is very easy to use. First, we specify the type of source for our datasheet. Use an Access intrinsic constant for this. For example, designate a table with `acOutputTable` and a view with `acOutputServerView`. After specifying the type of database object acting as a source for the datasheet, name the database object. A simple string with the name of the object works here. Then, we indicate the type of publication that we want (we use another Access intrinsic constant for this), either `acFormatHTML` or `acFormatASP`.

`acFormatIIS` is also available for the older `idc/htx` technology.

There is just one more required argument. We have to indicate the output file that will hold our published datasheet. The output file argument is actually a full path and file that we specify with a string expression. The next two arguments are optional. The first of these allows you to automatically open the web page with the datasheet after publication. This option only works for statically published datasheets. The final possible argument is a template filename with formatting that you want to apply to your published datasheet. Again, this is a string expression. It evaluates to the full path and filename for the template file.

Microsoft made it so easy to publish datasheets programmatically! The most significant challenge is not with getting the syntax right for the `OutputTo` method, but in how the method is actually invoked. The level of this challenge can vary wildly depending on how you structure your task. The following three procedures work together to publish all tables and views in the database associated with an Access project that have the word "title" in their name. The sample database for this example is the pubs database on the cabarmada server. Three tables and views meet the criterion. These are titleauthor, titles, and titleview. The first procedure, launch_publish_proc, invokes the second procedure and passes it a Boolean argument that designates whether to publish the datasheet statically.

The second procedure, publish_title_tables_views, passes through the return set with the names of all tables and views in the current project. When it finds one that meets the criterion for publication, it checks to see if a datasheet for that database object already exists in a designated folder. A third function procedure helps it to determine if the file exists already. If it does, then it leaves the existing datasheet there without copying over it. In the process, it issues a message saying that the file already exists. Finally, if the datasheet does not exist already, then the second procedure publishes it.

This procedure assumes a local web server. This is how it can check the files on the server.

```
Sub launch_publish_proc()
publish_title_tables_views True
End Sub

Sub publish_title_tables_views(Statically As Boolean)
Dim rst1 As New ADODB.Recordset

'Create recordset of tables and views in database
'associated with the Access project
```

```
rst1.ActiveConnection = CurrentProject.Connection
rst1.Open "exec sp_tables"

'Loop through recordset
Do Until rst1.EOF
'If user-defined table or view contains "title"
  If (rst1(3) = "TABLE" Or rst1("TABLE_TYPE") = "VIEW") _
    And InStr(rst1("TABLE_NAME"), "title") = 1 Then
'Publish it either statically or dynamically
    If Statically = True Then
'Unless the .htm file already exists...
      If Not file_exist _
        ("c:\inetpub\wwwroot\adss", rst1("TABLE_NAME") & ".htm") Then
        DoCmd.OutputTo acOutputTable, rst1("TABLE_NAME"), _
          acFormatHTML, _
          "c:\inetpub\wwwroot\adss\" & rst1("TABLE_NAME") & ".htm", True
      Else
        MsgBox rst1("TABLE_NAME") & ".htm already exists."
      End If
    Else
'Or the .asp file already exists
      If Not _
        ("c:\inetpub\wwwroot\adss", rst1("TABLE_NAME") & ".asp") Then
        DoCmd.OutputTo acOutputTable, rst1("TABLE_NAME"), _
          acFormatASP, _
          "c:\inetpub\wwwroot\adss\" & rst1("TABLE_NAME") & ".asp"
      Else
        MsgBox rst1("TABLE_NAME") & ".asp already exists."
      End If
    End If
  End If
  rst1.MoveNext
Loop

End Sub

Function file_exist(path As String, fn As String) As Boolean
On Error GoTo exist_trap
Dim fso1 As FileSystemObject
Dim str1 As String
Dim filespec As String

'Compose file specification and
'instantiate reference to the FileSystemObject
filespec = path & "\" & fn
Set fso1 = New FileSystemObject

'If you can get file report it exists
fso1.GetFile filespec
file_exist = True

exist_exit:
Exit Function

exist_trap:
```

```
If Err.Number = 53 Then
'If you cannot get file report it does not exists
  file_exist = False
  Resume exist_exit
Else
  MsgBox "Unknown error happened.", vbCritical
End If

End Function
```

Why bother checking for whether the datasheet file already exists? Well, we might want to save it before publishing over it. In any event, if we invoke the OutputTo method and specify the destination for a file that already exists, then the DoCmd object silently copies over the old file. Therefore, checking whether a file already exists is critical if we want to preserve the preceding version of a datasheet. Of course, we could just back up the old file before copying over it. This would be a minor extension of the logic in the preceding sample.

The next pair of event procedures demonstrates how easy it can be to apply the OutputTo method in a meaningful application. The application re-publishes a datasheet every 10 minutes. This happens with only 7 lines of code, and one of those is just for monitoring purposes – it is not essential to the task. Regularly re-publishing a static datasheet enables our web server to work with static datasheets but still have fresh data to issue to clients when they connect. The procedure actually publishes the datasheet behind the form, frmtitleview. The form was created with the AutoForm Wizard and the titleview view. We can see from the Immediate window below the Code window that the Form_timer event goes off every 10 minutes (or 600,000 milliseconds).

The form's TimerInterval property can assume values up from 0 through 2,147,483,647 milliseconds. This is a range of over 24 days, but it is also very granular since we specify time in milliseconds. In addition, the sample re-publishes the datasheet behind the form. However, we can just as easily re-publish any collection of data sources as datasheets on web pages with this same technique. The only requirement is to leave an Access session open with the form open in the session.

509

Summary

This chapter is the book's introduction to web development techniques for SQL Server and Access. Among the technologies gaining focus in this chapter are HTML, Active Server Pages, VBScript, and VBA for manipulating FrontPage and Access object models. The chapter is nominally on publishing datasheets, and it covers this topic from many different angles. We learn how to deliver numbers, text, and pictures in datasheets on web pages. The chapter provides both manual and programmatic techniques for achieving this task. However, the review of the techniques is at least as important as the actual context in which they appear. For example, this chapter introduces Active Server Pages. The next chapter builds on the foundation provided with this chapter as it highlights how to process forms over the web with Active Server Pages.

Creating Forms with Active Server Pages

This chapter equips us to build forms for Web applications that permit users to browse, query, add, update, and delete data. Since many Web applications can maintain the interest of visitors and engender desired behavior via images, the chapter closes with a pair of techniques for presenting images on forms. The enabling technology for all the Web-based data access in this chapter and the preceding one is Active Server Pages (ASP). In the interest of broad applicability, this chapter and the preceding one restrict their development focus to ASP and HTML. Study the techniques from this chapter in combination with those from the preceding chapter to develop a rock-solid foundation for building Web applications that work in a range of browsers.

The presentation in this chapter has three legs. First, we learn the basics of ASP. Its quick introduction exposes us to the kinds of data-based tasks that ASP performs best as well as the main ASP objects with selected prototypical uses for them. The second and third legs illustrate a succession of practical Web-based form applications for working with SQL Server data sources. These samples aim to get us developing Web applications like those we are likely to need in any Web project we undertake. The second leg presents the user interfaces for building robust Web applications that perform data access and maintenance functions. The third leg takes us through the ASP, HTML, and FrontPage design tools to create these applications.

> *Remember that details on starting the Web Server, and finding root folders for Web Servers, is contained in Chapter 9.*

Sample Database for this Chapter

Both of the first two examples in this chapter for the FrontPage Database Wizard will work with any copy of the Northwind or NorthwindCS databases. These examples merely report data from the standard employees table. However, some special tables come into play with the next samples in this chapter.

If you want to download the database, the database and log files are under the names Chapter10Northwind.mdf and Chapter10Northwind.ldb (see below for comments on their format). The samples for this chapter were run on a Windows 2000 server running SQL Server 2000 (hence using IIS 5.0). The following stored procedure shows the paths for the database files. Due to the path length, the @filename1 and @filename2 assignment lines appear split on two lines. In the original stored procedure, they are on a single line. Keep in mind that all stored procedures listed in this book are for input and running from Access projects (unless we specifically note otherwise).

```
Create Procedure attach_chapter10_db
As
EXEC sp_attach_db @dbname = N'Chapter10Northwind',
    @filename1 = N'c:\Program Files\Microsoft SQL
                    Server\MSSQL\Data\Chapter10Northwind.ldf',
    @filename2 = N'c:\Program Files\Microsoft SQL
                    Server\MSSQL\Data\Chapter10Northwind.mdf'
```

The sample database for this chapter, Chapter10Northwind, uses a SQL Server 2000 file format. This format can cause failures with SQL Server 7 and the MSDE that ships with Office 2000. Therefore, you need to use another database than Chapter10Northwind if your database server is either of these latter two. You can use either the Northwind database that installs with SQL Server 7 or the database that installs with the NorthwindCS.adp file. The NorthwindCS.adp file ships with Office 2000. It is not part of the default installation, but the instructions for installing it appear in Chapter 2. It will create a database named NorthwindCSSQL. If you do use either the Northwind or NorthwindCSSQL database, add three sample stored procedures to your substitute sample database. The stored procedure names are create_guest_book_table, create_picture_addresses, and insert_into_guestbook_from_parameters – however, be patient and only add them as you encounter them in the chapter; this way, they will actually mean something when you look at the code!

The listing for this stored procedure exists in the sample database for easy reference. Keep in mind, however, that we cannot run this stored procedure from the sample database. This is because SQL Server will not recognize any contents in the database prior to it attaching the database. Therefore, type the values into a new stored procedure template for an Access project that has a connection to an existing database. Both the pubs and Northwind databases are routinely available with a normal SQL Server installation.

Before running the first set of HTML form samples for this chapter, we may care to re-create the GuestBook table in Access – the following stored procedure listing achieves that. It begins by deleting any prior version of the table. Then, it runs a CREATE TABLE statement to define a table with four columns – one of which has an IDENTITY property and serves as a primary key. Since the database for this chapter includes only a couple of new database objects, we can download the script for this table and several other database objects into any version of the Northwind database that we have conveniently available.

```
Alter Procedure "create_guest_book_table"
As
if exists (select * from sysobjects where id = object_id(N'[dbo].[GuestBook]') and
OBJECTPROPERTY(id, N'IsUserTable') = 1)
drop table [dbo].[GuestBook]


CREATE TABLE [dbo].[GuestBook] (
    [reg_id] [int] IDENTITY (1, 1) NOT NULL ,
    [f_name] [nvarchar] (10) NULL ,
    [l_name] [nvarchar] (20) NULL ,
    [e_address] [nvarchar] (50) NULL
) ON [PRIMARY]


ALTER TABLE [dbo].[GuestBook] WITH NOCHECK ADD
    CONSTRAINT [PK_GuestBook] PRIMARY KEY  NONCLUSTERED
    (
        [reg_id]
    )  ON [PRIMARY]
```

An Introduction to Active Server Pages

ASP is a server-side scripting language that, among other things, enables the creation of dynamic content for Web pages. The technology offers an object model tied to Microsoft Internet Information Server capabilities. Personal Web Server can also interpret ASP scripts. We can use the object model with SQL Server data sources that we create and manage through Access projects to retrieve values from and store values to a database. ASP can handle any OLE DB and ODBC data source, but that is beyond the scope of this book.

Whole books are available about ASP. In order to add value to this huge body of literature, this chapter's objectives are very precise. First, this chapter builds on our initial experiences with ASP from Chapter 9. In that chapter, we learned how to use ASP for publishing datasheets without focus on the ASP object model. The extension in this chapter reviews important elements of the ASP object model. In the process, this chapter introduces new scripting elements that will expand our opportunities for developing with ASP. Second, this chapter specifically focuses on building Web-based forms that tie to SQL Server data sources.

The chapter offers a rich selection of samples that target a very wide range of tasks, purposefully illustrating multiple approaches. For example, in addition to scripting-based techniques, we will also find illustrations of how to use the FrontPage Database Wizard to extract information from SQL Server databases and insert into HTML forms. Of course, we could use other programs than FrontPage to do this – if we already have a knowledge of HTML or ASP then Notepad is a simple but effective program to allow us to achieve our aims. However, within this chapter, we will focus on using FrontPage: it is part of the Office suite, so it will look familiar with the typical Windows controls we all know and love, but it helps us with our Web development techniques without relying on us having an extensive knowledge of HTML or ASP.

ASP delivers three important benefits to Access developers working with SQL Server data sources.

First, we should build applications that work in any browser. This is because ASP scripting executes on the server to create HTML pages. Then, the Web server sends those pages to a browser. Any browser that reads HTML – this is an inherent browser feature – can read Web pages created with ASP scripts.

While it is true that we can embed non-HTML elements in ASP-generated Web pages, developers will frequently build .asp files with just HTML and either VBScript or JScript. Other Microsoft Web technologies, such as Office Web Components, rely inherently on ActiveX objects that are not compatible with most non-IE browsers. Indeed, some Office Web Component functionality depends on the availability of a specific IE browser version.

Second, ASP creates Web pages based on server-side scripts. Since the scripts execute on the server, our code is secure from those who browse our Web pages. Client-side scripting takes advantage of computing power on client computers, but it will expose our scripts to examination by others. In any event, client-side scripting necessarily makes our code available on client workstations. In addition, by writing to a server-based scripting engine, such as ASP, organizations minimize the administrative burden of upgrading to the most recent scripting interpreter. This administrative benefit grows as the number of users grows and the control of browser selection for users diminishes.

Third, ASP enables scripting in multiple languages, including VBScript. Many who are reading this book will have some proficiency in VBA, VB, or VBScript. Since VBScript is largely a subset of VB, Access developers will feel comfortable developing Web applications. In addition, since the code executes on the server, experienced VBA and VB developers experience no diminishment in the compatibility of Web pages with browsers that do not interpret VBScript. Beyond data manipulation, our ASP scripts can also run stored procedures. Stored procedures are pre-compiled T-SQL, and they run on the server. When our ASP projects take advantage of stored procedures, they will be especially fast – also, by running scripts on the server, we will greatly reduce the amount of data going over the Internet, as the filter will occur on the server and not the client.

This presentation on ASP is to expose us to ASP basics that are sufficient to enable us to create HTML forms and use them with SQL Server data sources that we design and maintain with Access projects. Since many Access developers will be using FrontPage for Web assignments because it is a part of Office and ties in nicely with their development background, the ASP review relates to it where appropriate. The presentation does not aim to turn Access developers into experienced Web developers.

ASP Object Model and Selected Components

ASP exposes its functionality through seven objects. Database developers building Web applications with ASP and SQL Server can get by with a subset of these objects (and their methods). The full list of objects is:

- ❑ `Application` object
- ❑ `Server` object
- ❑ `Session` object
- ❑ `Request` object
- ❑ `Response` object
- ❑ `ASPError` object
- ❑ `ObjectContext` object

The last two objects, used for error trapping and processing transactions, are beyond the scope of this book and the first three are touched upon only lightly. More information can be seen in *Beginning Active Server Pages 3.0,* from Wrox Press, ISBN 1-861003-38-2. The focus of the next section, however, lies with the Request and Response objects, which are the main objects we will be using to build Web applications with ASP and SQL Server. First, though, a brief introduction to the Application, Server and Session objects.

The Application Object

The **Application Object** enables the sharing of information among all the users of a custom Web application. Recall from Chapter 9 that the FrontPage Database Wizard automatically creates a global.asa file. Whether we use the global.asa created by the Database Wizard or we create our own, it can work with Application level variables and events to control the behavior of a custom Web application. Variables set at the application level apply to all sessions using an application.

The Application object can serve many specific purposes in Web applications (see the ASP Help file that comes with Microsoft Internet Information Server for more in-depth examination of its uses). One of its uses is for sharing anything across all the users of an application. Database applications can use the Application object to define connection strings and various timeouts. The following event procedure for an application denotes the connection string for the **Database1** connection. This event procedure fires the first time a user starts the application. FrontPage 2000 automatically creates a procedure like this whenever we use the Database Wizard to create a new connection. It places the global.asa file in the root folder for an application. We can use this as a model for our own custom settings pertaining to database connections. If we decide to leave a user name and password in the event procedure for the Application object, then we may care to secure the file so that unauthorized users cannot view it.

```
Sub Application_OnStart
   '==FrontPage Generated - startspan==
   Dim FrontPage_UrlVars(1)
   '--Project Data Connection
      Application("Database1_ConnectionString") = "DRIVER={SQL
Server};SERVER=cab2000;DATABASE=Northwind;UID=sa"
      Application("Database1_ConnectionTimeout") = 15
      Application("Database1_CommandTimeout") = 30
      Application("Database1_CursorLocation") = 3
      Application("Database1_RuntimeUserName") = "sa"
      Application("Database1_RuntimePassword") = ""
   '--
   Application("FrontPage_UrlVars") = FrontPage_UrlVars
   '==FrontPage Generated - endspan==
End Sub
```

The Server Object

The **Server Object** exposes selected Web server capabilities. As we studied the ASP samples from Chapter 9, you probably noticed the CreateObject method. This Server method facilitates the creation of ActiveX Data objects, such as connections, recordsets, and commands. The samples in this chapter will reinforce the earlier ones and reveal the flexibility of the objects in different contexts. In general, recordset sources referencing stored procedures run faster than T-SQL strings. However, we may find it easier and faster to submit T-SQL strings in some contexts. The best choice depends on our project objectives, our programming preferences, the volume of site traffic, and the amount of use that a particular recordset receives within an application. We can also use the `CreateObject` method to set a reference to the File Access Component. Using this component we can read and write directly to files on a Web server. Database developers are likely to prefer databases objects instead of files for storing and retrieving results.

The Session Object

Use the **Session Object** to persist variable values across the page views within a session. `Session` variables can retain their values for the duration of a session. They go out of scope when a session expires (which can be after a set amount of time of inactivity) or a user actively terminates it. We can store database objects as well as both scalar values and stored arrays of values in `Session` variables. Database applications often use `Session` variables to hold database objects, such as connections and recordsets. This speeds performance by allowing the reuse of existing objects from prior visits to a page. Instead of having to re-create objects, our application can check and see if it already has an instance of an object available within a session.

The Request and Response Objects

The `Request` and `Response` objects cover the details of client requests and server responses in ASP.

- ❑ The **Request Object** permits an application to retrieve values passed to a page from an HTML form. This mode of passing data exposes it to users in the HTTP request header. Developers can find it useful when they are debugging an application because it gives them feedback about variables that one page passes to another.

- ❑ The **Response Object** is used to control output to a client workstation from a server. The `Write` method of this object enables a developer to enter content on a Web page. The method writes contents to the page on the Web server before the page returns to the browser. Consequently, users do not see the instructions used to prepare that content.

The more detailed information that we will need to know to use these objects in this chapter follows in the next sections.

The Request Object

The `Request` object provides a number of collections that we can use to access all kinds of information about the client's request to the Web server. However, in this chapter, we will only look at two of them, the `Form` and `QueryString` collections.

Collection Name	Description
Form	A collection of the values of all the HTML control elements in the <FORM> section that was submitted as the request, where the value of the METHOD attribute is POST. Each member is read-only.
QueryString	A collection of all the name/value pairs appended to the URL in the user's request, or the values of all the HTML control elements in the <FORM> section that was submitted as the request where the value of the METHOD attribute is GET or the attribute is omitted. Each member is read-only.

So, what is the difference between these collections?

The Form Collection

If our client-side Web page contains a <FORM> like this:

```
<FORM ACTION="show_request.asp" METHOD="POST">
    FirstName: <INPUT TYPE="TEXT" NAME="FirstName">
    LastName: <INPUT TYPE="TEXT" NAME="LastName">
    <INPUT TYPE="SUBMIT" VALUE="Send">
</FORM>
```

– we can access the values that are entered into the controls by accessing the Form collection:

```
strFirstName = Request.Form("FirstName")
strLastName = Request.Form("LastName")
```

We can see that the METHOD attribute within the <FORM> was set to POST – this means that information is being submitted to the Web server. By using POST, the browser wraps the values being submitted within the HTTP headers it sends to the server. This method is recommended, as it prevents important or sensitive information being exposed in the URL.

The QueryString Collection

If we append one or more name/value pair to the URL we're requesting, they become the querystring for the request, and so are exposed in the QueryString collection. The querystring appears after a question mark (?) placed after the 'main' URL, and each name/value pair is separated by the ampersand (&) character.

The QueryString collection uses the GET method – clicking on a hyperlink, typing an address into the Address box and hitting *Return*, or clicking on, for example, the Favorites button in the browser, all use the GET method to request information from the server to get the information we want. When using GET, however, the browser bundles up the values in all the controls on a form into a querystring, which is appended to the URL of the page being requested. This means that the form values are exposed in the Address box, which can be a security issue if the values are of a sensitive nature.

The QueryString collection is accessed in the same way as the Form collection. The URL and querystring combination:

http://mysite.com/process_page.asp?FirstName=John&LastName=Smith

provides values in the QueryString collection that we can access as:

```
strFirstName = Request.Querystring("FirstName") 'Returns "John"
strLastName = Request.Querystring("LastName") 'Returns "Smith"
strRaw = Request.Querystring 'Returns "Firstname=John&LastName=Smith"
```

The Response Object

An especially interesting Response method is the Redirect method (although this is only one method of many). This method enables an application to redirect an HTTP request to a different page. If our site retires a page, we can leave the page on the server and use a Response.Redirect "new URL" to transfer control to anther page for processing. This practice enables a site to retain visitors who came to a site via an obsolete link.

The following screen presents a page created with multiple invocations of the `Write` method for the `Response` object. It centers a line of text that starts "foo centered with" on a page in several different Heading tags. There are six Heading tags. These typically have diminishing font sizes from the H1 tag through to the H6 tag. Text appears between a pair of tags as follows: `<H1>This is my text.</H1>`. Within a Heading tag we can assign an **align** attribute to center content horizontally within a browser.

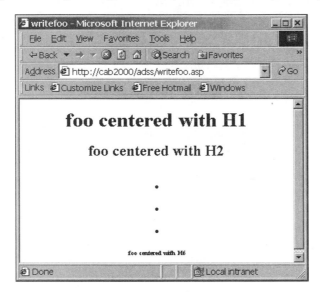

The server-side ASP script for the page appears in the next script segment. The code segment is from the HTML tab in FrontPage; it reveals all the contents on the tab. The HTML tab reveals the syntax for the `Response.Write` method within a `.asp` file, such as `writefoo.asp` in the preceding page. Notice the argument for the `Write` method is a string constant in the script. We can also use a string expression or any variant. However, the invocation of the method must appear within `<%` and `%>` delimiters. Failing to specify the delimiters will generate a failure instead of the output.

The code for the `writefoo.asp` page is very simple, but it appears differently in the browser from on the HTML tab of FrontPage. This is because the `Response.Write` method calls execute on the server and generate HTML that the server then passes to a browser that initiated an HTTP request to a Web server for a `.asp` file.

```
<html>

<head>
<meta http-equiv="Content-Type" content="text/html; charset=windows-1252">
<meta name="GENERATOR" content="Microsoft FrontPage 4.0">
<meta name="ProgId" content="FrontPage.Editor.Document">
<title>writefoo</title>
</head>

<body>
<%
Response.Write ("<H1 align=""center"">foo centered with H1</H1>")
Response.Write ("<H2 align=""center"">foo centered with H2</H2>")
%>
<H1 align="center">
```

```
.<BR>
.<BR>
.<BR></H1>
<%
Response.Write ("<H6 align=""center"">foo centered with H6</H6>")
%>

</body>

</html>
```

We can choose View | Source in an Internet Explorer browser to expose the code for the `writefoo.asp` page – of course, make sure that PWS or IIS is running at the time. Notice that there are no instances of `Response.Write`. However, the arguments for the three `Write` method calls do appear in the HTML for the page:

```
<html>

<head>
<meta http-equiv="Content-Type" content="text/html; charset=windows-1252">
<meta name="GENERATOR" content="Microsoft FrontPage 4.0">
<meta name="ProgId" content="FrontPage.Editor.Document">
<title>writefoo</title>
</head>

<body>
<H1 align="center">foo centered with H1</H1>
<H2 align="center">foo centered with H2</H2>
<H1 align="center">
.<BR>
.<BR>
.<BR></H1>
<H6 align="center">foo centered with H6</H6>

</body>

</html>
```

The FrontPage Database Wizard does Forms

The prior chapter confirmed that the FrontPage Database Wizard earned its title when it came to publishing datasheets. By responding to just five dialogs, we can publish a datasheet of our choice for any database for which we have a connection. If our Web site does not have a connection to a database that we want to use, the wizard makes it very easy to create one. The FrontPage Database Wizard also facilitates the design of forms and a special type of form control.

One of the most popular form controls is the drop-down list, and the wizard makes creating one of these as simple as generating a datasheet. These controls are popular because they automatically enumerate the items in their data source, which can be the employees on a shift, the products in a category, or whatever. The FrontPage Database Wizard, with just a little more work, enables the creation of custom search forms. This type of form enables a user to specify one or more search fields that determine a return set. The search field control is a one-line text box on the form. If our search form has multiple search criteria, then it will have a corresponding number of one-line text boxes. Curiously, the wizard doesn't readily allow users to have a drop-down list control on a search form, but the chapter demonstrates a workaround to this issue later in a more extended treatment of HTML forms.

Adding a Drop-down List Control.

You may recall from the prior chapter that the Database Wizard publishes only dynamic datasheets. Its drop-down list controls are similarly dynamic. This is because the wizard always uses Active Server Pages as a basis for its database reports. While this feature is often, but not always, attractive for datasheets, it is nearly always attractive for drop-down list controls. In general, designers want a list to show all the items in its underlying data source. If database administrators add, remove, or edit items in that source, the drop-down list should instantly reflect it.

The following screen shows a drop-down list generated by the wizard:

We can use the list as either a stand-alone control to itemize the individual elements of a data source or as a control on a form. Here the example shows the list on a Web page by itself. In this mode, it is just a quick reminder of the items in a list (and their properties, such as the spelling for employee names). We can select any item in the list to have it show in the control. This action assigns a value to the drop-down list control when it is on a form. For example, in the screenshot an EmployeeID value is assigned to the control after the selection of an item from the list. While there is actually no way to tell this in the screenshot, we can take advantage of this feature when we use the control in HTML forms. A return visit to this control with a sample later in the chapter will illustrate this capability.

Creating a Control

We can create a control by starting with a blank new Web page in FrontPage. Next, choose Insert | Database | Results to start the Database Wizard. In the first dialog, select a database connection that references the Northwind database. If we do not have such a connection, create a new one (see Chapter 9 for detailed instructions on how to accomplish this).

In the second dialog, select the Employees table. Progress to the fourth dialog by clicking Next on the intermediate screen. Our selection on this dialog uniquely specifies our drop-down list control. Start by highlighting the Drop-down List – one record per item in the top control on the dialog. As mentioned previously, the control has the capability to list one field value, but store another field value after a user makes a selection. In the preceding example, the control lists Lastname field values, but it stores EmployeeID field values. We can choose any fields that we want for displaying and storing from drop-down controls on the wizard's fourth dialog. After making our selections on the fourth dialog, click Next to advance to the final dialog and Finish to close the wizard. The following screen reveals the unique selections in the fourth dialog for creating the preceding drop-down list control:

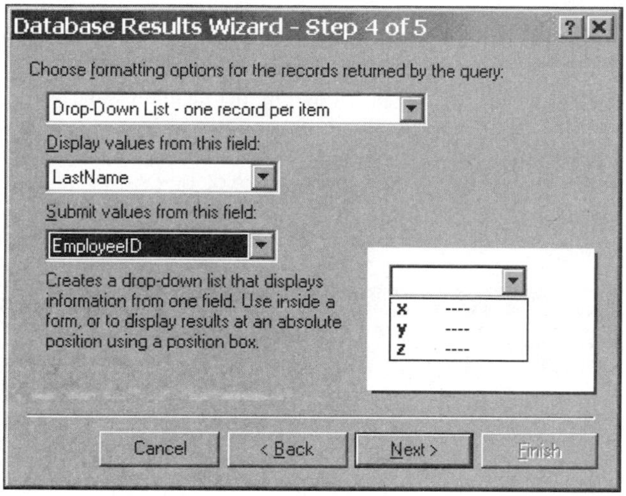

Adding a Search Form

One of the most popular things to do with a database is to look up data. The FrontPage Database Wizard facilitates this kind of task through its ability to generate search forms automatically. These forms enable Web site visitors to enter values into one or more text box controls that, in turn, govern the records that the form returns to a datasheet below the form.

The following search form example demonstrates a form that lets users input a last name and click the button labeled Submit Query to return the contact information for that employee:

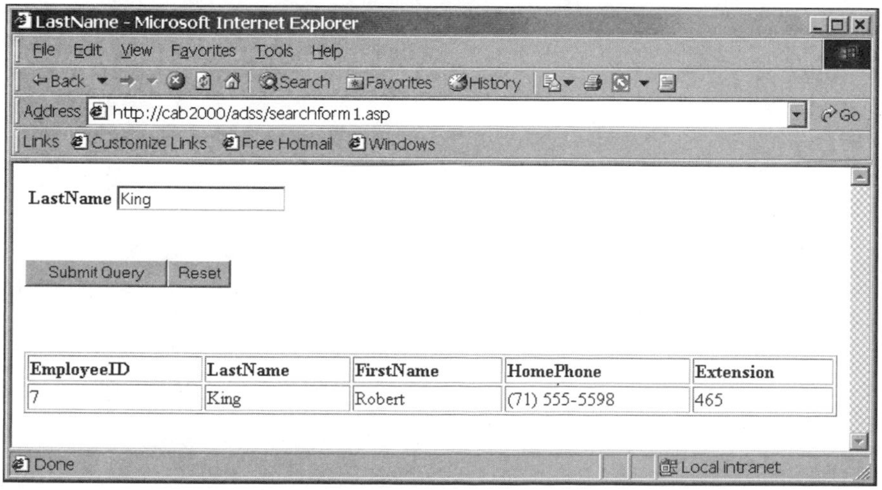

In the example, a user entered King into the LastName control before clicking Submit Query. The list of records below the Submit Query button can contain one record (as in the example) or multiple records. The rows of the list are rows in a standard datasheet that the Database Wizard routinely produces, except that its entries depend on the value(s) in one or more search controls.

Creating a Search Form

Create a new page, start the wizard and complete its first two dialogs as we did for the drop-down list example. On the third dialog, we can edit, optionally, the list of columns that our return set shows below the Submit Query button. Click the Edit List to open a dialog that facilitates this task. The following two screenshots illustrate how we can control which columns a search form returns. The top screen depicts the third wizard screen just before a click to the Edit List. Clicking this control opens the Displayed Fields dialog that appears in the second screen. Initially, the Displayed fields box shows all the column names. We can remove columns from this box to the Available fields box by selecting them and clicking Remove. The second screenshot shows the dialog just before the removal of Photo from the Displayed fields.

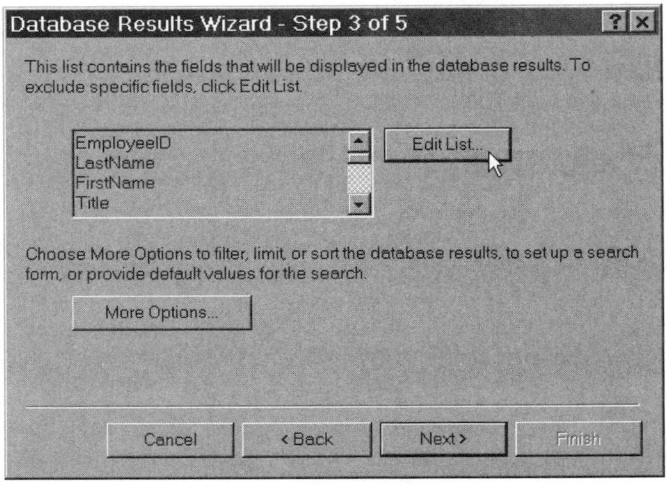

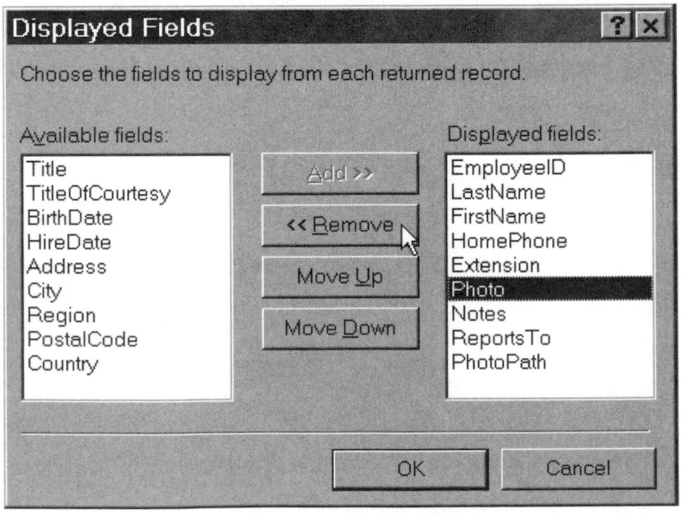

The distinguishing step for publishing a search form instead of a datasheet or drop-down list control is the use of More Options on the third dialog (see corresponding screenshot above). Click this button and then click Criteria to open the Criteria dialog.

This dialog and a sibling dialog enable us to design graphically the criteria for our search form. Start by clicking Add on the Criteria dialog. This, in turn, presents the Add Criteria dialog. Use the controls on this dialog to designate a search criterion field, select a comparison operator that specifies how the form reacts to user input, or designate a default value for a field. We can additionally specify how this criterion relates to any other criteria that we choose to add. Two or more criteria can combine with And and Or operators. The And operator is the default so that it appears even if there is only one criterion as in the example above.

The following pair of dialogs show the settings for the preceding search form. As we can see from the top Criteria dialog, there is one criterion field.

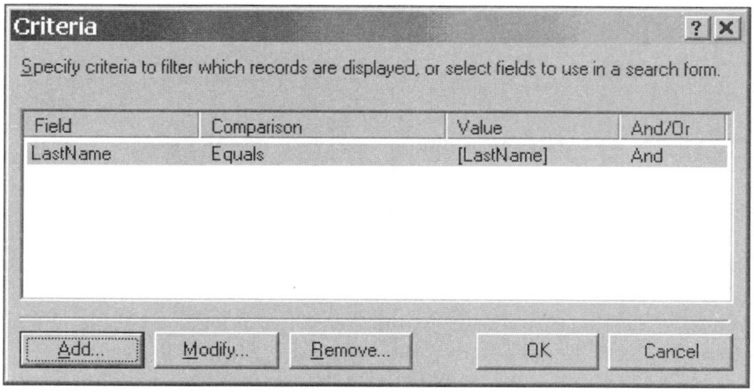

It is the LastName field. It uses an Equals comparison operator so the form returns records matching the value a user enters into the LastName field on the form.

The second form has a Modify Criteria title:

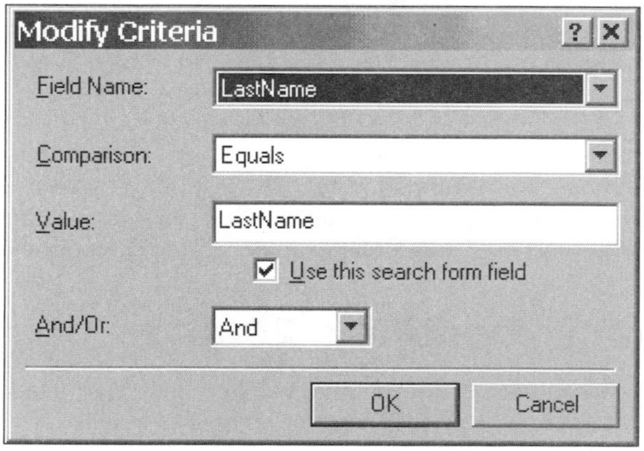

This is because the criterion has already been entered. When initially creating a form, the second dialog has an Add Criteria caption. In any event, the controls are the same as for the Modify Criteria dialog that appears above. Notice the dialog offers drop-down list controls for specifying the criterion field name and its comparison operator. Use the Value text box to designate a default value for the criterion field. If we are going to designate a second criterion field for the search form, we can specify how it combines with the preceding criterion with the drop-down And/Or list control. There is also a check box for specifying when a search field appears on the search form. If we clear this box, then we can specify a default value for a criterion that does not appear on the form.

If we review the instructions carefully, we will discover that they accept the default of 5 rows in the table showing the return set. However, with the Northwind Employees table, we will get just one row for each last name. Won't this look stupid? The answer is no because the Database wizard automatically shows just one row if there are no more rows. The same holds true for 2 through 5 rows. If there are more than five rows, the return set appears with navigating buttons for moving through pages of 5 rows each, and the last page reveals the exact number of remaining rows without any empty rows.

To finish the wizard in this case, OK the options we have just specified and accept the default on the remaining options.

An Introduction to Working with Forms

This section introduces you to the basics of processing HTML forms with ASP. If you are new to HTML (as are many Access and SQL Server developers), then you can benefit from an introduction to form design. Even if you are experienced at Web development, please skim this section because subsequent samples in this chapter will build on the core techniques presented here. The section introduces HTML by describing techniques for graphically creating forms with FrontPage. We also learn a couple of required code-based techniques. The section presents the techniques in the context of instructions for creating a form and then revising it. We additionally gain exposure to ASP script statements for processing form field values. A sample that permits Web site visitors to register by inserting their name and e-mail address concludes the section. This sample inserts form field values into a SQL Server table.

Processing HTML forms with ASP drives home the point that building Web applications is client-server development. The user completes a form on the client workstation in a browser. Since we are using HTML forms, any browser that reads HTML is suitable for this purpose. The form has fields that accept user input. After completing a form, the user must send the form field values from the browser on the client to a program on the Web server that knows how to process them. When we are using ASP to process HTML forms, the server-based program will be a file with an `.asp` extension. It can echo the results back to the user, perform some database operation, such as add a new record to a table, or both.

While ASP obviously does not restrict us to performing database operations in response to form field values, since we're exploring how to build SQL Server solutions with Access this chapter will focus on that kind of activity. The next section illustrates the basics of designing a form so that we can read its values with ASP.

Designing a Form in FrontPage 2000

FrontPage 2000 enables us to graphically design an HTML form on a Web page. From the Normal tab, choose Insert | Form | One-Line Text Box. This adds a rectangle, denoted by a dashed line, which surrounds three controls to the Web page:

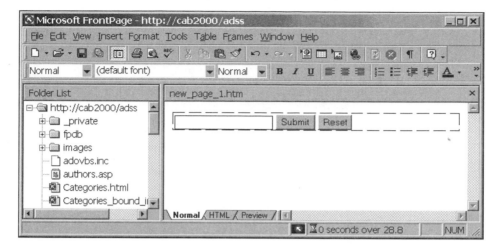

The dashed line represents the form control. The controls include a one-line text box and two buttons labeled Submit and Reset. These buttons are standard buttons on HTML forms. When we click Submit, it transfers the form field's contents from the client's browser to a program on the Web server. This button is essential to the purpose of a form. The Reset button is common, but not essential. It removes user input from form fields and returns them to the original value of the form's field, most likely an empty text box. This action happens locally in the client's browser. It does not involve the server. The one-line text box is a user-defined control. It is our job to create a caption for the text box control and to assign a name to it.

A Simple Address Form

Now let's design a form to enable visitors to register at a Web site by submitting their first name, last name, and e-mail address. Position the cursor just before the text box, then, type "First name:" followed by a space. While pressing *Ctrl*, press the forward arrow key (→) on the keyboard so that our cursor rests just before Submit. Press *Enter* a couple of times to add a blank line between the First name control and the two buttons. Add two more one-line text boxes to the form – one for last name and the other for e-mail address. Then, select the Reset button by clicking it, and choose Edit | Delete to remove the control from the form. This will be one of several steps to simplify the form. After these steps, our form should have an appearance like the following one in the Normal tab:

527

Before doing anything else, reset one of the form's default properties. Right-click inside the dashed rectangle, and choose Form Properties from the context menu. By default, FrontPage creates forms that write their form field contents to a file in the _private folder of a Web site. However, we want a custom ASP script to process the form. Therefore, click Send to other on the Form Properties dialog and select the option that includes a custom ASP script. This selection appears below:

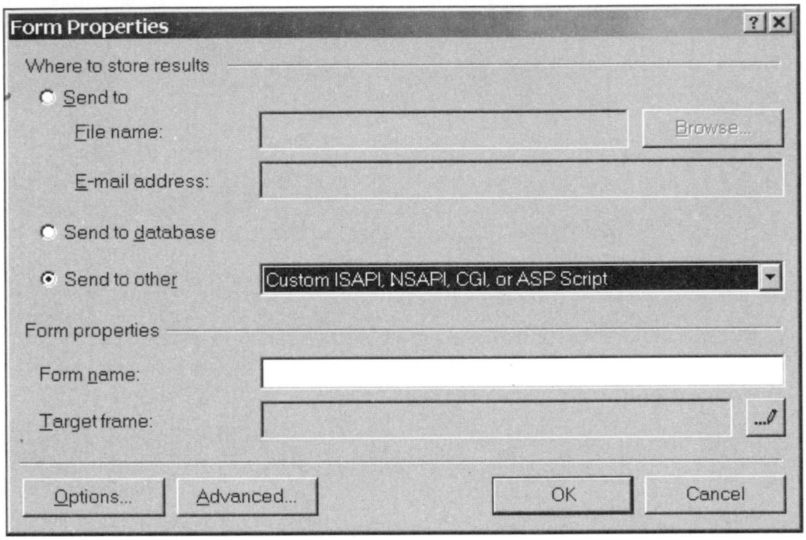

We are now ready to start editing the HTML for the form. In fact, our actions on the Normal tab created a first draft of the HTML that we will ultimately want for our form. Click the HTML tab to expose the HTML source code. The tab should expose some HTML that looks like the following:

```
<html>

<head>
<meta http-equiv="Content-Language" content="en-us">
<meta http-equiv="Content-Type" content="text/html; charset=windows-1252">
<meta name="GENERATOR" content="Microsoft FrontPage 4.0">
<meta name="ProgId" content="FrontPage.Editor.Document">
<title>New Page 1</title>
</head>

<body>

<form method="POST">
    <p>First name: <input type="text" name="T1" size="20"></p>
    <p>Last name: <input type="text" name="T2" size="20"></p>
    <p>e-mail: <input type="text" name="T3" size="20"></p>
    <p><input type="submit" value="Submit" name="B1"></p>
</form>

</body>

</html>
```

The only part that really pertains to our immediate needs is that between the opening `<form>` and closing `</form>` form tags. This code references four controls. Three of these are input controls with a text type. The fourth is an input control. The input control has a type attribute setting of `submit`. This HTML is for the form's Submit button that we saw in the earlier example. The value attribute determines the label that appears on the form as it is viewed in the browser – in this case, just the standard Submit. The HTML for each control resides within a paragraph of its own (notice the opening and closing paragraph tags):

```
<p>First name: <input type="text" name="T1" size="20"></p>
<p>Last name: <input type="text" name="T2" size="20"></p>
<p>e-mail: <input type="text" name="T3" size="20"></p>
<p><input type="submit" value="Submit" name="B1"></p>
```

These paragraph tags result from the use of the Return *key in the instructions for FrontPage to position controls on a form. A subsequent sample will demonstrate a technique that gives us more precise placement control over the position of form fields.*

Modifying the Form

We need to make several edits to the starter HTML that FrontPage writes:

1. We will want to designate an ASP file path for the form's contents to be posted to for processing.

2. It will be useful to rename the text box controls with something more meaningful in terms of our application. For example, the field named T1 collects the first name of registrants. Since the `GuestBook` table that this form will eventually populate assigns values to a column of first names, we could conveniently change T1 to f_name. We can rename the other two text boxes so they correspond with the database table that we will use in the form: l_name and e_address.

3. We will want to resize the text boxes so that they accept no more than the maximum number of characters for a field. Since some fields can have a maximum width that is well beyond the width of most fields, we may prefer to distinguish between display width and maximum input width. When we add a maxlength attribute setting to a text box control, it controls the upper limit of characters in a text box. The size control determines the display width of a text box. If a user inputs more than the display width then the text box window scrolls up to the maxlength setting.

The code below shows the edited HTML:

```
<form method="POST" action="gotform.asp">
    <p>First name: <input type="text" name="f_name" size="10" maxlength="10"></p>
    <p>Last name: <input type="text" name="l_name" size="15" maxlength="20"></p>
    <p>e-mail: <input type="text" name="e_address" size="30" maxlength="50"></p>
    <p><input type="submit" value="Submit" name="B1"></p>
</form>
```

HTML allows two legitimate settings for a form's method attribute; The preceding example uses the **POST** setting. The other setting is **GET**.

The POST method transfers the form's field values in the body of an HTTP transmittal to a Web server. We can use the Form collection of the Request object to extract form field values with a .asp file from a form submitted to a Web server. Examples of the syntax appear in several examples throughout the remainder of this chapter. These examples give us a chance to see the forms with their corresponding Request object syntax.

The GET method transfers a form's field values after the URL in an HTTP transmittal. The URL and its trailing form field values appear in the **Address** box of a browser. Web developers frequently refer to this string as the HTTP request header. Recall that we can use the QueryString collection of the Request object to extract information from after the URL. When working with forms, we will often want to use the POST method, since it can keep our passed form field values out of a browser's **Address** box. For the sake of completeness, a sample in this chapter demonstrates the use of the QueryString collection for capturing form field values.

First, we'll assign a destination file to process the form's contents. We use the attributes of the form tag to determine where and how the information is sent once the user clicks the **Submit** button in the browser. The action attribute points at an .asp file in the same folder as the form. Its name is gotform.asp. We'll be looking at this file in just a moment. The main point is that we must use the action attribute to point at the .asp file that will process the form.

Second, the name attributes of the three text boxes have now been renamed in accordance with the columns in the GuestBook table. This makes it easy to know which text box values belong in which columns.

Third, the edited form has new size attribute settings that reflect common entries in their fields. In addition, each text box field has a **maxlength** attribute setting that matches the maximum number of characters its corresponding GuestBook column permits. We can review the T-SQL for creating the GuestBook table to confirm this.

Finally, after making these changes to the original HTML, save our Web page as reg_input.htm.

Viewing the Form

We can open the form in a browser by clicking the **Preview in Browser** control on the HTML toolbar. If we fill out the form with our name and an e-mail address, the form will look something like the following screenshot:

The form field controls will permit users to enter values into them and click Submit. The Submit button will transfer the form field values to a file called gotform.asp that processes them. This won't work at the present stage, however, because we have yet to build gotform.asp.

Before we move on, we can tidy up the form by aligning the form controls and giving the form a more appropriate title.

Aligning the Form Controls

Form Controls can be aligned giving the form a neater appearance that encourages users to complete it. There are a number of techniques for the alignment of form controls. Placing the form controls and their captions in separate table cells is one of the easiest and most universally applicable ways of achieving this result with browsers.

Open reg_input.htm in FrontPage and position the cursor just before the first caption. Then, choose Table | Insert | Table. Use the Insert Table dialog to specify a table with 4 rows and 2 columns. In general, we will want a separate row for each control and two columns – one for the label captions and a second one for text box controls.

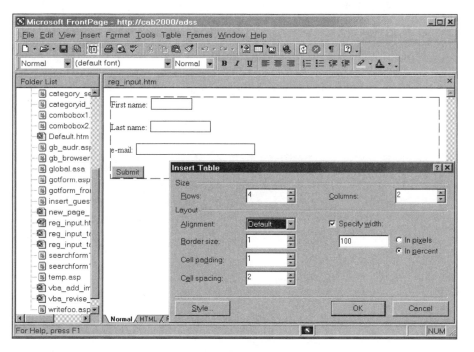

As the screenshot reveals, the dialog enables the setting of several other table attributes. We can reset the table's border size to 0 from the default setting of 1. This modification makes the table's border invisible when users view the form in a browser, but we can still see and manipulate its overall table and cell boundaries from the Normal tab in FrontPage.

After adding the table to the form by clicking OK on the Insert Table dialog, we can cut and paste the text box controls into the table's second column. Reserve the table's first column for the text box captions and the Submit button. FrontPage permits us to graphically re-size column widths by dragging the line between columns. After repositioning the controls, we will have four blank lines just below the table. We can remove these by positioning our cursor in the first blank line and choosing Edit | Delete. Repeat this for the other three blank lines to remove them as well (or just select them in one step for deletion).

We can further refine the appearance of the form by right-aligning the contents of the first column. Select the whole column by positioning the cursor just above the top cell in the table. The mouse cursor turns to a down arrow. Click the mouse to select the whole column and highlight its cells (see the following screen). Then, click the Right Align control on the Formatting toolbar in the Normal tab to make the contents of the first column flush with the right border. The following screen shows the column selected, but not yet right-aligned. The screenshot after the one below reveals the text in the selected column as right aligned.

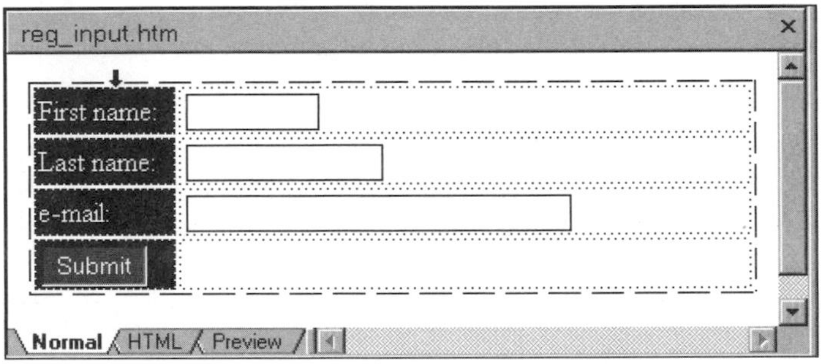

There is one last task to perform from the Normal tab – change the page's title from the one that FrontPage automatically assigned. Right-click anywhere in the form, and choose Page Properties from the context menu. Then, enter a new title on the General tab of the Page Properties dialog, such as "Informative Title created by the Great Web Development Company".

The following screen shows the re-designed form in the `reg_input_table.htm` file:

Notice that the text boxes align on their left edge. These controls are aligning with the left edge of the table cells that contain them. This is the default alignment for a text box. In addition, the captions for the text boxes and the Submit button right-align. This alternative alignment positions the captions closer to their values in the text boxes. The instructions for creating the form include a special alignment setting to achieve this result. Notice the title in the browser; this reflects the page title assignment for the revised form.

Reading Form Field Values

As we mentioned before, Clicking Submit on the preceding form in a browser or from the Preview tab of FrontPage transfers control to the `gotform.asp` file on the Web server. This was the destination file we set for the form's action attribute. The output to a browser from this file appears next:

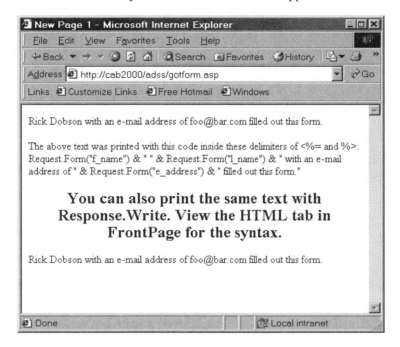

Notice that this page essentially displays the contents of the user's form within some surrounding text. In addition, the ASP script for the page illustrates how to retrieve form field values. We will need this critical capability when we use forms in coordination with databases.

The code for the body section from the `gotform.asp` page follows:

```
<body>
<!-- Start of Body section -->

<!-- Use Request.Form("fieldname") inside of special delimiters to expose form
field values on a page -->
<%= Request.Form("f_name") & " " & Request.Form("l_name") & " with an e-mail
address of " & Request.Form("e_address") & " filled out this form." %>
<BR><BR>The above text was printed with this code inside these delimiters of
&lt;%= and %&gt;: <BR>
Request.Form("f_name") & " " & Request.Form("l_name") & " with an e-mail address
of " & Request.Form("e_address") & " filled out this form."


<!-- You can alternatively use Response.Write(Request.Form("fieldname")) -->
<%
Response.Write ("<H2 align=""center"">You can also print the same text with
Response.Write. View the HTML tab in FrontPage for the syntax.</H2>")
```

```
Response.Write (Request.Form("f_name") & " " & Request.Form("l_name") & " with an
e-mail address of " & Request.Form("e_address") & " filled out this form.")
%>
</body>
```

Notice from the code in the bottom portion of the page that we can also mix `Request.Form` output with HTML code. The argument for the last `Write` method in the lower portion of the page illustrates the mixing of `Request.Form` with standard HTML. In this case, the HTML appears as text strings, but we can mix `Request.Form` with HTML tags as well.

`Write` method calls must be embedded within <% and %> delimiters.

Recall that the argument for the `Write` method can be any variant value or expression. As we can see from the preceding example, the expression can even include a `Request.Form` value.

Submitting the Form Fields – the Method Attribute

The form's `Method` attribute enables the transfer of user information entered into the form's fields over the server to the `gotform.asp` file. The setting for this form attribute can impact on the design of the program that processes the form's field values. The settings of `POST` and `GET` are the only two legitimate ones for a form's `Method` attribute.

Recall that the default is `POST` and currently our example uses this setting. We're now going to change this to `GET` to compare the two method settings.

There are two impacts of switching from `POST` to `GET`. First, the `GET` method transfers form field values by appending them after the URL of the destination file. This means that the values appear in the **Address** box. When we are debugging an application, we may find it convenient to be able to view the passed form field values in the **Address** box. However, when we go live, it does mean that everyone can see the information passed, so if there is any sensitive information passed which has been generated by the site, `GET` is not an advisable method.

Second, when our application accesses the form's field values, it uses the `QueryString`, rather than the `Form`, collection for the `Request` object. The application must extract values with `Request.QueryString` instead of `Request.Form`. After presenting sample output in a browser window based on `Request.QueryString`, we will see the code that generates the browser contents.

Neither of these consequences directly impacts on the Web page containing the form unless that page also processes the form's field values.

In this example, we need to update the form's action attribute setting from "gotform.asp" to "gotform_from_get.asp" as we will be creating a new `.asp` page to process the form fields' contents via the `QueryString` collection. After modifying the method attribute of the form to `get`, re-save the Web page containing the form with a new name – for example, `reg_input_table.htm`.

Clicking the **Submit** button on the new page's form in the browser replaces it with the output from the corresponding new form processor, `gotform_from_get.asp`, which is shown opposite.

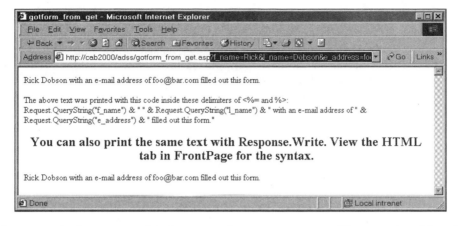

Notice the content in the page matches the content from `gotform.asp`. However, the address box includes a querystring – a series of form field names and values after the URL for the `.asp` file. A question mark (?) intervenes between the URL for the `.asp` file and the querystring. The names and values appear in the address due to switching the form's `Method` attribute setting from `POST` to `GET`.

The following excerpt from `gotform_from_get.asp` illustrates the syntax for using `Request.QueryString` to generate the sample output in the preceding browser screen :

```
<body>
<!-- Start of Body section -->

<!-- Use Request.Form("fieldname") inside of special delimiters to expose form
field values on a page -->
<%= Request.QueryString("f_name") & " " & Request.QueryString("l_name") & " with
an e-mail address of " & Request.QueryString("e_address") & " filled out this
form." %>
<BR><BR>The above text was printed with this code inside these delimiters of
&lt;%= and %&gt;: <BR>
Request.QueryString("f_name") & " " & Request.QueryString("l_name") & " with an e-
mail address of " & Request.QueryString("e_address") & " filled out this form."


<!-- You can alternatively use Response.Write(Request.QueryString("fieldname")) --
>
<%
Response.Write ("<H2 align=""center"">You can also print the same text with
Response.Write. View the HTML tab in FrontPage for the syntax.</H2>")
Response.Write (Request.QueryString("f_name") & " " &
Request.QueryString("l_name") & " with an e-mail address of " &
Request.QueryString("e_address") & " filled out this form.")
%>
</body>
```

Inserting a New Registrant

So we've seen alternative techniques for formatting a form and both methods for processing its information, but neither sample performs any database tasks, such as inserting a record in a table. However, the form clearly targets the insertion of a new registrant in a table. This section illustrates how to pass the form field values on to the GuestBook table in the Chapter10Northwind database.

The sample code assumes the availability of a DSN named **Chapter10Northwind** that points at the **Chapter10Northwind** database from the Web server. If you are using one of the two alternative sample databases for this chapter, namely **Northwind** or **NorthwindCSSQL**, create a DSN named **Chapter10Northwind** that points at your alternative sample database. That will let you use the chapter's program listings with your alternative database.

In order for the form application to work, two functions need to take place.

First, our application needs to have a Web page that gathers input from a form. The sample form file for this demonstration uses `reg_input_table_insert.htm` (see below).

The file that gathers input must pass it off to a second file, which can process the information and use it to update the **GuestBook** table. Two form attribute settings control this – namely, the `Action` attribute and the `Method` attribute. The `Action` attribute points at the file that processes the form field values. The `Method` attribute sends the file in either the HTTP request header or body.

The following code excerpt presents the body HTML for the `reg_input_table_insert.htm` file. As we can see, the code deposits the form's field values to `insert_guest.asp` in the same Web folder as the form file. In addition, it has a `POST` method setting. This means that `insert_guest.asp` must use `Request.Form` to extract form field values.

```
<body>

<form method="post" action="insert_guest.asp">
    <table border="0" width="100%">
        <tr>
            <td width="20%" align="right">First name: </td>
            <td width="80%"> <input type="text" name="f_name" size="10"
                                                maxlength="10"></td>
        </tr>
        <tr>
            <td width="20%" align="right">Last name: </td>
            <td width="80%"> <input type="text" name="l_name" size="15"
                                                maxlength="20"></td>
        </tr>
        <tr>
            <td width="20%" align="right">e-mail: </td>
            <td width="80%"> <input type="text" name="e_address" size="30"
                                                maxlength="50"></td>
        </tr>
        <tr>
            <td width="20%" align="right"><input type="submit" value="Submit"
                                                name="B1"></td>
            <td width="80%"></td>
        </tr>
    </table>
</form>

</body>
```

The `insert_guest.asp` file accepts the form field values with `Request.Form`. It relies on a stored procedure to add the new record to the **GuestBook** table. The stored procedure has the name `insert_into_GuestBook_from_parameters`. The T-SQL code for the stored procedure appears below:

```
Alter Procedure insert_into_GuestBook_from_parameters
@f_name nvarchar(10),
@l_name nvarchar(20),
@e_address nvarchar(50)
As
INSERT GuestBook Values(@f_name, @l_name, @e_address)
```

The code merely invokes an `INSERT` statement. Aside from that core feature, its most important characteristic is that it relies on parameters. These parameters enable an application to gather input from an HTML form and then pass it on to the procedure as parameters for insertion into the table.

This technique of using stored procedures that rely on parameters is a powerful one for updating SQL Server data sources. Stored procedures run very quickly since SQL Server runs compiled code. There is no need to pass a T-SQL string, compile it, and execute it to generate a return set. Instead, an application can just accept passed parameters and generate a return set.

> *Passing parameters to a stored procedure can sometimes lead to some tedious ADO code. In order to keep the remaining samples (after the next one) in this chapter easy to follow and highlight the ASP elements of coding, stored procedures with parameters aren't being used.*
>
> *As we saw Chapter 6, in selected production applications, we can save time with by using stored procedures. These time savings are most evident when a stored procedure is called many times in a short interval.*

The code for `insert_guest.asp` appears next (don't forget to put `adovbs.inc` with the rest of the files):

```
<!-- Declare language and constants file -->
<%@ LANGUAGE = VBSCRIPT %>
<!-- #include file="adovbs.inc" -->

<html>

<head>
<meta http-equiv="Content-Type" content="text/html; charset=windows-1252">
<meta name="GENERATOR" content="Microsoft FrontPage 4.0">
<meta name="ProgId" content="FrontPage.Editor.Document">
<title>New Page 1</title>
</head>

<body>
<!--Start of custom ASP script -->
<%
'Create connection
'Change the DSN, userid, and password for your needs
set cnn1 = Server.CreateObject("ADODB.Connection")
cnn1.open "Chapter10Northwind","sa",""

'Create a command for the stored procedure
set cmd1 = Server.CreateObject("ADODB.Command")
set cmd1.ActiveConnection = cnn1
```

```
cmd1.CommandText = "insert_into_GuestBook_from_parameters"
cmd1.CommandType = adCmdStoredProc

'define the stored proc's parameter and value
cmd1.Parameters.Append cmd1.CreateParameter("f_name",adVarChar,adParamInput,10)
cmd1.Parameters("f_name") = Request.Form("f_name")
cmd1.Parameters.Append cmd1.CreateParameter("l_name",adVarChar,adParamInput,20)
cmd1.Parameters("l_name") = Request.Form("l_name")
cmd1.Parameters.Append cmd1.CreateParameter("e_address",adVarChar,adParamInput,50)
cmd1.Parameters("e_address") = Request.Form("e_address")

'Run stored procedure to insert values in form into GuestBook table
cmd1.Execute

'Cleanup
set cmd1 = Nothing
cnn1.close
set cnn1 = Nothing

'Develop string for feedback
Dim str1
str1 = "Record for <BR> f_name: " & Request.Form("f_name") & "<BR>"
str1 = str1 & "l_name: " & Request.Form("l_name") & "<BR>"
str1 = str1 & "e_address: " & Request.Form("e_address") & "<BR>"
str1 = str1 & " successfully inserted."
Response.Write(str1)
%>

</body>

</html>
```

Its first two lines include a comment and a directive that specifies VBScript as the language for creating ASP script code in the sample. The third line references the adovbs.inc file that permits the use of constant names when scripting ADO objects in an ASP file. Chapter 9 describes the use of this file in ASP scripts.

```
<!-- Declare language and constants file -->
<%@ LANGUAGE = VBSCRIPT %>
<!-- #include file="adovbs.inc" -->
```

The insert_guest.asp expects the include file to be in the same folder as the one that it also occupies.

The main part of the ASP script does not begin until the initial body tag. This code passes sequentially through a series of segments. For example, the initial segment makes a connection to the Chapter10Northwind database:

```
<%
'Create connection
'Change the DSN, userid, and password for your needs
set cnn1 = Server.CreateObject("ADODB.Connection")
cnn1.open "Chapter10Northwind","sa",""
```

First, it uses the CreateObject method for the ASP Server object to instantiate a variable that points at a connection. Then, it uses the Open method for the Connection object to reference the same database at which the Chapter10Northwind DSN points.

The next three segments work together to run the `insert_into_GuestBook_from_parameters` stored procedure from the `insert_guest.asp` file:

```
set cmd1 = Server.CreateObject("ADODB.Command")
set cmd1.ActiveConnection = cnn1
cmd1.CommandText = "insert_into_GuestBook_from_parameters"
cmd1.CommandType = adCmdStoredProc
```

The first segment creates an ADO Command object. It sets properties for this object so that it uses the `Connection` previously created, and it specifically references the `insert_into_GuestBook_from_parameters` stored procedure. By itself, this is insufficient to run the stored procedure. That's because the procedure requires parameters. Therefore, the next code segment creates the `Parameter` objects for the stored procedure:

```
cmd1.Parameters.Append cmd1.CreateParameter("f_name",adVarChar,adParamInput,10)
cmd1.Parameters("f_name") = Request.Form("f_name")
cmd1.Parameters.Append cmd1.CreateParameter("l_name",adVarChar,adParamInput,20)
cmd1.Parameters("l_name") = Request.Form("l_name")
cmd1.Parameters.Append cmd1.CreateParameter("e_address",adVarChar,adParamInput,50)
cmd1.Parameters("e_address") = Request.Form("e_address")
```

The code requires three of these – one for each form field value. Notice the use of the `Request.Form` statement to assign form field values to the stored procedure parameters.

In the third segment, the code executes the `Command` object. This invokes the stored procedure with the parameters assigned in the preceding segment:

```
cmd1.Execute
```

If the ASP successfully executes the `Command` object, we are ready to exit the `.asp` file after a little housekeeping. While the scope of the `Command` and `Connection` objects is just for the current page, it is always good practice to close objects where appropriate by setting them to `Nothing` when they are no longer necessary:

```
set cmd1 = Nothing
cnn1.close
set cnn1 = Nothing
```

Users normally appreciate some feedback about the outcome of their actions. If the `Execute` command fails (for example, because the connection to the server is not open), then an error message appears automatically. However, if the `Execute` command succeeds, ASP provides no feedback beyond what we provide through our custom code. Therefore, the sample concludes with a message to confirm the insertion of the new registrant into the database:

```
Dim str1
str1 = "Record for <BR> f_name: " & Request.Form("f_name") & "<BR>"
str1 = str1 & "l_name: " & Request.Form("l_name") & "<BR>"
str1 = str1 & "e_address: " & Request.Form("e_address") & "<BR>"
str1 = str1 & " successfully inserted."
Response.Write(str1)
%>
```

By the way, this final segment reveals one approach to handling long lines without a continuation character. It simply builds the string message confirming the new record incrementally before using it as the argument of a Response.Write *statement. The string message in this sample includes HTML code (namely, the* BR *tag) and ASP script (namely,* Request.Form*) concatenated with standard text. Building statements in this way makes it easier to maintain them.*

The following series of four screens chronicles the operation of the application to insert a new record. It starts with a view of the GuestBook table from the Chapter10Northwind Access project before inserting a new registrant named Elvis Presley:

Next, it shows the reg_input_table_insert.htm file with a form populated with data for Mr. Presley:

The third screen reveals the feedback that insert_guest.asp sends back to a browser:

The final member of the set reveals the `GuestBook` table from Access after the insertion of Mr. Presley:

reg_id	f_name	l_name	e_address
1	Rick	Dobson	foo@bar.com
2	Tony	Hill	foo@foo.com
3	Virginia	Dobson	foo2@bar.com
4	Glen	Hill	foo2@foo.com
5	Shelly	Hill	foo3@foo.com
6	Delores	Simmons-Edelstein	foo@barnyc.com
7	Elvis	Presley	blue@suede.com
(AutoNumber)			

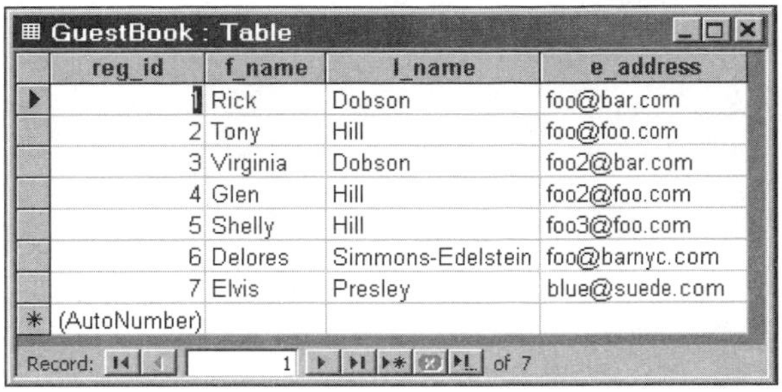

HTML Forms for Browsing and Editing SQL Server Data

All the custom forms to this point in the chapter relied on two files. One file collects data. This is a standard Web page with an `.htm` extension. The second file with an `.asp` extension processes data that the first form passes to it. The search form created by the FrontPage Database Wizard does create a somewhat richer experience. In this instance, a user specifies a criterion on one page and views the return set on the same page. The wizard uses a single `.asp` file for this application. However, developers are restricted to designing this form through the wizard's custom development interface, and that interface yields strictly search forms. In addition, we cannot edit or update the data returned by the search form any way. This section shows workarounds to both of these issues. Namely, it describes how we can develop a Web page that views and manipulates data. This section focuses on browsing and database maintenance operations, but we can use the same design for search tasks. The chapter's concluding section demonstrates this use for the technology.

Browsing Data with HTML Forms

One typical service that a form can provide for a data source is to let users browse through its records. Access and SQL Server users are used to doing this with four controls that move to the first record, the previous record, the next record, or the last record. We can readily implement this with HTML forms in an `.asp` file. The file can read the button pressed previously and update the record it displays. It is necessary to use an `.asp` file for this since we are managing a relationship with a data source, and a standard `.htm` or `.html` file cannot do this.Since an `.asp` file can hold standard HTML as well as ASP script, it can perform both functions.

The following screen depicts a browser view of the `gb_browser.asp` file:

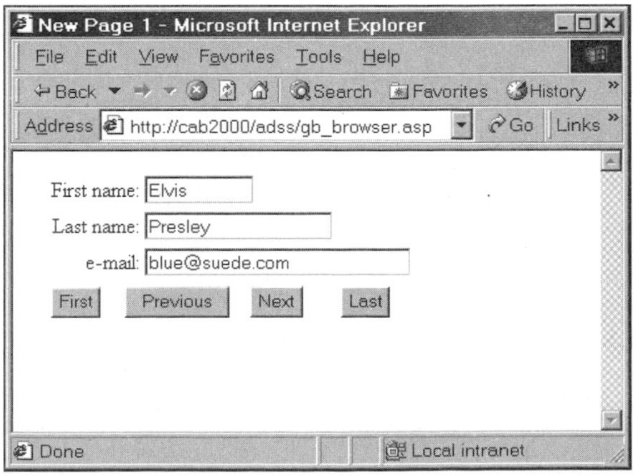

The page is open to the last record in the recordset. Recall that the prior application just added this record to the GuestBook table in the Chapter10Northwind database. The preceding datasheet view of the GuestBook table from that application shows all of its records. The four buttons below the three form fields enable a user to navigate through the rows in the GuestBook table. For example, users would be able to navigate to the displayed record by clicking Last. Clicking First opens the form to Rick Dobson with an e-mail address of foo@bar.com. Clicking Next from a form showing Rick Dobson advances the view to data for Tony Hill. If a user tries to move beyond the first or last record by clicking either Previous or Next, the file traps the error and prints a warning message.

There are a couple to tricks to making a form like the proceeding one work with an .asp file. First, the file has to call itself. This gives the user the impression of working with a single bound form. In fact, it is a single form, but its fields are not bound to a data source. Second, when a form opens, its page has to read the prior button selection to determine to which record to navigate. Third, the form has to display the record currently active after navigating to it. The following ASP script illustrates one approach to implementing these steps :

```
<!-- Declare language and constants file -->
<%@ LANGUAGE = VBSCRIPT %>
<!-- #include file="adovbs.inc" -->

<html>

<head>
<meta http-equiv="Content-Type" content="text/html; charset=windows-1252">
<meta name="GENERATOR" content="Microsoft FrontPage 4.0">
<meta name="ProgId" content="FrontPage.Editor.Document">
<title>New Page 1</title>
</head>

<body>

<%
'Set Session Direction variable
Select Case Request.Form("cmd_browse_button")
   Case ""
      Session("Direction") = ""
   Case "Next"
      Session("Direction") = "Next"
   Case "Previous"
      Session("Direction") = "Previous"
   Case "First"
      Session("Direction") = "First"
   Case "Last"
      Session("Direction") = "Last"
End Select
%>

<%
'Re-use or create a connection
if isobject(Session("Chapter10_cnn1")) then
   set cnn1 = Session("Chapter10_cnn1")
else
   set cnn1 = Server.CreateObject("ADODB.Connection")
   cnn1.open "Chapter10Northwind","sa",""
   Set Session("Chapter10_cnn1") = cnn1
end if
```

```
%>

<%
'Re-use or create a recordset
dim str1
if isobject(Session("gb_rs")) then
    set rs = Session("gb_rs")
    if Session("Direction") = "Next" then
        rs.MoveNext
        if rs.EOF then
            rs.MovePrevious
            str1= "<font color=red size=3><b><i>"
            str1 = str1 & "Already at end of recordset."
            str1 = str1 & "</i></b></font>"
            Response.Write (str1)
        end if
    elseif Session("Direction") = "Previous" then
        rs.MovePrevious
        if rs.BOF then
            rs.MoveNext
            str1= "<font color=red size=3><b><i>"
            str1 = str1 & "Already at beginning of recordset."
            str1 = str1 & "</i></b></font>"
            Response.Write (str1)
        end if
    elseif Session("Direction")= "Last" then
        rs.MoveLast
    else
        rs.MoveFirst
    end if
else
    str1 = "SELECT * FROM GuestBook"
    set rs = Server.CreateObject("ADODB.Recordset")
    rs.open str1, cnn1, adOpenStatic, adLockOptimistic
    Set Session(("gb_rs")) = rs
end if
%>

<form method="post" action="gb_browser.asp">
<table border="0" width="69%">
    <tr>
        <td width="40%" align="right">
        First name:</td>
        <td width="60%"> <input type=text name=f_name value=<%= rs("f_name")
                                            %> size=10 maxlength=10>
        </td>
    </tr>
    <tr>
        <td width="40%" align="right">
        Last name:</td>
        <td width="60%"> <input type=text name=l_name value=<%= rs("l_name")
                                            %> size=20 maxlength=20>
        </td>
    </tr>
    <tr>
        <td width="40%" align="right">
```

```
            e-mail:</td>
            <td width="60%"> <input type=text name=e_address value=<%=
                            rs("e_address") %> size=30 maxlength=50>
        </td>
    </tr>
    <tr>
        <td width="100%" align="center" colspan="2">
            <table border="0" width="100%">
                <tr>
                    <td width="25%">
                    <p align="center"><input type="submit" value="First"
                                        name="cmd_browse_button"></td>
                    <td width="25%">
                    <p align="center"><input type="submit" value="Previous"
                                        name="cmd_browse_button"></td>
                    <td width="25%">
                    <p align="center"><input type="submit" value="Next"
                                        name="cmd_browse_button"></td>
                    <td width="25%">
                    <p align="center"><input type="submit" value="Last"
                                        name="cmd_browse_button"></td>
                </tr>
            </table>
        </td>
    </tr>
</table>

</form>

</body>

</html>
```

This script builds on many techniques previously described, and it introduces some new ones. As in previous code samples, it commences with a directive to use VBScript for server-side scripting and a reference to the `adovbs.inc` file.

```
<!-- Declare language and constants file -->
<%@ LANGUAGE = VBSCRIPT %>
<!-- #include file="adovbs.inc" -->
```

The next important block of original code uses `Request.Form` and `Select Case` statements to decipher which button a user clicked. Each of the four buttons on the form assigns a value to `cmd_browse_button`. If a user navigates to the page without clicking one of the four buttons, then the value for `cmd_browse_button` will be a zero-length string. The `Select Case` statement stores the value for `cmd_browse_button` in a `Session` variable.

```
<%
'Set Session Direction variable
Select Case Request.Form("cmd_browse_button")
    Case ""
        Session("Direction") = ""
    Case "Next"
        Session("Direction") = "Next"
```

```
        Case "Previous"
            Session("Direction") = "Previous"
        Case "First"
            Session("Direction") = "First"
        Case "Last"
            Session("Direction") = "Last"
    End Select
    %>


    <%
```

The next block of ASP script either creates a new connection or re uses an existing one if it is available from a prior page view in the same session.

```
    <%
    'Re-use or create a connection
    if isobject(Session("Chapter10_cnn1")) then
        set cnn1 = Session("Chapter10_cnn1")
    else
        set cnn1 = Server.CreateObject("ADODB.Connection")
        cnn1.open "Chapter10Northwind","sa",""
        Set Session("Chapter10_cnn1") = cnn1
    end if
    %>
```

This connection serves as the `ActiveConnection` property for the recordset in the next block of code. This code creates or re uses a recordset. If the recordset does not exist from a previous session, then the code creates a recordset based on the **GuestBook** table and saves the recordset. This action navigates by default to the first record in the recordset. If the recordset did exist previously, then the application deciphers where to move next by reading the value of `Session("Direction")`. The procedure uses an `If...Then...ElseIf` statement to conditionally execute code appropriate for each legitimate `Session("Direction")` value.

When the `Session("Direction")` variable equals **"Next"**, the code invokes the `MoveNext` method on the `rs` object. If the outcome of this action makes `rs.EOF` equal `True`, then the application performs two actions. First, it moves back to the last record in the recordset. Second, it prints an error message on the screen letting the user know that the recordset is already at the last record. A `Session("Direction")` value of **"Previous"** results in the application of the `MovePrevious` method to the recordset object. If this makes `rs.BOF` equal `True`, then the code restores the former position and prints a warning message on the Web page.

The only remaining values that `Session("Direction")` can assume are **"Last"** and **"First"**. In the case of **"Last"**, the code invokes the `MoveLast` method for the recordset object. There is no need for error trapping in this case. Finally, the only remaining value for `Session("Direction")` is **"First"**. A simple `ELSE` clause is sufficient to transfer control to the `rs.MoveFirst` statement appropriate in this circumstance.

```
    <%
    'Re-use or create a recordset
    dim str1
    if isobject(Session("gb_rs")) then
        set rs = Session("gb_rs")
        if Session("Direction") = "Next" then
```

```
      rs.MoveNext
      if rs.EOF then
         rs.MovePrevious
         str1= "<font color=red size=3><b><i>"
         str1 = str1 & "Already at end of recordset."
         str1 = str1 & "</i></b></font>"
         Response.Write (str1)
      end if
   elseif Session("Direction") = "Previous" then
      rs.MovePrevious
      if rs.BOF then
         rs.MoveNext
         str1= "<font color=red size=3><b><i>"
         str1 = str1 & "Already at beginning of recordset."
         str1 = str1 & "</i></b></font>"
         Response.Write (str1)
      end if
   elseif Session("Direction")= "Last" then
      rs.MoveLast
   else
      rs.MoveFirst
   end if
else
   str1 = "SELECT * FROM GuestBook"
   set rs = Server.CreateObject("ADODB.Recordset")
   rs.open str1, cnn1, adOpenStatic, adLockOptimistic
   Set Session(("gb_rs")) = rs
end if
%>
```

The next screenshot illustrates the form when the user clicks Next from the last record in the GuestBook table. Notice the message in the top left corner of the screen reads Already at end of recordset. In addition, the form displays the last record in the table – not a cryptic ASP error message.

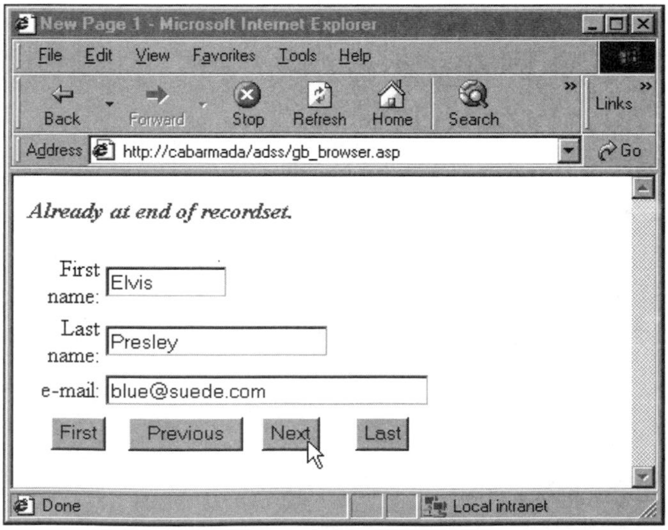

The next block of code is mostly HTML. The first line of this code makes an assignment for the action setting to the form on gb_browser.asp. However, the assignment sets the attribute to the name of the current file, gb_browser.asp. In other words, the Web page calls itself. This is how the current Web page can process the responses to the previous version of the page. The basic layout of the form depends on a pair of nested tables. The first three rows in the table consist of two columns – one for the control captions and the other for the text box controls. The fourth row has a single-rowed table within it. This row contains four columns – one for each navigation button.

```
<form method="post" action="gb_browser.asp">
<table border="0" width="69%">
    <tr>
        <td width="40%" align="right">
        First name:</td>
        <td width="60%"> <input type=text name=f_name value=<%= rs("f_name")
                                        %> size=10 maxlength=10>
        </td>
    </tr>
    <tr>
        <td width="40%" align="right">
        Last name:</td>
        <td width="60%"> <input type=text name=l_name value=<%= rs("l_name")
                                        %> size=20 maxlength=20>
        </td>
    </tr>
    <tr>
        <td width="40%" align="right">
        e-mail:</td>
        <td width="60%"> <input type=text name=e_address value=<%=
                        rs("e_address") %> size=30 maxlength=50>
        </td>
    </tr>
    <tr>
        <td width="100%" align="center" colspan="2">
            <table border="0" width="100%">
                <tr>
                    <td width="25%">
                    <p align="center"><input type="submit" value="First"
                                    name="cmd_browse_button"></td>
                    <td width="25%">
                    <p align="center"><input type="submit" value="Previous"
                                    name="cmd_browse_button"></td>
                    <td width="25%">
                    <p align="center"><input type="submit" value="Next"
                                    name="cmd_browse_button"></td>
                    <td width="25%">
                    <p align="center"><input type="submit" value="Last"
                                    name="cmd_browse_button"></td>
                </tr>
            </table>
        </td>
    </tr>
</table>

</form>
```

See the layout of the controls in the following screen from the Normal tab of FrontPage :

We develop this form like the previous samples: first, add the controls; second, add the tables; third, position the controls in the tables. The text box cells show the ASP expressions for their value settings. The next paragraph focuses on this, but some readers may find it helpful to receive guidance on the design of nested tables in FrontPage. In this sample, create a table with 4 rows and two columns. Choose Table | Insert | Table to open the Insert Table dialog. Then, complete the dialog to create the desired outer table. Next, select the two columns in the table's bottom row and choose Table | Merge Cells. With the bottom row still selected, choose Table | Insert | Table and specify a new table with one row and four columns. This adds a new table within the outer table in a row before the last one. Complete the formatting by selecting the table's last row with the merged cells and deleting it (choose Table | Delete Cells).

The application assigns values to the text boxes from the active row of the recordset by assigning recordset values to the text box controls. Use the <%= and %> delimiters to mark our recordset expressions. These expressions appear in the preceding design view of the form and in the script for the page's .asp file.

The final trick for the design of this form is the assignment of a single value to the cmd_browse_button form field value based on which of four buttons a user clicks. The solution is to use four buttons, each with the same name setting but a different value setting. The form returns the value setting for whichever button a user clicks. In this case, the name setting is cmd_browse_button. The value settings are First, Previous, Next, and Last.

Editing Data with HTML Forms

The prior sample primarily targets browsing static SQL Server data over a Web. It never permits change from its form, but it can operate in some circumstances when the underlying data changes. In particular, the form will reflect updates to fields for records that are already in the database. However, it does not reflect additional records that other users add to a database (unless we reload the application into the browser after someone else adds a new record). More critically, if someone else deletes a record, such as the last record in a database, when the user moves to the last record, it does not automatically show the new last record. Instead, the IE 5 browser says the page cannot be displayed. We can change this behavior by altering the type of cursor our application uses when it opens a recordset on GuestBook (or whatever data source our needs dictate), but the form will still not permit updates to the data source. This section shows how to resolve these two issues – namely, reflecting changes by others and permitting changes directly from the form.

The `gb_audr.asp` file in the browser includes controls for adding, updating, and deleting records:

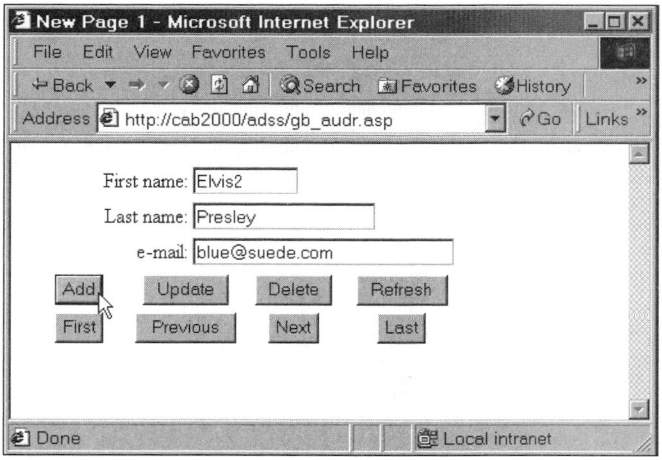

By clicking the button with a caption of **Refresh**, users can update the browser's data source for a form to view changes made by others since the form initially loaded or was last refreshed. The new form application retains the navigational controls of the previous sample (namely, `gb_browser.asp`). The amount of functionality that the new form provides depends on cursor type; we should use a cursor of `adOpenDynamic` for the most flexibility (although the `adOpenStatic` cursor from the previous sample provides some data modification support). For example, with the `adOpenDynamic` cursor, browsers can view new records added by another user without having to refresh the form. However, the `adOpenStatic` cursor forces a user to refresh a form to view changes made by other users.

Clicking the **Add** button in the previous screen adds a new record to the database with column values that match the form field values. This happens with either the `adOpenStatic` cursor type or the `adOpenDynamic` cursor type. When a developer designates an `adOpenStatic` cursor for the recordset behind a form, then users must click **Refresh** to view the new record. If a user clicks **Add** in the preceding screen, their browser will not detect the new record until after the user clicks **Refresh**. If a developer specifies an `adOpenDynamic` cursor type, then it is not necessary to click **Refresh** to view the new record.

To add a new record, type the new data into the three form fields and click **Add**. The **Update** button also revises the underlying data source for a form, but its behavior is different. Clicking **Update**, instead of **Add**, changes the first name for the last record from **Elvis** to **Elvis2**. The update behavior is independent of the cursor type. When a user clicks **Delete**, the action removes the current record in the browser from the recordset underlying the form. The application moves the current record to the first record in the form.

The code for the `gb_audr.asp` appears below:

```
<!-- Declare language and constants file -->
<%@ LANGUAGE = VBSCRIPT %>
<!-- #include file="adovbs.inc" -->

<html>

<head>
<meta http-equiv="Content-Type" content="text/html; charset=windows-1252">
<meta name="GENERATOR" content="Microsoft FrontPage 4.0">
```

```
<meta name="ProgId" content="FrontPage.Editor.Document">
<title>New Page 1</title>
</head>

<body>

<%
'Set Session Direction variable
Select Case Request.Form("cmd_browse_button")
    Case ""
        Session("Direction") = ""
    Case "Next"
        Session("Direction") = "Next"
    Case "Previous"
        Session("Direction") = "Previous"
    Case "First"
        Session("Direction") = "First"
    Case "Last"
        Session("Direction") = "Last"
End Select
%>

<%
'Re-use or create a connection
if isobject(Session("Chapter10_cnn1")) then
    set cnn1 = Session("Chapter10_cnn1")
else
    set cnn1 = Server.CreateObject("ADODB.Connection")
    cnn1.open "Chapter10Northwind","sa",""
    Set Session("Chapter10_cnn1") = cnn1
end if
%>

<%
'Re-use or create a recordset
dim str1
if isobject(Session("gb_rs")) then
    set rs = Session("gb_rs")
    If Request.Form("cmd_audr") = "" then
        if Session("Direction") = "Next" then
            rs.MoveNext
            if rs.EOF then
                rs.MovePrevious
                str1= "<font color=red size=3><b><i>"
                str1 = str1 & "Already at end of recordset."
                str1 = str1 & "</i></b></font>"
                Response.Write (str1)
            end if
        elseif Session("Direction") = "Previous" then
            rs.MovePrevious
            if rs.BOF then
                rs.MoveNext
                str1= "<font color=red size=3><b><i>"
                str1 = str1 & "Already at beginning of recordset."
                str1 = str1 & "</i></b></font>"
```

```
                           Response.Write (str1)
                     end if
              elseif Session("Direction")= "Last" then
                     rs.MoveLast
              else
                     rs.MoveFirst
              end if
         Else
              if Request.Form("cmd_audr") = "Add" then
'Create a command for the stored procedure
                  set cmd1 = Server.CreateObject("ADODB.Command")
                  set cmd1.ActiveConnection = cnn1
                  cmd1.CommandText = "insert_into_GuestBook_from_parameters"
                  cmd1.CommandType = adCmdStoredProc
'define the stored proc's parameter and value
                  cmd1.Parameters.Append
                  cmd1.CreateParameter"f_name",adVarChar,adParamInput,10
                  cmd1.Parameters("f_name") = Request.Form("f_name")
                  cmd1.Parameters.Append
                  cmd1.CreateParameter"l_name",adVarChar,adParamInput,20
                  cmd1.Parameters("l_name") = Request.Form("l_name")
                  cmd1.Parameters.Append
                  cmd1.CreateParameter"e_address",adVarChar,adParamInput,50
                  cmd1.Parameters("e_address") = Request.Form("e_address")
'Run stored procedure to insert values in form into GuestBook table
                  cmd1.Execute
              elseif Request.Form("cmd_audr") = "Update" then
                  rs("f_name") = Request.Form("f_name")
                  rs("l_name") = Request.Form("l_name")
                  rs("e_address") = Request.Form("e_address")
                  rs.Update
              elseif Request.Form("cmd_audr") = "Delete" then
'Delete code illustrates use of ado rather than stored procedure
                  rs.Delete
                  rs.Requery
              else
'Else refresh and move to first record
                  rs.Requery
              end if
         end if
    else
       str1 = "SELECT * FROM GuestBook"
       set rs = Server.CreateObject("ADODB.Recordset")
'Use with adOpenDynamic to view added records
'without having to click Refresh
       rs.open str1, cnn1, adOpenStatic, adLockOptimistic
'    rs.open str1, cnn1, adOpenDynamic, adLockOptimistic
       Set Session(("gb_rs")) = rs
    end if

'Cleanup
    set cmd1 = Nothing
    cnn1.close
    set cnn1 = Nothing

%>
```

```
<!-- Form design -->
<form method="post" action="gb_audr.asp">
<table border="0" width="73%">
   <tr>
      <td width="40%" align="right">
      First name:</td>
      <td width="65%"> <input type=text name=f_name value=<%= rs("f_name")
                                              %> size=10 maxlength=10>
      </td>
   </tr>
   <tr>
      <td width="40%" align="right">
      Last name:</td>
      <td width="65%"> <input type=text name=l_name value=<%= rs("l_name")
                                              %> size=20 maxlength=20>
      </td>
   </tr>
   <tr>
      <td width="40%" align="right">
      e-mail:</td>
      <td width="65%"> <input type=text name=e_address value=<%=
                      rs("e_address") %> size=30 maxlength=50>
      </td>
   </tr>
</table><table border="0" width="73%">
   <tr>
      <td width="25%">
      <p align="center"><input type="submit" value="Add"
                                name="cmd_audr"></td>
      <td width="25%">
      <p align="center"><input type="submit" value="Update"
                                name="cmd_audr"></td>
      <td width="25%">
      <p align="center"><input type="submit" value="Delete"
                                name="cmd_audr"></td>
      <td width="25%">
      <p align="center"><input type="submit" value="Refresh"
                                name="cmd_audr"></td>
   </tr>
</table><table border="0" width="73%">
   <tr>
      <td width="25%">
      <p align="center"><input type="submit" value="First"
                             name="cmd_browse_button"></td>
      <td width="25%">
      <p align="center"><input type="submit" value="Previous"
                                name="cmd_browse_button"></td>
      <td width="25%">
      <p align="center"><input type="submit" value="Next"
                             name="cmd_browse_button"></td>
      <td width="25%">
      <p align="center"><input type="submit" value="Last"
                             name="cmd_browse_button"></td>
   </tr>
</table>
```

```
    </form>

    </body>

    </html>
```

The code for `gb_audr.asp` differs from `gb_browser.asp` in two main respects. First, `gb_audr.asp` has more complicated logic for specifying the form's recordset. Second, the design of the form is different. This sample code below includes both cursor type settings (see specifically the two comment lines just before the close of the section creating a new recordset). Insert an apostrophe at the beginning of the line for the cursor type setting that we do not want to use. Chapter 12 includes additional commentary about cursor type settings.

```
    str1 = "SELECT * FROM GuestBook"
    set rs = Server.CreateObject("ADODB.Recordset")
'Use with adOpenDynamic to view added records
'without having to click Refresh
    rs.open str1, cnn1, adOpenStatic, adLockOptimistic
'   rs.open str1, cnn1, adOpenDynamic, adLockOptimistic
    Set Session(("gb_rs")) = rs
end if
```

The code specifying a recordset in `gb_audr.asp` includes the `gb_browser` code for designating a recordset, but this code appears as a branch in an `If...Then...Else` statement. In particular, if the `cmd_audr` form field value is a zero-length string, then `gb_audr.asp` executes the same code as `gb_browser.asp` for specifying a recordset behind the form.

```
<%
'Re-use or create a recordset
dim str1
if isobject(Session("gb_rs")) then
    set rs = Session("gb_rs")
    If Request.Form("cmd_audr") = "" then
        if Session("Direction") = "Next" then
            rs.MoveNext
            if rs.EOF then
                rs.MovePrevious
                str1= "<font color=red size=3><b><i>"
                str1 = str1 & "Already at end of recordset."
                str1 = str1 & "</i></b></font>"
                Response.Write (str1)
            end if
        elseif Session("Direction") = "Previous" then
            rs.MovePrevious
            if rs.BOF then
                rs.MoveNext
                str1= "<font color=red size=3><b><i>"
                str1 = str1 & "Already at beginning of recordset."
                str1 = str1 & "</i></b></font>"
                Response.Write (str1)
            end if
        elseif Session("Direction")= "Last" then
            rs.MoveLast
        else
            rs.MoveFirst
        end if
    Else
```

The cmd_audr form field acts like the cmd_browser_button form field. Namely, the application passes it as a single form field that can assume any of four values. Its four possible values are Add, Update, Delete, and Refresh. If cmd_audr has one of these values, then the Else branch of the outer If...Then...Else statement passes control to an inner If...Then...ElseIf statement. This statement, in turn, passes control to instructions that perform one of the four updating functions. The code for the Add button is similar to the previous sample that permitted the insertion of a record into the GuestBook table. Its major differences are that it does not clean up objects (because the application may still need them), and it does not echo the information for the added record. With the browsing capabilities of the current application, a user can just browse to a newly added record.

The code for the Update button is new. It simply copies the form field values from the form to the recordset before invoking the Update method. This is easy to code. Recall from earlier comments that we may want to use a stored procedure instead of ADO programming in a production environment. The same comment applies to the code for the Delete operation.

The code for the Delete function is even easier than for updating a record. All the application does is invoke the Delete method for the recordset. Then, it re-queries the recordset. This refreshes the data source for the form.

If cmd_audr is not Add, Update, or Delete and the cmd_audr form field value is not a zero-length string, cmd_audr must be Refresh. In this case, all the application needs to do is invoke the Requery method for the recordset behind the form. This captures any revisions made to the form's data source since the browser initially loaded gb_audr.asp or the last refresh, whichever is more recent. The invocation of the Requery method also moves the recordset to the first record.

```
if Request.Form("cmd_audr") = "Add" then
'Create a command for the stored procedure
        set cmd1 = Server.CreateObject("ADODB.Command")
        set cmd1.ActiveConnection = cnn1
        cmd1.CommandText = "insert_into_GuestBook_from_parameters"
        cmd1.CommandType = adCmdStoredProc
'define the stored proc's parameter and value
        cmd1.Parameters.Append
        cmd1.CreateParameter("f_name",adVarChar,adParamInput,10)
        cmd1.Parameters("f_name") = Request.Form("f_name")
        cmd1.Parameters.Append
        cmd1.CreateParameter("l_name",adVarChar,adParamInput,20)
        cmd1.Parameters("l_name") = Request.Form("l_name")
        cmd1.Parameters.Append
        cmd1.CreateParameter("e_address",adVarChar,adParamInput,50)
        cmd1.Parameters("e_address") = Request.Form("e_address")
'Run stored procedure to insert values in form into GuestBook table
        cmd1.Execute
    elseif Request.Form("cmd_audr") = "Update" then
        rs("f_name") = Request.Form("f_name")
        rs("l_name") = Request.Form("l_name")
        rs("e_address") = Request.Form("e_address")
        rs.Update
    elseif Request.Form("cmd_audr") = "Delete" then
'Delete code illustrates use of ado rather than stored procedure
        rs.Delete
        rs.Requery
    else
'Else refresh and move to first record
        rs.Requery
    end if
  end if
else
```

Reviewing the HTML code for the buttons in gb_audr.asp versus gb_browser.asp shows a couple of significant differences. First, there are four more buttons. Second, the new buttons all share the name cmd_audr. This strategy of using one button name for multiple buttons is how the code detects which control a user clicks from a set of related controls.

Search Forms for Graphic Images on HTML forms

This section presents two different approaches to searching for graphic images. One approach relies on the drop-down list control generated by the FrontPage Database Wizard. The second approach uses a standard HTML Select tag. The second approach also reveals how to store image addresses directly in a database. This is the first sample in the book that shows us how to store image addresses in and retrieve them from a SQL Server data source. The browser can take an address found by a search form and use it as the src setting for an img tag. This is a more immediate approach for displaying images that integrates more tightly with a SQL Server database than other image processing samples covered previously in this book.

Even if your needs do not pertain to displaying graphic images, this section may have content of interest to you. For example, it reveals two contrasting approaches to including drop-down list boxes on HTML forms. Second, it reveals strategies for building custom search forms that we can edit without going through the manual interface that FrontPage offers for search forms.

Displaying Images with the FrontPage Database Wizard

The following screen reveals a single form that lets a user look up the image for a product:

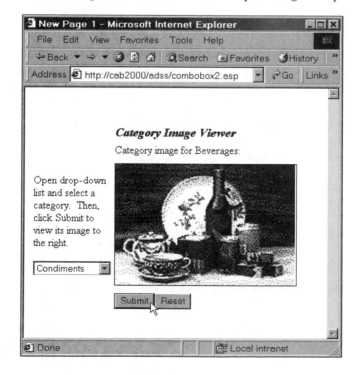

Clicking the drop-down arrow presents all the categories in the Categories table. When a user makes a selection the drop-down list saves the CategoryID value but displays the CategoryName. Clicking Submit passes the drop-down list selection to the same page via a round-trip to the Web server so that ASP script can manage the return of the image that corresponds to the selected category. In the previous screen, when the user clicks Submit, the image changes from the default one of beverages to the selected category of condiments. It is possible to change the image automatically whenever a user changes the selection in the combo box. This alternative approach restricts the generality of the Web page since not all browsers respond to the change event for an HTML select control in the same way. Using the Submit control ensures a more robust solution.

This application is really a search form. The user selects a criterion with the drop-down list control on the left, and the application responds by updating the title for the picture and by inserting a picture of the selected category on the form. After updating the image, the drop-down list automatically restores to show the first category in the Categories table from the Chapter10Northwind database. The application is particularly easy to develop since it uses the FrontPage Database Wizard. While the wizard does not permit the creation of its standard search forms with drop-down lists, it does enable the creation of drop-down list controls without any code. We can readily use this control on our own custom search form. This discussion of this sample will demonstrate how.

We can start the process of creating the custom search form with a new page in FrontPage.

> **Before starting, make sure that you have a connection to the database containing the Categories table (Chapter10Northwind in the example). In addition, you need a folder with your images for the categories. This example stores category images in the images folder of the root directory for the application. You can download the sample code from the Wrox Press Web site, at http://www.wrox.com**

Begin the creation of the custom search form by choosing Insert | Form | Picture. Select any category image as the source for the picture, which is just an img tag on the Web page. It does not matter what image we select since our application will ultimately assign the src setting for the img tag dynamically based on user selections from the drop-down list of categories. After assigning a picture to the img tag, FrontPage shows a form with the image, a Submit button, and a Reset button. Next, press *Home* to move our cursor to before the image. Then, add a table to the form with four rows and two columns. We can complete the preliminary steps for creating the form by right-clicking in the form and choosing Form Properties. Click Send to Others and select Custom ISAPI, NSAPI, CGI, or ASP Script.

The preceding steps generate an infrastructure that we need to complete the form. The following screen shows the status of the form on the Normal tab after completing the following actions. Drag the picture to the third row of the second column. Move the Submit and Reset buttons to the last row of the second column. Delete the blank line below the table. Use the Table command to merge the two cells in the top row and type "Image Category Viewer". After selecting the text, make menu selections to center the text with a font size of 14, a bold face and a slant. Complete our editing in the Normal tab by adding a drop-down list in the cell opposite the picture. A previous section in this chapter describes the steps for accomplishing this. Replace the Employees table in that example with the Categories table for this example.

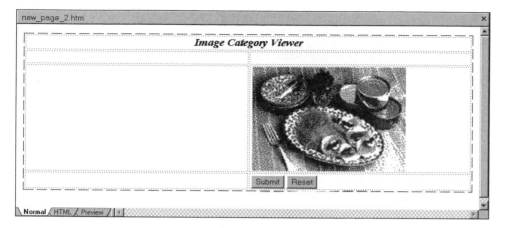

We are now ready to start editing the form on the HTML tab. After opening that tab, save the file with an
.asp extension (for example, as combobox2.asp). We need to name the file so that we can assign the
action attribute for the form. Use the file's name for this purpose so that the Web page with the form calls
itself. Now that the Web page calls itself, we can add some code to decipher the value of the drop-down list
control. The goal of this code is to take the numeric CategoryID values and translate them to addresses for
the image files corresponding to the CategoryID value. For example, the beverages category has a numeric
value of 1, and its image is at images/beverages.gif in the root folder for the Web site. The other
category pictures are also in the images folder. Some of the addresses for these images have names with
embedded spaces. HTML requires the encoding of the spaces as %20 when we use them as the src setting
for an img tag.

The following ASP script creates two Session variables based on the value of the drop-down list control,
which the form passes as CategoryID. The picture_file variable denotes the location of the image file
for the category that a user selected from the drop-down list. The category_name variable is the name of
the category a user selected. This variable will help to document the picture. If CategoryID is a zero-length
string because someone calls the page initially or refreshes the page, the code assigns default values to the
category_name and CategoryID Session variables. Insert the following block of code after the body
tag but before the form tag.

```
<%
if Request.Form ("CategoryID") = "1" then
    Session("picture_file") = "images/beverages.gif"
    Session("category_name") = "Beverages"
elseif Request.Form ("CategoryID") = "2" then
    Session("picture_file") = "images/condiments.gif"
    Session("category_name") = "Condiments"
elseif Request.Form ("CategoryID") = "3" then
    Session("picture_file") = "images/confections.gif"
    Session("category_name") = "Confections"
elseif Request.Form ("CategoryID") = "4" then
    Session("picture_file") = "images/dairy%20products.gif"
    Session("category_name") = "Dairy Products"
elseif Request.Form ("CategoryID") = "5" then
    Session("picture_file") = "images/grains%20and%20cereals.gif"
    Session("category_name") = "Grains and Cereals"
elseif Request.Form ("CategoryID") = "6" then
    Session("picture_file") = "images/meat%20and%20poultry.gif"
    Session("category_name") = "Meat and Poultry"
```

```
    elseif Request.Form ("CategoryID") = "7" then
       Session("picture_file") = "images/produce.gif"
       Session("category_name") = "Produce"
    elseif Request.Form ("CategoryID") = "8" then
       Session("picture_file") = "images/seafood.gif"
       Session("category_name") = "Seafood"
    'assign a default image
    else
       Session("picture_file") = "images/beverages.gif"
       Session("category_name") = "Beverages"
    end if
    %>
```

Now that we have the code that deciphers the value of the **CategoryID** control on the form to both a category name and the address for the image file, we need to use the two `Session` variables. From the HTML tab, insert the following code between the `<td>` and `</td>` tags for the second cell on the second row of the table inside the form.

```
    Category image for <%= Session("category_name") %>:
```

This line allows the label over the image to change each time the user makes a new selection by clicking **Submit**. When we use an ASP `Session` variable in HTML, it requires delimiters. The most typical delimiters for embedding ASP values directly into HTML are `<%=` and `%>`.

Next, scroll down the page to the `img` tag. The `src` setting for the tag is "http://cab2000/adss/images/seafood.gif" (though obviously this URL will be different depending on where we have saved our images). This URL points at the image initially selected for the `img` tag when creating it (see the preceding screen). The application requires the `img` `src` setting to be conditional on the category a user selects. We can achieve this result by replacing the URL with the following ASP expression.

```
    <%= Session("picture_file") %>
```

After making these changes, we have the basic functionality but not the final appearance of the form complete. The image will change according to a user's selection in the drop-down list box, and the caption above the image updates also to reflect the contents of the img tag below it. The screen on the rifght depicts the current version of the form immediately after a user selected **Confections** from the drop-down list and clicked **Submit**. Notice both the image and its caption reflect the selected item.

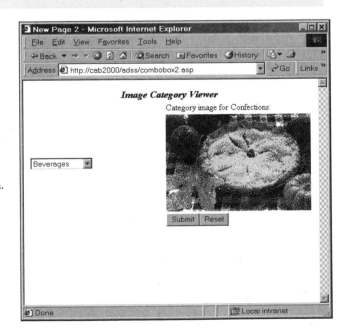

The final two steps involve re-sizing the columns of the table in the form. By default, FrontPage makes the columns even, but we may prefer the first column to be smaller than the second one that exposes the image. In addition, we may wish to have some text in front of the drop-down list control to instruct users how to make the search form work. The following ASP script shows the completed version of `combobox2.asp`. It includes all the editing touches described throughout this section as well as the two alluded to in this paragraph. This listing is useful because it shows how all the parts fit together into a custom ASP search form. As this section describes all the code, we can adapt any portion of it as our individual needs dictate. This is not true for the FrontPage wizard-generated search form. In that case, we must manually re-execute the steps for creating the form whenever we want to make any kind of change to the form.

```
<html>

<head>
<meta http-equiv="Content-Language" content="en-us">
<meta http-equiv="Content-Type" content="text/html; charset=windows-1252">
<meta name="GENERATOR" content="Microsoft FrontPage 4.0">
<meta name="ProgId" content="FrontPage.Editor.Document">
<title>New Page 2</title>
</head>

<body>
<%
if Request.Form ("CategoryID") = "1" then
    Session("picture_file") = "images/beverages.gif"
    Session("category_name") = "Beverages"
elseif Request.Form ("CategoryID") = "2" then
    Session("picture_file") = "images/condiments.gif"
    Session("category_name") = "Condiments"
elseif Request.Form ("CategoryID") = "3" then
    Session("picture_file") = "images/confections.gif"
    Session("category_name") = "Confections"
elseif Request.Form ("CategoryID") = "4" then
    Session("picture_file") = "images/dairy%20products.gif"
    Session("category_name") = "Dairy Products"
elseif Request.Form ("CategoryID") = "5" then
    Session("picture_file") = "images/grains%20and%20cereals.gif"
    Session("category_name") = "Grains and Cereals"
elseif Request.Form ("CategoryID") = "6" then
    Session("picture_file") = "images/meat%20and%20poultry.gif"
    Session("category_name") = "Meat and Poultry"
elseif Request.Form ("CategoryID") = "7" then
    Session("picture_file") = "images/produce.gif"
    Session("category_name") = "Produce"
elseif Request.Form ("CategoryID") = "8" then
    Session("picture_file") = "images/seafood.gif"
    Session("category_name") = "Seafood"
'assign a default image
else
    Session("picture_file") = "images/beverages.gif"
    Session("category_name") = "Beverages"
end if
%>
<form method="POST" action="combobox2.asp">
    <table border="0" width="100%">
        <tr>
```

```
            <td width="20%" colspan="2">
            <p align="center"><font size="4"><b><i>Image Category
                                    Viewer</i></b></font></td>
      </tr>
      <tr>
            <td width="20%"></td>
            <td width="50%">Category image for <%= Session("category_name")
                                                %>:</td>
      </tr>
      <tr>
            <td width="20%"><p>Open drop-down list and
            select a category.  Then, click Submit to view its image to
            the right. </p><nobr><!--webbot bot="DatabaseRegionStart"
            startspan
            s-columnnames="CategoryID,CategoryName,Description,Picture"
            s-columntypes="3,202,203,205" s-dataconnection="Database1"
            b-tableformat="FALSE" b-menuformat="TRUE"
            s-menuchoice="CategoryName"
            s-menuvalue="CategoryID" b-tableborder="TRUE" b-tableexpand="TRUE"
            b-tableheader="TRUE" b-listlabels="TRUE" b-listseparator="TRUE"
            i-ListFormat="0" b-makeform="TRUE" s-recordsource="Categories"
            s-displaycolumns="CategoryID,CategoryName,Description,Picture"
            s-criteria s-order s-sql="SELECT * FROM Categories"
            b-procedure="FALSE"
            clientside SuggestedExt="asp" s-DefaultFields
            s-NoRecordsFound="No records returned." i-MaxRecords="256"
            i-GroupSize="0" BOTID="0" u-dblib="_fpclass/fpdblib.inc"
            u-dbrgn1="_fpclass/fpdbrgn1.inc" u-dbrgn2="_fpclass/fpdbrgn2.inc"
            local_preview=" &lt;span style=&quot;color: rgb(0,0,0); background-
            color:
rgb(255,255,0)&quot;&gt;Database&lt;/span&gt; "
      preview=" &lt;span style=&quot;color: rgb(0,0,0); background-color:
rgb(255,255,0)&quot;&gt;Database&lt;/span&gt; " --><!--#include
file="_fpclass/fpdblib.inc"-->
<%
fp_sQry="SELECT * FROM Categories"
fp_sDefault=""
fp_sNoRecords="No records returned."
fp_sDataConn="Database1"
fp_iMaxRecords=256
fp_iCommandType=1
fp_iPageSize=0
fp_fTableFormat=False
fp_fMenuFormat=True
fp_sMenuChoice="CategoryName"
fp_sMenuValue="CategoryID"
fp_iDisplayCols=4
fp_fCustomQuery=False
BOTID=0
fp_iRegion=BOTID
%>
<!--webbot bot="DatabaseRegionStart" i-CheckSum="31226" endspan -->
```

```
        <select NAME="CategoryID" SIZE="1">
        <!--webbot bot="AspInclude" startspan CLIENTSIDE
        U-INCFILE="_fpclass/fpdbrgn1.inc" --><!--#include

file="_fpclass/fpdbrgn1.inc"--><!--webbot
        bot="AspInclude" i-CheckSum="62210" endspan -->
        <option

VALUE="<%=FP_FieldHTML(fp_rs,"CategoryID")%>">
<%=FP_FieldHTML(fp_rs,"CategoryName")%></option>
        <!--webbot bot="AspInclude" startspan CLIENTSIDE
        U-INCFILE="_fpclass/fpdbrgn2.inc" --><!--#include

file="_fpclass/fpdbrgn2.inc"--><!--webbot
        bot="AspInclude" i-CheckSum="62218" endspan -->
        </select><!--webbot bot="DatabaseRegionEnd" startspan
        b-tableformat="FALSE" b-menuformat="TRUE"
        u-dbrgn2="_fpclass/fpdbrgn2.inc" i-groupsize="0" clientside
        local_preview=" &lt;span style=&quot;color: rgb(0,0,0); background-
        color:

rgb(255,255,0)&quot;&gt;Results&lt;/span&gt; "
        preview=" &lt;span style=&quot;color: rgb(0,0,0); background-color:

rgb(255,255,0)&quot;&gt;Results&lt;/span&gt; " --><!--webbot
        bot="DatabaseRegionEnd" endspan -->
        </nobr></td>
        <td width="50%"><input border="0" src="<%= Session("picture_file") %>"

name="I2" width="270" height="184" type="image"></td>
        </tr>
        <tr>
        <td width="20%"></td>
        <td width="50%"><input type="submit" value="Submit" name="B1"><input
                          type="reset" value="Reset" name="B2"></td>
        </tr>
    </table>
</form>

</body>

</html>
```

Linking a Select Tag to a Database for Displaying Images

The preceding sample enables a user to do a search. However, the database plays a relatively minor role in the overall process. The drop-down control derives its value from the database, but code inside the `.asp` file generates the image address and the category name corresponding to the drop-down list value. Some database users may prefer a solution that ties more tightly to the database. This section shows that approach, and the section additionally demonstrates how to programmatically link a `Select` tag, which is a drop-down list box in HTML, to a data source.

In order for the data to provide the image addresses, we need to maintain them inside the database. One obvious way to do this is with a table. The following stored procedure creates a table named picture_addresses and populates it with values. The table has just two columns – one for linking its contents to the Categories table in the Chapter10Northwind database and the other to store the picture addresses. These addresses have an nvarchar data type with a maximum length of 50. Since the addresses include the path and filename, we may require a longer maximum size if we have long path names for our image files.

The ALTER TABLE statement for the foreign key links the picture_addresses table with the Categories table. The ALTER TABLE statement for adding the primary key constraint is marginally necessary depending on how we plan to update the list of address files. For example, we need it to manually alter table values from the Access user interface, but we can add and change values programmatically without a primary key. The stored procedure ends with a series of INSERT statements for populating the picture_addresses table with values. Database administrators can readily update the list of image addresses by modifying these INSERT statements as their needs dictate.

```
Alter Procedure create_picture_addresses
As

--Drop the table if it already exists
if exists (select * from dbo.sysobjects where id =
object_id(N'[dbo].[picture_addresses]') and OBJECTPROPERTY(id, N'IsUserTable')1)=
drop table [dbo].[picture_addresses]

--Create the new version of the table
CREATE TABLE [dbo].[picture_addresses] (
    [CategoryID] [int] NOT NULL ,
    [Address] [nvarchar] (50) NOT NULL) ON [PRIMARY]

--Designate a Primary Key for the table
ALTER TABLE [dbo].[picture_addresses] WITH NOCHECK ADD
    CONSTRAINT [PK_picture_addresses] PRIMARY KEY  CLUSTERED
    (
        [CategoryID],
        [Address]
    )  ON [PRIMARY]

--Designate a Foreign Key for the table
ALTER TABLE [dbo].[picture_addresses] ADD
    CONSTRAINT [FK_picture_addresses_Categories] FOREIGN KEY
    (
        [CategoryID]
    ) REFERENCES [dbo].[Categories] (
        [CategoryID]
    )

--Populate the table with values
INSERT picture_addresses
VALUES (1, 'images/Beverages.gif')
INSERT picture_addresses
VALUES (2, 'images/Condiments.gif')
INSERT picture_addresses
VALUES (3, 'images/Confections.gif')
```

```
INSERT picture_addresses
VALUES (4, 'images/Dairy%20Products.gif')
INSERT picture_addresses
VALUES (5, 'images/Grains%20and%20Cereals.gif')
INSERT picture_addresses
VALUES (6, 'images/Meat%20and%20Poultry.gif')
INSERT picture_addresses
VALUES (7, 'images/Produce.gif')
INSERT picture_addresses
VALUES (8, 'images/Seafood.gif')
```

We will return to this table later, but for now let's switch our focus to the completed application that uses the table. This application has two screens. The first of these is a drop-down list; it lets a user pick an item from the list of categories. When a user clicks the Submit button, control transfers to a second page that does a lookup based on the value of the drop-down list control, and it returns three columns of information – the category name, description, and image. The application exposes the Submit button with a caption of Select Category. The table does not maintain the images per se, just their address. However, this is all the img tag needs to display an image. The addresses for the images come from the picture_addresses table in the Chapter10Northwind database. The second screen is just a table with two columns – one for the return value captions and the other for the return values. The table additionally starts with a title row, and the Web page holding the table includes a link to transfer control back to the initial screen to permit another selection.

The two screens for the final sample in this chapter appear next. The file controlling the first screen has the name category_selector.asp. Its status as an .asp file enables it to update automatically whenever a database administrator changes the list of categories. The first screen below shows the drop-down list open to the Dairy Products category :

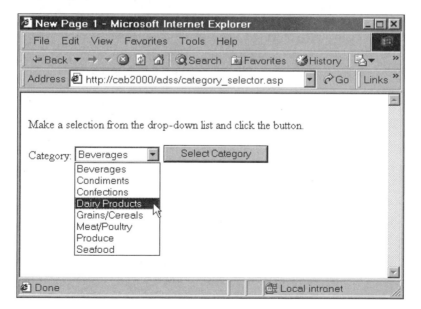

Clicking the category and Select Category opens the second screen. This screen displays the category name, description, and image corresponding to the selected item from the first screen.

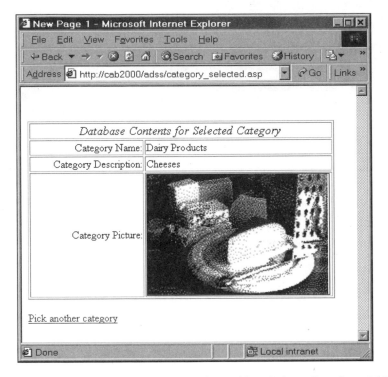

The code for implementing these two pages is extremely basic although they offer substantial functionality together. The code for the first page shows how to link a `Select` tag to a database. It starts as normal with a directive to use VBScript and a reference to the `adovbs.inc` file so that we can use constant names instead of values.

```
<!-- Declare language and constants file -->
<%@ LANGUAGE = VBSCRIPT %>
<!-- #include file="adovbs.inc" -->
```

Two additional scripts create a database connection to the Chapter10Northwind database and open a recordset based on the Categories table.

```
<%
'Re-use or create a connection
if isobject(Session("Chapter10_cnn1")) then
    set cnn1 = Session("Chapter10_cnn1")
else
    set cnn1 = Server.CreateObject("ADODB.Connection")
    cnn1.open "Chapter10Northwind","sa",""
    Set Session("Chapter10_cnn1") = cnn1
end if
%>

<%
'Create a new recordset
str1 = "SELECT * FROM Categories"
set rs = Server.CreateObject("ADODB.Recordset")
rs.open str1, cnn1, adOpenStatic, adLockOptimistic
%>
```

After the declaration of a form that points at the second file in the application with its action attribute, the HTML specifies a caption, namely **Category**, for the drop-down list control. In addition, it starts the process of creating the control with a `Select` tag. We must give the `Select` tag a name so that we can retrieve its value later. Next, the code launches a `Do` loop to pass through all the rows in the `Categories` table. Then, an option tag assigns pairs of value and display expressions for the drop-down list to expose. The `Option` tag can take up to two values. If we want to display one value and store another in the drop-down list control, our application requires two values. The first `Option` tag argument is a value attribute. Designate the value to store with this argument. The second argument reveals the value to display. In this sample, the control stores the **CategoryID** value, but it displays the **CategoryName** value. The balance of the code for the page completes the loop and designates the **Submit** button for the form.

```
<!-- Start form -->
<form  method="post" action="category_selected.asp">
<p>Make a selection from the drop-down list and click the button.</p>

<!-- Start drop-down list control in form -->
Category: <select name=cat_selector>

<%
'Start loop to iterate through recordset for control options
do while not rs.eof
%>

<!-- Enumerate option value and display  fields -->
    <option value=<%= rs("CategoryID") %>><%= rs("CategoryName") %>

<%
'Advance to next record and close loop
rs.MoveNext
loop
%>
</select>
<input type = "submit" value = "Select Category">
</form>
```

The complete listing for `category_selector.asp` as it should appear in the FrontPage HTML tab appears below.

```
<!-- Declare language and constants file -->
<%@ LANGUAGE = VBSCRIPT %>
<!-- #include file="adovbs.inc" -->

<html>

<head>
<meta http-equiv="Content-Type" content="text/html; charset=windows-1252">
<meta name="GENERATOR" content="Microsoft FrontPage 4.0">
<meta name="ProgId" content="FrontPage.Editor.Document">
<title>New Page 1</title>
</head>

<body>
<%
'Re-use or create a connection
if isobject(Session("Chapter10_cnn1")) then
```

```
    set cnn1 = Session("Chapter10_cnn1")
else
    set cnn1 = Server.CreateObject("ADODB.Connection")
    cnn1.open "Chapter10Northwind","sa",""
    Set Session("Chapter10_cnn1") = cnn1
end if
%>

<%
'Create a new recordset
str1 = "SELECT * FROM Categories"
set rs = Server.CreateObject("ADODB.Recordset")
rs.open str1, cnn1, adOpenStatic, adLockOptimistic
%>

<br>
<!-- Start form -->
<form  method="post" action="category_selected.asp">
<p>Make a selection from the drop-down list and click the button.</p>

<!-- Start drop-down list control in form -->
Category: <select name=cat_selector>

<%
'Start loop to iterate through recordset for control options
do while not rs.eof
%>

<!-- Enumerate option value and display  fields -->
    <option value=<%= rs("CategoryID") %>><%= rs("CategoryName") %>

<%
'Advance to next record and close loop
rs.MoveNext
loop
%>
</select>
<input type = "submit" value = "Select Category">
</form>

</body>

</html>
```

The code for the second page appears next. Like the first page in the application, this page re-packages much of what we already know to perform the behavior of showing the category name, description, and image. The special feature of this page is a T-SQL statement for a recordset that designates an inner join between the Categories and picture_addresses tables. This statement provides a recordset with just the three fields to populate the right-hand column of the table. In addition, the recordset has a single row that corresponds to the category selected on the first form. A simple WHERE clause in the T-SQL statement designates the row.

```
<%
    str1 = "SELECT Categories.CategoryID, Categories.CategoryName, "
    str1 = str1 & "Categories.Description, picture_addresses.Address "
    str1 = str1 & "FROM Categories INNER JOIN  picture_addresses ON "
    str1 = str1 & "Categories.CategoryID = picture_addresses.CategoryID "
    str1 = str1 & "WHERE Categories.CategoryID = " &
                  Request.Form("cat_selector") & ""
```

```
    set rs = Server.CreateObject("ADODB.Recordset")
    rs.open str1, cnn1, adOpenStatic, adLockOptimistic
%>
```

After opening a `Recordset` object based on the T-SQL statement, all the application needs to do is place values from the recordset in the second column of the table. The following code shows three different approaches to this task. They are interchangeable. Self-documenting code, such as `rs.Fields("fieldname").Value`, is often attractive, but short and cryptic code, such as `rs(indexnumber)`, is inviting when we are just trying ideas out to explore a possible solution strategy. The three different formats that the page illustrates are

❑   `rs(indexnumber)`

❑   `rs.Fields("fieldname")`

❑   `rs("fieldname")`

For reference, the complete listing for the `category_selected.asp` page from the HTML tab in FrontPage appears below.

```
<!-- Declare language and constants file -->
<%@ LANGUAGE = VBSCRIPT %>
<!-- #include file="adovbs.inc" -->

<html>

<head>
<meta http-equiv="Content-Language" content="en-us">
<meta http-equiv="Content-Type" content="text/html; charset=windows-1252">
<meta name="GENERATOR" content="Microsoft FrontPage 4.0">
<meta name="ProgId" content="FrontPage.Editor.Document">
<title>New Page 1</title>
</head>

<body>
<%
'Re-use or create a connection
if isobject(Session("Chapter10_cnn1")) then
   set cnn1 = Session("Chapter10_cnn1")
else
   set cnn1 = Server.CreateObject("ADODB.Connection")
   cnn1.open "Chapter10Ñorthwind","sa",""
   Set Session("Chapter10_cnn1") = cnn1
end if
%>


<%
   str1 = "SELECT Categories.CategoryID, Categories.CategoryName, "
   str1 = str1 & "Categories.Description, picture_addresses.Address "
   str1 = str1 & "FROM Categories INNER JOIN  picture_addresses ON "
   str1 = str1 & "Categories.CategoryID = picture_addresses.CategoryID "
   str1 = str1 & "WHERE Categories.CategoryID = " &
                 Request.Form("cat_selector") & ""
   set rs = Server.CreateObject("ADODB.Recordset")
   rs.open str1, cnn1, adOpenStatic, adLockOptimistic
%>
```

```
<p> </p>
<table border="1" width="455">
   <tr>
      <td width="443" align="right" colspan="2">
      <p align="center"><i><font size="4">Database Contents for Selected
                                    Category</font></i> </td>
   </tr>
   <tr>
      <td width="169" align="right">Category Name: </td>
      <td width="274"><%= rs(1) %></td>
   </tr>
   <tr>
      <td width="169" align="right">Category Description: </td>
      <td width="274"><%= rs.Fields("Description").Value %></td>
   </tr>
   <tr>
      <td width="169" align="right">Category Picture:</td>
      <td width="274"><img border="1" width="270"  height="184" src=<%=
                                    rs("Address") %>></td>
   </tr>
</table>

<p><a href="category_selector.asp">Pick another category</a></p>

</body>

</html>
```

Summary

The main substantive focus of this chapter is the building of forms for Web-based applications. Nearly all the forms in the chapter prepare us to work with SQL Server databases over the Web. A broad range of samples equip us to create solutions for searching, browsing, adding, updating, and deleting words, numbers, and images via forms.

The main technologies that this chapter taps are ASP and HTML forms. With ASP, we can build database connectivity into an application. With HTML forms, we can build robust Web solutions that work in nearly every browser. The numerous code samples and step-by-step instructions equip us to adapt the solutions presented here to our own custom data-based Web projects.

This chapter and the preceding one explore mature technologies that are easy to use, broadly applicable, or both. Adopt them with confidence that they will work in the broadest possible range of browsers without the need for extensive (or any) browser sniffing techniques. The next chapter explores alternative Web technologies that deliver special benefits, but at the expense of broad browser applicability. Nevertheless, their leading-edge capabilities and development features make them worth investigating.

11
Data Access Pages

Data access pages represent a step forward in enabling Office developers to Web-enable their solutions; along with **Office Web Components**, they offer much of the functionality of Microsoft Office in a web-friendly environment. Even if we aren't an Office/Access developer, but a database analyst with a different background, this environment is easy to use. While Active Server Pages (ASP) technology offers substantial power and is compatible with many different types of browsers, developing with it is a code-intensive exercise. Office has always been about making things easy. Data access pages continue that tradition by enabling the graphical development of web solutions. Since Office 2000 uses MSDE as one of its two standard database engines, data access pages enable us to develop full-featured web-based solutions for SQL Server data sources without having to write any code ourselves. However, if we prefer, we can enrich the capabilities of these pages through VBScript, as we discuss later in the chapter.

This chapter introduces the user interface for creating and using data access pages. We'll learn how to create bound forms as well as to work with unbound controls, which require coding. The chapter also includes code samples demonstrating VBA and VBScript techniques for managing and empowering data access pages. These pages support form-like functionality, and additionally enable report-like functionality. As the chapter explores these capabilities, it illustrates the innovative, interactive report style introduced with data access pages in Office 2000. The section on reporting reveals how to control page size, sort items within a report, and calculate results on data access pages. The chapter closes by drilling down on Office Web Components. Multiple samples demonstrate how to create and use the **Spreadsheet**, **Chart**, and **PivotTable List** components on data access pages. In addition, their treatment highlights how to extend data access page capabilities through these components.

So, the main sections in this chapter are as follows:

- ❑ What are Data Access Pages?
- ❑ Creating a Data Access Page with the Page Wizard
- ❑ Creating a Data Access Page in Page Design View

❑   Creating Interactive Grouping and Sorting Reports
❑   Using Office Web Components with Data Access Pages

The samples in this chapter were developed on a SQL Server 2000 database server, so its database file format is not usable on either MSDE or SQL Server 7. However, we can copy the scripts for procedures into an MSDE or SQL Server 7 database to add custom objects to a standard version of the Northwind database or the NorthwindCS database as discussed later. Since all examples are developed with Access projects, we'll be using an Access project unless otherwise stated.

What are Data Access Pages?

A **data access page** (**DAP**) is a web page with a special Microsoft Office Web Component to facilitate working with data sources. This component is one of the four Office Web Components (we examine each of them later in the chapter). The component for managing data is an ActiveX control that Microsoft calls the **Data Source** control. Data access pages deliver graphical form and report design for web applications through this control.

The Office Web Components install as part of Office 2000. We can also install them automatically on the client browser with data access pages by including a codebase setting that points to a network installation source for the Microsoft Office Web Components cab file. Their installation can require as much as 30 MB of disk space, but only 5 MB is directly a part of the Office Web Components. The balance is for related components, such as the Microsoft Data Access Components, version 2.1. The Office 2000 Resource Kit includes instructions for installing the Office Web Components cab files from a network location.

DAP's don't work too well for general web publishing, because not everyone who may want to use them has IE 5 and Office 2000. However, a corporate Intranet setting is fine, because in this case the client workstation can be guaranteed to have the requisite software. We need to know, though, that each workstation requires a license for Office 2000, whether it has Office 2000 installed or only the Office Web Components. This level of control over client workstations is uncharacteristic for Internet applications.

Second, the graphical design features for data access pages make them especially easy to develop when contrasted with ASP or HTML techniques. In fact, there are some strong, but not perfect, parallels between creating Access forms or reports versus data access pages. This lowered difficulty of development through bringing the development tools closer to traditional Access tools makes data access pages more cost-effective for intranet applications.

Third, client workstations can connect with data access pages on a web server or via the file system. We can even e-mail data access pages to clients. However, the client must have a network file path connection to the database server. This network file path permits the client to open a database connection through the data access page. ASP, on the other hand, requires HTTP requests for opening them as they are intended for Web applications. This contrast enables us to use data access pages in offices whether or not they have a web server.

> Fourth, the security model for data access pages in two-tier models will typically require cross-domain database access (meaning that each separate tier will reside on a different domain to the other). This can expose data in ways that can compromise security to unacceptable levels for Internet applications. However, applications behind a firewall are more likely to be able to tolerate the security risk associated with data access pages.

This chapter explores data access pages from the perspective of two-tier deployments on intranets. Deploying applications built with data access can involve many issues – particularly, if we focus on Internet-based three-tier deployment models. A white paper available from MSDN serves as an excellent starting point for those who want to create sophisticated data deployment environments for distributing data access pages. This paper is available from **msdn online** *at (HTTP://msdn.microsoft.com/library/techart/deploydap.htm).*

Accessing a Data Access Page

Users can refer to data access pages from IE 5, an Access project, or an Access database file created with Access 2000 (one with a .mdb extension). If we distribute Access projects or Access database files as the route to our pages, they will contain links in their database window that point at the actual data access pages. As we create and save data access pages, Access by default creates links in its Database window that point to **local drives** instead of **UNC** (**Universal Naming Convention**) paths. Either method (local drives or UNC paths) will permit the retrieval of pages from the computer used to create them. However, other computers will not be able to use links automatically in an Access project that point at a local drive, unless they all have the same drive mappings. This can be an issue because no special warning pops up to remind developers to save data access pages with UNC path specifications. This is less of an issue in an intranet environment where all machines have the same drive mappings, but it is good practice to use UNC paths anyway. Since IE 5 directly accesses data access pages, the link specification is not an issue when opening pages with an IE 5 browser as the data access page has a full HTTP address. Instead, we must get the browser security settings right. The remainder of this section drills down on this point.

The ability of a user to open a data access page from an IE 5 browser depends on the browser's security setting. If a browser has a Medium security setting for a site, then it will not be able to open data access pages from that site. With a Medium-low setting for the site, the browser can open the site, but only after the user replies correctly to a prompt. Users can avoid this message by appropriate browser security settings, which we look at next. However, it is relevant to point out that opening data access pages from Access projects or Access database files does not depend on IE browser security settings. Therefore, these routes open data access pages more robustly.

Two methods are particularly well suited to making it easy to open data access pages across domains with IE 5 browsers. First, we can include a web site in the set of trusted sites. From the IE 5 browser menu, choose Tools | Internet Options and select the Security tab of the Internet Options dialog. Highlight the Trusted sites icon and choose Sites. Then, follow the instructions for adding a trusted site. If our site publishing data access pages is not using HTTPS protocol, clear the check box requiring this protocol for all sites in the zone.

The following pair of dialogs shows the transition from the Security tab of the Internet Options dialog to the Trusted sites dialog. Notice that we click Sites on the Security tab to open the Trusted sites dialog. In the Trusted sites dialog, enter the URL for a new site we want trusted in the top text box.

Click Add to move that cell from the top text box to Web sites, a list box for trusted sites. There is a "gotcha" in this process that is not obvious. Notice the check box at the bottom of the dialog is not selected. When this dialog is selected, which happens to be its default setting, we cannot enter a URL without an HTTPs prefix. Since it is highly likely that URLs behind a firewall on an intranet will not be secure sites, we have to remember to clear the check box to add unsecured, intranet URLs to the trusted web sites list.

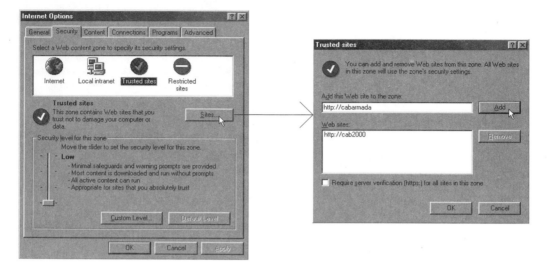

Second, if we want a browser to open data access pages from any site on an intranet, then choose the Local Intranet icon instead of the Trusted Sites icon on the Security tab. Next, click Custom Level. Scroll down the Security Settings until the Miscellaneous group appears. The first item here refers to accessing data sources across domains. Click Enable and OK twice to close the open dialogs. The following dialog shows the route to enabling the accessing of data across domains from an IE 5 browser. This setting for the local intranet allows a browser to open, without prompts, a data access page that connects to a database on any database server within the intranet.

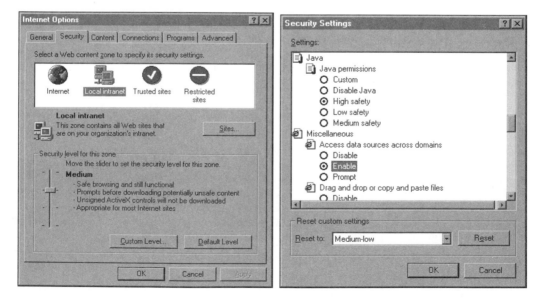

We can use FrontPage as a vehicle for performing some formatting to Web pages, but Access is the default editor for data access pages. In addition, selected formatting options from FrontPage do not apply to data access pages. For example, themes apply, but page transitions do not. Page transitions work for web pages like slide transitions work slides in a PowerPoint presentation. However, we can also apply themes programmatically from Access. Therefore, this chapter focuses on IE as a vehicle for viewing data access pages, and Access as a vehicle for browsing and editing pages.

Data Access Pages versus ASP and HTML

Since the last two chapters dealt with ASP and HTML, it may be instructive to contrast data access pages with them.

The first differentiating factor relates to the type of web page that ASP creates relative to data access pages. With data access pages, we are creating Dynamic HTML (DHTML) pages in contrast to what are normally HTML pages from ASP. The DHTML dialect used by data access pages is specific to IE 4+ browsers. This is one reason why data access pages are less suited for applications that require many different types of browser as Netscape Navigator uses a different dialect of DHTML.

> **Data access pages *require* IE 5, but ASP will work equally well with any browser that reads HTML.**

Another major distinction is that ASP technology always works with unbound forms, but forms in applications built from data access pages are normally bound. Bound forms can dramatically reduce the amount of code necessary to create an application, although we can still use unbound forms with data access pages.

A third distinction is that data access pages enable us to design forms and reports entirely graphically. ASP, which will typically interact with HTML forms, doesn't support this graphical design approach. With FrontPage, we can design a form's interface in a mostly graphical way, but any processing behind the form – even to the point of navigating between records – requires programming. Data access pages include a built-in navigation bar that accommodates sorting, filtering, and updating functions as well as navigation. While developers can programmatically and manually restrict the navigation bar's functionality, it takes no special actions to tap all its features.

Creating a Data Access Page with the Page Wizard

Getting started creating data access pages can be very simple. Although data access pages do not require manual coding, as is essential for ASP, we can take advantage of the Page Wizard to further simplify the process. While this wizard does not expose the full range of capabilities, it can generate customized data access pages. As data access pages are bound to their data source, they offer a high degree of functionality, including the ability to add, update, and delete records as users navigate through a record source. In order to facilitate the management and access of data access pages from Access projects, our `Database` window requires page links pointing at the page files, which are stand-alone web pages. Properly managing these links is essential – especially when our environment calls for designers with different computers having to open and edit the same page.

This section demonstrates the Page Wizard. It also introduces us to the basic functionality of data access pages that enables the editing of data on a page. In addition, we will discover some workarounds for potential weaknesses of the Page Wizard in environments where multiple page authors will need to manage the content on a page from different computers. We do this in three parts:

❏ Creating a Simple Bound Form on a Data Access Page

❏ Using our Custom Pages

❏ Administering Pages with VBA

Creating a Simple Bound Form on a Data Access Page

To start with we need to open an Access project with a connection to a database (in this illustration we use Chapter11.adp). It connects to the SQL Server data source from the preceding chapter, Chapter10Northwind. Select Pages on the Objects bar of the Database window and double-click Create data access page by using wizard. This opens the Page Wizard. Our initial task is to designate a data source for the form. The wizard enables us to choose from any table or view for the project.

The following screen shows the Shippers table highlighted so that, once we select it, it will serve as the source for a form. The Page Wizard dialog appears to the right and below the Database window with Pages selected in its Objects bar and Create data access page by using wizard selected within the window. Clicking the table completes the selection and arranges the Shippers table's columns in the Available Fields box (the drop-down list exposing the tables and views in the current project hides the box). Developers can use arrow controls to move fields from the Available Fields to the Selected Fields box. For this example, select all three fields by clicking on the double-headed arrow. This moves all the Available Fields to the Selected Fields box. Then, click Next three times to confirm our field selection in the first dialog and accept the default settings on the second and third dialogs.

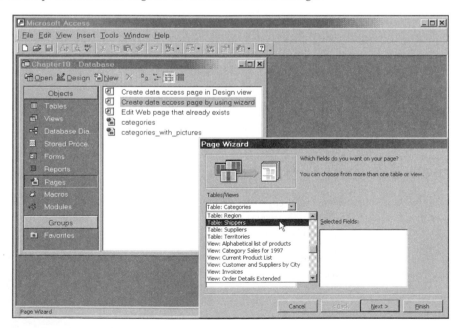

This opens the final Page Wizard dialog (see opposite). Access automatically suggests a default name for the page file caption based on the data source that we select (here Shippers is suggested), although this can be overridden. We can also select from the final dialog whether to open the page in Page view or

Design view – just as with Access forms and reports. One feature about the final dialog is unique to data access pages: it lets us choose to apply a theme to our page. If we check the box, then when Access opens the page in Design view, it exposes a dialog for assigning a theme to the page. (If we do choose a theme, a sub-folder containing various image files etc. is also created). Clicking Finish on the final dialog opens the data access page in either Design or Page view.

If we are doing web work with Access, then we should seriously consider installing FrontPage on our workstation and FrontPage Extensions on our web server. Microsoft shares a similar view about the desirability of FrontPage for web work – shown by the fact that version 5 of its IIS web server automatically installs FrontPage Extensions.

The caption on the wizard's last form does not serve as the object's name as is true for both forms and reports. It is strictly a title, or caption, for the web page. We assign a name to the data access page when we choose File | Save As. Until then, Access assigns a provisional, default name to the page, such as Page1.

File Saving Considerations

When we do save the file, we will be saving two things: the actual data access page, and a link to it from the Access project. Using the Save As menu command presents two Save As dialogs, meaning that we can specify the name for the link as being different to the name for the page. If we simply Save the data access page, then both the page and the link have the same name.

Access developers used to the Access form creation wizard may be a little frustrated if they close a data access page that has never been saved. A message box appears asking us if we want to save our changes. If we click No in response, we will lose all our work on the page. We must save a data access page if we want to be able to access the page later.

Just as when we save the data access page we save two things, deleting the page can result in deleting two things. Access gives us the choice whether to delete the link, or the link and the page, and the option to cancel the delete.

When we save the file, just giving it a file name will result in the link pointing at a mapped drive, which, as we pointed out earlier could cause problems. In order to prevent different drive mapping on the client computer meaning that the link doesn't work properly, we have to specify a UNC path in the file name box when we initially save the page. Of course, we have to ensure that the drive that our files are to be saved upon has a share name appropriately set up.

The following screen illustrates the use of a UNC specification, although as we can see it is too long to show properly. Since we are running this example as the system administrator of a Windows 2000 Server operating system, the full entry in this instance is \\CAB2000\C\Documents and Settings\Administrator\My Documents\Page2.htm. CAB2000 is the name of the computer, C denotes the share name for the C:\ drive, and the rest is just like the normal mapped file path.

As part of the sample Access project for this chapter (Chapter11.adp), two data access pages were created for the Shippers form generated by the Page Wizard in the preceding example. One points at a local drive and path (which we have already saved as Page1.htm). The second one references a different file name, Page2.htm, and a UNC path. The following screen shows the Save As dialog settings. The full entry in the file name box for the Save As Data Access Page is \\CAB2000\C\Documents and Settings\Administrator\My Documents\Page2.htm.

Again, CAB2000 denotes the computer's name, and C denotes the share name for the C:\ drive. Page authors connecting to the file from another computer can successfully reference this second page, but not the first one, for the reasons described in the preceding paragraph.

The difference between the two methods of saving shown above is only really apparent when the link is used from a different computer from the one on which it was created. For example, if we had created two pages, one for each method, they would both work fine on the computer they were created on. However, if a user from a second computer attempts to open the page with the mapped drive file name, the link won't connect. Instead, they'll get the following message box telling them that Access doesn't know where the page they want is. Clicking the Locate button will allow the user to graphically browse to the location of the file they seek, assuming they know where to look. Following this option rewrites the path associated with the pointer to UNC format, preventing this happening the next time it is opened.

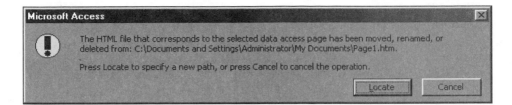

Before leaving the topic of local drive versus UNC format specifications for page links, let's consider one more case. In this scenario, we create a third data access page from the second computer. However, the page points at the Shippers table in the Chapter10Northwind database on the first computer. If we try to create a new data access page and save it in the same folder as the initial two pages, the page link will automatically have a UNC format. What this means is that a developer from any computer on the network will be able to open and edit the file. These exercises indicate that we will find it more convenient to create data access pages on a remote computer. This approach makes it easier to get the benefit of the UNC file specification. If we save a data access page to a local computer, then we have to manually enter the full, correct UNC format specification.

Using Our Custom Pages

All the pages have the same design once we finally open them – they include three text boxes above a navigation bar. We can see the text boxes and the navigation bar below. One significant benefit of the form is that it is bound to the data source through the Microsoft Data Source control.

The navigation bar exposes first, previous, next, and last browsing capabilities. Between the previous and last controls – marked by backward and forward arrows – a window indicates the data source name for the form, the absolute record position, and the total number of records. To the right of the "last" button are some controls that offer enhanced functionality.

The control just to the right of Last lets us add a new record. The next control deletes the current record, just like in an Access form. If we start to edit a record, Access enables the next two controls. The first of these allows a user to commit a data change, and the next one lets a user throw away a change and return to showing the initial data value. If we make a change to field, but then don't commit the change before closing the form, the change is not saved. However, if we move to a new record, it automatically commits the change.

The A-to-Z and Z-to-A controls sort the records in ascending or descending order for the values in the currently selected field. The control containing a funnel and a lightning bolt enables filter by selection. When we click it, only other records with matching field values to the one we were in when we clicked the control remain available for browsing with the form. Users can further restrict the subset that a form displays by invoking the filter-by-selection control for a different value in another field. Access enables the feature through a control with a funnel followed by a lightning bolt. Click the control while the cursor is in a field, and only other records with a matching value display in the form. Users can restore browsing for all the records in the data source behind a form by choosing the control with a funnel and no lightning bold behind it. The final button opens a viewer for help on data access pages. This viewer includes guidance for page designers as well as users, just like an Access form.

Data access pages create a local store for the data behind a form on the browsing computer. Data changes, such as edits, additions, and deletions, transfer immediately to the remote data server, if it can connect, and refresh the local store. However, changes by other users do not appear until we reload the page. Within an Access project, we can open and close the page – with a browser, we can just click Refresh. Other changes, such as new sort orders and filters, occur exclusively for the local cache. Filtering a local cache has no impact on the availability of records from a database server. Another instance of the page on a new computer can open to expose all the records or filter on a different subset from the initial instance.

Administering Pages with VBA

Two administrative tasks for data access pages include managing page links and controlling the paths at which those links point. With just a few VBA techniques and Access object model elements, we can administer data access pages to control the links that appear in the Database window of an Access project. Furthermore, these design techniques apply generally to managing related kinds of Access objects, such as forms and reports. To help us understand what is going on, we'll break these tasks down into three sections:

- ❑ Managing Page Links
- ❑ Updating Page Links
- ❑ Renaming Page Links

Managing Page Links

The AllDataAccessPages collection is hierarchically dependent on the CurrentProject. This collection has limited information on all data access pages, including critically whether they are open. The IsLoaded property has special significance for exposing the members of the DataAccessPages collection. This collection belongs to the Access object model Application object. The members of the DataAccessPages collection are open data access pages. Each of its members has 10 properties and 1 method. By using the AllDataAccessPages and DataAccessPages collections together, our applications can manage their data access pages to the full extent possible with VBA. As we will discover later in this chapter, there is another major programmatic interface as well.

To find out more about these collections, use the Object Browser in the VBE window to tap the built-in Microsoft Help file documentation for programmers. The following screenshot depicts the Object Browser with the ApplyTheme *method selected for a* DataAccessPage *object. Clicking the* Help *control in the Object Browser opens a Microsoft Access Help screen with documentation on the method and links to related information.*

The following short sample illustrates how to loop through all the members of the AllDataAccessPages collection. This sample prints the IsLoaded, Name, and FullName properties for each member. Each member of this collection corresponds to a link in the **Database** window for a data access page. The Name property is the name that appears in the **Database** window. The FullName property is the path and filename for the data access page. This FullName property appears in either UNC or local drive format, depending on how the link points at its data access page.

```
Sub enumerate_pages_in_db_win()
Dim obj As AccessObject

'List select properties of AllDataAccessPages members
For Each obj In CurrentProject.AllDataAccessPages
    Debug.Print obj.IsLoaded, obj.Name, obj.FullName
Next
End Sub
```

Notice that we declare members of the AllDataAccessPages collection with an AccessObject data type. Access projects include other collections of AccessObject types, such as AllForms and AllReports. Refer back to Chapter 7 and Chapter 8, respectively, for descriptions of these collections. A simple For Each...Next loop efficiently iterates through the members of the AllDataAccessPages collection.

The following listing shows the output for the `Chapter11.adp` file. It includes the three page links discussed so far as well as a couple not mentioned yet. The lines for `Page3`, `Page2`, and `Page1` wrap onto a second line. Notice the return value of `IsLoaded` is `False` for each link. No page links point to an open data access page when the `enumerate_pages_in_db_win` sub procedure runs. As we can see, the `Page1` link points to its associated data access page with a local drive. This is because it hasn't been located and changed into a UNC filename yet. In addition, another link named `categories_with_pictures` also designates its data access page with a local drive specification. That link points to a web folder named `Chapterxx` that is just below the root folder for the **cab2000** web server.

```
False        Page3            \\Cab2000\c\Documents and Settings\Administrator\My
Documents\Page3.htm
False        Page2            \\cab2000\c\Documents and
Settings\Administrator\Page2.htm
False        categories       \\cab2000\c\Inetpub\wwwroot\Chapterxx\categories.htm
False        categories_with_pictures
C:\Inetpub\wwwroot\Chapterxx\categories_with_pictures.htm
False        Page1            C:\Documents and Settings\Administrator\My
Documents\Page1.htm
```

Updating Page Links

As it's easy to create page links that point at their matching data access pages on local drives, a program for automatically converting from local drive to UNC drive designations may be found useful. The following sample illustrates how to programmatically convert any individual page link from one referencing its data access page via local drives to one using a UNC file specification to point at its web page. As the code is so easy to follow, it is also simple for us to adapt its logic for iterating through all, or any subset of, the links in an Access project.

The sample actually consists of a pair of sub procedures. The first one, `call_change_link_path`, just passes an existing link name and new file specification for the link to the second procedure. This second procedure, `change_link_path`, removes the old link before creating a new one that uses the passed file format for specifying a link. Whether the program fails or succeeds, it provides feedback about the attempt to update the file format specification.

```
Sub call_change_link_path()

'Assign UNC path spec for link
change_link_path "Page1", _
    "\\cab2000\c\Documents and Settings\Administrator\My Documents\Page1.htm"

'Restore local drive path spec for link
'by commenting out the previous sub procedure call
'and replacing it with the following one that is commented out
'change_link_path "Page1", _
    "C:\Documents and Settings\Administrator\My Documents\Page1.htm"

End Sub


Sub change_link_path(link_name As String, new_link_path As String)
On Error GoTo change_link_path_trap

'Attempt to remove old link
```

```
    DoCmd.DeleteObject acDataAccessPage, link_name

    'Create a new link pointing at the existing file
    Application.CreateDataAccessPage new_link_path, False

    'Save the new link
    DoCmd.Close acDataAccessPage, link_name, acSaveYes
    MsgBox "Change succeeded."

change_link_path_exit:
Exit Sub

change_link_path_trap:
Debug.Print Err.Number, Err.Description
If Err.Number = 7874 Then
    MsgBox "Link does not exist. Therefore, I cannot change it."
Else
    MsgBox "Failure for unknown reason. Did not change link path."
End If
Resume change_link_path_exit

End Sub
```

The Access DoCmd object offers a rich mix of methods that can assist in managing page links. For example, its DeleteObject method can eliminate an existing page link in an Access project. The Close or Save methods can save a data access page. We can programmatically generate a new data access page with the CreateDataAccessPage method for the Application object. While the CreateDataAccessPage method does technically create a new page object and place its link in the **Database** window for an Access project, the page must physically exist before we invoke it.

In the preceding sample code, the DeleteObject method deletes the page link for Page1.htm, but it does not affect the physical file (the data access page exists outside the Access project: for example, we can open it with a browser or another Access project). Therefore, the page is still available for use with a new link. Invoking the CreateDataAccessPage method takes advantage of this as it creates a new page link for an existing data access page.

The preceding sample specifically targets updating the link for an existing file. It does not handle renaming a link – just creating a new link. However, the next sample, which is somewhat more complex, specifically addresses renaming page links. We can run the upcoming application before the preceding one to change a page link's name and the way that it references a data access page.

Renaming Page Links

The following pair of procedures demonstrates one approach to changing page link names in a **Database** window. While it is relatively easy to perform this kind of task manually, web sites can contain hundreds, or even thousands, of pages. Therefore, it can dramatically reduce the cost of web site maintenance if developers prepare custom development tools, such as this one to manage page link names.

Whether or not you want to perform the specific function demonstrated in the sample, the code does illustrate one broadly applicable technique – how to reference an open data access page by finding a match in the AllDataAccessPages collection. Recall that this collection includes the set of all pages whether or not they are open.

```
Sub call_change_link_name()

'Print original list of pages and their links
Debug.Print "Original List of Page Links"
enumerate_pages_in_db_win

'If Change worked print a revised list
If change_link_name("Page1", "Page11") Then
    Debug.Print vbCrLf & "Updated List of Page Links"
    enumerate_pages_in_db_win
End If

End Sub

Function change_link_name(original_link_name As String, _
    new_link_name As String) As Boolean
Dim obj As AccessObject
Dim bln_open_in_design_view As Boolean

'Loop to orginal_link_name
For Each obj In CurrentProject.AllDataAccessPages
    If obj.Name = original_link_name Then
'Is page for link loaded
        If obj.IsLoaded = True Then
'Save whether open in design or page view
            If Application.DataAccessPages(obj.Name).CurrentView = 0 _
                            Then bln_open_in_design_view = True
'Rename link while it is closed
            DoCmd.SelectObject acDataAccessPage, original_link_name, False
            DoCmd.Close acDataAccessPage, original_link_name
            DoCmd.Rename new_link_name, acDataAccessPage, original_link_name
'Restore initial view
            If bln_open_in_design_view Then
                DoCmd.OpenDataAccessPage new_link_name, acDataAccessPageDesign
            Else
                DoCmd.OpenDataAccessPage new_link_name, acDataAccessPageBrowse
            End If
            change_link_name = True
        Else
'If page for link is not open, just rename link
            DoCmd.SelectObject acDataAccessPage, original_link_name, True
            DoCmd.Rename new_link_name, acDataAccessPage, original_link_name
            change_link_name = True
        End If
    End If
Next

End Function
```

The main purpose of the first sub procedure, call_change_link_name, is to pass two parameters to the second procedure, change_link_name. This second procedure is a function procedure that returns a Boolean value depending on whether it succeeded in updating the name of the page link. If the link for which we want to change the name does not exist, then the function procedure obviously can not change its name. In addition to passing parameters to the second procedure, the first procedure gives as many as two snapshots of the page links. The first one is before the change, and the second listing of page links occurs after the change if the second procedure does revise a link name. The procedure calls the enumerate_pages_in_db_win procedure discussed above to generate the listings.

The second procedure uses the DoCmd object's Rename method to assign a new link name. By itself, this command takes just one line. However, we have to first locate the page link before we can invoke the method. A For Each...Next loop on the members of the AllDataAccessPages collection facilitates this goal.

We can only invoke the Rename method for links pointing at closed pages. An If...Then statement within the loop tests the IsLoaded property of the AllDataAccessPages member we have just located, to assess if the pages for links are open or closed. For links pointing at closed pages, the procedure selects the link, invokes the method, and assigns a True value to the function procedure.

If the page for a link is open, the procedure performs the same tasks but it must take a more convoluted route. This is because it has to close the page before invoking the method. However, it is proper etiquette to restore environments after we make changes. Therefore, the procedure re-opens the page. The page can initially be open in either Page view or Design view, and the sample code uses the CurrentView property of members in the DataAccessPages collection to determine in which view a page is open. If this property equals 0, then it restores the page to a Design view; otherwise the procedure re-opens using Page view to show the page.

Creating a Data Access Page in Page Design View

Creating data access pages in Design view is straightforward and has strong similarities to creating forms in Access. For example, there is a Field List control to help us populate a page with fields from a database object in the current connection. We also have a Toolbox control for adding controls to a page. We have to assign a field reference to bind these controls, or we can use them as unbound controls when our application requirements call for them. While creating new pages from Design view is more involved than using the Page Wizard, it offers more functionality. Most developers will find the extra features well worth the extra work. For example, this section indicates how to edit the behavior of the navigation bar in a form on a data access page. Beyond that, we learn how to use Design view to create forms that behave as if they had bound images and controls with custom event procedures.

Creating a Data Access Page Based on a Table

We can create a form for data entry and browsing from Design view. This approach grants more flexibility in the design and function of our data access pages than we get with the Page Wizard. For example, we can create a data access page for the categories table in the Chapter10Northwind database. Recall that this database serves double duty as the sample database for this chapter and the preceding one.

We're going to go through the procedure for creating a Data Access Page based on a table in three easy steps.

- ❑ First, we'll create the table.
- ❑ Secondly, we'll customize the layout of the objects.
- ❑ And thirdly, we'll add a title and change the dimensions of the page.

After we've created the table, we'll have a look at what it does.

Creating the Data Access Page

We are now ready to construct a data access page based on the Categories table. Start by highlighting Pages in the Objects bar if it is not already selected. Then, double-click Create data access page in

Design View: this opens a blank data access template in Design view. Next, make sure that the Field List dialog is available. If it doesn't appear, click the Field List control on the Page Design toolbar (this control looks like the Field List control in an Access report or form Design view). This control opens the Field List dialogs with four data folders on its Database tab. By default, these folders let us select a data source from table, view, or stored procedure objects in the current connection. A fourth folder has the label Database Diagrams. It offers access to the same table data sources available from the Tables folder. The Database Diagrams folder organizes the tables by the collection of database diagrams associated with an Access project. From the Database Diagrams folder, we can select from a subset of tables within a particular diagram instead of all the tables within a project.

These four folders extend from a Connection object. By default, this object connects to the database for the current Access project. However, we can open the Connection object and designate an alternative SQL Server or Access database file source for the data access page. Unlike ASP, data access pages are restricted to connecting to SQL Server and Jet 4.0 databases. The Connection object opens to an interface that is very similar to the Data Link properties dialog for an Access project.

The following screenshot depicts an open Tables folder with the Categories table dragged from the Field List dialog to the empty data access page. The rectangle around the grid below the Section: Unbound label denotes the table; the small box within the rectangle denotes the position of the cursor.

Releasing the mouse opens the Layout Wizard. This enables developers to choose a classic form layout or a PivotTable List control. The PivotTable List control will gain focus later in the chapter. For now, just choose Individual Controls on the Layout Wizard dialog, which will add three controls for the CategoryID, CategoryName, and Description fields. The Layout Wizard automatically rejects the data in the Picture column because there is no HTML control for the data type in that column, as the message Access will display tells us. Selecting the columns from a table can also be done individually, allowing us to choose which we have on the page.

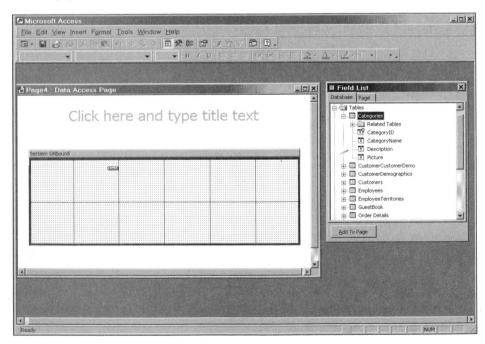

After the completion of these steps, we have the rough layout of a form. For example, we can click the View control on the Page Design toolbar and see what the page looks like. The exact position of controls will depend on where we position the Layout Wizard dialog when choosing Individual Controls by clicking OK.

Customizing the Page Layout

It is highly likely that we will want to rearrange the controls on the page. While we can do this manually without any assistance, the Alignment and Sizing toolbar is available to ease the task. If the toolbar is not already open, we can expose it by choosing View | Toolbars | Alignment and Sizing. Then, we drag any control to where we want the other controls to align.

Next, click one of the tools on the Alignment and Sizing toolbar. Our selection includes tools for left, right, top, and bottom aligning. In addition, it includes three other tools for matching controls on height, width, or height *and* width. The following screen depicts the mouse pointer over the CategoryName control (we have highlighted this by drawing a circle around it – the circle will obviously not appear on the actual screen!). Notice that it looks like the Left Align control, which is the selected button. Clicking the control aligns the left edge of the CategoryName control with the CategoryID control. We can repeat the process for the Description control. This can require selecting a base control (CategoryID), highlighting an alignment or sizing control, and clicking a control targeted for change.

If we have several controls that require the same type of alignment with a base control, we can simplify the process. Start by selecting the base control. Then, select the alignment or sizing tool that you want to use repeatedly with a double-click. This action persists the selection for more than one use. Finally, just click each control that you want to re-align.

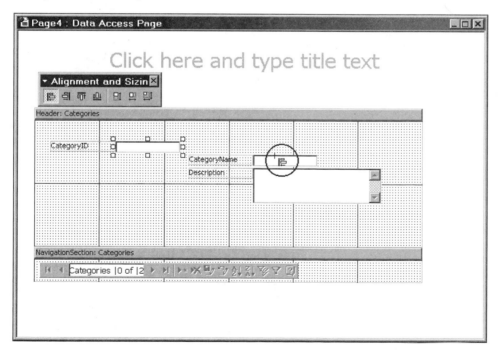

Notice that the Layout Wizard automatically selects a multi-line text box for the Description field values. The multi-line text box is more flexible than a manually expanded single-line box since it includes a scroll bar for viewing multiple lines.

Adding a Title

Data access page templates include a pre-formatted title area above the form. This area has an HTML H1 tag. We can type any heading we like into it, such as a title or brief instructions for the form. We will use this area as a title for the page, calling it A Customized Form for the Categories Table. We can also type additional text below the pre-formatted H1 title area. This additional text will initially appear in an HTML normal font, but we can re-format the text with the aid of the Formatting toolbar. This approach may be more appealing to Access users because of its graphical nature.

Nevertheless, the entire process relies on HTML and DHTML in the background. We can expose the raw HTML and DHTML for a page by choosing Tools | Macro | Microsoft Script Editor (the keyboard shortcut is *Alt+Shift+F11*). Subsequent examples will illustrate how to work in this environment. We can return to Page Design view by choosing File | Exit from the new window that appears when we select the Microsoft Script Editor. If you're comfortable with writing web documents, you can of course use any text file editor to write HTML, although you will need to have saved the file before doing so. The Microsoft Script Editor represents a more integrated approach, as we don't need to save the data access page before editing the HTML and DHTML it is built on.

We can control the page dimensions by dragging the boundaries of the section containing the controls. Click anywhere inside the area that isn't an existing control. This exposes handles around the edge of the area; drag any of these handles to make the area larger and smaller.

After re-arranging the controls and performing any other appropriate editing, we may be ready to save our page. If the page will have multiple authors on multiple machines, be sure to use a UNC format for specifying the destination path.

What our Page Does

Before we start talking about how to edit the navigation bar functions, lets look at the data access page we just created. We can open the page by double-clicking it from the Database window. This page contains a basic form that allows users to edit the underlying data. We can create a form like this one with the graphical steps described above. Notice that the category description has the letter z appended five times to the end of the category description: this is so we can see how the Page reacts to the user. The cursor rests on the control that can update the database with the new content if the user clicks it. Notice that not all of these controls are enabled when the page loads. Only after we have added something to one of the text boxes do the Save and Undo buttons cease to be grayed out.

When we select a page link we want to remove and click Delete on the Database window frame, Access responds by presenting a prompt that asks if we want to delete the data access page. When we click Yes, Access responds with another pop-up dialog that gives us the option to remove just the link, the link and the page file at which it points, or abort altogether. We should click Yes if we want to delete both the link and its underlying page.

Editing Navigation Bar Functions

Many applications will benefit from all the "extra" functions that the Navigation bar control provides. However, some applications will want to restrict at least some of its capabilities. For example, we may care to restrict the ability of users to edit data in one or several ways. We can selectively limit the ability of users to delete or edit values for existing records. In addition, we can eliminate the capability to add new records.

There are two ways we can restrict what the user can accomplish with the Navigation Bar:

- ❑ Disabling Navigation Bar Buttons
- ❑ Stopping the Data Access Page Updating the Database

Disabling Navigation Bar Buttons

We can edit Navigation bar control display properties by manipulating its properties. The Design view for data access pages enables us to accomplish this task manually. Start by selecting the bar. Then, click the Properties tool on the Page Design tool bar. For the page we've just created, this opens a dialog with a caption of Object: CategoriesNavigation.

This dialog organizes properties for the Navigation bar on the page with four tabs. Click the Other tab and scroll down to expose all the properties whose name begins with Show. These properties start with ShowDelButton and end with ShowUndoButton. Each of the properties prefixed by Show determines the visibility of some element on the Navigation bar. With the default setting of True, users can see the element. To remove a control from the Navigation bar change the property setting for the corresponding control from True to False.

If a requirement for a form was that it disabled the ability to delete records, we could do this by changing the ShowDelButton property from True to False. There is no need to move off the property setting to confirm the choice. In fact, Access shows the new appearance of the Navigation bar in Design view. The Delete control disappears from the Navigation bar.

Four controls enable the editing of data via a form on a data access page. The property names corresponding to these controls are ShowNewButton, ShowDelButton, ShowSaveButton, and ShowUndoButton. The first two properties determine the visibility of controls for adding and deleting records. The ShowSaveButton property sets the visibility of the control that commits to the database any edits that users make to the contents of a record in a form. The ShowUndo property determines the visibility of the control that discards changes to the record displaying in a form and restores the original data in the display. When we start to customize the display of controls on a form, we will probably want to set the ShowHelpButton property to False. This will suppress the display of *all* Help dialogs, including those for the features that we eliminated.

The following screen depicts the settings to remove all special data-editing controls from a form. All four properties for data editing controls have settings of False. In addition, the ShowHelpButton property is False so users cannot learn that we are suppressing features built into the form automatically. The dialog on the right shows the settings. The form on the left shows the edited Navigation bar. Notice that it contains fewer controls than with previous samples. This new form contains controls to view data locally, but it has no controls to change data. While users can sort and filter it locally, these manipulations do not impact on the use of the form's data source by other users.

It would obviously be nice to be able to provide Help for only those features that are included, but the method of doing this is beyond the scope of the book. This example is here to show how the control form's appearance can be changed by manipulating its properties at Design time.

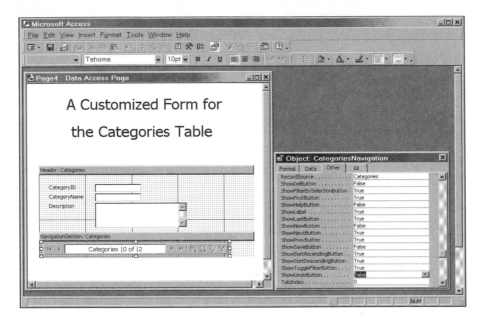

The updated property settings in the preceding example do not entirely remove editing capabilities. These new settings just eliminate the visibility of controls on the Navigation bar. In the case of add and delete functions, removing the controls is the same as removing the capability. This is because the control fully exposes the capability. However, users can normally update a record in a bound form without relying on the Save control. All they have to do is make a change, and then navigate off the record. The data access page automatically commits the change to the database.

Stopping the Data Access Page Updating the Database

The RecordsetType property of a page can eliminate fully the capability of users to edit data. We can expose this property by clicking a page's title bar in Design view, opening the Properties dialog, and selecting the Data tab. The property has two possible settings. The default setting is dscUpdatableSnapshot. This setting creates a local cache and causes updates to the cache to propagate to the database server.

Change the setting to dscSnapshot if we need to totally prevent data editing capabilities within a form on a data access page. After making the change, users will no longer be able to edit records at all. In fact, this update means that users can't even alter the text in the record, so there is no need for the Save button to appear. Changing the setting of ShowSaveButton to True causes the Save button to appear on the Navigation bar, but it remains permanently disabled whenever the RecordsetType property for the page is dscSnapshot.

The following screen depicts a data access page with the four properties for editing buttons set to False. In addition, the settings suppress the visibility of the Help control. Finally, the page's RecordsetType property has a dscSnapshot assignment. These settings remove data editing controls and they eliminate the ability to edit via the record navigation controls. We cannot even make a change to a value in a form field.

The screen shows the whole Description field value highlighted, but the form will not permit any changes to the field value. Recall that we could make changes with the earlier version of the page showing fields from the Categories table. This earlier version accepted the default property settings for the Navigation bar and the page's RecordsetType property.

Forms with Images on Data Access Pages

If you followed the instructions for the example that created a form based on the Categories table, you will recall the error message for the Picture column in the table. The column has an image data type that does not fit into HTML controls for display on web pages. Unless we need the picture in the application, this is not a problem. However, many applications do benefit from the ability to display pictures on forms. This is possible with data access pages. The next sample demonstrates how to do this.

The approach involves building a stored procedure with a return set that includes the addresses for the image files denoting categories. The return set will also include the CategoryID, CategoryName, and Description columns from the Categories table. Since the Design view for data access pages permits referencing stored procedures, this database object can serve as a source for a form.

We need two resources to make this work. First, we need a folder of category images. This example takes advantage of the collection of category images developed in Chapter 10. These images reside in the \\cab2000\c\inetpub\wwwroot\adss\images folder within the local intranet on which this example was created. We will need to update this path for our particular computing environment.

Second, we need a stored procedure to assist in the maintenance of the image file addresses. Chapter 10 gave us a stored procedure that created a table of picture addresses, called create_picture_addresses. However, we can't use that stored procedure, because the ASP sample performed HTML encoding for the image names and it used relative addresses. Neither of these techniques is appropriate when dealing with data access pages. On the other hand, the addresses for the image files in the data access page application are longer. These addresses use UNC notation. The ASP example uses relative addresses. Therefore, the Address column receives a width of 128 in the example for data access pages. This contrasts with a maximum width of only 50 characters for the ASP example.

Knowing Where to Find the Image

The following stored procedure assists in the maintenance of the picture_addresses_dap table. This procedure creates the table, but it erases any prior version, if one already exists. The table has two columns – one to hold CategoryID values and a second to hold addresses for image files. As it creates the table, it defines a primary key based on both columns and a foreign key that ties the picture_addresses_dap table to the Categories table via referential integrity. The procedure closes with a series of INSERT statements that populate the table with values. Don't forget to specify a UNC path that your computer can reach when you run this procedure yourself.

If we have a relatively short list of images that do not change very often, we can use a file very similar to this to maintain our images. If we have many images that change frequently, we may require a more advanced stored procedure and table for holding the image addresses. Nevertheless, we can still use the same general principles.

> *As we pointed out previously, the samples in this chapter were developed on a SQL Server 2000 database server, so its database file format is not usable on either MSDE or SQL Server 7. However, we can, by using the stored procedure below, copy the scripts for procedures into an MSDE or SQL Server 7 database to add custom objects to a standard version of the* Northwind *database or the* NorthwindCS *database.*

```
Alter Procedure create_picture_addresses_dap
As

--Drop the table if it already exists
if exists (select * from dbo.sysobjects where id =
object_id(N'[dbo].[picture_addresses_dap]')
and OBJECTPROPERTY(id, N'IsUserTable') = 1)
drop table [dbo].[picture_addresses_dap]

--Create the new version of the table
CREATE TABLE [dbo].[picture_addresses_dap] (
    [CategoryID] [int] NOT NULL ,
    [Address] [nvarchar] (128) COLLATE SQL_Latin1_General_CP1_CI_AS NOT NULL
) ON [PRIMARY]

--Designate a Primary Key for the table
ALTER TABLE [dbo].[picture_addresses_dap] WITH NOCHECK ADD
    CONSTRAINT [PK_picture_addresses_dap] PRIMARY KEY  CLUSTERED
    (
        [CategoryID],
        [Address]
    )  ON [PRIMARY]

--Designate a Foreign Key for the table
ALTER TABLE [dbo].[picture_addresses_dap] ADD
    CONSTRAINT [FK_picture_addresses_dap_Categories] FOREIGN KEY
    (
        [CategoryID]
    ) REFERENCES [dbo].[Categories] (
        [CategoryID]
    )

--Populate the table with values
INSERT picture_addresses_dap
VALUES (1, '\\cab2000\c\inetpub\wwwroot\adss\images\Beverages.gif')
```

```
INSERT picture_addresses_dap
VALUES (2, '\\cab2000\c\inetpub\wwwroot\adss\images\Condiments.gif')
INSERT picture_addresses_dap
VALUES (3, '\\cab2000\c\inetpub\wwwroot\adss\images\Confections.gif')
INSERT picture_addresses_dap
VALUES (4, '\\cab2000\c\inetpub\wwwroot\adss\images\Dairy Products.gif')
INSERT picture_addresses_dap
VALUES (5, '\\cab2000\c\inetpub\wwwroot\adss\images\Grains and Cereals.gif')
INSERT picture_addresses_dap
VALUES (6, '\\cab2000\c\inetpub\wwwroot\adss\images\Meat and Poultry.gif')
INSERT picture_addresses_dap
VALUES (7, '\\cab2000\c\inetpub\wwwroot\adss\images\Produce.gif')
INSERT picture_addresses_dap
VALUES (8, '\\cab2000\c\inetpub\wwwroot\adss\images\Seafood.gif')
```

The sample code below shows the stored procedure that joins the Categories and picture_addresses_dap tables. The name of the stored procedure is categories_and_addresses_dap. The return set from this stored procedure includes the non-image data type fields from the Categories table merged with the Address column values from the picture_addresses_dap table. The Query Designer that permits the graphical designs of views makes it a natural candidate for creating the record source for our sample. However, using stored procedures serves a couple of purposes: firstly, the graphical designer is not working properly with the beta version of SQL Server 2000 (Microsoft promises it will work by the time the product ships); and secondly, using a stored procedure confirms that we have more flexibility when manually creating a form from Page Design view than with the Page Wizard, which restricts record sources to tables and views.

```
Alter Procedure categories_and_addresses_dap
As
SELECT Categories.CategoryID, Categories.CategoryName,
    Categories.Description, picture_addresses_dap.Address
FROM Categories INNER JOIN
    picture_addresses_dap ON
    Categories.CategoryID = picture_addresses_dap.CategoryID
```

Putting the Image on the Data Access Page

With the preceding two stored procedures built, we are ready to start graphically designing our form on the data access page that will display text, numeric, and image data. The page uses the categories_and_addresses_dap stored procedure as its data source. Start by opening a blank page in Design view. Then, open the Stored Procedures folder in the Field List dialog. Next, drag the icon for the categories_and_addresses_dap stored procedure to the page. Click OK to accept the Individual Controls layout from the Layout Wizard.

Since the Address column has an nvarchar data type, Access automatically assigns it to a text box control. We'll want to remove this control, unless we want the user to see where we keep our picture files. Then, open the Toolbox. Select the Image control and drag an area for the size that we want our category pictures.

The following screen depicts this step in the process. Releasing the mouse control opens the Insert Picture dialog to the default folder for images. Select any image file. Leave the Image control selected, and open its Properties dialog to the Data tab. Click at the right end of the ControlSource property box to open a drop-down list with the fields in the record source for the page. Select Address. This selection causes the image control to display the image for the file address in the Address field. Use the Alignment and Sizing tool bar to position the image control so that its left edge aligns with the other controls on the form. Now, add a label for the Image control. Drag a label control from the Toolbox to the page. Open its Properties dialog to the Other tab. Assign an appropriate caption for the category images, such as Picture, by entering it in the InnerText property box.

The instructions to add the image control direct us to select "any" image file. The "any" part is true, but it isn't really good practice. We need to specify the address of an image to tack the image control on the page. However, as a data access page opens, it briefly populates the image control with the "any" image file we select. Therefore, our form will look better if we use as our "any" image the one that should initially appear. In the example above, this is the Beverages image at \\cab2000\c\inetpub\wwwroot\adss\images\Beverages.gif. Alternatively, use an image that is the same as the background, or even an appropriate logo. This kind of attention to design detail makes for better appearing data access pages.

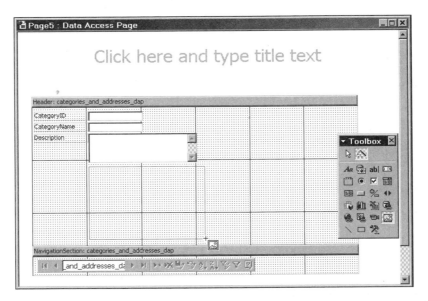

There is just one more property to edit. Select the Navigation bar and open its Properties dialog. Scroll to the RecordsetLabel property box on the Other tab. Replace the first instance of "categories_and_addresses_dap" with "Category Pictures". This puts a meaningful label, Category Pictures, in the Navigation bar label. The following screen shows the highlighted text ready for replacement. After replacing the label, drag the Navigation control's right edge until we can view the whole label in the label's window. Before viewing the page in Page view, we may care to add a custom title for our form.

The following screen reveals the finished form on a data access page in Page view. We can perform any of the additional customizations mentioned above to it. For example, we can re-size the image control to make it bigger. If we want multiple authors to work with the file, remember to save it with a UNC file designation.

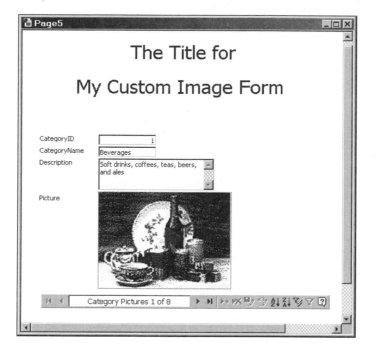

Before launching into a discussion of the Microsoft Script Editor, let's review the third way to create a data access page in a project. This method links a web page that already exists. Recall that Access projects merely hold page links. The data access page exists as stand-alone `.htm` *file. When we delete a page from an Access project, we have the option of deleting just the page link or the page link and its associated* `.htm` *file. Therefore, it is easy to have data access pages on our computer or an intranet for which there is no page link in a particular project. This feature is potentially useful to build a series of "template" DAPs that can then be used to help create new pages more quickly.*

We can create a data access page within a project by double-clicking Edit Web page that already exists *from the* Database *window with* Pages *selected in the* Objects *bar. This technique for building new page links to previously disconnected pages works as well for pages created by other authors or by you in other Access projects. Double-clicking the item opens the* Locate Web *Page dialog. Highlight a desired page file and click* Open *to open it within the current Access project. Then, choose* File | Save *to re-save the page with any changes that we made as well as create a page link for it in the current project.*

Working in the Microsoft Script Editor

The Design view for pages and the object model for manipulating pages offer some attractive features. Nevertheless, these development environments do not support many typical development tasks. For example, there has been no mention of event procedures to this point. By using the Microsoft Script Editor, we can expose another realm of programmatic features. This editor exposes the elements on a web page, and it does richly support event procedures. This section introduces the Microsoft Script Editor and event programming within it. We'll do this in the following sections:

❑   Creating a Form with a Click Event

❑   Using our Form

❑   Making a Text Box Read-Only

❑   Writing an `AfterUpdate` Event Procedure

Creating a Form with a Click Event

We can layout the form we're going to use by opening a new page in Design view. These instructions work from the `Chapter10.adp` file (or any Access project with a connection to the Northwind database). Once we've got our blank page, open the Toolbox if it isn't already open. Add to the form a text box control and command button control. Each of these controls will require us to manually position and size it. Select the control type we want by clicking it in the Toolbox, then click and drag to establish its position and size on the page.

Next, select the Control Wizard control on the Toolbox if it isn't already selected. Then, add a Dropdown list control to the form below the text box. This opens the Combo Box Wizard (see below). Then, just follow the wizard screens. We want to create a combo box based on the Categories table that displays the CategoryName column value, but stores the CategoryID column value. The selections we have to specify to the wizard are as follows:

❑   Select I want the combo box to look up the values in a table or view

❑   Select the Categories table

❑   Select CategoryID and CategoryName, in that order using the Select button (\)

❑   Adjust the column width if desired

❑   Give our combo box a label

We can add an unformatted combo box to the form and then assign properties with the Properties dialog, but it is simpler and faster to use the wizard. Complete the basic layout of the form by opening the Alignment and Sizing toolbar. Use it to size and align controls as appropriate.

At the end of this task, we have a basic form with three controls. However, there is no interaction between them. The combo box does open and allow users to select a category, but that's all.

It assigns a CategoryID value based on the selection, but users cannot see this since the combo box displays the CategoryName value corresponding to a user selection. A click event procedure for the button can copy the value from the combo box to the text box. Then, users can click the button to see the CategoryID value that corresponds to a CategoryName value.

Adding the Click Event

To add an event procedure, open the Microsoft Script Editor (Tools | Macro | Microsoft Script Editor). This opens a new window titled with the concatenation of our page name and Microsoft Development Environment. Choose View | Other Windows | Script Outline. Expand the Client Objects & Events folder in the Script Outline window, if it is not already open. Then, expand the command button icon to view all the events that we can select for it. Double-click onclick. This leaves onclick highlighted, but it transfers control to an empty event handler in the Code window. The event handler is properly set up for the command button's onclick event. We can enter code to achieve whatever action we prefer to happen when the event fires.

Selected events require parameters that the Microsoft Script Editor in Access 2000 does not write automatically. The Current event for the Microsoft Data Source Control object is an example of this. In these cases, we need to manually revise the automatically generated event handler. Programming using the Microsoft Script Editor can be very similar to VBA programming within Access, but there are some important differences to learn that are beyond the scope of this chapter. See an excellent white paper on programming techniques for data access pages at HTTP://msdn.microsoft.com/library/techart/programdap.htm.

The following screen highlights the onclick event handler for the button's onclick event. The Script Wizard automatically inserts it in the Head block of the web page. Notice the selection of the onclick event icon in the Script Outline window. Clicking that icon created the function outline, ready for us to add assignment statement. For ease of reading, the event handler code appears in text after the screenshot.

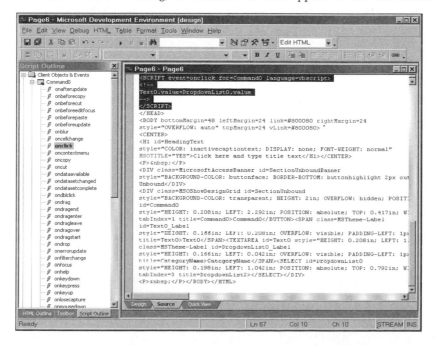

```
<SCRIPT event=onclick for=Command0 language=vbscript>
<!--
Text1.value=DropdownList2.value
--|
</SCRIPT>
```

The syntax for declaring the event handler follows VBScript conventions. Notice that we might see `language=vbscript` appearing adjacent to the `SCRIPT` keyword – the case or the positioning of the `language`, `for`, and `event` identifiers doesn't matter so long as they are inside the `<SCRIPT>` tag. Since the event handler is a client-side script, it appears in HTML block comment markets (`<!--` and `-->`). This suppresses the text for the code for browsers that do not know how to process VBScript. These comment markers are not strictly necessary in this case since data access pages only run in IE 5 browsers, and these interpret VBScript. The body of the event handler is a single line that copies the value in the combo box, with the name DropdownList2, into the text box control, with the name Text1.

After creating this event procedure, our command button will work. We'll need to switch to Page view to see the button working, or we could save the page and open it to view from the Database window. We can select an item from the combo box, click the button, and populate the text box with the CategoryID value corresponding to the CategoryName value in the combo box. There is another way of making this page perform the same way, which is to use the `onchange` event procedure, which we'll be looking at in a short while. However, this sample has the virtue of showing us how to program a `click` event procedure for a button – a task that is very typical for Access applications.

Using our Form

The following screen shows the data access page we've just created in Design view. The title added explains the function of the form. It updates the text box based on a selection from the combo box when the user clicks the button. This page demonstrates the basics of a button's click event procedure. The event procedure copies the value from the combo box and places it in the text box. The combo box saves CategoryID but shows CategoryName from the Categories table. Since the page is not bound to a data source, there is no Navigation bar. We can populate the text box with any expression we wish.

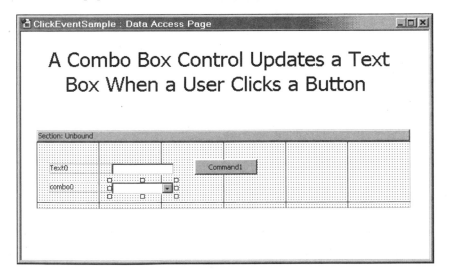

The next progression of three screens demonstrates the basic behavior of the form on the page. As the page opens in Page view, it shows Beverages in the combo box. Recall that this is the first category in the Categories table. Clicking the button at this point transfers the value "1" into the text box. The first screen on the right depicts the form immediately after the page opens.

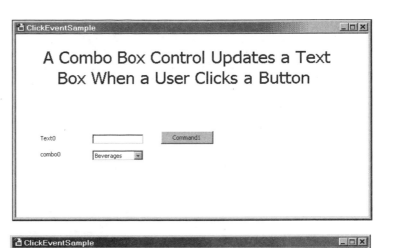

The next screen reveals the appearance of the screen after the user has performed two actions. First, the user opened the combo box and selected Confections. This is the third category in the Categories table. The text box remains blank after a user updates the value in the combo box. It is not until the user clicks the button that the text box value updates to "3".

The third and final screen in the progression reveals the appearance of the form after a user has performed another action. This time, the user clicked the combo box to select the Seafood category. Again, the combo box is unsynchronized with the text box. This is because the Seafood category has a CategoryID value of 8, but the text box shows a "3". A user can synchronize the text box with the combo box by clicking the button.

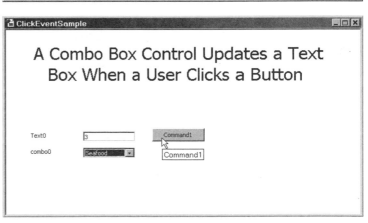

Making a Text Box Read Only

We can readily accomplish many other objectives from the Microsoft Script Editor. For example, it is especially easy to make individual controls read-only. This is a more granular level of control than we have in the Design view window for a page. In Design view, we can make the whole form read-only, but not individual controls.

Toggle back to Microsoft Script Editor (if you left it) and choose View | Properties to open the Properties window. This window acts like a Properties dialog in the Design view for a page. Then, choose View | Other Windows | Document Outline. We can select individual controls on a page from the HTML Outline window. The Properties window exposes the properties for the selected item in the HTML Outline window. In the following screenshot, the HTML Outline window shows the Text0 control selected. In the Properties window, developers can examine and update properties for objects within a page. In the screen below, the readOnly property for the text box is in the process of changing from its default value of False to True. The event handler will still be able to update the text box's value, but users will not be able to overwrite values inserted by the event handler.

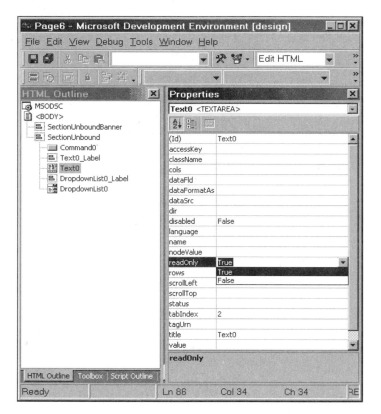

Writing an AfterUpdate Event Procedure

Access developers should be familiar with the AfterUpdate event. It lets us run a procedure to perform some action after the data changes in a control. Many developers would naturally look for this event in the preceding click event sample to simplify the operation of the form. With the AfterUpdate event, a developer can revise the text box value automatically whenever a user makes a selection from the combo box. Unfortunately, intrinsic HTML controls, such as the combo box on the form, do not support an AfterUpdate event.

When working with HTML controls, look to the onchange event to support our traditional AfterUpdate event processing requirements. This event fires after the contents of a control change. It performs similarly to the AfterUpdate event on Access forms. We can create the framework for a custom event handler for a combo box named DropdownList0 by double-clicking onchange for the control in the Client Objects &

Events folder of the Script Outline window. Then, just type our expression into the function outline Microsoft Script Editor has just created. The following sample code illustrates the procedure for copying the contents of a combo box control to a text box immediately after the user selects a new item from the combo box list.

```
<SCRIPT event=onchange for=DropdownList0 language=vbscript>
<!--
Text0.value=DropdownList0.value
-->
</SCRIPT>
```

The following screen depicts the data access page with the form immediately after the user selected Confections from the combo box list. The above event procedure automatically updated the text box. Using the onchange event like this can make our forms more interactive and require less work on the part of users. For example, using the onchange event in this case eliminates the need to require a click event for the button to transfer a value from the combo box to the text box.

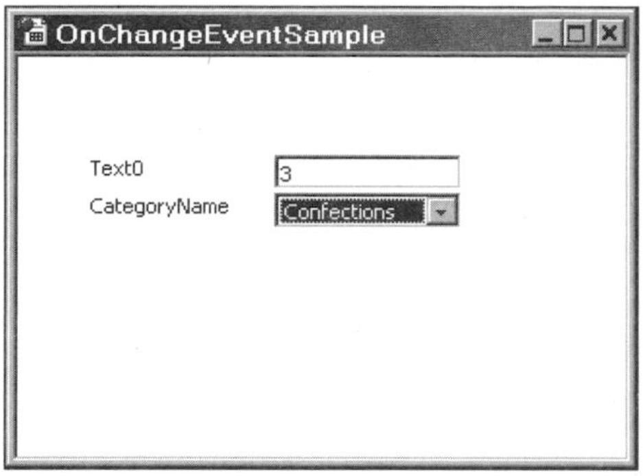

Notice the absence of the button from the above form. This form is smaller than the preceding one in another way. The caption at the top of the page is missing. When Access creates a blank page in Design view, it is not really blank. In fact, it includes an H1 tag at the top of the body section, and the H1 tag has a blank line separating it from the form design grid and its header. The H1 tag is convenient for a page title or instructions, but sometimes we just need the form.

We can make our forms more compact by eliminating the H1 tag and the blank line immediately after it. To do this, just highlight them in Design view and choose Edit | Delete. It may require more than one execution of the Delete command until the space for the tag and its trailing line disappear from the page. The number of times we must invoke Edit | Delete depends on the exactly what we select (and this is not always obvious from Design view). We can accomplish this task more precisely in the Microsoft Script Editor. Just highlight the elements that we want to remove from the Code window and choose Edit | Delete once. The Microsoft Script Editor is superior because we can view the exact items selected for removal in the Code window. If you are not handy with HTML and you find the look and feel of the Microsoft Script Editor an unfamiliar, unfriendly looking place, then perform the task as described in Design view.

Creating Interactive Grouping and Sorting Reports

The data access pages presented so far in this chapter all demonstrated how to create forms. In many ways, these forms emulated the ease of development and power of Access forms – except forms on data access pages work over a web. While the capability of Access to create powerful forms is one reason for its immense popularity as a database development tool, Access is also highly regarded for its ability to generate reports.

We can readily create data access pages that have a strong resemblance to Access reports. In particular, data access pages support banded report sections.

They also offer grouping and sorting capabilities. Reports are inherently read-only and so are reports on data access pages.

Finally, data access pages add a new interactive feature that permits users to expand and contract report sections dynamically as they view them over a web. This section examines techniques for using expressions on data access pages. Data access pages permit the use of expressions in either forms or reports.

We'll be breaking this discussion on reports down into four easier-to-handle sections. These sections are as follows:

❑   Reporting Products within Categories

❑   Working with Bound HTML Controls and Caption Sections

❑   Sorting Records and Controlling Page Size

❑   Calculating in a Report

Reporting Products within Categories

The Northwind database view named Alphabetical list of products combines data from both the Categories and the Products tables. Due to this, the data source serves as a good model for a grouping report. This is because categories group together collections of similar products – for example, all the products in the Beverages category are for drinking.

Using the techniques that we learned so far, it is relatively simple to create a data access page that might serve as the basis for a future report. Our form could list CategoryName, ProductName, UnitPrice, and UnitsInStock. This is the kind of report that can serve multiple purposes, including price and stock-on-hand lookups. As the view is built from two tables, users cannot update any of the fields unless we set the UniqueTable property to the "most-many" table, which is the Products table in this example.

The UniqueTable property can be found on the Data tab of the Properties dialog for the Navigation section. The following example builds the data access page without setting the property. This is sufficient since we want this form to act like a report anyway – and users cannot update report field values. This UniqueTable property came up previously in Chapter 7 in the discussion of forms. The property is the same for both Access forms and data access pages. To update record values within a form based on two or more tables the UniqueTable property must be set properly. We can do this by referencing with the property the table that has its values repeated the most in the recordset for the form or data access page.

Setting up our Page

Start with a blank data access page in Design View. Then, open the Field List, and double-click several fields from below the icon for the Alphabetical list of products view. Double-clicking automatically stacks the fields in the default control type one below the other within the data access page. The default control type is a text box. This type of control serves both viewing and updating purposes. This text box control is an HTML text box. Access automatically transforms the control type to match the data type for a field. For example, if we are working with a bit data type, Access automatically returns a check box control. In any event, select CategoryName, ProductName, UnitPrice, and UnitsInStock. Access automatically adds a Navigation bar control to complete the form. The following screenshot depicts the form at the completion of these steps.

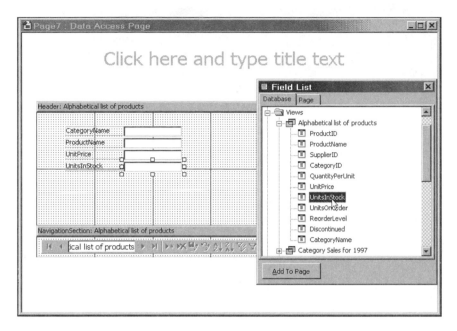

As we use this page, we will note two things. First, the navigation bar may not show the full name of the record source; selecting the Navigation bar in Design view and dragging it to the right size easily remedies this.

The second thing to note is that it permits us to browse the 69 products. These exclude rows from the discontinued items from the Products table. That is a consequence of the definition from the underlying record source. The data access page allows us to browse the records in their natural order – namely, ordered by ProductID. While users can override this by sorting the records with the help of the Navigation bar, this requires an extra step. If the main emphasis of the page is to show products within a category, it is unproductive to require users to perform a sort to obtain that order. Also, if users want to find a particular record, they must either browse the records sequentially or filter the recordset on a field value that is in their target record to help narrow the search. These requirements are not efficient.

Grouping our Products Records by Category

By now, you should be wondering just how you do group product records by category. The answer is to click the Promote control on the Page Design toolbar. This appears as a left-pointing arrow, as in the following screen overleaf. First, we have to select the field to promote over the others. This enables the Promote control on the toolbar (it is disabled until we select a control). Second, click the Promote control. This action moves the control we had selected to above the other controls, in a section of it's own. Access adds an expand indicator next to the grouping field. This new type of control enables users to expand and contract grouped records. This will be demonstrated shortly. If we want to add other controls to the new header section, we can just drag them into it.

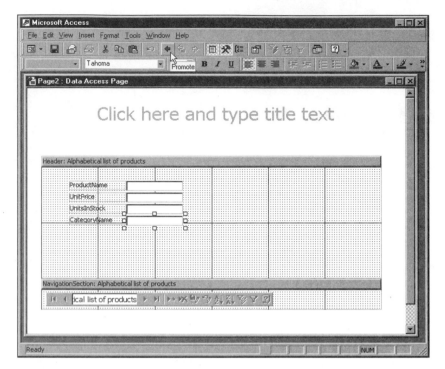

Promoting a field adds a second Navigation bar to the page, with a different name. In this example, the new Navigation bar has the text Alphabetical list of products – CategoryName. With this second bar, users can move across sets of values for the grouping field. By default, Access creates a page size of 5 records for both the grouping field and the grouped fields. However, we can override the default setting independently for the grouping field values and the grouped records, which is what we'll be doing later in this section.

Selecting the CategoryName field from our previous data access page in Design view and clicking the Promote control creates a page layout like the one opposite above. The layout was adjusted in two ways:

- ❑ First, the height of the design grid area below the CategoryName section was shrunk to make the field values easier to examine in Page view. Other solutions exist for this issue, and we consider one in a subsequent sample.

- ❑ Second, the right edges of the Navigation bars were dragged to make it easier to read their labels. It is necessary to read the Navigation bar labels since we have two of them and their labels start with the same set of characters.

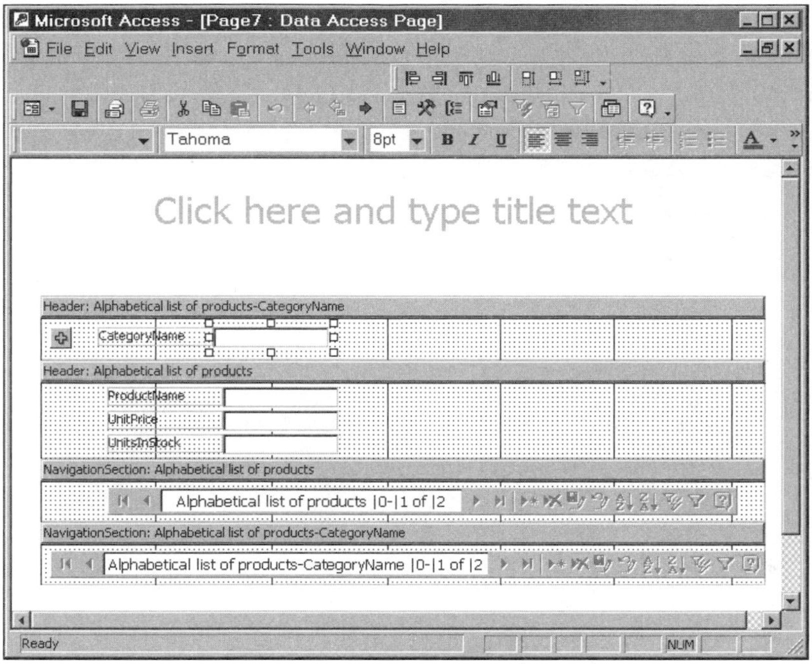

The expand indicator appears as a plus sign on a button next to the CategoryName field. Furthermore, the field has its own section on the page. Below the CategoryName section are the remaining fields in another section. In Page view, the fields in this second section appear grouped as records below the CategoryName field values. The two Navigation bar controls allow users to page independently through CategoryName field values and the records grouped within these values. Recall that the default page size is 5 records.

The next screen reveals the preceding data access page in Page view. Notice that there are five CategoryName values showing. We can view the remaining CategoryName values by clicking the Next control on the bottom Navigation bar. Notice that its label includes the field name for the grouping field, CategoryName. Four of the five expand indicators show a plus sign (+), but the one for Dairy Products has a minus sign (−) on its indicator. This category is expanded to show the individual product records within it. Click the indicator once to view the records grouped for a CategoryName field value, and a second time to contract them.

Notice the Navigation bar below the expanded records. We can use its controls to browse, sort, and filter the records within a group. With this type of design, data access pages do not enable any data maintenance functions – even if we are working with a single table. The same is true for the grouping field values. The nested Navigation bar appears only if we have the records for at least one group expanded. If no groups are expanded, then users only see the Navigation bar for the grouping field, which is CategoryName in this example.

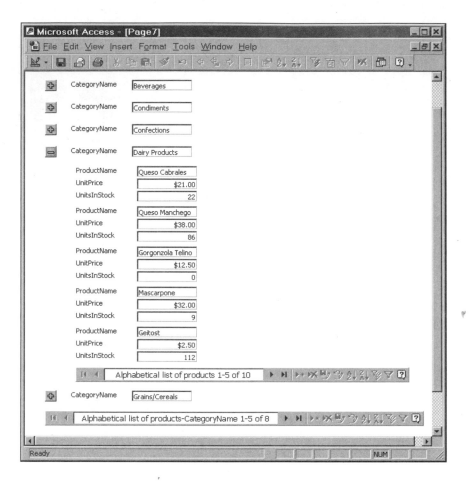

Working with Bound HTML Controls and Caption Sections

There are two issues that emerge from the preceding sample. First, the example uses text box controls, but a simpler control that just displays data is sufficient. This is because the controls on the page are read-only. In fact, the Toolbox for data access pages does offer a Bound HTML control that is just for viewing data. That is, it does not permit data editing. In addition to fitting the role more precisely, this control enables data access pages to load faster. Therefore, we should always consider the Bound HTML control when it matches the needs of an application.

Second, the length of the expanded records is longer than necessary because it displays fields in a columnar format. This requires three rows for every record. However, a tabular layout displays the three fields for a record across a single row. Therefore, the default 5-record page size takes 15 rows with the columnar layout, but it would require just 5 rows with a tabular layout. This will make it easier to view all the CategoryName values on a page and at least one expanded category page on a single computer screen. We'll be taking a look at how to do this in this section.

Data access pages support a Caption section for each nested section. This caption section for the records that expand and contract is particularly well suited to working with nested data in a tabular format. To add a Caption section for the records that expand, switch to Design view for the page and choose View | Sorting and Grouping. Continuing from the preceding example, this opens the Sorting and Grouping dialog with two entries in its Group Record Source section. These entries have labels that match the Navigation bar labels.

Selecting the row for an entry in the Group Record Source pane of the Sorting and Grouping dialog allows us to control several aspects of the way records form a Navigation bar display. This is done in the lower half of the dialog, Group Properties, and includes the availability of a Caption section.

The objective here is to add a Caption section for the display of the records with the nested Navigation bar. Therefore, highlight the row with the label that reads Alphabetical list of products. Then, click the right edge of the Caption Section box in the property list below the dialog's Group Record Source section. Change the setting from its default value of No to Yes. This immediately adds a Caption section to the page between the top Header section for CategoryName and the Header section for the nested records. The following screen presents the new data access page design with the Caption section. We can also see the Sorting and Grouping dialog with the settings that created the new section.

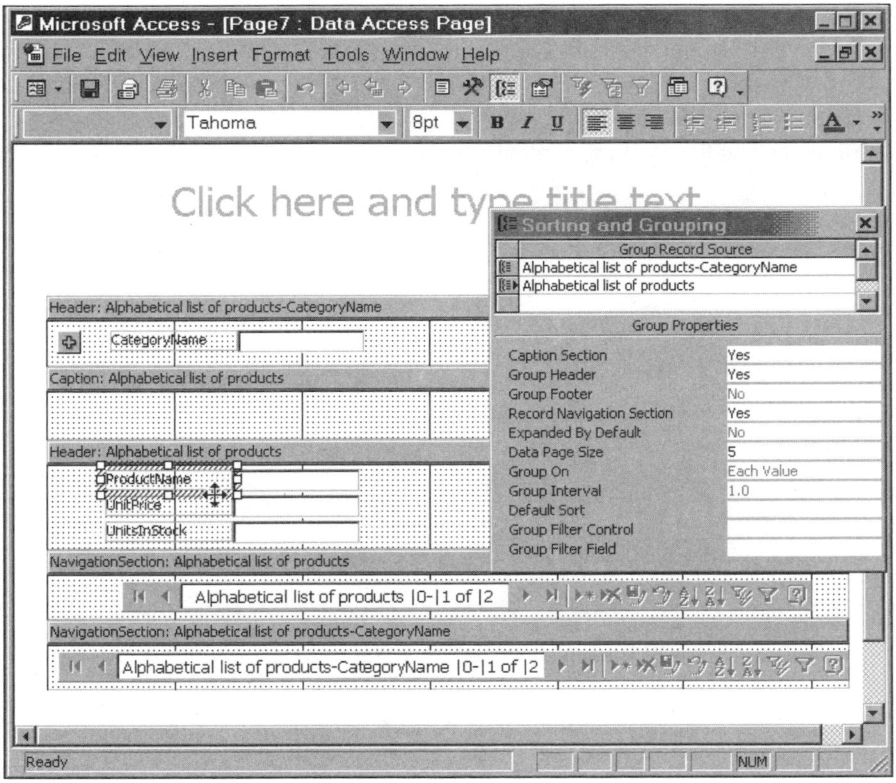

In the previous screenshot, we can see the caption for the first nested field has been selected and is about to be moved. For the next step in our example, we're going to need to move all three nested field captions into the Caption section. This is because when we add the Bound HTML controls, they don't create their own captions in the Header or Caption sections. If we don't have the text box caption controls, we can add label controls from the Toolbox to name the columns in the tabular display we're creating. Either way, we'll have to delete the text box controls in the Header section, which we can do by selecting them and pressing the *Delete* key. Select the captions for UnitPrice and UnitsInStock individually and right-align their contents with the Align Right control on the Formatting toolbar. This is desirable because the UnitPrice and UnitInStock field values automatically appear with a right alignment since they are numeric.

Adding Bound HTML Controls

We are now ready to add and layout the three Bound HTML layout controls for the ProductName, UnitPrice, and UnitsInStock fields. Open the Toolbox and double-click the Bound HTML control, enabling the instruction to add a Bound HTML control for multiple uses.

Next, drag and drop from the Field List dialog the three field names from the Alphabetical list of products view. After adding the controls for the fields, click again the Bound HTML control in the Toolbox to free the mouse cursor for other purposes.

Use the Alignment and Sizing toolbar to position the newly added Bound HTML controls below the caption controls in the Caption section and horizontally to one another in the Header section. In addition, re-size the Bound HTML controls so that they do not overlap one another, and have enough space for the text they will be containing.

The following screen displays the newly formatted report for nesting ProductName, UnitPrice, and UnitsInStock within CategoryName (the vertical extent of each section has been purposely reduced – this has the benefit of making it easier to present more expanded sections on a single computer screen).

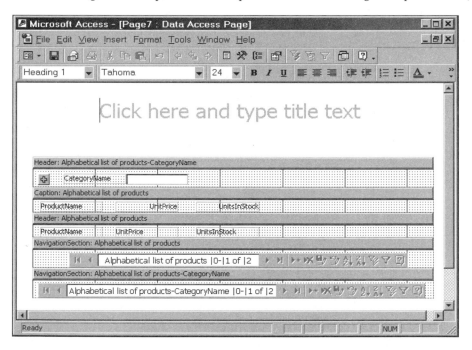

The next display shows the preceding data access page in Page view. Notice how efficiently it presents information. In just 10 rows, this page presents 5-record pages for both the Confections and Dairy Products categories. The previous page design required 5 more rows to present just one page for the Dairy Products category. Minimizing the vertical extent of each section also contributes to the efficient use of screen space, although some users might find it harder to read.

The steps to perform the transformation from the preceding Page view to the one below were manual. We did not have to program the layout. This is in marked contrast to building ASP solutions, which are code intensive. There was no need for an HTML table although the data appears in a tabular format. In fact, the general layout approach was similar, but not identical, to how we manually lay out forms and reports in Access. Developers who are more familiar with the Access graphical development techniques, and others who want to graphically build web solutions, can substantially speed up their development time by using data access pages.

Sorting Records and Controlling Page Size

There are many ways to customize reports on data access pages. Two of these permit us to modify the page size and the sort order of items on a nested page. The Sorting and Grouping dialog helps us to manage these aspects of a report. By reducing the page size, we make it easier to open two or more nested pages on the same computer screen without scrolling. We can independently set the page size for both the outer field used for grouping and as the inner records that are nested. The overleaf screen shows the Sorting and Grouping dialog with the inner, nested rows selected. Notice the Data Page Size setting is 3. This means that the data access page will display the data in groups of three, instead of five, which is the default setting. We can type any number to indicate how many records we want to show on a page.

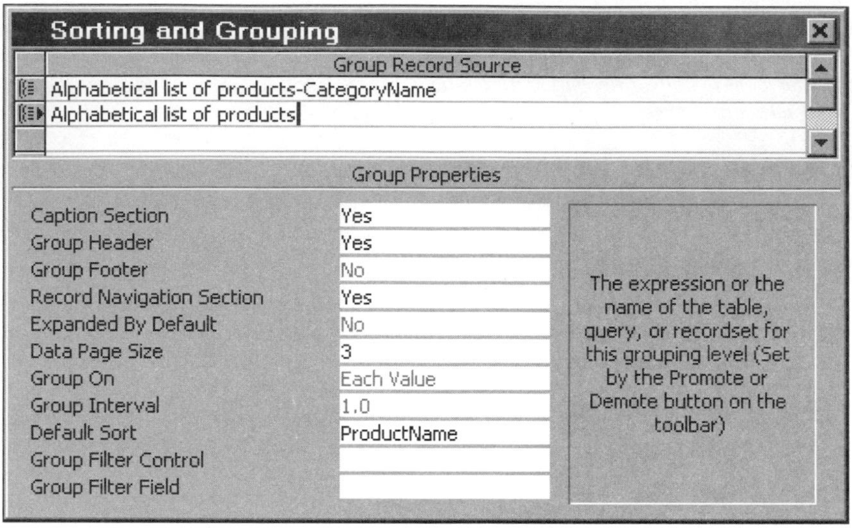

Sorting and Grouping

Group Record Source
Alphabetical list of products-CategoryName
Alphabetical list of products

Group Properties

Caption Section	Yes
Group Header	Yes
Group Footer	No
Record Navigation Section	Yes
Expanded By Default	No
Data Page Size	3
Group On	Each Value
Group Interval	1.0
Default Sort	ProductName
Group Filter Control	
Group Filter Field	

The expression or the name of the table, query, or recordset for this grouping level (Set by the Promote or Demote button on the toolbar)

In addition, notice the entry of ProductName in the Default Sort box for this dialog. This box is null by default for nested records. Unless we specify a value for it, reports display records in the natural sort order for the record source behind a report. In this series of examples on the Alphabetical list of products view, the natural sort order is ProductID. By changing to ProductName, the report lists items in alphabetical order by product name. We can use ASC and DESC to vary the direction of a sort. The default sort order is consistent with an ASC setting. We can additionally sort on multiple fields. Separate field names by commas, but make sure that the sort order is contained within the same commas as the field name to which they apply. Thus, "ProductID ASC, ProductName DESC", and not "ProductID, ASC, ProductName, DESC", which would cause an error.

The grouping field, which is CategoryName in this example, uses the CategoryName field as the Default Sort field. Access enters the value in the Default Sort box automatically. In fact, Access makes up an alias name for the field starting with the string GroupOf and ending with the name of the field. In the current example, this rule results in an alias name for the sort field of GroupOfCategoryName.

To help organize the progression of changes, this version of the data access page was saved as list_of_products_grouped_pagesized_sorted.htm. In addition, one more design change was made to the report: the text box control for the CategoryName field was swapped with a Bound HTML control. Since the report does not let users edit the field, this is a better design anyway (recall the page loads faster with Bound HTML controls versus text box controls). We may have to add a label manually.

The following screen shows the new version of the report with all three nested recordsets open on the first page. The products within each category appear in alphabetical order. This was not true in previous reports based on the Alphabetical list of products view. Notice just three categories appear on the screen. Within each category, only three records show at any one time. These design elements are consistent with the changes to the Sorting and Grouping dialog. Finally, observe that the CategoryName field values do not appear in a text box. Instead, they blend in with the rest of the report. We can format the instances of CategoryName field values with the Formatting toolbar in Design view or in the Microsoft Script Editor window.

Some readers may find value in viewing the same page within a browser. Recall that we will typically do this over an intranet. The file for the web page was saved in the Chapter11 web site on the cab2000 web server. While this information is not strictly necessary for a user to open a data access page from an Access project, we will need it to open a web page from a browser. The reason it is not necessary in an Access project is that the page link encapsulates it. Users traverse the address path to the page by clicking the page link in the Access project Database window. Within a browser, users must enter the address in the Address box. Of course, we can create a hyperlink that points at a data access page, but this is an extra step beyond creating and saving the web page file. Aside from this minor addressing inconvenience, the page looks identical when we open it in a browser as when we open it from within Access. The screenshot overleaf depicts the preceding page in a browser.

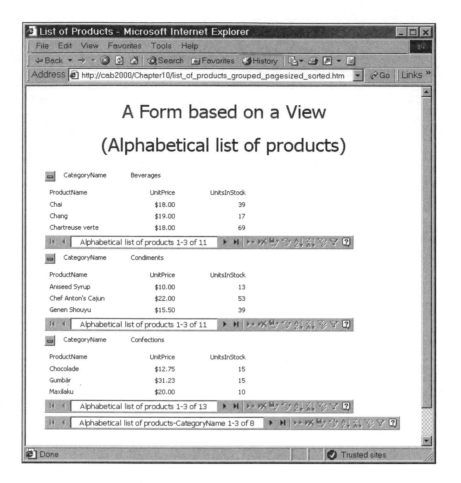

Calculating in a Report

Performing calculations on data access pages is straightforward. This section presents a sample that includes two types of typical calculations for a report:

❑ First, it computes a result in a nested section based on other field values in the section

❑ Second, it computes results within the grouping section based on aggregates of field values and expressions in the nested sections

We learn two solutions to this task that tackle the issue for computing based on fields and expressions in the nested section.

Laying out the Report

The following screen presents a report with a couple of expanded sections. By looking at the bottom Navigation bar, we can tell that this page reports on the sixth, seventh, and eighth categories out of eight categories. Since the sixth and seventh categories have just 2 and 4 nested records, respectively, the display shows those categories expanded. The GrossInStock column in the nested records section is a computed value based on the product of the UnitPrice and UnitsInStock columns. The Records in category result in the grouping section counts the number of nested records in the category. While users can obtain this value from the Navigation bar of the nested records, they have to expand a category to discover the number of records for products within a category. The Records in category result is simply a count of the ProductName field values in a category group. The Gross In Stock result in the grouping section sums the individual GrossInStock expression values for each product within a category group. This demonstrates that we can build one computed field on another.

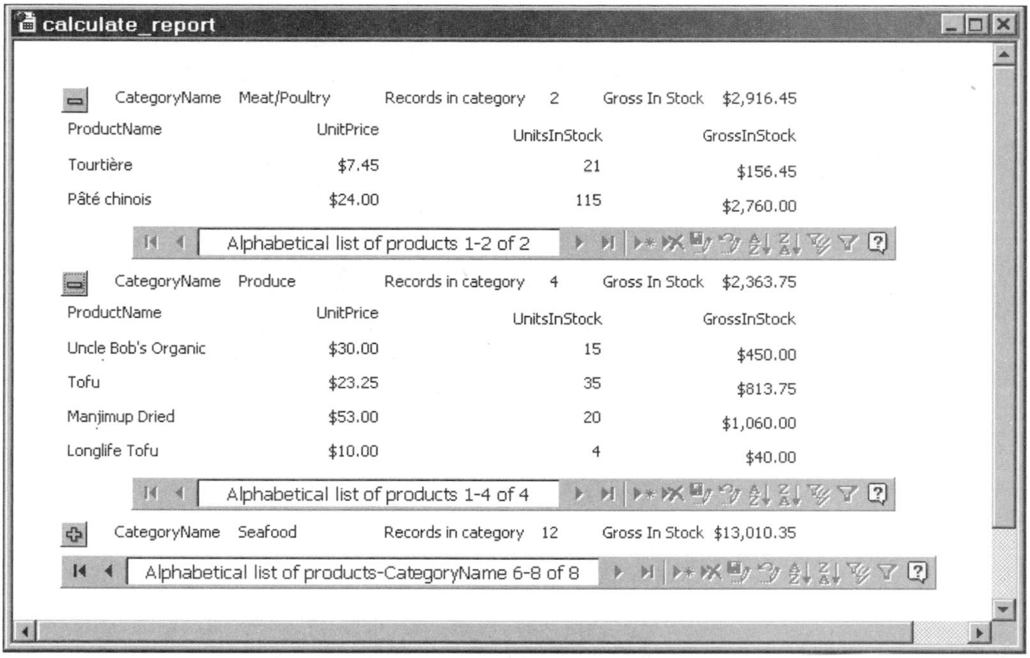

As we can tell by looking at the sample report, the computed fields all show from Bound HTML controls. Therefore, the first step in generating a report like the preceding one is to add the controls to the page. As we add Bound HTML controls, we may want to assign meaningful names to them so we can recognize the values they represent in Design view. By default, Access names controls with serial numbering (the first is BoundHTML1, the next BoundHTML2, etc.). Two properties exist for referencing Bound HTML controls. These are the ID and InnerText properties. The InnerText property setting shows inside the control in Design view. The ID property is the identifier for the control in Design view and in the Script Outline window in the Microsoft Script Editor. The ID property setting is the name of the control as it appears in the Script Outline window. We can assign both of these properties from the control's Properties dialog. Type whatever string value you care into the ID and InnerText boxes on the Other tab of the Properties dialog.

The following screenshot reveals the Properties dialog for the GrossInStock control in the Header section. Notice that the InnerText property is GrossInStock. This text string appears inside the control in Design view. The ID property setting is bht_nested_gross. Notice that that name appears as the name for the object in the Properties dialog window caption. While bht_nested_gross is the name of the control, the text in this section refers to it as GrossInStock because that is what we see when we view the control in Design view.

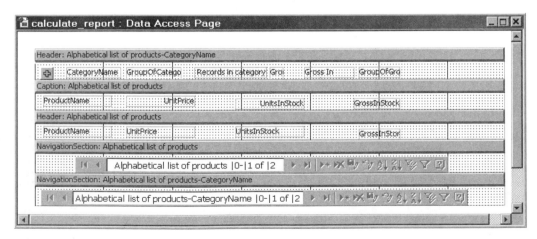

We will also need three new label controls. One new label appears in the Caption section to identify the computed field values in the nested records section. Another pair of labels belongs in the grouping section to identify the count of records in a category group and the sum of expression values in the GrossInStock column within the nested section. Labels on data access pages do not have a Caption property as they do for Access forms and reports. Instead of assigning the string value that a label shows with its Caption property, we must set its InnerText property to the string value. For example, set the InnerText property for the far right label in the Caption section to "GrossInStock". Assign the InnerText property for a label control the same way we do for a Bound HTML control.

The following screen depicts the completed layout for the labels and Bound HTML control:

Adding Calculations to the Report

After adding our controls and positioning them, we can start to define expressions for them. We can enter expressions for the GrossInStock control in the products Header using the ControlSource property box of the control's Property dialog. This setting is available on the Data tab. The expression must have two parts. The first part is a label, which is how we refer to the expression value if we want to use it in another expression. Although we can give an expression any name we like, it makes it easier to follow what is happening if we name it after the control in which it appears. In other words, use the InnerText property setting for the control as the label for the expression in the control.

The second part is the actual expression. This can contain field names in the report and other expression values at the time that we develop the expression. After creating an expression, we can remove or hide one or more of its terms so they do not appear in the report. However, the terms must show in the report at the time that we develop the expression. The following line shows the expression for the GrossInStock control in the sample report.

```
GrossInStock: UnitPrice*UnitsInStock
```

When we create expressions for a grouping section, we need to specify settings for the ControlSource and TotalType properties. The ControlSource property can designate a field name or expression from a nested section. The TotalType property points to one of a handful of aggregate functions, such as Count, Sum, and Avg. It is easy to assign the ControlSource and TotalType properties since we can make our settings with a drop-down list. The following dialog shows the settings for the Records in category result.

Notice that it uses the Count aggregate function with the ProductName field. The settings for the Gross in category result are GroupOfGrossInStock: GrossInStock and Sum, respectively, for the ControlSource and TotalType properties. GrossInStock was selected, but Access automatically converted it to GroupOfGrossInStock: GrossInStock. Recall that GrossInStock was the name of the expression in the nested report.

Using Office Web Components with Data Access Pages

Office Web Components (OWC) is a collection of ActiveX controls that ships with Office 2000. Whether or not we have Office 2000 physically installed on each workstation, all workstations using the OWC must have a license for Office 2000 in order to use them legally. The Microsoft Data Source ActiveX control is one of the four components. The full collection adds the Spreadsheet, Chart, and PivotTable List ActiveX controls. The Data Source control is the only one that requires IE 5 for its operation, but the others offer enhanced capabilities when we use them with IE 5 instead of IE 4.

Developers can mix and match these components in their web applications. For example, the Microsoft Data Source Control is a database power tool. If we have databases as a significant part of our intranet application, we definitely want to consider a solution that relies on the Data Source Control through data access pages. On the other hand, if our application involves substantial computations, then consider putting the Spreadsheet control to work in it. When we need to graphically display data, the Chart component is a great resource. The PivotTable List control appeals to many business professionals with heavy analytical requirements. This control offers a feature set similar to the PivotTable functionality available from Excel and Access.

> *The Microsoft OWC ship as two* .cab *files,* msowncin.cab *and* msowc.cab. *These components install by default with the Microsoft Office 2000 Developer, Premium, Professional, and Standard editions. The Microsoft Office 2000 Resource Kit contains detailed instructions on installing the Office Web Components without Office 2000 on a workstation, including how to install them over the web.*

Having used the Data Source Control to power our Data Access Pages, we're now going to look at the remaining Office Web Components. Each of these components receives a section of its own:

❑ Using the Spreadsheet Component

❑ Using the Chart Component

❑ Using the PivotTable List Component

Using the Spreadsheet Component

The Spreadsheet component includes a calculation engine, a function library, and a single worksheet interface. Unlike Excel, the Spreadsheet component enables just a single worksheet at a time. Since this component creates a spreadsheet on a standard web page, our applications can link with others pages to simulate the availability of multiple worksheets in a workbook. Many Office developers will appreciate the fact that they can start creating a Spreadsheet component application from within Excel. We can also insert a spreadsheet on a web page from FrontPage 2000 and Access 2000. Developers who enjoyed learning about VBScript earlier in this chapter and in prior chapters may welcome the opportunities to automate the Spreadsheet component with VBScript.

One of the most obvious applications for the Spreadsheet component is as a calculator. While we can use them to display data via ADO and VBScript programming, some users will most likely prefer data access pages or ASP to work with databases. We can include a spreadsheet on a web page to help the managers and technicians perform standard computations essential to the running of an organization's business. As many business analysts work in Excel, and we can use Excel as a stepping stone to Spreadsheet component solutions, systems professionals can work with business analysts to move business processes to the web rapidly through the Spreadsheet component. Due to the ease of connecting to a web server from anywhere in the world, this kind of solution can be global in reach.

> *If we have the Spreadsheet component installed on our browser's workstation, then we can connect to a web page with a spreadsheet from anywhere in the world. For example, the ProgrammingMSAccess.com web site has a sponsoring ISP in College Park, Maryland within the USA. However, if our browser workstation has the Spreadsheet component installed, then we can open these pages from anywhere in the world. Two URLs that we can open and with which we can perform calculations are HTTP://www.programmingmsaccess.com/samples/sapplanner.htm and HTTP://www.programmingmsaccess.com/samples/rooter.htm.*

Don't worry too much that we seem to be moving away from talking about Access and SQL Server. In the next section, when we look at the Chart component, we'll be moving back to databases. Before we do this, though, there are a few basics we need to learn about the spreadsheet component.

The Spreadsheet component does not require IE 5. It also does not necessarily require a connection to an external data source. Therefore, we can readily deploy solutions built with the Spreadsheet component to anyone on the Internet who connects via IE 4 or later. Recall, however, that the Spreadsheet component relies on an ActiveX control; therefore, it does not work with non-IE browsers.

An Interest Calculator

The solution we're going to build takes advantage of Excel's function library to compute interest payments due on a loan in either of two ways – with payments due at the end of the month or at the beginning of the month. The Excel function library includes an expression that computes the payment either way. Users can specify the loan amount, term in years, and interest rate to have the spreadsheet compute the payment and selected other items, such as total payments and the portion of those payments that are interest payments. The latter two simple calculations are very easy to perform in a spreadsheet. We can specify each of these with point-and-click simplicity. Finally, formatting cell values to appear with currency and percent format is a menu-based operation – no code is required.

We can start to build this interest calculator from Access with a blank data access page, either by choosing Insert | Office Spreadsheet, or by selecting the Office Spreadsheet from the Toolbox. Next, start to populate our spreadsheet with labels and default values for display when the spreadsheet opens.

The next screenshot depicts the spreadsheet, as it appears while we are in the process of building it. The labels for the first interest calculation appear along with default values for amount, years, and rate. Cell B5 shows the output of the first interest payment expression. Notice that we can build an expression by simply pointing at cell locations. The complete expression appears in cell B7 as a string expression.

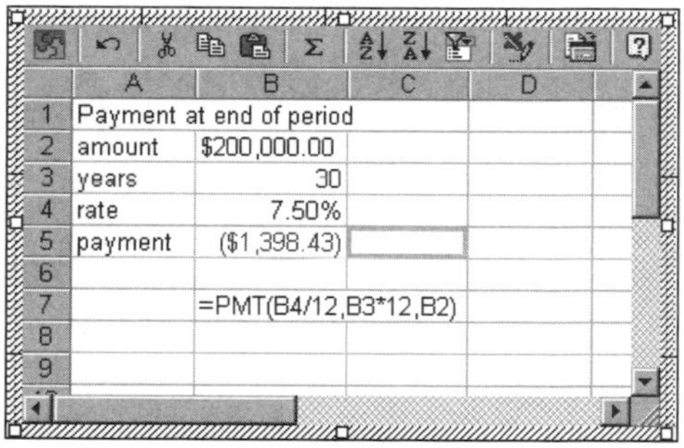

After completing the entry of labels and default values for both sets of interest payment calculation models (see their layout in the following screenshot), we will typically want to edit the look of our spreadsheet and edit the protection for selected cells. Choose the Property Toolbox control on the Spreadsheet's toolbar. This control is next to the Help button at the right edge of the toolbar. After clicking the control, the Spreadsheet Property Toolbox dialog appears. This dialog has a set of collapsing menus.

The screenshot overleaf depicts the Show/Hide and Protection menus open. Use the Show/Hide menu to control the spreadsheet design elements to appear in our solution. The following screen, which exposes the Spreadsheet Property Toolbox, shows all the spreadsheet design elements, including the Title bar. We can remove an element by clicking its toggle control on the Show/Hide menu. The screenshot depicts the dialog just before preparing it to hide the Title bar.

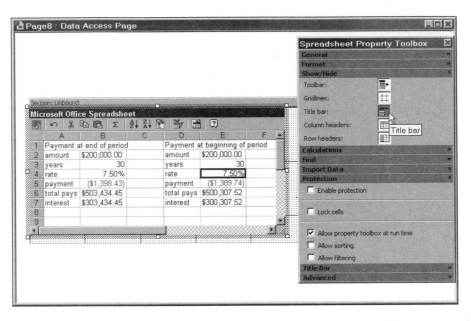

The Protection menu in the Spreadsheet Property Toolbox dialog lets us control two aspects of a spreadsheet's performance. First, we can use it to protect all or a subset of the cells in a spreadsheet. By default, the Spreadsheet component selects all cells for protection. If we want to protect the whole sheet, and also prevent it from providing functionality for the user, just click Enable protection. Alternatively, we can sequentially highlight one or more cell ranges and clear the Lock cells check box. Then, highlight Enable protection. This locks all cells except those for which we cleared the Lock cells check box. In the sample we are developing, the input cells need to be unlocked. These are cells B2:B4 and E2:E4.

Second, we can also use the Protection menu to restrict the functionality of an application. For example, we can make the Property Toolbox unavailable to users opening it from a browser. If we do elect to expose it, users get only a subset of the menu commands. For example, the Property Toolbox for users does not allow them to specify or change protection.

Notice that the amount and rate cells appear in currency and percent formats. The default format for spreadsheet cells is General Number. We can assign a different format by opening the Format menu within the Spreadsheet Property Toolbox. Next, highlight the cell range that we want to format and make a selection from the drop-down Number format control. The Spreadsheet component automatically displays the expression values in cell ranges B6:B7 and E6:E7 with a currency format based on the format for cells B2 and E2, although it is worthwhile setting this format manually.

If we elect to hide the toolbar, the Spreadsheet will suppress its visibility in user and author displays. Page authors can make it appear by opening the page in Design view and clicking the component until a striped line appears around the control. Then, they can right-click the control, which will expose a menu that includes Property Toolbox. Choosing this item opens the Property Toolbox in Design view (but users will not be able to view the toolbar with the Property Toolbox control from a browser).

After making our menu selections, we may want to add HTML to the web page that titles our application and instructs users as to how it works. The Spreadsheet component application saves as an .htm file. We can store it on a web server or in a local file directory. The web server has a potentially further reach. This is one significant attraction of the solution strategy. While it is phenomenally easy to build Spreadsheet component solutions, we can use them worldwide. Since spreadsheets are so ubiquitous in business, the significance of this capability can have profound impact – especially, for large multi-national corporations (along with their suppliers and clients).

Enabling Two-way Communication between a Spreadsheet Component and a Data Access Page

The Spreadsheet component is great because of the wide range of calculations that it performs, and the ease with which it lets developers and business analysts write expressions. However, the component is not as powerful as forms and reports on data access pages for accepting inputs and displaying results. It would be great if we could take the best of each of our application development projects. Gaining this advantage requires three techniques not presented yet.

❏ First, we need to learn how to pass data collected with form controls on a data access page to spreadsheet cells

❏ Second, we need to discover how to accept results computed in a spreadsheet and display them in controls on a data access page

❏ Third, we need to learn how to use VBScript to manage interactions between a Spreadsheet component and the controls on a data access page

We'll be looking at this example in the following three sections:

❏ Building a Spreadsheet Component Ready for Two-way Communication with a Data Access Page

❏ Managing the Communication

❏ Important Things to Note about this Example

Building a Spreadsheet Component Ready for Two-way Communication with a Data Access Page

In this section we'll create an example for calculating interest payments that takes advantage of controls on a data access page to collect data items, display results based on them, and control when an update occurs. Three text boxes collect user input for the loan amount, the term in years, and the interest rate. When a user clicks a button labeled Calculate!, the application displays the payment on the web page. It populates a Bound HTML control with an event procedure to accomplish this task. The trick to making this application work is two-way communication between the Spreadsheet component and the controls on the data access page.

The next screen depicts the Design view of the data access page before the Spreadsheet component is initialized. Before we initialize a Spreadsheet component that depends on control values from a data access page, the spreadsheet will often show #VALUE! markers in one or more cells (as it does in the following example). If our data access page has default values for the controls set in its Design view, giving the Spreadsheet component focus will cause the replacement of #VALUE! markers with these default data values. Otherwise, we will have to wait until a user enters a value in a control in Page view or from a browser.

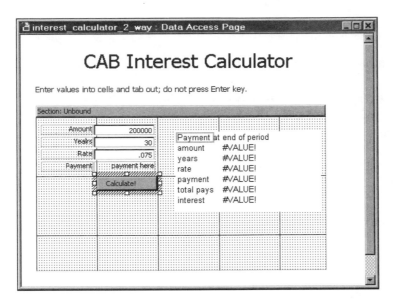

The three text boxes have ID property settings of txt_amount, txt_years, and txt_rate. Since the text boxes exist on the web page document, the Spreadsheet component can refer to their values through the document object (for example, document.textbox_name.value). The following screen shows the Spreadsheet component after it has gained focus with the cell next to amount open to show its expression. This expression points back to the txt_amount text box on the data access page. Its formulation illustrates how a Spreadsheet component can receive values from the controls on a data access page.

```
Payment at end of period
amount     =document.txt_amount.value
years                 30
rate               0.075
payment      ($1,398.43)
total pays $503,434.45
interest   $303,434.45
```

The expressions for the cells next to the years and rate labels in the spreadsheet appear below:

```
=document.txt_years.value
=document.txt_rate.value
```

The area of the data access page that reads payment here in the preceding Design view is a Bound HTML control. The name for this control is bht_payment. Its Design view value of payment here shows the default InnerText property setting. When the page opens, an onload event for the browser window replaces that value with Click Calculate!. Then, when a user clicks the button in Page view, a computed interest payment transfers from the spreadsheet to the Bound HTML control through its InnerText property setting.

The working web page enables a user to enter a new value in the Amount, Years, or Rate text boxes and click the Calculate! button to compute a new interest payment. The instructions above the text boxes remind users how to use the sample. Click into a cell and enter a new value. They must tab out instead of pressing the Enter *key.*

For example, to change the interest rate from the default value of 7.5% to 10.0%, start by clicking in the Rate *text box. Next, select the contents of the text box. Then, enter .1. An event procedure will automatically convert it to 10.0%. This event procedure fires when the cursor exits the text box. A user achieves this by following the instructions above the text boxes and tabbing out of the box.*

Managing the Communication

As suggested in the preceding instructions for using the data access page, there are actually several event procedures that help to manage communication between the data access page and the Spreadsheet component as well as perform selected other functions. The following listing shows these event procedures. As we can see, a little bit of code goes a long way. The most straightforward way to prepare our event procedures is using the techniques illustrated earlier for the Microsoft Script Editor.

```
<SCRIPT event=onload for=window language=vbscript>
<!--
txt_amount.value=formatcurrency(txt_amount.value)
txt_rate.value = formatpercent(txt_rate.value)
bht_payment.InnerText="Click Calculate!"
-->
</SCRIPT>

<SCRIPT event=onchange for=txt_rate language=vbscript>
<!--
me.value = formatpercent(me.value)
-->
</SCRIPT>

<SCRIPT event=onchange for=txt_amount language=vbscript>
<!--
me.value = formatcurrency(me.value)
-->
</SCRIPT>

<SCRIPT event=onclick for=Calculate language=vbscript>
<!--
bht_payment.InnerText=formatcurrency(Spreadsheet0.Range("b5").Value)
-->
</SCRIPT>
```

When the data access page loads into a browser, four activities take place. First, it formats the txt_amount control value as a currency. Without the use of the `formatcurrency` function, the page would open with txt_amount showing 200000 (instead of $200,000).

```
txt_amount.value=formatcurrency(txt_amount.value)
```

The `formatpercent` function displays the interest rate as a percent instead of an unformatted floating point value.

```
txt_rate.value = formatpercent(txt_rate.value)
```

The last assignment statement in the first block of code sets the Bound HTML control to show Click Calculate!. The expression appears overleaf.

```
bht_payment.InnerText="Click Calculate!"
```

Whenever the application revises the contents of the text boxes for either amount or rate, they lose their format settings. Therefore, the second and third activities are onchange event procedures for the txt_amount and txt_rate text boxes. In each case, the onchange event procedure re-formats the text box.

```
<SCRIPT event=onchange for=txt_rate language=vbscript>
<!--
me.value = formatpercent(me.value)
-->
</SCRIPT>

<SCRIPT event=onchange for=txt_amount language=vbscript>
<!--
me.value = formatcurrency(me.value)
-->
</SCRIPT?
```

The final event procedure is for the button below the **Bound HTML** control. Its **ID** property setting is **Calculate**, which is why its event handler contains for=Calculate. The assignment statement in this event procedure copies the computed interest payment from cell B5 in the spreadsheet to the **Bound HTML** control after first formatting it as a currency value.

```
<SCRIPT event=onclick for=Calculate language=vbscript>
<!--
bht_payment.InnerText=formatcurrency(Spreadsheet0.Range("b5").Value)
--|
</SCRIPT>
```

Important Things to Note about this Example

We've covered the main points governing two-way communication between a Spreadsheet component and controls on a data access page, but there are just a few points about this specific implementation. The most important of these is why the spreadsheet does not show in the initial **Page** view of the application. The example does not set the Spreadsheet's visibility property to **hidden**. Doing that would cause it to fail. However, we can collapse the perimeter of the Spreadsheet component on itself by dragging its sides so there is no space within the spreadsheet. We may also need to disable showing the scrollbars, as well as hiding the other elements of the spreadsheet. The screenshot on the right depicts the spreadsheet in this way next to the button.

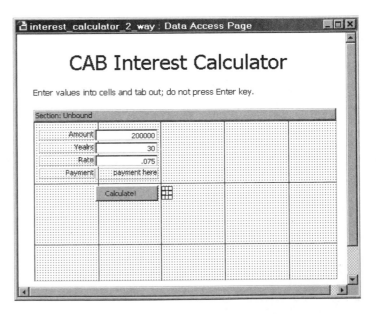

The second point relates to the instruction for completing the form. Notice that it says do not press Enter key. The reason is that VBScript does not process a press of the *Enter* key as a move to the next text box or control on the page. Instead, it enters a couple of character codes at the end of the entry to the cell (the codes are for a carriage return and linefeed). We could code our way out of this problem, and we may want to do that in a production application – however, that code is not included here so that we could keep the example's focus on the basic processing issues of having data access page controls and the Spreadsheet component communicate with one another.

Although this example shows the title property for the button (on the end of the mouse pointer) and the button's value property (label on button) having the same setting, we can set them differently using the button's Properties dialog. After the click, the area with Click Calculate! changes to display the computed payment based on the inputs in the text boxes. Notice that the Spreadsheet component is not visible, yet, it is on the data access page facilitating the computation.

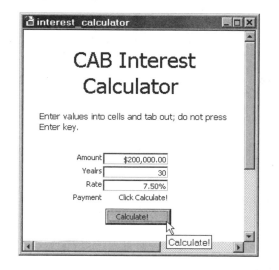

Using the Chart Component

The Chart component enables developers to display static and dynamic charts of data from spreadsheets and database tables. We can also use the Chart component to display data in a PivotTable List control. A separate section drills down on this type of control. Like the Spreadsheet component, the Chart component has manual and programmatic interfaces. Due to the highly interactive process for designing graphic objects, such as form and report layouts as well as charts, this section focuses on the manual interface for generating charts on data access pages. The Chart component does not require a data access page as a container – any web page will suffice. However, putting a chart on a data access page enhances its graphical communication.

Using the Chart component on data access pages opens the possibility of a "virtual gallery of charts". Analysts and decision-makers can browse through collections of charts with the help of a network of hyperlinks to view whole recordsets in charts, or they can view charts based on the contents of a single record in the data source.

Creating a Bar Chart Based on a Table

One of the easiest ways to put the Chart component to work on a data access page is to present a static chart of the data in a table. When using a database as a record source through the manual interface, the database will only use tables as a source. Since we can readily base tables on stored procedures, this can make them more dynamic. For example, if a stored procedure updated the data in a sales table daily, weekly, monthly, or quarterly, then our chart could be more dynamic.

Creating a data access page like this involves two major steps.

❏ First, we have to create our table and populate it with data. As mentioned, a stored procedure is a great way to make the data source for the table dynamic.

❏ Second, we need to insert the Chart component on a data access page and point it at the table.

Creating the Table

The following stored procedure listing creates the table for the chart we'll be building in a moment. The stored procedure has three major sections.

❏ It drops the old version of the table if one exists already.

❏ The stored procedure creates a new version of the table. The structure for the table includes just three columns and no primary key.

❏ An INSERT statement populates the new table based on an aggregation of data from the Employees, Orders, and [Order Details] tables in the sample database for this chapter.

We can run this stored procedure in any copy of the Northwind database.

```
Alter Procedure create_tbl_employee_sales_1997
As

-- Drop sales table if it already exists
if exists (select * from sysobjects where id =
object_id(N'[dbo].[tbl_employee_sales_1997]') and OBJECTPROPERTY(id,
N'IsUserTable') = 1)
drop table [dbo].[tbl_employee_sales_1997]


-- Create the sales table
CREATE TABLE [dbo].[tbl_employee_sales_1997] (
    [employeeid] [int] NOT NULL ,
    [lastname] [nvarchar] (20) NULL ,
    [salesamount] [money] NULL
) ON [PRIMARY]


-- Populate the sales table
INSERT tbl_employee_sales_1997
SELECT Employees.EmployeeID, Employees.LastName,
    SUM(CONVERT(money,
    [Order Details].UnitPrice * [Order Details].Quantity * (1 - [Order
Details].Discount)
    / 100) * 100) AS SalesAmount
FROM Employees INNER JOIN
    Orders ON
    Employees.EmployeeID = Orders.EmployeeID INNER JOIN
    [Order Details] ON
    Orders.OrderID = [Order Details].OrderID
GROUP BY Employees.EmployeeID, Employees.LastName,
    DATEPART(yyyy, Orders.OrderDate)
HAVING (DATEPART(yyyy, Orders.OrderDate) = 1997)
```

Creating the Bar Chart

After creating our data source as a table, open a blank data access page and choose Insert | Office Chart. This opens the Microsoft Office Chart Wizard. It lets us create a first draft of a chart in just three steps. We'll refine the design of the chart later.

To follow this example, select a Clustered Bar design in the first step. This type of design is one of the horizontal bar chart options.

In the second step, designate a table as the data source for the chart. A list box shows all the tables in the database connected to the current project. Scroll through the list entries to highlight the one we want to use, in this case dbo.tbl_employee_sales_1997.

The third step has two wizard screens. Step 3a lets us select an orientation for extracting data for the chart. We can often use whichever default orientation the wizard suggests. In this case, make sure we choose Entries for the legend are in one column, as shown in the following screenshot. Don't worry about the information the wizard shows in the Sample pane – it shows this whatever source we have selected for the chart.

Step 3b lets us designate data values to chart and categories for representing the data. Our chart uses the salesamount field for values and the lastname field for Category (Y) axis labels. Developers can pick these selections from drop-down lists. The screenhots present the selections from Step 3b that start to create our chart:

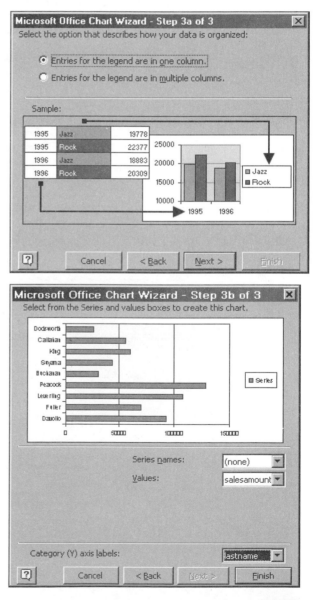

Clicking Finish on this dialog creates a first draft of the chart for the data access page. After re-sizing the chart to suit our preferences, there are still several design choices available. Aside from the page label (which we've set to Employee Sales in 1997), our chart has two edits to the default chart.

First, it removes the legend description. Since the chart has just one series, there is no need for a legend. Just click the legend and press the *Delete* key to remove it.

Second, the chart formats the salesamount field values to appear as currency. We can do this by selecting the Chart component, right-clicking it, and choosing Property Toolbox from the context menu. From a drop-down box in the General section, choose the chart element that we want to edit. For this example, we choose Chart 1 Value Axis 1. The Chart Property Toolbox changes at that point to reveal a series of sub-menus, names from which we can select. In the case of this chart element, the sub-menus are Axis, Format, Font, Ticks and Gridlines, Scale, and Split Axis. Open the Font sub-menu and change the Number format from General Number to Currency. The following screenshot illustrates this edit as it is about to occur:

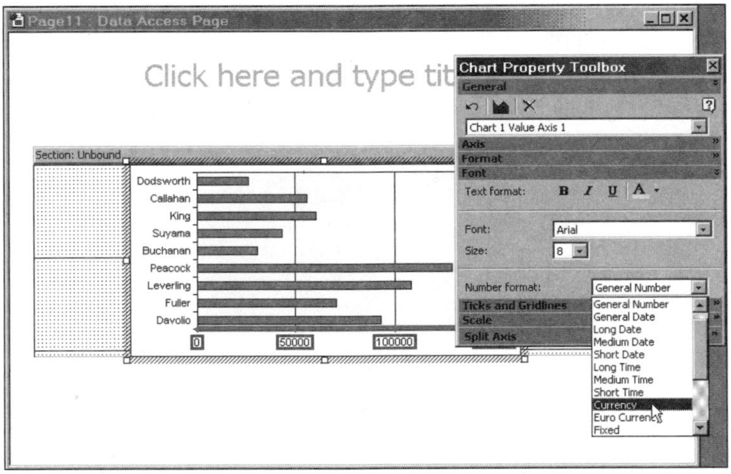

Now that we've created a bar chart, what does it do? In this case, nothing until the table it draws its data from is updated. Before we learn how to make a chart more dynamic, let's see our creation:

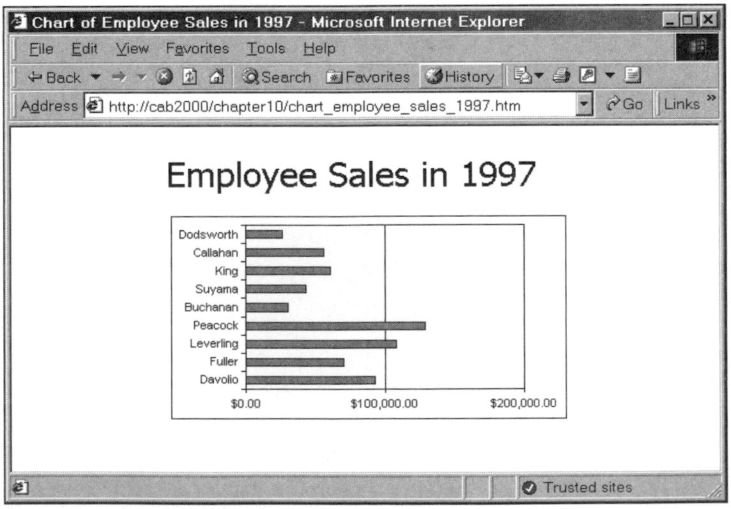

Creating a Line Chart Based on a Spreadsheet

The preceding sample can generate many different types of charts besides a bar chart, but the main point is that updates depend on when we revise the data source for the chart. We can create charts that are even more dynamic by basing them on spreadsheet values that extend the values in a database record. With this approach, the Chart component generates a new chart every time a user navigates to a new record.

The data access page we're going to create now illustrates this design. Three text boxes on the page expose sales data for employees from the tbl_employee_sales_1997 table. A Spreadsheet component on the page projects the 1997 sales into 1998, 1999, and 2000. Finally, a Chart component takes the spreadsheet values and plots them as a line chart. As users navigate through the recordset, the chart updates automatically for each record!

Setting up our Data Access Page

This chapter has already explained all we need to know to build a data access page like the one we're going to build now. Start by creating a data access page that binds to the tbl_employees_sales_1997 table. The following screen shows the arrangement of all the controls and components for the page in Design view. This chapter has covered how to work with all these components. What it has not done to this point is show us how to use them together.

The first step is to add the three bound text boxes, from the Field List dialog. Adding these this way will also cause a Navigation bar to be added.

We can next add the Bound HTML control to the page. The only requirement for adding this control to a page is that the page be bound to a data source. That's because the control's ControlSource property depends on the data source. Recall that the ControlSource setting has two parts. The first part is a label that it is recommended be set to the InnerText property for the control, which is page_title in this case (see the Bound HTML control at the top of the next screenshot). The second part is an expression that concatenates the LastName column value from the current record in the form to the end of a string expression that appears below.

```
page_title: "Sales for " & LastName
```

Next, insert the Spreadsheet component. It is advisable to add the Spreadsheet component after we add the text box for the salesamount field since the spreadsheet depends on the value in this field. We need the text box for the salesamount field on the data access page first because the top right cell contains an expression that directly references the text box.

After entering values and expressions in the spreadsheet cells (see below), we can insert the Chart component. By waiting until after we populate the spreadsheet cells with values and expressions, we will be able to preview our chart's appearance. We'll show the chart component being added when we've learned what we need to know about the spreadsheet.

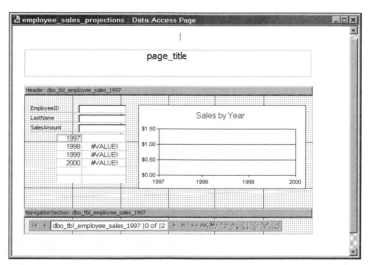

The spreadsheet has numbers down its first column for the successive years that it shows sales. The years appear in cells A1:A4. The sales values are the result of expressions in cells B1:B4. These expressions appear below. The first one ties the spreadsheet to the current record on the data access page in the text box control for the salesamount field. The remaining three cells simply use growth factors to project sales through 2000.

Cell	value
B1	=document.txt_salesamount.value
B2	=1.1*B1
B3	=1.15*B2
B4	=1.2*B3

We are not limited to this approach. Instead, we can use the full extent of the Spreadsheet component's function library. Additionally, we can invoke event procedures to populate the spreadsheet's cells dynamically based on a change in value of the EmployeeID field. While it is true that just changing the record can update the values without an event procedure, the event procedure opens a broader range of options, including making the formatting of the spreadsheet conditional on the value it contains.

We can search the entire list of Spreadsheet functions by clicking within a spreadsheet component in Design view so that it gains focus. Then, press Help (F1) to open the Microsoft Spreadsheet Help dialog. We can also open the dialog from Page view as well. Select the Search tab and type "functions" into the Type in the keyword to find text box. Clicking List Topics returns a list of all the available spreadsheet functions along with selected other Help screens for using functions in a spreadsheet on a web page.

Linking the Line Chart to the Spreadsheet

Start to add the Chart component to the page with the Insert I Office Chart command in Design view. Select a line chart in Step 1. Highlight Microsoft Office Spreadsheet in Step 2 and then specify the spreadsheet that the chart references. In this case, there is only one spreadsheet, named Spreadsheet0. The following screen depicts this selection:

In the third Office Chart Wizard step, reference the spreadsheet cells that we want to chart. Designate cells B1:B4 in the Values text box and cells A1:A4 in the Category (X) axis labels text box. The following screen depicts these entries for the current sample. Finish formatting the chart as described previously. As we can see from the Property Toolbox dialog in the preceding chart example, developers can manipulate many formatting specifications for the charts they display on data access pages.

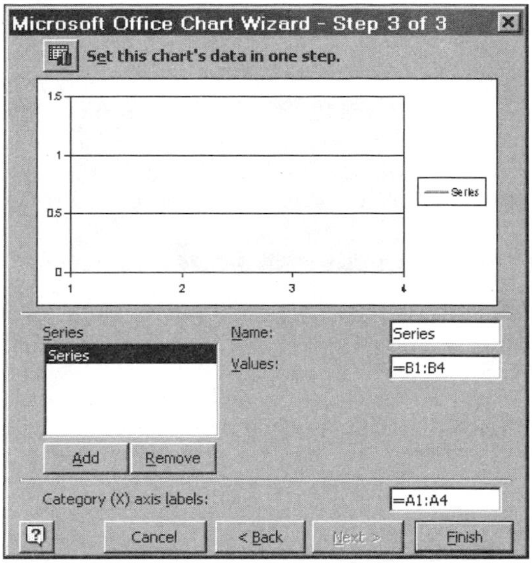

Now that we've built the page, we can watch as it works. The following screenshot shows the finished page, after the user navigates to the second employee.

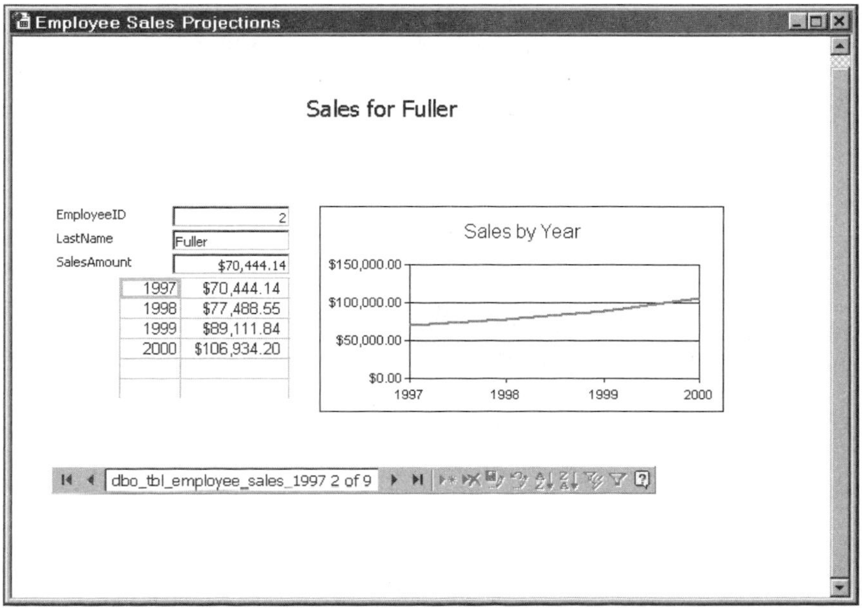

Using the PivotTable List Component

Pivot tables get their name from the fact that they enable us to pivot or virtually move the rows and columns of a spreadsheet without physically changing the spreadsheet. In addition, we can specify filters, sort criteria and directions, and create subtotals and grand totals. All of this power is available through manual as well as programmatic features.

Microsoft initially introduced pivot tables for Excel spreadsheets. Later, Access acquired a PivotTable form. With Office 2000, Microsoft expanded to browsers with the introduction of the **PivotTable List** control. Developers can use this control with IE 4 and IE 5 browsers. Since not all PivotTable features are available to IE 4 browsers, we should upgrade to IE 5 if the PivotTable List control feature set is important for meeting our application development requirements. This is a less dramatic step than it may at first appear since we require a license to Office 2000 to use the PivotTable List control in any event, and IE 5 ships with Office 2000.

Publishing Datasheets on Data Access Pages

Up to this point in the chapter, we have learned many different ways to populate a data access page with form controls. However, publishing datasheets on data access pages has not been mentioned; the PivotTable List control is how we do this. When we add a control from the Field List to a blank data access page, the Layout Wizard initially asks if we want Individual controls or a PivotTable List. The PivotTable List control initially appears as a standard spreadsheet. However, it is much more.

The samples for PivotTable List controls use the Product Sales for 1997 view. This database object sums a computed field by CategoryName and ProductName. The computed field is extended price. It multiplies unit price by quantity for line items in orders and then multiplies that product by 1 minus the discount. The following SELECT statement shows the T-SQL for the view. The statement includes an expression that shows how to compute extended price using the UnitPrice, Quantity, and Discount columns from the [Order Details] table in the sample database for this chapter. Notice that the expression also applies the CONVERT function to format the outcome with a money data type. The SELECT statement also reveals the syntax for joining the Categories, Products, Orders, and [Order Details] tables in its FROM clause. The WHERE clause restricts data to 1997, and the GROUP BY clause designates elements into which to aggregate the computed values.

```
SELECT Categories.CategoryName, Products.ProductName,
    SUM(CONVERT(money,
    [Order Details].UnitPrice * [Order Details].Quantity * (1 - [Order
Details].Discount)
    / 100) * 100) AS ProductSales
FROM Categories INNER JOIN
    Products ON
    Categories.CategoryID = Products.CategoryID INNER JOIN
    Orders INNER JOIN
    [Order Details] ON
    Orders.OrderID = [Order Details].OrderID ON
    Products.ProductID = [Order Details].ProductID
WHERE (Orders.ShippedDate BETWEEN '19970101' AND
    '19971231')
GROUP BY Categories.CategoryName, Products.ProductName
```

The view has 77 rows in its return set. The following screen shows an excerpt from the view from expanding it in the Database window. For users who do not require access to the whole database, distributing the datasheet for the view in a browser makes sense.

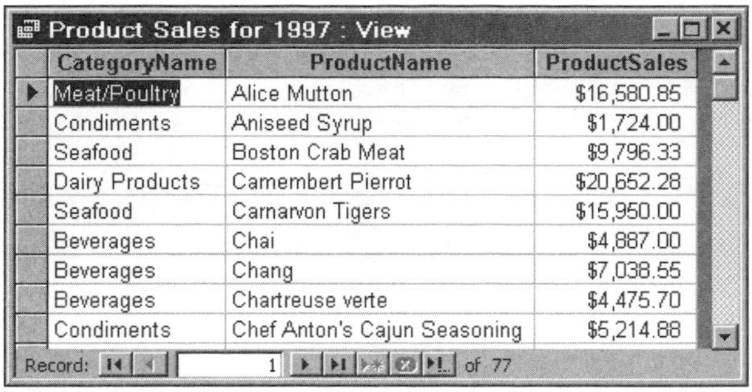

To publish the view as a datasheet on a data access page, drag the view from the Field List dialog to a blank data access page. Instead of selecting Individual Controls on the Layout Wizard, select PivotTable List before clicking OK. Then, drag the control so that it shows all columns (or as many as possible). Click inside the resulting control until a striped line surrounds it. then, right-click the area inside the striped line to open the PivotTable Property Toolbox. Highlight the ProductSales column and open the Format menu on the PivotTable Property Toolbox. Change the Number format setting from General Number to Currency. Finally, save the data access page.

The following screen illustrates a published datasheet for the Product Sales for 1997 view on a data access page. Notice that the address box points at a local file and path. This reminds us of one of the advantages of data access pages: we can use them with or without a web server. Of course, we still have to be careful when dealing with local drives, so it's always good practice to save files with UNC paths. Access automatically adds a scroll bar to the datasheet so users can view all the rows. The following path to the data access page designates the address with a UNC specification. It specifies the page in the c share of a computer named cab2000. This more general specification makes the page accessible from any computer with permission to open the c share on the cab2000 computer.

```
\\cab2000\c\Documents and Settings\Administrator\My Documents\
                        datasheet_product_sales_for_1997.htm
```

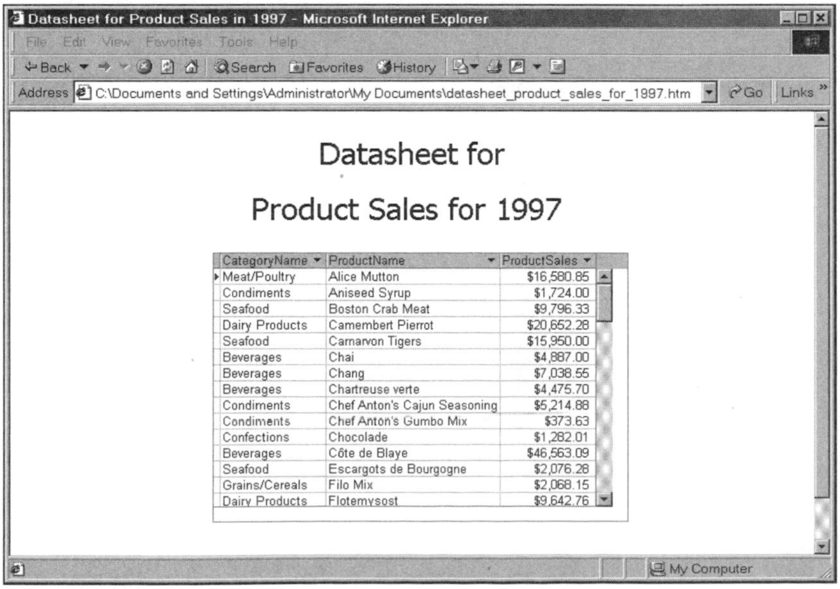

For users who understand how to use Pivot tables, the advantages of publishing datasheets this way can be significant. Computing a total for the ProductSales column is as easy as right-clicking the column header, and choosing AutoCalc | Sum from the context menu. The following screen depicts the ProductSales sum developed from a browser. The ProductSales column remains selected from the right-click to its column header.

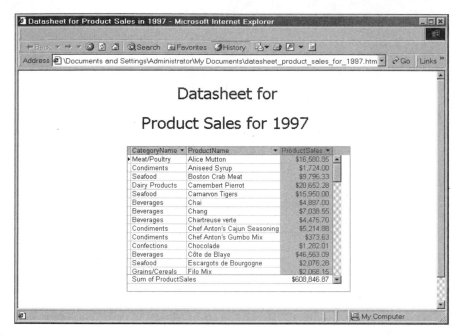

After choosing to calculate a sum of the ProductSales column, computing subtotals for product categories is as easy as successively choosing Move to Row Area from the context menus for the CategoryName field. The following screenshot depicts the CategoryName field selected with its Move To Row Area context menu item highlighted.

After clicking the menu item, the PivotTable List control automatically displays the subtotals. The subtotals for categories are in the table, but they show the detail for other fields within them. In this instance, that is the **ProductName** field. We can individually collapse the detail within a subtotal category. The following screen reveals the subtotals for the Beverages, Condiments, and Confections categories collapsed. We can see all the detail for the Dairy Products category and a portion of the product detail for the Grains/Cereals category. The cursor rests on the control for contracting the detail within the Dairy Products category.

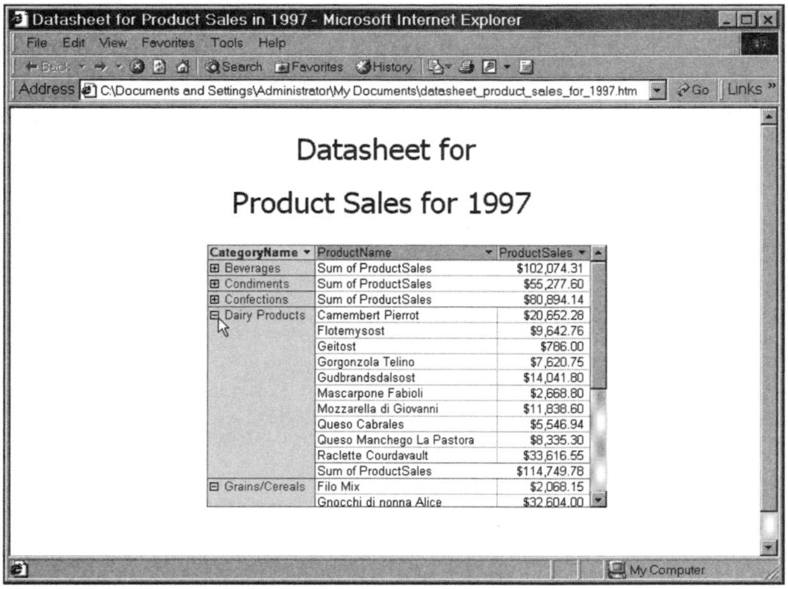

We can contract all product detail within the table. Right-click the **CategoryName** column header in the table and clear the **Expand** selection. This completes the steps to create a summary table like the one below.

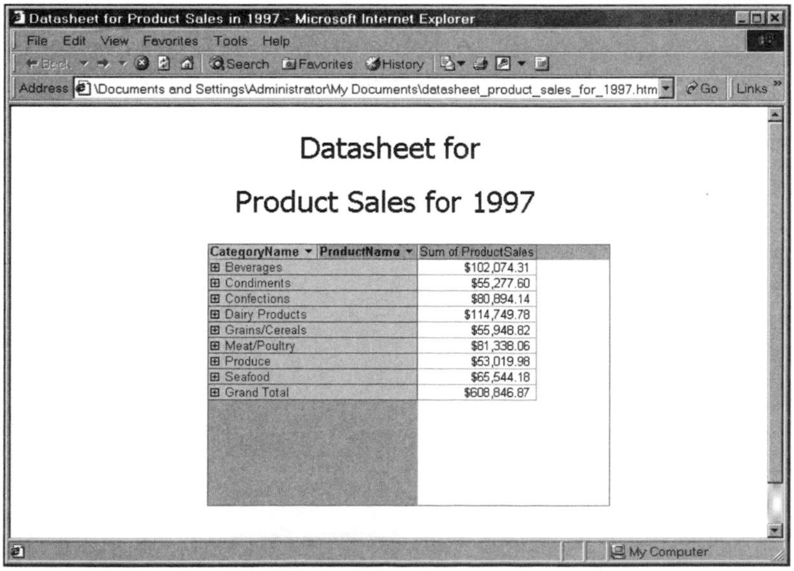

Recall that a browser can make both revisions with the help of the PivotTable List control. The changes are not permanent. They remain in effect just for the current browser session. If a user re-opens the data access page, they can start over again from a fresh copy of the datasheet. The ability of users to manipulate data within the confines of limits sets by database analysts is a liberating outcome. It frees database analysts to manage more databases while it increases the demands for their services by empowering more users to manipulate their own data.

The PivotTable List control enables developers and database analysts to better serve a community of users. By strategically publishing a few broad datasheets with PivotTable List controls, users can easily make many different types of data reports for their own unique needs. Developers can restrict the level of detailed access that users have to data by restricting the ability to expand detail. Set the AllowDetails property on the Other tab of the pivot table's Properties dialog to False to restrict the overall ability of a pivot table to permit drilling down to more detail with the Expand menu command. In addition, we can create summary reports that simultaneously wrap up results for two or more fields simultaneously. Since PivotTable List controls always re-calculate whenever a user opens them in a browser, we can be assured our database clients will always get fresh data.

End users can permanently save their changes by making them from the Design view for a data access page in an Access project. All end users have to do is open the web page from an Access project instead of an IE browser. For this reason, Information System departments may care to publish carefully crafted datasheets based on PivotTable controls in read-only directories or browse-only folders. End users will still be able to save their own custom datasheets based on ones initially created by the Information Systems department, but they will not be able to save over the original datasheets.

Summary

This is the third and final chapter on web development techniques. Your feelings about the material covered in this chapter probably depend on your computing environment, and your web development needs. If your organization stays current with the latest Microsoft innovations, then data access pages and their sibling Office Web Components should make a lot of sense to you. This is especially true for computing environments where ease or speed of development is a critical requirement. If your organization is heavily committed to Office, then data access pages are the way to go for internal web applications and those with partners that also stay current with Office innovations and the latest Microsoft browsers.

If you do a lot of application development work that must embrace many different browsers and your client workstations are not likely to have Office 2000 installed or licensed, you should consider another technology, such as ASP. If you find a need for ASP, you'll need to become familiar with VBScript and HTML. In such circumstances you may find the FrontPage 2000 Database Wizard becomes very useful.

Programming Access for SQL Server

Access 2000 is a great development platform for building a front end for SQL Server solutions. This chapter takes a step back and reviews some fundamental issues for programming Access 2000. So far we've demonstrated many examples of using stored procedures, active data pages, and using data within Access controls. In this chapter we will be looking at running Access macro commands with SQL Server, spreadsheets, reports, sending data access pages, an in depth discussion on ADO, and also how to import from an Access database file.

Beyond just Access programming, this chapter drills down on techniques that any SQL Server developer who also works with Access is likely to find useful. In particular, the chapter demonstrates Access development methods that can increase your productivity when working with SQL Server databases. It highlights mechanisms for exchanging data between SQL Server databases and Access database files. We also integrate and extend the presentation of ADO programming techniques from earlier chapters. The focus throughout this final chapter is developing an appreciation of how Access programming skills can assist you to develop better SQL Server solutions.

To meet this objective we've split the chapter into two major sections:

- ❑ The DoCmd object – the object we use to perform macro commands or Access actions from inside VBA

- ❑ Programming ADO objects in modules – this section should consolidate our previous coverage and provide further insights on how to effectively use ADO

The DoCmd Object

This section will begin our discussion of using VBA code to get more out of Access for SQL Server. When developers begin to work with VBA code in Access, the DoCmd object is often a useful object to use. DoCmd contains a wide selection of methods that correspond to Access macro actions. In fact, only eight of the forty-seven methods for the DoCmd object do not correspond to an equivalent Access Macro. They are, AddMenu, MsgBox, RunApp, RunCode, SendKeys, SetValue, StopAllMacros, and StopMacro. Therefore, developers migrating from macros to VBA will find this object contains many of the programming concepts with which they are familiar. Because macros are so easy to use, developers who are new to Access are likely to find this command friendly as well. The humble origins of the DoCmd object should not dissuade you from using it. In fact, its versatility and simplicity combined with its ability to manipulate SQL Server objects adds to its significance as a powerful development tool.

> *Just to recap; a macro is a grouping of actions and contains, essentially, a list of things for Access to do, in a given order. These actions can be made conditional, and can include other macros.*

In this section, we'll be looking at the following DoCmd methods:

❑ OpenTable and OpenStoredProcedure

❑ Close

❑ PrintOut

❑ Quit

❑ TransferText, TransferSpreadsheet, and TransferDatabase

❑ SendObject

Getting to Know the DoCmd Object

One major reason for the DoCmd object's importance is its huge collection of methods that are easy to apply. The **Object Browser**, is a particularly convenient tool for familiarizing ourselves with the scope of these methods. The following screen shows the DoCmd object selected in the **Classes** window of the **Object Browser** and an excerpt of the methods for the object in the **Members of** window:

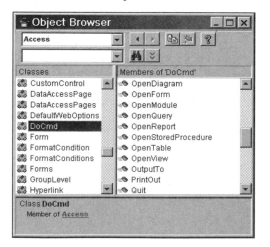

In Chapter 7 there was a demonstration of the operation of the OpenForm methods. In Chapter 8, you saw the OpenReport method demonstrated. To recap, with the OpenReport method, our application can print a report or preview it within our application, prior to printing.

However, DoCmd does not restrict us to working with Access forms and reports. The excerpt above depicts DoCmd methods for opening tables, views, stored procedures, database diagrams, and more. Selected DoCmd methods apply to either, but not both, of the two database engines with which Access 2000 can work. Consequently, some methods apply to one database engine, but not the other. Be very careful here; the OpenQuery method pertains exclusively to the Jet database engine. The OpenDiagram method, however, only works with SQL Server.

The **Object Browser** is not a great tool for learning about DoCmd, as this relates to macros more than methods or properties. Therefore, a parallel set of **Help** screens go into more depth on each macro action. The first sentence or two of a DoCmd method description offers a hyperlink to a matching macro action **Help** screen.

DoCmd methods can sometimes take many parameters; perhaps one of the best examples is the OpenForm action demonstrated in Chapter 7. In a few cases, it may not be clear how to assign parameters to them from the Help screen. In these situations, Access developers familiar with macros may sometimes find it easier to create a macro that uses the method in the way they want. Then, they can convert the macro to a VBA module. The module will demonstrate the syntax and appropriate argument values. Convert a macro to a module by choosing File | Save As from the Macro Design window and selecting Module from the drop-down As control in the Save As dialog. Then, confirm your choice by choosing Convert in the next Convert macro dialog.

Working with the Open Methods for Database Objects

A series of four Open methods for the DoCmd object permit your Access applications to open SQL Server database objects. Take care here, as you may recognize OpenTable as a Jet object as well. The names for these methods are OpenTable, OpenView, OpenStoredProcedure, and OpenDiagram. The OpenDiagram method opens a database diagram exclusively in **Design** mode, but the other three methods allow you to specify **Datasheet**, **Design**, or **Print Preview** modes for an object.

The OpenTable, OpenView, and OpenStoredProcedure methods take three similar arguments:

❑ The first argument (Procedure Name) is the name of the object that you want to open, tablename, viewname, or storedprocedurename; this is true for the OpenDiagram method as well where you need to supply the diagramname. This is the only argument required for OpenDiagram.

❑ The second argument, View, designates the mode for opening an object.

❑ The third argument is the Data Mode. It designates the kind of access we have to the data source.

The View argument has four options to choose from:

❑ The acViewNormal mode corresponds to clicking the **Open** button on the **Database** window for tables, views, and stored procedures.

❑ The second is acViewDesign mode, where the relevant object is opened ready for any design alterations. This is probably the least likely option as it's unlikely you'll want users altering the design of any objects

639

❑ The third mode is `acViewPreview`. This is the equivalent of choosing File | Print Preview with a table, view, or stored procedure selected in the Database window. In this mode, you can view the table or return set, but the object does not actually print. That requires an additional step of using the `DoCmd.PrintOut` method.

❑ The default way the method opens a row-returning stored procedure, view, or table is `acViewDatasheet` mode.

Similarly, the `Data Mode` argument has three settings to choose between:

❑ The default mode, `acEdit`, permits users to view and edit data as well as add and delete records.

❑ The `acReadOnly` mode permits you to expose a data source so users can view it without being able to change it in any way.

❑ The third data mode, `acAdd`, opens a data source so users can add data to it without being able to view any of the existing records.

The `table_opener` sub procedure below, which should be placed in an empty module, demonstrates the syntax for specifying the arguments for the `OpenTable` method. Most of the procedure's lines are commented out because their sole purpose is to show syntax. However of course, you can uncomment these depending on which methods you wish to try.

The first three `DoCmd` statements demonstrate the syntax for setting the mode for opening a table. The last of these three lines is uncommented. It opens the Employees table from the NorthwindCS database in Print Preview mode.

The second batch of three statements with the `OpenTable` method appears with comment prefixes. These lines illustrate the syntax for specifying the way a table opens – `ReadOnly`, the normal `Edit`, or just `Add` new records. The same arguments and settings apply to the `OpenView` and `OpenStoredProcedure` methods. Notice that there is a place marker for the `View` argument in this second set of three `OpenTable` method samples. It is necessary to leave a place marker when you accept the default value for one argument, but designate a value for a subsequent argument.

```
Sub table_opener()

'You can open tables in
'Design view to purposely expose table design
'Normal view for exposing data for browsing and maintenance
'PrintPreview for viewing what they look like before printing

'For SQL Server 2000, prefix object name with object owner
'For example, "dbo.employees"

'DoCmd.OpenTable "employees", acViewDesign
'DoCmd.OpenTable "employees", acViewNormal
DoCmd.OpenTable "employees", acViewPreview
'DoCmd.Close actable, "employees", acSaveNo


'A second OpenTable argument lets you restrict the
'uses for a database as you open it;
'default is acEdit for browsing and maintenance
```

```
'DoCmd.RunCommand acCmdPrint
'DoCmd.OpenTable "employees", , acReadOnly
'DoCmd.Close actable, "employees", acSaveNo
'DoCmd.OpenTable "employees", , acEdit
'DoCmd.Close actable, "employees", acSaveNo
'DoCmd.OpenTable "employees", , acAdd
'DoCmd.Close actable, "employees", acSaveNo

'Same options with arguments are available for
'views with OpenView method and
'stored procedures with OpenStoredProcedure method

End Sub
```

After opening a database object with one of the Open methods, the object remains open until our application closes it with the DoCmd.Close method, which is why we clean up behind ourselves after each example. The following sample demonstrates this feature along with syntax for printing a database object that is open in Print Preview mode. The sample additionally confirms the syntax for specifying how to view a stored procedure.

```
Sub sp_opener()

'OpenStoredProcedure offers viewmode and datamode arguments for stored
'procedures that have return sets; the following sample shows view
'mode syntax for a stored procedure

'Again, prefix object names with owner name for SQL Server 2000

'DoCmd.OpenStoredProcedure "Ten Most Expensive Products", acViewDesign
'DoCmd.OpenStoredProcedure "Ten Most Expensive Products", acViewNormal
DoCmd.OpenStoredProcedure "Ten Most Expensive Products", acViewPreview

'Print return set from stored procedure; then, close its return set
'By calling a sub procedure, this means that any print request
'can call this

print_current_preview
DoCmd.Close acStoredProcedure, "Ten Most Expensive Products"

End Sub


Sub print_current_preview ()

'Prints all of the currently open PrintPreview document
DoCmd.PrintOut acPrintAll

End Sub
```

The first procedure above, sp_opener, opens the Ten Most Expensive Products stored procedure from the NorthwindCS database. It reveals the syntax for designating the View argument setting, but only the last of these for Preview is uncommented. Notice the comparability of the syntax for the OpenStoredProcedure and OpenTable methods.

After opening the stored procedure, sp_opener calls print_current_preview. This second sub procedure introduces the DoCmd.PrintOut method. With this method, an application can print many different objects open in Print Preview mode. The sp_opener procedure concludes by invoking the Close method. This method takes two arguments. The first of these designates the type of argument to close. The second argument specifies the name of the database object to close.

The samples to this point in the chapter hard code both a database object and the arguments for a DoCmd method. This is not very flexible and would probably not be used in a real production situation. However, the DoCmd object in combination with simple If...Then...Else logic and other conditional VBA statements, or perhaps using parameters for the name of the object and what the object is, can give our solution a much greater amount of flexibility. Let's have a look at this flexibility in our examples.

Choosing What to Print and Whether to Print

In the following pair of procedures, the second procedure will work with any table in a data source. The first procedure shows how you would call the procedure to preview the table. The second procedure, table_previewer_printer, opens the designated table in Print Preview mode, and then goes on to prompt users with a Msgbox function if they want to print the table. Three different outcomes can follow from the reply to the prompt.

❑   First, the table can remain open without it printing

❑   Second, the table can close without printing

❑   Third, the table can close after printing

The second procedure in this sample draws on the print_current_preview sub procedure from the preceding sample. It also demonstrates the syntax for closing a table. The documentation for the Close method includes a list of specific constants for designating different types of SQL Server and Access objects.

```
Sub call_table_previewer_printer()

'Specify data source to preview and print
table_previewer_printer "employees"

End Sub


Sub table_previewer_printer(tbl_name As String)
Dim byt1 As Byte

'Open table in PrintPreview mode
DoCmd.OpenTable tbl_name, acViewPreview

'Ask if the table should be printed
byt1 = MsgBox("Print it?", vbYesNoCancel)

If byt1 = vbCancel Then
'If user clicks Cancel, leave table open
    Exit Sub
ElseIf byt1 = vbNo Then
'If user clicks No, just close table
    DoCmd.Close acTable, tbl_name
Else
```

```
'Otherwise, print table before closing it
    print_current_preview
    DoCmd.Close acTable, tbl_name
End If

End Sub
```

Quitting Access with DoCmd

The DoCmd object can also be used to quit Access, perhaps placed within an Error routine where you don't wish to pass control up to the calling module. A more common way to leave Access is to use the DoCmd object on the Access project control form. Access developers frequently refer to a form with controls for launching many different actions as a **switchboard**. A control to quit Access often appears on this kind of form and offers users a way to exit the application and Access. The Quit action, which the DoCmd.Quit method invokes, exits Microsoft Access and offers a clean and careful way of stopping any Access built system. After successfully executing the Quit method, no additional actions can take place inside Access until you re-start Access. Invoking the Quit method is the same as choosing File | Exit from Access.

The Quit method takes an optional argument, AcQuitOption. The setting for this argument determines what Access does with unsaved Database objects as it exits. The three intrinsic constants for this method's arguments are acQuitPrompt, acQuitSaveAll, which is the default option, and acQuitSaveNone. With the acQuitPrompt setting, the Quit method prompts separately whether a user wants to save each unsaved Database object before closing Access. Using the acQuitSaveAll setting automatically saves any unsaved database objects before closing the session. The acQuitSaveNone setting causes the Quit method to exit Access without saving any changes.

The following VBA procedure quits Access without saving any unsaved Database objects. It uses the acQuitSaveNone setting for the DoCmd.Quit method's argument. If we wanted to use the quitter() method, but wanted to save any unsaved objects first, then we should invoke the DoCmd Save method before launching the quitter() procedure.

```
Sub quitter()

'Quit Access without saving changes
DoCmd.Quit acQuitSaveNone

End Sub
```

Actually, it is not likely that we will run the Quit method within a sub procedure of a stand-alone module. This is because we can easily put the method in the Click event procedure for a button on a form, probably labeled Exit. However, if we permit quitting Access from more than one form, then there may be some value in having the Quit method in a sub procedure that two or more different forms call. It is very simple to call a procedure that is not contained in the form or module that you are currently within. Assuming the quitter() sub procedure resides in a module named Module1, then we can invoke it from one or more event procedures with the syntax Module1.quitter. It is always worth being very careful when we allow more than one module to quit Access. Unless our program is well structured, we could end up confusing the user and leave them not knowing how our application works. This example calls quitter() when Command0 is clicked.

```
Private Sub Command0_Click()

Module1.quitter

End Sub
```

This syntax for calling sub procedures within a module from elsewhere in Access is very useful. Using this approach allows you to place a useful procedure in one module, and rather than write it again each time you want to use it somewhere else in your program, simply call it from whichever other module needs to use that code.

Importing and Exporting from Access with DoCmd

Several DoCmd methods support importing and exporting Database objects into and out of SQL Server databases that you maintain with an Access project, and are available for use. Three interrelated methods are TransferDatabase, TransferSpreadsheet, and TransferText. The SendObject method is also handy for emailing Database objects, such as reports and data access pages, to others. This section commences with a brief overview of the transfer methods. Then, it drills down on the TransferDatabase method with a couple of samples. In addition, it gives a couple of samples illustrating the use of the SendObject method for Access reports and data access pages.

Using TransferDatabase, TransferSpreadsheet, and TransferText

Now that we are comfortable with the basics of the DoCmd, it is time to move on to more advanced features. Three transfer methods for the DoCmd object facilitate exchanges between SQL Server databases managed by Access projects and other applications or other SQL Server data sources.

The TransferText Method

For example, the TransferText method enables SQL Server databases maintained by Access projects to import text and HTML files into their tables or export tables, views, and stored procedures to text and HTML files. This method permits an Access project to share a data source with a word processing program or any application that can read HTML-formatted content. If you export from an Access project to a text file, Access creates a new text file. Access projects (.adp) do not link to these external text data sources, but it is possible to link these text files with Access database files (.mdb) Keep in mind this subtle difference. Nearly all programs can exchange data in one kind of text format or another, and so using a text file as a basis can allow basic exchange of information between many otherwise incompatible systems. For these reasons, it is likely that text files will continue to be a popular format for the import and export of data from database applications, such as Access with SQL Server.

If we take a look at an example where we are transferring data out in HTML format from the Customers table that is within the current Northwind Access project file we have open, you can see that the commands are very straight forward.

```
Sub export_text_from_ss_db()

'Export text from an Access project, from the Customers table

DoCmd.TransferText acExportHTML, , "Customers", "c:\Customers.htm", True

End Sub
```

An extract from the HTML file created in the instance above would look like this. Obviously this is a static set of data, which has no data links.

```
<HTML DIR=LTR>
<HEAD>
<META HTTP-EQUIV="Content-Type" CONTENT="text/html; charset=Windows-1252">
<TITLE>Customers</TITLE>
</HEAD>
<BODY>
<TABLE DIR=LTR BORDER>
<CAPTION>Customers</CAPTION>
<TR>
<TH>CustomerID</TH>
<TH>CompanyName</TH>
<TH>ContactName</TH>
<TH>ContactTitle</TH>
<TH>Address</TH>
<TH>City</TH>
<TH>Region</TH>
<TH>PostalCode</TH>
<TH>Country</TH>
<TH>Phone</TH>
<TH>Fax</TH>
</TR>
<TD DIR=LTR ALIGN=LEFT>ALFKI</TD>
<TD DIR=LTR ALIGN=LEFT>Alfreds Futterkiste</TD>
<TD DIR=LTR ALIGN=LEFT>Maria Anders</TD>
<TD DIR=LTR ALIGN=LEFT>Sales Representative</TD>
<TD DIR=LTR ALIGN=LEFT>Obere Str. 57</TD>
<TD DIR=LTR ALIGN=LEFT>Berlin</TD>
<TD></TD>
<TD DIR=LTR ALIGN=LEFT>12209</TD>
<TD DIR=LTR ALIGN=LEFT>Germany</TD>
<TD DIR=LTR ALIGN=LEFT>030-0074321</TD>
<TD DIR=LTR ALIGN=LEFT>030-0076545</TD>
</TR>
<TR>
<TD DIR=LTR ALIGN=LEFT>ANATR</TD>
<TD DIR=LTR ALIGN=LEFT>Ana Trujillo Emparedados y helados</TD>
<TD DIR=LTR ALIGN=LEFT>Ana Trujillo</TD>
```

Lets see how this would look in an Internet browser. As you see, a very good result is achieved.

The TransferSpreadsheet Method

With the `TransferSpreadsheet` method, our Access applications for SQL Server data sources can import data from and export data to Excel and Lotus spreadsheet packages. This method permits us to work with an individual worksheet in a workbook file or even a range within a worksheet. The `TransferSpreadsheet` feature is particularly attractive for sharing the results of a view or stored procedure return set with a population of spreadsheet users who do not have either Access or SQL Server. The capability is also valuable for upgrading applications that formerly relied on spreadsheets, but now require management via a database application. As with the previous example, it is a very simple method to use. Again from the Access project, we will be exporting from the **Customers** table, to an Excel 5 spreadsheet.

```
Sub export_spreadsheet_from_ss_db()

'Export a spreadsheet from an Access project, from the Cusomters table

DoCmd.TransferSpreadsheet acExport, acSpreadsheetTypeExcel5, "Customers", _
    "c:\Customers.xls", True

End Sub
```

Taking a look at the spreadsheet that is created, again this is a static result of the above command.

The TransferDatabase Method

We can use the `TransferDatabase` method to exchange data with other database applications, including ODBC data sources, such as Oracle or other SQL Server databases, and ISAM data sources, such as dBase and earlier versions of Jet. This method is similar to the File | Get External Data | Import command when we are importing data from another application or SQL Server data source. When we use this method, we'll probably find it a friendly, convenient VBA interface for exchanging data from an Access project with other applications. Within an Access project, this method only exports tables (and not views or stored procedures).

> The `TransferDatabase` method inherits the same limitation as the File | Get External Data | Import command. If the command does not work from the menu interface, you will get the same

kind of error with the `TransferDatabase` *method. In these circumstances, use an alternative approach for achieving your transfer, for example the* `TransferText` *method.*

The syntax for the `TransferDatabase` command is very straightforward – even if it does involve a long list of arguments. These arguments enable our custom applications to fine-tune how they exchange data with other applications. The following procedure reveals the syntax for importing a table from another SQL Server data source. Before you run this, ensure that you have an ODBC connection ready to the pubs database, as we saw in Chapter 9.

```
Sub import_table_from_ss_db()

'Import from an ODBC data source
'use the pubs dsn to identify the data source
'capture a table from the imported data source
'the table's name is Authors
'name the imported table NorthwindCS_Authors in this database
DoCmd.TransferDatabase acImport, _
    "ODBC Database", _
    "ODBC;DSN=pubs;uid=sa;pwd=", _
    acTable, _
    "Authors", _
    "NorthwindCS_Authors"

End Sub
```

The `DoCmd.TransferDatabase` method has the following syntax:

```
DoCmd.TransferDatabase ([TransferType as AcDataTransferType = acImport],
[DatabaseType], [DatabaseName], [ObjectType As AcObjectType = acTable], [Source],
[Destination], [StructureOnly], [StoreLogin])
```

Let's look at how we've used this method in the preceding example:

- ❑ The first argument in the listing (`[TransferType as AcDataTransferType = acImport]`) declares the direction of the data transfer – from the remote data source into the current SQL Server data source.

- ❑ The second argument (`[DatabaseType]`) denotes the type of data source with which the method programs an exchange. The sample uses ODBC Database since the procedure seeks to import a table from another SQL Server database.

- ❑ The third argument (`[DatabaseName]`) is the connection string. This can take any of several forms depending on how your application references the remote data source. As you can see, if you use a DSN, your connection string syntax can be very simple. It merely names the DSN, the user ID, and password. In this case, the pubs DSN points at the pubs database on the current computer. The procedure uses the sa user with a blank password (you will typically want another user and password for production applications, but the exact value of these settings should be unique for each application).

- ❑ The fourth argument (`[ObjectType As AcObjectType = acTable]`) denotes the type of database object to import – a table. This could be any number of options from query, stored procedure, table, etc.

- ❑ The fifth argument (`[Source]`) designates the specific table in the database from which the statement imports data.

❑ The sixth argument (`[Destination]`) designates a name for the table in the current database, to which the data is imported.

❑ The seventh argument (`[StructureOnly]`) is not used, as we want to transfer the data not just the structure.

❑ The eighth argument (`[StoreLogin]`) is also not used, because we don't want to store the login information we've used to access the data.

You can check the contents of the **Database** window for the NorthwindCS sample Access project that this chapter uses. If it contains a table named NorthwindCS_Authors, delete it. Then run the preceding sub procedure named `import_table_from_ss_db`. Return to the **Database** window. Notice that it shows a NorthwindCS_Authors table. This table contains identical contents to the Authors table in the pubs database. If you run the sub procedure a second time without deleting the current version of NorthwindCS_Authors, the procedure generates another copy of the table in the **Database** window with the name NorthwindCS_Authors1. If the Authors table in the pubs database changes between running the procedure the first and the second time, then the NorthwindCS_Authors and NorthwindCS_Authors1 tables will have different contents. This may be a desirable result, however, there are circumstances when it won't be. If this was your method of completing a backup, and you wanted the table name to remain constant, then the best option would be to call a stored procedure first, to drop the required table.

It is similarly easy to export a table from a SQL Server data source managed by an Access project (`.adp`) to a traditional Access database file (`.mdb`). The `export_table_to_access_db` procedure in the next listing illustrates the syntax to accomplish this task. Notice the method exports data; it does not provide a link. However, we can publish exported tables on a frequent basis, so that the client Access database file always has a relatively fresh copy of the original data source. Since exported tables overwrite prior versions of the table in the destination database, there is only one table to examine for the most recent data. Recall that imports add new versions of a table to a database. To perform this example, it is necessary to have exclusive use of the Access database.

```
Sub export_table_to_access_db()

'Export a database object from this SQL Server database
'to a Microsoft Access database file
'named Chapter12.mdb in the designated location
'the database object should be a table
'named Categories in this database
'and exported_Categories in Chapter12.mdb
DoCmd.TransferDatabase acExport, _
    "Microsoft Access", _
    "C:\Documents and Settings\Administrator\" & _
        "My Documents\Chapter12.mdb", _
    acTable, _
    "Categories", _
    "exported_Categories"

End Sub
```

As before, let's take a look at the arguments we're using in this example. The syntax is the same as the method is the same, but since we're using it to achieve a different goal, we're using different arguments:

❑ In contrast to the prior sample, the first argument for this instance of the `TransferDatabase` method is acExport. This establishes the direction of data transfer from the current database and towards a destination database.

❑ The second argument ("Microsoft Access") denotes the type of the destination data source, which is an Access database file in this case.

❑ The third argument ("C:\Documents and Settings\Administrator\" & _ "My Documents\Chapter12.mdb") designates the path and file name for the destination database.

❑ The fourth argument in this case (acTable) refers to the type of database object whose contents you want to export.

❑ The fifth argument ("Categories") points to the name of the object to export from the current database.

❑ The sixth argument ("exported_Categories") specifies a name for the table the method creates in the destination database.

The following sample demonstrates one case and refers to another in which you should not try to use the TransferDatabase method. The syntax mimics the preceding samples. However, notice the following sample differs in that it tries to import a table from an Access database file to the sample database for the chapter.

When we run this example, the program generates a Visual Basic run-time error. If we try to perform the Import manually with the File | Get External Data | Import command, Access returns an identical error. This confirms its status as either a bug or a documentation error (because the documentation gives no clue that this result is likely). The TransferDatabase method also fails when you try to export from the current database to an ODBC data source, such as another SQL Server database. This bug is less of a problem than it appears, since we can use ADO programming techniques to accomplish the objective. The final sample in this chapter demonstrates the approach.

```
Sub import_table_from_access_db()

'It does not work; same result for export to
'ODBC data source from Access project
DoCmd.TransferDatabase acImport, _
    "Microsoft Access", _
    "\\cab2000\c\Documents and Settings\Administrator\" & _
        "My Documents\Chapter12.mdb", _
    acTable, _
    "exported_Categories", _
    "imported_Categories"

End Sub
```

Sending Snapshots of Access Reports

Access reports represent a powerful vehicle for conveying the contents of an Access project. We have shown numerous examples in Chapter 8 demonstrating the power and flexibility of this tool. However, what do we do when the client workstation to which we want to send a report does not have Access installed? Or how can we distribute a report to a client workstation that does not have a connection to the LAN with the data?

While traditional interactive Access reports will not work in either of these situations, there is a solution. We can send a **snapshot** of the report from the Access project that does have the connection to the data, to another workstation via e-mail.

Our applications can use the `DoCmd` object to send Access objects to other users via e-mail with the `SendObject` method. If the recipient has a connection to the data, then the report need not be a snapshot, but could remain dynamic. Using the `SendObject` method also enables us to transport reports in multiple formats, for example HTML, RTF, or Excel spreadsheets. One example of using this method is for sending a product catalog that exists as an Access report to clients who request it. To use the `SendObject` method requires the installation of a MAPI-compliant (Microsoft Mail Applications Programming Interface, which is what Outlook uses) or a VIM-compliant (Vendor Independent Mail, which is what Lotus cc:Mail uses) e-mail client application on the workstation that will be sending the report. If you have Outlook or ccMail or a mail program that uses one of the two compliant mail interfaces, then `SendObject` should work.

> If you are using a VIM compliant mail package, then to use **`SendObject`** you must have installed the **`Mapivi32.dll`** library on the machine.

When we create a snapshot of the report, this is a particularly attractive format because it represents the report with full fidelity and the same user interface as if the client had Access running on their workstation. However, it does not require either Access or a live link to the data source for a report.

By using the `SendObject` method, the snapshot travels as an attachment to a standard e-mail message. Microsoft offers a free viewer for snapshot files, called Microsoft Access Snapshot Viewer. This viewer enables workstations without Access to read Access reports, once they have the viewer installed. You can obtain the free snapshot viewer from http://www.microsoft.com/accessdev/prodinfo/snapshot.htm. From the download, there is a snapshot viewer help file, and the snapshot OCX which also needs to be installed to view the reports. In addition, users can install the snapshot reader with Office 2000.

If the idea of sending and working with snapshots appeals to you, ProgrammingMSAccess.com offers a tutorial on snapshot files. The tutorial includes a collection of samples, showing different kinds of uses for snapshots of reports as well as instructions for creating and manipulating snapshot files for e-mail clients and browsers. The tutorial can be found at: www.programmingmsaccess.com/Snapshots/default.htm.

The following code sample shows a pair of procedures that work together to mail the Alphabetical List of Products report from the sample `NorthwindCS.adp` file for this chapter, to an e-mail address. This report is a standard NorthwindCS report that comes when you install the NorthwindCS sample Access project example. The first program passes an e-mail address in to the second procedure, which is trying to mimic what may be found in a production environment. When you use the sample application, insert a valid e-mail address in the first procedure, as the mail address in the code clearly doesn't exist. This is the address to mail a snapshot file to.

The second procedure accepts this address, creates the snapshot, and mails the snapshot as an attachment to an e-mail message. The `SendObject` method, like the equivalent `Send` method in Outlook, takes a long list of arguments, such as the type of object, a report, a query, or different output formats like HTML, `.txt` files, etc.

Because `SendObject` just interfaces with a workstation's mail client, it is easy to use and learn. The following example will demonstrate how easy this is. However, don't forget, as we discussed earlier in this chapter, in the `DoCmd` section, you have to have an e-mail client application installed on the workstation in order for this method to function properly. You may find however, that you do have to log on, or be logged on to the mail client.

```
Sub call_send_snapshot_of_product_list()

'Pass recipient's email address as string
    send_snapshot_of_product_list "someone@somewhere.com"

End Sub


Sub send_snapshot_of_product_list(recipient As String)
Dim str1 As String

'Send the Alphabetical List of Products report
'as a snapshot file
'to recipient string with
'trailing cc and bcc arguments blank
'with a subject line of Our product list
'subject line ends with blank
'a message that says thanks
'and forward it immediately without waiting for editing

str1 = "Thanks for your request. We look forward to " & _
    "helping you in any way possible."
DoCmd.SendObject acSendReport, _
    "Alphabetical List of Products", _
    acFormatSNP, _
    recipient, , , _
    "Our product list ", _
    str1, _
    False

End Sub
```

The DoCmd.SendObject method has the following syntax:

```
DoCmd.SendObject(ObjectType As AcSendObjectType, [ObjectName As Variant],
[OutputFormat As Variant], [To As Variant], [Cc As Variant], [Bcc As Variant],
[Subject As Variant], [MessageText As Variant], [EditMessage As Variant],
[TemplateFile As Variant])
```

The second procedure specifies seven arguments for the SendObject method, and it leaves place markers for two others. When unspecified arguments have other arguments following them, then we need to denote the unspecified argument with commas. This sample does not assign values to the cc and bcc arguments, but it does use three arguments that appear after the bcc field marker.

- ❑ The first argument (ObjectType As AcSendObjectType) is an intrinsic constant. It designates that the method will be sending a report. Other options include objects such as a data access page, a table, or the datasheet behind a form. You cannot mail views and stored procedures with this method, but you can create tables based on their return sets and then mail those.

- ❑ The second argument ([ObjectName As Variant]) names the specific report for which the method should generate a snapshot.

- ❑ The third constant ([OutputFormat As Variant]) designates the use of a snapshot format for sending the report. Selected other formats include Rich Text Format, HTML, and standard MS-DOS Text.

651

❑ The fourth, fifth, and sixth arguments appear on the same line in this example. The procedure passes the recipient's e-mail address as the fourth argument ([To As Variant]), and the fifth and sixth arguments are blank for the cc and bcc fields.

❑ The seventh argument ([Subject As Variant]) is the subject for the e-mail message.

❑ The eighth argument ([MessageText As Variant]) is the body of the message for your e-mail. If your message is more than a line, it will probably be convenient to assign it to a string variable. Then, reference the string variable in the argument list for the SendObject method.

❑ By setting the ninth argument ([EditMessage As Variant]) to False, you direct the workstation to mail the message immediately. Using a value of True causes your e-mail program to pause and open the message for editing. Only after a user closes the message will it mail. By the way, the default value for this argument is True. Therefore, set the argument to False if you want it to mail immediately.

❑ The final tenth argument ([TemplateFile As Variant]) is left blank, as we aren't using an HTML file as a template for our message.

The following screen shows an Outlook e-mail client with a snapshot report attachment about to be sent, generated by the preceding sample with the ninth argument set to True. The SendObject method, as you will find in Outlook, does not permit us to specify a sending e-mail account. This is because the e-mail client takes an ID of the logged on and default account. If the sending workstation supports multiple e-mail accounts, we have to make sure the default account is the one we want to use. Alternatively, do not send the e-mail message immediately (set the ninth argument to True). During the pause for editing the message, we can assign the sending e-mail message that we wish to use for forwarding the snapshot file. Notice the subject and message body fields. They are directly from the SendObject argument list. The e-mail client application will automatically convert the recipient's address from its name@yourdomain.com format to a literal name for a person, if they are found in your contacts folder within Outlook.

The attachment area of the preceding message includes an icon for the snapshot file, followed by the name of the attachment file, which in this instance, is the name of the report.

The following screenshot depicts an excerpt from the snapshot file in the viewer. Notice the title bar. It lists the name of the application, namely Snapshot Viewer, and the file the viewer is showing, which is

Alphabetical List of Products in this case. Notice the interface looks very similar to the Access report interface. Scroll bars allow us to move a viewing window vertically and horizontally on a particular page, and a navigation control enables us to move between pages in the normal way. In addition, the Snapshot Viewer features a Print command on the File menu, so we can print a report.

Sending Data Access Pages

When an application relies on data access pages for displaying the contents of a SQL Server database, we can mail these to recipients as well. The main advantage of this approach is that the page arrives in a recipient's Inbox instead of requiring them to browse to some URL. Being able to mail data access pages enables marketing and financial analysts within an organization to make sure that their clients become aware of the latest new reports on a web site. Recall that data access pages require recipients to have an Office 2000 license and an IE 5 browser. For these reasons, it is likely that you will be using them behind firewalls on company intranets. In any event, mail recipients of data access pages should have a LAN-based connection to the data source for the data access page when you have them set up for two-tiered use. See Chapter 11 for more detailed discussion of data access pages.

When we send a data access page to a recipient, we will again use the SendObject method of the DoCmd object. Unlike with snapshot files, we do not require a special reader – other than the IE 5 browser that our recipient workstation should be using. This browser installs by default with Office 2000, and is a compulsory component for Help. Therefore, if the recipient has Office 2000, they must have Internet Explorer 5. The order of the arguments is the same as for mailing snapshots, and the settings are same, except for three arguments. We go in to these after the example code, but the arguments are the ObjectType, the ObjectName, and the OutputFormat. The following sample code illustrates the syntax for sending a page named employee_sales_projections_from_cab2000 to a recipient. This is being sent from a module within an Access project, and so the connection to the data is live, therefore there is no need to actually complete any connection information.

```
Sub call_send_employee_sales_page()
```

```
'Pass recipient's email address as string
    send_employee_sales_page "cab@ix.netcom.com"

End Sub


Sub send_employee_sales_page(recipient As String)
Dim str1 As String

'Send the employee_sales_projections_from_cab2000
'as a data access page
'do not use acFormatDAP to specify output format
'as documentation suggests; instead use
'"MicrosoftAccessDataAccessPage(*.htm;*.html)".
'Send data access page to recipient string
'with a subject line of "The answer to your data request"
'a message that says the attachment contains a dap
'and forward it immediately without waiting for editing

str1 = "The attachment to this message contains " & _
    "a data access page with the answer to your data request."

DoCmd.SendObject acSendDataAccessPage, _
    "employee_sales_projections_from_cab2000", _
    "MicrosoftAccessDataAccessPage(*.htm;*.html)", _
    recipient, , , _
    "The answer to your data request", _
    str1, _
    False

End Sub
```

Let's look at how sending a data access page differs from sending a snapshot.

The differences start with the first argument for the SendObject method. We use the intrinsic constant acSendDataAccessPage to signal that you want the SendObject command to forward a data access page to the recipient. In this situation, you must have previously created the page before you can send it. Recall that in the case of a snapshot for a report, the SendObject method automatically generated the snapshot file.

The second argument is the name of the link for the data access page in the **Database** window. You cannot send a page with the SendObject method unless the current Access project already has a link to the page. Recall that data access pages can exist even without links from Access projects (.adp) or database files (.mdb), but the SendObject method cannot forward these pages to recipients. Chapter 11 describes programmatic and manual means for linking a data access page to an Access project.

The third argument is a string denoting the type of file that the SendObject method is to forward.

All the remaining arguments are the same between sending snapshots and data access pages. The exact values for these arguments changes in some cases from the preceding sample, but the modifications are merely cosmetic. In fact, as you can see, the basic format for the command is identical in both cases.

The third argument's value highlights a documentation error in the Access online Help files. These indicate that you should use acFormatDAP as the setting for the third argument when forwarding a data access page with the SendObject *method. In fact, this intrinsic constant results in a 2282 run-time error. Instead, use the string in the preceding code listing to avoid this error.*

Programming ADO Objects in Modules

We have already reviewed ADO programming heavily in many of the preceding chapters. This section takes one last look at the area to cover selected issues deliberately excluded from earlier treatments of the ADO topic. In particular, we briefly review the Connection object and the syntax for selected connection strings. Next, the discussion shifts to a focus on use of the Recordset and Command objects, with a comparison of using stored procedures versus T-SQL text to create SQL Server database objects. Finally, the section and chapter close with a sample that offers a workaround to the inability of the TransferDatabase method to import data from an Access database file to an Access project.

Making the Connections

Many of our earlier discussions of the ADO Connection object simply referenced the Connection property for the CurrentProject object. This was reasonable since those discussions dwelt on using the connection to point at another object in the current project. More generally for Access and SQL Server, the Connnection object represents a unique client session with a different database. We can also use the Connection object to link an Access project to ISAM data sources, such as Access database files. In order to use other ADODB objects, such as Recordset and Command objects, we must assign a Connection object to their ActiveConnection property. We can also create the connection and place it directly into the ActiveConnection property, but this is not recommended as we then have no object with which to close the connection effectively. Also, it is not good programming practice when creating flexible solutions.

During the presentation of web techniques, the samples typically used a DSN to specify a connection. It is common for Internet Service Providers (ISPs) to offer a fixed number of DSNs to accounts with database privileges. System DSNs process very quickly and their syntax is very simple. With a DSN, we are free to reference any database within a SQL Server, not just the database associated with the current project. However, if we ever wish to connect to a SQL Server through our Access project, we will need a means of accessing the ODBC Data Source Administrator. ISPs typically set these up for the client accounts, but since they allow access to any database on SQL Server there is a security issue with this. Within a firm, the web server administrator can manage these for webmasters in different business units.

A third approach to creating Connection object references is with the ConnectionString property and the Open method of the Connection object. The ConnectionString property contains the information to connect with a data provider, such as a SQL Server database engine or a Jet database engine. We will typically set the ConnectionString property for a connection by using the ConnectionString argument for the Open method.

Using the Open method makes the connection live with the argument that we specify for it. After invoking the Open method, a connection becomes ready for use with the ActiveConnection property for Command and Recordset objects. The ConnectionString can contain the name of a provider and a string that points to a valid data source for the provider. To clarify, lets take a look at an example of the syntax for the ConnectionString property. We will demonstrate this with a full example in a few moments.

In the following snippet, we are opening the connection by defining the data engine Provider (in this instance, the Jet OLEDB provider) and what the Data Source is (where it resides). This is combining the setting of the ConnectionString, with the Open command. We've assumed the creation of Connection object cnn1.

```
cnn1.Open "Provider=Microsoft.Jet.OLEDB.4.0;" & _
    "Data Source=\\cab2000\c\Program Files\Microsoft Office" & _
    "\Office\Samples\Northwind.mdb;"
```

The code above could be defined just as easily as follows:

```
cnn1.ConnectionString "Provider=Microsoft.Jet.OLEDB.4.0;" & _
    "Data Source=\\cab2000\c\Program Files\Microsoft Office" & _
    "\Office\Samples\Northwind.mdb;"
cnn1.Open
```

The `ActiveConnection` property would then be set after either of the code snippets above, by using this code: The combination of a designator for the provider type (`Provider=`) and a specific data source (`Data Source=`) constitute the `ConnectionString` specification for two-tier applications, such as Access projects. This two-tier type of design is simpler and easier to manage than three-tier designs, which have additional essential parameters for specifying `Connection` objects. The simplicity of the two-tier data access model is one of the factors that contribute to making Access projects a rapid application development tool.

The following pair of procedures shows the syntax for making connections to Jet and SQL Server data sources using the `ConnectionString` property and `Open` method. The `open_mdb` procedure illustrates the syntax for making a connection to an Access database file from an Access project. The `open_ss_db` procedure shows the parallel syntax for linking an Access database to a SQL Server data source. This syntax is appropriate for any SQL Server data source – whether or not you have a connection to it through an Access project. However, you will typically use it when there is no such connection available for use with a `Command` or `Recordset` object. We'll discuss the `open_mdb` procedure first, then move on to `open_ss_db`.

```
Sub open_mdb()

'Don't worry about Errors,just quit out
On Error GoTo EndSub

'Declare cnn1 as our Connection object
Dim cnn1 As ADODB.Connection

'Instantiate cnn1 object
Set cnn1 = New ADODB.Connection

'Open an Access database file (.mdb)
cnn1.Open "Provider=Microsoft.Jet.OLEDB.4.0;" & _
    "Data Source=\\cab2000\c\Program Files\Microsoft Office" & _
    "\Office\Samples\Northwind.mdb;"

'Print name of provider for confirmation the procedure has worked
Debug.Print cnn1.Provider

'Cleanup before exit
cnn1.Close
```

```
Set cnn1 = Nothing

EndSub:

End Sub
```

Leaving the very basic error handling out of this discussion, the open_mdb procedure commences by declaring a data type for the variable that points at the new connection. The use of the ADODB prefix is optional, but it is good form. It unambiguously designates the Connection object for the ADODB object model; also, if for some reason we had another type of connection possible through the Project References, for example DAO, it defines which connection object is to be used. This declaration by itself does not make the object available for the assignment of properties and the invocation of methods.

Before our application can do this, we must first instantiate the object. The New keyword accomplishes this task. Access permits us to insert the New keyword in a Dim statement so that our applications can declare and instantiate an object in a single statement. Many developers suggest not following this convention. They suggest instead that you reserve instantiating an object until just before you need it, through a Set statement. There is no difference in speed or efficiency gains in either method, but it is recommended that the New keyword is placed with the Set statement, rather than the Dim

After instantiating a Connection object, we must make it live. Invoking the Open method with a ConnectionString argument accomplishes this goal. When working with the Jet database engine for Access 2000, we'll need to use the Jet 4.0 OLE DB driver, just like we saw in the snippets before this example. The Provider assignment shows the syntax for making this reference. The Data Source element of the ConnectionString argument must refer to an .mdb file when working with a Jet 4.0 database. The source specification must include the path to the database file and the file name. If we enter either the Provider or the Data Source specifications incorrectly, the Open method will fail. We will get different run-time errors for incorrectly specifying either element of the ConnectionString argument. When our application completes its use of the Connection object, we'll release the resource as soon as possible. This is a two-step process. First, we close the Connection object using its Close method. Second, we Set the Connection object to have a value of Nothing, which is the command that releases the memory which has been held for that connection. However, you may wish to keep the memory if the connection object is to be immediately reused as a connection to another data source. It is better to use the same object again, rather than using a new Set statement to re-create the memory allocation.

> *The ADO interpreter will sometimes silently fix up an incorrect Connection string argument. This is especially an issue when you are reusing a Connection object. In this circumstance, a faulty specification of the new ConnectionString argument can cause the Connection object to revert to using an earlier ConnectionString argument. Therefore, you may care to print out the ConnectionString argument (using Debug.Print) for reused Connection objects to assure yourself that they update correctly, so that during testing, you can ensure that the settings are correct.*

Now here is the procedure for opening a SQL Server database. See how similar it is to the previous code.

```
Sub open_ss_db()

'Don't worry about Errors, just quit out
On Error GoTo EndSub
```

```
'Declare and instantiate connection object
Dim cnn1 As New ADODB.Connection


'Open connection
str1 = "Provider=sqloledb;" & _
    "Data Source=cab2000;Initial Catalog=pubs;User Id=sa;Password=;"
cnn1.Open str1

'Print name of provider for confirmation the procedure has worked
Debug.Print cnn1.Provider

'Cleanup before exit
cnn1.Close
Set cnn1 = Nothing

EndSub:

End Sub
```

The open_ss_db procedure creates a connection to a SQL Server data source. This sample inserts the New keyword into the Dim statement so that it declares and instantiates the Connection object in a single statement. The Open method operates on a string argument in a way comparable to the preceding procedure. Both samples contain Provider and Data Source elements in their ConnectionString argument for the Open method. However, the details of the ConnectionString argument are different. The Provider element in this sample references a different OLE DB driver to that in the preceding sample. The sqloledb provider is a specific provider for SQL Server 7 and SQL Server 2000. We can also use a generic ODBC driver, but Microsoft optimized the sqloledb driver for SQL Server.

The elements of the Data Source string are also different. Access developers migrating from Jet to SQL Server need to understand that you do not reference database files (as is the practice with Access database files). Instead, you reference a database server, a database name (set by Initial Catalog), and a login account, comprising a username and password. The names for the database server and database identify the source of the database. The login account determines the permissions that a connection to a database enjoys. It takes the proper specification of these four details in order to gain access to a SQL Server database.

Programming a Recordset

The Recordset object provides us with a means of referencing a collection of records within a database. With a SQL Server database, this collection can come from tables and return sets for views and stored procedures. We can specify the source for a Recordset by the name of the underlying database object or a T-SQL string that generates its own return set. A Recordset encapsulates meta-data about the collection of records that it references, as well as the raw records. For example, we can enumerate the field names in a Recordset, and we can additionally return one or more specific field values. The field values correspond to column values in the underlying record source of a Recordset, and the records in a Recordset align with the rows of the underlying record source.

The CursorType property designates the type of functionality that a Recordset provides. It does this by setting the type of **cursor** we will use to retrieve data from the Recordset. A cursor is a means of keeping track of where our application has got to in the Recordset, and can allow us to pick our way through the Recordset data rather than being presented with it all in one lump.

There are four possible CursorType settings. These are adOpenForwardOnly, adOpenKeyset, adOpenDynamic, and adOpenStatic.

❑ The default setting of adOpenForwardOnly allows us to travel through a Recordset in one direction – from the first to the last record. A Recordset with an adOpenForwardOnly cursor does not have a MovePrevious method, and because of this it is the fastest method of returning and accessing data.

❑ The adOpenKeyset setting enables us to move back and forth in a Recordset. In addition, this type of cursor enables us to view changes by other users, including deletions. However, any additions made by any other users are not visible until the Recordset is refreshed. In the case of deletions, the records just appear as unavailable.

❑ The adOpenDynamic cursor includes the functionality of adOpenKeyset cursor, but it doesn't require the Recordset to be refreshed to view additions, changes, and deletions made by other users.

❑ The adOpenStatic cursor is a static copy of the records from a source, so it does not show any changes by other users. Full movement back and forth is available. By having this type of cursor, we are in fact dealing with a snapshot of the data, taken at the time the data retrieval was requested.

Our cursor can reside on either the client (adUseClient) or server (adUseServer). Depending on volume of data, and what is happening within our code at the time, we may change where we want the cursor to reside. If in doubt, leave the cursor on the server. With an adUseClient setting for the CursorLocation property, the only possible CursorType is adOpenStatic.

The LockType is another important property that can impact significantly on the behavior of a Recordset. The possible settings for this Recordset property are adLockReadOnly, adLockPessimistic, adLockOptimistic, and adLockBatchOptimistic.

❑ With LockType set to adLockReadOnly, we can only view record values. This setting does not allow updates regardless of the cursor type defined.

❑ The adLockPessimistic setting reserves the record we are using for changes as soon we start to edit it. After the lock is in place, other users cannot gain write access to the record; until after the update has been applied, they can only read the data. The adUseClient setting for the CursorLocation property does not support the adLockPessimistic LockType setting, as this is a snapshot of the data.

❑ The adLockOptimistic setting also enables database updates, but it does not reserve a record until it is time to write the change to the record. This can lead to conflicts in the situation where a second user completed a change to a record after a first user opened a record for editing. This is because the change by the first user is to a different record to the one that it started from (because the other user changed it). When this happens, you will need to create code to resolve the conflict that has occurred. This is not covered in this book.

❑ The fourth setting of adLockBatchOptimistic is for when you are running a batch where updates need not be immediate, which will then allow the batch to run faster. It provides a mechanism to update several records on a server in a single pass from a local cursor. The CursorLocation property for the Recordset should be adUseClient in this circumstance.

It is highly likely that procedures processing Recordsets will be performing loops. This is because a Recordset exposes values for a single current record at a time. A procedure processing a Recordset can access each record in that Recordset by moving from one record to the next and exposing each record through the current record of the `Recordset`. The same guidelines relate to the `Fields` collection for a `Recordset`. We can loop through the `Fields` collection for a `Recordset` to enumerate the field names.

The following sample demonstrates both of these techniques, as it reinforces our skills in managing `Connection` objects from the previous two samples:

```
Sub loop_through_authors()

Dim cnn1 As ADODB.Connection
Dim rst1 As ADODB.Recordset

Set cnn1 = New ADODB.Connection

'Set the ConnectionString, and open  our connection
str1 = "Provider=sqloledb;" & _
    "Data Source=cab2000;Initial Catalog=pubs;User Id=sa;Password=;"
cnn1.Open str1

'Instantiate our recordset object
Set rst1 = New ADODB.Recordset

'Point the recordset at the authors table and gather
'the data to fill the recordset
rst1.Open "authors", cnn1, adOpenForwardOnly, adLockReadOnly

'Enumerate fileld names for recordset
Dim fld1 As ADODB.Field
For Each fld1 In rst1.Fields
    Debug.Print fld1.Name
Next

'Enumerate selected fields for recordset
Do Until rst1.EOF
    Debug.Print rst1("au_fname"), rst1("au_lname"), rst1("phone")
    rst1.MoveNext
Loop

rst1.Close
cnn1.Close

Set rst1 = Nothing
Set cnn1 = Nothing

End Sub
```

Since there is a lot happening in this code, let's go through it a section at a time so we don't miss anything. This first section is much the same as for the previous example, except it also declares our `Recordset` object, `rst1`:

```
Sub loop_through_authors()

Dim cnn1 As ADODB.Connection
Dim rst1 As ADODB.Recordset
```

```
Set cnn1 = New ADODB.Connection

str1 = "Provider=sqloledb;" & _
    "Data Source=cab2000;Initial Catalog=pubs;User Id=sa;Password=;"
cnn1.Open str1
```

Now that we have the connection, we can create the `Recordset` object that will hold the returned data:

```
'Instantiate our recordset object
Set rst1 = New ADODB.Recordset
```

It is now time to open up our `Recordset` object and create a collection based on the information we want to return. In this instance, we want to return all the rows and information from the authors table.
We inform the `Recordset` of the connection we made earlier so it knows from where to return the data. As you can see, we are now using some of the options discussed earlier. We want to process the data as fast as possible, and we won't be moving around the records, so we have chosen `adOpenForwardOnly`. Finally, there will be no updates, so the code will set in place that this `Recordset` is read-only.

```
'Point the recordset at the authors table and gather
'the data to fill the recordset
rst1.Open "authors", cnn1, adOpenForwardOnly, adLockReadOnly
```

Now that our `Recordset` is open and the data has been returned, we can use it. In the next section of code, we will be printing out just the names of the fields in the `Recordset`.

```
'Enumerate field names for recordset
Dim fld1 As ADODB.Field
For Each fld1 In rst1.Fields
    Debug.Print fld1.Name
Next
```

This section now takes all of the data returned, and one record at a time displays the information in the Immediate window. Note that the only movement of data is through the `MoveNext` command, which moves the data forward one record. The loop continues until the end of the `Recordset` is reached, denoted by `rst1.EOF`.

```
'Enumerate selected fields for recordset
Do Until rst1.EOF
    Debug.Print rst1("au_fname"), rst1("au_lname"), rst1("phone")
    rst1.MoveNext
Loop
```

Don't forget to close the connections, `Recordset` first, and then remove the variables from memory, as they won't be used any more.

```
rst1.Close
cnn1.Close

Set rst1 = Nothing
Set cnn1 = Nothing

End Sub
```

This screenshot shows an extract from the Immediate window after the execution of our sample:

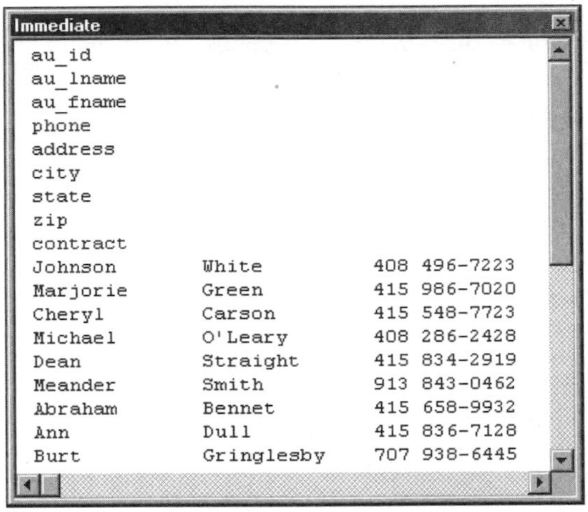

Performing SQL Server Data Definition with ADO

Several samples throughout this book have demonstrated how to use Command objects to manipulate SQL Server databases from Access. One of the most exciting features of Access 2000 is programmatic data definition. With the introduction of Access 2000, we can not only extract and manipulate data in a SQL Server data source, but we can also create and drop Database objects. Using Command objects, we have two ways to accomplish this kind of task.

❑ First, we can invoke a stored procedure on the database server. This is fast and efficient. However, we have to have a stored procedure that performs the task we want to perform. While it is possible to create a custom stored procedure manually or programmatically, not all Access developers will have this permission available to their login accounts.

❑ Second, we can base a Command object on a T-SQL statement. Using this method of creation of custom stored procedures permits us to test ideas and easily modify and refine those ideas, before we commit them to stored procedures.

The next sample demonstrates both approaches. It relies on a stored procedure to create a table, which is named imported_categories. There is nothing very special about the stored procedure. Notice, however, that it does drop the table if it exists already. The stored procedure's use here is just to review how to invoke a data definition stored procedure from a VBA procedure in an Access module. The T-SQL for the stored procedure appears below:

```
Alter Procedure create_imported_categories
As
If Exists (SELECT * from dbo.sysobjects
      WHERE id = object_id(N'[dbo].[imported_categories]')
      AND OBJECTPROPERTY(id, N'IsUserTable') = 1)
Drop table [dbo].[imported_categories]

CREATE TABLE [dbo].[imported_categories] (
   [CategoryID] [int] .IDENTITY (1, 1) NOT NULL ,
   [CategoryName] [varchar] (15),
```

```
        [Description] [text],
        [Picture] [image] NULL
   ) ON [PRIMARY] TEXTIMAGE_ON [PRIMARY]


   ALTER TABLE [dbo].[imported_categories] WITH NOCHECK ADD
      CONSTRAINT [PK_imported_categories] PRIMARY KEY  CLUSTERED
      (
          [CategoryID]
      )  ON [PRIMARY]
```

The following VBA procedure demonstrates how to invoke the create_imported_categories stored procedure with a Command object. It also shows how to remove the table that it creates, using a second Command object that relies on a T-SQL test string for its source. The sample aims to teach you about the availability of Database objects and the syntax for referencing them. The best way to run this VBA procedure is to step through it one line at a time, using the **Debug | Step Into** command, or pressing *F8*. This is because it purposely creates an error, and has a built-in trap to detect the error and recover from it. By stepping through the code, you will be able to see the recovery logic in action.

```
Sub command_create_and_drop_table()

'Set up error trapping procedure
On Error GoTo create_drop_trap

Dim str1 As String
Dim cmd1 As ADODB.Command
Dim rst1 As ADODB.Recordset

'Create the imported_categories table with
'a stored procedure; look at the syntax
Set cmd1 = New ADODB.Command
cmd1.ActiveConnection = CurrentProject.Connection
cmd1.CommandText = "create_imported_categories"
cmd1.CommandType = adCmdStoredProc
cmd1.Execute

'Open and close a recordset for imported_categories
Set rst1 = New ADODB.Recordset
rst1.ActiveConnection = CurrentProject.Connection
rst1.Open "imported_categories"

'Display the number of records returned to prove
'that the recordset has returned
Debug.Print rst1.Fields.Count

'Now close the recordset
rst1.Close

'Store T-SQL text to drop imported_categories table
'and run it with a command object; look at the syntax.
'Because we re-use the command object
'we don't have to specify the connection again
str1 = "If Exists (SELECT * From dbo.sysobjects " & _
    "WHERE id = object_id(N'[dbo].[imported_categories]') " & _
```

```
        "AND OBJECTPROPERTY(id, N'IsUserTable') = 1)"
str1 = str1 & "Drop table [dbo].[imported_categories]"
cmd1.CommandText = str1
cmd1.CommandType = adCmdText
cmd1.Execute


'Attempt to re-open recordset based on
'the imported_categories table
rst1.Open "imported_categories"

'Re-create imported_categories table
'next commented line not necessary because re-using command
'cmd1.ActiveConnection = CurrentProject.Connection
cmd1.CommandText = "create_imported_categories"
cmd1.CommandType = adCmdStoredProc
cmd1.Execute

'Attempt again to re-open recordset based on
'the imported_categories table
rst1.Open "imported_categories"
MsgBox "See, you can open table after re-creating it."

create_drop_exit:
Set cmd1 = Nothing
Set rst1 = Nothing
Exit Sub

create_drop_trap:
If Err.Number = -2147217865 Then
    MsgBox "Cannot open table after droping it."
    Resume Next
Else
    Debug.Print Err.Number, Err.Description
    Resume create_drop_exit
End If

End Sub
```

Step through the `command_create_and_drop_table` procedure code down to the `rst1.Close` statement. By this point, the procedure has performed two data definition tasks. After instantiating the `Command` object, the procedure initially creates the **imported_categories** table with that ADO object:

```
Set cmd1 = New ADODB.Command
cmd1.ActiveConnection = CurrentProject.Connection
cmd1.CommandText = "create_imported_categories"
cmd1.CommandType = adCmdStoredProc
cmd1.Execute
```

As you can see here, the VBA procedure does this by invoking the **create_imported_categories** stored procedure. Before invoking the `Execute` method for the `Command` object, the code sets three properties. First, it sets the `ActiveConnection` property to the current project's `Connection`. Next, it points the `CommandText` property at the name of the stored procedure. Therefore, the stored procedure `Database` object must reside in the database for the current project. The third property setting specifies the type of source we are using for the `Command` object. The sample uses the intrinsic constant `adCmdStoredProc` to designate a stored procedure.

To confirm the availability of the imported_categories table, the procedure opens a Recordset on it. Again, the process starts by instantiating an object. In this case, it is the rst1 Recordset object:

```
Set rst1 = New ADODB.Recordset
rst1.ActiveConnection = CurrentProject.Connection
rst1.Open "imported_categories"

Debug.Print rst1.Fields.Count

rst1.Close
```

Next, the code sets the ActiveConnection property for the object so that it is now ready for use. In the next line, the procedure invokes the Open method for the rst1 object. The format of the Open method is simple because the code previously assigned the ActiveConnection property for the Recordset, and the Open method accepts the default values for the CursorType and LockType properties. The default CursorType setting is adOpenForwardOnly as this cursor is on the server, and the default setting for LockType is adLockReadOnly. These settings are fine in this case since all we want to do is verify that a Recordset can open on the data source, namely the imported_categories table that the Command object just created. After confirming the availability of the table, the procedure prints the number of fields in the Recordset, as there would be no other way to see that it had actually opened. When this has been done, the procedure closes the Recordset for its reuse later.

The next several lines reuse the cmd1 Command object. This reuse involves a T-SQL text string as the source for the Command object instead of a stored procedure:

```
str1 = "If Exists (SELECT * From dbo.sysobjects " & _
    "WHERE id = object_id(N'[dbo].[imported_categories]') " & _
    "AND OBJECTPROPERTY(id, N'IsUserTable') = 1)"
str1 = str1 & "Drop table [dbo].[imported_categories]"
cmd1.CommandText = str1
cmd1.CommandType = adCmdText
cmd1.Execute
```

The str1 string stores the string that conditionally drops the imported_categories table if it exists. Then, the procedure assigns that string to the CommandText property for the cmd1 Command object. In this case, the procedure sets the CommandText property to adCmdText to signify that the ADO interpreter should process the CommandText property as a string.

After executing the cmd1 Command object, the procedure again invokes the Open method for the rst1 Recordset object:

```
rst1.Open "imported_categories"
```

However, the procedure just removed from the database the source for the Recordset. Therefore, the Open method fails.

Control transfers to the error trap we put at the end of the procedure. It tests for an invalid object name with an error number of −2147217865:

```
create_drop_trap:
If Err.Number = -2147217865 Then
    MsgBox "Cannot open table after dropping it."
    Resume Next
```

```
Else
    Debug.Print Err.Number, Err.Description
    Resume create_drop_exit
End If
```

If the trap detects this error, it alerts the user to the problem with a message box, and it resumes processing with the next line in the main procedure. This particular error does not impact on the operation of the rest of the procedure. Therefore, continuing with the next line of code in the main procedure is an acceptable response to the error in this instance. In a production environment, our error trapping has to be more robust. However, the error trap logs any other error to the **Immediate** window before exiting by transferring control to the `create_drop_exit` label:

```
create_drop_exit:
Set cmd1 = Nothing
Set rst1 = Nothing
Exit Sub
```

This creates a graceful exit in response to the error so that our application remains in control instead of control passing to default Access error processing procedures. If you have been wondering how to construct conditional processing for different kinds of errors, this example should help you to construct your logic. One word of warning, however; a robust error handler is a godsend to creating professional applications, and giving the users confidence that when something goes wrong, there are no knock-on effects. Care and time should be set aside for dealing with error handling.

After the user responds to the message box that the error trap presents, the procedure resumes by re-creating the `imported_categories` table and attempting to open a `Recordset` based on it again.

```
cmd1.CommandText = "create_imported_categories"
cmd1.CommandType = adCmdStoredProc
cmd1.Execute
```

However, this time the `Open` method succeeds because the data source for the `Recordset` is in the database.

```
rst1.Open "imported_categories"
MsgBox "See, you can open table after re-creating it."
```

After informing the user of this result with a message box, the procedure closes by setting the `cmd1` and `rst1` objects to `Nothing` to free their resources. This practice helps to avoid memory leaks that can occur with the repeated use of procedures that fail to close their resources.

Adding and Dropping Tables using T-SQL Text or Stored Procedures from ADO

The next sequence of three VBA procedures contrasts adding and dropping a table via stored procedures versus T-SQL text. The prior samples did not explicitly mention one short stored procedure, but it is an excerpt from the **create_imported_categories** stored procedure. The **drop_imported_categories** stored procedure merely extracts the first two lines that conditionally remove the **imported_categories** table from the database. Don't forget to create this stored procedure before you run the second example:

```
Alter Procedure drop_imported_categories
```

```
As
IF Exists (SELECT * from dbo.sysobjects
    WHERE id = object_id(N'[dbo].[imported_categories]')
    AND OBJECTPROPERTY(id, N'IsUserTable') = 1)
Drop table [dbo].[imported_categories]
```

The most important issue for this sample is to contrast two different approaches for performing the same pair of tasks – namely, adding and dropping a table. The three VBA procedures for this sample each serve a distinct role.

Adding and Dropping a Table using T-SQL Text from ADO

First, the add_and_drop_by_text procedure illustrates how to create and drop a table with a primary key for a SQL Server database with ADO code. Just about anything you can do with T-SQL is possible with ADO Command objects.

```
Sub add_and_drop_by_text()
'Store T-SQL text to drop imported_categories table
'and run it

Dim str1 As String
Dim cmd1 As ADODB.Command

'Text to conditionally drop table if it already exists
str1 = "If Exists (SELECT * from dbo.sysobjects " & _
    "WHERE id = object_id(N'[dbo].[imported_categories]') " & _
    "AND OBJECTPROPERTY(id, N'IsUserTable') = 1)"
str1 = str1 & "Drop table [dbo].[imported_categories]"

'Text to create table
str1 = str1 & "CREATE TABLE [dbo].[imported_categories] (" & _
    "[CategoryID] [int] IDENTITY (1, 1) NOT NULL ," & _
    "[CategoryName] [varchar] (15) ," & _
    "[Description] [text] ," & _
    "[Picture] [image] NULL" & _
    ") ON [PRIMARY] TEXTIMAGE_ON [PRIMARY]"

'Text to create primary key for the table
str1 = str1 & "ALTER TABLE [dbo].[imported_categories] " & _
    "WITH NOCHECK ADD " & _
    "CONSTRAINT [PK_imported_categories] " & _
    "PRIMARY KEY  CLUSTERED " & _
    "( [CategoryID] ) ON [PRIMARY]"

'Instantiate command object to create table
Set cmd1 = New ADODB.Command
cmd1.ActiveConnection = CurrentProject.Connection
cmd1.CommandText = str1
cmd1.CommandType = adCmdText
cmd1.Execute

'Store T-SQL text to drop imported_categories table
'and run it
str1 = "If Exists (SELECT * from dbo.sysobjects " & _
    "WHERE id = object_id(N'[dbo].[imported_categories]') " & _
```

```
        "AND OBJECTPROPERTY(id, N'IsUserTable') = 1)"
str1 = str1 & "drop table [dbo].[imported_categories]"
cmd1.CommandText = str1
cmd1.CommandType = adCmdText
cmd1.Execute

End Sub
```

The `add_and_drop_by_text` procedure design is straightforward. First, it constructs a string. Second, it executes a `Command` object based on the string. The procedure performs this cycle twice – once to create the `imported_categories` table, and a second time to drop the table. In the first cycle to create the table, the procedure builds the T-SQL string in three phases. This is not essential, but it can make the code easier to read.

Adding and Dropping a Table using Stored Procedures from ADO

Second, the `add_and_drop_by_sp` procedure shows a parallel approach to the same task with stored procedures in place of several T-SQL text strings. Stored procedures are generally faster since they reside on the server already and SQL Server has already compiled their code.

```
Sub add_and_drop_by_sp()
Dim cmd1 As ADODB.Command

Set cmd1 = New ADODB.Command
cmd1.ActiveConnection = CurrentProject.Connection
cmd1.CommandText = "create_imported_categories"
cmd1.CommandType = adCmdStoredProc
cmd1.Execute

cmd1.CommandText = "drop_imported_categories"
cmd1.CommandType = adCmdStoredProc
cmd1.Execute

End Sub
```

The two stored procedures this ADO procedure uses are the ones we've seen already, create_imported_categories and drop_imported_categories. The design of the add_and_drop_by_sp procedure illustrates another advantage of referencing stored procedures versus running T-SQL strings. It takes dramatically fewer lines of code to build ADO procedures that invoke stored procedures than to duplicate the stored procedures in T-SQL text strings. In addition, it is just easier to reference a stored procedure's name than to write T-SQL to duplicate the functionality of a stored procedure. Finally, by altering the contents of the stored procedure, we can produce different results from running the add_and_drop_by_sp procedure. This happens even though the VBA code remains unchanged.

Comparing the Relative Speed for T-SQL Text and Stored Procedures

Third, the add_drop_speeds procedure runs both of the other two procedures a fixed number of times and reports the time savings of performing the tasks with stored procedures:

```
Sub add_drop_speeds()
Dim int1 As Integer
Dim dt1 As Date
Dim dt2 As Date
Dim dt3 As Date
Dim dt4 As Date
```

```
dt1 = Now()
For int1 = 1 To 150
    add_and_drop_by_text
Next int1
dt2 = Now()

dt3 = Now()
For int1 = 1 To 150
    add_and_drop_by_sp
Next int1
dt4 = Now()

Debug.Print "Number of seconds for text is: " & DateDiff("s", dt1, dt2)
Debug.Print "Number of seconds for sp is: " & DateDiff("s", dt3, dt4)
Debug.Print "Percent saving is: " & _
    Round((1 - (DateDiff("s", dt3, dt4) / DateDiff("s", dt1, dt2))) * 100, 1)
End Sub
```

The add_drop_speeds test procedure gives you a model for running performance comparisons between alternative ways of coding tasks. As you build solutions, you often encounter design options. A procedure like this can help you develop objective criteria for choosing one design approach over another. The procedure calls the add_and_drop_by_text and add_and_drop_by_sp procedures 150 times each, to give a fair assessment of time rather than a one-off snapshot. Immediately before and after each series of executions, it stores the current time. After completing both sets of iterations, the procedure computes the duration of performing the tasks via T-SQL strings and stored procedures. It also computes the percent savings from using stored procedures. The results will vary from system to system, but the stored procedure approach should always be faster, or at least as fast, as the technique using T-SQL text.

This excerpt from the Immediate window shows the outcome of running the procedure three times. In these cases, using stored procedures delivered a performance time saving of between 20 and 33.3 percent.

```
Immediate                                    [X]
 Number of seconds for text is: 6      [▲]
 Number of seconds for sp is: 4
 Percent saving is: 33.3
 Number of seconds for text is: 5
 Number of seconds for sp is: 4
 Percent saving is: 20
 Number of seconds for text is: 6
 Number of seconds for sp is: 4
 Percent saving is: 33.3
                                       [▼]
 [◄][                              ][►]
```

Importing from an Access Database File

There are two reasons why we're looking at this next sample. First, the TransferDatabase method for the DoCmd object doesn't perform the task, as discussed earlier in this chapter. Second, we can readily perform this task with our knowledge of ADO programming techniques, learned in the previous sections on ADO.

This example copies a file from the sample Chapter12.mdb file used earlier in the chapter. Make sure the file is available, and that it has an exported_categories table. The last sample using the Access database file creates that table in the database file.

The basic design of this sample is to make a `Connection` to a remote database file. Then, it forms a `Recordset` based on a table in that file. Finally, it copies the values from that `Recordset` into another `Recordset` based on an empty table in the SQL Server database associated with the current Access project. One unfortunate side effect of this approach is that the **Database** window does not update – even if you invoke the `RefreshDatabaseWindow` method after adding the new table based on the one in the Access database file. However, the inability of users to view the table in the **Database** window does not block their ability to work with the new table. The sample confirms this. In any event, we can still view the new table by manually invoking a **View | Refresh** command from the **Database** window menu.

The following procedure shows the detailed code for the sample. It copies the values from the exported_categories table in the Access database file to the imported_categories table in the current project.

```
Sub import_table_from_access_db_2()
Dim cnn1 As ADODB.Connection
Dim cmd1 As ADODB.Command
Dim rst1 As ADODB.Recordset
Dim rst2 As New ADODB.Recordset
Dim int1 As Integer
Dim rst3 As ADODB.Recordset

'Instantiate cmd1 object
Set cmd1 = New ADODB.Command

'Point cmd1 at drop_imported_categories stored proc
'and execute it
With cmd1
    .ActiveConnection = CurrentProject.Connection
    .CommandText = "drop_imported_categories"
    .CommandType = adCmdStoredProc
    .Execute
End With

'Instantiate cnn1 object and point it Chapter12.mdb
Set cnn1 = New ADODB.Connection
cnn1.Open "Provider=Microsoft.Jet.OLEDB.4.0;" & _
    "Data Source=C:\Documents and Settings\Administrator\" & _
    "My Documents\Chapter12.mdb;"

'Open exported table in Chapter12.mdb
'Make sure you populated Chapter12.mdb with exported_categories
Set rst1 = New ADODB.Recordset
rst1.Open "exported_categories", cnn1

'Run stored procedure to create structure for new table
With cmd1
    .ActiveConnection = CurrentProject.Connection
    .CommandText = "create_imported_categories"
    .CommandType = adCmdStoredProc
    .Execute
End With

'Now we can open a recordset against the new table
With rst2
    .ActiveConnection = CurrentProject.Connection
    .CursorType = adOpenKeyset
```

```
        .LockType = adLockOptimistic
        .Open "imported_categories"
    End With

    'Copy the contents of the exported_categories table from
    'Chapter12.mdb into imported_categories table in this Access project
    Do Until rst1.EOF
        With rst2
            .AddNew
            For int1 = 1 To rst1.Fields.Count - 1
                rst2(int1) = rst1(int1)
            Next int1
            .Update
            rst1.MoveNext
        End With
    Loop

    'The RefreshDatabaseWindow method fails, but the table is there
    'Choose View | Refresh to see it in the database window or just use it
    Application.RefreshDatabaseWindow

    'Although you cannot see imported_categories in the DB window,
    'you can open it programmatically
    Set rst3 = New ADODB.Recordset
    rst3.Open "imported_categories", CurrentProject.Connection

    'Display the number of records returned to prove
    'that the recordset has returned
    Debug.Print rst1.Fields.Count

    'Clean up before exiting. We could move the Close statements
    'to when each recordset is finished with. Either solution is fine
    rst1.Close
    rst2.Close
    rst3.Close
    Set rst1 = Nothing
    Set rst2 = Nothing
    Set rst3 = Nothing
    Set cmd1 = Nothing
    cnn1.Close
    Set cnn1 = Nothing
End Sub
```

The procedure starts by dropping any existing version of the imported_categories table. Then, it opens a connection to the Access database file, Chapter12.mdb.

```
Set cmd1 = New ADODB.Command

With cmd1
    .ActiveConnection = CurrentProject.Connection
    .CommandText = "drop_imported_categories"
    .CommandType = adCmdStoredProc
    .Execute
End With
```

```
Set cnn1 = New ADODB.Connection
cnn1.Open "Provider=Microsoft.Jet.OLEDB.4.0;" & _
    "Data Source=C:\Documents and Settings\Administrator\" & _
    "My Documents\Chapter12.mdb;"

Set rst1 = New ADODB.Recordset
rst1.Open "exported_categories", cnn1
```

Once it is connected to Chapter12.mdb, the procedure opens a Recordset on the **exported_categories** table. This Recordset will be used later.

After forging a link to the remote data source, the procedure re-creates the **imported_categories** table:

```
'Run stored procedure to create structure for new table
With cmd1
    .ActiveConnection = CurrentProject.Connection
    .CommandText = "create_imported_categories"
    .CommandType = adCmdStoredProc
    .Execute
End With
```

This new version of the **imported_categories** table is in the SQL Server database behind the current project. Having created the table, the procedure now opens a second Recordset object and points it at the new table:

```
With rst2
    .ActiveConnection = CurrentProject.Connection
    .CursorType = adOpenKeyset
    .LockType = adLockOptimistic
    .Open "imported_categories"
End With
```

This Recordset, which is returned from the **imported_categories** table, has to be editable, since we are going to be adding values to it. Therefore, its CursorType and LockType properties are, respectively, adOpenKeyset and adLockOptimistic.

The next pair of nested loops are especially important to the performance of the procedure:

```
Do Until rst1.EOF
    With rst2
        .AddNew
        For int1 = 1 To rst1.Fields.Count - 1
            rst2(int1) = rst1(int1)
        Next int1
        .Update
        rst1.MoveNext
    End With
Loop
```

The outer loop passes through each record in the remote **exported_categories** table from the Access database file. The inner loop passes through each column within a row of the **imported_categories** table. After copying the values from the remote table to the Recordset for the local table, it adds the copied values to the table. The combination of the AddNew and Update methods for the rst2 object performs the copy of the Access database field values to the SQL Server database.

The remaining lines in the procedure do not deal with the copying of values. Instead, they focus on the status of the **Database** window. First, the code invokes the `RefreshDatabaseWindow` method. However, if you check the **Database** window at the conclusion of this procedure, you will notice that there is no trace of an imported_categories table. The absence of the table's appearance in the **Database** window does not deny the application from using the table. As you can see, the last few lines before the code to clean up object resources open a `Recordset` based on the imported_categories table. This is only possible because the table is in the database. To show that we can use the table, the procedure prints to the **Immediate** window how many fields are in the `Recordset`.

Summary

We are now at the end of the book. By this point, you should be comfortable and experienced in using Access and SQL Server or MSDE together to provide an ideal solution in your environment. In this last chapter we have pulled together and revisited certain areas covered throughout the book, to cement and progress those areas that were inappropriate to cover at an earlier time.

We have drilled down on Access programming issues. This chapter introduced the flexible, powerful, and easy-to-use `DoCmd` object. With the examples and the individual sections, the `DoCmd` should have become a much more powerful tool in your arsenal in developing solutions for your customers.

We've also looked at linking the database behind an Access project to other SQL Server data sources and Access database files. This chapter closed with another look at ADO programming, and how `Recordsets` are used within ADO solutions. This presentation complements and extends earlier treatments of the topic in prior chapters. This chapter also contrasted alternative approaches for creating database objects with ADO programming.

Database Security

The key issue to consider in database security for SQL Server is who you allow to access your data. In any given environment, there will be people who need to be able to access different parts of the database, and will have no need to use data from other parts of a database. Some people will need to update the information contained in the database, and others won't. You could achieve some of this by only distributing the relevant database objects, which could mean that everybody gets a different set of tables and views. However, the easiest and most secure way to restrict access to the database is to use the SQL Server security model.

SQL Server security uses a different kind of model from the one that most Access developers already know. Nevertheless, the SQL Server security model has a consistent design and simple interface that will make the transition easy. On top of that, the Access project user interface for security is similar to the user interface Enterprise Manager uses for this task. With the Access project security interface, you can define logins, create users, and assign permissions. The interface offers a variety of vehicles for assigning database and server permissions to user accounts.

SQL Server represents a major security upgrade from traditional Access database files in terms of power, scope, and ease of use. SQL Server has a rich, powerful, easy-to-use security model. You can readily determine database access and server administration permissions. The SQL Server security model works well with both Windows NT servers and on a stand-alone basis. This appendix dwells mostly on the aspects of the model that are especially easy to administer through the graphical user interface in Access projects. It also devotes some space to alerting you to problems not clearly documented in the SQL Server documentation, such as Books Online.

In this appendix, we'll take a look at the concepts you need to understand, and then put them into practice. We'll do this in the following sections:

- ❑ SQL Server Database Concepts
- ❑ Logins

❑   User Accounts

❑   Roles and Permissions

SQL Server Database Concepts

The SQL Server security database model is substantially different from the model for traditional Access databases; for example, there is no workgroup information file. As SQL Server couples tightly with Windows NT and Windows 2000, developers designing security for their SQL Server solutions can take advantage of **NT Authentication**, if they choose and the system allows. In addition, since SQL Server doesn't always run on a Windows NT or Windows 2000 server, SQL Server supports **SQL Server Authentication**.

Beyond the issue of authentication, you will want to grasp concepts such as **logins**, **users**, **roles**, and **permissions**. Some special roles and users can profoundly affect your ability to lock down a database. Before you create logins and users for your SQL Server databases, let's have a quick look at what these concepts represent:

❑   **Login** – an account name that allows access to the SQL Server

❑   **User** – an account name that allows access to a database on the SQL Server

❑   **Role** – a collection of permissions that can be assigned to one or more users

❑   **Permission** – specifies what a role allows a user to do in the database

In order to get to grips with these new concepts, we'll be looking at them in order, and tying them all in to the same example. So, we're going to create a couple of fictional users for our database, assign a login and a user account, which belongs to a couple of roles, and has some other permissions. The users we are going to create security for will be called cabxli and foo.

Unfortunately, because these security concepts and structures are so interdependent upon one another, there will be times when we tell you that you can do one thing if you have something that we haven't explained properly yet. You'll just have to bear with it until you reach the appropriate section for what we're talking about, as most of this is quite simple once you get into it.

> The samples and examples up to this point in the book used the **sa** login without a password. This was done so that the discussion of database security could be deferred to this appendix. Developers in larger organizations will often design security as part of a team, and it may be the database administrator or the network administrator, rather than the developer, who has the final authority and responsibility for database security administration. However, in smaller working units, the developer will likely have more authority over database security.

Logins

Login accounts belong to the outer layer of SQL Server security. If a user cannot designate a legitimate login account, then they cannot enter the SQL Server. Any member of the sysadmin or securityadmin fixed server roles can manage login accounts. We'll come on to what these are in the section on *Roles* *and Permissions.* While a sysadmin or securityadmin member can recognize a Windows user account as a SQL Server login account, Windows user accounts do not automatically have SQL Server login accounts associated with them. When we install SQL Server on a Windows NT or 2000 server, we will have two additional automatic logins besides sa. These are BUILTIN\Administrators and ServerName\Administrator. If our Windows server name is CAB2000, the second name appears as CAB2000\Administrator. All three of these login accounts belong to the sysadmin fixed server role.

We can create and manage logins, user IDs, and roles from the same SQL Server Security dialog. This dialog is opened by choosing Tools | Security | Database Security from the Access project Database menu.

The SQL Server Security dialog has three tabs named Server Logins, Database Users, and Database Roles. As the name implies, the Server Logins entries apply to the database server. Once we create a login for a server, we can use it with any database on that server. The entries on the Database Users and Database Roles tabs are specific to a database, namely the one for which our Access project has a connection. If we want to examine or edit the users and roles for another database with the dialog, then we need to change the connection for the Access project. We can do this with the Data Link Properties dialog for the Access project, with which we should by now be familiar.

We'll come back to user IDs and roles in subsequent sections. For now, let's look at some authentication issues, and then we'll start creating our logins.

Authenticating a Login

When we create logins, we can create them with either **Windows NT authentication** or **SQL Server authentication**. Windows NT authentication uses the Windows user account name and password to connect to the SQL Server. This contrasts with the SQL Server authentication method, which requires its own user name and password.

Windows NT Authentication

With Windows NT authentication, we will typically specify our login name with a two-tier name convention.

- ❑ First, we denote the **domain** for the Windows server.
- ❑ Second, we designate the **user name**. We separate the first and second names with a backslash.

For example, if our Windows user account named cabxli existed on a Windows 2000 server named cab2000, then we would designate its login as cab2000\cabxli.

After successfully designating a Windows user account as a SQL Server login, it can connect to a SQL Server and enjoy all the permissions of the guest user account in any database, once it has been authenticated (and, of course, if the domains trust each other and if there are the proper privileges in place). The guest user account is something we'll talk about in the *User Accounts* section, although it will be mentioned in this section.

SQL Server Authentication

When we choose SQL Server authentication, it is necessary to designate a password at the time that we create a login. This is because the SQL Server manages the authentication in this case. This type of authentication is the only authentication support when SQL Server is running on a Windows 95/98 computer. It is particularly appropriate for SQL Server solutions that must operate at least some of the time disconnected from a network server.

This type of authentication is also appropriate for solutions running against the Microsoft Data Engine (MSDE) when it is running on a laptop computer with a Windows 95/98 operating system. Developers who are developing a solution on more than one computer may find special value in the ability to switch back and forth between the two types of authentication.

Creating a Login

The screen on the right depicts the SQL Server Security dialog with the Server Logins tab exposed. The entries on the tab are the default ones for a SQL Server installation. The first two logins are from the Windows server (we won't see these if we are running a Windows 95/98 machine). The sa login is from SQL Server. The Add, Edit, and Delete controls enable the management of logins. This section drills down on the Add control. The Delete control lets us remove any login except sa. The Edit control permits us to assign a login as a member in an existing fixed server or database role as well as a custom role.

After we click Add on the Server Logins tab, Access responds by opening the SQL Server Login Properties – New Login dialog (we may also get a number of messages previous to the dialog opening that inform us that the only database accessible is the one we are connected to). This same dialog works for logins that we specify to have either Windows NT authentication or SQL Server authentication.

Creating a Login using Windows NT Authentication

The following screen shows the settings to create a login named cab2000\cabxli that links initially to the pubs database on a SQL Server. This two-tier name refers to the cabxli user on a Windows 2000 server named cab2000. Since the database administrator wants to use Windows NT authentication, there is no need to specify a password. The Windows NT or Windows 2000 server authenticates the account when a user logs on to their computer.

Notice that we can specify a default database. This is relevant when we are using the login with Query Analyzer. When we use the login with an Access project, the default setting does not matter since we must explicitly designate a database on the Data Link Properties dialog. We'll only be able to connect to that database, however, if there is either an explicit user account for that login, or there is a guest account set up on that database.

> **If we're creating a new login on a Windows 95 or 98 system, the Windows NT authentication section is grayed out.**

After clicking OK on the preceding screen, the Server Logins tab shows a new login named cab2000\cabxli. The cabxli user on the Windows 2000 server can now connect to the SQL Server with the Data Link Properties dialog displayed on the right. If there is an explicit user account for the login or a guest user account, then the login connects to the database with all the permissions for the union of those accounts. Notice that the Data Link Properties dialog explicitly references the pubs database. However, we can reference any other database on the SQL Server that has either an explicit account for the login or a guest account.

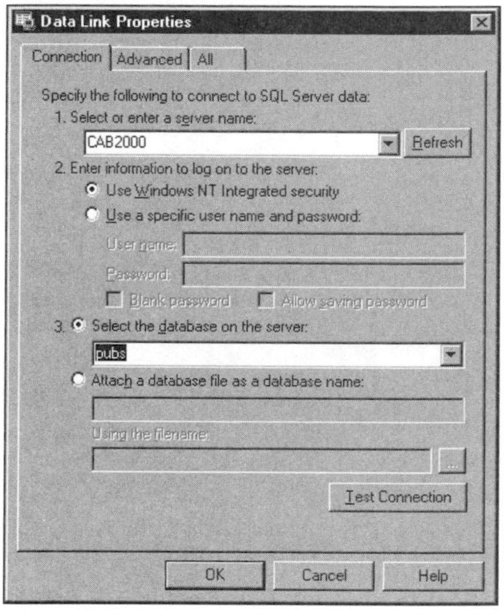

Creating a Login using SQL Server Authentication

For completeness, and for those who can't use NT Integrated security, the following screenshot depicts the setting for creating a SQL Server login using SQL Server authentication. The name of the login is foo. Notice that we use the same dialog for SQL Server authentication as with Windows NT authentication, just specifing Use SQL Server authentication. The name in this case has no prefix designating a server. In addition, we must specify a password. When we click OK, Access prompts us to confirm the password.

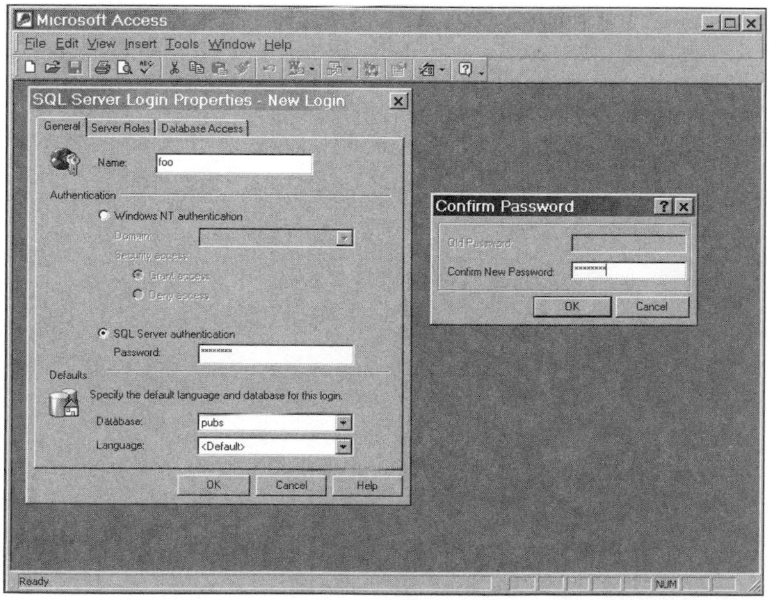

The person creating a login account is responsible for managing the password of the account, and this will generally be a member of the sysadmin fixed server role. The login's user will need this password so they can use it to complete their Data Link Property dialog when they connect via an Access project using the login account. SQL Server administrators with membership in the sysadmin role can change the password for SQL Server logins with the sp_password system stored procedure.

The syntax of this stored procedure is pretty straightforward:

```
sp_password [[@old =] <'old password'>,]
            [@new =] <'new password'>
            [,[@loginame =] <'login'>]
```

The new and old password parameters work just as we would expect, where we accept them from the user and pass them into the stored procedure. The login, however, is an optional parameter – if a login isn't supplied, it will be assumed that the change of password applies to the current connection.

> *The sp_password system stored procedure doesn't check for the new password twice, as we have come to expect from other password-changing experiences – instead, this functionality is left up to us to develop (which, of course, would be in place well before anybody attempted to use sp_password!).*

Users can also update their own password with this system stored procedure. Of course, we only need to do these things if we assign the user ID a password, which is optional but strongly recommended.

The next screenshot reveals the Data Link Property dialog settings for using the foo login. Notice we must choose Use a specific user name and password when connecting to a database via SQL Server authentication. This selection offers text boxes for the login name and its password. Both of these must be correct for an Access project to connect correctly to a SQL Server. The same principles regarding user accounts apply equally to logins with Windows NT authentication and to those with SQL Server authentication. Therefore, the foo login will connect to the pubs database via the guest user account unless there is an explicit account defined for foo. Don't forget we'll be creating user accounts in the next section.

If there is no guest user account and no explicit account for the foo login, then the login to the server for the connection to the pubs database fails. However, the login can connect to any other database on the server with a guest account, such as the master database.

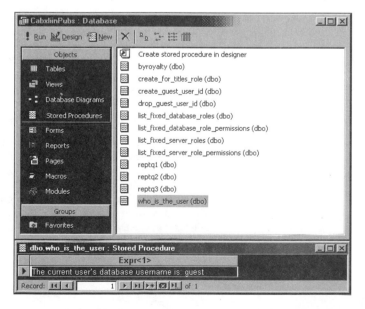

Using Logins

The screenshot below portrays the Database window after the cabxli user opens an Access project connected to the pubs database. Database objects appear with a (dbo) after their name. This name designates the user account that owns the object. It will frequently, but not necessarily always, be the case that all database objects belong to the dbo user. Recall that this user name applies to objects created by any member of the sysadmin role. The dbo in parentheses after an object's name only appears when that user is not a member of the sysadmin role.

Notice the highlighted stored procedure, who_is_the_user. The cab2000\cabxli login has permission to run this stored procedure, which returns the user account that it is run from. This stored procedure appears below the screen shot. We can see the output from the procedure below the Database window. In this case, the login uses the guest user account. Therefore, that login must have EXEC permission for the stored procedure either through an explicit permission to the guest user account or by virtue of the guest user's membership in the public role. We'll find out more about these roles later.

Here is the T-SQL for the who_is_the_user stored procedure. It declares a local variable, and then it uses that variable to store the output from the user function. This function returns the name of the current user account. A SELECT statement presents the value stored in the local variable. The following procedure is handy whenever we need to verify by which user account a login account connects to a database.

```
Alter Procedure who_is_the_user
As
DECLARE @usr char(30)
SET @usr = user
SELECT 'The current user's database username is: '+ @usr
```

User Accounts

A **user** is another type of account on a SQL Server, the next layer of SQL Server security. The user account grants permission to perform operations in a database. Login accounts derive permissions to operate within a database through their association with a user account. While login accounts belong to a SQL Server or SQL Servers, user accounts belong to a particular database on a SQL Server. We can explicitly create user accounts, but databases can have as many as two built-in user accounts. These are the dbo user ID, and the guest user ID, both of which we'll look at after we've created new user accounts for cabxli and foo.

It will typically be more efficient to create roles and then assign users to them rather than to directly assign permissions to users. This type of security model permits an administrator to add and drop permissions from users by adding and dropping their membership in roles. Don't worry if this doesn't make sense to you now, we will be talking about roles and permissions later. For now, all you need to know about a role is that it is a fast way of assigning a set of permissions to a user. Permissions, as their name would imply, specify what database activities can be performed by a user with that permission.

Creating User Accounts

As we will remember, there are two ways to authenticate a login to a SQL Server – using Windows NT authentication, or letting SQL Server do the authentication. Due to the difference in login authentication, there are some slight differences in the way we create user accounts for logins. Consequently, we're going to look at creating user accounts for both a Windows NT authenticated login and a SQL Server authenticated login. Also bear in mind that user accounts get assigned roles and permissions, which we are going to talk about after we've done with user accounts.

Creating a User Account for a Windows NT Authenticated Login

To create a user account for the cab2000\cabxli login, open the SQL Server Security dialog to the Database Users tab. Then, click Add to make the Database User Properties - New User dialog available. Click the drop-down control for Login name and select cab2000\cabxli. Access responds by inserting cabxli in the User name dialog. We can override this default name if we so choose. Click the db_datareader checkbox to make the cabxli user a member of this role, which grants SELECT permissions. See the section on *Roles and Permissions* for more details on what this means. Finish the process of creating the user account by clicking OK. This adds a new user to the Database Users tab named cabxli. The following screen reveals the Database User Properties - New User dialog just before the click on OK.

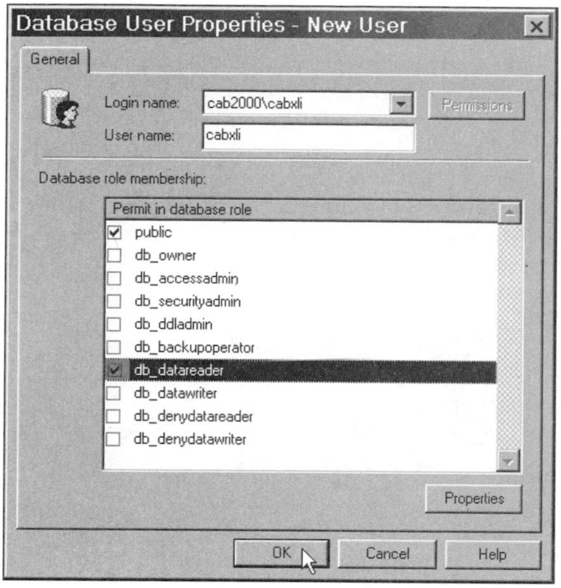

With this setting, the cabxli user can open any table or view in the database, but it cannot add or delete anything in them. The following screenshot depicts the authors table in the pubs database opened by the cab2000\cabxli login. Since this login connects with the cabxli user account, it has membership of the db_datareader role. Notice from the title bar that Access precedes the table name with the dbo prefix. This occurs because cabxli is not a member of the sysadmin role. While the cabxli user can open the table, notice that an attempt to edit the table results in a Microsoft Access error message that explains the user has no permission to update the table.

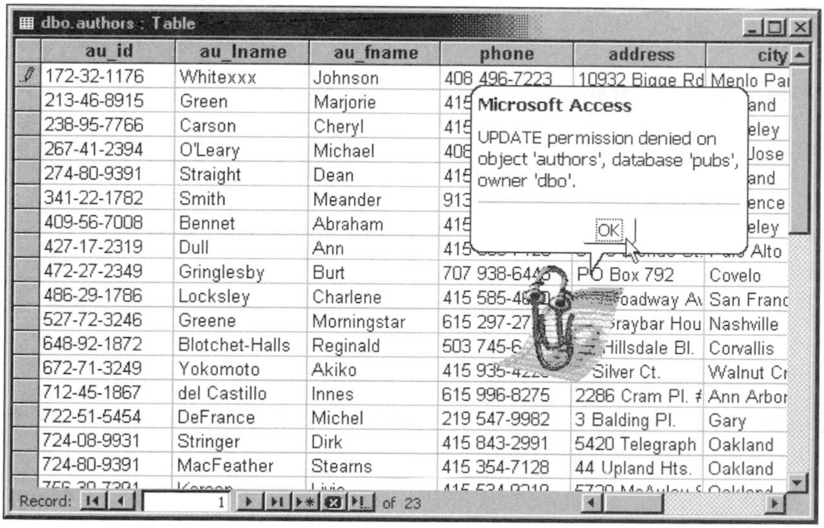

Creating a User Account for a SQL Server Authenticated Login

The next screenshot shows how to create a user for the foo login that can both SELECT and maintain the entries in any table or view within the database. The db_datawriter fixed database role grants permission to update, insert, and delete rows in tables and views. However, this role by itself is not sufficient for most purposes since users with just this role will not have the ability to SELECT from database objects. Therefore, we need to assign **both** db_datareader and db_datawriter when we want to permit updating. Otherwise, users will not be able to select a record that they need to update. The following dialog shows these fixed database role selections for a new user named foo. This user is for the foo login. These settings enable an Access project for the foo login to SELECT, INSERT, UPDATE, and DELETE rows from database objects. This means that foo won't be presented with the error message when they try to add something to a database column.

Built-in User Accounts

Earlier, we said there can be as many as two built-in user accounts for a database. One of these will always be the dbo account, which is connected to the login that created the database. The other is the guest account, which is used by every login that connects to the database, whether they have their own user account or not.

The dbo User Account

The creator of the database is also considered to be the owner, or dbo. Whatever object they create within the database will have an ownership, or prefix, of dbo, rather than their user name, whereas objects created by anybody else will have an ownership of that user's login name.

To help us see this more clearly, let us look at an example. I am a user of the database (but not the creator) and my user name is JDoe — I am allowed to create tables, so I create a table called ThisTable. The name for this object would then be JDoe.ThisTable. Since ThisTable has a specific owner, it must always be referred to as JDoe.ThisTable by whoever wants to use it.

Another user, with a user name of JSmith, is the creator, and therefore owner, of the database. If JSmith created a table called ThisTable, in exactly the same way as JDoe did, the table created by JSmith would be called dbo.ThisTable. However, as dbo is the default owner, anybody wishing to use this particular table could just refer to it as ThisTable, rather than dbo.ThisTable.

The dbo user ID maps automatically to the sa login, which means that database objects created by any member of the sysadmin fixed server role automatically have dbo assigned as the user qualifier (prefix) for an object, regardless of whether they actually own the database or not. As we add other users to the sysadmin fixed server role, they assume this user ID as well. We'll see how to add users to a role later.

The Guest User Account

The guest user account is standard with the pubs and Northwind databases. When a login does not have a user ID assigned explicitly to it, then the login can connect to a database through the guest user account. The guest user ID isn't assigned to any particular login account. The guest account passes on to the login accounts that use it whatever permissions it inherits by virtue of its membership in roles, which we'll talk about in the next section. New databases we create do not have a guest user ID by default. Adding it graphically is just the same as we've seen, only we don't need to link it to a login. The T-SQL statement to add a guest user ID to a database is as follows:

```
EXECUTE sp_grantdbaccess guest, guest
```

The T-SQL statement to remove a guest user ID from a database is

```
EXECUTE sp_dropuser guest
```

We can assign custom users to logins either programmatically with T-SQL or SQL-DMO or manually with the menu commands of an Access project. Those using the SQL Server client tools can manipulate all the security elements, including logins, user IDs, and permissions, with Enterprise Manager. With the exception of the guest user ID, we must always designate a login for each user ID that we specify.

Roles and Permissions

Creating a user account can involve assigning roles to the user, but we haven't looked at these yet. This is where we look at roles, what they do, and how to create them. As we've already seen, assigning them is a matter of ticking a box on the **Database User Properties** dialog. So why are we talking about permissions here? Unfortunately, permissions are so closely bound up in roles that it would be very confusing to try to talk about roles without talking about permissions. Creating a role is a process of assigning permissions, and there's no point assigning something if we don't know what it does.

Roles are used to assign groupings of permissions to users. This means that all users who are members of the same role have the same permissions to act upon the database and SQL Server. We'll look at the types of role that SQL Server has, then we'll look at creating our own.

Types of Role

SQL Server has three types of role. There are **server** roles, **database** roles, and **application** roles. Each of these roles has a different purpose, as we might expect.

Server roles are used to grant permissions to users so that they can perform server-related tasks, such as creating databases and managing linked servers. The server roles are specific to the SQL Server, not a given database.

Database roles are similar to server roles, in that they used to grant permissions to a user. This time, though, the permissions are only valid for the particular database for which the database role is granted.

The third type of role is the application role. This type of role differs from the others quite a bit, and is used in a different way. Rather than assigning members to an application role, it is used to provide a different set of security options for a given user.

Both the server roles and the database roles are known as fixed roles. This means that they come with SQL Server, and they can't be changed. We'll take a closer look at each of these types of role, and then look at assigning them to our examples cabxli and foo.

Server Roles

There are seven fixed server roles in SQL Server 7, and eight in SQL Server 2000. These roles, as we know, are for assigning permissions for tasks beyond the scope of an individual database. We can enumerate these with the sp_helpsrvrole system stored procedure. This will ask us to enter a parameter value for srvrolename. Leaving the box blank and clicking OK will result in the procedure returning a table with the server role name and a description. Since these descriptions aren't very detailed, the following table has better descriptions for each server role.

Role	Description
sysadmin	Members of this role can perform any activity on the SQL Server.
serveradmin	Members of this role can configure server-wide settings or shut down the server.
setupadmin	Members of this role can manage extended stored procedures for managing linked servers and startup procedures.
securityadmin	Members of this role can manage the logins for the server, including reading error logs.
processadmin	Members of this role can manage the processes running in SQL Server, being able to kill any that run for too long.
dbcreator	Members of this role can create and alter databases.
diskadmin	Members of this role can manage disk files, which means attaching databases, managing what filegroup things are assigned to, etc.
bulkadmin	Members of this role are Bulk Insert administrators. This is a new role with SQL Server 2000.

We can enumerate the permissions associated with each fixed server role with the sp_srvrolepermission system stored procedure, and much like the sp_helpsrvrole system stored procedure, it will prompt for a srvrolename. The following screen shows an excerpt that selected permissions for the securityadmin, serveradmin, setupadmin, and sysadmin roles. Notice that the sysadmin roles grant permissions to add members to other fixed server and fixed database roles.

```
list_fixed_server_role_permissions ...  _ □ X
  ServerRole        Permission                        ▲
  securityadmin   sp_revokelogin
  serveradmin     Add member to serveradmin
  serveradmin     dbcc pintable
  serveradmin     RECONFIGURE
  serveradmin     SHUTDOWN
  serveradmin     sp_configure
  serveradmin     sp_tableoption
  setupadmin      Add member to setupadmin
  setupadmin      Add/drop/configure linked servers
  setupadmin      Mark a stored procedure as startup
  sysadmin        Add extended procedures
  sysadmin        Add member to dbcreator
  sysadmin        Add member to diskadmin
  sysadmin        Add member to processadmin
  sysadmin        Add member to securityadmin
  sysadmin        Add member to serveradmin
  sysadmin        Add member to setupadmin
  sysadmin        Add member to sysadmin
  sysadmin        Add/drop to/from db_accessadmin
  sysadmin        Add/drop to/from db_backupoperator  ▼
Record: I◄ ◄        1  ► ►I ►* ⊘ ►I. of 150
```

Database Roles

There are nine fixed database roles. We can enumerate these with the sp_helpdbfixedrole system stored procedure. Again, there is a brief description of each of these roles in the following table, although some are quite obvious from their names.

Role	Description
db_owner	Members of this role can perform all the tasks that members of the other database roles can. This means that members of this role can perform the same functions that the database owner can.
db_accessadmin	Members of this role can perform similar activities to the securityadmin server role, restricted to the database. This means that they can create new users, but not new logins.
db_datareader	Members of this role can issue SELECT statements against all user tables in the database.
db_datawriter	Members of this role can use INSERT, UPDATE, and DELETE statements with all user tables in the database. Note that they can't SELECT them though.
db_ddladmin	Members of this role can manipulate objects in the database through use of the Data Definition Language. They cannot use GRANT, REVOKE, or DENY, so cannot influence permissions.
db_securityadmin	Members of this role can manage roles and members of database roles, including statement and object permissions.
db_backupoperator	Members of this role can back up the database.

Table continued on following page

Role	Description
db_denydatareader	Members of this role cannot SELECT any table in the database.
db_denydatawriter	Members of this role cannot use INSERT, UPDATE, or DELETE statements on any table in the database.

These names are shorthand names for referring to collections of permissions to perform different tasks. We can enumerate the tasks for each fixed database role with the sp_dbfixedrolepermission system stored procedure. As with the two system stored procedures mentioned earlier, we will be prompted for a rolename. In total, 89 permissions exist across all fixed database roles. The following excerpt shows a selection of five of these from the output from the sp_dbfixedrolepermission system stored procedure. Notice that it shows 105 records. This is because some permissions are held by more than one role.

Sample stored procedures enumerating the fixed server roles, the fixed database roles, and the permissions that go with either appear in the sample Access project and database for this appendix. The project's name is AppendixA.adp. *The sample database is an updated version of the pubs database.*

A tenth database role is not fixed at all. This is the public role. Developers or administrators can assign permissions to this role, according to what they are prepared to let everyone have permission for. All user IDs with database access for an application are a member of the public role. We cannot remove any user ID from this role. In addition, the guest ID inherits permissions assigned to the public role.

If we want to severely restrict access to an application, one useful strategy is to strip all permissions from the public role. If an application has a small community of users where all users should enjoy the same permissions, then we can use the public role to enable those permissions. If the application grows, we will almost certainly want to revise this strategy. In fact, we might not want to use the public role in this way at all.

If we need to ensure that users outside the group do not enjoy these same permissions then drop the guest account for the database and make sure that any legitimate user of the database has a login and user account. We can define database roles ourselves, unlike server roles. This means that we can create custom roles that allow us to specify, say, that only certain tables can be selected from.

Application Roles

Application roles are an emerging SQL Server technology. Application roles are something that we create ourselves, and which are used in a given application. The application role will grant permissions that are required for the application to function, regardless of what permissions the user might have if they logged in to the SQL Server through another method.

For example, suppose our user cabxli is logged into the SQL Server with the permission to SELECT from the Sales table. Their normal combination of roles means that they can't SELECT from the Author table. If they now run an application connected with the Author table, which doesn't need the Sales table, an application role will be used. In this case the application role will mean that they will no longer be able to SELECT from the Sales table, but will instead now be able to SELECT from the Author table.

Users activate the role with the **sp_setapprole** system stored procedure, or we can do it for them in an application. This system stored procedure requires a role name and a password for activating the role. Once we've been assigned an application role, our security settings are those specified by that role until we log out of the SQL Server. We can add and drop application roles similarly to other custom roles, but they require different stored procedures when we perform the tasks. With application roles, we can more precisely control how certain permissions perform by programmatically restricting their behavior with application roles.

> Unfortunately, application roles do not work from the Access project stored procedure template or ADO code in VBA modules. However, we can invoke them successfully from either Visual Basic code, or Query Analyzer (if we have SQL Server rather than MSDE).

Types of Permission

Before we move on to creating new roles, we need to take a look at permissions. As we've already said, roles are collections of permissions. Creating a role without knowing what its permissions do would be like building a machine from parts we don't understand. It may work fine for a while, but we never know when it will stop doing what it is supposed to do. Due to this, we need to understand how permissions work.

There are three states for a permission to be in. A permission can be **granted**, it can be **denied**, or it can be neither. While this may seem slightly strange, there is a difference between denying a permission and not granting it. When we grant a permission to a role, the custom role gains the right to perform that task. If we deny a permission to a role, then the role explicitly forbids that task.

> Users can belong to more than one role. These roles can have conflicting permission assignments. User IDs receive the union of the permission assignments to all the roles to which they belong. A deny action overrides any other assignment.

To expand on this a little further: a user may belong to a number of roles, each having different permissions for particular objects. If a user was part of role1, which grants INSERT permission for Table1 to its members, but also a member of role2, which denies INSERT permission for Table1 to its members, then the union of the permission assignments of the roles to which the user belongs would mean that the user is denied INSERT permission on Table1: the deny action takes precedence over any other action. This is the way in which permission conflicts are resolved.

There are six permissions we can use, some of which don't apply to all objects. Tables can have SELECT, INSERT, UPDATE, DELETE, and DRI permissions. The first four permissions correspond to the T-SQL statements of thee same names. The DRI permission on the **Database Role Properties** dialog is the same as the REFERENCES permission we may be more used to. The DRI permission allows a user to enter a value in one table that has a foreign reference to another table for which the user has no other permission. Since SQL Server checks foreign reference constraints before accepting new data, the user would not be able to enter data into one table unless he also had datawriter permissions for the table to which the reference refers. The DRI permission enables a user to enter a row into one table even if they have no permissions for a second table to which the table they are using refers.

Views can have also have SELECT, INSERT, UPDATE, and DELETE permissions. Stored procedures offer an EXEC permission that designates the permission to run the procedure. The stored procedures always show in the Database window whether or not they have an EXEC permission.

Creating Roles

We can use custom user-defined roles just like the fixed database roles, but we can tailor them to our own unique requirements. For example, the db_datawriter fixed database role grants UPDATE, INSERT, and DELETE statement permission for all tables and views. However, what if our application needed a role with UPDATE, INSERT, and DELETE permissions exclusively for just the authors table, but not any other table? A custom role can fill this need nicely.

The use of a custom role is a two-step process. First, we have to create the role. Second, we can assign a user to the role. When we create a custom role, we need to give it a name, and then assign permissions to it. This section illustrates this process for a new login named foo2. The login needs SELECT permission for all database objects, but it requires UPDATE, INSERT, and DELETE permissions just for the authors table. The following discussion assumes the creation of the foo2 login with a user account of the same name. Like foo, foo2 uses SQL Server authentication, but because roles are assigned to users, it doesn't matter what authentication method the login uses. Initially, though, the foo2 user is a member of no roles.

To create a new role also involves two steps. First, we have to create the role, and second we have to assign it permissions. To do this, open the SQL Server Security dialog, select the Database Roles tab, and click Add. This opens the Database Role Properties New Role dialog. Enter the name for our custom role in the Name text box. Since we are using a standard role rather than an application role in this sample, make sure you select the Standard role radio button. We can optionally add users to the role by clicking Add. Since the example assigns the foo2 user to this custom role and a fixed database role later, we defer this option until then. By assigning all the roles they're going to get to a user at one time, we get a better overview of permission assignments for that user. Notice that Access disables the button to the right of the role's name. The label for this button is Permissions (and it is grayed out because we can't assign permissions to a role that doesn't yet exist!). Click OK to create the role. The following screenshot depicts the Database Role Properties New Role dialog just before the creation of the datawriters_authors_only role. The click to OK creates the role, but the new role is empty. It has no permissions.

After control returns to the SQL Server Security dialog, select the new role, and this time click Edit. On the Database Role Properties dialog, click the Permissions button next to the role's name. Notice that the button is enabled after we have created the role. Clicking the button opens another Database Role Properties dialog. This dialog is for the datawriters_authors_only role.

We can grant, revoke, or deny permissions for any object in the database with this dialog. The boxes within columns denote permissions for a specific object on the row. Each box can show a blank, check mark, or red x mark. The check mark indicates that the permission is granted, and the red x mark represents the denying of a permission for an object. We can revoke either a granted or a denied permission. Just click it to clear the check mark or the red x mark.

The screen on the right reveals the Database Role Properties dialog for the datawriters_authors_only role. The display reveals the dialog right after the selection of the DELETE permission for the authors table. As we can see, the screen shows the prior selection of the INSERT and UPDATE permissions. Clicking OK saves the custom role with its assigned permissions. We are now able to use the custom datawriters_authors_only role just like any fixed database role.

We are now ready to complete the definition of the foo2 user. Open the SQL Server Security dialog to the Database Users tab. Select foo2, and click Edit. In the Database User Properties dialog for foo2, select the datawriters_authors_only and the db_datareaders roles. This allows the foo2 user to exercise the permissions of both roles – namely, SELECT for all tables and views and UPDATE, DELETE, and INSERT for the authors table only. The screenshot on the right depicts these selections on the Data User Properties dialog.

Working with Application Roles

Application roles aren't quite as straightforward as normal fixed roles or custom defined roles. We design an application role just like a custom standard role, except that we select the Application role radio button on the Database Role Properties New Role dialog. We must also give the role a password.

The difference comes in using an application role. As we've already said, we don't assign users to application roles. Rather, we use application roles to grant permissions for an application. Remember we can invoke the application role with the **sp_setapprole** system stored procedure and its password.

> **Unfortunately, this system stored procedure does not work from Access projects. If we attempt to invoke the system stored procedure from within an Access project it generates the error message that appears in the following screen.**

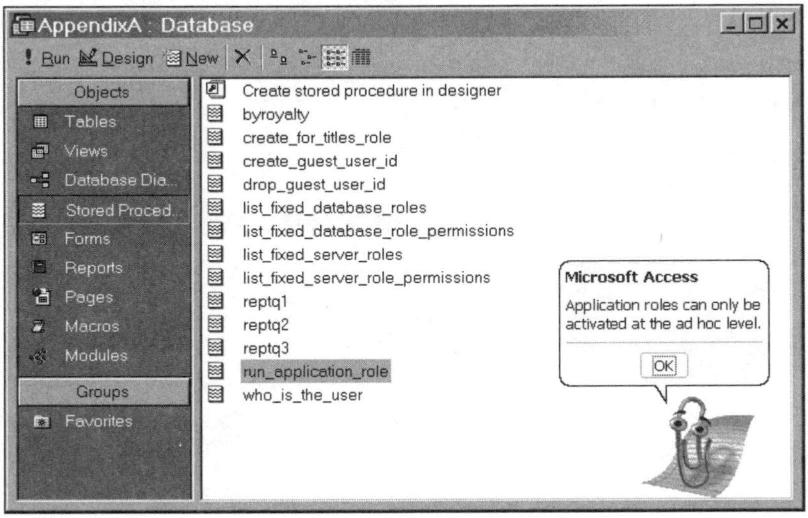

The code inside the run_application_role appears below. As we can see, it simply invokes the select_all_write_authors application role with a password of password.

```
Alter Procedure run_application_role
As
--Does not run from Access stored procedure template
--Does run from Query Analyzer
EXEC sp_setapprole 'select_all_write_authors', 'password'
```

As we can see, the same line of code executes properly from Query Analyzer – SQL Server's ad hoc environment for running T-SQL statements. The ability to run the application role is independent of fixed server and fixed database roles. To launch an application role, all a user has to do is run the **sp_setapprole** system stored procedure with the name of the application and the proper password. If we are building our own applications to handle SQL Server interaction, then we can run the application role from inside the application.

```
Query - cab2000.pubs.foo - (untitled) - EXEC sp_setappr...*     _ □ ×

EXEC sp_setapprole 'select_all_write_authors', 'password'

The application role 'select_all_write_authors' is now active.

Results
Query batch completed.                Exec time: 0:00:00   0 rows      Ln 2, Col 1
```

Summary

In this appendix, we've looked at the key issues in SQL Server security, and how to implement them. We've looked at:

❑ logins

❑ users

❑ roles and permissions

We saw what these concepts mean, and also how to use them. We've found that there are two ways of authenticating access to the SQL Server, which is the front line of SQL Server database security. We then looked at how to control access to, and behavior in, databases, by means of users and roles.

Securing your information is important, as it is essential that confidential or sensitive information does not get into the wrong hands. By setting the appropriate permissions and roles for each user, you can ensure that you are doing your best to prevent this from happening. Although throughout this book the sa login is used, it is imperative that this is changed in a real-world situation – otherwise, your information would not be secure.

By thinking carefully about what each user needs to do, and what information they actually have to work with, you can set the appropriate roles and permissions to make sure that they can't do something you don't want them to do. Security is a big issue and needs to be thought out very carefully – it should be worked in throughout the whole of the development process, and not just be an afterthought.

Converting Access Database Files to SQL Server Databases

This book focuses on creating and using Access projects to manage SQL Server databases. In the end, the easiest way to build SQL Server solutions with Access projects is with new systems. This frees us from any design trade-offs optimized for Access database files instead of SQL Server. However, the reality is that many developers will have solutions based on Access database files from Access 2000 (or even earlier versions) that they want to upgrade to SQL Server and an Access project. For these situations, this appendix explores two tools.

First, the **Access Upsizing Wizard** integrates fully with Access 2000. The Access Upsizing Wizard has been available for Access developers since Access 95. In its latest incarnation, it adds the capability to upgrade from an Access database file to an Access project. It still has the other capabilities introduced with earlier versions of Access. When you want to upgrade an Access database file from an earlier version, an excellent preliminary step is to migrate the solution to Access 2000 and then use the Access Upsizing Wizard integrated into Access 2000.

Second, this appendix demonstrates how to use the SQL Server **Data Transformation Wizard**. This wizard does not target migrating solutions. Instead, it focuses on moving database contents from one format, such as that for an .mdb file, to a SQL Server database. This tool is generally more powerful than the Access Upsizing Wizard for moving data from one source to another. The presentation in this appendix restricts its focus to moving data from Access database files to SQL Server databases. This limitation is consistent with the objectives of the book. Every section has at least one example to illustrate a technique.

Using the Access Upsizing Wizard

The Access Upsizing Wizard exists to transfer database objects from an Access database file to a SQL Server database (and, with Access 2000, to an Access project). The target database can be new or existing, but the wizard will always create a new Access Project if that is what you want. The Upsizing Wizard in Access 2000 targets SQL Server 7 and SQL Server 6.5 databases.

> **At the time of writing this appendix, Microsoft did not have the Upsizing Wizard working for SQL Server 2000 databases, but you should be able to download an update from the OfficeUpdate site (http://officeupdate.microsoft.com) when one becomes available.**

There are three main options for upsizing an Access database file using the Upsizing Wizard. A brief description of each option now follows. In the following sections, we will take a closer look at the process of upsizing an Access database using each method in turn.

❑   Option 1: Simply upsize the data definitions with or without the actual data. Since the Upsizing Wizard is a mature product, it is extremely effective at reading Access database files and transferring them to their SQL Server table equivalents. Thus, when we transfer the tables, we actually convey the full database schema from an Access database file to a SQL Server database. This is much more powerful than just transferring the table names and their column names along with the data. Note that we can choose to upsize just the data definitions without any data. This is especially useful for larger databases where it is more efficient to upsize the schema using the Upsizing Wizard but to transfer the data using other means (see later).

❑   Option 2: Create a Front-End/Back-End Application. Here, we create a front-end/back-end application that uses the Access queries, forms, and reports as the front-end with the upsized SQL Server database tables as the back-end. Any data access pages in our application also reference the new upsized tables. The good part of this upsizing scenario is that we retain our original queries, forms, and reports while we gain the power of a SQL Server database to maintain our tables. The bad part of this upsizing scenario is that we end up with an .mdb file that must link tables whenever it works with data. This is an inherently less forward-looking design than the OLE DB connection that underlies an Access project.

❑   Option 3: Create a Full Client-Server Application. This third option creates a full client-server solution with an Access project acting as the client interface to a SQL Server database. This takes full advantage of Microsoft's latest technology for using Access 2000 with SQL Server, as has already been described in this book.

Whichever option we choose, the Upsizing Wizard generates a detailed report on the upsizing process. The wizard automatically generates this report in a snapshot format. This report fully documents the overall conversion process, as well as each individual converted object. Its snapshot format facilitates e-mailing the report to others so that you can receive input from those in a position to assist in refining the conversion or enhancing a database's functionality through the addition of new features. Database developers interested in improving their T-SQL programming skills will find the report a valuable source for samples that illustrate how to code triggers for referential integrity, cascading deletes, and updates, as well as column constraints.

For a variety of reasons, you can sometimes expect the upsizing of an Access database file to SQL Server database to be incomplete. Variations in design practices and database specification differences, along with conversion limitations, lead to this outcome. Therefore, you should plan to manually tweak the final design of the SQL Server database when the conversion is not complete. The previous paragraph mentions the **Upsizing Wizard report**. *This is a critical tool for tracking down problems so that you can forge remedies. Go to the* Comparing Access Projects to Access Databases *under* Working with Access Projects *in the Access Help files to examine multiple tables comparing and contrasting the differences between Access database files and SQL Server databases.*

Upsizing Option 1 – Upsizing a Database Schema with Data

The simplest way to upsize an Access database file is to transfer just the schema from the database file to the SQL Server to form a new database. When choosing this option, the Upsizing Wizard makes it very easy to send the data from the database file as well. If your database is not too large, sending the data along with the schema is attractive. In contrast, if we have a medium to large database, it is advisable to keep the two parts of the upsizing task separate from one another. In such cases, the Access Upsizing wizard is still used to transfer the database schema. However, the transfer of data is best dealt with using the **Data Transformation Services** (**DTS**) Wizard that comes with both SQL Server and Access. The DTS Wizard is optimized for transferring data between sources. Overall, this approach allows us to take the best feature from each tool, and minimizes the time to upsize medium to large databases. Another reason for using the DTS Wizard for data transfer is that it allows us, for example, to combine data from two or more fields and to check for inconsistencies in your data. This can often be very useful. The DTS Wizard gains focus later in this appendix.

Running the Upsizing Wizard

No matter which Upsizing Wizard option we select, we can start, run, and learn about the option in the same way. Start by choosing Tools | Database Utilities | Upsizing Wizard from the Database window menu for the database you wish to upsize. The Wizard only works on an open database and provides onscreen instructions about how to use its services. Furthermore, each dialog has an associated Help screen that explains the impact of each control on that wizard screen. After making all our choices through the dialogs, we click Finish to execute the upsizing task that we specified.

After invoking the Upsizing Wizard, Access prompts us for whether we want to work with a new or existing database. When we begin to work with the wizard, we will typically want to start a new database. Although two of the three wizard options will preserve the original database, it is always good practice to make a backup copy of the database in any case. The following screen shows the `Northwind.mdb` file Database window above the screen that lets us specify the name and owner of a new database. In the following wizard screen, the new database name is NorthwindUpsize. This new database will reside on the SQL Server named CAB2000, which will have to be running for the upsizing to proceed. The database owner will be dbo since sa is a member of the sysadmin group, and SQL Server represents the members of this group with the dbo qualifier. See Chapter 3 for more commentary on SQL Server's use of the dbo qualifier, and Appendix A for more information on the sysadmin group.

The next Wizard screen permits us to select one or more tables for upsizing from the Access database file to the SQL Server database. This dialog appears with two list boxes and some arrow controls for moving entries from the left box labeled Available Tables to the right box labeled Export to SQL Server. One advantage of transferring all tables is that the wizard can convey our database schema from the Access database file to SQL Server. When we designate a table for export, this does not mean that we will actually copy its data from the Access database file to the SQL Server database. Instead, designating a table for export to SQL Server merely means that we want the table in the new SQL Server database design.

The next screen allows us to specify how table attributes transfer between the Access database file and tables in the new SQL Server database. We can also designate whether to upload the database schema and the data or just the schema. If we only want to create the table schema on the new SQL Server database, we should select Only create the table structure; don't upsize any data. For obvious reasons, this won't transfer any data. Except when linking SQL Server tables to an .mdb file, you may want to consider changing the Add timestamp fields to tables control value from its default setting of Yes, let wizard decide to No, never. The purpose of the timestamp is to synchronize the linked table in the Access database file and its server version after an update through the interface in the database file. Note that failing to use the timestamp field can slow performance for tables containing columns with image or text data types – for more information on this issue, see the later discussion on *Upsizing Option 2*.

When we upsize a database, we will normally want to preserve the relationships and referential integrity. With the Table Relationships box checked, we have two options: Use DRI and Use triggers. DRI, which stands for Declared Referential Integrity, works in the same way as Access referential integrity and will preserve relationships and referential integrity. However, it does not preserve any cascading updates or deletes. If we need to maintain cascading updates and deletes, we should make sure that the Use Triggers option is selected instead.

Aside from the preceding discussion, the defaults for this screen are robust and serve multiple purposes. The following settings transfer the data, but do not create any timestamp fields. The reason we've declined the creation of timestamp fields is because we're going to upsize the data just once to populate the schema without updating the Access database file to make it link to the SQL Server database. After the upsizing, the Access database file and its upsized SQL Server database can diverge as users make independent changes to each database.

The next screen lets us select one of three upsizing options. The following screenshot uses the default No application changes. This leaves the Access database file unchanged as it upsizes the database. Consequently, there are no links between the Access database file and the SQL Server database after the upsizing. This absence of a tie permits the divergence between the two databases after the upsizing. After confirming that this screen indicates No application changes, we click Finish to start the upsizing process. Access responds by building a SQL Server database based on the Access database file and displaying the Upsizing Wizard report at the conclusion of the upsizing process. We could print the report to examine it carefully. Access also creates a copy of the snapshot file for the report in the same folder as the original database.

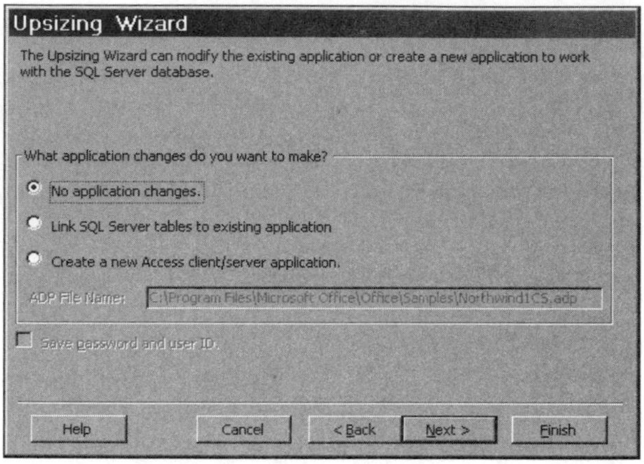

Completing the Upsizing Process

At the conclusion of the preceding upsizing example, we have two independent databases. While they contain the same data, and they have the same relationships between tables, there are differences between the two databases in two areas. A simple inspection of the Errors section in the Access Upsizing report indicates where these differences lie. The Errors section appears immediately after the report summarizes its source and destination databases, as shown in the next screenshot.

First, the Upsizing Wizard fails to convert several validation rules from the [Order Details] table in the Access database file to its corresponding NorthwindUpsize database on the SQL Server.

Second, the HomePage column in the Supplier table for the SQL Server database does not contain active hyperlinks.

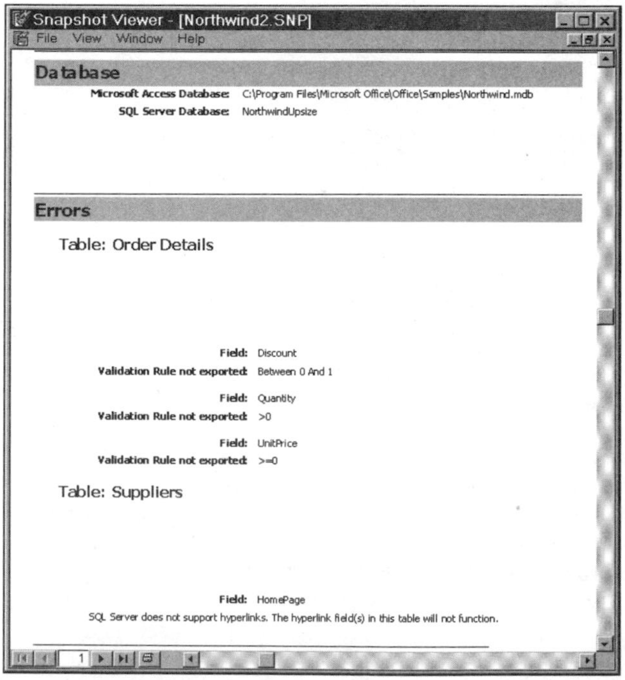

The addition of simple check constraints can resolve the [Order Details] errors. The next shot demonstrates the Access project graphical interface displaying a manually created check constraint to force Quantity column values to exceed 0. Similar constraints can resolve the other errors in the [Order Details] table conversion. We reviewed check constraints in Chapter 3 and Chapter 4.

Upsizing Option 2 – Linking an Access Database File to a SQL Server Database

The second style of upsizing an Access database file changes the design of the database. Although the change retains the original data tables, it is still a good idea to make a backup copy before starting the Upsizing Wizard. This precaution is not necessary with either of the other upsizing options since they do not alter the original Access database file. However, it is good practice to make backup copies in these cases as well.

At the conclusion of the second upsizing option, we will have a front-end/back-end solution. A modified version of the original Access database file serves as the front-end, and a SQL Server database is the back-end. The front-end Access database file links the SQL Server database for the tables that the upsizing process transfers from the Access database file to the SQL Server database. These linked tables are the data sources for the forms and reports in the revised application. In addition, the queries and data access pages point at the new linked tables in the SQL Server database instead of the original local tables. The modified front-end Access database file contains the original local tables and links for the tables in the new SQL Server database. The linked table names are the same as the original table name, and the original tables have _local appended as a suffix to their names. These two sets of tables have identical contents immediately after the conversion. As database users add, delete, and modify information in the database application, the SQL Server and local tables diverge.

The Option 2 Upsizing Process

The process for the second upsizing option is nearly identical to the first style of upsizing. Our example for the second upsizing option creates a new database named NorthwindUpsize2 on the CAB2000 server. As with the first example, this upsizing uses all the tables from the original `Northwind.mdb` file. After indicating that we want a new database, designating a name for the upsized database, and specifying the tables to go into it, we can use the next wizard screen to specify the addition of timestamp fields. This step can improve the performance for updating image and text fields from the front-end file to the back-end database.

Without a timestamp field, Access unconditionally updates the whole record on a server whenever any field changes. With a timestamp field for image and text fields, Access can check the timestamp field to determine if there was an update before copying a potentially large field from the application to the server. With a setting of Yes, let wizard decide, the wizard creates timestamp fields for `Memo`, `OLE Object`, and `float-point` fields in Access database files as it upsizes them to SQL Server. The following display shows the screen where you let the wizard decide about adding timestamp fields when using the second upsizing option.

The next wizard screen, as in the following screenshot, lets us choose an upsizing option. For this example, we'll select the second one that reads Link SQL Server tables to existing application. This selection causes the wizard to insert linked tables named after the original tables, and rename the existing tables in the application with the _local suffix. The Save password and user ID control determines if the user ID and password for the SQL Server database get stored with the application file. Without saving the user ID and password, users have to log into the SQL Server database each time they open the application file. If we save the user ID and password, then anyone who can open the application file can also get into the SQL Server with the identity of the user ID and password for the upsized database. Since you will often create databases with a member of the sysadmin role, this can extend extremely broad authority over a SQL Server and is not good practice. As we saw in Appendix A, you can never be too careful where security is concerned.

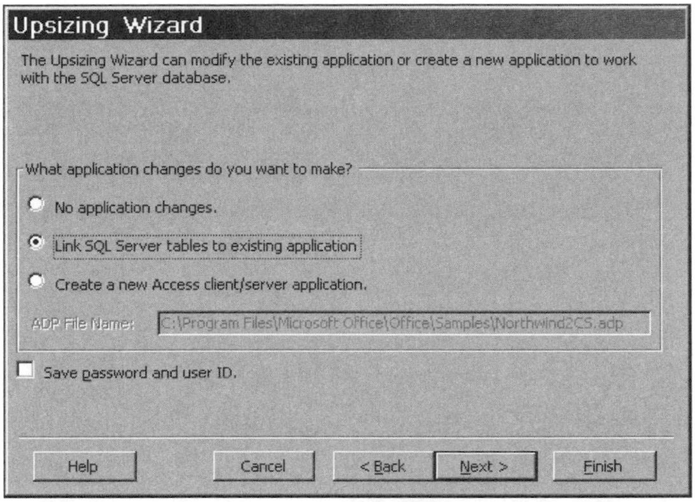

Note that the **Save password and user ID** control was disabled when we reviewed Option 1 for upsizing earlier on. This was because there was no application file with which to save a password with the first upsizing option.

After choosing the second option, click **Finish** to start the creation of a new SQL Server database to which the Access database file is linked. At the conclusion of the process, our **Database** window in the original Access database file changes to show the linked ODBC files on the SQL Server. The following screenshot depicts the new revised **Database** window for the `Northwind.mdb` file. We still need to check the Access Upsizing report, and make any necessary modifications to fix errors in the resulting conversion. For example, we'll have to add check constraints to selected fields in the [Order Details] table. We need to do this through a SQL Server interface, such as Enterprise Manager, or by creating an Access project that points at the SQL Server database to which the Access database file links.

Some developers prefer this second option for upsizing because it allows them to create tables locally even while they work with a SQL Server back-end. On the other hand, Access projects enable you to save local recordsets and retrieve them with the ADO `Recordset` *object. Therefore, even without the ability to create tables locally, Access projects enable you to save data that does not reside on the server for reuse. With the growing hardware power of computers running database servers, the need to save data locally is less significant than previously. Others like the second approach because it is so easy to convert to a SQL Server back-end and still maintain a familiar* `.mdb` *file as a front-end. However, keep in mind that the resulting design does not expose the full extent of SQL Server capabilities available from an Access project. For example, if you want to edit a table's design, you need to use Enterprise Manager or an Access project pointing at the SQL Server to which the* `.mdb` *file connects.*

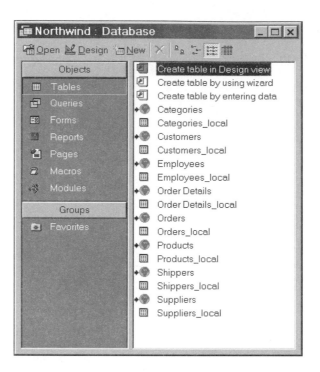

Upsizing Option 3 – Creating an Access Project Based on an Access Database File

The third upsizing option generates an Access project and SQL Server database derived from an Access database file. Unlike the second option, the third option does not modify the original Access database file. Instead, it creates an entirely new Access project that links via an OLE DB connection with the new SQL Server database upsized from the Access database file. This third option converts the forms, reports, and data access pages from the Access database file into the Access project. The third option also attempts to convert the Access query objects automatically into SQL Server stored procedures and views. Importantly, the conversion techniques do not work for all Access query objects. Therefore, you should carefully study the Upsizing Wizard report not only for conversion errors with tables but also for conversion errors with queries. Then, you can use Chapters 5 and 6 from this book to develop views and stored procedures that meet your needs.

> *A wide mix of issues can lead to unconverted Access queries in a new Access project. The Access Help files remain an excellent source of general background documentation on factors that can cause a failed query conversion. Go to the Comparing Access Projects to Access_Databases section, under Working with Microsoft Access Projects in the Access Help files for details. The page titled Comparison of Microsoft Access and SQL Server SQL syntax is particularly helpful. With respect to any particular upsizing, the Upsizing Wizard report is the definitive source for details of conversion errors for Access query objects.*
>
> *It will not take you too much testing to discover that the conversions for forms, reports, and data access pages are not perfect either. Unfortunately, the Upsizing Wizard report does not provide any guidance about conversion errors for these objects. You'll need to discover them manually. Despite*

these difficulties, the conversion does provide many working features – particularly those related to record sources. The sample `NorthwindCS.adp` *file that ships with Access 2000 is an excellent resource for viewing a working version of the forms and reports of the* `Northwind.mdb` *Access database file functioning in an Access project. You can use its fixes relative to the upsized forms and reports as a guide for developing fixes in your own custom upsizing tasks.*

The Upsizing Wizard does not attempt to perform conversions for macros and modules. You need to update your code to remove references to DAO objects since Access projects do not work with DAO objects but work exclusively with ADO objects. This is a manual process. Many samples throughout this book can equip you for the conversion, but Chapter 12 especially targets working with VBA modules in Access projects. The Programming MS Access site (www.programmingmsaccess.com) also includes numerous code samples that can help you with this process.

The Option 3 Upsizing Process

The process for generating an Access project and SQL Server database from an Access database file is nearly identical to the one for creating a SQL Server database by itself. The example for this option creates a new SQL Server database named NorthwindUpsize3. Although only one of the wizard screens requires a different response from the settings used with the first upsizing option, think carefully about what settings you use for the login ID and password on the second wizard dialog. These will then be set for the Access project that this upsizing process creates. Appendix A deals with these security issues.

As you might expect, the screen on which we need to specify a different option is the one on which we choose our upsizing option. First, we'll need to select the radio button for the third option. The label is Create a new client/server application.

Second, we can either accept the default path and name for the Access project or designate an alternative. The following screen shows that the default path is the same as for the Northwind sample Access database file. The name of the .adp file is normally the name of the Access database file with a CS suffix. In this case, the wizard supplies the name Northwind1CS.adp because there is already a NorthwindCS.adp file in the path for the new Access project. Recall that a sample Access project that ships with Access 2000 has this name. After deciding on a path and name for the new Access project, we can click Finish to start the creation of the SQL Server database and the Access project that connects to it.

Completing the Upsizing Process Manually

At the conclusion of the potentially long upsizing process, after we close the Access Upsizing report, the new Access project replaces the Access database file on your monitor. The new Access project has the user name and password in its OLE DB connection string that we specify for the creation of the SQL Server database. Although the Access project replaces the Access database file on the screen, the Upsizing Wizard does not alter the original Access database file on disk.

The following excerpt from the Upsizing Wizard report shows the feedback for two queries from the original `Northwind.mdb` file. The query named **Alphabetical List of Products** converts successfully to a view. The query named **Product Sales for 1997** does not upsize. While the Upsizing Wizard fails to make the automatic conversion of the query to a view, a conversion is still possible. You just need to perform it manually. The T-SQL for the [Product Sales for 1997] view is readily available in the sample **NorthwindCS** database and you can view it in the sample `NorthwindCS.adp` Access project file. For your convenience, the T-SQL for the [Product Sales for 1997] view appears after the excerpt from the Access Upsizing report.

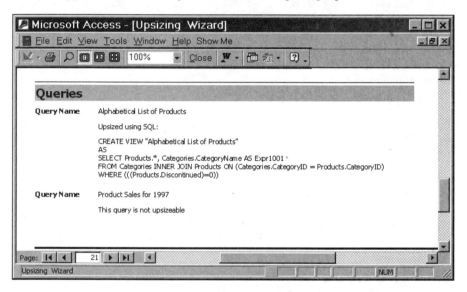

```
SELECT Categories.CategoryName, Products.ProductName,
    SUM(CONVERT(money,
    [Order Details].UnitPrice * [Order Details].Quantity *
    (1 - [Order Details].Discount)
     / 100) * 100) AS ProductSales, 'Qtr ' + DATENAME(qq,
    Orders.ShippedDate) AS ShippedQuarter
FROM Categories INNER JOIN
    Products ON
    Categories.CategoryID = Products.CategoryID INNER JOIN
    Orders INNER JOIN
    [Order Details] ON
    Orders.OrderID = [Order Details].OrderID ON
    Products.ProductID = [Order Details].ProductID
WHERE (Orders.ShippedDate BETWEEN '19970101' AND
    '19971231')
GROUP BY Categories.CategoryName, Products.ProductName,
    'Qtr ' + DATENAME(qq, Orders.ShippedDate)
```

This concludes the discussion of the three upsizing options using the Access 2000 Upsizing Wizard. The remainder of this Appendix now focuses on the use of the versatile Data Transformation Wizard to assist in the transfer of data from Access database files to SQL server databases.

Using the Data Transformation Services Wizard

The Data Transformation Services (DTS) Wizard is a SQL Service component that also ships with Microsoft Office 2000. The DTS Wizard becomes available in Microsoft Office after you install the Microsoft Data Engine (MSDE). In order to use the DTS Wizard, your workstation must have MSDE, SQL Server 7, or SQL Server 2000 installed on it. We can use the DTS to import, export, and transform data from a source format to a destination format. While the DTS is appropriate for working with many different data types (for example, Oracle and dBASE), the presentation here examines the DTS Wizard for moving data from Access database files to SQL Server databases. The DTS Wizard in SQL Server 2000 supports the saving of a DTS Package in a Visual Basic file. This saved package enables developers to replicate programmatically the operations performed manually with the DTS Wizard. In fact, Access developers can use the DTS packages like macro recorders to replay selections made when manually operating the DTS Wizard. In addition, SQL Server 2000 introduces other more subtle enhancements.

Because many Access developers will not have the SQL Server 2000 version of the DTS Wizard, we'll start with a couple of examples using the initial DTS wizard, and then add an example with the latest version.

The DTS Wizard contrasts with the Upsizing Wizard in that it does not transfer the schema from the original Access database file. Instead, the DTS Wizard creates tables in a destination SQL Server database based on the data in the tables from the Access database file. This means we have to add primary keys and IDENTITY settings for columns after the DTS Wizard has transferred the data, a task that the Upsizing Wizard does for you automatically. The DTS Wizard transfers the data efficiently, but it does not capture relationships between the tables. The Upsizing Wizard does capture these relationships.

The two wizards can complement one another by using the Upsizing Wizard to move the schema from an Access database file to a SQL Server database without moving any data. Then, we can follow the schema-building activity of the Upsizing Wizard with the data migration services of the DTS Wizard. While the DTS Wizard cannot build a schema based on the relationships among tables in an Access database file, it can very efficiently move large quantities of data, which is not a strong point for the Upsizing Wizard.

Populating a Schema with the DTS Wizard

Populating an empty SQL Server schema with data from an Access database file via the DTS Wizard is a two-step process. First, we create the schema. One especially easy way to do this is with the Upsizing Wizard, as has already been demonstrated. Second, we run the DTS Wizard with an Access database file as the source and the empty SQL Server schema as the destination. This approach is particularly appropriate whenever the Access database is large because of the speed advantage that the DTS Wizard has over the Upsizing Wizard for migrating data. Another very good use of this method is to update an existing test SQL database with live data ready for further testing or for final migration of the data to SQL Server. There are various options within DTS to automatically delete existing data while leaving the schema intact, as we shall see later.

Creating the Empty Database Schema

Creating an empty SQL Server schema based on an Access database is identical to the first upsizing option for using the Upsizing Wizard, except for one check box on the dialog setting the overall specifications for the upsizing. The following screenshot displays the Upsizing Wizard screen that lets you create an empty SQL Server schema based on an Access database file. Notice that the check box for Only create the table structure; don't upsize any data is chosen. This selection creates an empty database schema on the SQL Server. In the example to demonstrate populating an empty schema with the DTS Wizard, we create a database named NorthwindUpsize4 by running the Upsizing Wizard in the sample Northwind.mdb file that ships with Access.

Running the DTS Wizard

After creating the empty SQL Server database schema, we can use the DTS Wizard to populate it with data. The DTS Wizard lets you specify a source and destination for your data migration. The DTS Wizard also offers options to control how the migration works. For example, you can graphically specify a query to filter the source data before migration. If we are creating a new table in the destination (as opposed to appending data to an existing table), we can edit the T-SQL that the DTS Wizard automatically generates to create the new table. This means that we can specify a constraint for a primary key. We can also designate that the DTS Wizard conditionally drop an existing table if there is already one in the database.

The SQL Server 2000 DTS Wizard has a marginally different interface, but it provides the same functionality along with some new features. In any event, the DTS Wizard is invoked from the Windows Start button menu. Highlight the menu item for the version of SQL Server or MSDE that you are running, and then choose the submenu item named Import and Export Data. This opens the welcome screen for the DTS Wizard. Click Next to advance to the first functional DTS Wizard screen.

The following screenshot displays the DTS Wizard dialog for specifying the source for the example to populate a schema. It designates Microsoft Access as the source. When we select Microsoft Access in the Source drop-down box, the Wizard reconfigures the screen to prompt for a file name and optional username and password entries. The file name points to the Access database file from which we want to transfer data. A button next to the file name box lets us navigate to the location of the Access database file serving as the source. The username and password entries are for Jet database security (in case we're using it). We'll click Next to open another wizard screen that allows us to specify the source for the data migration.

The following DTS Wizard screen shows the settings for selecting the destination for the data transfer. As we are migrating data from an Access database file to a SQL Server database, Microsoft OLE DB Provider for SQL Server is selected from the destination drop-down list. In this instance, the destination database resides on the local server, although for you it could just as easily be elsewhere – the drop down box will let you select from the SQL Servers to which you have access. After designating a SQL Server and a username for the SQL Server, we can select a target database on the server. The wizard screen also offers a drop-down box to let us pick one of the databases already on the server. You may have to click the Refresh button first to get a list of databases on your server. For the example, we highlight NorthwindUpsize4, the empty database schema created by the Upsizing Wizard earlier in this example.

In the next DTS Wizard screen, we can specify whether to copy tables directly from the source Access database file or to use a query as the source. The example calls for using all the tables from the source Access database file.

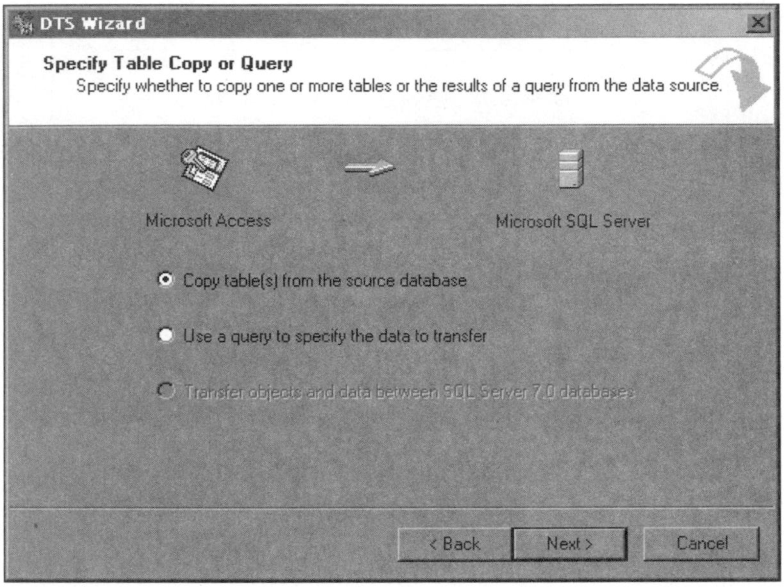

After making the appropriate selection, click Next so that that we can specify the database objects that contribute directly to the data migration. This opens the Select Source Tables screen in SQL Server 7. Note that the SQL Server 2000 version of the screen also includes queries that return rows. Select all the tables we want to transfer data for, as in the following screen, before clicking Next.

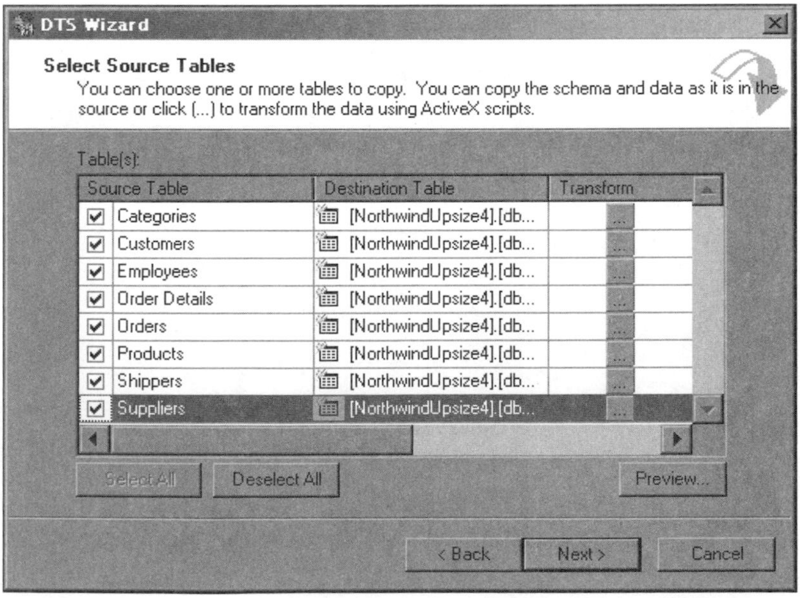

After designating your source table, you can accept the defaults for the Save, Schedule and Replicate Package screen. The important one for this sample is the selection of Run immediately. We'll discuss this screen in more depth in the example for the SQL Server 2000 version of the DTS Wizard. The display below shows the SQL Server 7 version of the screen. Notice that it lets you save the DTS Package for reuse in SQL Server, the Repository, or a File. The SQL Server 2000 version of the DTS Wizard adds to these options by permitting you to save it to a VB project. You can import this into a module within the VBA project associated with an Access project. Clicking Next on the screen below opens a DTS Wizard screen that summarizes your selections to that point. If the summary of your choices reflects your intent, launch the data migration by clicking Finish. Otherwise, click Back to navigate to the wizard screen that requires revision.

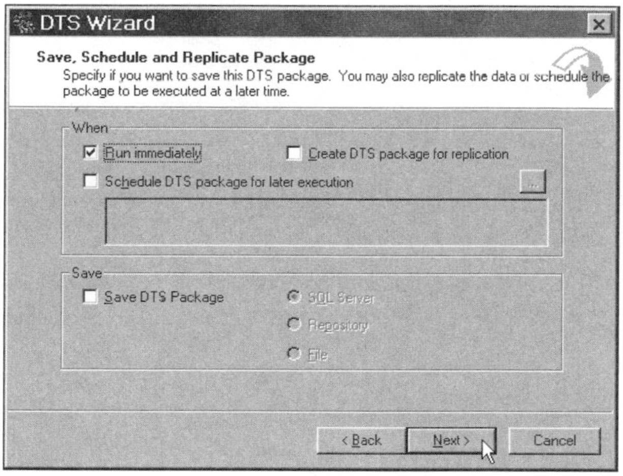

Viewing the Results of the DTS Data Migration

The following screen depicts an Access project opened on the newly populated NorthwindUpsize4 database. The Access project name is adp6 because we didn't change it from the default, but the important point is that it connects to the NorthwindUpsize4 database. The Database window below shows the Shippers table open within it. Notice that the ShipperID column shows (AutoNumber). This indicates that the column serves as an IDENTITY column that automatically populates whenever users enter new records. Notice also that the table appears with the New Record control enabled. We'll show in a moment that the DTS Wizard does not automatically provide this functionality. The reason that we have the capability in this example is that the DTS Wizard populates a schema previously created by the Upsizing Wizard.

711

Transferring Data Without the Schema

Sometimes it is not necessary or desirable to move the schema from another application, like when your requirements call for just the values in the database. For example, your need may just be to pump data from one or more remote databases to a central database. Another scenario is one where you have data from several different data sources to aggregate for a new application that will replace the systems providing data. Another variation calls for periodically pumping data from subsystems that support data input and lookup functions into a master database for analysis and reporting purposes. In any of these circumstances, the DTS Wizard can operate very effectively without the benefit of the Upsizing Wizard. However, at the end of the process, you must keep in mind that all you have done is to move data. You may very well need to modify your table design to make the data user friendly. One way to appreciate the benefits of just moving data is to transfer the tables from the `Northwind.mdb` to a new SQL Server database, say NorthwindUpsize5.

The process for copying just data from an Access database file to a SQL Server database does not require the running of the Upsizing Wizard first to transfer the schema to a SQL Server. This has several advantages:

❑   First, you have fewer steps to perform.

❑   Second, you just have to work with one wizard.

❑   Third, you can automate the data migration process since the DTS Wizard lets you package and save DTS settings and then re-run them later. This re-running feature is particularly convenient for Access developers since they can manage it with VBA. It can also be useful to save the packages and email them to a remote site or sites where a local administrator can perform the data migration at a suitable time.

Options for Moving Data with the DTS Wizard

When you are moving data from Access tables to tables in a SQL Server database, the DTS Wizard offers a variety of options. This section focuses on those available with the SQL Server 7 version of the wizard. This is the version also available with the MSDE installation from Access 2000. The discussion for a subsequent sample highlights some capabilities that the DTS Wizard in SQL Server 2000 introduces.

The first way to move data from Access to SQL Server is to create a new SQL Server database for the table contents you are copying. This is convenient for a one-time transfer of data from one source to another.

Second, you can copy data from an Access database file into a new table in an existing database. This saves you the step of creating a new SQL Server database. It also makes your migrated data readily available with other data sources that your new application may need. If a table with the name that you specify already exists, your DTS settings to create a new SQL Server table will fail, but the copying to the source data can succeed or fail. It will succeed so long as your new data meet the existing table's constraints. However, the new data can violate a primary key or other kind of constraint.

For this reason, the DTS Wizard offers a third option that automatically deletes and recreates a new table based on your data source. This option is attractive when you have not created many indexes and other refinements for the existing table.

However, if the target table is highly crafted, you may prefer to keep the table design, discard the old data, and populate the table with new data. A fourth option supports this capability.

Sometimes, you need to add data to an existing table. The DTS Wizard supports this capability with a fifth option for appending data from a source table to a destination table.

If all these options are insufficient to satisfy your needs, the DTS Wizard offers an option called Edit SQL. With this option, you can design the table in any way that T-SQL supports.

Moving your Data

Here, we will examine in detail the option of using the DTS wizard to create a new SQL Server database based on some or all of the tables from an Access database file. The DTS Wizard steps for doing this are very similar to those you use when populating a schema. First, you designate the source Access database file. In the second step, complete the dialog as in the preceding example, except do not reference an existing SQL Server database. Instead, tell the wizard to create a new database by selecting the <new> option in the Database drop-down box on the Choose a Destination screen. This, in turn, pops up the Create Database dialog. Enter a database name along with the size of the primary database file and the log file in MB. If you inadvertently name an existing database, an error results. However, you can recover by entering a new database name that does not already exist in the database. This example uses a database name of NorthwindUpsize5. You can specify any size for the data and log file sizes, although 2 MB is the default. The following screenshot shows the <new> selection in the Database drop-down box and the settings for the pop-up Create Database dialog. When you click OK on the Create Database dialog, the DTS Wizard replaces <new> in the Database drop-down box with the name of the new database.

If you are going to copy all the table contents from the sample Northwind database file to the NorthwindUpsize5 database, you can duplicate the settings for the remaining DTS Wizard screens from the preceding sample. At the end of the process, you can open an Access project on the new database. The screen overleaf shows the adp6 Access project open on the NorthwindUpsize5 database with the Shippers table nestled inside the Database window. This screenshot parallels one from the preceding sample that populates an existing schema instead of creating new tables. Notice that the New Record control appears disabled. This is because the table does not have a primary key. Consequently, users cannot manually add records to the table. SQL Server does permit the addition of records under programmatic control, and the DTS Wizard can append records to the table.

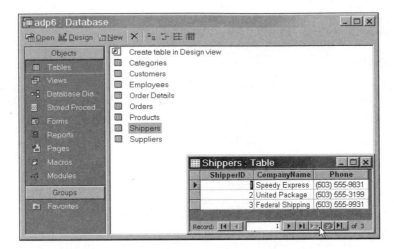

If your application calls for users being able to add data manually, you have several remedies. From within the Database window of an Access project, you can open the table in Design view and designate a primary key. See Chapter 3 for instructions on how to do this.

Second, you can modify the table's design before the DTS Wizard builds it. When you are working with SQL Server 7, you must specify the primary key with T-SQL code. You can create the opportunity to do this by clicking the Transform control for a table, say Shippers, on the Select Source Tables screen. This opens the Column Mappings and Transformations dialog for the Shippers table. Select the Column Mappings tab to expose the Edit SQL control. The following screenshot reveals the control just before a click:

Clicking Edit SQL opens the Create Table SQL Statement dialog. The sample dialog opposite illustrates the edited SQL for the Shippers table. The box reveals two edits to the automatically generated code. The display highlights the second edit. It adds a constraint to the Shippers table that designates the ShippersID column as a primary key.

The IDENTITY specification at the end of the second line is also not standard. This addition causes SQL Server to add one to the ShipperID column whenever a user enters a new row. The combination of these two edits enables users to enter values without having to specify values for the ShipperID column. In order to enjoy this result for every table, you need to make corresponding changes in the T-SQL for each of the eight tables the DTS Wizard transfers from the Access database file to the SQL Server database named NorthwindUpsize5.

These two changes make the tables created by the DTS Wizard behave like those populated for the schema generated by the Upsizing Wizard. The behavior correspondence is for data entry. The DTS-generated tables still do not reflect the relationships between tables in the original Access database file. Nevertheless, in some circumstances, the absence of this feature is irrelevant.

Create Table SQL Statement

You may modify the default create table SQL statement that is generated by the DTS Wizard. Further modifications to the column mappings will not change the below SQL statement.

SQL statement:

```
CREATE TABLE [NorthwindUpsize5].[dbo].[Shippers] (
[ShipperID] int NOT NULL IDENTITY(1,1),
[CompanyName] nvarchar (40) NOT NULL,
[Phone] nvarchar (24) NULL,
CONSTRAINT [PrimaryKey_Shippers] PRIMARY KEY ([ShipperID])
)
```

Auto Generate   OK   Cancel

The DTS Wizard in SQL Server 2000

The SQL Server 2000 DTS Wizard reflects the same ease-of-use features that characterize the wizard's introduction with SQL Server 7. In addition, Microsoft adds some new features to make the DTS Wizard more powerful and user-friendly. Specifically, the DTS wizard for SQL Server 2000 allows us to select any queries that return rows in the database. It shows these as SQL Server views in its Select Source Tables and Views dialog. The other major difference is that the SQL Server 2000 DTS wizard allows us to save our DTS package as a Visual Basic file.

We can import the VB code that the DTS wizard creates into a VBA project and run it from an Access form. The VB code that the DTS Wizard generates is essentially a macro recording of the settings made during a manual execution of the DTS Wizard. When we properly expose the main routine in the VB code, we can build a form so that a database administrator can re-run a DTS Package with a single click of a button. This drastically simplifies using the DTS wizard since one click replaces having to repeat all the DTS Wizard screen settings to specify an export. This technique exports successfully to SQL Server 2000 and SQL Server 7 database servers, but we have to define the initial DTS Package and run the VBA code on a SQL Server 2000 server.

This section presents an example that exports the Ten Most Expensive Products query from the sample Northwind.mdb Access database file to the NorthwindUpsize database on the CAB2000 server. Recall that the CAB2000 server in this appendix is running SQL Server 7. Therefore, we need a SQL Server 2000 server to run and save the DTS Package – like CAB2200 in this Appendix. The presentation of this sample comprises three parts:

❏ First, we demonstrate how to create and save a DTS Package based on a query in an Access database file

❑ Second, we show how to adapt the VB code that expresses the DTS Package for use in an Access module and with Access forms

❑ Third, we illustrate the sample application

Part 1 – Creating and Saving the DTS Package

There are three major elements to the DTS Package. First, it must export the return set from a query in an Access database file. Recall that the DTS Wizard always exports a table to its destination. Therefore, the DTS Wizard converts the return set from the query to a table for export.

Second, the table needs to be unique in the destination database, which is the NorthwindUpsize database on the CAB2000 server in this example. We can ensure this by dropping any prior versions of the exported table as you create the new version in this package.

Third, it is desirable to have a primary key for the exported table so users can edit the data if they want.

The process for creating and saving a DTS Package is almost identical to running the DTS Wizard normally. We make the DTS settings as normal, but we have to think about them so that they will be suitable for automatic use. With the SQL Server 2000 version of the DTS Wizard, we can save our settings to a Visual Basic File. This file contains VBScript code suitable for import and running from a module in the VBA project associated with an Access project. With the SQL Server 7 version of the DTS wizard, we can save a DTS package for later reuse from within the wizard, but we save the DTS package as a VB file with this earlier version of this wizard.

We'll start the example by specifying the source as in the preceding sample. Recall this includes designating a Microsoft Access data source type and navigating to the Northwind.mdb sample file on the CAB2000 computer from the CAB2200 computer on which the example runs. It is, of course, highly likely that your computers will not be the same as those in this example so you will need to change server designations if you wish to work through the example.

It is important to understand that the reason the DTS Wizard runs from the CAB2200 computer is because that computer has SQL Server 2000 installed on it. The example must run from a computer running SQL Server 2000.

On the first DTS Wizard screen, we'll point the wizard at the Northwind.mdb file on the CAB2000 computer because that's where the source file is. Similarly, the second DTS Wizard screen, which appears on the right, is pointed at the NorthwindUpsize database also on the CAB2000 server since that's where we want to add a new table based on the Ten Most Expensive Products query in the Northwind.mdb file.

When we click Next on the preceding screen, we are asked to specify whether we use a query or existing tables. After specifying to copy from tables, we click Next to open the Select Source Tables and Views screen in the DTS Wizard. This example calls for exporting a single database object – the Ten Most Expensive Products query. Consequently, we select the query's name at the bottom of the list in the Table(s) and Views(s) window, and click its Transform control. The adjacent screen depicts the selected source and the Transform control just before a click to it.

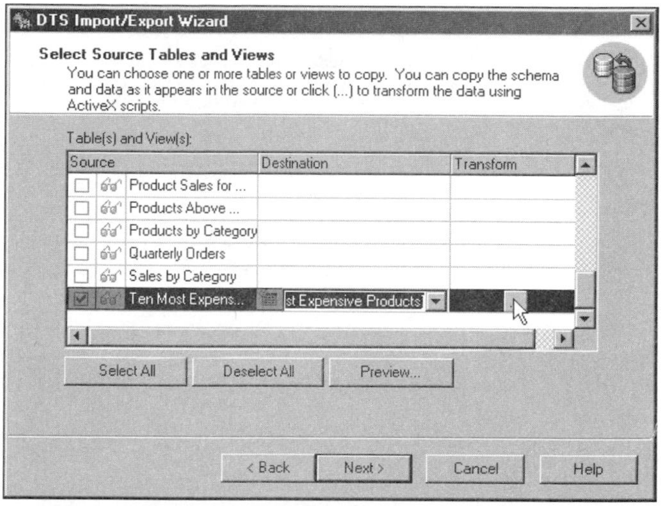

When the Column Mappings and Transformations dialog opens in response to a click of the Transform control, we will need to make changes or at least verify settings on two tabs. First, we'll deal with the Column Mappings tab. The safe way to run this application is to drop any old versions of the table in the target database before creating a new version. Therefore, we select Create destination table and Drop and recreate destination table. We need a primary key for the table that the wizard creates. The only candidate for this is the first column named TenMostExpensiveProducts. Therefore, we need to make sure the Nullable control for this column is blank. The UnitPrice column cannot serve as a primary key since more than one row in the query's return set can contain the same price. The adjacent screen reveals the settings for the Column Mappings tab.

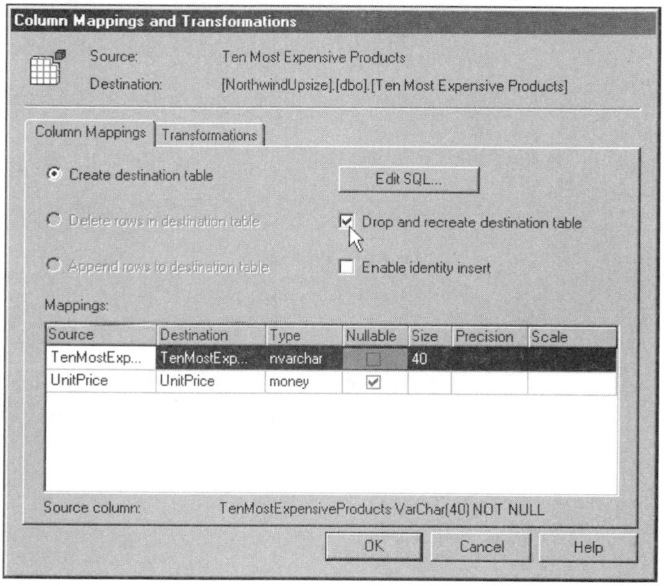

By making the settings described and demonstrated for the previous screens in this example, we have defined the elements of our DTS Package. However, we have not yet instructed the wizard to create a package and designated where to save it. The next two DTS Wizard screens offer these options. On the Save, schedule, and replicate package screen, you need to click Save DTS Package. For this example, we save the package as a Visual Basic File. This makes it possible to import the package into an Access project as a VBA module. The following screen illustrates the settings that make the example work. The mouse points at the Visual Basic File radio button after it has been selected.

717

When we click Next on the Save, schedule, and replicate package screen, the DTS Wizard opens the Save DTS Package screen. This screen lets us name and specify a storage location for the Visual Basic File. As we want to use the file containing the DTS package again, it is useful to give it meaningful filename.

The following sample settings save the package to the My Documents folder for the Administrator on the CAB2000 computer. The Save As dialog shows the package being save over a former version named Refresh_Top_Ten. This file has a VBScript file type. It appears with a .bas extension in the Windows Explorer.

Part 2 – Using the DTS Package in an Access Project

Once you have a saved DTS Package, it takes just six steps to attach the package to a button on an Access form. With the form open, a database administrator can refresh a connection from an Access database file to a SQL Server database with just the click of a button. As you see in the next section, even normal database users can take advantage of this form to refresh their data on demand.

> This section assumes a basic familiarity with VBA programming and the **VBE** window for an Access project.

To start the process of attaching the package to a button, all you need is an Access project. This example uses the adp3 Access project. It resides on the CAB2000 computer, but the computer developing the project is CAB2200. The adp3 Access project does not even require a connection to a database. The only purpose of the Access project is to offer a `Forms` collection and a VBA project. The `Forms` collection provides a vehicle for adding a form that contains a button. This button has to have an event procedure that launches the package. The VBA project serves has a container for the code from Visual Basic File in which we previously saved the DTS Package. We will also store our event procedure for the button in the VBA project. The six steps to attach the DTS package to a button on an Access form are as follows:

Step 1

The first step in using a DTS Package previously saved as a Visual Basic File is to add a reference to the VBA project. We start this by choosing Tools | References to open the References dialog. Then, we scroll down in the Available References list box until we reach Microsoft DTSPackage Object Library. We select the check box next to the entry, and add the object library to our VBA project by clicking OK and closing the dialog.

Step 2

Next, we need to import the previously saved Visual Basic File as a module into our VBA project. Choose File | Import File from the VBE. Then, we use the Import File dialog to navigate to folder containing our Visual Basic File with the DTS Package. The following dialog shows the selection of the Refresh_Top_Ten file in the My Documents in which we saved it previously. After we click Open, Access adds a new module to its Modules collection. If this is the first module in the VBA project, Access names the new module Module1 (otherwise, it is Module2, Module3, and so forth).

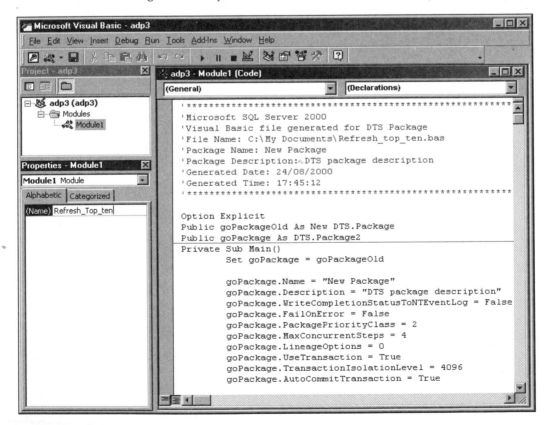

Step 3

It is a good idea to rename the module from its default name to one that has meaning in terms of your project. We can rename the module from the **Database** window in the Access project, or from the **Properties** window in the VBE. In the **Properties** window, we simply select the name for the module and give it a new value. Our task is similarly easy from the Database window, where we click on the name of the module until it allows us to change the text. The screenshot below illustrates the **Properties** window immediately after the entry of a new name for the module. Pressing the *Enter* key will rename Module1 to the new setting in the **Name** property box.

Step 4

The next step is to re-specify the Main sub as Public rather than Private. The Main sub procedure appears just to the right of the Properties window in the preceding screen shot. This sub is the entry point for launching the DTS Package. If we wanted to invoke the package from a form module outside of the Refresh_Top_Ten module, then we would need to expose the procedure. The best way to do this is by changing its declaration from Private to Public. We can accomplish this change by replacing Private with Public just before Sub Main.

Step 5

The fifth step is to design a form with a button on it that launches the DTS Package. If you require a refresher in designing forms, have another look at Chapter 7. We start making this form by adding a blank form in our Access project. Then, we add a button to the form and give it a descriptive Caption property assignment (like the form below). Next, we'll add a label to remind its user of the form's purpose, and we've completed the layout of the form. You can see a graphic layout of the form below.

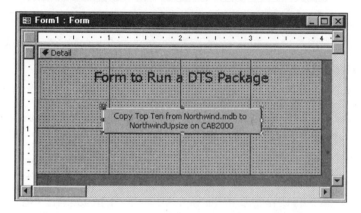

Step 6

Finally, we need to create the event procedure to launch the DTS Package. Begin by selecting the Event tab of the Properties dialog for the command button. Click the Build button next to the On Click event.

Then, double-click Code Builder in the pop-up Choose Builder dialog (which we're not showing since it's so small). This transfers control back to the VBE window with the shell for a click event for the command button object. The name of the command button in this example is Command3. The name of the event procedure is Command3_Click.

Next, type `Refresh_Top_Ten.` into the event procedure shell, and don't forget the " . " at the end. Access presents a pop-up list of all publicly exposed references to the module. Select Main and press *Enter* or *Tab*, and we've got our completed event procedure:

This completes the construction of the form and its event procedure. Make sure that you save all your changes to the Access project.

Part 3 – Illustrating the Sample Application

The application in the adp3 Access project can operate on any computer that is running SQL Server 2000 and can make a connection to the NorthwindUpsize database on the CAB2000 computer. The Access project containing the application does not require a connection, but the application itself must be able to make a connection from the Access project to the CAB2000 SQL Server. Remember from our previous discussions that the CAB2000 computer is running SQL Server 7. We can use the features of this application with a database maintained by a SQL Server 7 server. However, you can only run the DTS Package and the VBA software that operates it on a computer running SQL Server 2000. Microsoft did something very cool here! This means that by installing one SQL Server 2000 computer on a network, we can enjoy its DTS Wizard benefits on other servers throughout the network even if they are not running SQL Server 2000. In addition, this particular application is interesting because any computer running SQL Server 2000 can operate it. This means database administrators and users can update on demand a SQL Server application with data from a legacy application, such as one based on an Access database file.

To demonstrate the versatility of the application and the feature set that it uses, we'll look at the application on the Cabarmada computer running SQL Server 2000. It uses two Access projects:

❑　The adp3 Access project contains the form with the button to refresh the data in the NorthwindUpsize database on the CAB2000 SQL Server. The event procedure behind the button copies data from the Ten Most Expensive Products query in the `Northwind.mdb` file to the [Ten Most Expensive Products] table in the NorthwindUpsize database.

❑　The Cabarmada computer then runs the second Access project named adp6. For the purposes of this example, the adp6 Access project has a connection to the NorthwindUpsize database on the CAB2000 server. A stored procedure named sorted_top_ten sorts the rows on the [Ten Most Expensive Products] table in descending order by the values in its UnitPrice column. This stored procedure provides a mechanism to display the row values in order by price. The natural order for rows is by the table's primary key, which is a column of string values naming the products with an nvarchar data type. The T-SQL for the sorted_top_ten stored procedure appears below:

```
Alter Procedure sorted_top_ten
As
```

```
SELECT * FROM [Ten Most Expensive Products]
ORDER BY UnitPrice Desc
```

The following screen depicts the sorted_top_ten stored procedure open with an edit in process. We've changed the value of the least expensive value to the most expense value – from $45.60 to $4599.60. After choosing Records | Refresh, the return set displayed by the stored procedure changes to show Rössle Sauerkraut at the top of the list.

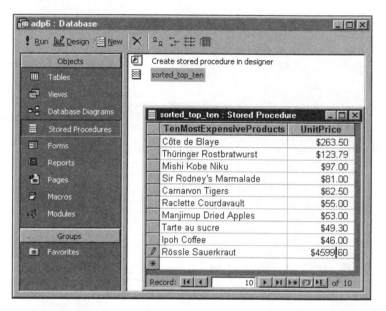

The change after the Records | Refresh command occurs in the NorthwindUpsize database. The original query in the Access database file still has its original value (unless someone else changed it). Therefore, running our sample application with the command button can refresh the [Ten Most Expensive Products] table in the NorthwindUpsize database with the original value from the legacy Access database file. The following screen shows the form with the button in the adp3 Access project. The screen depicts the form just before a click to the button.

After the click to the button in the preceding screen, the [Ten Most Expensive Products] table refreshes with the most recent value in the query from the Access database file. If users of the Access database file change the values of products in the query, then those new values transfer over to the SQL Server table. The sorted_top_ten stored procedure does not reflect the refreshed values until you refresh the stored procedure relative to the [Ten Most Expensive Products] table. One way to do this is by invoking the Records | Refresh command again. The following screen depicts the stored procedure nestled in the adp6 Database window with the refreshed, original values.

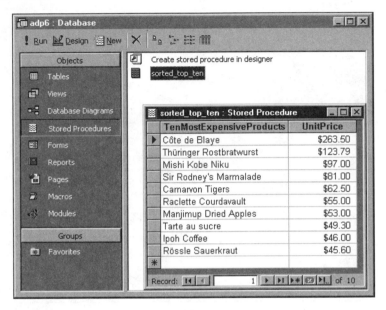

Summary

So, there we are – the Upsizing Wizard that ships with Access 2000 and the DTS Wizard that ships with SQL Server. Each of these tools offers distinct advantages for transferring data from an Access database to a SQL Server database. When we need to transfer the schema from an Access database file to a SQL Server database, the Upsizing Wizard represents an easy solution. If we also need to transfer data as well as the schema, we can use either the Upsizing Wizard to transfer data from the Access database file to a SQL Server or we can use the DTS Wizard. If the database is not very large, say on the order of the Northwind database, the Upsizing Wizard is fine. For much larger databases, we can generate faster copying performance by using the DTS Wizard to transfer the data. The DTS Wizard is great when all we need to do is transfer data. In addition, it includes a kind of macro recorder that enables us to replay DTS settings from the VBA project associated with an Access project by saving the process as a Visual Basic file.

C
Copying Databases Between Servers

This appendix aims to show how you can attach a database from another SQL Server to your SQL Server or MSDE. This is particularly useful for attaching the downloadable databases from www.wrox.com. Although the aim here is to show you how to attach a database to your server, there is also some discussion of copying from one database to another. In the case of the downloadable databases, the first part (detaching the database) has already been done.

If you are an Access developer using MSDE, you will not have pubs. This section covers two methods for transferring a copy of the pubs database to a server running MSDE. The first method relies on a short SQL-DMO procedure that copies the database from a server with pubs to a server running MSDE.

The second method illustrates a way to accomplish the same task manually, using an Access project. Both techniques have their merits.

In any event, developers frequently encounter a need to transfer a database from one server to another. This appendix equips you with two methods to accomplish the task. People who have not used SQL Server before will be unacquainted with this classic sample database that the Books Online uses heavily.

SQL Server 2000 adds a little something to our checklist when attaching databases to our servers. Databases created on a SQL Server 2000 can't be attached to SQL Server 7 or MSDE servers, although you can attach SQL Server 7 databases to SQL Server 2000.

Attaching a Database to a New Server Using SQL-DMO

The following sample for copying pubs between servers relies on both the Scripting.FileSystemObject library and the SQL-DMO library. You'll need to create a reference in your VBA project to both of these libraries before attempting to run the code. The sample below starts by declaring new instances for the File System and the SQLServer objects. The code uses fso1, a File System object, to copy the database files from one server to another. The srv1 SQL-DMO object instance actually has a dual function in the sample. At the beginning, it helps to manage the copy of pubs on a server that we want to copy to another server. This approach permits us to retain an original version of pubs on one database server while we have an updated version with custom extensions on another server. Later, the program uses srv1 to manage the attachment of the copied database files to the second server.

In order for this to run successfully on your computer or network, you'll have to change the names of the servers and possibly the locations for the files. This procedure is run on the cabarmada server, and references the cabxli server using a Universal Naming Convention filename, which includes the path.

```
Sub copy_pubs_from_cabarmada_to_cabxli()
Dim fso1 As New Scripting.FileSystemObject
Dim srv1 As New SQLDMO.SQLServer
Dim str1 As String

'Connect to 7.0 server with pubs
'and detach pubs temporarily
srv1.Connect "cabarmada", "sa", ""
srv1.DetachDB "pubs"

'Copy database files from current
'machine to target computer
fso1.CopyFile "c:\mssql7\data\pubs*.*", _
  "\\cabxli\c\DataPlace\"

'Re-attach pubs database and print
'outcome to Immediate window
str1 = srv1.AttachDB("pubs", "c:\mssql7\data\pubs.mdf," & _
  "c:\mssql7\data\pubs_log.ldf")
Debug.Print "Result from attempt to re-attach:"
Debug.Print str1

'Disconnect from cabarmada and
'point SQLServer object at target server
srv1.Disconnect
srv1.Connect "cabxli", "sa", ""

'Attach pubs database files to
'the target server
str1 = srv1.AttachDB("pubs", _
  "\\cabxli\c\DataPlace\pubs.mdf," & _
  "\\cabxli\c\DataPlace\pubs_log.ldf")
Debug.Print "Result from attempt to attach " & _
  "for new server:"
Debug.Print str1


End Sub
```

After creating instances of two objects, the sample connects `srv1` to the `cabarmada` server. This server has a version of **pubs** that we want to copy to another server, and is also the computer from which this example is run. Access developers transitioning to SQL Server must get used to the idea that servers manage databases. Indeed, a server manages a folder of database files. One implication of this active database management by a server is that our applications have to detach a database from a server before they can manipulate its files.

```
Sub copy_pubs_from_cabarmada_to_cabxli()
Dim fso1 As New Scripting.FileSystemObject
Dim srv1 As New SQLDMO.SQLServer
Dim str1 As String

'Connect to 7.0 server with pubs
'and detach pubs temporarily
srv1.Connect "cabarmada", "sa", ""
srv1.DetachDB "pubs"
```

The sample uses the `DetachDB` method for the `SQLServer` object to release the **pubs** database from the `cabarmada` server. This then allows us to move the two files that comprise the database. In the case of the **pubs** database, the file names are `pubs.mdf` and `pubs_log.ldf`. The `mdf` file contains the data in a database, and the `ldf` file holds the log of transactions. Every SQL Server database must have a log file. It stores the log of transactions used to recover a database. If you do not copy the **pubs** log file from the original server, the server receiving the copy of **pubs** will create a new log file.

> *The log file, while your SQL Server is running, represents an integral part of the database. Without the log file, you only have the data that has been written to the database in the past. The log file represents something of a temporary storage area for transactions and other database activity, which will be written into the database .mdf file at certain time – namely when a **checkpoint** is issued. A checkpoint is just that, a point at which any data in the cache is written to the physical disk. As you might expect, a checkpoint occurs when you shut down your SQL Server normally. Any more about the SQL Server log is out of the scope of this book.*

After detaching a database from a server, we can copy the files from one server to another.

```
'Copy database files from current
'machine to target computer
fso1.CopyFile "c:\mssql7\data\pubs*.*", _
  "\\cabxli\c\DataPlace\"
```

The sample uses the `CopyFile` method for the `FileSystem` object to perform the copy. By using a wildcard, the code picks up both **pubs** files from the connected server, `cabarmada`. Notice the destination is not in the **MSSQL7\Data** folder on the `cabxli` server. The procedure does not have permission to write to the **Data** folder on that server. This is because the second server is still actively managing its **Data** folder. Therefore, the procedure writes the files to another folder not actively managed by the `cabxli` server. At a suitable point, when the server is not being used, you should move the files to a folder that will be actively managed by the server. You'll have to stop the service on the server, and then reconnect the database files after you've moved them. As you adapt this procedure for your installation, you will want to change the server names and the alternative folder destination on the second computer.

Before disconnecting from the `cabarmada` server, the procedure re-attaches the **pubs** database files to this server.

```
'Re-attach pubs database and print
'outcome to Immediate window
str1 = srv1.AttachDB("pubs", "c:\mssql7\data\pubs.mdf," & _
  "c:\mssql7\data\pubs_log.ldf")
Debug.Print "Result from attempt to re-attach:"
Debug.Print str1
```

The AttachDB method for the SQLServer object takes two arguments. First, you must specify the database name – pubs in this case. Second, your code must designate a string that contains all the files you want to attach. In this case, the procedure specifies the mdf and ldf files for pubs. SQL Server also permits the designation of secondary files to hold data that do not fit in the primary mdf file. If you adapt this sample for databases with secondary files (these have an ndf extension), you must include them in the second parameter for the AttachDB method. This method returns a string value reporting the success of the attempt to attach the database. We must save this string value if we want to check on the success of our procedure. The sample writes it to the Immediate window.

In its final set of actions, the procedure shifts its attention from the cabarmada server to the cabxli server.

```
'Disconnect from cabarmada and
'point SQLServer object at target server
srv1.Disconnect
srv1.Connect "cabxli", "sa", ""
```

The sample commences the shift by disconnecting srv1 from cabarmada and connecting it to cabxli. In a busy, productive system care must be taken when doing this kind of work. If you disconnect a database that is in use, problems could arise.

```
'Attach pubs database files to
'the target server
str1 = srv1.AttachDB("pubs", _
  "\\cabxli\c\DataPlace\pubs.mdf," & _
  "\\cabxli\c\DataPlace\pubs_log.ldf")
Debug.Print "Result from attempt to attach " & _
  "for new server:"
Debug.Print str1
```

Then, it invokes the AttachDB method of the SQLServer object to attach the copied files to the cabxli server. This allows the server to know about and manage the files. Before attachment, the files are unmanaged, and anyone can delete them. After attachment, the cabxli server protects them from deletion through the file system. You can only delete the files through SQL Server.

In order to build an Access application for our new copy of the pubs database on cabxli, we require an Access project that points at it. The following screen depicts the Data Link Properties dialog for opening a new Access project. The dialog specifies a connection to the copied version of pubs on the cabxli server. This dialog becomes available as a result of opening a new Access project that is to connect to an existing server. See Chapter 2 for the details on creating Access projects to connect with previously existing databases.

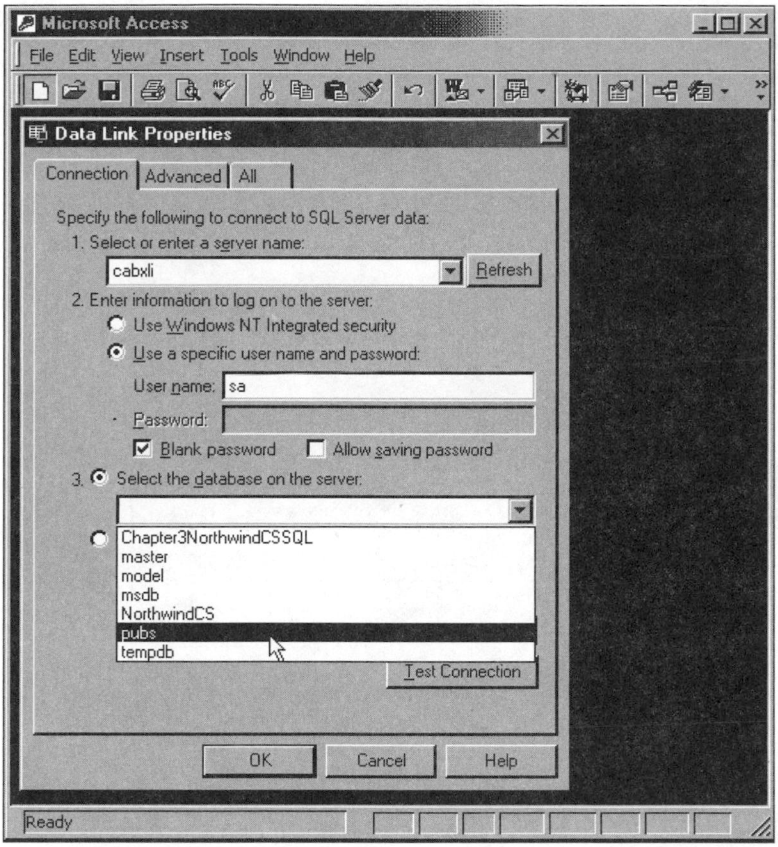

Attaching a Database to a New Server Using an Access Project

The above procedure, appropriately edited, fully automates copying and installing database files from one server to another. If you just have a database to copy and install very infrequently, you may prefer a manual approach. Here's one with just two steps! The technique is also handy when the computer receiving the database file is not on a LAN with the one that has the original database file.

First, start the manual approach by copying the mdf file from one computer to another. You will need to stop the server with the original database if you want to copy the file manually. If it is not convenient or possible to stop the database server, run the detaching and copying part of the preceding procedure, stopping the code just before making the connection to the second computer. Also, be sure to delete the ldf file from the computer to which the procedure copies. This technique fails if there is already a log file because it automatically creates a new one.

Second, open a new Access project as if it were to connect to an existing database. In fact, the database does not yet exist on the second server, but the Access project can attach to it, and also attach it to the server. Use settings for the Data Link Properties dialog like those in the following screen. Notice that the dialog requests that the Access project **Attach a database file as a database name**, and specifies a filename for that database. This is the file we copied from the other computer. Click OK to have Access attach the database file to the server and open the Access project with a link to the database.

Setting Up A Connection

With the growth of the Internet, people want the information they seek to be available, accurate, and, more importantly, as up-to-date as possible. Companies often achieve this by linking their web pages to a data store (which can be a database, a spreadsheet, in fact anywhere that information is kept) – the data store is kept as up-to-date as possible, meaning that every time an outside user accesses the company's web pages, they will get the most recent information available.

However, in order for us to link our web pages to the most recent information, we must know where it can be found. This is done by creating a connection to the data store; but just what is a connection, and what are its benefits?

What is a Connection?

This might seem pretty obvious, but a connection is what links our code to the data store. Our connection ties us to the data store and shows us the way to what we want to work with without getting us lost.

> *A connection, however, is not always tied to just the one data store it – can be untied from one data store and attached to another, or it can even point to several data sources at once.*

Once we have a way of connecting to the data store, we need to know how to identify it – but this identifying information will depend on what we are connecting to, and how. For example, an Access database is just identified by the .mdb file; SQL Server, on the other hand, is designed to handle more (and larger) databases, and there is often more than one machine running SQL Server, so in order to uniquely identify a database, you have to use the name of the server as well as the name of the database.

Every data store that we connect to will have some form of connection – although sometimes we might create the connection ourselves, and other times we might allow the system to create a connection for us.

Before we can connect to a data store, we need some way of knowing *what* it is and *where* it is – there are a number of ways to do this, and this appendix covers:

❑ ODBC Data Source Names (DSN)
❑ Connection Strings

ODBC Data Source Names

Open DataBase Connectivity was the precursor to OLEDB and ADO, and still plays a large part in development issues. A Data Source Name (DSN) is simply a pointer to a particular source of data, and allows us to reference this data source just by a name, rather than by the physical location. This allows the location of the data to change without any changes to the code, because the code points to the DSN.

There are three types of DSN:

❑ **User DSN**, which is only visible to a single user. Other users on the machine cannot use this DSN.

❑ **System DSN**, which is visible to all users who use the machine, including the operating system.

❑ **File DSN**, which is a DSN stored in a file, and is visible to all users.

For Active Server Pages we only need to concern ourselves with a System DSN.

To create a DSN we use the **ODBC Data Sources** applet in the **Control Panel**. Opening this gives the Administrator dialog:

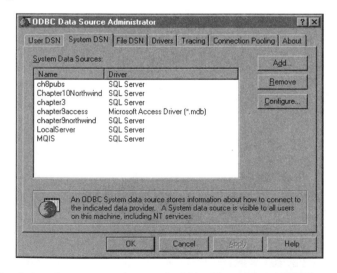

This shows a list of existing data sources (you probably will not have all of those shown in the screenshot). To create a new DSN click the **Add...** button, where we will see a list of data stores drivers that we can connect to:

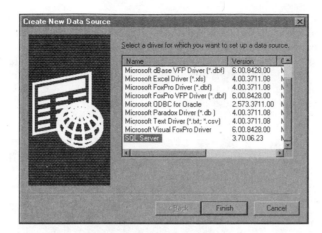

*A **driver** is what ODBC uses to connect us to the actual source of the data. There is a driver for each type of data that ODBC can handle.*

We'll need a SQL Server DSN, so make sure the correct driver is selected, then press the Finish button to take us to the SQL Server DSN setup dialog:

This is where we get a chance to enter the name and description of the data source. These can be anything, so it's best to make them fairly descriptive. We also need to choose which SQL Server we want to connect to:

Click the Next button. The following screen asks us for some login details for the SQL Server (as this process was carried out on a Windows 98 machine, Windows NT authentication is not available; obviously, we would have a choice between the two if the machine we were on did allow NT authentication). We can also specify which Login ID we wish to obtain the default settings for – if we specify a login that isn't used on the SQL Server, we will get an error, so make sure that the login you choose is correct. Also, make sure that if you choose this option, the SQL Server you want to connect to is running; if it isn't, clicking on the Next button will throw up an error, because the dialog won't be able to connect to verify the login:

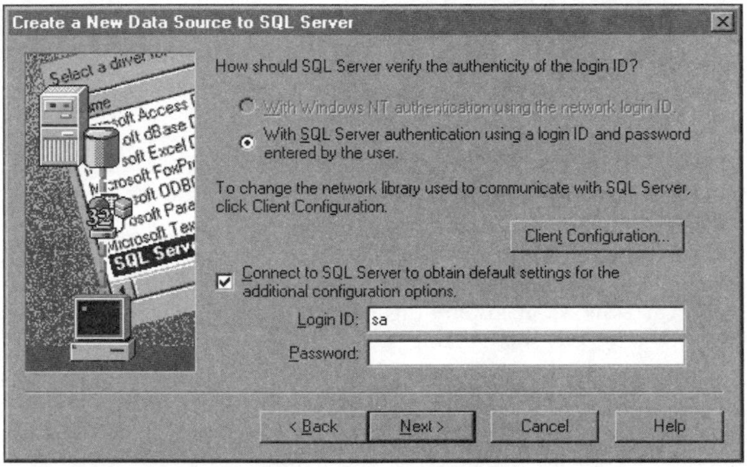

Click the Next button. This screen allows us to specify which database on the SQL Server we wish to connect to, or we could attach a database by using its filename. We will make the DSN reference the Northwind database, so change the default database to Northwind:

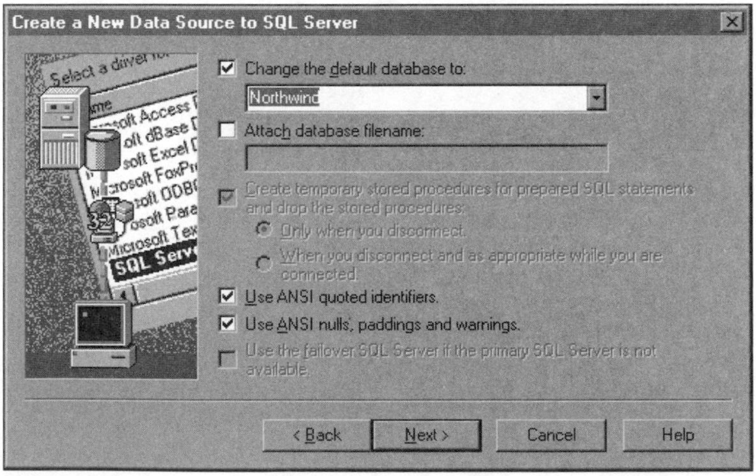

Click the Next button. The following screen allows us to set other options for the DSN – the default options provided by the dialog are usually sufficient, so accept these by pressing the Finish button:

After clicking the Finish button, the dialog presents us with a summary screen of the options we have specified. Notice the Test Data Source button at the bottom of this dialog – it is worth testing that the DSN works before we rely on it in our code, so press this button:

If we have set everything up correctly, we should be presented with the following dialog:

If something is wrong, the dialog will reflect this and so we have the opportunity to fix it by going through the steps again.

Click OK on the Data Source Test dialog, and also on the summary screen. We should now see the following screen again, only this time with ourDSN listed:

Creation of the DSN is now complete, so we can close this dialog by pressing the OK button.

Although using a DSN is the preferred way for the purposes of this book, we will now look at another possible way of connection to a data store – using a Connection String.

Connection Strings

A Connection String is just a combination of all the information needed to connect to a source of data.

First of all, we need some key pieces of information:

- ❏ `Provider` – the type of OLE DB provider. If we omit this, then the default OLE DB provider for ODBC is used.

- ❏ `Driver` – identifies the ODBC driver (such as Access or SQL Server).

- ❏ `Server` – specifies which server we are connecting to.

- ❏ `DSN` – the name of the data source, as we created earlier.

- ❏ `Database/DBQ` – identifies the actual database name.

- ❏ `UID` – specifies the user name with which to connect to the database.

- ❏ `PWD` – the user's password.

As we have already set up a DSN, we have already provided some of this information – for example, in setting up the data source, we have already specified the driver and the database. To get a connection string, we just join the various pieces of information together, so for a connection string that uses a DSN, we might use:

```
DSN=Orange
```

which assumes that we have filled in the `Database` and user details in the `DSN` called `Orange`. We can also add more details, if needed:

```
Provider=MSDASQL; DSN=Orange; UID=sa; PWD=
```

This just adds the `Provider` and the user name and password. This means that we can set up a DSN to hold just the bare minimum and then add other information in our ASP script at a later date. This is particularly useful when setting up the user details, since we may want to ask the user for them, rather than store them in the DSN. If we're using the OLE DB provider for ODBC we can leave out the `Provider`, since this is the default, but we must add it for other providers.

DSN-Less Connection Strings

We can also create DSN-less connection strings, which don't use a DSN, but we must include the information that would have been stored in the DSN. So, for example, an Access database would have a connection string like this:

```
Driver={Microsoft Access Driver (*.mdb)};
DBQ=C:\Inetpub\wwwroot\companyxyz\Orange.mdb
```

For a SQL Server database, this is slightly different:

```
Driver={SQL Server}; Server=ourServer; Database=MainCompany; UID=sa; PWD=
```

This is exactly the same information that would be needed if this company set up a DSN to their data source. The database name used here would be the one that held the information that the company wanted to manipulate.

Reporting on Log Files

We often find that reporting needs develop for situations where there are no nicely developed relational models. In fact, it is very common to encounter situations where data is stacked together in no particular order in a text file or a worksheet. For this type of assignment, developers must get the data into SQL Server and then extract some useful information from it.

A web log file is a classic example of a rich data source that does not come neatly packaged as a relational model. This data source is a text file that logs hits at a web site. Each hit is a reference to a file or resource at a web site. The log file contains information about each hit, including such items as its date and time, the client IP address, and the URL stem within the site for the referenced resource. These resources can include .htm and .html files, .asp files, and image files, as well as a host of command files, such as script files, .exe files, and .dll files. The data for all types of files from all users appears sequentially in a log file. The log file does not come with maps for translating the text data into a relational model before we start to prepare reports documenting web site traffic.

For a site with even a modest number of visitors, log file data can grow to massive proportions quickly. The sample log file examined in this section is for a site with slightly more than 300 visits on a single day. Its log file contains 3200 hit records. At this rate, hit records accumulate to about 100,000 per month or 1,200,000 per year – and a site with 300 visitors is by no means a high traffic site. Due to the potential usefulness of log file data for many different audiences within an organization for a web site, reports for log files represent an important database development topic. This section illustrates how we can start to develop custom SQL Server solutions with Access for this kind of resource.

Importing the Log File into SQL Server

Web log files vary in format from one server to another. An excerpt from a Microsoft Internet Information Server 4.0 log file appears below. This excerpt is for hits to a server on May 1, 2000. Notice that the first three lines and the beginning of the fourth line contain explanatory information for the file's content. The fourth line includes the field names for the data in the log file. The actual log of hit data begins on the fifth line. You can see the date and time of each hit as well as the originating IP address for the hit. This excerpt shows hits from two different IP addresses, namely 12.37.130.111 and 216.120.69.197. At the right edge of the window, you can see part of the URL stem for the web resource associated with each hit. The screen depicts several other fields for hit data.

Database consultants tackling log file analysis for small and medium-sized businesses will typically perform two steps as they import a log file to SQL Server. First, they will use ftp or another protocol to move the log file for a date from a web server to another computer with SQL Server for analysis. Second, they will import the text file into SQL Server. The Data Transformation Services Wizard is a user-friendly tool for importing the log file into SQL Server.

Analyzing a Log File Database

Rather than take you through the process of importing the log file into a SQL Server database using the Data Transformation Services, we're assuming that you've got the log files imported into a database, and are using the logfiles.mdf database available to download from the Wrox site, along with the logfiles.ldf file. The logfiles database contains two tables, and some other objects we'll see later. These tables are called session_changes and ex000501, and contain all the data from the log file for the web site.

The following screen shows an excerpt from the ex000501 table. The table's status bar reveals that the table contains 3200 rows. The screenshot rearranges the table's columns to display the fields we will be using most often in this appendix. Some of the fields we will be using are the date, time, client IP address (c-ip), and stem of the URL for the visited resource (cs-uri-stem). The analysis in this appendix works with these important columns. Note that for simplicity we are using single sites in the cs-uri-stem field. A log file may have multiple sites listed in this field and if the log came from an IIS 5 server the default directories/log file sites will be different. The table contains 20 columns in total.

Analyzing Log Files with Views

We can gain a basic understanding of site behavior by analyzing this table. For example, the following view, named unique_visitors, returns the unique IP client addresses to a site. This captures the unique visitors to a site. The IP number is what uniquely identifies the local machine from where the user is logging in.

```
SELECT DISTINCT [c-ip]
FROM ex000501
```

An IP address can occur multiple times within and between sessions. For example, the ex000501 table contains separate rows for each hit. A single viewing of a web page may involve multiple hits for the web page file, as well as image and script files associated with the web page. Each of these hits shows the client's IP address. As IP addresses repeat for multiple hits with a single page view as well as views of multiple pages within a session, we must use the DISTINCT keyword in the SELECT statement to list the unique visitors to a site. We then invoke a COUNT aggregate function to the preceding view to total the number of unique visitors to a site. The following T-SQL statement presents the T-SQL for that view, called unique_visitors_count. It returns a single value with the total number of unique visitors to the web site in the day covered by the log file. Notice that it builds on the return set from the preceding view.

```
SELECT COUNT([c-ip]) AS [Total Unique Visitors]
FROM unique_visitors
```

Another especially useful view is one that returns the total number of views for each page. This view is also available in the logfiles database, called views_by_page. We can base page views on hits for pages. For example, web pages can have the extensions .htm and .html as well as .asp. In addition, a visitor can navigate a browser to the default page for the site or one of its directories. The following T-SQL statement shows the syntax for counting the views per web page in a log file. By capturing the rightmost three characters of the cs-uri-stem field, the statement filters hits just for web pages or to the default page for a directory, including the root directory for the web site.

```
SELECT [cs-uri-stem] AS Pages, COUNT(*) AS Views
FROM ex000501
GROUP BY [cs-uri-stem]
HAVING (RIGHT([cs-uri-stem], 3) = 'htm') OR
    (RIGHT([cs-uri-stem], 3) = 'asp') OR
    (RIGHT([cs-uri-stem], 3) = 'tml') OR
    (RIGHT([cs-uri-stem], 3) LIKE '%%/')
```

For ease of understanding, we may prefer to label the Views column as Hits. As we can see in the following excerpt from the view, the return set has a limitation characteristic of views: it does not show its return set sorted. Recall that users can manually perform the sort with toolbar buttons in Datasheet view, but sometimes an application calls for initially presenting items sorted by a specific rule. Reports based on views can use their internal sorting capabilities to rearrange the order in which rows appear in a return set. Our log file analyses can take advantage of this feature to return pages in descending order based on the number of hits.

Enumerating Sessions with a VBA Procedure

Visitors can interact with the web server for a site at multiple times within a day. In one sense, each hit to the site is unique, or we can configure our server to group hits together from the same IP address within a certain time frame. For example, we can group hits within 20 minutes of the last hit from the same IP address as belonging to the same session from that IP address. With these criteria in mind, we need just two columns from the ex000501 table to enumerate a list of sessions. These columns are the c-ip and time columns. Values from the c-ip column designate the IP addresses making hits on a web site. The time column returns the hour, minutes and second during which hits occur. A high hit rate for a single IP address often indicates access to the sited from a corporate firewall using NAT or a proxy server.

The log signals the potential start of a new session and end of an existing session whenever the c-ip column value changes. However, the transition from one IP to another does not guarantee the start of a new session. If that new IP address is the initial instance of the address in the log, then it clearly signals a new session. If the IP address for a record is not new, then the instance can designate a new potential ending time for a session or the start of a new session. If the time for a hit is within 20 minutes of the last hit from an IP address, then that hit refreshes the ending time for a session. If the hit is longer than 20 minutes from the last hit by that IP address, then it designates the beginning of a new session. We will also have a problem with ISP's like AOL where we'll get a number of IP addresses from the same person.

While a web server can maintain concurrent sessions, each session has just one immediately preceding session in the log file. Our sample application tracks sessions from the last hit for the immediately preceding session to the last hit from the current session. The difference between the first time for a session and the last time for that same session defines the duration of that session. The last time for the initial session is also the first time for the second session. Similarly, the last time for the second session is the beginning of the third session. The sample application demonstrates how to use these relationships to compute the duration of any session in a log file.Due to the complex nature of the events defining a session, we need to create a table to track sessions and populate its values with a VBA procedure. The sample for this section uses a table named session_changes with five columns. The first two columns are the IP addresses for the immediately preceding session to the current session and the current session. These column names are strlastip and strthisip, respectively. The second pair of column contains the times for the final hits to both sessions. These columns, named lasttime and thistime, have a Datetime data type. The fifth column is a number denoting the sequence in which sessions start.

Both the ex000501 and session_changes tables are available in the logfiles database to which the logfiles.adp file connects. These are sample materials for this Appendix. We can create the session_changes table graphically, but it includes a primary key and a couple of indexes. The following T-SQL script succinctly describes the design for the session_changes table. We can run this as is from Query Analyzer or we can run it from an Access stored procedure template after removing the GO keywords. The GO keywords are used in SQL Server to start the execution of T-SQL commands. This does the same thing as running a stored procedure in Access, so we don't need to include the GO in Access. This T-SQL is also available, suitably edited, as a stored procedure called create_session_changes in the logfiles.adp Access project.

```
if exists (select * from sysobjects
    where id = object_id(N'[dbo].[session_changes]')
    and OBJECTPROPERTY(id, N'IsUserTable') = 1)
drop table [dbo].[session_changes]
GO
```

```
CREATE TABLE [dbo].[session_changes] (
    [strlastip] [varchar] (255) NOT NULL ,
    [strthisip] [varchar] (255) NOT NULL ,
    [lasttime] [datetime] NOT NULL ,
    [thistime] [datetime] NOT NULL ,
    [intsession_count] [int] NOT NULL
)
GO


ALTER TABLE [dbo].[session_changes] WITH NOCHECK ADD
    CONSTRAINT [PK_indx_session_changes] UNIQUE  CLUSTERED
    (
        [intsession_count]
    ) ON [PRIMARY]
GO


CREATE  INDEX [indx_thistime] ON [dbo].[session_changes]([thistime]) ON [PRIMARY]
GO


CREATE  INDEX [indx_strthisip] ON [dbo].[session_changes]([strthisip]) ON
[PRIMARY]
GO
```

The following VBA procedure populates the five columns of the session_changes table. We can run this from a module in the logfiles Access project, and indeed there is a module already containing this procedure in logfiles.adp. The procedure uses three Recordsets which it instantiates at the beginning of the procedure.

The first Recordset (rst1) links to a view that contains just the c-ip and time columns from the ex000501 table. The name of the view is sequential_visitor_ips_hits, which can be found in the sample logfiles database.

The second Recordset (rst2) connects to the session_changes table. The procedure uses this recordset to add new sessions to the table.

The third Recordset (rst3) is a utility recordset that serves two different purposes.

❑   First, the procedure uses this Recordset to initially clear the session_changes table of any existing records before populating it with new records from the log file.

❑   Second, the third Recordset helps to find the most recent previous hit from an IP address.

```
Sub enumerate_sessions_from_log_file()
Dim rst1 As ADODB.Recordset
Dim strlastip As String
Dim strthisip As String
Dim lasttime As Date
Dim thistime As Date
Dim i As Long
Dim intsession_count As Long
Dim rst2 As ADODB.Recordset
Dim rst3 As ADODB.Recordset
Dim str1 As String
```

```
'Instantiate recordset for log file
Set rst1 = New ADODB.Recordset
rst1.ActiveConnection = CurrentProject.Connection
rst1.Open "sequential_visitor_ips_hits"

'Instantiate recordset to store a history of sessions
Set rst2 = New ADODB.Recordset
rst2.ActiveConnection = CurrentProject.Connection
rst2.CursorType = adOpenKeyset
rst2.LockType = adLockOptimistic
rst2.Open "session_changes"

'Instantiate working recordset
'before starting clear session_changes
Set rst3 = New ADODB.Recordset
rst3.ActiveConnection = CurrentProject.Connection
rst3.CursorType = adOpenKeyset
rst3.LockType = adLockOptimistic
rst3.Open "DELETE FROM session_changes"

'Initialize local variables for first record in
'log file with ip address and time
'also initialize session counter variable
strlastip = rst1(0)
strthisip = strlastip
lasttime = rst1(1)
thistime = lasttime
intsession_count = 0

'Move to second record in log file
rst1.MoveNext

'Start a loop through all records in the log file
For i = 1 To rst1.RecordCount - 1

'If ip address changes in log file it could signal
'the beginning of a new session; search session_changes
'for the last previous incident of the ip address
   If rst1(0) <> strthisip Then
      strlastip = strthisip
      strthisip = rst1(0)
      lasttime = thistime
      thistime = rst1(1)
      str1 = "SELECT MAX(thistime) AS thistime_from_db " & _
          "FROM session_changes GROUP BY strthisip " & _
          "HAVING (strthisip = '" & strthisip & "')"
      rst3.Open str1

'If there is no prior instance of the ip address,
'add the new ip address
      If rst3.EOF Then
         intsession_count = intsession_count + 1
         rst2.AddNew
            rst2("strlastip") = strlastip
            rst2("strthisip") = strthisip
            rst2("lasttime") = lasttime
```

```
                rst2("thistime") = thistime
                rst2("intsession_count") = intsession_count
            rst2.Update

    'If there is a prior instance of the ip address from more than
    '20 minutes ago, add the ip address as a new session
            ElseIf DateDiff("n", rst3("thistime_from_db"), thistime) > 20 Then
                intsession_count = intsession_count + 1
                rst2.AddNew
                    rst2("strlastip") = strlastip
                    rst2("strthisip") = strthisip
                    rst2("lasttime") = lasttime
                    rst2("thistime") = thistime
                    rst2("intsession_count") = intsession_count
                rst2.Update

    'If there was a prior instance within the past 20 minutes,
    'update the prior instance
            Else
                strmaxthistime = rst3("thistime_from_db")
                rst3.Close
                str1 = "SELECT TOP 1 * FROM session_changes " & _
                    "WHERE (strthisip = '" & strthisip & "') " & _
                    "ORDER BY thistime DESC"
                rst3.Open str1
                rst3("strthisip") = strthisip
                rst3("thistime") = thistime
                rst3.Update
            End If
        rst3.Close
        End If
    rst1.MoveNext
    Next i

End Sub
```

After instantiating the `Recordsets`, the procedure performs some preliminary processing to prime the `session_changes` table with an initial set of values and positions `rst1` at the second hit. Next, the procedure starts a `For` loop that cycles through all the records in the log file `Recordset`. This `Recordset` contains a row for each hit to a web site. Recall that each row contains just the IP address and time for a hit. These are the values we need to populate the first four columns of the `session_changes` table. The `intsession_count` variable and column hold the unique number for each session.

A pair of nested `If` statements within the loop examine each record in `rst1` to determine if it starts a new record, updates the end time for an existing record, or does not need processing. Only records that have a different IP address from the IP address for the current session (`strthisip`) require processing. The outer `If` statement detects these transitions.

When an IP address changes, the hit can mark the beginning of a new session in either of two cases, or the update of a prior session in a third case:

❑   First, if the new IP address is not already in the strthisip column of session_changes, then it clearly denotes a new session for the IP address.

749

❏ Second, if the address is already in the strthisip column, but the last hit was more than 20 minutes ago, it also denotes a new session.

❏ Third, if the transition does not mark a new session, then it at least identifies an update to an existing session end time.

The inner If statement detects one of these three scenarios. If either the If or ElseIf conditions is True, the procedure adds a record to the session_changes table. If neither of these conditions are True, the procedure revises the end time for the most recent record in the session_changes table matching the c-ip column in the sequential_visitor_ips_hits view. This view serves as the record source for the rst1 recordset.

The following screen presents an excerpt of the output to the session_changes table from the preceding VBA procedure. A transition from the 12.37.130.111 to 216.120.69.197 IP addresses marks the first session. This session started at 12:10:04 AM and concluded at 12:12:55 AM. The next two sessions happen sequentially and run from 12:12:55 AM through 12:16:15 AM and 12:16:15 AM through 12:20:01 AM, respectively. These sessions are for IP addresses 216.120.69.197 and 38.28.3.160.

strlastip	strthisip	lasttime	thistime	intsession_count
12.37.130.111	216.120.69.197	12:10:04 AM	12:12:55 AM	1
216.120.69.197	38.28.3.160	12:12:55 AM	12:16:15 AM	2
38.28.3.160	203.101.127.50	12:16:15 AM	12:20:01 AM	3
203.101.127.50	24.200.44.175	12:20:01 AM	12:44:58 AM	4
24.200.44.175	209.156.146.213	12:39:36 AM	12:43:48 AM	5
24.200.44.175	24.13.106.244	12:44:58 AM	12:47:27 AM	6

The fourth session is for the 203.101.127.50 IP address: before its session ends at 12:44:58 AM, another session starts at 12:39:36 AM. This session is for IP address 24.200.44.175, and it ends before the conclusion of the session for IP address 203.101.127.50. The conclusion of that session marks the opening of a new session for IP address 24.13.106.244.

Creating Reports for Log Files

The following three sample reports will show us how to perform aggregations of data with Access report sections, which will help when analyzing log files. Many readers of this book will be more familiar with Access report writing than T-SQL syntax for creating custom views. Therefore, the capability to perform log file analyses with Access report sessions can be an attractive option. This section also examines two different approaches to grouping data on an hourly basis.

Creating a Report to Show Session Changes

In this example we will be using the session_changes table to base our report on. Start the AutoReport wizard by selecting Reports in the Objects bar and clicking New on the Database Window. This opens the New Report dialog that exposes AutoReport: Tabular as an option. If we select this option, we must specify a source before we can click the OK button on the dialog. Click the drop-down arrow for the control below the box listing options for creating a report. This drop-down arrow will automatically expose all tables and views in the database to which our Access project connects. This list doesn't distinguish tables from views, a good reason to name our database objects consistently with a scheme that identifies what they are. Select session_changes as our source and click OK to have the wizard generate a tabular report in landscape mode for us. The following New Report dialog shows the settings for creating a default report based on the session_changes table from the logfiles database. Clicking OK will generate a draft of the report.

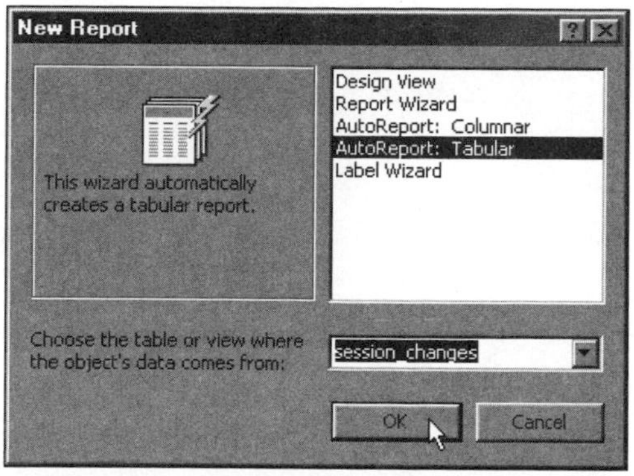

The following screenshot displays the report in **Print Preview** mode. We may find that the formatting on our report appears slightly differently – the numbers in the intsession_count column may be blue and underlined. The wizard automatically opens the report in **Print Preview** mode. The report spreads column labels across the top of the report in the order that they appear in the data source definition. Column labels appear in the **Page Header** section, so that each page of the report starts with the column headings. If there are more labels than the wizard can fit on one page, it continues on to subsequent pages until it enumerates all the columns in the report's data source. The wizard automatically assigns a report title with the name of the data source. The label holding the report's title is in the **Report Header** section. Therefore, this label appears just once at the beginning of the report on the report's first page. The **Detail** section includes a text box for each field in the underlying data source for the report. These text boxes populate the pages of the report until there are no more records to display. The data for a record spreads across pages in a layout that follows the arrangement of the report's column headings. The wizard automatically adds a date stamp and a page indicator for each page in a report. This content appears in text boxes in the report's **Page Footer** section.

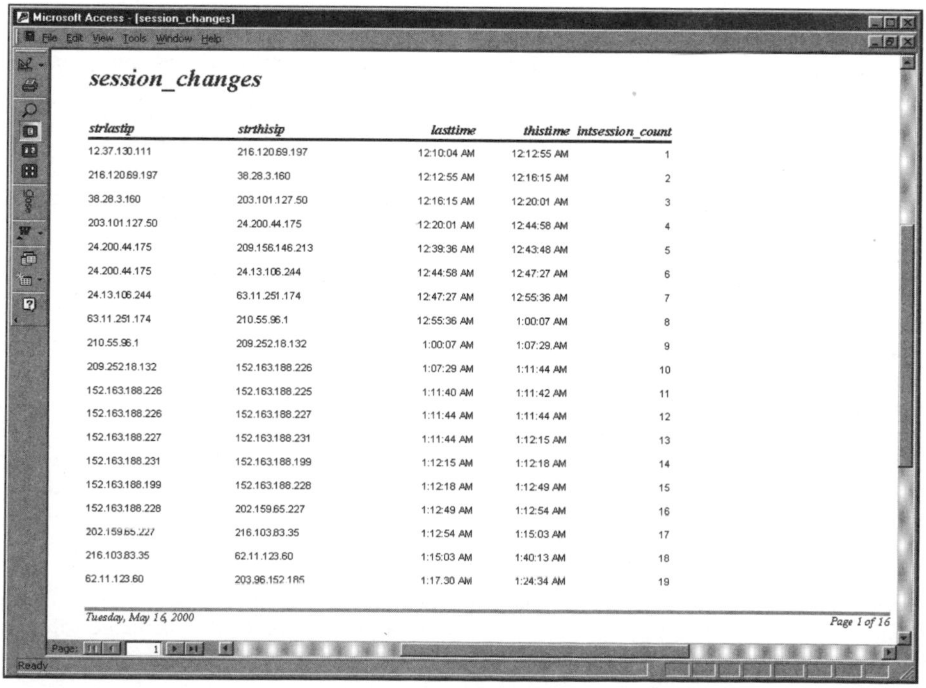

The next screenshot presents a pair of reports in Design view. The top panel presents the Design view for the preceding report, named rptsession_changes_1 in the logfiles.adp. The bottom panel presents a modified version of this report, named rptsession_changes_2 in the logfiles.adp. The report in the bottom panel makes a series of design changes from the top panel report that make the report easier to view and more meaningful to users.

The initial report for the session_changes table lays out controls for columns in the same order as they appear in the underlying table. In addition, the initial report lays out all the columns in the underlying data source. Neither of these conditions is likely to be appropriate for many custom reports.

The bottom panel shows a modified version of the initial report based on the session_changes table. In particular, it leaves out the intsession_count column, and it rearranges the remaining columns so that the beginning time for a session associated with an IP address appears next to that address. We can accomplish this kind of design update by dragging text boxes and labels around a report. The Format menu is our friend when we are performing this kind of chore. In particular, we are likely to get a lot of use from the Format | Align and Format | Size commands on the Report Design menu, which will automatically align a selection of objects for us. If we hold the *Shift* button down as we click on multiple text boxes and labels, we can select them all. Any commands we issue while they are all selected will be applied to all of them.

The labels contain column titles, and appear in the Page Header area. The text boxes display actual values from their underlying sources, and are in the report's Detail section. The labels for the lasttime column and the strthisip column were swapped around, as were their corresponding text boxes. In particular, the Text Align property is set to Right for all the labels serving as column headings. The two text boxes for IP addresses also have the Text Align property set to Right. These IP addresses appear as four-part number sequences, but SQL Server saves them as VARCHAR data types. The text boxes for the Datetime fields automatically right align. The report updates also revise the contents of the label holding the report's title. This change does not alter its default left alignment. The specific Text Align property setting for the control is actually General. This varies according to the data type. As you have seen, dates and times automatically align to the right, while labels automatically align left.

A third report for the session_changes table (rptsession_changes_3) takes advantage of the design improvements from the second version as it adds an unbound text box with a calculated value. The calculation shows the duration in seconds for the strlastip sessions based on the difference between the beginning time for the **strlastip** session minus the beginning time for the **strthisip** session. The report is less crowded because there are fewer rows per page. We can accomplish this by adding more space between each line; to do this, we drag the bottom border of the **Detail** section to make it taller. In any event, this report includes 19 pages instead of the 16 pages in the initial version of the report. If we altered the page orientation for this report, from landscape to portrait, we could make the report fit on less pages. We could maintain the space between the lines, but still save paper. Of course, if we were to alter the orientation of the page after we've generated the report we could find that parts of the report stretch pointlessly onto a second sheet. If we drag the right-hand edge of the report background in **Design** view, we can change the width of the report.

The `Control Source` property setting for the **Duration (sec)** text box uses the `DateDiff` function with the SQL Server **lasttime** and **thistime** fields. The syntax follows VBA as opposed to T-SQL conventions. For example, we can represent the duration for a session with the following expression. Notice the designation of the basis for computing a difference is in quotes – it is `"s"` for seconds. T-SQL syntax does not require the date part in quotes. Use the expression as the `Control Source` property setting for an unbound text box.

```
=DateDiff("s",TimeValue([lasttime]),TimeValue([thistime]))
```

This general approach works for any situation where we have to compute a value for each row in a report. By default, Access construes an argument's name as referring to a SQL Server column value as opposed to a control value. This is potentially confusing if the control and column have the same name. This is why it is good practice to have naming conventions that make it easy to identify data types. For example, starting all text variables with `txt`, or starting all string variables with `str`.

Sorting a View and Computing Aggregates

It is exceptionally easy to sort Access reports by one or more fields. Since Access reports can readily use views from SQL Server databases as the record source, reports can readily compensate for the inability of views to sort data automatically. The views_by_page view from earlier in the Appendix sums the hits to all web page resources at a web site. However, the view cannot ensure the presentation of the results in descending or ascending order. An Access report based on the views_by_page view can readily present the pages listed in ascending or descending order by the count of the views per page. Beyond that, our application gains all the formatting advantages associated with Access reports when we present a view via a report.

The following screen presents the first page from a report based on the views_by_page view. The view's return set appears in descending order according to Views value. This makes it easy for a site-planning analyst or marketing analyst to tell which pages are most popular with users.

Microsoft Access - [views_by_page]	
Pages	Views
/Default.htm	169
/Samples/Default.htm	112
/Samples/VBAProcs/vba_code_sample_menu.htm	76
/Contests/default.htm	76
/Access2000Seminar/default.htm	55
/FAQs/default.htm	34
/Samples/telelookup.asp	27
/The+Book/default.htm	26
/Samples/vba_code_sample_menu.htm	23
/Contests/EZDeveloperSuite.htm	18
/The+Book/ADOExcerpt/ADO+Overview.htm	17
/Samples/telereturn.asp	16
/IWLA99/default.htm	16
/Snapshots/default.htm	13
/Favorites.htm	13
/Presentations/SnapshotTutorialIE_files/outline.htm	12
/IWLA99/shippers.asp	11
/Samples/VBAProcs/VBAProcToOpenAView.htm	11
/Presentations/default.htm	10
/FAQs/SQLServer.htm	10
/The+Book/TOC.htm	9

Tuesday, May 16, 2000   Page 1 of 6

It is amazingly easy to sort the return set from the view. We can generate a report with the AutoReport: Tabular Wizard. This creates a report in tabular format with no sorting. Before we save the report created by the wizard, we'll open it in Design view. Then, we click the Sorting and Grouping control on the Report Design toolbar. From the Sorting and Grouping dialog, we click the drop-down arrow under Field/Expression. We highlight Views, which is the name of the column containing the page view counts. On the same row, we then click the drop-down arrow in the Sort Order column, and select Descending. Then, when we open the report in Print Preview mode, the report shows the web pages in descending order.

The following screenshot depicts the Sorting and Grouping dialog completed for the preceding report. We can see the Sorting and Grouping control highlighted on the Report Design toolbar. These two minor changes are all we need to create the sorted report of pages by views. If our application needs to sort by the values in more than one column, we can select those column names in the Field/Expression column of the Sorting and Grouping dialog along with a sort order for each successive sort field.

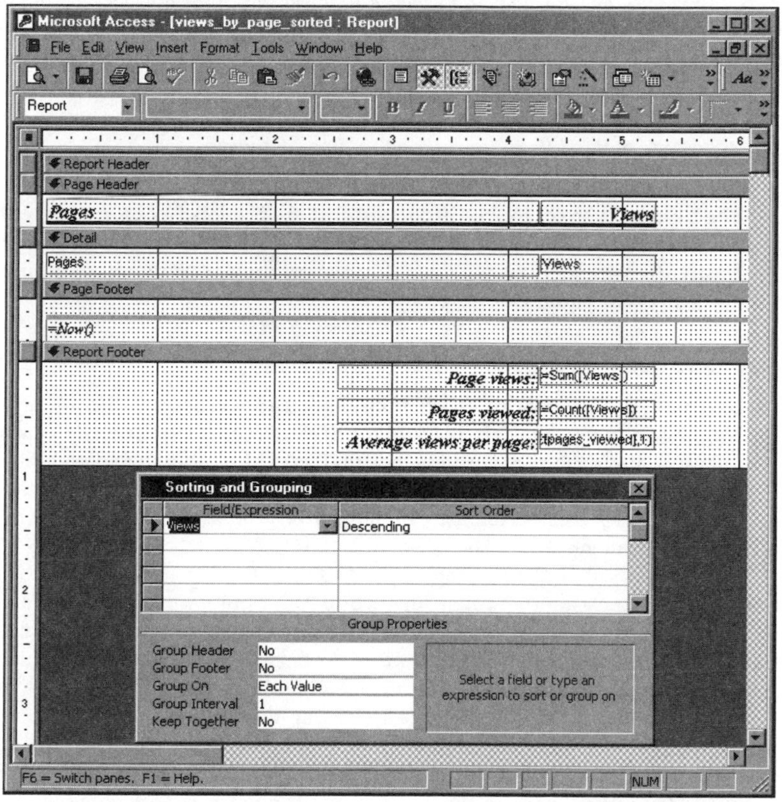

As we can see, we've added three extras to our report in the Report Footer section. These are: counts of the number of page views, the number of pages viewed, and an average number of viewings per page. Now we are going to add the aggregate functions: Page Views, Pages Viewed, and Average Veiws per page to our report.

The top text box in the Report Footer section sums the values in the Views column of the views_by_page view; it does this by applying the Sum function to the Views column.

The next text box counts the number of rows in the view underlying the report; it does this by applying the Count function to the Views column.

The last text box computes the average views per page, rounded to the first place after the decimal. It derives this result with the following expression, which we assign to the Control Source property for the bottom text box in the Report Footer section.

```
=Round([txtpage_views]/[txtpages_viewed],1)
```

The arguments for the `Control Source` in the bottom text box do not reference the underlying view for the record source. Instead, it derives its results indirectly from the view by computing the ratio of the values for two text boxes. The names txtpage_views and txtpages_viewed reference the first and second text boxes, respectively, in the Report Footer section.

While we made this point before, it is important enough to repeat. Access wizards for reports and forms assign names for text box controls that are identical to their underlying data source. Therefore, the name of a text box based on the Views column is Views. By default, Access will use the underlying field value instead of the control value when our application has an expression on a report that refers to Views. If we want to explicitly reference the control value like we do in this example, assign a name to the control, such as txtpage_views, that is different from the underlying data source.

The positioning of the three text boxes in the Report Footer section lets Access compute the aggregations for all rows in the underlying view. We can have Access sum and count across custom groupings of the data as the next example illustrates. This finer level of detail for our computations requires nothing more than positioning unbound text boxes within custom groups.

Aggregating for Custom Groups

The Sorting and Grouping dialog supports the definition of custom groups within a report. This can be very convenient for developing subtotals. This kind of tool for SQL Server is exceptional because it permits the graphical design of complicated reports against enterprise data. This ability to generate many different report styles easily and quickly has always been an Access hallmark. The improved data definition and connectivity that Access projects have for SQL Server databases relative to earlier versions multiplies the value that Access reports can deliver to organizations.

The following screenshot portrays another report (rptgroup_by_hour_with_thistime) based on the session_changes table. This version includes custom groups of hour intervals, based on thistime column values. Recall that the thistime column marks the end of the session with the strlastip value on a row. The Sorting and Grouping dialog appears in the lower right corner of the display. It shows that the thistime column serves as a sorting column, but it also serves as a grouping column.

The selection of Yes for the Group Footer property for the thistime column makes it a value for grouping records. The Group Footer assignment also opens a new section in the report from which we can display custom summary results. Access automatically detects the data type of column values selected for grouping and varies the options that it offers for forming groups based on a column. In the case of the `Datetime` data type, Access permits grouping based on year, quarter, month, week, day, hour, and minute. We can select a grouping factor from a drop-down arrow in the `Group On` box. Using the `Group Interval`, we can specify blocks of a grouping factor. For example, if we chose Hour for `Group On` and 6 for `Group Interval`, our report would return data grouped into 4 day-parts. Leaving the `Group Interval` at its default value of 1 causes Access to create a report that groups data into 24 day-parts.

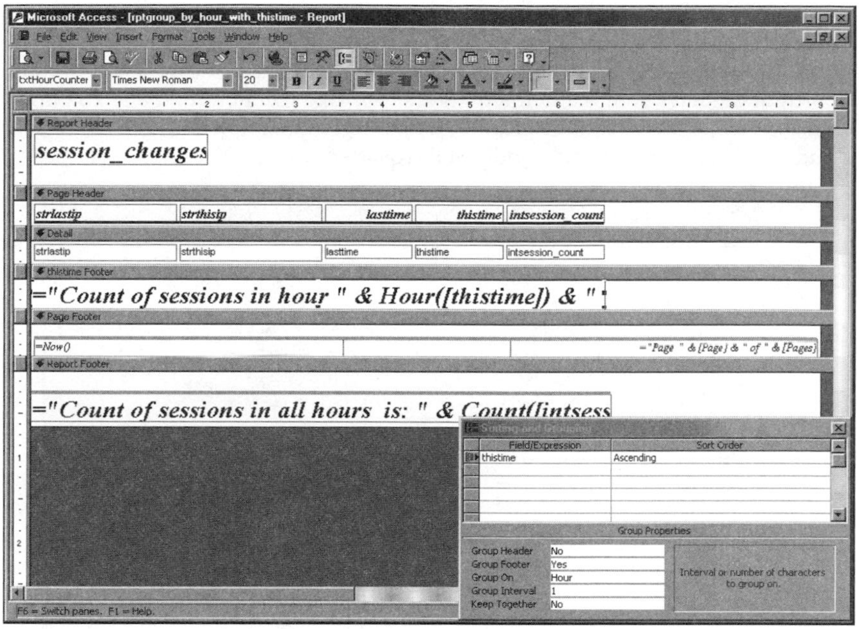

The preceding report Design view also shows two text boxes in footer sections. These show the counts for sessions in an hour group, and total sessions in the report. The first of these is in the custom thistime Footer section. This appears after the Detail section and before the Page Footer section in Design view. The second text box is in the Report Footer section.

Both of these text boxes contain expressions for counting the intsession_count column values. However, the Count aggregate function behaves differently in the thistime Footer section from in the Report Footer section. In the thistime Footer section, the aggregate function counts the records within hourly groups. In the Report Footer section, the function counts the instances of intsession_count across all groups.

The expression for the Control Source property of the thistime Footer text box is:

```
="Count of sessions in hour " & Hour([thistime]) & " is: " &
Count([intsession_count])
```

This expression concatenates string constants, a time function based on a serial number, and an aggregate function based on a column from the Record Source property for the report. Access converts the SQL Server Datetime data type for thistime column values to Access serial numbers. The Hour([thistime]) function in the expression returns the hour value from the thistime column for the last row in a group.

The text box in the Report Footer section has a slightly different expression as its Control Source property, as shown below. Nevertheless, both expressions concatenate the Count aggregate function for the intsession_count column with a string constant. However, the aggregate function in the Report Footer section returns the total number of sessions for the log file, while the aggregate function within the thistime Footer section returns the count of sessions within a particular hour.

```
="Count of sessions in all hours is: " & Count([intsession_count])
```

The following screen presents an excerpt from the report defined by the preceding report specification. Notice that it includes just three records in the first hourly group. These are all sessions finishing before 12:29:59 AM. Records with thistime values after that time count in the second hourly group. This grouping rule splits records into hourly groups, but the splits are from one half hour to the next. Other grouping functions do not work this way. For example, the quarterly grouping function collects data for a group through the end of the quarter – not the middle of the quarter.

session_changes

strlastip	strthisip	lasttime	thistime	intsession_count
12.37.130.111	216.120.69.197	12:10:04 AM	12:12:55 AM	1
216.120.69.197	38.28.3.160	12:12:55 AM	12:16:15 AM	2
38.28.3.160	203.101.127.50	12:16:15 AM	12:20:01 AM	3
Count of sessions in hour 0 is: 3				
203.101.127.50	24.200.44.175	12:20:01 AM	12:44:58 AM	4
24.200.44.175	209.156.146.213	12:39:36 AM	12:43:48 AM	5
24.200.44.175	24.13.106.244	12:44:58 AM	12:47:27 AM	6
24.13.106.244	63.11.251.174	12:47:27 AM	12:55:36 AM	7
63.11.251.174	210.55.96.1	12:55:36 AM	1:00:07 AM	8
210.55.96.1	209.252.18.132	1:00:07 AM	1:07:29 AM	9
209.252.18.132	152.163.188.226	1:07:29 AM	1:11:44 AM	10
152.163.188.226	152.163.188.225	1:11:40 AM	1:11:42 AM	11
152.163.188.226	152.163.188.227	1:11:44 AM	1:11:44 AM	12
152.163.188.227	152.163.188.231	1:11:44 AM	1:12:15 AM	13
152.163.188.231	152.163.188.199	1:12:15 AM	1:12:18 AM	14
152.163.188.199	152.163.188.228	1:12:18 AM	1:12:49 AM	15
152.163.188.228	202.159.65.227	1:12:49 AM	1:12:54 AM	16
202.159.65.227	216.103.83.35	1:12:54 AM	1:15:03 AM	17

Tuesday, May 16, 2000

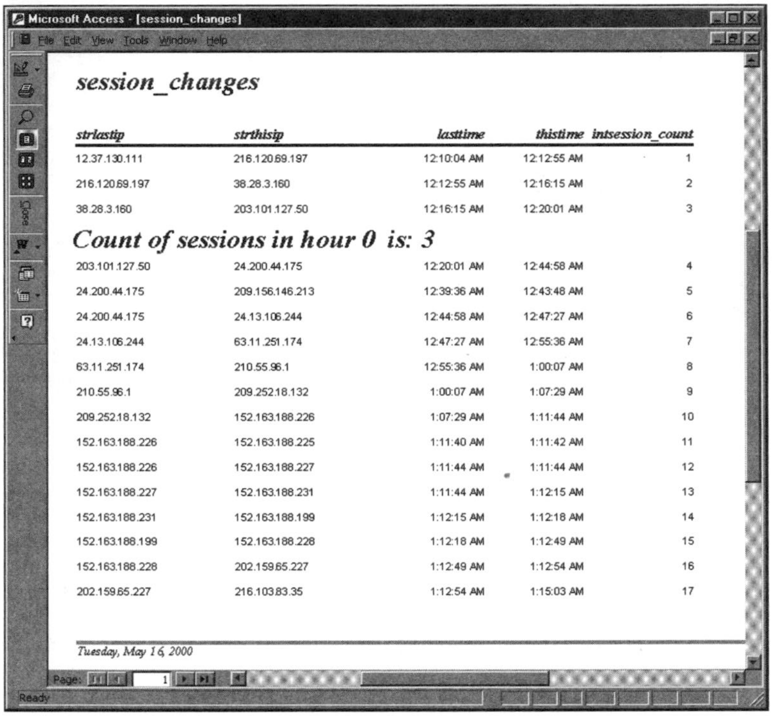

The problem with the half-hour splits derives from the way Access and SQL Server represent time as a fraction. By contrast, the days in a quarter are whole integer numbers. An Access report can pass integer hourly numbers to the grouping function by using the `DatePart` function on the thistime column values to define a new column. We can develop a T-SQL statement with the extra column directly from the preceding report. We should be in Design view, and then bring up the Properties dialog. From here, we click the Query Builder button next to the `Record Source` property for the report. Rather than specify the session_changes table as the Record Source for the report, we instead specify a T-SQL statement. This T-SQL statement, which appears below, creates a new column from the table for the report to us. This column extracts the hour from the thistime column as an integer. The `DatePart` function with an `hh` argument can achieve this result:

```
SELECT *, DATEPART(hh, thistime) AS Hour
FROM session_changes
```

The following screenshot shows the report based on the new T-SQL statement. Notice that it displays an extra column named Hour. We'll have to manually add this column to the report, although the sample shows it for tutorial purposes. The sample report in the database does not show the Hour field. We are using the screenshot as an illustration for the example. If we choose not to display the Hour column in our report, we can still make use of it as a base for the grouping. Recall that aggregate functions refer back to fields in the record source for a report – they do not depend on a field appearing in a text box. The main point to note is that grouping occurs on the hour – instead of the half-hour as in the previous report. Below the screenshot is the `Control Source` property statement for the grouping shown in the screenshot.

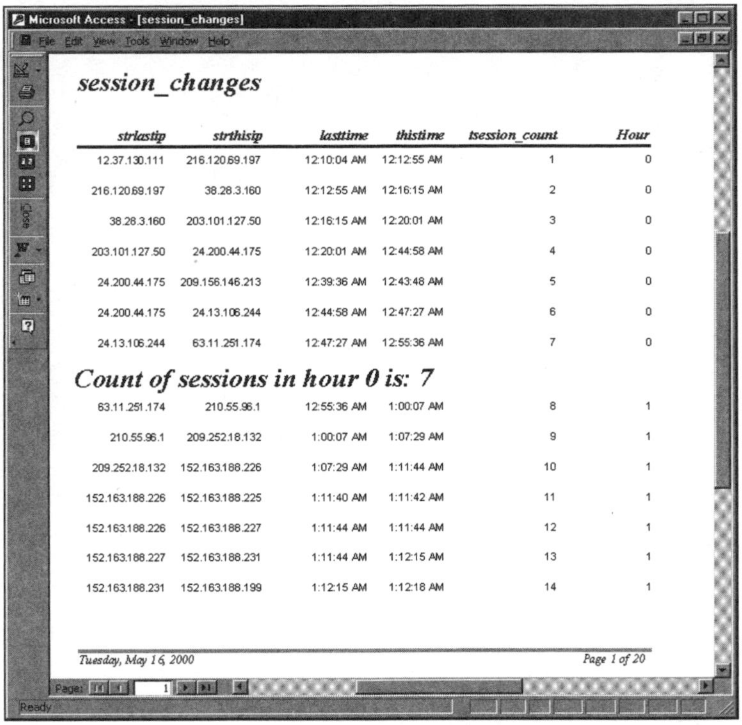

Here is the `Control Source` property expression for the new report with grouping by hours:

```
="Count of sessions in hour " & [Hour] & " is: " & Count([intsession_count])
```

We also have to set the Sorting and Grouping dialog to group on the Hour column. Because the Hour column has integer contents, the Grouping and Sorting dialog appears a little different, as shown in the screenshot on the right:

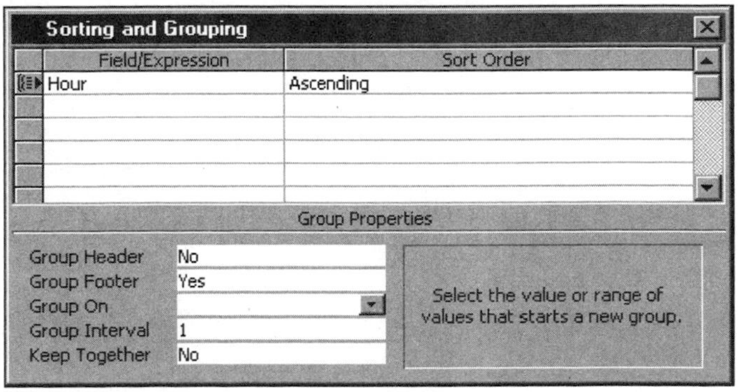

Summary

In this appendix we have covered how to create reports that we can use to help analyze web log files. We have covered topics such as sorting and computing aggregates, aggregating for custom groups, and enumerating sessions with VBA procedures.

ADO 2.1 Object Model

All properties are read/write unless otherwise stated.

Objects

Name	Description
Command	A Command object is a definition of a specific command that you intend to execute against a data source.
Connection	A Connection object represents an open connection to a data store.
Error	An Error object contains the details about data access errors pertaining to a single operation involving the provider.
Errors	The Errors collection contains all of the Error objects created in response to a single failure involving the provider.
Field	A Field object represents a column of data within a common data type.
Fields	A Fields collection contains all of the Field objects of a Recordset object.
Parameter	A Parameter object represents a parameter or argument associated with a Command object based on a parameterized query or stored procedure.

Table continued on following page

Name	Description
Parameters	A Parameters collection contains all the Parameter objects of a Command object.
Properties	A Properties collection contains all the Property objects for a specific instance of an object.
Property	A Property object represents a dynamic characteristic of an ADO object that is defined by the provider.
Recordset	A Recordset object represents the entire set of records from a base table or the results of an executed command. At any time, the Recordset object only refers to a single record within the set as the current record.

Command Object

Methods

Name	Returns	Description
Cancel		Cancels execution of a pending Execute or Open call.
CreateParameter	Parameter	Creates a new Parameter object.
Execute	Recordset	Executes the query, SQL statement, or stored procedure specified in the CommandText property.

Properties

Name	Returns	Description
ActiveConnection	Variant	Indicates to which Connection object the command currently belongs.
CommandText	String	Contains the text of a command to be issued against a data provider.
CommandTimeout	Long	Indicates how long to wait, in seconds, while executing a command before terminating the command and generating an error. Default is 30.
CommandType	CommandTypeEnum	Indicates the type of Command object.
Name	String	Indicates the name of the Command object.
Parameters	Parameters	Contains all of the Parameter objects for a Command object.

Name	Returns	Description
Prepared	Boolean	Indicates whether or not to save a compiled version of a command before execution.
Properties	Properties	Contains all of the Property objects for a Command object.
State	Long	Describes whether the Command object is open or closed. Read-only.

Connection Object

Methods

Name	Returns	Description
BeginTrans	Integer	Begins a new transaction.
Cancel		Cancels the execution of a pending, asynchronous Execute or Open operation.
Close		Closes an open connection and any dependent objects.
CommitTrans		Saves any changes and ends the current transaction.
Execute	Recordset	Executes the query, SQL statement, stored procedure, or provider-specific text.
Open		Opens a connection to a data source, so that commands can be executed against it.
OpenSchema	Recordset	Obtains database schema information from the provider.
RollbackTrans		Cancels any changes made during the current transaction and ends the transaction.

Properties

Name	Returns	Description
Attributes	Long	Indicates one or more characteristics of a Connection object. Default is 0.
CommandTimeout	Long	Indicates how long, in seconds, to wait while executing a command before terminating the command and generating an error. The default is 30.

Table continued on following page

Name	Returns	Description
ConnectionString	String	Contains the information used to establish a connection to a data source.
ConnectionTimeout	Long	Indicates how long, in seconds, to wait while establishing a connection before terminating the attempt and generating an error. Default is 15.
CursorLocation	CursorLocationEnum	Sets or returns the location of the cursor engine.
DefaultDatabase	String	Indicates the default database for a Connection object.
Errors	Errors	Contains all of the Error objects created in response to a single failure involving the provider.
IsolationLevel	IsolationLevelEnum	Indicates the level of transaction isolation for a Connection object. Write-only.
Mode	ConnectModeEnum	Indicates the available permissions for modifying data in a Connection.
Properties	Properties	Contains all of the Property objects for a Connection object.
Provider	String	Indicates the name of the provider for a Connection object.
State	Long	Describes whether the Connection object is open or closed. Read-only.
Version	String	Indicates the ADO version number. Read-only.

Events

Name	Description
BeginTransComplete	Fired after a BeginTrans operation finishes executing.
CommitTransComplete	Fired after a CommitTrans operation finishes executing.
ConnectComplete	Fired after a connection starts.
Disconnect	Fired after a connection ends.
ExecuteComplete	Fired after a command has finished executing.
InfoMessage	Fired whenever a ConnectionEvent operation completes successfully and additional information is returned by the provider.
RollbackTransComplete	Fired after a RollbackTrans operation finishes executing.

Name	Description
WillConnect	Fired before a connection starts.
WillExecute	Fired before a pending command executes on the connection.

Error Object

Properties

Name	Returns	Description
Description	String	A description string associated with the error. Read-only.
HelpContext	Integer	Indicates the ContextID in the help file for the associated error. Read-only.
HelpFile	String	Indicates the name of the help file. Read-only.
NativeError	Long	Indicates the provider-specific error code for the associated error. Read-only.
Number	Long	Indicates the number that uniquely identifies an Error object. Read-only.
Source	String	Indicates the name of the object or application that originally generated the error. Read-only.
SQLState	String	Indicates the SQL state for a given Error object. It is a five-character string that follows the ANSI SQL standard. Read-only.

Errors Collection

Methods

Name	Returns	Description
Clear		Removes all of the Error objects from the Errors collection.
Refresh		Updates the Error objects with information from the provider.

Properties

Name	Returns	Description
Count	Long	Indicates the number of Error objects in the Errors collection. Read-only.

Table continued on following page

Name	Returns	Description
Item	Error	Allows indexing into the `Errors` collection to reference a specific `Error` object. Read-only.

Field Object

Methods

Name	Returns	Description
AppendChunk		Appends data to a large or binary `Field` object.
GetChunk	Variant	Returns all or a portion of the contents of a large or binary `Field` object.

Properties

Name	Returns	Description
ActualSize	Long	Indicates the actual length of a field's value. Read-only.
Attributes	Long	Indicates one or more characteristics of a `Field` object.
DataFormat	Variant	Write-only.
DefinedSize	Long	Indicates the defined size of the `Field` object. Write-only.
Name	String	Indicates the name of the `Field` object.
NumericScale	Byte	Indicates the scale of numeric values for the `Field` object. Write-only.
OriginalValue	Variant	Indicates the value of a `Field` object that existed in the record before any changes were made. Read-only.
Precision	Byte	Indicates the degree of precision for numeric values in the `Field` object. Read-only.
Properties	Properties	Contains all of the `Property` objects for a `Field` object.
Type	DataTypeEnum	Indicates the data type of the `Field` object.
UnderlyingValue	Variant	Indicates a `Field` object's current value in the database. Read-only.
Value	Variant	Indicates the value assigned to the `Field` object.

Fields Collection

Methods

Name	Returns	Description
Append		Appends a `Field` object to the `Fields` collection.
Delete		Deletes a `Field` object from the `Fields` collection.
Refresh		Updates the `Field` objects in the `Fields` collection.

Properties

Name	Returns	Description
Count	Long	Indicates the number of `Field` objects in the `Fields` collection. Read-only.
Item	Field	Allows indexing into the `Fields` collection to reference a specific `Field` object. Read-only.

Parameter Object

Methods

Name	Returns	Description
AppendChunk		Appends data to a large or binary `Parameter` object.

Properties

Name	Returns	Description
Attributes	Long	Indicates one or more characteristics of a `Parameter` object.
Direction	Parameter DirectionEnum	Indicates whether the `Parameter` object represents an input parameter, an output parameter, or both, or if the parameter is a return value from a stored procedure.
Name	String	Indicates the name of the `Parameter` object.
NumericScale	Byte	Indicates the scale of numeric values for the `Parameter` object.
Precision	Byte	Indicates the degree of precision for numeric values in the `Parameter` object.

Table continued on following page

Name	Returns	Description
Properties	Properties	Contains all of the Property objects for a Parameter object.
Size	Long	Indicates the maximum size, in bytes or characters, of a Parameter object.
Type	DataTypeEnum	Indicates the data type of the Parameter object.
Value	Variant	Indicates the value assigned to the Parameter object.

Parameters Collection

Methods

Name	Returns	Description
Append		Appends a Parameter object to the Parameters collection.
Delete		Deletes a Parameter object from the Parameters collection.
Refresh		Updates the Parameter objects in the Parameters collection.

Properties

Name	Returns	Description
Count	Long	Indicates the number of Parameter objects in the Parameters collection. Read-only.
Item	Parameter	Allows indexing into the Parameters collection to reference a specific Parameter object. Read-only.

Properties Collection

Methods

Name	Returns	Description
Refresh		Updates the Property objects in the Properties collection with the details from the provider.

Properties

Name	Returns	Description
Count	Long	Indicates the number of Property objects in the Properties collection. Read-only.
Item	Property	Allows indexing into the Properties collection to reference a specific Property object. Read-only.

Property Object

Properties

Name	Returns	Description
Attributes	Long	Indicates one or more characteristics of a Property object.
Name	String	Indicates the name of the Property object. Read-only.
Type	DataTypeEnum	Indicates the data type of the Property object.
Value	Variant	Indicates the value assigned to the Property object.

Recordset Object

Methods

Name	Returns	Description
AddNew		Creates a new record for an updateable Recordset object.
Cancel		Cancels execution of a pending asynchronous Open operation.
CancelBatch		Cancels a pending batch update.
CancelUpdate		Cancels any changes made to the current record, or to a new record prior to calling the Update method.
Clone	Recordset	Creates a duplicate Recordset object from an existing Recordset object.
Close		Closes the Recordset object and any dependent objects.
CompareBookmarks	CompareEnum	Compares two bookmarks and returns an indication of the relative values.

Table continued on following page

Name	Returns	Description
Delete		Deletes the current record or group of records.
Find		Searches the Recordset for a record that matches the specified criteria.
GetRows	Variant	Retrieves multiple records of a Recordset object into an array.
GetString	String	Returns a Recordset as a string.
Move		Moves the position of the current record in a Recordset.
MoveFirst		Moves the position of the current record to the first record in the Recordset.
MoveLast		Moves the position of the current record to the last record in the Recordset.
MoveNext		Moves the position of the current record to the next record in the Recordset.
MovePrevious		Moves the position of the current record to the previous record in the Recordset.
NextRecordset	Recordset	Clears the current Recordset object and returns the next Recordset by advancing through a series of commands.
Open		Opens a Recordset.
Requery		Updates the data in a Recordset object by re-executing the query on which the object is based.
Resync		Refreshes the data in the current Recordset object from the underlying database.
Save		Saves the Recordset to a file.
Seek		Searches the Index of a Recordset to locate a row that matches a value, and changes the current row to the found row. This feature is new to ADO 2.1.
Supports	Boolean	Determines whether a specified Recordset object supports particular functionality.
Update		Saves any changes made to the current Recordset object.
UpdateBatch		Writes all pending batch updates to disk.

Properties

Name	Returns	Description
AbsolutePage	PositionEnum	Specifies in which page the current record resides.
AbsolutePosition	PositionEnum	Specifies the ordinal position of a Recordset object's current record.
ActiveCommand	Object	Indicates the Command object that created the associated Recordset object. Read-only.
ActiveConnection	Variant	Indicates to which Connection object the specified Recordset object currently belongs.
BOF	Boolean	Indicates whether the current record is before the first record in a Recordset object. Read-only.
Bookmark	Variant	Returns a bookmark that uniquely identifies the current record in a Recordset object, or sets the current record to the record identified by a valid bookmark.
CacheSize	Long	Indicates the number of records from a Recordset object that are cached locally in memory.
CursorLocation	CursorLocation Enum	Sets or returns the location of the cursor engine.
CursorType	CursorTypeEnum	Indicates the type of cursor used in a Recordset object.
DataMember	String	Specifies the name of the data member to retrieve from the object referenced by the DataSource property. Write-only.
DataSource	Object	Specifies an object containing data to be represented as a Recordset object. Write-only.
EditMode	EditModeEnum	Indicates the editing status of the current record. Read-only.
EOF	Boolean	Indicates whether the current record is after the last record in a Recordset object. Read-only.
Fields	Fields	Contains all of the Field objects for the current Recordset object.
Filter	Variant	Indicates a filter for data in the Recordset.

Table continued on following page

Name	Returns	Description
Index	String	Indicates the name of the current Index for the Recordset. This property is new to ADO 2.1.
LockType	LockTypeEnum	Indicates the type of locks placed on records during editing.
MarshalOptions	MarshalOptions Enum	Indicates which records are to be marshaled back to the server.
MaxRecords	Long	Indicates the maximum number of records to return to a Recordset object from a query. Default is zero (no limit).
PageCount	Long	Indicates how many pages of data the Recordset object contains. Read-only.
PageSize	Long	Indicates how many records constitute one page in the Recordset.
Properties	Properties	Contains all of the Property objects for the current Recordset object.
RecordCount	Long	Indicates the current number of records in the Recordset object. Read-only.
Sort	String	Specifies one or more field names the Recordset is sorted on, and the direction of the sort.
Source	String	Indicates the source for the data in a Recordset object.
State	Long	Indicates whether the recordset is open, closed, or executing an asynchronous operation. Read-only.
Status	Integer	Indicates the status of the current record with respect to match updates or other bulk operations. Read-only.
StayInSync	Boolean	Indicates, in a hierarchical Recordset object, whether the parent row should change when the set of underlying child records changes. Read-only.

Events

Name	Description
EndOfRecordset	Fired when there is an attempt to move to a row past the end of the Recordset.
FetchComplete	Fired after all the records in an asynchronous operation have been retrieved into the Recordset.

Name	Description
FetchProgress	Fired periodically during a lengthy asynchronous operation, to report how many rows have currently been retrieved.
FieldChangeComplete	Fired after the value of one or more Field object has been changed.
MoveComplete	Fired after the current position in the Recordset changes.
RecordChangeComplete	Fired after one or more records change.
RecordsetChangeComplete	Fired after the Recordset has changed.
WillChangeField	Fired before a pending operation changes the value of one or more Field objects.
WillChangeRecord	Fired before one or more rows in the Recordset change.
WillChangeRecordset	Fired before a pending operation changes the Recordset.
WillMove	Fired before a pending operation changes the current position in the Recordset.

Constants

AffectEnum

Name	Value	Description
adAffectAll	3	Operation affects all records in the recordset.
adAffectAllChapters	4	Operation affects all child (chapter) records.
adAffectCurrent	1	Operation affects only the current record.
adAffectGroup	2	Operation affects records that satisfy the current Filter property.

BookmarkEnum

Name	Value	Description
adBookmarkCurrent	0	Default. Start at the current record.
adBookmarkFirst	1	Start at the first record.
adBookmarkLast	2	Start at the last record.

CEResyncEnum

Name	Value	Description
adResyncAll	15	Only invoke the Resync for each row that has pending changes.
adResyncAutoIncrement	1	Default. Only invoke Resync for all successfully inserted rows, including their AutoIncrement column values.
adResyncConflicts	2	Only invoke Resync for which the last Update or Delete failed due to a concurrency conflict.
adResyncInserts	8	Only invoke Resync for all successfully inserted rows, including their Identity column values.
adResyncNone	0	Do not invoke Resync.
adResyncUpdates	4	Only invoke Resync for all successfully updated rows.

CEResyncEnum is new to ADO 2.1.

CommandTypeEnum

Name	Value	Description
adCmdFile	256	Indicates that the provider should evaluate CommandText as a previously persisted file.
adCmdStoredProc	4	Indicates that the provider should evaluate CommandText as a stored procedure.
adCmdTable	2	Indicates that the provider should generate a SQL query to return all rows from the table named in CommandText.
adCmdTableDirect	512	Indicates that the provider should return all rows from the table named in CommandText.
adCmdText	1	Indicates that the provider should evaluate CommandText as textual definition of a command, such as a SQL statement.
adCmdUnknown	8	Indicates that the type of command in CommandText unknown.

CompareEnum

Name	Value	Description
adCompareEqual	1	The bookmarks are equal.
adCompareGreaterThan	2	The first bookmark is after the second.

Name	Value	Description
adCompareLessThan	0	The first bookmark is before the second.
adCompareNotComparable	4	The bookmarks cannot be compared.
adCompareNotEqual	3	The bookmarks are not equal and not ordered.

ConnectModeEnum

Name	Value	Description
adModeRead	1	Indicates read-only permissions.
adModeReadWrite	3	Indicates read/write permissions.
adModeShareDenyNone	16	Prevents others from opening connection with any permissions.
adModeShareDenyRead	4	Prevents others from opening connection with read permissions.
adModeShareDenyWrite	8	Prevents others from opening connection with write permissions.
adModeShareExclusive	12	Prevents others from opening connection.
adModeUnknown	0	Default. Indicates that the permissions have not yet been set or cannot be determined.
adModeWrite	2	Indicates write-only permissions.

ConnectOptionEnum

Name	Value	Description
adAsyncConnect	16	Open the connection asynchronously.
adConnectUnspecified	-1	The connection mode is unspecified.

ConnectPromptEnum

Name	Value	Description
adPromptAlways	1	Always prompt for connection information.
adPromptComplete	2	Only prompt if not enough information was supplied.
AdPromptComplete Required	3	Only prompt if not enough information was supplied, but disable any options not directly applicable to the connection.
adPromptNever	4	Default. Never prompt for connection information.

CursorLocationEnum

Name	Value	Description
adUseClient	3	Use client-side cursors supplied by the local cursor library.
adUseClientBatch	3	Use client-side cursors supplied by the local cursor library.
adUseNone	1	No cursor services are used.
adUseServer	2	Default. Uses data provider driver supplied cursors.

CursorOptionEnum

Name	Value	Description
adAddNew	16778240	You can use the AddNew method to add new records.
adApproxPosition	16384	You can read and set the AbsolutePosition and AbsolutePage properties.
adBookmark	8192	You can use the Bookmark property to access specific records.
adDelete	16779264	You can use the Delete method to delete records.
adFind	524288	You can use the Find method to find records.
adHoldRecords	256	You can retrieve more records or change the next retrieve position without committing all pending changes.
adIndex	8388608	You can use the Index property to name an index. This value is new to ADO 2.1.
adMovePrevious	512	You can use the ModeFirst, MovePrevious, Move, and GetRows methods.
adNotify	262144	The recordset supports Notifications.
adResync	131072	You can update the cursor with the data visible in the underlying database with the Resync method.
adSeek	4194304	You can use the Seek method to find a row in a Recordset. This value is new to ADO 2.1.
adUpdate	16809984	You can use the Update method to modify existing records.
adUpdateBatch	65536	You can use the UpdateBatch or CancelBatch methods to transfer changes to the provider in groups.

CursorTypeEnum

Name	Value	Description
adOpenDynamic	2	Opens a dynamic type cursor.
adOpenForwardOnly	0	Default. Opens a forward-only type cursor.
adOpenKeyset	1	Opens a keyset type cursor.
adOpenStatic	3	Opens a static type cursor.
adOpenUnspecified	-1	Indicates an unspecified value for cursor type.

DataTypeEnum

Name	Value	Description
adBigInt	20	An 8-byte signed integer.
adBinary	128	A binary value.
adBoolean	11	A Boolean value.
adBSTR	8	A null-terminated character string.
adChapter	136	A chapter type, indicating a child recordset.
adChar	129	A String value.
adCurrency	6	A currency value. An 8-byte signed integer scaled by 10,000, with 4 digits to the right of the decimal point.
adDate	7	A Date value. A Double where the whole part is the number of days since December 30 1899, and the fractional part is a fraction of the day.
adDBDate	133	A date value (yyyymmdd).
adDBFileTime	137	A database file time.
adDBTime	134	A time value (hhmmss).
adDBTimeStamp	135	A date-time stamp (yyyymmddhhmmss plus a fraction in nanoseconds).
adDecimal	14	An exact numeric value with fixed precision and scale.
adDouble	5	A double-precision floating point value.
adEmpty	0	No value was specified.
adError	10	A 32-bit error code.
adFileTime	64	A DOS/Win32 file time. The number of 100 nanosecond intervals since Jan 1 1601.

Table continued on following page

Name	Value	Description
adGUID	72	A globally unique identifier.
adIDispatch	9	A pointer to an IDispatch interface on an OLE object.
adInteger	3	A 4-byte signed integer.
adIUnknown	13	A pointer to an IUnknown interface on an OLE object.
adLongVarBinary	205	A long binary value.
adLongVarChar	201	A long String value.
adLongVarWChar	203	A long null-terminated string value.
adNumeric	131	An exact numeric value with a fixed precision and scale.
adPropVariant	138	A variant that is not equivalent to an Automation variant.
adSingle	4	A single-precision floating point value.
adSmallInt	2	A 2-byte signed integer.
adTinyInt	16	A 1-byte signed integer.
adUnsignedBigInt	21	An 8-byte unsigned integer.
adUnsignedInt	19	A 4-byte unsigned integer.
adUnsignedSmallInt	18	A 2-byte unsigned integer.
adUnsignedTinyInt	17	A 1-byte unsigned integer.
adUserDefined	132	A user-defined variable.
adVarBinary	204	A binary value.
adVarChar	200	A String value.
adVariant	12	An Automation Variant.
adVarNumeric	139	A variable width exact numeric, with a signed scale value.
adVarWChar	202	A null-terminated Unicode character string.
adWChar	130	A null-terminated Unicode character string.

EditModeEnum

Name	Value	Description
adEditAdd	2	Indicates that the AddNew method has been invoked and the current record in the buffer is a new record that hasn't been saved to the database.
adEditDelete	4	Indicates that the Delete method has been invoked.
adEditInProgress	1	Indicates that data in the current record has been modified but not saved.
adEditNone	0	Indicates that no editing is in progress.

ErrorValueEnum

Name	Value	Description
adErrBoundToCommand	3707	The application cannot change the ActiveConnection property of a Recordset object with a Command object as its source.
adErrDataConversion	3421	The application is using a value of the wrong type for the current application.
AdErrFeatureNot Available	3251	The operation requested by the application is not supported by the provider.
adErrIllegalOperation	3219	The operation requested by the application is not allowed in this context.
adErrInTransaction	3246	The application cannot explicitly close a Connection object while in the middle of a transaction.
adErrInvalidArgument	3001	The application is using arguments that are the wrong type, are out of the acceptable range, or are in conflict with one another.
adErrInvalidConnectio n	3709	The application requested an operation on an object with a reference to a closed or invalid Connection object.
adErrInvalidParamInfo	3708	The application has improperly defined a Parameter object.
adErrItemNotFound	3265	ADO could not find the object in the collection.
adErrNoCurrentRecord	3021	Either BOF or EOF is True, or the current record has been deleted. The operation requested by the application requires a current record.
adErrNotExecuting	3715	The operation is not executing.
adErrNotReentrant	3710	The operation is not reentrant.

Table continued on following page

Name	Value	Description
adErrObjectClosed	3704	The operation requested by the application is not allowed if the object is closed.
adErrObjectInCollection	3367	Can't append. Object already in collection.
adErrObjectNotSet	3420	The object referenced by the application no longer points to a valid object.
adErrObjectOpen	3705	The operation requested by the application is not allowed if the object is open.
adErrOperationCancelled	3712	The operation was cancelled.
adErrProviderNotFound	3706	ADO could not find the specified provider.
adErrStillConnecting	3713	The operation is still connecting.
adErrStillExecuting	3711	The operation is still executing.
adErrUnsafeOperation	3716	The operation is unsafe under these circumstances.

EventReasonEnum

Name	Value	Description
adRsnAddNew	1	A new record is to be added.
adRsnClose	9	The object is being closed.
adRsnDelete	2	The record is being deleted.
adRsnFirstChange	11	The record has been changed for the first time.
adRsnMove	10	A Move has been invoked and the current record pointer is being moved.
adRsnMoveFirst	12	A MoveFirst has been invoked and the current record pointer is being moved.
adRsnMoveLast	15	A MoveLast has been invoked and the current record pointer is being moved.
adRsnMoveNext	13	A MoveNext has been invoked and the current record pointer is being moved.
adRsnMovePrevious	14	A MovePrevious has been invoked and the current record pointer is being moved.
adRsnRequery	7	The recordset was requeried.
adRsnResynch	8	The recordset was resynchronized.
adRsnUndoAddNew	5	The addition of a new record has been cancelled.

Name	Value	Description
adRsnUndoDelete	6	The deletion of a record has been cancelled.
adRsnUndoUpdate	4	The update of a record has been cancelled.
adRsnUpdate	3	The record is being updated.

EventStatusEnum

Name	Value	Description
adStatusCancel	4	Request cancellation of the operation that is about to occur.
adStatusCantDeny	3	A Will event cannot request cancellation of the operation about to occur.
adStatusErrorsOccurred	2	The operation completed unsuccessfully, or a Will event cancelled the operation.
adStatusOK	1	The operation completed successfully.
adStatusUnwantedEvent	5	Events for this operation are no longer required.

ExecuteOptionEnum

Name	Value	Description
adAsyncExecute	16	The operation is executed asynchronously.
adAsyncFetch	32	The records are fetched asynchronously.
adAsyncFetchNonBlocking	64	The records are fetched asynchronously without blocking subsequent operations.
adExecuteNoRecords	128	Indicates CommandText is a command or stored procedure that does not return rows. Always combined with adCmdText or adCmdStoreProc.

FieldAttributeEnum

Name	Value	Description
adFldCacheDeferred	4096	Indicates that the provider caches field values and that subsequent reads are done from the cache.
adFldFixed	16	Indicates that the field contains fixed-length data.
adFldIsNullable	32	Indicates that the field accepts Null values.

Table continued on following page

Name	Value	Description
adFldKeyColumn	32768	The field is part of a key column.
adFldLong	128	Indicates that the field is a long binary field, and that the AppendChunk and GetChunk methods can be used.
adFldMayBeNull	64	Indicates that you can read Null values from the field.
adFldMayDefer	2	Indicates that the field is deferred, that is, the field values are not retrieved from the data source with the whole record, but only when you access them.
adFldNegativeScale	16384	The field has a negative scale.
adFldRowID	256	Indicates that the field is some kind of record ID.
adFldRowVersion	512	Indicates that the field time or date stamp used to track updates.
adFldUnknownUpdatable	8	Indicates that the provider cannot determine if you can write to the field.
adFldUpdatable	4	Indicates that you can write to the field.

FilterGroupEnum

Name	Value	Description
adFilterAffectedRecords	2	Allows you to view only records affected by the last Delete, Resync, UpdateBatch, or CancelBatch method.
AdFilterConflicting Records	5	Allows you to view the records that failed the last batch update attempt.
adFilterFetchedRecords	3	Allows you to view records in the current cache.
adFilterNone	0	Removes the current filter and restores all records to view.
adFilterPendingRecords	1	Allows you to view only the records that have changed but have not been sent to the server. Only applicable for batch update mode.
adFilterPredicate	4	Allows you to view records that failed the last batch update attempt.

GetRowsOptionEnum

Name	Value	Description
adGetRowsRest	-1	Retrieves the remainder of the rows in the recordset.

IsolationLevelEnum

Name	Value	Description
adXactBrowse	256	Indicates that from one transaction you can view uncommitted changes in other transactions.
adXactChaos	16	Default. Indicates that you cannot overwrite pending changes from more highly isolated transactions.
AdXactCursorStability	4096	Default. Indicates that from one transaction you can view changes in other transactions only after they have been committed.
adXactIsolated	1048576	Indicates that transactions are conducted in isolation from other transactions.
adXactReadCommitted	4096	Same as adXactCursorStability.
AdXactReadUncommitted	256	Same as adXactBrowse.
adXactRepeatableRead	65536	Indicates that from one transaction you cannot see changes made in other transactions, but that requerying can bring new recordsets.
adXactSerializable	1048576	Same as adXactIsolated.
adXactUnspecified	-1	Indicates that the provider is using a different IsolationLevel than specified, but that the level cannot be identified.

LockTypeEnum

Name	Value	Description
AdLockBatchOptimistic	4	Optimistic batch updates.
adLockOptimistic	3	Optimistic locking, record by record. The provider locks records when Update is called.
adLockPessimistic	2	Pessimistic locking, record by record. The provider locks the record immediately upon editing.

Table continued on following page

Name	Value	Description
adLockReadOnly	1	Default. Read-only, data cannot be modified.
adLockUnspecified	-1	The clone is created with the same lock type as the original.

MarshalOptionsEnum

Name	Value	Description
adMarshalAll	0	Default. Indicates that all rows are returned to the server.
adMarshalModifiedOnly	1	Indicates that only modified rows are returned to the server.

ObjectStateEnum

Name	Value	Description
adStateClosed	0	Default. Indicates that the object is closed.
adStateConnecting	2	Indicates that the object is connecting.
adStateExecuting	4	Indicates that the object is executing a command.
adStateFetching	8	Indicates that the rows of the recordset are being fetched.
adStateOpen	1	Indicates that the object is open.

ParameterAttributesEnum

Name	Value	Description
adParamLong	128	Indicates that the parameter accepts long binary data.
adParamNullable	64	Indicates that the parameter accepts Null values.
adParamSigned	16	Default. Indicates that the parameter accepts signed values.

ParameterDirectionEnum

Name	Value	Description
adParamInput	1	Default. Indicates an input parameter.
adParamInputOutput	3	Indicates both an input and output parameter.

Name	Value	Description
adParamOutput	2	Indicates an output parameter.
adParamReturnValue	4	Indicates a return value.
adParamUnknown	0	Indicates parameter direction is unknown.

PersistFormatEnum

Name	Value	Description
adPersistADTG	0	Default. Persist data in Advanced Data Table Gram format.
adPersistXML	1	Persist data in XML format.

PositionEnum

Name	Value	Description
adPosBOF	-2	The current record pointer is at BOF.
adPosEOF	-3	The current record pointer is at EOF.
adPosUnknown	-1	The Recordset is empty, the current position is unknown, or the provider does not support the AbsolutePage property.

PropertyAttributesEnum

Name	Value	Description
adPropNotSupported	0	Indicates that the property is not supported by the provider.
adPropOptional	2	Indicates that the user does not need to specify a value for this property before the data source is initialized.
adPropRead	512	Indicates that the user can read the property.
adPropRequired	1	Indicates that the user must specify a value for this property before the data source is initialized.
adPropWrite	1024	Indicates that the user can set the property.

RecordStatusEnum

Name	Value	Description
adRecCanceled	256	The record was not saved because the operation was cancelled.
adRecCantRelease	1024	The new record was not saved because of existing record locks.
adRecConcurrencyViolation	2048	The record was not saved because optimistic concurrency was in use.
adRecDBDeleted	262144	The record has already been deleted from the data source.
adRecDeleted	4	The record was deleted.
adRecIntegrityViolation	4096	The record was not saved because the user violated integrity constraints.
adRecInvalid	16	The record was not saved because its bookmark is invalid.
adRecMaxChangesExceeded	8192	The record was not saved because there were too many pending changes.
adRecModified	2	The record was modified.
adRecMultipleChanges	64	The record was not saved because it would have affected multiple records.
adRecNew	1	The record is new.
adRecObjectOpen	16384	The record was not saved because of a conflict with an open storage object.
adRecOK	0	The record was successfully updated.
adRecOutOfMemory	32768	The record was not saved because the computer has run out of memory.
adRecPendingChanges	128	The record was not saved because it refers to a pending insert.
adRecPermissionDenied	65536	The record was not saved because the user has insufficient permissions.
adRecSchemaViolation	131072	The record was not saved because it violates the structure of the underlying database.
adRecUnmodified	8	The record was not modified.

ResyncEnum

Name	Value	Description
adResyncAllValues	2	Default. Data is overwritten and pending updates are cancelled.
adResyncUnderlyingValues	1	Data is not overwritten and pending updates are not cancelled.

SchemaEnum

Name	Value	Description
adSchemaAsserts	0	Request assert information.
adSchemaCatalogs	1	Request catalog information.
adSchemaCharacterSets	2	Request character set information.
adSchemaCheckConstraints	5	Request check constraint information.
adSchemaCollations	3	Request collation information.
adSchemaColumnPrivileges	13	Request column privilege information.
adSchemaColumns	4	Request column information.
adSchemaColumnsDomainUsage	11	Request column domain usage information.
AdSchemaConstraintColumn Usage	6	Request column constraint usage information.
AdSchemaConstraintTable Usage	7	Request table constraint usage information.
adSchemaCubes	32	For multi-dimensional data, view the Cubes schema.
adSchemaDBInfoKeywords	30	Request the keywords from the provider.
adSchemaDBInfoLiterals	31	Request the literals from the provider.
adSchemaDimensions	33	For multi-dimensional data, view the Dimensions schema.
adSchemaForeignKeys	27	Request foreign key information.
adSchemaHierarchies	34	For multi-dimensional data, view the Hierarchies schema.
adSchemaIndexes	12	Request index information.
adSchemaKeyColumnUsage	8	Request key column usage information.

Table continued on following page

Name	Value	Description
adSchemaLevels	35	For multi-dimensional data, view the Levels schema.
adSchemaMeasures	36	For multi-dimensional data, view the Measures schema.
adSchemaMembers	38	For multi-dimensional data, view the Members schema.
adSchemaPrimaryKeys	28	Request primary key information.
adSchemaProcedureColumns	29	Request stored procedure column information.
adSchemaProcedureParameters	26	Request stored procedure parameter information.
adSchemaProcedures	16	Request stored procedure information.
adSchemaProperties	37	For multi-dimensional data, view the Properties schema.
adSchemaProviderSpecific	-1	Request provider specific information.
adSchemaProviderTypes	22	Request provider type information.
AdSchemaReferential Contraints	9	Request referential constraint information.
adSchemaSchemata	17	Request schema information.
adSchemaSQLLanguages	18	Request SQL language support information.
adSchemaStatistics	19	Request statistics information.
adSchemaTableConstraints	10	Request table constraint information.
adSchemaTablePrivileges	14	Request table privilege information.
adSchemaTables	20	Request information about the tables.
adSchemaTranslations	21	Request character set translation information.
adSchemaTrustees	39	Request trustee information. This value is new for ADO 2.1.
adSchemaUsagePrivileges	15	Request user privilege information.
adSchemaViewColumnUsage	24	Request column usage in views information.
adSchemaViews	23	Request view information.
adSchemaViewTableUsage	25	Request table usage in views information.

SearchDirectionEnum

Name	Value	Description
adSearchBackward	-1	Search backward from the current record.
adSearchForward	1	Search forward from the current record.

SeekEnum

Name	Value	Description
adSeekAfter	8	Seek the record after the match.
adSeekAfterEQ	4	Seek the record equal to the match, or if no match is found, the record after where the match would have been.
adSeekBefore	32	Seek the record before the match.
adSeekBeforeEQ	16	Seek the record equal to the match, or if no match is found, the record before where the match would have been.
adSeekFirstEQ	1	Seek the first record equal to the match.
adSeekLastEQ	2	Seek the last record equal to the match.

StringFormatEnum

Name	Value	Description
adClipString	2	Rows are delimited by user defined values.

XactAttributeEnum

Name	Value	Description
adXactAbortRetaining	262144	The provider will automatically start a new transaction after a RollbackTrans method call.
adXactAsyncPhaseOne	524288	Perform an asynchronous commit.
adXactCommitRetaining	131072	The provider will automatically start a new transaction after a CommitTrans method call.
adXactSyncPhaseOne	1048576	Performs a synchronous commit.

Method Calls Quick Reference

Command

*Command.*Cancel

*Parameter = Command.*CreateParameter(*Name As String, Type As DataTypeEnum, _
    Direction As ParameterDirectionEnum, Size As Integer, [Value As Variant]*)

*Recordset = Command.*Execute(*RecordsAffected As Variant, Parameters As Variant, _
    Options As Integer*)

Connection

*Integer = Connection.*BeginTrans

*Connection.*Cancel

*Connection.*Close

*Connection.*CommitTrans

*Recordset = Connection.*Execute(*CommandText As String, RecordsAffected As Variant, _
    Options As Integer*)

*Connection.*Open(*ConnectionString As String, UserID As String, Password As String, _
    Options As Integer*)

*Recordset = Connection.*OpenSchema(*Schema As SchemaEnum, [Restrictions As Variant], _
    [SchemaID As Variant]*)

*Connection.*RollbackTrans

Errors

*Errors.*Clear

*Errors.*Refresh

Field

*Field.*AppendChunk(*Data As Variant*)

*Variant = Field.*GetChunk(*Length As Integer*)

Fields

*Fields.*Append(*Name As String, Type As DataTypeEnum, DefinedSize As Integer, _
    Attrib As FieldAttributeEnum*)

*Fields.*Delete(*Index As Variant*)

*Fields.*Refresh

Parameter

*Parameter.*AppendChunk(*Val As Variant*)

Parameters

*Parameters.*Append(*Object As Object*)

*Parameters.*Delete(*Index As Variant*)

*Parameters.*Refresh

Properties

Properties.Refresh

Recordset

Recordset.AddNew(*[FieldList As Variant]*, *[Values As Variant]*)
Recordset.Cancel
Recordset.CancelBatch(*AffectRecords As AffectEnum*)
Recordset.CancelUpdate
Recordset = *Recordset*.Clone(*LockType As LockTypeEnum*)
Recordset.Close
CompareEnum = *Recordset*.CompareBookmarks(*Bookmark1 As Variant, Bookmark2 As Variant*)
Recordset.Delete(*AffectRecords As AffectEnum*)
Recordset.Find(*Criteria As String, SkipRecords As Integer, _*
    SearchDirection As SearchDirectionEnum, [Start As Variant])
Variant = *Recordset*.GetRows(*Rows As Integer, [Start As Variant], [Fields As Variant]*)
String = *Recordset*.GetString(*StringFormat As StringFormatEnum, _*
    NumRows As Integer, ColumnDelimiter As String, RowDelimeter As String, _
    NullExpr As String)
Recordset.Move(*NumRecords As Integer, [Start As Variant]*)
Recordset.MoveFirst
Recordset.MoveLast
Recordset.MoveNext
Recordset.MovePrevious
Recordset = *Recordset*.NextRecordset(*[RecordsAffected As Variant]*)
Recordset.Open(*Source As Variant, ActiveConnection As Variant, _*
    CursorType As CursorTypeEnum, LockType As LockTypeEnum, Options As Integer)
Recordset.Requery(*Options As Integer*)
Recordset.Resync(*AffectRecords As AffectEnum, ResyncValues As ResyncEnum*)
Recordset.Save(*FileName As String, PersistFormat As PersistFormatEnum*)
Recordset.Seek(*KeyValues As Variant, SeekOption As SeekEnum*)
Boolean = *Recordset*.Supports(*CursorOptions As CursorOptionEnum*)
Recordset.Update(*[Fields As Variant], [Values As Variant]*)
Recordset.UpdateBatch(*AffectRecords As AffectEnum*)

Index

A Guide to the Index

The index is arranged hierarchically, in alphabetical order, with symbols preceding the letter A. Most second-level entries and many third-level entries also occur as first-level entries. This is to ensure that users will find the information they require however they choose to search for it.

W

p2p.wrox.com

The programmer's resource centre

A unique free service from Wrox Press
with the aim of helping programmers to help each other

Wrox Press aims to provide timely and practical information to today's programmer. P2P is a list server offering a host of targeted mailing lists where you can share knowledge with your fellow programmers and find solutions to your problems. Whatever the level of your programming knowledge, and whatever technology you use, P2P can provide you with the information you need.

ASP
Support for beginners and professionals, including a resource page with hundreds of links, and a popular ASP+ mailing list.

DATABASES
For database programmers, offering support on SQL Server, mySQL, and Oracle.

MOBILE
Software development for the mobile market is growing rapidly. We provide lists for the several current standards, including WAP, WindowsCE, and Symbian.

JAVA
A complete set of Java lists, covering beginners, professionals,and server-side programmers (including JSP, servlets and EJBs)

.NET
Microsoft's new OS platform, covering topics such as ASP+, C#, and general .Net discussion.

VISUAL BASIC
Covers all aspects of VB programming, from programming Office macros to creating components for the .Net platform.

WEB DESIGN
As web page requirements become more complex, programmer sare taking a more important role in creating web sites. For these programmers, we offer lists covering technologies such as Flash, Coldfusion, and JavaScript.

XML
Covering all aspects of XML, including XSLT and schemas.

OPEN SOURCE
Many Open Source topics covered including PHP, Apache, Perl, Linux, Python and more.

FOREIGN LANGUAGE
Several lists dedicated to Spanish and German speaking programmers, categories include .Net, Java, XML, PHP and XML.

How To Subscribe

Simply visit the P2P site, at **http://p2p.wrox.com/**

Select the 'FAQ' option on the side menu bar for more information about the subscriptio process and our service.

Programmer to Programmer